Sarge

Sarge

The Life and Times of Sargent Shriver

Scott Stossel

Foreword by Bill Moyers

Smithsonian Books
Washington

Copy editor: Joanne S. Ainsworth
Production editor: Joanne Reams
Designer: Brian Barth

Library of Congress Cataloging-in-Publication Data
Stossel, Scott.
    Sarge : the life and times of Sargent Shriver / Scott Stossel.
      p. cm.
    Includes bibliographical references and index.
    ISBN 1-58834-127-5 (alk. paper)
    1. Shriver, Sargent, 1915– 2. Politicians—United States—Biography. 3. Democratic Party
(US)—Biography. 4. Kennedy family. 5. Businessmen—Illinois—Chicago—Biography.
6. Lawyers—United States—Biography. 7. Ambassadors—United States—Biography.
8. United States—Politics and government—1945–1989. 9. United States—Politics and
government—1989– I. Title

British Library Cataloging-in-Publication Data available

Manufactured in the United States of America
09 08 07 06 05 04   1 2 3 4 5

For Susanna

CONTENTS

FOREWORD BY BILL MOYERS

He changed my life.

But that is the least of it. I can think of no American alive today who has touched more lives for the better than Sargent Shriver. Reel off the names of the organizations he inspired, led, or created and you have a sense of his multiplying legacy: Peace Corps, Head Start, VISTA, Job Corps, Community Action, Upward Bound, Foster Grandparents, Special Olympics. To each he brought the passionate conviction that no one need be spiritually unemployed when there is so much to be done in the world.

He is the radical I would like to have been if only I had met earlier his inner circle: Maritain, Teilhard, Merton, Dorothy Day. He is the Christian who comes closest, in my experience, to the imitation of Christ in a life of service. Not for him what Archibald MacLeish, the poet laureate he often quoted, called "the snake-like sin of coldness-at-the-heart." This book could well have been entitled, *A Leap of Faith*, for Shriver has lived his life as a great gamble that what we do to serve, help, and care for our fellow human beings is what ultimately counts.

He redefined patriotism for us. Love of country, yes—and he had five years in the navy to show for it. But he carries two passports—one stamped American, the other human being. To one group of departing Peace Corp volunteers after another he would proclaim, in essence, that all of us are members of the same great human endeavor but that our tents are pitched on different ground, causing us to look out on the passing scene from different angles. This, he said, means you go abroad cautious about the help you can be to others; the only change that really matters must come from within. But you go because the world is your home.

He is the one man I know who, if he had obtained the White House, might truly have transformed how we Americans see ourselves and how we see the world. A few millimeters of tilt in the political wheel of fortune and he might have become president. In 1964 Lyndon Johnson had to choose a vice presidential nominee and only two men were in the running in LBJ's mind, the only precinct that counted. One was Senator Hubert Humphrey of Minnesota, with whom LBJ had served in the Senate and who he believed could secure the labor, liberal, and civil rights constituencies that were still nervous about Johnson's own progressive credentials.

The other was Shriver, JFK's brother-in-law. That kinship intrigued Johnson: Could this be the way to keep the Kennedys in the tent without having Robert Kennedy on the ticket? That was not the only reason, however, that LBJ meditated on Shriver as a possibility. The two had spent considerable time together in 1961 when Johnson, then vice president, had "tutored" Sarge in how to sell the Peace Corps to Congress, whose powerful barons considered the idea naive if not hare-brained. I had worked in the Kennedy-Johnson campaign and served briefly in the new vice president's office before wrangling myself a place on the team Shriver was putting together to turn the Peace Corps into a going concern. After Sarge and I left our first lengthy tutorial at Johnson's knee, the vice president called me and said that the way to sell the Peace Corps was to sell Shriver: "They won't be able to resist him."

And they weren't. Over the next few months Sarge and I called on every member of Congress—House and Senate—to pitch the Peace Corps. Most were dazzled to be courted by the president's charismatic brother-in-law, of course, but what turned the tide was not his glamour but his passion. He was the Apostle Paul and they were the gentiles of Asia Minor; the theology paled in comparison with the intense ardor and appeal of the messenger. I saw jaded, world-weary, cynical politicians begin to pay attention as Shriver talked about America's revolutionary ideals, about our mission in the world—not to go abroad in search of monsters to destroy, he would say, paraphrasing some Founding Father, but to demonstrate that Americans are down-to-earth, believable, card-carrying idealists who can show that democracy begins with a teacher in a classroom and clean water coming from a new pump in the village square. There was one particular megalomaniacal, unreconstructed Southern racist whose chairmanship of a key House subcommittee meant life or death to our appropriations. He was aghast that volunteers living and working abroad under official American auspices might not only "practice miscegenation" but bring it home with them. Sarge never blinked. "Congressman," he said, "surely you can trust young Americans to do abroad exactly what they do back in your district in Louisiana." We left the man scratching his head, and much later a member of his staff quoted him as saying, "I was had." Indeed. While the chairman remained recalcitrant, Shriver plucked off a majority of the full committee above him and mitigated his obstructionism.

LBJ chose Humphrey, whom I also revered, and Sarge soldiered away at the war on poverty until he went to Paris as ambassador. He still had a presidential race ahead of him—as George McGovern's belated running mate—and then he turned to those pursuits that mark the character of a man who believes in public service without the aura, power, or reward of public office. I have often wondered, though, what the history of the last thirty-five years might have been if he had been president. Even now, as the journalist Colman McCarthy writes, Shriver "can look back on four decades of public service and a record of successful innovation unmatched by any contemporary leader in or out of government." But imagine him populating the White House and the government with the astounding array of unconventional citizens he brought to the Peace Corps and the Office of Economic Opportunity—journalists, public interest lawyers, psychologists (I have not been able to confirm it but McCarthy believes Sarge hired the first psychiatrist ever to be employed by a federal agency), business executives, poets, physicians, and imaginative career civil service officers who were frustrated by the ossified bureaucracies where they worked. To run our programs in India he recruited the American authority in high-altitude medicine who had himself been a leader in the first assaults on K-2 in the Himalayas. To Nepal he dispatched another climber who was a noted professor of English at Phillips Exeter Academy. The West Coast head of the NAACP, the Agency of International Development's most creative bureaucrat, a seasoned practitioner of West Virginia politics—not since the early days of FDR's New Deal had such a critical mass of unconventional talent descended on Washington.

Colman McCarthy's story is typical and instructive. In the summer of 1966, having left a Trappist monastery, McCarthy was roving the country writing articles about civil rights and the antiwar movement. One of his articles in the *National Catholic Reporter* was somewhat critical of a Shriver poverty project in Harlem. Shriver tracked him down and said he had a job opening for "a no man because I already have enough yes men." They met for dinner. For four hours. Not a word was said about the job. Instead, they talked about philosophers and theologians, about Tolstoy, Thomas Merton, and Flannery O'Connor. Only once did McCarthy get lost in the conversation—"when Shriver began talking about the nuanced differences between the early, middle and late Maritain." Shriver asked questions about the Trappists. "He said he could probably handle the silence, early rising and manual labor well enough, but the obedience would be a killer. Then he exclaimed, 'Welcome aboard, you're hired.'"

He did not have to recruit me. I lobbied for the job, having to overcome the reluctance of LBJ to let me leave his staff and the opposition of the White House mafia, who wanted me to continue to serve as a liaison between them and Johnson's Texans, as I had done in the campaign. Shriver braved both Johnson and Kennedy to take me aboard. I still possess the neat blue stationery on which later he made me the offer, at age twenty-eight, to become his deputy director. They were the best days of my life.

He was more than a leader, more than my boss. He was a one-man ecumenical society, as curious about my training in a conventional Baptist seminary as I was about his deep roots in Catholic spirituality. He had once been an altar boy to a cardinal; the only place other than the Peace Corps he would have wanted to be, he once told me, was somehow serving close to John XXIII, and on a long plane ride he discoursed in detail how he thought Pope John's "science of the heart" could transform the Church from a medieval institution into a powerful progressive force in a world polarized by hard-crusted ideology, implacable militarism, and rampant materialism. There was an opening, no doubt about it. Shriver came to national prominence after a long season during which young Americans had been nurtured in cold-war passions and subjected to the poisons of the Red Scare years. It was widely said that they welcomed the complacency and comfort of the good life in a booming economy. I once gave him a cartoon depicting Uncle Sam with his arm around a youthful American. They were looking at students demonstrating in some foreign country as Uncle Sam said: "We want our young people reading history, not writing it." He studied it, broke into that great broad-chinned grin, and said: "We'll give them a chance to make it."

They were ready, and from all walks of life they responded. They came from their own motives and with their own aspirations and ideals, and Sarge believed in them. Once he told a gathering of them: "The politics of death is bureaucracy, routine, rules, status quo. The politics of life is personal initiative, creativity, flair, dash, a little daring. The politics of death is calculation, prudence, measured gestures. The politics of life is experience, spontaneity, grace, directness. The politics of death is fear of youth. The politics of life is to trust the young to their own experiences."

To serve with such a man is a life-defining experience. One never forgets the personal touches of a friend who had a wife and five children himself and a rollicking extended clan. When my wife, Judith, experienced a miscarriage, he showed up at the hospital with a copy of Harper Lee's *To Kill a Mockingbird*. When our infant son was struck by a strange, undefined affliction, Sarge intervened, insisted that we take the boy to Johns Hopkins University Hospital for the scrutiny of one of the world's leading pediatricians, a Shriver friend.

I did not think a book could do justice to the man. To his accomplishments and exploits, yes. But to the whole dimension of a remarkably composed life—very unlikely. I was wrong, and Scott Stossel's work achieves what I thought impossible. He has captured in these pages the full measure of a great humanitarian. Reading it over the weekend, I thought back to a book Sarge gave me decades ago, in the early flowering of our friendship—Chaim Potok's *The Promise*. There it is written:

> Human beings don't live forever, Reuven. We live less than the time it takes to blink an eye, if we measure our lives against eternity. So it may be asked what value there is to human life. There is so much pain in the world. What does it mean to have to suffer so much if our lives are nothing more than a blink of the eye . . . I learned a long time ago, Reuven, that a blink of the eye is nothing. But the eye that blinks, that is something. A span of life is nothing. But the man who lives that span, he is something. He can fill that tiny span with memory, so that its quality is immeasurable.

And so he has.

ACKNOWLEDGMENTS

This project has been many years in the making. It would never have come to fruition without the assistance and guidance of many individuals and institutions.

The archival research for this book was conducted primarily in four places: the John F. Kennedy Library, in Boston, Massachusetts (where I pored through 170 cubic feet of uncatalogued Shriver material, much of it still sprinkled with rodent droppings from the Shriver family attic); the Lyndon Baines Johnson Library, in Austin, Texas; the National Archives, in College Park, Maryland; the Chicago Historical Society; and the Kennedy Foundation archives, in Washington, DC. I greatly taxed the photocopying machines and drew heavily on the wisdom of librarians and archivists in all of these places. Particular thanks are due to Megan Desnoyers at the JFK Library and Allen Fisher at the LBJ Library. Yale University, the Canterbury School, the Browning School, and the Carroll County Historical Society were also generous in providing access to archives and historical materials.

The Shriver family was generous in providing photos from their private family collection. I'm greatful to the archivists at the JFK Library (in particular, Allan Goodrich, James Hill, Mary Rose Grossman, and Nova Seals) for helping to produce additional photos. The entire library staff, it should be noted, was extremely tolerant of the three-month-old research assistant that my wife brought along with her on her trips here.

The Blue Mountain Center, in the Adirondack Mountains of New York, provided the time and space for me to begin writing in the summer of 2001. Both the *Atlantic Monthly* and the *American Prospect* magazines were generous in allowing me protracted leaves-of-absence for research and writing. Special thanks to Cullen Murphy and David Bradley at the *Atlantic*—and to Toby Lester, Amy Meeker, Don Peck, Corby Kummer, and others—for covering for me during my absence.

Through the years that I worked on this book, I relied on the research and editing assistance of several talented individuals. Katherine Arie and Julie Parker helped get me started by transcribing interviews. Jessica Chapel's excellent research memos helped me fill in the factual gaps in Shriver's life before 1960. (I think I still owe Jessica some overdue library books.) Kathy Crutcher deserves combat pay for providing library research, interview transcriptions, administrative work, and good company through the long, hot summer of 2003, when I worked out of a third-floor walk-up office without air conditioning in Boston's North End. (In July we measured the temperature inside the office at 102 degrees.) And Jessica Dorman provided emergency editing services when I was still wrestling with a 1,300-page manuscript; Jess's sympathy, judgment, and—most important under the circumstances—ability to read quickly made this a better book.

Ron Golfarb, agent extraordinaire, deserves much of the credit for keeping this project afloat when it had begun to take on water in the spring of 2002. Ron took firm hold of the rudder and navigated the ship to calmer seas. Once arriving in port at Smithsonian Books (to belabor the metaphor), the book found itself in the hands of an expert editorial team. Caroline Newman, my editor, understood my vision for the book and championed it with passion. Director Don Fehr also understood what the book was about—and made Smithsonian into the natural home for this biography. Carolyn Gleason and Joanne Reams managed to cope with my missed deadlines through the fall of 2003, after I had returned to full-time magazine work. Joanne Ainsworth did the copy editing; I have worked with many copy editors over the years, and Joanne is among the very best. Emily Sollie has held my hand through the editing and production process, patiently answering all of my questions. Brian Barth deserves credit for the cover design, the typeface, and the layout.

Of all the many people who contributed to this project, several deserve particular mention. Members of the Shriver family—and especially Sargent Shriver—were generous with their time and hospitality. Jeannie Main, who has been Shriver's deputy for more than thirty years, was not only an invaluable source of information and guide to all things Shriver but also helped get me through many dangerous thickets that otherwise might have permanently entangled me. And this book would almost certainly never have made it through to publication without the wisdom, advice, legal expertise, shrewd editorial eye, and steady exhortations of William Josephson. (Another biographer—Nancy Milford, the award-winning author of books on Zelda Fitzgerald and Edna St. Vincent Millay—once described Josephson as her Virgil, leading her through the circles of hell and purgatory. If Dante should ever return to this earth and if Virgil should be unavailable, he should consider calling on Bill Josephson to be his guide.)

Finally my wife, Susanna, has gone far beyond the call of spousal obligation in her contribution to this book. She tolerated my extended research travels, my long hours of work, and the financial debt this project incurred on the family. She performed countless hours of research and administrative work over the years, right up to the very day she gave birth to our first child. (And she was back at the research and fact-checking by the time our daughter was two weeks old.) She also edited, tracked down photo rights, and contributed to the book in numerous additional ways. But the hardest and most important task she performed was to keep me sane throughout this arduous journey; no one else could have done that.

INTRODUCTION

In early 1964 it looked as though Sargent Shriver would become the next vice president of the United States. After a successful three years directing the Peace Corps, Shriver had just returned from a round-the-world tour on behalf of President Lyndon Johnson. His stewardship of the Peace Corps work had made Shriver enormously popular, and his portrait, handsome and statesman-like, had recently graced the cover of *Time* magazine. For Johnson, a Shriver vice presidency would send a powerful symbolic message about the continuing place of the Kennedy family in the executive branch.

Rumors that Johnson might select Shriver as his running mate for the 1964 election had swirled around for weeks, but without confirmation. When reporters queried Shriver about the prospect of the vice presidency, he deflected the questions by saying Johnson hadn't asked him. Privately, however, he wondered. The day after President Kennedy was shot, Johnson had cornered Shriver in the foyer of the White House Cabinet Room and said, "Sarge . . . I'm completely overwhelmed, but I do want to say that I've always had a very high regard for you. It hasn't been possible for me to do anything about it until now, but I intend to." Shriver wondered what Johnson had meant by that.

In fact, Johnson did want Shriver to be his vice president, for reasons both exalted and Machiavellian. Having seen Shriver in action, Johnson had a high regard for the Peace Corps director's abilities; he particularly admired Shriver's talent for charming Congress. And he certainly saw the symbolic appeal of bringing a Kennedy family member onto the Democratic ticket. But the president's strongest motivation for selecting Shriver was more personal: He loathed Bobby Kennedy. (Bobby, if anything, loathed Johnson even more.) Naming Shriver to the ticket would allow him to avoid putting Bobby on it—something there was strong pressure for him to do—yet still claim that he was allowing the "Kennedy Era" to continue. In short, naming Shriver to the ticket would be a way for Johnson to score political points while simultaneously sticking it to his nemesis. So Johnson's aides leaked Shriver's impending nomination to Rowland Evans and Robert Novak, who published the story in their influential *Washington Post* column. The *Post*'s editors thought the column of sufficient interest that they took the unusual step of running the column on page one of the newspaper.

Shriver had been out of town when the *Post* column ran, and to avoid press questioning he retreated to the Kennedy family compound in Hyannis Port. There, he did evade the press, but he couldn't avoid Bobby. "What's this about the vice presidency?" Bobby asked him when he got Sarge alone. "Did you plant that story with Evans and Novak?" Shriver said that he hadn't—that in fact he had been out of town and had spoken to no one in the Johnson administration about the vice presidency. But Bobby, still fueled by grief at Jack's death, grabbed Shriver by the lapels and moved in close to his brother-in-law's face. "Let me make something clear," Bobby growled. "There's not going to be a Kennedy on this ticket. And if there were, it would be me."

Shriver both knew and didn't know what he was getting into when he married into the Kennedy family in 1953. He knew that he was hitching his fate to that of a large, powerful, overweening, exciting family, and that it would be a challenge to maintain his own identity among such a formidable clan. What he *didn't* know, in 1953, was that he was joining what would become an American political dynasty, the closest thing America has ever had to royalty. This would have tremendous costs and benefits for Shriver's own political ambitions, as it involved constantly negotiating the proper balance between serving his own interests and deferring to the family's.

For the most part, Shriver managed this balance deftly. He successfully contributed to and shared in the Kennedy triumphs—without ever being sullied by the Kennedy scandals. Many who entered the Kennedy orbit, whether as lovers or advisers or employees, never really emerged again as independent entities. From the moment of their association with the family, their identities became fixed as "Kennedy acolytes" or "Kennedy in-laws." Shriver was willing, at times, to dim his own bright star to accommodate the whole shimmering constellation of Kennedys; but in the firmament of history, his star glows with its own inner luminosity—not just reflected Kennedy light. It took a strong man to marry one of Joseph P. Kennedy's daughters and not be overwhelmed. Shriver survived, however, and in a family of outsized personalities, he held on to his own.

Shriver was, it might be said, "the Good Kennedy": in his idealism, heart-felt Catholicism, and commitment to Democratic politics and public service, he was perhaps more Kennedy than the Kennedys—and yet he was also, in his personal rectitude, moral probity, and gentle kindness, less Kennedy than they were. He was *in* the Kennedy family without being fully *of* it.

Shriver's achievements in his own right make him one of the major figures of the second half of the twentieth century. His period of greatest prominence in American public life—1960 to 1972—corresponds neatly with the rise and decline of New Frontier-Great Society liberalism; the arc of his political career closely paralleled the waxing and waning of an important era. Shriver's life therefore provides an illuminating window on a significant chapter of American history.

Shriver was one of the reasons John F. Kennedy defeated Richard Nixon in 1960. (Some have plausibly argued that Shriver was *the* reason Kennedy won, citing in particular Kennedy's telephone call to Mrs. Martin Luther King that Shriver had urged the candidate to make.) He was the man most responsible (besides Kennedy himself) for stocking the Kennedy administration's cabinet, and the executive branch generally, with "the best and the brightest." He created, legislated, and ran the Peace Corps, one of the most unusual—both in its function and in its administrative culture—agencies in the history of American government.

The impact and significance of this creation should not be understated. Tens of thousands of American Peace Corps volunteers have served abroad; even today, volunteers who have never met the man feel a personal affection for the Peace Corps' founding father, whose spirit still infuses the organization's mission. More remarkably, millions of citizens in developing countries have been indirectly touched by Shriver's presence. On several occasions, I have witnessed current African leaders come up to Shriver and tell him that they owe their careers to him: It was Peace Corps teachers, they said, who gave them their education in the early 1960s. When Shriver launched the Peace Corps he was, in effect, planting the seed of an idea; that idea continues to flower and bear fruit more than forty years later. After the terrorist attacks of September 11, 2001, one of the first things President George W. Bush did was to call for an expansion of the Peace Corps program.

As head of the War on Poverty under President Johnson from 1964 to 1968, Shriver created a host of programs—such as Head Start, the Job Corps, VISTA, Foster Grandparents, and Legal Services for the Poor—each of which rivals the Peace Corps in historical significance. These and other programs started by Shriver's Office of Economic Opportunity (OEO) still exist, and Shriver's spiritual presence continues to animate them. I have been at national Head Start conferences where Shriver has been mobbed like a rock star, surrounded by Head Start parents and teachers (many of them Head Start alumni) wanting to thank him and shake his hand. Shriver's programs affected not only those who were served by them but also those who ran them. Many members of Bill Clinton's cabinet and top-level staff had worked in programs started and led by Shriver (several were former Peace Corps volunteers, several had worked on his 1972 or 1976 election campaigns, and several had been in the first generation of lawyers working for Legal Services for the Poor). Shriver cultivated a generation of dedicated public servants who will continue to exert a powerful influence on American history for years to come.

By the time Shriver stepped down from heading the OEO in 1968, after miraculously preserving the antipoverty program from what seemed like certain extinction, he was a minor legend. Although he had suffered through difficult times at the OEO, when it seemed as if every constituency in the world was attacking him, he emerged with his reputation for political salesmanship, imaginative policymaking, and personal integrity intact. Indeed, it was partly Shriver's great popularity—and the political clout it conferred—that led Lyndon Johnson to dispatch Shriver to Paris as ambassador to France: Johnson worried that if Shriver had stayed stateside to campaign for Bobby Kennedy in the 1968 primaries, Bobby's momentum would be unstoppable.

Shriver's arrival in Paris coincided with such momentous events as the famous Paris riots of 1968 and the Paris peace talks on Vietnam, and Shriver once again found himself at the center of history. The relationship between the United States and France was then at its postwar chilliest. Charles de Gaulle was outspokenly critical of US foreign policy, and he was threatening to withdraw France from NATO. But Shriver, through his personal relationship with de Gaulle, did as much as anyone to thaw relations between the two countries.

Returning to the United States in 1970, Shriver headed the successful 1970 midterm elections for the Democrats. Then, in 1972, he joined the doomed presidential campaign of George McGovern as the vice presidential nominee after scandal caused the original nominee to bow out. Having been present at the creation of New Frontier-Great Society liberalism, Shriver was now present at its evident demise—the trouncing of the Democratic ticket, 49 states to 1.

In some ways, Shriver always seemed to be just missing his moment. In the 1950s and 1960s, Shriver's reputation in Chicago was such that, had family obligations not drawn him to Washington, he very likely would have become a senator from Illinois or its governor—and from there, he would have had a plausible launching pad for the presidency. In 1964, if Bobby Kennedy hadn't scuttled Shriver's vice presidential hopes, it might have been Johnson and Shriver, not Johnson and Hubert Humphrey, who trounced Barry Goldwater—and consequently Shriver, not Humphrey, whom the Democrats selected to take on Richard Nixon in 1968.

In August 1968, as the Democratic Convention began, it looked as though Humphrey would select Shriver as his vice president. Once again the "Kennedy wing" of the Democratic Party intervened. Polls showed Shriver faring better head-to-head than Maine senator Edmund Muskie against Republican vice presidential nominee Spiro Agnew; but the Kennedy wing, afraid that Shriver would jump ahead of Ted Kennedy in the line of family succession, put pressure on Humphrey to keep Shriver off the ticket. Given the less than 1 percent margin by which Humphrey lost, it's easy to imagine a Humphrey-Shriver combination winning the 1968 election, making the last quarter of twentieth-century American history vastly different from how it played out.

By the time Shriver did grace a presidential ticket, as George McGovern's running mate in 1972, the timing was wrong; the moment had passed. When Shriver ran in the Democratic presidential primaries in 1976, he was seen by some in the party as a relic of a bygone time. He got into that race late and then, although he was running as the "Kennedy candidate," failed to secure the absolutely critical endorsement of his own brother-in-law, Senator Ted Kennedy.

Shriver's relationship with the Kennedys was complex. They buoyed him up to heights and achievements he would never otherwise have attained—and they held him back, thwarting his political advancement. In 1959, standing alongside the sunbathing Joe Kennedy by the ocean in Palm Beach, Shriver ventured to his father-in-law that political operatives in Illinois were asking him to run for governor. Mr. Kennedy told Shriver in no uncertain terms that he was not to run; to have three Catholics on the Democratic ticket in Illinois (Dick Daley for mayor, Shriver for governor, and JFK for president) would spell doom for Jack Kennedy's presidential hopes. No, Mr. Kennedy said, he should forget about being governor for now; Jack needed Shriver to help with his campaign. Shriver dutifully agreed, and he went on to manage key parts of Jack's 1960 presidential campaign.

Clearly, the Kennedy brothers at times overshadowed Shriver. Bobby and Ted, in particular, were slow to take him seriously, the legacy both of his long courtship of their sister Eunice (which they found touching, if bathetic) and of his starry-eyed idealism (which led them to call him the family "Boy Scout").

Shriver's relationship with Bobby was especially complicated. "Bobby always spat on Sarge," recalled Charlie Peters, who, after working with Bobby during Jack's campaign for president, went to work for Shriver at the Peace Corps. "His people considered Sarge weak, a nonplayer. . . . That was what he had bought into by marrying Eunice." Relations with Bobby became even more strained when Shriver stayed on after President Kennedy's assassination to take command of Lyndon Johnson's War on Poverty. Shriver was often caught in the crossfire between the Kennedy and Johnson camps; with one foot in each camp, he often *was* the crossfire, a (mostly) unwilling weapon in the war between the two.

But to see Shriver purely as a victim of his association with the Kennedy family is to oversimplify grossly what was in fact a complex and often mutually rewarding relationship. Forgone election campaigns notwithstanding, his eminent career in public life after 1960 could not have been achieved absent his association with the Kennedy family. Moreover, the obvious respect that the hard-to-please Joseph P. Kennedy had for Shriver's abilities was eventually shared by Jack. Over the years, in fact, Shriver became a rock of the Kennedy family. Jacqueline Kennedy picked Shriver to organize her assassinated husband's funeral. Indeed, although the family's support for him was sometimes uneven, he was their stalwart supporter through everything, bailing them out of crises and unsavory predicaments without judgment or complaint.

Some have seen Shriver's association with the Kennedy family as a kind of Faustian bargain. Perhaps, but only to a point: The balance sheet is long on both sides. What he gained by hitching his fate to the Kennedys may well have been greater than what he lost by doing so.

Today, the heady idealism of the early 1960s, of Jack Kennedy's New Frontier, seems like ancient history. The cynicism that infected public life in the late 1960s and deepened after the Watergate scandal in 1974 has metastasized, as other scandals have continued to undermine our confidence in the major institutions of our society—government, organized religion, the corporate sector. Yet it was not so long ago that men like Kennedy and Shriver convinced the American people that anything was possible: We could put a man on the moon, defeat communism, end poverty, achieve peace in our time.

Throughout his life, Shriver has been a powerful magnet to talented, creative, idealistic, iconoclastic personalities. In this, Shriver was like Jack Kennedy. Shriver's style was very different from the president's, yet the two men shared a great gift: the ability to expand the horizons of the possible, to change our sense of what we can accomplish as individuals and as a nation. In ushering in the New Frontier, President Kennedy helped the United States change its conception of itself, giving its citizens a sense of a grander, more hopeful, more idealistic future. In part it was Shriver's ability to instill this same idealism and hopefulness in those he encountered that enabled him to fit so neatly into the New Frontier, and that helped make the Peace Corps its most representative illustration.

Not long ago a former colleague of Shriver's from the War on Poverty, Colman McCarthy, wrote an article about him for the *National Catholic Reporter*. Shriver, McCarthy wrote, "is a man of grace and goodness whose life of service has arguably touched more lives than any living American." Shriver can "look back on four decades of public service and a record of successful innovation unmatched by any contemporary leader in or out of government. The list of programs he started, defended and expanded, and which remain in place as necessary and productive while seven presidents have come and gone, is long."

Yet beyond the concrete legacy represented by the policies and programs he started is the joy and optimism he instilled in a whole generation. "What Sarge has always had is the ability not to be deterred by the enormity of the task," recalled Edgar May, one of his colleagues from the War on Poverty. "Nothing was impossible. And I think that was the hallmark of those days. We really believed that we were changing this country. And we did change it. Did we change it all in one fell swoop? Did we fix all the problems? Did we fix even half of the problems? The answer is no, we didn't, but we sure as hell changed people's lives."

In the winter of 1997, Sargent Shriver, whom I had never met, called me out of the blue one day and told me he was looking for someone to ghostwrite his autobiography. For years, he said, his family had been pressuring him to do this for his grandchildren and their descendants, as well as for the historical record. Now that he was eighty-one years old he figured he had better get down to work on the project. "Why me?" I asked him. I was twenty-seven years old at the time, working as an editor for *American Prospect,* a small political magazine.

Shriver explained that he specifically wanted someone young, someone whose generational perspective could balance his own. And, he continued, he wanted to write something that would be forward looking, something that would be of value to his grandchildren's generation in working toward achieving peace in the world.

In February 1997 I flew down from Boston to the headquarters of the Special Olympics, in Washington, DC, where Shriver was then serving as chairman of the board. He kept me waiting in the reception area, sitting under pictures of all of Joseph P. Kennedy's children (Joe Jr., Rosemary, Kathleen, Eunice, Jack, Bobby, Pat, Jean, and Ted), for more than an hour. I would later learn this was standard practice for Shriver. When he came out to introduce himself he was apologetic and warm, and we went on to spend several hours eating lunch and talking in a conference room.

As I had noted in our phone conversation, he seemed much less interested in talking about the events of his life than about his vision for the future. Also, he kept summoning other people to the conference room to talk to me *about* him while he was out of the room. He seemed to have little interest in talking about himself or in sitting down to talk about his life. At one point, I looked on awkwardly as Shriver and his son Timothy, who had recently taken over as president and CEO of the Special Olympics, shouted at each other. "Daddy," Timothy said, "if you're going to do this book, *you* have to focus on it. You can't have other people do it for you."

I flew back to Boston and the following weekend wrote Shriver a long letter, explaining that it seemed to me he wasn't really committed to writing an autobiography. "If you are to write something worthwhile," I suggested, "you need to figure out exactly what it is you want to write, and for what audience you are writing it, and what your rationale for writing is."

He wrote back to me a few days later, telling me that he had shared my letter with members of his family and that they agreed I was right: He needed to think some more about what kind of book he wanted to write and about whether, in fact, he really wanted to put in the time and introspection necessary to produce a good autobiography.

I assumed that was the last I would hear from him. Based on my limited interaction with the man, I thought that Shriver seemed too temperamentally unsuited to the processes that go into autobiographical writing and thinking, and too strongly oriented toward the future rather than the past, to commit himself to the project.

To my surprise, six months later he called me again. "I've decided to go forward with it," he told me, "and I've decided I'd like you to work with me on it." My circumstances had changed, however. I had just taken over as executive editor at the *American Prospect,* and I didn't feel I could take on an additional job. When I explained this to him, he said, "Well, why don't you just come down to Hyannis Port this weekend and help me get started. Just talk to me a little bit about how I might approach this."

I went down the first weekend in August 1997, intending to spend the weekend. Five weeks later, I had spent much of August at the Shrivers' house overlooking the Atlantic Ocean, and several hours of each day tape recording interviews with Sargent Shriver. (Much of the rest of each day I would spend on the telephone with my office, trying to put out a magazine from afar.) When I left after Labor Day, I had accumulated some sixty hours of interview tape. Somehow, without ever accepting a job—and without ever being paid a cent—I had been "hired" to be the ghostwriter of Sargent Shriver's autobiography.

I spent parts of 1998 and 1999 doing many additional interviews with Shriver and his friends and former colleagues and composing a proposal for a Shriver autobiography, to be written by me in his voice. Beginning in the summer of 2000, I took a leave of absence from my job and spent nearly six months engaged in full-time research at the John F. Kennedy Library in Boston; the Lyndon Baines Johnson Library in Austin, Texas; the National Archives in College Park, Maryland; and the Chicago Historical Society in Illinois. What I found in these places—and especially among the Shriver papers at the Kennedy Library, to which no other scholar had ever been granted access—was a treasure trove of material. Not only did I find the full (and heretofore partly secret) histories of the founding of the Peace Corps and the War on Poverty, but also considerable documentary evidence of Shriver's complex relationship with the Kennedy family.

Complications arose. There was plenty of interesting and historically relevant material here—but it was material that, in its richness of detail, would be hard to fit into a conventional autobiography. Also, Shriver's incorrigible habit of deflecting credit for his accomplishments to other people made composing a historically credible autobiography very difficult. As my intuition had told me from the start, Shriver had little interest in writing an autobiography or memoir, properly speaking, but was more interested in building "a vision for the future," as he put it.

William Josephson, a Peace Corps colleague of Shriver's, proposed to me that perhaps the material I had unearthed would be better suited for a biography than an autobiography. Shriver expressed his enthusiasm for this idea in the summer of 2000 and officially signed off on my writing an "authorized" biography. (Mr. Josephson has served as Shriver's designated representative for purposes of this book.)

"Authorized," in this case, meant that I had unvarnished access to all Shriver materials at the JFK Library, at the Special Olympics, and at the Joseph P. Kennedy Foundation as well as to other partially closed collections at the JFK Library. It has also meant that, when I've approached Shriver's old friends and former colleagues for interviews, most of them have been eager to talk to me. It does not mean, however, that members of Shriver's family, or the extended Kennedy family, necessarily agreee with everything I have written. I have relied heavily on Shriver materials and on conversations with the subject (who has himself read and commented on multiple drafts of this book), as well as on hundreds of other corroborating accounts, but the interpretations and judgments contained herein are my own; there are places where other people (including members of the Kennedy and Shriver families) with different perspectives disagree with them.

Early in 2003 Shriver was diagnosed with the early symptoms of Alzheimer's disease. (For this biography, I haven't used anything from conversations with Shriver conducted after December 2000 unless what he said could be corroborated by additional sources.) By the spring of 2003, as his memory deterioration accelerated and as my work on his biography progressed, a strange kind of alchemic transfer took place; I became, in effect, his external hard drive. Many of the memories, stories, and facts that had once been in his head were gone and had by now been downloaded into *my* head, or into the book. To capture, and to render accurately, the memories and the life story of a great man and an important historical figure before they dissipate is daunting to say the least. I hope I have served him justice.

PART ONE

Youth (1915–1945)

CHAPTER ONE

States' Rights, Religious Freedom, and Local Self-Government

⁓

If you drive out Route 27 north from the suburbs of Washington, DC, toward southern Pennsylvania, it is possible—if you ignore the occasional eruption of housing developments and commercial sprawl—to imagine the Maryland of 1915. Rolling farmland begins at the road's edge and extends to the horizon in all directions. Churches of traditional denominations abound. The architecture of many of the farmhouses, sturdy and square, bespeaks the simple values of an earlier time. And the flags—about every third house flying the Stars and Stripes, and about every fourth flying the yellow Maryland state emblem—reveal the distinctive commingling of American patriotism and state pride unique to the southern border states. These are the values and the architecture and the landscape that formed Sargent Shriver.

Shriver came into this world at a historic time: 1915. The technological advances of the Industrial Revolution were being harnessed and consolidated. The Ford Motor Company had just implemented mass production. Manufacturers were just beginning to use electric power in their factories. The structure of the atom was being discovered. The first X-rays and rocket ships had just been tested; the first machine guns were about to be. *Tarzan of the Apes* had recently fallen from the bestseller list. The silent film era was in full blossom, providing a new form of popular entertainment. Ragtime was hot; jazz was just beginning to be. The *New Republic* magazine, championing the progressivism of Teddy Roosevelt, had just been launched. The Baltimore Orioles, of baseball's International League, had just sold Babe Ruth and three other players to the Boston Red Sox for $20,000. In Brookline, Massachusetts, Joseph and Rose Kennedy had just celebrated their first wedding anniversary; Joe's exploits as a banking prodigy were being covered in the Boston papers; and their son Joe Jr. had just been born.

Most important, of course, the Great War had broken out in Europe, inaugurating the modern era in a torrent of bloodshed. Most Americans, although they supported the Allied powers, still considered the war to be only a distant concern. The Democrat Woodrow Wilson was president. A German submarine had sunk the *Lusitania*, an American passenger ship, in May, but Wilson was avowing American neutrality. "There is such a thing as being too proud to fight," Wilson said. But a countervailing interventionist sentiment was growing. As the death toll in Europe rose into the tens and then hundreds of thousands, former president Theodore Roosevelt—an occasional visitor to the Shriver household in Maryland—was preaching that "our country should not shirk its duty to mankind" by failing to get involved in the war. In 1915, however, the Shrivers agreed with Wilson: Steeped in the lore of their immigrant ancestors, they felt that the clash of the European powers vindicated their forebears who had emigrated to America to *escape* endless European wars.

The first Shrivers—or Schreibers, as they were then called—to come to the New World were a family of noble descent hailing from the southeastern region of Germany, along the Rhine River. Weary of the European wars that had devastated the area, and mesmerized by shipping-company advertisements touting the verdant promise of North America, Andrew and Anna Margareta Schreiber and their four children set off across the Atlantic in 1721. Atlantic crossings in that era could be harrowing; often many weeks long, they involved churning seas that produced wretched seasickness; storms that sank ships; cramped quarters; and rampant disease. But the Schreibers were hardy and fortunate; arriving safely in Philadelphia, they walked several miles along the Schuykill River, their scant possessions in hand, to the village of Goshenhappen, one of the first German settlements on American shores. There they set themselves up as tanners and lived peacefully among the local Native American tribes.

The Shriver bloodline's powerful aversion to the affairs of Europe was strengthened when Andrew Schreiber's grandson David Shriver married Rebecca Ferree in 1761. Rebecca was the great-granddaughter of Mary Ferree, a leader of the Huguenots, the French Protestants who had fled France to escape the persecutory policies of Louis XIV. (In 1685 Louis had revoked the Edict of Nantes, which had previously granted political rights and freedom of worship to Protestants in Catholic France.)

David and Rebecca Shriver moved across the southern border of Pennsylvania into Frederick County, Maryland. On the banks of Little Pipe Creek, David Shriver built a home and cleared land around the house to build a mill. The couple enjoyed a biblical fecundity: they had 8 children, 64 grandchildren, and at least 265 great-grandchildren. (When David's grandson William Shriver and his wife had their thirteenth child in the mid-nineteenth century, William joked that he wanted to name it "Enough.") By 1790 the first US Census listed fifty Shrivers as heads of families.

For David Shriver, as for his descendants, America represented the promise of freedom from religious and political tyranny, and in the 1770s he emphatically declared himself a Whig in opposition to the British monarchy. On November 8, 1774, he was among those selected to help form the government agreed upon by the First Continental Congress. In 1776 he was elected to Maryland's Constitutional Convention, in Annapolis, where he helped draft Maryland's Declaration of Rights (which served as a model for the Declaration of Independence) and became a signatory to the colony's first constitution. Growing up, Sargent Shriver and his cousins, taught to revere David Shriver's bold, independent spirit, would visit the state house in Annapolis where David's name was engraved on the wall.

In 1797, as George Washington served out the final weeks of his second term in office, David Shriver's sons Andrew and David Jr. bought 400 acres of land near their father's home on Little Pipe Creek. Together, they built a new brick mill, which they called the "Union Mills," in honor of the "union their partnership represented." Growing up, when Sargent Shriver spent his summers in the town of Union Mills, the first thing he would see outside his window at dawn each day was horse-drawn wagons driving past the mill built by Andrew and David.

Until 1826 all the Shrivers in America were Protestant. That changed when William Shriver, the fourth of Andrew Shriver's sons, wed Mary Josephine Owings, a devout woman from a prominent Maryland Catholic family. William at first declined to convert to his wife's faith, but Mary Owings raised her children as Catholics, among them Sargent's grandfather Thomas Herbert, known as Herbert. After his wedding, William Shriver assumed management of his father's mill and built a new home for himself across the road from the mill, where he lived until the end of his life. In this home were born both Sargent Shriver's grandfather and Sargent's mother, Hilda, Herbert's daughter. Sargent himself spent his childhood summers in this house and was baptized in the chapel that Maria Owings had had consecrated in the living room.

During the Civil War, Maryland lay on the border between North and South, and although officially on the side of the Union, its citizens were divided in their sympathies: The county that included Union Mills sent about 600 soldiers to the North, 200 to the South. Neighbors in adjacent houses took opposing sides. Families turned against each other.

The Shrivers were no exception. William Shriver, although he was opposed to slavery, was a great champion of states' rights and ardently supported the Southern cause. Six of his nine sons would serve in the Confederate army. Just across the road lived William's brother Andrew, who, despite being a slave owner, was a staunch Unionist; his son was serving in the Twenty-sixth Emergency Regiment of Pennsylvania Volunteers. "My four cousins, C. Columbus, A. Keiser, Mark O. and T. Herbert Shriver, joined the Confederate army, while my own brother, H. Wirt Shriver, went to the defense of the Stars and Stripes," wrote Louis Shriver years after the war. "Our two families lived close together and although we continued to visit back and forth, social intercourse was always strained and often resulted in unhappy arguments."

On the eve of the Battle of Gettysburg, the Shriver family became divided as never before. On June 27, 1863, Gen. Robert E. Lee's cavalry commander, J. E. B. Stuart, entered Maryland with 5,000 Confederate cavalry and two days later arrived in Westminster, 7 miles south of Union Mills. On the morning of Tuesday, June 30, General Stuart arrived for breakfast at the Union Mills home of William Shriver, setting up his headquarters in the home where Sargent Shriver would be born fifty years later.

As Stuart began making preparations to lead his troops north toward Gettysburg, he took aside William Shriver's son Herbert, who was sixteen years old, and asked him if he could lead him through the backwoods country roads to Pennsylvania. When Herbert said he could, Jeb Stuart asked permission of William and Mary Shriver to take their son as a guide. When they consented, General Stuart promised to keep him safe and to enroll him at the Virginia Military Institute. After breakfast the whole family—William Shriver's family on one side of the road, Andrew Shriver's family on the other—gathered on the front porch to watch Jeb Stuart's cavalry ride north toward Pennsylvania, with Herbert Shriver riding directly alongside the general. Herbert led Stuart's cavalry 4 miles north through the back roads of Maryland into Pennsylvania to Gettysburg, where General Lee's Army of Northern Virginia was already engaged with the Army of the Potomac. During the final day of the Battle of Gettysburg, Herbert stood alongside General Stuart amid a grove of hickory trees, watching the green of the fields become obscured by piles of the dead, and clear streams turning opaque with blood. When a Confederate soldier fell back into Herbert's arms, mortally wounded by a rifle shot, he gasped, "for God's sake, Shriver, tell them I was facing the enemy."

Hours after the last of Stuart's cavalry had disappeared from view over the hills to the north of Union Mills, Gen. George Sykes's Fifth Corps of the Army of the Potomac appeared from the south. Sykes's men marched directly into Union Mills, pitching their tents all along the hills above Pipe Creek. Andrew and William Shriver now switched roles: Andrew's family swelled with pride at the Union blue; across the road, the Confederate-gray hearts of William's family fell. Whereas General Stuart had made his staff headquarters at William Shriver's house, Gen. James Barnes, a Union commander, now made his staff headquarters across the road in Andrew's house. The following morning the Fifth Corps broke camp and marched north, arriving on the morning of July 2 at Gettysburg, where it helped the Army of the Potomac seal victory.

As North and South clashed at Gettysburg, the sound of gunfire shook the windows and rattled the dishware at Union Mills. "We heard the cannon of the battle," wrote Andrew's daughter Kate Shriver in her memoir, "and soon the wounded and prisoners began to go down the pike toward Westminster." The wounded soldiers made great demands on both Shriver families. Whereas the Andrew Shrivers were robbed and vandalized by the Confederate soldiers, the

William Shrivers were robbed and vandalized by the Union soldiers. "There has been a sort of bitter feeling between the two families," wrote Frederick Shriver a few days later, "but there is hardly any doubt but that it will soon wear off."

One evening during the Battle of Gettysburg a drunken soldier began raising a ruckus in front of the Shrivers' mill. When an officer arrived to discipline him, the soldier shot him dead. The bullet tore right through the officer's body and lodged in the wall of the mill, 2 feet from its front door. The bullet remained lodged in the wall of the mill, still there when Sargent Shriver was a boy, a tangible memento of Union Mills's Civil War days.

As General Stuart had promised, Herbert Shriver returned home safely several months later and shortly thereafter enrolled as a cadet at the Virginia Military Institute (VMI). On May 15, Herbert Shriver and some 280 of his fellow VMI cadets were called upon to assist the embattled Gen. John C. Breckenridge, who was pinned down by Union troops at the sleepy crossroads town of New Market, Virginia. Herbert was shot and wounded, but the VMI cadets routed the Union soldiers of the Thirty-fourth Massachusetts Army, helping to produce a Confederate victory at the Battle of New Market. Herbert Shriver was decorated for his efforts, and he served out the remainder of the war in the First Maryland Cavalry.

The lore of the Shrivers' service during the war permeated the culture of Union Mills. The Civil War, although it ended fifty years before his birth, was a living part of Sargent Shriver's childhood. Enmity over the war lingered long into the twentieth century and colored the relations between the residents of Sargent's house (William Shriver's Confederate household) and the residents of his cousin Louis's house across the street (Andrew Shriver's Union household). As William H. Shriver, Sargent Shriver's uncle, would later recall, the Civil War stories of Herbert Shriver's generation "echoed throughout the home, year after year, to hosts of friends and guests even . . . up to the departure of those who lived during these times of cherished memories." The "hurrahs and songs" of Jeb Stuart at the Union Mills Steinway piano "re-echo through long memories" and were passed on to later generations. To the young Sargent Shriver, the Civil War was not some abstract fact from the history books but, rather, a tangible part of the culture that surrounded him.

Herbert Shriver—one of the last surrendering Confederates—returned to Maryland to take over the business of running the family mill, with the help of his older brother, Benjamin Franklin Shriver. They remodeled the mill and upgraded its equipment with machinery produced by the Industrial Revolution. In 1869 the two brothers founded the B. F. Shriver Canning Company.

In addition to working at the canning company, Herbert continued the Shriver family political tradition, representing Carroll County for one term each in the Maryland House of Representatives and the Maryland Senate. In 1908 he was a delegate to the Democratic National Convention in Denver, which nominated William Jennings Bryan; in 1912 he was a delegate at the Baltimore convention that nominated Woodrow Wilson. According to *Men of Mark in Maryland*, published in 1912, "Lately [T. Herbert Shriver] has been frequently mentioned as the next nominee for governor of Maryland of the Democratic party."

Hilda, the eldest of T. Herbert and Elizabeth Lawson Shriver's four children, was born in 1882. She debuted in Baltimore society in 1900 and graduated at the top of her class from Notre Dame College in Baltimore in 1902. In 1907, at a party at the family homestead in Union Mills, she was introduced to a second cousin, Robert Sargent Shriver. Robert, the fourth of Henry and Sarah Van Lear Perry Shriver's ten children, had been raised in Cumberland, Maryland. Superficially, the cousins appeared ill matched: Robert's family was Republican and Protestant and had been staunchly pro-Union. Hilda's family was Democratic and Catholic and had been avowedly pro-Confederacy. But Robert found himself powerfully attracted to Hilda's good looks, broad intellectual interests, and striking self-confidence. The two were married on June 1, 1910—although not before Hilda received special dispensation from the cardinal archbishop of Baltimore, who was a close friend of her father's, to marry a non-Catholic. They moved into a rented home at 196 Green Street in Westminster, where Robert was working as an officer of a local bank. Their first son, Herbert, was born in 1911. And on November 9, 1915, their second son, Robert Sargent Shriver, was born in his mother's bedroom on the second floor of his parents' house 7 miles south of the Shriver family homestead in Union Mills, on the Pennsylvania border.

For young Sarge, the world revolved around his mother. That wasn't surprising: Her force of personality was so strong that anyone who came in contact with her tended to find themselves in orbit around her. The patriarchal T. Herbert Shriver had doted on Hilda, his only daughter, instilling in her a confidence and independent-mindedness that were rare in women in the 1920s. Her political principles were fiercely held—she had campaigned strongly for women's suffrage—but she was so warm and social in her demeanor that everyone (and men in particular) melted in her presence.

In 1914 Robert and Hilda Shriver, at the urging of the Catholic Church hierarchy in Baltimore, agreed to take in a Belgian woman, a refugee from the fighting in Europe. Before the war drove her out of her country, Louise Thiele Carpentier had been an opera singer in Antwerp. She became the nursemaid to the infant Sarge and his older brother. Aside from Hilda, no one—not even his father or brother—exerted a stronger formative influence on young Sargent Shriver than Louise Carpentier. Under Louise's influence, Sargent was speaking fluent Flemish before he spoke English; by the time he was five years old he could sing along with Enrico Caruso on the records she played for him on the family Victrola. His earliest career aspiration was to be an opera singer.

Sargent's father was more reserved than Hilda and more distant in his relationship with his two sons. But Robert, like his son, felt Hilda's force powerfully. He left banking and went to work for his father-in-law as a vice president at the B. F. Shriver Canning Company. As the two brothers grew older, Sargent took after his mother, becoming garrulous and outgoing, with a zest for political discussion and public life; Herbert, meanwhile, took after his father, becoming taciturn and reserved, with a yen for Wall Street finance.

Although Robert Shriver was a Protestant when he married Hilda, he soon converted to Catholicism. This was not a conversion for mere appearance's sake; Robert became devout in his faith. He later joined or founded many Catholic aid societies: In 1922 he and Hilda founded Baltimore's Catholic Evidence League (whose purpose was to help Catholics apply Church teachings to their daily lives), and in the 1930s the Shrivers would found a Catholic bookstore in New York City. Robert also founded the National Catholic Convert League, later renamed the Society of St. Vincent de Paul, which gave money to support married Protestant clergymen who converted to Catholicism. Robert also made weekly forays into the Baltimore slums to distribute food to the poor.

It is impossible to overstate the presence of religion in Sargent Shriver's childhood. Maryland had been founded on the principle of religious toleration by Lord Baltimore, a convert to Catholicism who set out to establish an American colony whose inhabitants might worship freely, according to their consciences. The years preceding Sargent's birth had seen Baltimore become "the Catholic capital of the United States." The city of Baltimore had been the first Catholic diocese in the United States, and by 1860, the archdiocese had 120,000 Catholics and 127 priests and was continuing to grow fast. The councils of the American Catholic Church were based in Baltimore, and much of the communication between the Vatican and the American bishops came through the Catholic hierarchy in the city. Maryland's large Catholic population was still rapidly growing when Sargent was born. The Smith & Reifsnider men who delivered coal to his house would warn the young Sargent to "watch out for the Ku Klux Klan," alluding to the organization's virulent anti-Catholic bias—but as far as he knew, practically the whole world (except for his grumpy cousins at Union Mills) was Catholic.

Upon his discharge from the Confederate army, Sargent's grandfather T. Herbert Shriver had believed his true calling to be the priesthood. Twice he had entered St. Mary's Seminary in Baltimore, run by the Sulpician Fathers, intending to become a priest; twice, after falling gravely ill, he had been compelled to leave. After Herbert's second illness, Father François Lhomme, the superior at St. Mary's, told him, in effect, "You are clearly a good Catholic and have a sincere desire to become a man of the cloth. But maybe God is telling you that you are meant for other things." Herbert agreed and went on to become a successful businessman and politician, as well as one of Maryland's leading Catholic laymen.

During one of Herbert's sojourns at St. Mary's, he roomed with a skinny young Irishman named James Gibbons, who would go on to become the archbishop of Baltimore and, a few years after that, the first American priest to be designated a cardinal. Herbert's sister Mollie Shriver lived year-round in Union Mills, and whenever Cardinal Gibbons wanted to escape the press of city life in Baltimore, he would retreat to her rural home—the same home where Sargent's family spent its summers. Sargent and Herbert Shriver were surely the only boys in America who slept next to a cardinal every night during their summer vacation.

"In the simple and dignified atmosphere of this Catholic family Cardinal Gibbons felt thoroughly at home," Gibbons's biographer has written. "He frequently remarked that he knew of no finer Catholic family than the Shrivers. At Union Mills . . . the Shriver girls served him as temporary secretaries and prepared the dishes he relished, while their brothers drove him back and forth to the city, discussed current baseball or horse-racing news, and sometimes accompanied him on his walks or afforded him competition at horseshoes."

Hilda Shriver spent each summer as the cardinal's full-time secretary, helping him with the administrative affairs of the archdiocese. Sargent and his older brother and their cousins would serve as altar boys at Mass in the family chapel, which Gibbons himself had consecrated in the late 1800s at the behest of Sargent's great-grandmother Mary Shriver. It's a striking picture: Five-year-old "Sarge"—as everybody called him—and his cousins would be playing baseball in the rolling fields beside the creek in Union Mills. A bell would ring, signaling evening Mass. Throwing balls, bats, and gloves aside, the boys would run into the house, rustle through the closet for their acolyte vestments, and then stand silently as they prepared to assist with the pouring of the wine.

When stricken with his final illness, the cardinal went to Miss Mollie's to rest; he spent all but his very last days in her home. Sarge and his cousin William served as altar boys at the last Mass ever served by the cardinal, on December 9, 1920. Soon thereafter, Gibbons was confined by illness to his bedroom at Mollie Shriver's, and he was anointed with the last rites of the Catholic Church there on December 17. But a week later his health momentarily improved, and he was able to attend the Christmas Midnight Mass.

That Midnight Mass made an indelible impression on Sarge Shriver. The cardinal, for the first time in the last fifty-two Christmases, was too ill to celebrate a pontifical Mass, so another local priest was sent for. The cardinal had been sick for several days, too weak even to rise from his Union Mills bed, where he was tended to round the clock by Hilda and Mollie. But on Christmas Eve, Sarge's Belgian nursemaid, Louise Carpentier, stood on the stairs between the first and second floors and, with her beautiful voice, sang Christmas carols to the cardinal; the nursemaid's beau, a fellow Belgian, accompanied her on the organ from the chapel downstairs. Some forty Shrivers looked on. Lying in bed, Gibbons smiled, and Sarge could see the color returning to his face and the strength to his body. Unable to descend the stairs to the chapel, Gibbons asked to have his bed pushed out onto the upstairs landing, from which he could peer over the railing and participate in the Mass. This was the first time in his life that five-year-old Sarge contemplated the power of religion as a potentially miraculous force.

The Catholic religion was woven into the fabric of Shriver's daily life. Baptized by the cardinal himself, Shriver was accustomed to the regular presence of nuns, priests, monsignors, bishops, and seminary students, who were always coming by the house, often staying overnight. On Sundays after the cardinal died, all the Catholic members of the extended Shriver clan would pile into two Model T Fords and four or five horse-drawn wagons and travel 7 miles in a convoy from Union Mills to Westminster to attend Mass.

Although he spent his summers in Union Mills, Sarge lived the first few years of his life in Westminster, in the rented home on Green Street where he was born. That house, a square, brick structure, two stories tall, still stands, its exterior not noticeably changed in eighty-five years.

Green Street was at the edge of the town proper; the Shrivers' backyard ran down an incline a few hundred yards to where Westminster's "Negro" population, ex-slaves or the descendants of slaves, lived in small shacks clustered together in the dirt. Every afternoon after school, Sarge would run into his backyard, halfway between his house and the Negro shacks, and meet his friends to play baseball. Sometimes he would go home with one or another of his Negro friends for dinner, and he'd come home marveling at the exotic foods he had eaten there. "Why don't *we* slaughter hogs in the backyard and hang the pigs in the house until it's time to eat them?" he would ask his parents.

After a few years, the Shrivers moved to a larger house at the corner of Willis and Center Streets, a little closer to the center of town. There were Shrivers everywhere: Sarge and his family lived at 100 Willis Street; Joseph Nicholas Shriver (one of Hilda's younger brothers) lived up the road in a big, gray clapboard house at 145 Willis Street; and just across the street from that, William H. Shriver (another of Hilda's younger brothers) lived in a large, white colonial house at 131 Willis. The parish priest, who was a close family friend and frequent visitor, lived at 54 Main Street, just around the corner from Sarge's house. And the Shriver family plot was in the cemetery on East Green Street, adjacent to St. John's Church, where Sarge attended a school staffed by stern but kindly nuns.

In Westminster, everybody knew almost everybody else; people lived on their front porches in the evenings, talking to one another and waving at passing wagons and the occasional automobile. Neighbors looked on benignly as Sarge, Herbert, and their legions of cousins tore up and down Willis Street on their bicycles. When snow made the roads impassable for autos, they used their sleds to get around town.

But for Sarge, the most exciting social life was at Union Mills. Driving from Westminster to the family estate, the Shrivers would pass the acres of open fields where the B. F. Shriver Canning Company grew its crops. The family's first car, a Model T, could barely manage to crest the hill that rose just before Union Mills. At the base of the hill, on the right side of the road as the family drove in from Westminster, was the old mill, built by Andrew and David Shriver in 1797, still in operation when Sarge was a child. Alongside it was the Union Mills homestead, where the Union army had made its headquarters for a night on its way to Gettysburg. The homestead was now inhabited by Sarge's uncle Lou, still bitter that Confederate troops had stolen his horse, Charley.

Across the road from the homestead stood the home of Sargent's aunt Mollie. Built by William Shriver in 1826, this was where the flamboyant Gen. Jeb Stuart had stopped for a night and belted out tunes on the Steinway that still stood in the parlor next to the chapel below Sarge's bedroom. Aunt Mollie still bitterly recalled the damage done to her family's crops by the trampling Union army.

Life at Union Mills had an easy rural rhythm. A typical summer evening might have, as Sarge's cousin Frederic Shriver Klein recalled in 1957, a "family of ten or twelve gathered on rocking chairs on the lawn near the front porch, as the rumbling of the mill wheel died away, leaving the entire valley quiet and poised for dusk, with only the music of crickets, treefrogs, birds, and the occasional bass grunt of a bullfrog." A porch stretched all the way across the front of Mollie's house, and every night in summertime, Sarge and his family would sit on that porch, watching the wagons go by. Every evening, Uncle Lou would limp across the road, leaning on his cane, to play whist with Aunt Mollie. As he played, he would regale the children with stories of the Civil War—the story, for instance, of how he had snuck off to Gettysburg as a twelve-year-old to hear Lincoln's address. Always, at some point in the evening, Lou and Mollie would fall into arguing about the War Between the States (or the War of Northern Aggression, as Mollie called it). Every night, Lou would throw down his cards and stalk back across the street as fast as his aging legs would carry him, yelling over his shoulder that he would never, ever again lay a foot in Mollie's Confederate household. The next night, of course, he would be back.

After the Catholic Church and the Shriver family, the Democratic Party was the most integral part of Sarge's identity. The Shrivers had played a significant role in Maryland politics since the state's beginning as a colony in the eighteenth century—they were founders of Maryland's Democratic Party—

and Sarge was taught to revere his ancestor David Shriver's crusade for American independence.

Hilda succeeded early on in converting her husband to Catholicism, but changing his politics took slightly longer. For years Hilda Shriver had actively campaigned for women's suffrage, and in August 1920 Tennessee became the thirty-second state to ratify the Nineteenth Amendment to the Constitution, making a woman's right to vote the law of the land. Having finally won the right to vote, Hilda planned to exercise it. As a Democrat, she supported James M. Cox, who was the governor of Ohio, and his running mate Franklin Delano Roosevelt in the presidential election. Her husband, a Republican, was campaigning on behalf of Warren G. Harding, who promised a more isolationist "Return to Normalcy" after the strains of the Great War. The discussions across the Shriver family dinner table that election season were heated and intense. "How can a wife cancel out her own husband's vote?" Shriver recalled his father demanding.

In 1924 Robert Shriver again succumbed to his wife's gravitational force and switched his party allegiance. After that, the Shriver household became a regular venue for Democratic Party meetings. The neighbors became accustomed to the sight of the big black car, belonging to Maryland's four-term governor Albert Cabal Ritchie, parked in front of the Shrivers' house.

"States' rights, religious freedom, local self-government." That was the three-plank platform on which Shriver was always to remember Ritchie campaigning. Elected to the governor's mansion in Annapolis in 1920, and reelected in 1924 and 1928, Governor Ritchie dominated Maryland politics, an oasis of Democratic rule during the Republican stranglehold on the Roaring Twenties. The Shriver family would sometimes travel with the governor around the state as he made campaign speeches—almost all of them boiling down to those same three planks: "states' rights, religious freedom, and local self-government." In the germinal political sensibility of Sarge Shriver, already sympathetic to the Confederacy's Lost Cause of States' Rights, and to his ancestors' desire for religious freedom, Ritchie's message found ready lodgment.

Later in life, between 1956 and 1976, Sargent Shriver would play an important role in several Democratic National Conventions. He got his first taste of convention excitement, however, through the technical ingenuity of his brother, Herbert, in 1924. That year, the Democratic Convention was held in Madison

Square Garden, in New York City. The 1924 convention saw Al Smith, the Tammany Hall candidate who was governor of New York, competing for delegates with Southern-born William Gibbs McAdoo, the favorite son of the Ku Klux Klan. With the convention deadlocked, delegates looked to alternatives: John W. Davis, a conservative lawyer from West Virginia; Oscar Underwood, a senator from Alabama; and the Shrivers' friend Albert Ritchie, known as the great "wet hope" for his opposition to Prohibition. Unable to reach a decision, the convention stretched on for more than two weeks.

The Shrivers were not at the convention, but they followed its every twist and turn from their living room. Earlier that year, thirteen-year-old Herbert had bought a kit for a "7.2 superheterodyne receiver" radio. He assembled it himself, as Sarge looked on in wonder. In 1924 radios were still a rarity, so there were not many radio stations. But KDKA in Pittsburgh had just four years earlier become one of the first commercial stations, broadcasting for hundreds of miles around the eastern part of the United States. Herbert's giant receiver could pick up its transmission clearly. The first time Sarge heard a voice coming out of the machine, saying, "This is KDKA in Pittsburgh," he nearly fell over from astonishment.

During the 1924 convention, Herbert set up his radio in the living room, where it broadcast updates from the voting in New York twenty-four hours a day. The Shrivers and their neighbors took turns wearing the headphones and jotting down the latest delegate counts on a pad of paper. Everyone on the block, and all the local Democratic politicians, would gather in the Shriver living room, talking politics and waiting for the next round of voting. To nine-year-old Sarge, this was thrilling: the camaraderie and discussion, the suspense—who would come out ahead on the next ballot? It almost matched baseball for sheer excitement.

When Governor Ritchie fell out of contention, the Shrivers hoped Al Smith, the governor of New York, would be named the Democratic presidential nominee. Smith was a political hero to the family, not only because he was a Democrat who was firmly against Prohibition, but also because he was a Catholic— the first serious Catholic candidate in American national politics.

Although Smith's candidacy eventually fell short, his strong showing set the stage for him to try again in 1928. When he won the nomination that year, he announced that he would make his formal acceptance speech at the governor's mansion victory party in Albany a few weeks later. Hilda Shriver and her two sons traveled with Albert Ritchie to New York for the event. In a large room in the New York state house in Albany, where there were too few seats for everyone to sit down, thirteen-year-old Sarge watched Smith's acceptance speech with a mixture of pride and embarrassment from his perch on Governor Ritchie's lap. Afterward, Shriver and his cousin Mollie wandered among the cars parked outside of the state house, sticking chewing gum on any automobile without a Smith-for-President placard.

Alas, November 6, 1928, was a dark day in Catholic Democratic households across America. Herbert Hoover, campaigning on the prosperity of the Harding-Coolidge years, defeated Smith by more than 6 million votes. Worse, Smith had lost parts of the "Solid South," a Democratic stronghold since the Civil War, suggesting to expert observers that Catholicism had made him unelectable. This remained a political article of faith for thirty-two years, until Sargent Shriver's brother-in-law demolished it.

CHAPTER TWO

The Education of a Leader

Sargent Shriver began his education at the St. John's Catholic Parochial School, in downtown Westminster, where he was taught by nuns from the Sisters of Notre Dame de L'Amour, a French order. He would have continued at St. John's but a family feud at the B. F. Shriver company caused Robert Shriver to decide it was time to leave the cannery business and return to banking. By 1923 Sarge's family had sold the house on Willis Street and moved to a Georgian-style house at 641 University Parkway in Baltimore, when his father got a job as vice president of the Baltimore Trust Company. Sarge, beginning the third grade, was sad to leave Westminster, but Union Mills was only 28 miles away, so Pipe Creek picnics remained a regular part of his life.

In Baltimore, Sarge quickly settled into a comfortable routine. He attended the Cathedral School, which was affiliated with the Baltimore Cathedral, across the street, where he served as an altar boy. In the morning, Louise Carpentier would walk him the four blocks from his house to school. On his way home from school, when he was old enough to walk on his own, Sarge might stop to pick something up for his mother at Hopper McGraw's, a grocery store, or he would go across the street to browse in Remington's Books. His parents believed in the importance of reading and let their sons charge one book per week to the family account. Sarge read books from the Wizard of Oz series and plowed through all the Tom Swift books. He also loved the Dr. Doolittle books, reading and rereading until he had them nearly memorized.

Sarge's best friend during these years was an Italian boy named Emil Goristidi, whose family ran the Lexington Market; they sold fish caught fresh in the Chesapeake Bay. A German family, the Matthais, lived next door to the Shrivers; their two boys, Worth and Bruce, joined Emil and Sarge. Together, these four made the core of a gang, the Maryland Military Club, with Sarge as the ringleader. The Maryland Military Club would play baseball with other gangs on the field at Johns Hopkins University. After games they would walk to the local druggist for chocolate malted milks.

The highlight of living in Baltimore was baseball. As with just about everything in Maryland, the Shrivers were involved with the game from the beginning. The first national professional baseball league was established in the United States in 1857—and in 1860, Hervey Shriver became its vice president and first non–New York officer. Hervey, a cousin of Sarge's grandfather, had been the founding second baseman and the secretary of the Baltimore Excelsiors since 1859.

A half century after Hervey Shriver's career ended, Sarge Shriver began his life as a fan by following the Baltimore Orioles. In the 1920s, the Orioles played in the International League of the "High Minors," the equivalent of what today would be a Triple-A team. Sarge came of age at probably the best time in history to be an Oriole fan. Playing in Oriole Park, at the corner of Greenmount and Twenty-ninth Streets in Baltimore, the team went on a tear between 1919 and 1926, winning the International League pennant in seven consecutive years—more than any other team, in any other professional league, had ever won. Sarge went to as many games as he could, usually with his brother, his cousin Nick Shriver, and his family's driver, John Caesar, a tall, distinguished-looking African American. If Sarge ever received any stares for attending the game with a black man, he never noticed; he was too riveted by the game. Many spring and fall days through the 1920s, John Caesar would pick Sarge up at school at 2:30 and they would buy fifty-cent tickets and sit in the bleachers together, a tall black man and a slightly corpulent white boy, watching the great Lefty Grove pitch. Life was good.

In a stroke of bad timing, however, Robert Shriver and his colleague Eugene Norton decided the late winter of 1929 would be a good time to become founding partners of a new investment bank in New York. So the Shrivers sold their house in Baltimore and moved into a three-bedroom apartment in the Madison Hotel, at the corner of Sixty-ninth Street and Madison Avenue in Manhattan. Because it was late winter, Sarge immediately enrolled in the seventh grade at the Browning School, a private boys school just seven blocks up Madison Avenue. There, despite being the new kid, he soon asserted his leadership, launching Browning's first student newspaper and starring on the athletic fields.

Hilda and Robert continued the Catholic social work they had been doing in Baltimore. They worked with Richard Dana Skinner to found *Commonweal*, which remains today a distinguished progressive Catholic magazine. They also opened a Catholic bookstore, the St. Paul's Guild, on the north side of Fifty-seventh Street, between Park and Madison Avenues, an incongruously low-rent storefront among all the fancy clothing shops. Hilda ran the day-to-day operations and ordered the books for the shelves; Herbert and Sarge both helped out in the afternoons after school.

New York in the late 1920s still had a Jazz Age glimmer, although in retrospect this pleasant sheen obscured portents of the dark times to come. But for a while the halcyon days continued. The Shrivers lived a modestly glamorous existence, establishing themselves among Catholic society in the city; after a few months, they moved from the Madison Hotel to a brand-new apartment at 1215 Fifth Avenue, on the corner of 102nd Street. Soon after they arrived, a winter storm hit the city, covering the streets in a blanket of white. The roads were impassable. Sarge got his skis and trudged up to the apartment of some friends who lived on Park Avenue, and they spent a giddy afternoon skiing down the Park Avenue boulevard all the way from Ninetieth Street to the Waldorf-Astoria, some fifty blocks away.

On October 24, 1929, the stock market crashed and Robert Shriver's new investment firm was hit hard immediately. Hoping the downturn was temporary, Robert struggled to keep the company afloat. But his savings dwindled and he had to move his family to a smaller apartment, at 1170 Park Avenue, and then, not much later, to an even smaller apartment down the street at 1070 Park Avenue. The Shrivers remained residents of the Upper East Side, so they could still consider themselves part of upper-class Catholic society, but they were coming down in the world.

As the market fell further over the ensuing months, the economy slid into a depression, and in 1930 Robert Shriver's company went belly up. He and his partner soon signed on with another investment firm, the Cyrus J. Lawrence Company. But that firm, too, was ailing, and Robert moved on to yet another firm, Wickwire & Company. And then Robert Shriver went bankrupt.

Although Sarge's parents never said anything to him, he knew something was amiss. At night in bed, he could hear his parents talking in hushed, urgent voices about finances. His father, almost overnight, looked ten years older. Departed servants were not replaced; dinners became plainer and smaller, guests less frequent.

Coming home from school one day, Sarge found his mother sitting with her head in her hands, her forehead glistening with perspiration. She had gone down to Fifty-seventh Street on the bus to shop for groceries. At the store, she spent the few dollars she had left and did not have a nickel left over to catch a bus home. So she walked the thirty blocks, groceries in hand. Seeing his beloved mother, his existential anchor in this world, in this condition, made a profound impression on Sarge.

His father was hit even harder. Robert Shriver was a different man after 1929. Not having been in New York long enough to have the job security of some of his peers, Robert had to take a series of decreasingly important jobs on Wall Street. Over just a few months, he went from being a vice president of a big Baltimore bank and a man of influence in local politics to being a fifty-year-old hawker of stocks that no one any longer wanted to buy. The flow of distinguished guests to the Shriver household slowed to a trickle. Robert Shriver felt he was an embarrassment, a failure to himself and his family. He would live for twelve more years, long enough to see the Depression ending, but he would never fully recover from the crash.

The economy, spurred by massive military spending during World War II, eventually would recover, but not before Franklin Delano Roosevelt transformed American politics completely. By the time Roosevelt's presidential successor,

Harry S. Truman, left office in 1952, the size and functions of the US government had changed dramatically. From the minimalist government of the GOP-dominated Harding-Coolidge-Hoover era (when Calvin Coolidge could say, with only slight hyperbole, "If the Federal Government should go out of existence, the common run of people would not detect the difference in the affairs of their daily life for a considerable length of time"), FDR's New Deal fashioned a government juggernaut that millions of Americans relied on to subsidize their education, their livelihood during hard times, and their retirement in old age. FDR—with the help of the Depression that swept him into the Oval Office and the world war that happened while he occupied it—changed forever the US government's relationship with American citizens, with the American economy, with American business, with the American court system, and even with American culture.

Sarge Shriver was sixteen years old when FDR took office in March 1932. And with his strong bias for the prerogatives of local government, he was initially skeptical of the president's ambitious plans for the federal government. But the strain the Depression put on his parents became forever linked in Shriver's mind with the helpless, do-nothing approach of Herbert Hoover. And though he didn't recognize it at the time, his own politics were subtly changing. The influence of Governors Albert Ritchie and Al Smith remained evident (even as Sarge watched, chagrined, as Smith in his later years became a cranky, demagogic critic of the New Deal policies of his former protégé FDR); Shriver, to be sure, retained a healthy respect for states' rights. But as a witness to the 1930s and '40s, he gained a deep appreciation for the power of the government to help its citizens, particularly the least fortunate.

On September 24, 1930, Hilda and Robert dropped their younger son off at the Canterbury School in New Milford, Connecticut, where he was to begin the ninth grade. Canterbury was like many prep schools throughout western Massachusetts and Connecticut: an all-boys boarding school based on the English model (schools like Eton and Harrow) that aspired to provide a college preparatory curriculum for students who would soon be matriculating at primarily Ivy League schools. Canterbury was also—like nearby Westminster, Kent, South Kent, St. Mark's, St. Paul's, and St. George's, among others—religiously oriented: Although basically secular in its main course of instruction, it also strove to ground students in the moral tenets of a religious faith. But

Canterbury was almost unique among these schools in that it was Catholic; all other prep schools in the country at that time, save Portsmouth Priory, in Rhode Island, were strictly Protestant. Indeed in 1915, when Canterbury was founded, "the domain of American—and this meant particularly New England—classical education was a citadel of reserved culture, the breaching of which by any intimation of 'Popery' was unthinkable."

There were, of course, Catholic schools before 1915. But these institutions were run by religious orders, like the Jesuits or the Dominicans, who would not—as a matter of principle—prepare students to enter non-Catholic colleges such as those in the Ivy League; therefore the priests at these schools would not teach their students the knowledge required to pass the College Entrance Examination. The Ivy League colleges, for their part, refused to waive the requirement that students pass this examination, even for graduates of Catholic schools. "This was a stalemate from which neither side would move" until 1914, when a group of affluent Catholic immigrant families from New York and New England banded together to start what theretofore would have been an oxymoron: a Catholic college-preparatory school.

With money and advice from prominent Catholics across the country, the school was officially established on the grounds of a former girls school in the rolling hills of southwestern Connecticut, overlooking the Housatonic River. Named after England's famous Canterbury Cathedral, where the Catholic martyr and saint Thomas More had been archbishop, the school appointed as its first headmaster Dr. Nelson Hume, a man of stern moral bearing and diverse background. Hume had trained briefly to be a priest, then done stints in business and the theater, before finally settling on teaching as his metier.

On full scholarship, Robert and Hilda's sons (Herbert was also at Canterbury) did not cost them anything in tuition or room and board. For spending money, Sarge relied on a summer job at the B. F. Shriver cannery and on the occasional small allowance from his parents. His letters home during prep school and college reveal a constant need for money that he strives to balance with his acute awareness of his parents' own financial straits. "When I wrote my last letter," Sarge wrote to his parents in the spring of 1934, I hated to [ask for money]. I did not know where the money was coming from, but I hoped, and as usual you came through. . . . If we were worth millions, nothing you would have done would have been more appreciated. . . . Promise that if it will mean a hard struggle through all the summer, you will not send the money. If I thought that it was meaning a long summer for you, I know that I should not get much pleasure out of [my summer vacation]."

For the most part, Canterbury insulated Sarge from the tribulations of the Depression. As the 1930s progressed, Sarge could tell on his visits home that all was not well with his father—as his economic state continued to erode so did his emotional well-being. But at Canterbury itself, life was not much changed from the more halcyon, pre-crash days. The sons of Catholic affluence went to Mass, attended classes, played sports, and socialized under strictly circumscribed—almost Victorian—behavioral standards.

Shriver's parents visited him nearly every weekend during his first semester of boarding school. Noted alongside "Mr. and Mrs. Robert S. Shriver, of New York City" in the log of visitors to the school those first few weekends at Canterbury is another couple: "Mr. and Mrs. Joe P. Kennedy, of Bronxville, New York." Joe and Rose Kennedy were—like the Shrivers—the parents of a new Canterbury student that autumn, dropping off a second former (or eighth grader), John F. Kennedy, their second-eldest son. The crash had bankrupted Robert Shriver, but it had catapulted Joe Kennedy—who had taken short positions in the market—to vast wealth.

If a visitor to Canterbury in 1930–1931 had been asked to guess which boy, of Sarge Shriver and Jack Kennedy, would one day be president of the United States, he would surely have named the former. Although both Shriver and Kennedy appeared on the honor roll when first-term marks were posted that November 11, it would be just the first of many such appearances for Shriver, the sole one for Kennedy.

Academics aside, Shriver quickly established himself as a boy to watch, making the junior football squad as an end in the fall season and earning the starting catcher's position on the varsity baseball team during the spring season. Sarge was growing tall and fit, his physical stature catching up with his already charismatic presence. His classmates seemed naturally to gravitate to him. He was becoming a leader.

Jack Kennedy, in contrast, a year younger than Shriver, was small and wan and apparently unhappy. In his history of the school, Edward Mack, who taught history to both Shriver and Kennedy, recalled "little Jack Kennedy . . . a shock of auburn hair, a Boston accent, highly reserved and somewhat on the defensive, not quite certain of himself." Shriver watched Kennedy trying to play football without much strength or skillfulness.

Shriver knew Kennedy only slightly at Canterbury, but he could tell that his future brother-in-law did not like it there. Jack found the school too strict, too regimented—it didn't provide a ready outlet for the mischief that would later make him legendary at the Choate School. (*School Life at Canterbury,* a promotional catalog from the 1930s, says that "the kind of boys that attend Canterbury is another outstanding feature of the school. Boys that do not appreciate or respond to the idea of self-discipline are not kept in the school.") Although Kennedy came from an important family, he was neither athletically strong nor an academic standout, and he was not a boy of much status. He left after one year.

Unlike Jack, Sarge thrived in the regimented environment. He had attended Mass every day almost since birth, so the daily religious rituals were a comfort, not a burden, and the strictness of the faculty was nothing new to a boy who had previously been educated by the no-nonsense nuns at St. John's and the Cathedral School. He loved the camaraderie and the discipline, and he excelled academically, athletically, and socially.

The strict school discipline reflected the character of its headmaster. Hume believed in a correlation "between manners and virtues, between cleanliness and Godliness," and therefore demanded civilized comportment at all times from his students. A single instance of being late or untidily dressed—clothes (white shirt, dark suit, black shoes) clean and pressed, shoes shined, four-in-hand neatly tied—would result in the dreaded "days on bounds": A boy "on bounds" could not leave campus to go downtown.

Although there was no priestly religious instruction, and in fact no full-time chaplain on campus during Shriver's four years at Canterbury, Headmaster Hume ensured that the lay teaching of religion was woven into the curriculum. He personally taught the sixth formers a religion class, in which he tried to impress on the graduating seniors "the atmosphere of secularism, of agnostic indifference, of sectarian hostility which he knew they would encounter in non-Catholic colleges and universities."

In the 1930s, Canterbury advertised that students would acquire both "a reasonable knowledge of the doctrines of the faith" and a "love" of the "actual practice of the Christian faith." The boys would receive lessons "in doctrine, in morals, in ethics, in liturgy, in history, and in apologetics." Religion would

become, Canterbury promised, an integral part of its boys' natures, "a mould
of their characters, a firm foundation of their lives." An item in the February
17, 1931, school newspaper gives the flavor of how Canterbury may have been
somewhat different from other prep schools:

**School Hears Pope Speak—Time Taken from Classes to Hear
Radio Address of His Holiness**
Pope Pius XI was heard in a radio broadcast from Vatican City. The program was
heard on the radio in the common room of Middle House. . . . Although the boys
could not understand the Latin tongue as spoken by the Pope, few of them could
help being moved by the gravity and impressiveness of the occasion.

Beginning in 1932, during his junior year at Canterbury, weekends would often
find Shriver and his friends at the Noroton School of the Sacred Heart, a convent school in Connecticut where Shriver's first love, Eleanor Hoguet, was
enrolled.

In the 1930s, Eleanor's parents, Robert Louis Hoguet and his wife, Louise,
stood atop New York Catholic society. Robert was descended from an old
French Catholic family; his grandfather had made millions of dollars investing in real estate in Manhattan. Robert's father, in turn, had frittered many of
those millions away on bad investments and a spendthrift lifestyle. But Robert
Hoguet was cut from his grandfather's cloth. After graduating from Harvard
Law School, he diligently ascended through the ranks of New York law and
banking. He met Louise Lynch at a debutante party in 1902 and married her
in a Catholic ceremony in Paris in 1907. In 1927 the Hoguets took up residence
in grand style in an enormous brownstone at 45 East Ninety-second Street, just
around the corner from where the Shrivers would soon move.

By the 1930s Robert Hoguet had reached the empyrean of the New York
banking establishment. As president of the Emigrant Industrial Savings Bank
and as a board member of other important institutions, he commanded respect
within both the banking profession and Catholic social circles. When Hilda and
Robert Shriver moved to New York in 1929, they were quickly assimilated into
New York's Catholic society, much of which was centered on the Shrivers' local
church, St. Ignatius Loyola, at 980 Park Avenue. The Hoguets and Shrivers were
introduced to each other by one of the grandes dames of New York society,

Effie Wyatt (her extravagant full name was Euphemia Van Wenschler Wyatt), who in addition to running a fancy rooming house for single Catholic girls from the Midwest was a prominent drama critic. Before long, the Hoguets and the Shrivers were sitting on many of the same Catholic boards, working together to support *Commonweal* magazine, and working for the same charities and relief organizations. The two families soon became close.

The Hoguets had eight children, the seventh of whom, Eleanor, was born in 1918. Off at their respective boarding schools, Sarge and Eleanor did not meet until 1932, at a small dinner party at the Shrivers' apartment. Eleanor was initially intimidated by Sarge. She was only thirteen, somewhat timid and shy. Sarge was three years older, and tall and handsome. He talked with the adults as confidently as if they were his peers. Eleanor was struck on this first visit to the Shriver apartment by how big the furniture was relative to the size of the apartment. The Shrivers had brought with them all their furniture from their house in Baltimore, and as each successive apartment got smaller, the furniture seemed disproportionately bigger, more packed in. Sarge seemed that way, too—his presence was so large the apartment could hardly contain him. Before long, however, Sarge and Eleanor had become smitten with one another. They would remain romantically involved on and off for the next seven years.

As they became upperclassmen, Sarge and his friends from Canterbury would sometimes drive over to Noroton to surprise Eleanor and her schoolmates. Eleanor's best friend at Noroton was Kathleen Kennedy, Jack Kennedy's younger sister. Thus in visiting Eleanor at Noroton, Shriver continued a pattern established when he and Jack Kennedy had enrolled at Canterbury at the same time: orbiting in and out of the Kennedy family galaxy into which he was ultimately to fix his star.

Marriage, for the moment, was out of the question. Shriver had to finish his education, and Eleanor wanted to finish hers—and besides, there was the problem of money. Sarge didn't have any, and he was not inclined to propose as a pauper.

In the evenings, after a date, Sarge would walk Eleanor back to her family's brownstone on Ninety-second Street. The most distinctive feature of the home was a semicircular driveway running around the house to a garage in the back, which accommodated the Hoguet family Packard. Standing in the shadows on the long brick semicircular driveway that ran around the great house, Sarge and

Eleanor would say good night, talking softly and kissing. If the kissing went on too long, Eleanor's mother would begin banging on the window, ringing a bell, and yelling, "That's enough, Ellie! Good night, Sarge. Good *night*, Sarge!"

In the 1930s, New England prep schools joined together to form an organization called the Secondary School Society of International Cooperation (SSSIC). Each year students from a dozen schools would gather in the spring for a meeting to talk about international relations. Guest speakers would lecture for a few hours, and then all the delegates from the various schools would break into smaller groups to talk about how better cooperation among nations might be achieved.

In the spring of 1934 the SSSIC meeting was to be held at a girls school, Avon-Old-Farms, in Avon, Connecticut. The Canterbury headmaster, Nelson Hume, who knew that Shriver's charisma would reflect well on the school, asked if he would serve as the school's senior delegate to the SSSIC and deliver a fifteen-minute speech to the meeting on the League of Nations. The text of the speech Shriver gave that Sunday at Avon-Old-Farms is lost to history, but the response to it is not.

"Dear Mr. Shriver," Nelson Hume wrote to Sarge's father,

Sargent did such a good job for us today at the meeting of the S.S.S.I.C. that I think that you and Mrs. Shriver should share the pleasure that I had when I heard a report. . . . Sargent had written the paper and prepared himself under great diffi- culties, for he was very busy with his lessons, "The Tabard" [the school newspaper, of which Sarge served as editorial chief], and the captaincy of the baseball team. . . . Well, apparently he ran away with the meeting. . . . He was the last speaker called upon . . . and he was greeted at the end with a real round of sincere applause. Then, according to custom, a discussion of his ideas began from all over the hall. . . . Sargent didn't falter a bit, and answered questions from all sides without any hesitation. Later in the afternoon, Mr. Riddle, a former ambassador to Russia, whose money was responsible for the founding of [Avon-Old-Farms], came around . . . and said that he wanted to meet Sargent and congratulate him on the fine show- ing he had made in his speech in the morning. . . . [This] was evidence of a fine impression having been made by the boy on a mature man.

This may be a little incident in the general school life but it is an important indication and shows that Sargent has a good deal of courage and determination, for it took both to go up in front of that meeting and make such a good impression. There was no question that his performance reflected a good deal of credit on his school.

A week or so later, Hume summoned Shriver to his office after dinner. When Shriver got to Hume's office, the headmaster was waiting for him with a middle-aged woman. After Hume made introductions, during which Sarge learned that the woman came from a foundation in Massachusetts that gave money to international causes, the woman turned to Sarge. "Sargent," she said to him, as he recalled it, "I was at the SSSIC the other week, and I was *very* impressed with your speech on the League of Nations and the importance of international cooperation." Shriver beamed. The woman continued, "Have you ever heard of the Experiment in International Living?"

Three years earlier, in 1931, Donald Watt, a thirty-eight-year-old Pennsylvania Dutchman hailing originally from Lancaster, Pennsylvania, had conceived a simple idea that he believed would foster peace among nations: If young people from different countries could be exposed to other cultures, folkways, lifestyles, values, and attitudes, the mutual understanding that would be generated would inhibit war. This was neither an isolated nor an original idea. The air after the Great War was thick with schemes to prevent future such conflicts; many religious groups, in particular, had espoused such ideas for decades, if not centuries. But Watt was convinced that by putting this simple idea—having young people of different national cultures interact deeply with one another—into practice on a small scale and then letting it spread, it would lead ultimately to, as the novelist Pearl Buck, a great supporter of the program, was later to put it, "peace on earth, goodwill toward men."

Calling his program the Experiment in International Living, Watt brought together a group of German boys and a group of American boys at a camp in the Swiss Alps over the summer of 1932. Although he succeeded in cementing some friendships among the boys, Watt found the camp environment too artificial, too divorced from the real German life that he wanted his American youth to experience. So the following year, he placed participants (now consisting of boys and girls) in the homes of German families, where they could experience life as it was actually lived in a foreign culture. Soon there were groups of Experimenters living with families all over Europe, as well as in South America and India.

In the spring of 1934, the Experiment was still in its germinal stages, and Watt and his associates were recruiting American students who they thought would represent the United States well. The first groups of students to go overseas with the Experiment were required to have some background in the German language and to pay a $360 fee. In the spring of 1934, however, Sargent Shriver had neither any training in German nor, certainly, $360. But that, said the woman now sitting across from him in Nelson Hume's office, didn't matter. Based on his performance at the SSSIC, she said, Shriver was exactly the sort of boy they were looking for. Her foundation, which had helped launch the Experiment, would pay his fee. And the German requirement would be waived—he would just have to pick up as much German as he could on the ten-day passage across the Atlantic.

Shriver was thrilled at the opportunity. So a few days after his graduation from Canterbury, Shriver set sail from New York with a group of eighteen other young men and women. Dr. Elizabeth Zorb, a young professor of German from Vassar College who had traveled extensively abroad, was the group's director, and each day she led her charges through several hours of intensive German instruction. Shriver spent the summer living with a host family in Backnang, in the southeast corner of Germany, just north of Stuttgart.

Shriver's summer in Germany had a powerful formative effect on him. It exposed him to a new language, to a culture older than American history, and to a way of life different from his own. As William Peters wrote in his 1957 history of the Experiment in International Living, "The summer made a tremendous impression on [Shriver], gave him, in essence, a new view of the world, and sent him back to school . . . with new goals and a deeper understanding of the profits of scholarship." He would head to Yale that fall, filled with the spirit of international cooperation and global fellowship.

CHAPTER THREE

A Yale Man

⌒

B ack home in the United States in the fall of 1934, Shriver began college
at Yale University. During his years at Canterbury, Sarge had variously
considered Yale, Princeton, and the University of Maryland, but he ultimately
decided on Yale because, at least in Canterbury's Connecticut-centric universe, that institution was considered to be simply the best. (Canterbury sent
more graduates to Yale each year than to any other college.) There was, too,
an ineffable set of personal characteristics associated with a "Yale Man" in
those days; Shriver had read the novels of F. Scott Fitzgerald, in whose tax-
onomy of Ivy League men, Princeton's and Yale's stood far above Harvard's.
So in September, just back from his first summer in Germany, Shriver drove
with his mother to New Haven, where he and four of his Canterbury classmates were to begin their college careers.

Having been a very big man on a very small campus at prep school, Shriver
felt lost in the vaster landscape of a university. "It seems as though I have been
here a long time although it is only a week," he wrote home to his parents after
arriving. "I still feel like a fish out of water, and most of all I miss the intimacy

of Canterbury. I fear that it is going to take me some time to catch on to the college method of learning."

But Shriver did well in his classes, and he dove into a broad panoply of activities. Before his freshman year was out, he had joined the Elizabethan Club, a literary society; Delta Kappa Epsilon, a fraternity; the St. Thomas More Society, a Catholic organization in which Shriver served as secretary; and the freshman baseball team, for whom he played second base. He also began systematically reading through the complete works of Thomas Aquinas, which he had discovered in the Yale library.

To outward appearances he was thriving, but Shriver continued to find himself plagued by self-doubt. At Canterbury, he had been one of the best at just about everything: the best baseball player, a top student, the most accomplished debater, the captain of the football team, the editor of the school paper, the headmaster's favorite. At Yale, he was no longer the best at anything: There were better ballplayers, better debaters—and dozens of better students. This provided a bracing dose of humility to a young man who, in the years since he had set up the Maryland Military Club as an elementary school student, had automatically become a leader wherever he went.

As a freshman, Shriver also "heeled" for the *Yale Daily News*, the oldest college daily in the country. Freshmen seeking to become staff writers for the *Daily News* would join as cub reporters under the supervision of senior editors, and they would receive points in categories like writing ability, initiative, and dependability. The top point-getters would become members of the junior editorial board for the remainder of their freshman year and then join the senior board in their sophomore year. Shriver was named to the junior board in his first semester at Yale; in his sophomore year he was voted *Daily News* chairman. This was a position of great prestige on campus, equivalent to being captain of the football team or president of the class. The job also paid him several hundred dollars per year, helping to alleviate the strain of paying his way through college.

Money troubles were a recurring theme throughout his undergraduate and law school years. He was constantly in debt to the school's treasurer, struggling to make payments through a combination of scholarships, his father's meager earnings, gifts from rich Catholic friends, and money generated through jobs in the summer and the school year.

Worry about money was a constant refrain in letters home between 1934 and

1940. Expressions of concern for his parents' financial situation alternated with requests for money from them. "If by any chance you all are worried about these bills of mine up here, you can forget them," he wrote late in his freshman year. "What with the money I expect to make this summer and advances on my 'News' salary, if necessary, I can easily meet all of my bills myself. . . . If things turn out correctly, I should be able to contribute about $800 toward my maintenance next year." When his parents lacked the money to pay their rent, Sarge would send them what little he had. The constant worry about finances drove Sarge to wax philosophical. "Money means so awfully, awfully little to me" in comparison with higher values, he wrote to his mother after she had lamented that she and Robert could not provide him with more money for his education. My generation, Shriver wrote, is "tired of seeing the most honorable people we know, people like you & Dad, worn down by an inhuman and impossible struggle."

Two related facts exacerbated Shriver's vexed relationship to money. His family, like many affluent middle-class banking families who saw their net worth evaporate in the crash, had to struggle to retain their upper-middle-class existence and identity and social connections but without upper-middle-class money. Plenty of Americans (sharecroppers in the South, farmers in the dustbowl) were in circumstances far more dire, but the Shrivers nonetheless had to struggle mightily to pay rent, put food on the table, and put their sons through college. More than that, they struggled with what their financial decline in the world implied for their social standing.

Life at Canterbury and at Yale was relatively insulated from the effects of the Depression. For although the families of some of Shriver's friends were hurt by the Depression, many more hailed from high enough in the economic strata to be spared the hardships visited upon the rest of the country. As a scholarship student, living within fairly straitened financial limits, Shriver was, among his friends, somewhat of an unusual case. To keep up with them, he often found himself living beyond his means.

This compounded his peculiar relationship to money and class. His background was the Maryland Catholic aristocracy; his education was upper class; his friends were upper class—many of them extremely wealthy. And Shriver himself—with his fine clothes, skillful squash game, and friends in high places—lived a very upper-class existence: Ivy League education; weekends at extravagant house parties in Rhode Island, Massachusetts, or Long Island; European tours; escort at debutante balls. One weekend at Yale, he idly expressed an interest in playing golf but lamented that with all the work he had to do he hadn't the time to spare to get to a course. No sooner had he mentioned this than his friend Nick Frauchot proposed that they take his private plane and fly out to the links for a round—which they did.

Clearly, this was not a lifestyle of great hardship. Yet to sustain life in this high style required a combination of hard work (at all the various jobs he worked to generate income); uncomfortable reliance on the generosity of his rich friends; the carrying of debt; continuous negotiation with his parents about what bills should be paid first from the scant funds available; and constant anxiety about money.

This worry fueled Shriver's ambition to make a financial success of himself, so that he might lift himself and his parents above the wearying stress about how to pay the next month's rent or laundry bill. Whereas many of his friends were ambitious in their own way, wanting to make something of themselves in the world, their easier relationship to money allowed them more insouciant college careers: When they graduated, opportunity would simply await them. Shriver felt constantly driven to create his own opportunities. This clearly worried his mother. As he began his final semester of college he wrote to her, "You seem to feel sometimes, if not always, that I've turned into a self-contained, success-mad youngster. It's only that I've got a dream that hard work & application may give us" a place in the country, where the whole Shriver family could relax and be together.

Before his sophomore year, it looked for a time as though Shriver might have to withdraw from Yale because he could not afford it. "I must tell you," Yale treasurer George Day wrote to Sarge, "how much it means to all of us to have you make these payments at your first opportunity. . . . I shall hope with you that the award of the Samuel R. Betts fellowship of $1000 to you for this coming year, together with such additional funds as many come to you from the *Yale Daily News* and from your vacation earnings will enable you to carry on successfully your work here at Yale."

Back in New Haven in the autumn of 1935, Shriver moved to Pierson, one of Yale's residential colleges, where he inhabited Suite 1457, part of a block of rooms across two entry halls, with his friends Ed Bailly, Donald Keefe, Tom

Thatcher, John Woolsey, and Richard Day. With their friend Burton Maclean, the group made up the social epicenter of the Yale class of 1938. Shriver's suite in Pierson became a lively ongoing salon, where the problems of the world were discussed (and putatively solved). Hilda and Robert often sent the latest issue of *Commonweal* for Shriver and his friends to dissect.

In a letter to his parents later that year, Shriver described one of Yale's peculiar social rituals.

Tap Day was the outstanding event on yesterday's program. (Tap Day is the name given to the afternoon on which Senior Societies select their members from the Junior class.) All of the Juniors who think they have a chance stand around one of the Elm trees in Branford courtyard. While they are standing thus, huddled like wind-beaten sheep in a herd, the various fortunates of the Senior class, representing the societies that are tapping, lurk around, wandering in and out, always seeming to search for one particular person. Sometimes these members will walk around & around for as long as twenty minutes. Then suddenly, as if seized by divine inspiration, they will issue forth from behind someone, reach high into the air, and whack some poor, unsuspecting Junior a terrific blow on the shoulder, all the while spitting out the sonorous, "Go to your room."

The Junior decides immediately whether to cast his social lot as a Yale man with the society the tapper represents. If he does not, he merely stands still; if he does he sets off running to his own room where he is told when he may next meet the brotherhood en masse. The whole proceedings start exactly at five and finish exactly at six, the bells in Harkness Tower being used as starting and finishing guns. While the custom is exciting, it must be nerve-wracking for the Juniors & tragic for those who do not get what they wish or nothing at all. Essentially it is a rather barbaric custom but one that has its compensation. From what I understand, the three leading societies, Skull & Bones, Scroll & Key, and Wolf's Head, are the three wealthiest corporations in Connecticut.

The following spring, as a junior, Shriver himself endured this "barbaric custom." He was tapped by Scroll and Key, who would pay his senior year tuition.

In January of his sophomore year, Shriver ascended to the senior board of the *Yale Daily News*, which provided him a regular outlet for expressing his political views. "We begin work on the twentieth," he wrote his parents, "and from then on I'll be writing edits at least once a week. Prepare for the call to arms!" Shriver's ascension to the chairmanship of the *Daily News* the following January was reported in the *New York Times*, alongside a handsome picture of the college junior. "Robert S. Shriver, Jr., Takes Over Yale News" the *Times* headline declared.

It was a tradition at the *News* that each successive editorial board would begin its regime with a modest, one-column "Opening Editorial" saluting the previous board and quietly promising to expand on past goals. Shriver's first editorial—on January 25, 1937—was neither modest nor quiet: two full columns long, it boldly declared "in categorical terms" what would be the *News*'s "mental point-of-view" over the coming year. The only quiet note was a prefatory epigraph to his parents: *"To Mother and Dad, whose constant interest and loving guidance alone have made this editorial possible. From their loving son, Sargent."* Beyond that, everything was declamatory.

After briskly complimenting his predecessors for their work in "consolidating" many changes that had begun to be put into effect in earlier years, Shriver moved on to state his board's aims. "We shall be opinionated in the finest sense of that much despised word," he declared, and then defined the five categories by which the editorial board under his leadership would identify itself. Those categories are revealing.

"First, therefore, we are Christians," he began. "We wish to go on record as having no more preference for Godless Communism than for the adoration of the gods of the twentieth century, the saviors of humanity and preservers of culture, Hitler, Mussolini, and their ilk. We oppose their authoritarian or totalitarian states in any form." Second, he wrote, we are "democratists:—By that we assert our belief that democracy is the only order of society where even the possibility of free thought exists." Third, "in education we are Aristotelians," by which he meant that he opposed any efforts to roll back the more stringent academic requirements imposed by Yale's president.

Fourth, Shriver wrote, "we are Americans. The tradition of a government directly responsible to its people, the people's conviction that they in turn are responsible one to another as well as to their Maker, the realization that our standard of living is and will be the result of our productive powers—these are the qualities of America most worthy of our continued preservation."

And finally, "Fifth and last we are optimists:—In other words, we believe that things can be accomplished; that those who have ideals and are willing to work for them can often attain their ambitions; in short, that the world is not too much with us but by sincere and untiring effort can be made a better place to live in."

"There is a delight in accepting responsibility in a world of men who shun it," Shriver concluded. Shriver was barely twenty years old when he wrote these words—but his character had been formed at an early age. A Christian, a Democratist, an Aristotelian, an American, and an optimist: Shriver was ostensibly writing of his editorial board's point of view when he chose these terms, but the constellation of categorizations is pure Shriver, right down to the boldly declamatory tone.

THE NAZI MENACE

Donald Watt, the director of the Experiment in International Living, had been impressed with Shriver when he met the young Catholic on his visits to Germany in 1934, and so in 1936 he invited Sarge to visit Germany again, this time as an "assistant leader" of a group of Experimenters. Since being an assistant leader meant having his way paid, plus a small stipend, Shriver happily signed on.

Although his first trip to Germany had gained him valuable experience, it was—in the context of the second trip—an experience of a blessedly innocent kind. In January 1933, sixteen months before Shriver was first to set foot on German soil, Adolf Hitler had become Germany's chancellor. When Shriver had lived in Backnang in the summer of 1934, the Nazi Party's reach did not yet extend all over the country and had not penetrated fully to the individual family level. Thus Shriver could spend a whole summer happily oblivious to Hitler's growing impact on the country.

The difference two years made was striking. Indeed, as the world began to perceive that Hitler was a menace, many critics tried to argue Donald Watt into suspending the Experiment's programs in Germany. But Watt declined to bow to this pressure, telling his critics: "If your real interest is in peace, you do not turn your back on the first person you meet who disagrees with you. If you want to make peace, start to create understanding where your misunderstanding is greatest."

Shriver's group in 1936 consisted of nine college students, plus himself and Professor Zorb. Zorb had also recruited a friend from the University of Bonn to help with the teaching. Dr. Willy Kramp, twenty-seven years old that

summer, met the students at the port in Cuxhaven, on the northwestern coast of
Germany, and accompanied them on the train to Hamburg. Kramp took the
group sightseeing in Hamburg, but Shriver's attention was riveted on all the men
in uniform. In 1934 Shriver had seen the occasional Nazi swastika or picture of
Hitler; now they were everywhere. Every boy under eighteen wore a Nazi arm-
band; half of the adult men Shriver saw did, too. Parades marched continuously
through the streets, with soldiers goose-stepping in ramrod-straight formation.
Labor brigades of young men marched to work with picks and shovels. With
Kramp's assistance, Shriver was soon able to distinguish the SS from the SA, and
the SA from the Hitler Youth. Kramp became one of Shriver's two principal
guides through the snarled thickets of German politics that summer.

Shriver's other guide was Herr Schrimpf, the father of the host family he
stayed with in Weimar. Mr. Schrimpf was a Social Democrat who had at one
time been active in Weimar politics but had been forced into quiescence by the
rise of National Socialism. The Schrimpfs sensed that the end of freedom was
coming fast. They cut the family paintings out of their frames, rolled them up,
and inserted them behind the bricks of the chimney—they didn't want their
most prized possessions to be seized by the Nazis. At night, in his room on the
second floor of the Schrimpfs' house, Shriver would listen to the soldiers
goose-stepping past on the street below and shudder at what the sound fore-
bode for Germany.

Two other experiences crystallized Shriver's sense of the sickness in the
German soul that summer. In Weimar, Shriver attended Mass every Sunday at
the local Catholic parish. There, he took note of something he had also seen
two summers earlier in the Catholic Church near Backnang: the almost complete absence in the congregation of men between the ages of thirty and fifty.
When he saw a memorial with a long list of names at the back of the church,
he understood why: The Great War of 1914–1918 had decimated an entire generation of European men. Surely, he thought, Germany would never be so foolhardy as to subject its population to such mortal devastation again.

In 1936, however, as compared with two summers earlier, there were very
few people of *any* age or gender at Mass. A comment by one of the parishioners
confirmed his fear. The parishioner sidled up to Shriver after the service and
said in a hushed tone, "Thank you for coming to Mass this morning."

"I always attend Mass on Sundays," Shriver said.

The parishioner pulled him aside, away from the hearing of the congregation. "You don't understand. Many of our parishioners are now afraid to go to church. Members of the congregation who are too 'enthusiastic' about the Catholic religion get picked up by the Nazis. Last week, two local priests were taken away to a camp."

Shriver didn't know exactly what a "camp" was, but the basic meaning of what the man had told him was clear. Catholics were being persecuted, along with Jews and Communists, for what they believed.

Once, on an afternoon drive, the Schrimpfs' automobile rolled past what looked like a big farmhouse, partly concealed behind a tall, yellow stucco wall. Shriver asked what was behind the wall.

"That is Buchenwald, a work camp," said Schrimpf.

"Slow down, so we can see it," said Shriver.

"I don't dare," said Schrimpf, accelerating ahead.

Rounding a corner, they passed the front gate. Nazi soldiers with guns stood on either side of it. Through the gate, Shriver could for a moment see up to the big house. "Can't we please stop by the gate and look in?" he asked.

"It is not good to show curiosity about such things," said Schrimpf. But he agreed to drive past the camp again in the other direction. "This time," according to William Peters's account, "as they neared the gate, a group of perhaps fifty men in denim work clothes, their shaved heads bare to the sun, marched four abreast, guarded by soldiers. As the car passed, the men turned from the road into the open gate."

The image of those men seared itself into Shriver's consciousness. He would never forget their shaved heads, how they marched four abreast, not permitted to look to the left or the right, only straight ahead.

"Who are they?" he asked Schrimpf, gesturing toward the men.

"Those are political prisoners," Schrimpf replied, "people who did not agree with Herr Hitler and were not careful enough about who knew it."

As Buchenwald faded into the distance behind them, Shriver lapsed into silence. There was nothing to say. This was thousands of miles away from his happy-go-lucky life at Yale, but it felt a lot farther away than that. He had grown to love the German countryside, love the German people, in his two summers abroad—but he was of the growing conviction that the United States, if it knew what was good for it, would keep a prudent distance from the affairs of Europe.

Back in New Haven in the fall, when Shriver thought of the summer just past, his first memory was always of his host father, Herr Schrimpf, peering anxiously out from the back porch into the yard behind, scanning for Nazi spies. "There were two worlds in Germany that summer," William Peters wrote. "The unhealthy world of repression, uniforms and suspicion and the healthy world of green forests, German songs, and Goethe. Shriver was never quite able to reconcile the two in his mind."

INNOCENCE LOST

The summer of 1937 once again saw Shriver heading off to Europe, this time as a crew member on a cruise liner, where his primary responsibility consisted of keeping wealthy vacationers happy on their travels through the Mediterranean. Shriver was accompanied on this trip by his friend Greg Smith, who with his brother Gerard had been a few years ahead of Shriver both at Canterbury and at Yale. Shriver had enjoyed spending weekends with the Smith brothers at the lavish Long Island estate of their father, John Thomas Smith, who was the general counsel for General Motors and a fixture of New York's Catholic society. Over the next six weeks Sarge and Greg enjoyed a grand tour of southeastern Europe: Italy, Greece, Yugoslavia, Asia Minor.

In the Mediterranean, swaddled in the luxury of the *Odyssey*, Shriver perceived the specter of authoritarianism and war to be at a greater remove than it had been the previous summer in Weimar. Even in southern Europe, however, signs of the gathering storm would at times cloud the horizon: the German fleet off the coast of Portugal; the rebel Spanish airplane, manned by three men carrying conspicuous machine guns that circled the *Odyssey* as it approached Gibraltar; the houses nestled against the Rock of Gibraltar, "armed to every last inch . . . threatened by the German and Italian occupation of the African Pillar of Hercules," as Shriver wrote to his parents; Mussolini, *Il Duce* himself, recent conqueror of Ethiopia, speaking from Palermo over the radio while the Florentines gathered around cafés where "public radios blare forth the leader's words."

But these small harbingers did not disturb Shriver's relaxed equanimity. Only the usual angst over money clouded his mood. "I'm afraid I'll have to have some money in Rome," he wrote his parents. "I have about $85 in Lira & no

American money. . . . Laundry and pressing has made inroads I never anticipated; so, if possible, I wish you could send me something in Rome. But please don't worry about it! For if you can't manage it comfortably I can probably borrow some from Gregory & I can pay him back in the fall."

In the end, Smith subsidized most of Shriver's expenses. "Gregory is doing all in his power to make everything financially easy for me," Sarge wrote to his parents. "I'm going to pay him a lump sum covering the whole business & being no more than I should have spent had I traveled as cheaply as possible. He goes where he wishes & I pay what I can, & he takes care of the remainder. Isn't that generous of him? So don't worry about me: I'm in good company!"

Eleanor Hoguet had also gotten free passage across the Atlantic by serving on a different steamship as a librarian that summer and was traveling in Italy with her brother Joe.

Greg and Sarge arrived in Florence on August 16. Joe and Eleanor arrived the following day. On the evening of August 17, Sarge and Eleanor met privately for dinner. They had been courting more or less continuously for five years now. Eleanor had had other boyfriends over that period, but Sarge was, for almost all of that time, her "number one beau." Shriver, too, had entertained numerous admiring girlfriends over the years, but Eleanor was first in his heart. Over the years Sarge and Eleanor had expressed great affection for one another, but they had never had sexual relations.

Sargent Shriver, indeed, had never had sexual intercourse, nor would he until a relationship had been blessed by the sacrament of marriage. His devout Catholicism would not permit it. Although not sanctimonious in his conviction, Shriver had never wavered in his belief that sex outside of marriage was sinful; this was what he believed on the night of August 17, 1937, in Florence.

Sarge and Eleanor had dinner at a Florentine restaurant, recounting their European travels, exchanging news and gossip about mutual friends from the States, and talking about politics. But Sarge could tell something was amiss. When he walked Eleanor back to the apartment where she was staying, he asked her if anything was bothering her.

Eleanor was always a little shy, but she was also direct and courageous and when confronted with this question, as Shriver recalled, she looked him in the eye and conceded that something was wrong. She explained that being out of the convent in France and traveling around Europe with her brother had made her feel free and different somehow, more adventurous. She had met an American soldier, she told him, and had briefly fallen in love with him. Her relationship with the soldier was now ended—but before it had, she said, they had slept together.

Sarge felt as though he had been punched in the stomach. Stoically, without (he hoped) betraying how miserable he felt, he thanked her for telling him, told her that he still cared for her a great deal, and that he would see her tomorrow. He said good night and then exited briskly, closing the door behind him. Once in the hallway he ran to the balustrade and vomited out onto the street below, his convulsing gut a direct register of the emotional trauma he felt. His respect for Eleanor never wavered. Nor, in some sense, did his deep, abiding affection for her. But something in him changed that night and he knew that he would never marry her.

Greg and Sargent and the Hoguets spent five more days together in Florence before Greg and Sargent headed to Rome. During this time Shriver maintained a jaunty front; inside, however, he felt a great sense of loss, and he prayed for succor. ("I seem to have recouped some of my lost ability to pray," he wrote home on August 22, "and you can be sure St. Peter and St. Paul will get the works from me" in Rome.)

Sarge and Eleanor remained close friends. Their families, too, remained close, and Shriver concealed from even his closest friends how that evening in Florence had caused a rending of something within him. But one day Eleanor's mother came over to the Shrivers' apartment and asked Sargent to take a walk with her in Central Park. "Sarge," he recalls her saying to him, "you've been going out with my daughter for quite a long while now. Are you interested in marrying her?"

He knew what Mrs. Hoguet was driving at. In the 1930s the socially appropriate course of action for a woman of Eleanor's background was to marry soon after completing her education, if not before. Although Shriver's parents had fallen on hard times during the Depression, the Hoguets considered them a good Catholic family, and they perceived Sarge to be a young man with good prospects. They would have been very happy to have him marry their daughter. But if he wasn't going to marry Eleanor, Mrs. Hoguet implied, he should make that clear so she could marry somebody else.

Shriver responded that he had been interested in marrying Eleanor but that something had come up which now made it unlikely he would ever propose.

Mrs. Hoguet received the news with a look of stern disapproval, but then she thanked him for his candor and went home. Eleanor—who had been told by her father that she had one year to marry upon graduating from Manhattanville College if she did not want to get a job—began entertaining other suitors more seriously, even as Sarge continued to hang somewhat diffidently around. In the winter of 1941, after spending time in the hospital recovering from an operation for phlebitis, Eleanor announced her engagement to Paul DeGive, a young banker who had starred as a hockey goalie at Harvard. Paul and Eleanor were married in October 1941—Ensign Sargent Shriver, US Navy, was in attendance—and in 2001 they celebrated their sixtieth wedding anniversary. The night before her wedding, Eleanor regretfully burned all her letters from Sarge. But for years thereafter, Shriver and Eleanor continued to correspond fondly, in the manner of long-ago paramours and longtime friends.

In the fall of 1937 Shriver returned to New Haven to conclude his final year as a Yale undergraduate. Early that semester, still greatly shaken by his meeting with Eleanor in Florence, he wrote an affecting note to his parents.

> You will never know till you're in Heaven what you've meant to me, both of you. I can't ever tell you how much courage you've given me when I needed it most, how your example has been & is today the strength that keeps me moving forward. At times, when I have been lonely, yes, in Europe & at Yale, when I've felt there was no one standing with me and things were difficult . . . my thoughts have gone out to you & my knowledge of what you are. When I've felt that between God & me there was one great mighty space . . . then in those times you have been with me, guiding me, encouraging me, leading me right. You have never been physically with me at such a time, & it's impossible that a parent could be. But always when the cards were down & the pressure was on, when there was no escape and facts had to be faced, then the memory of your [model] lives was everything to me. God & his saints, though it may be sacrilegious to say it, were nothing to me in comparison to the positive, tangible example of true & righteous & happy living that you have given me.

As always, Shriver turned to his faith for consolation, spending much of his time working with Father T. Lawrason Riggs, the Catholic chaplain at Yale, to build the membership of the St. Thomas More Society. Like Shriver's father a Protestant convert, Riggs came from an old Maryland banking family who were friendly with the Shrivers. Heavyset and heavy-drinking, Riggs was a man of many talents—he was, among other things, a philosopher, a theologian, a singer, a writer, a wit, and a dramatist (in 1914, he had co-written a musical with Cole Porter). He was also, through access to his family's banking fortune, a man of considerable means. He used his money to buy a stately home in New Haven, which—because Yale had no Catholic chapel or student center when Shriver enrolled in the mid-1930s—served as the gathering place for the university's Catholic students. Riggs hosted regular Bible discussion sessions, and he would say Mass and hear confessions in his private chapel. Beginning in his junior year, Shriver spent as much time as he could at the home of this colorful, orotund priest.

Together, Shriver and Riggs established an annual ecumenical congress at Yale that would bring Catholics and Protestants together (along with the few Jews around) to discuss religious issues and to make common cause against what they perceived as the spread of secularism on campus and in the world at large.

As a result of Shriver's recruitment drive for the More Society in 1937, club membership doubled to 155 undergraduates, becoming (as Sarge wrote to his parents) "the largest Catholic Club in Yale history." For Shriver, the highlight of the More Society's activities in 1938 was the invitation to his heroine, Dorothy Day, the great Catholic social activist, for a Communion breakfast. Day's passion for social justice helped inspire much of the political, social, and religious work Shriver would do in the 1950s and 1960s.

As he finished his last set of final exams in May, Shriver wrote to his parents, "That ends little Sarge's undergraduate days, & on Friday he's going to pack books & rugs & clean up." Shriver's enjoyment of the final weeks of his undergraduate career was marred by concern for his father, who had suffered a heart attack and been admitted to Doctor's Hospital on the East River, where he remained for some time.

LAW SCHOOL

Upon graduation from college in June 1938—with a degree cum laude in English literature—Shriver's plan had been to enroll in Yale Law School the following autumn. But neither Shriver nor his parents had any money at all; law school, therefore, was out of the question. Through his college classmate Mac Muir Jr., whose father was the editor-in-chief of *Newsweek* magazine, Sarge approached that publication about getting an editorial job. He planned to live at home and supplement his family's income.

But when Greg and Gerard Smith learned about this, they told their father, John Thomas Smith, who called Shriver and asked him to come to Smith's Manhattan office for a talk. When Shriver arrived in Smith's office, Smith said that he had heard Shriver had decided not to attend law school. "If you could pay for law school, would you go?" Shriver recalled Smith asking. When Shriver said that he would, Smith declared that he would pay for whatever tuition and living expenses were not covered by scholarships and other funds.

Barely a week later Shriver was back in New Haven, readying himself to begin his first year of law school. It was too late for him to obtain a room on campus, so he and a classmate named Hart Spiegel, who was also enrolling late, rented a small apartment in downtown New Haven, just above a barbershop and a cheap diner. All year long, Shriver and Spiegel inhaled the aroma of grilling meat and aftershave as they studied the statutes.

If Shriver had had reason to be intimidated in his first year of college, he had even more reason to be intimidated in his first year of law school. Yale Law School's class of 1941 included a remarkable, perhaps unique, array of talent. Yale Law '41 produced, among others, Sargent Shriver; Gerald Ford, who would serve as House minority leader, vice president, and president of the United States; Cyrus Vance, who would serve as deputy director of defense under President Lyndon Johnson and as secretary of state under President Carter; Walter Lord, who would become a best-selling writer, the author of *A Night to Remember*, about the sinking of the *Titanic*; Peter Dominick, who would become a senator from Colorado; Raymond Shafer, who would serve as the lieutenant governor of Pennsylvania; William Scranton, who would become governor of Pennsylvania; Stanley Resor, who would serve as secretary of the army under LBJ; Richardson Dilworth, who would become president of the Rockefeller Foundation; and Potter Stewart and Byron "Whizzer" White, who would both become Supreme Court justices.

"Whizzer" White joined Shriver's class late in the first semester, having spent the early part of the fall playing pro football for the Detroit Lions. Sarge and his friend Bob Stuart, seeing White's prowess on the football team and finding him to be a very agreeable fellow, took it upon themselves to help White adjust to the rigors of law school life and to assist him with his academic work. White politely submitted to what Shriver and Stuart thought were patient and helpful explanations of the common law. But when the first semester's marks came out, White was at the top of the class—and Shriver and Stuart were struggling along in the bottom third. From that point on, Stuart and Shriver sought out White for academic assistance, not the other way around.

The class's other future Supreme Court justice, Potter Stewart, initially had trouble keeping up academically with his peers. Situated between Bob Stuart and Sarge Shriver in the alphabetical seating arrangements in class, Stewart grew frustrated when Shriver and Stuart scored higher than he did on some of the first-year exams. Resolving to do better, Stewart decided his problem was that he looked less "judicial" than his friends. He set out to rectify this by going to Woolworth's and buying a pair of ten-cent eyeglasses he deemed professorial in appearance, which he would then wave around for effect while talking during class. This seemed to produce the desired outcome. By the end of the second year, he was at the top of the class with Whizzer White.

Law school was an academic shock to Shriver. After years of garnering honors grades despite exerting only modest academic effort amid his myriad other activities, Shriver found himself working harder than ever but having less to show for it. He nearly failed Contracts his first semester. He was unaccustomed to struggling in this way. "I've been riding so high for so long," he wrote to his parents upon receiving his first set of marks, "that my ego was given a good jolt, which I presume was good for me spiritually but not too pleasant. . . . I suppose the real reason for my disappointment was . . . that everyone expected me to do 75 or better [in Contracts, where he got a 63]. If no one expects anything of you, I think it is easier to take a licking. When everyone wonders 'what happened to Shriver' it burns one's ego." He briefly contemplated dropping out of school. "I do feel I should do much better than I have. Certainly if I don't, I'll think twice before returning next year. Too much remains to be done in other ways; to clutter up the world with another dull lawyer would be almost anti-social!"

In 1939 he gained his initial exposure to the firsthand practice of law. "I am doing Legal Aid work here in New Haven & tomorrow appear with my first client at 9:30 in the City Attorney's office for a hearing!" he wrote to his parents. "It's a family squabble (hurrah for domestic relations) & I am giving advice on it. Me, the old family man with years of experience in human affairs! My poor client. It should be fun, however, for me, provided the client does not lose her birthright in the process." Shriver surely couldn't have predicted, at the time, that he would put his Legal Aid experience to work thirty-five years later, when he founded Legal Services for the Poor as part of the War on Poverty under Lyndon Johnson.

FRANCE BEFORE THE WAR

In June 1939 Europe was buzzing with diplomatic negotiations, trying to avert the outbreak of military action. Hitler's armies had entered Czechoslovakia in March, and Mussolini had invaded Albania in April. Donald Watt, of the Experiment in International Living, began making alternative arrangements for European students to be brought to Goddard College in Vermont, where they would live in a camp setting with American youth. But by the end of June, tensions in Europe seemed to be easing, so Watt decided to send American groups to Europe after all. The leader of one of the groups traveling to France, on his third Experiment trip, was Sargent Shriver.

Entrusted with the care of younger American college men and women, Shriver set off from New York, via Boston, on the French ocean liner *De Grasse* in early July. It arrived in a week's time in France, where the Experimenters met up with families for their home stays in the southern part of the country. Shriver stayed with Mme Batut, a professor of mathematics at a nearby lycée in Montaubau, just north of Toulouse, not far from the Spanish border. Mme Batut put him to work teaching English to her students.

Life in the South of France was extremely pleasant, but portents of the conflict to come lurked beneath the surface of daily life, sometimes erupting unpleasantly into view. For instance, when Shriver asked his hostess about "the mail planes" he saw flying overhead, she revealed that they were, as he wrote to his parents, "pursuit and observation squadrons out of Toulouse. Nightly they patrol the sky guarding against a possible raid of German and Italian bombers from Spain or even from Italy! The sensation is not at all pleasant. To sit in one's parlor & hear the drone of those monsters overhead constantly reminding one of the proximity of enemies is eerie & for the inhabitants an impossible condition in which to live."

In a long letter to his family on July 19, Shriver recounted some of what he had learned from a conversation with Mme Batut about the French state of mind toward a possible conflict. Mme Batut, he wrote,

> shares the universal fear of German aggrandizement directed at France & attempting to vassalize the country. Most of the French I've met are convinced the Germans wish to fight, & discussion of the truth of that fact is impossible. Of course, I'm still fond enough of the Germans to realize that the ordinary German has no more desire to fight than the ordinary Frenchman. The difference lies in the leaders. But the French hereabouts refuse to believe that. They are convinced that even the rank-and-file German is out for blood. . . . Mme. Batut's son, 30 years old, is an official of some importance in the war department, & he says France is about ready. *Everyone* in Paris has a place in the country assigned to them for refuge in case of attack by air or in the case of invasion. The productive capacities are now so organized that everything being done in Paris may be transferred to identical plants & facilities 100 miles south of the capital. People with country homes have been assigned the numbers & the exact persons now living in Paris whom they will be required to harbor in case of war. Paris itself is completely undermined with bomb-cellars, etc, & even the little faubourg shops have gas masks on display in the windows. Frankly it's ghastly & seems to me to be a situation which civilized people cannot countenance for a long time. Everyone agrees it is absurd, impossible, & necessary.

Shriver also noted that young French men were declining to marry, for fear of subjecting their would-be wives to excessive anxiety during wartime. This reluctance to wed had shrunk the French birth rate to such a distressingly low level that the French government was urging citizens to get married and have children. "God knows," Shriver wrote, "the world is in a queer condition when it is impossible for men to work, to marry, & therefore, in the final analysis, to live. I really feel Europe must be entering a period of disorganization, disorder, & decay. The next 20 to 50 years will disclose a history that would startle the most ruthless & pessimistic today."

Despite the ominous forebodings surrounding them, Shriver's American group embarked with thirteen French counterparts on an extended bicycle tour of the South of France. The first few weeks of the trip passed peacefully; the war retreated to the edge of Shriver's consciousness. Camping throughout the lush French countryside was, Shriver wrote to his parents, "a great life." In mid-

August, his French students returned home as planned, leaving Shriver with thirteen fewer young people to be responsible for.

Beginning in late August, however, Shriver observed that there seemed to be fewer people on the road. A few days later Shriver noticed that the local families he would see working in front of their farmhouses seemed to consist of women only; all the men seemed to have vanished. Alarmed, he asked a woman where all the men had gone. "Haven't you heard?" Shriver recalled her saying. "They've gone to join the army. The first call was the day before yesterday. The second call went out today."

Although Shriver wasn't supposed to return to Paris with his students for several days yet, he decided they would be wise to return to Experiment headquarters in the city and get a fuller picture of what the situation was. When Shriver and his charges arrived in Paris by train late in the evening of August 29, the City of Lights was dark. Many restaurants were closed. Those buildings that had lights on seemed to have them partially covered, so the illumination was dimmed. The Experiment's Paris office was located in a rented private home on the West Bank. It, too, looked dark. Shriver knocked softly on the door and, getting no response, banged louder. Finally, it opened slowly and a face peered around it. "Open the door," Sarge said. "It's Shriver."

The door swung open and an Experiment administrator barked, "Goddamnit, Shriver, where the hell have you been? Do you know how many cables from worried parents the home office has received?!" While Shriver and his group had happily cycled through the vineyards, the American papers had been full of the news that Hitler and Stalin had signed a nonaggression pact on August 23, and that as Germany rattled its saber at Poland, more French reservists had been called up. The Experiment's main office in Putney, Vermont, had been inundated with telegrams from parents (including Shriver's) demanding to know where their sons and daughters were.

Booking passage home for the Experimenters was not easy. The news of impending war had generated a stampede of American tourists to ships bound for the United States. Fortunately, the Experiment's French liaison was able to secure berths on the *Ile de France*, which was scheduled to depart from the port of Le Havre, northeast of Paris, on the following afternoon, September 1.

Shriver awoke early the next morning to a commotion of agitated French voices. Listening, he learned that at 4:45 that morning, Hitler's tanks had crossed the Polish border into Danzig; the German air force was streaking toward Warsaw.

Shriver roused his charges and shepherded them to the train station, where they were packed like cattle in among the thousands of other people desperate to escape the Continent. After arriving safely at the port of Le Havre and boarding the *Ile de France*, the Experimenters waited tensely to depart. A passage from a group log reported:

> The pier was crowded with people frantically trying to get last minute space on our boat, and we began to realize just how fortunate we were. We boarded the *Ile de France*. . . . Supposed to have sailed at 2 p.m., we were all pretty tense at dinner. Still in the harbor and not knowing when we would sail. The strain was not at all alleviated by the fact that we began our series of black-outs that night with nothing but blue lights for illumination. It was so hot in our cabins that a lot of Experimenters found it more bearable to sleep on deck. We spent Saturday in Havre, not knowing if and when it would sail, until late in the afternoon when a notice was posted saying that the boat would sail in a short while—which it did at 4:30. Passengers practically went mad—it was such a relief to know that we were actually going to start out for home. . . . We had another black-out that night plus a terrific electric storm; it was a frightful night.

The Experimenters were not yet home free. A few hours after the *Ile de France* set sail, the SS *Athenia*, a British ocean liner, was sunk by a torpedo from a German U-boat. The ship went down just offshore of England, so most of the 200 Americans aboard were saved; 28 of them, however, died in the initial explosion. Word of the sinking was quickly transmitted to the *Ile de France*, just 200 miles to the south. Shriver and the other sleepless passengers worried that a German torpedo or mine might bring the end at any moment. (At the same time, ashore in England, the *Athenia*'s surviving Americans were being interviewed by the twenty-two-year-old son of the US ambassador to Britain, Shriver's old Canterbury schoolmate Jack Kennedy.) With war officially declared, and a passenger ship just sunk, the Experimenters aboard the *Ile de France* were naturally convinced that the Germans were out to destroy all ships in the North Atlantic.

The first few days aboard the *Ile* were harrowing. News reports of the war crackled in over the ship's radio. The Nazis were taking Warsaw. Shriver was afraid not just for his own life but also for the lives of the students with whose well-being he had been entrusted. Finally, one crisp September afternoon, the *Ile* sounded its horn: the skyline of New York was in sight. Shriver and his fellow Experimenters were safely home.

Shriver's four years of experience as a participant in the Experiment in International Living had, initially, an apparently contrary effect. For the first and only time in his life, he became a dedicated isolationist. It was not that he believed cultural exchange between countries was bad (in fact he believed the opposite) or that he thought the United States should withdraw from world affairs forever; it was simply that what he had seen in Germany in 1936 and in France in 1939 had frightened and revolted him. Shriver knew that European wars had prompted his ancestors' emigration to America; he knew through his visits to Catholic churches throughout Europe the devastation visited on the combatants of the First World War; and thus he was firmly convinced that the United States should keep its nose out of any wars across the Atlantic.

But the longer-term effect of his experience abroad between 1934 and 1939 was to instill in him an unshakable belief that the more that citizens of different nations or cultures could be induced to interact with one another, the less likely they would be to go to war with one another.

As fate would have it, Shriver would find himself in a position some two decades later to draw directly on his experiences with the Experiment in International Living. In its can-do idealism, its emphasis on cross-national communication, its careful screening of participants, its respect for foreign cultures, and its ultimate aspirations, the Experiment bears a striking thematic resemblance to the Peace Corps. The Peace Corps, like the Experiment, was animated above all by a quest for world peace through intercultural cooperation. It is no wonder that, when ordered to set up the Peace Corps by President Kennedy in 1961, one of Shriver's earliest calls was to Gordon Boyce, Donald Watt's successor as director of the Experiment in International Living.

AMERICA FIRST

Convinced that the United States should keep an ocean's distance from Continental affairs, Shriver returned to law school in the fall of 1939 and watched developments across the Atlantic from afar. He wrote to his parents, "the news from Europe is most depressing. Certainly one can hardly help feeling the times are out of joint."

On April 9, 1940, the Germans invaded Norway and Denmark, and a month later blitzed Belgium, Holland, and France, the Dutch surrendering on May 15. Two days later, Shriver, who was preparing for law school exams, wrote a letter to his parents. "The news from Europe this evening is so appalling in many ways that I knew you would be troubled, & I hope this short letter will help you to realize that at least here we have some degree of protection and safety. This is a night when one wants to hold tightly to some one's hand & feel sure that everything is not in chaos. I hope that you feel that I am close by when this arrives, & that we four at least have unity and confidence."

As the Germans reached the English Channel on May 20, and Belgium appeared likely to fall imminently, Shriver lamented how meaningless and theoretical his law school work seemed to be. On May 26 he wrote, "I have only one week before exams—so the recurrent pressure is again here. In the midst of all that's taking place in the big, wide world our problems are not absorbing—I wish we could cease all the theorizing that is necessary here & get down to handling one real case where human beings are involved. School is stimulating but seems futile very often these days." As he finished his exams in mid-June, the Germans entered Paris.

To divert themselves, Shriver and Mac Muir traveled to Edgartown, on Martha's Vineyard, Cape Cod, for a sailing race, and then to Tom Thatcher's estate at Watch Hill, Rhode Island, for a weekend house party, where the drinking and carousing lasted for four days straight.

If this bout of libertinism for Shriver and his friends had a quality of urgency, it was because the drumbeat of war was growing louder. In Washington, the debates between the interventionists and the isolationists were intensifying. Political commentators, Congress, and FDR's administration were all divided among themselves over whether and how much to help England with money, materiel, and military support in its war with Germany.

In the spring and summer of 1940, Sarge felt profoundly divided. On the one hand, he felt the tug of his ancestry strongly. The earliest Shrivers had fled to America precisely to avoid these endless Continental wars and then had fought to throw off the yoke of Europe. Why, then, violate the spirit on which America was built by re-engaging with wars not of the nation's concern?

Europe was always fighting and always would be. He was also familiar with the tragic legacy of the Great War of 1914–1918. There was no reason to think that a second world war would be any less devastating.

On the other hand, however, was a competing set of considerations. Shriver's summers in Germany had exposed him to Hitler and the Nazis—his first experience with pure evil. He had seen the concentration camp at Buchenwald. He had also seen how the fascism of Mussolini was strangling Italy. If these men, these noxious regimes, were not worth fighting against, was anything?

The tug of his ancestry, Shriver came to see, pulled him in two directions. Yes, his forebears had sought to flee European wars—but they had also fought for what they believed in. Shrivers had fought for the country during the American Revolution, the War of 1812, and the Civil War. His parents had helped raise money for the American cause during the First World War, and he had imbibed from them the Wilsonian impulse toward noble interventions in foreign affairs. Was it not a Shriver's patriotic duty to do battle and risk death if circumstances called for it? War heroes had been venerated in Sarge's family from the time he was a young boy, and a small part of him—maybe even not so small—craved that veneration for himself.

In the end, Shriver arrived at perhaps the only workable solution to his conundrum. He vigorously and publicly opposed the war, helping to found the America First Committee. And at the same time—in a seemingly paradoxical move for an anti-interventionist—he enlisted in the Naval Reserve.

Reading through the *New York Times* in the Yale library one day in the early spring of 1940, Shriver had seen a small notice about a US Navy program called the V-7—for "volunteeers, seventh class"—designed to attract would-be officers into the armed forces. The V-7 program was aimed at college and graduate students, who would spend their summers being trained on navy ships while completing their education during the academic years. The very afternoon he read the advertisement, Shriver went down to the New Haven Navy Office and volunteered.

Shriver spent the summer of 1940 on the USS *Arkansas*, a World War I–era battleship. The *Arkansas* spent most of the summer in New York's harbor, rarely venturing more than a few dozen miles out to sea or up or down the eastern seaboard. Anchored in the Hudson River near 125TH Street, Shriver and his fellow V-7 volunteers went through a battery of training courses from the career officers and enlisted men, learning about naval history and about guns.

Navy life was at first a difficult adjustment. The living conditions on the *Arkansas* were spartan. In the navy, unlike at Yale, Shriver's place in the hierarchy was inscribed in his role—and as an apprentice seaman in the Naval Reserve, that role was lowly. "There is nothing lower than I was that summer," Shriver has said. Although he was mostly ashore or in the harbor, he felt figuratively at sea. He didn't know how anything worked and had to rely on his superiors to tell him what to do. He felt he was barely getting by, "just skimming through by the barest of margins," as he wrote his parents the following fall.

But Shriver slowly acquired not only the technical knowledge needed to do his job, but a knowledge of navy culture. The navy, he soon learned, wasn't all that different from Canterbury School: all male and highly structured about dress, punctuality, and comportment. Both environments fostered a great camaraderie. By the end of the summer he was growing to enjoy navy life.

And yet, returning to Yale in the fall, Shriver threw himself once again into active protest against American involvement in the war. Among his isolationist and non-interventionist friends, his military service made him a curiosity—and also gave him a certain credibility in debates against the interventionists. There were Anglophiles among his classmates who wanted the United States to give money, arms, and active military assistance to aid their beloved England; yet they themselves had not volunteered to fight. Shriver, in contrast, had declared himself willing to fight in a war in which he hoped his military would have no part.

In September 1940, as the Battle of Britain raged between England and Germany, Shriver arrived in New Haven for his final year of law school. "Dearest Mother & Dad," he wrote,

> Well tomorrow begins my seventh year in Yale University, & I realize, after talking to some of the freshmen & faculty members, just how fortunate I am. I wonder how many fellows entering Yale in the next few years, or maybe more, will be able to spend 7 uninterrupted years at Yale. Even fellows starting a professional education this year say they have little hope of finishing it regularly, in three or four years. They make me all the more thankful that I shall have my LL.B in June.

If law school had seemed stimulating but futile during his second year, it seemed even more futile now as the war spread. In late September, Germany, Italy, and

Japan had formed the Axis alliance; in September and October, Mussolini invaded Egypt and Greece; and by late June the war had taken its most dramatic turn, as Hitler launched Operation Barbarossa, the assault on Russia.

Throughout the fall of 1940, Shriver's attention was fixed decidedly less on his studies than on preventing American entry into the war. The debate about intervention swirled all around Shriver and his peers through their second and third years of law school. And though he considered and reconsidered his decision, it was with firm conviction that Shriver now joined his friend and law school classmate Bob Stuart in founding America First.

In the fall of 1940, R. Douglas Stuart Jr., the son of a vice president at the Quaker Oats Company in Chicago, was an idealistic New Dealer who ardently believed that by staying out of the war, the United States could help Europe achieve an acceptable peace settlement quickly. Stuart, who had studied international relations as a Princeton undergraduate, believed strongly that "the U.S. had gained nothing and lost a great deal through participation in World War I" and that "what turned out to be World War II was simply a renewal of the same nationalistic struggles [that had caused World War I]."

It was natural that Shriver and Stuart should become close friends. Both were handsome and charismatic, and Stuart, like Shriver, had spent a summer before law school traveling through Europe, attaining a touch of cosmopolitanism as well as learning firsthand about the mortal costs of the First World War. In 1939 Shriver joined the new student group Stuart organized to discuss the war and means of resisting American participation in it. As early as November 1939, just a few months removed from his harrowing escape from the Continent on the *Ile de France*, Shriver wrote a letter with Stuart to Charles Lindbergh, who was already an outspoken opponent of American involvement in the war, asking him to speak to their group. The letter was signed not only by Bob Stuart and himself, but also by Potter Stewart, Windham Gary, and Millard Brown, all members of Stuart's group. (Lindbergh did not respond.)

During the summer of 1940, while Shriver endured his concentrated military training on the *Arkansas*, Stuart was in the Midwest, where isolationist sentiment ran high. Using his father's business connections and his own considerable charm to round up business leaders and politicians, Stuart was attempting to found a national, anti-interventionist organization. His first important recruit was Gen. Robert E. Wood, the chairman of Sears, Roebuck and Company and a liberal Republican who had voted twice for Roosevelt and supported the New Deal. Wood had grown increasingly concerned about FDR's apparent drift toward intervention, and he agreed to become national chairman of the organization that Stuart was now calling America First. Stuart, only twenty-four years old, became the national director.

Stuart finally met Lindbergh in July in Chicago, where the aviator was in town to address 40,000 spectators at the Keep America Out of War Rally in Soldier Field along Lake Michigan. Stuart (like Shriver) had been an admirer of Colonel Lindbergh from childhood, when Lindbergh had become the first man to cross the Atlantic in an airplane. After dining with Lindbergh following the rally, Stuart recorded that he found the famous man "a most attractive guy and a very clear thinker," as well as "a sincere and courageous American who has the habit of sticking his neck out." But Lindbergh's conservatism made Stuart uncomfortable, and he worried about what would happen to his fledgling organization if it became publicly linked with the aviator. This led to a disagreement between Stuart and General Wood about whether or not to bring Lindbergh formally on to the America First national committee. Wood wanted Lindbergh to succeed him as national chairman, and Stuart preferred to keep the aviator at arm's length. Lindbergh finally did join the committee in April 1941 and became its most popular speaker.

The America First national committee formally announced itself on September 4, 1940, and began a national advertising campaign against intervention the following month. The committee's basic view was that America should build an impregnable defense and then retreat inside it. "American democracy," the America First founding document declared, "can be preserved only by keeping out of the European war."

In the fall, Lindbergh came to Yale. Kingman Brewster Jr., Shriver's successor as chairman of the *Yale Daily News* (and years later the university's president) organized the meeting, and on the evening of October 30, Shriver crowded into a packed auditorium in Woolsey Hall to hear Lindbergh speak for thirty-three minutes. The aviator got an enthusiastic response.

Yet Shriver had also determined that what Lindbergh (or anyone else) said was irrelevant: US involvement in the war was inevitable—and sooner rather than later. He ceased active participation in the America First organization, although he stayed in close contact with Stuart throughout his final year at Yale.

Posterity has looked unkindly on America First. America Firsters quickly became associated in the public mind with the head-in-the-sand isolationism of the Ohio senator Robert Taft, the North Dakota senator Gerald Nye, and the Chicago newspaper magnate William McCormick. Joe Kennedy Sr., then FDR's ambassador to England, was in the fall of 1940 locked in a tense battle with the president; Kennedy could see that Roosevelt's policies were stealthily laying the groundwork for greater American involvement and eventually military participation in the war, and he was convinced that was wrong. Roosevelt managed to cajole his ambassador into silence until after the 1940 presidential election, but Kennedy—a greatly reviled figure in some circles as the years went on—also became guilty by his association with the isolationist cause, and the America Firsters became guilty by association with him.

The harshest accusations leveled at America First charged it with being anti-Semitic or with harboring pro-German sympathies. It is true that some among America First's prominent figureheads (most notably Lindbergh) were demonstrated to have had anti-Semitic tendencies that may well have contributed to their noninterventionist conviction. Moreover, the truly isolationist stances of, for instance, Colonel McCormick and Senators Nye and Taft fed into the public impression that the America Firsters were blindly anti-European.

But simpleminded isolationism was not what motivated Shriver and the other Yale law students who launched America First. Rather it was the conviction that America's interests—namely, not sending its boys to be killed in another of Europe's endless wars—were not to be served by involvement. Yes, American intervention had helped bring closure to the First World War. But what had that produced? Another world war, not even twenty-five years later, which was shaping up to be every bit as bad as the first. What was more, America First's position was until December 1941 supported by most Americans. As late as August 1941, 74 percent of Americans favored staying out of war; a month later, 68 percent still did, even if that meant a German victory over England and Russia.

Shriver's enthusiastic contribution to the America First Committee's founding was born above all of his belief that staying out of the war was not only the most prudent course for America's interests but that it was also the best way of achieving peace in Europe. Although he recognized the evil of Hitler, Shriver believed a negotiated peace settlement, brokered by the United States, was the best way to stop the slaughter quickly and to protect and possibly restore what remained of the Continental democracies.

Later, when he had become a public figure of some renown, Shriver would occasionally receive letters, usually angry ones, asking why he had associated with such an ignominious group as America First. In a typical response, writing back to a man who decried Shriver's "guilt" by association with Lindbergh and company, Shriver explained his thinking. "Yes, I did belong to AMERICA FIRST," he wrote.

> I joined it because I believed at the time we could better help to secure a just settlement of the war in Europe by staying out of it. History proved that my judgment was wrong, neither for the first time nor the last. None of the people I knew in the organization expressed any views within my hearing that were either pro-German or anti-Semitic. I can see how people with such views might have supported AMERICA FIRST, just as people with pro-Russian or Communist views might have supported an interventionist organization at that time. I am a little surprised, however, at your willingness to assume that I am "guilty," on the basis you describe in your letter. The idea that guilt is personal and the presumption of innocence are two of the most fundamental ideas that distinguish our society from totalitarian societies.

"I wanted to spare American lives," Shriver told a journalist in 1964, by way of explaining his association with America First. "If that's an ignoble motive then I'm perfectly willing to be convicted."

Shriver's final months at law school were an afterthought, his attentions riveted on events overseas. By the spring of 1941 Shriver, although still opposed to American intervention, was resigned to it. He reported to the *Arkansas* the day after his final exam. As his classmates marched beneath Yale's Gothic spires to collect their diplomas, Sargent Shriver was aboard a US battleship.

CHAPTER FOUR

War

⟋

After finishing the bar exam on the third Friday in September 1941, Shriver donned his ensign's stripes and reported for active duty the following Monday. He had hoped for an assignment to the USS *Juneau*, a destroyer, but was assigned instead to desk duty in the Third Naval District, which extended along the eastern seaboard from Cape Hatteras, off South Carolina, to Nova Scotia, above the northernmost tip of Maine. Trapped in a small office in lower Manhattan, where the ten-story US Naval Building at 90 Church Street housed the Third Naval District Headquarters, Shriver was frustrated. He would much rather have been at sea, living aboard a ship. Instead, he spent his days shuffling paperwork at a desk.

As a newly commissioned ensign, Shriver was the lowest officer on the totem pole and thus was often relegated to weekend duty on watch at District Headquarters, with responsibility for monitoring the radio dispatches. In the unlikely event of an attack on American shores, it would fall to him to sound General Quarters, the alarm calling everyone to battle stations.

Through the autumn of 1941 Shriver endured a cloying mixture of boredom and nervous anticipation. Mostly, he was waiting: waiting not only to see what happened in the war, trying to determine when the United States would finally be compelled to join the conflict, but also waiting to learn whether he had passed the bar exam. Waiting drove him crazy, especially since there wasn't anything concrete he could do—so he sat at his government-issue desk and stewed, as he watched the country's nerves fray.

One Sunday morning, December 7, 1941, Shriver awoke in his cot at the District Naval Headquarters and, after breakfast and Mass, was installed at his desk by nine o'clock, prepared to endure another tedious day of waiting. At one o'clock, he switched the radio dial to WHN, which was broadcasting the New York Giants football game from the Polo Grounds.

Just after 2:22 p.m., with the Giants leading the Brooklyn Dodgers 14–0 in the fourth quarter, the Mutual Broadcasting System announcer Len Sterling abruptly interrupted the game to read a brief AP bulletin: "Flash: Washington—White House says Japs attack Pearl Harbor."

Shriver sat bolt upright in his chair. His first thought was that he had misheard. His second thought was of Halloween 1938, when Orson Welles had inadvertently pitched America into a panic with his radio adaptation of H. G. Wells's *War of the Worlds*, with its realistic simulation of a news broadcast announcing a Martian invasion. Could this Pearl Harbor bombing bulletin be simply another hoax, albeit a cruel and ill-timed one?

Unsure of what to do—not knowing whether to trust his own ears—Shriver picked up the phone and called the Brooklyn Navy Yard, where his brother Herbert was stationed as a junior naval officer. "Herbert," Sarge recalls saying when he got his brother on the phone. "Have you got the radio on?" Herbert said he did not. "Well turn it on, goddamnit," Sarge shouted, "turn it on! The Japs have attacked Pearl Harbor!" Herbert confirmed that he was hearing the same reports over his radio set.

With some trepidation, Shriver sounded General Quarters. In 1941 there was no Internet, no satellite communications, no CNN, no network television news—no way of knowing quickly or reliably what was going on 6,000 miles away. So when Shriver flipped the switch that sounded the alarm all up and down the East Coast, sending switchboard operators aflutter trying to reach officers at their weekend country homes, or on golf courses, or at family dinners, he was initiating the first communication that most of these men were to receive regarding the attack. Moreover, when they heard the General Quarters alarm, most of them had no way of knowing why it was being sounded. Thus, within minutes of the sounding of General Quarters, Shriver's telephone was ringing off the hook. "Shriver!" went the typical refrain. "What the hell is going on here? You better have a damn good reason for interrupting my Sunday afternoon."

He did. Bewildered officers, from ensigns up to admirals, began flowing into headquarters. Within twenty minutes of sounding General Quarters, Shriver was relieved of his duty as officer-on-call for the Third Naval District by a captain and was dispatched to comb through the building to make sure that all non-navy personnel were evacuated.

By the next day, the tragedy of Sunday's events had become clearer. The Japanese air force had crippled the US battle fleet in Pearl Harbor, killing nearly 2,500 American sailors. America's Pacific Fleet had been effectively destroyed. On December 8, President Roosevelt made his famous radio announcement: "Yesterday, December 7th, was a date which will live in infamy." America, scarcely two decades removed from involvement in the last world conflict, was once again at war.

For a while it looked to Shriver as though he would be assigned to military intelligence. This was a dreadful prospect—it meant more desk duty. The thought of being confined to an office, analyzing Japanese ship movements or studying German submarines while his peers were sailing off to the Pacific to fight, left Shriver feeling impotent. So he put in a request to be assigned to a ship— and was assigned to the USS *South Dakota*, a battleship still under construction in a shipyard in Camden, New Jersey.

Even though Camden was only a few dozen miles south of New York City, Shriver knew that it might be some time before he saw his family again, so he stopped in for a final visit at their apartment on the East Side, to say good-bye, collect a few belongings, and look at his mail. In a world made topsy-turvy by war, he opened a letter that under different circumstances might have set him to rejoicing, but which now he tossed aside, noting only briefly how insignificant it seemed: He had passed the bar exam and been admitted to the New York Bar. Despite sometimes daunting financial obstacles, Sargent Shriver had become a lawyer. For the moment, however, he didn't think of himself as such; he was an ensign, US Navy, and it was as an officer that he bid farewell to his family. It was the last time he was to see his father alive.

When Shriver reported for duty in Camden, the *South Dakota* was still in drydock. The vessel was enormous: 680 feet long and 108 feet wide, with a complement of more than 2,500 men. It seemed to Shriver almost like a small city. Shriver joined the Eighth Division on the starboard side of the ship, consisting of 95 men assigned to operate the 20- and 40-millimeter antiaircraft guns that ran from the bow of the boat about one-third of the way back toward the stern.

Thousands of miles away in the Pacific, the battle was not going well for the Allies. Japan had achieved landings in the Philippines, Burma, Malaya, Singapore, and the Dutch East Indies, and by the time the *South Dakota* was commissioned, the Japanese had not only sealed off China but had also secured almost the entire Pacific west of Midway Island and north of the Coral Sea; by May, the Americans in the Philippines had surrendered.

June 1942 brought some heartening news from the Pacific—in a stunning turn-around, the US Navy had won a decisive victory at the Battle of Midway—but some devastating news from home. On June 16, Shriver received a telegram from his brother: Their father, whose health had been in steady decline since the crash of 1929, had died. Shriver immediately set about trying to get a shore leave so he could attend the funeral. The *South Dakota* was docked that day at Annapolis, and it was only a short way up the Chesapeake Bay to Baltimore Cathedral, where his father's funeral was to be held. But, as Shriver recalled, when he asked his commanding officer for permission to leave the ship, the officer denied it.

Shriver was devastated. For a moment, he entertained the possibility of deserting. But he then banished the thought and proceeded stoically with his shipboard duties. Later, Shriver would concede the wisdom of his commanding officer's decision not to let him go off duty. Shriver understood the terrible anxiety that drove the navy brass: Most of the fleet's battleships had been sunk, if not at Pearl Harbor then in subsequent Pacific engagements, and the pressure to get ships into fighting condition quickly was enormous.

Unable to join his family at the funeral, Shriver instead wrote a letter that reveals the depth, and clarity, of his faith. "Dearest Mother," he wrote on June 16,

I just got Herbert's telegram about Dad today, the sixteenth, & I can't be with you right away, desperately as I would like to be. God alone knows what you must be suffering for it is enough for me. For you the loneliness after more than 30 years of your wonderful life together must be indescribable. Our best consolation is the certainty that Dad is at last completely happy & free of all the petty annoyances which a small world forced upon a great man. I am already praying to him, not only for him, & hoping that he is not too disgusted with his youngest son, now that he knows the miserable weaknesses which while he was alive I was able to keep to myself & the Lord.

The sensations you told me you underwent when your father died are now mine, I appreciate them for the first time. But you cannot know how much additional sorrow is caused by the knowledge that you are now alone, & I am helpless to change that immediately & permanently. I think of this—because you have more fortitude & courage than anyone I have ever known. I know you are taking this blow as you have all the others, & I feel if you can, I must, carry on with assurance & even joy. Not everyone has a husband nor yet a father of their own blood in heaven. (And as I write that line, I understand with a new insight what our Lord did for us when He gave us His Son to be our Father who art in heaven.)

Think, too, how pleased your father & the Cardinal [James Gibbons] must be . . . everyone who really knew Dad must be welcoming him. Saint Paul and Thomas More are rejoicing, & all that multitudinous army of heroes & heroines, all the people who have made and given us our Christian world are happy. We know all this is true. In my mind, so full of doubts & fears about a thousand inconsequential matters great and small, there is no question that Dad is where he belongs,—right in heaven. Even as I am sad, I smile inside to think of Dad meeting Saint Paul for the first time. What a thrill for him, & I'll bet too that Saint Paul himself was glad to see a man who embodied 1900 years later so many of his own qualities,—enthusiasm, perseverance, courage, highmindedness, devotion, charity, good, kindness, & vision. What a conversation they must have had! And most satisfying of all, they will all be there in the same joyful mood for you yourself some day. Of that I am as certain as I am thankful to God again for the two people who have meant more to me than all others or anything in the world. If I ever join you both in heaven, you will have brought me more than any other human beings. Tonight I am sorrowful, tonight I am rejoicing, tonight I am full of thanks, tonight I send you my deepest love. I shall be with you soon.

Sargent
R. S. Shriver, Jr
Ens, 8th Division

The battle in the Pacific raged on. In early August, the US Navy seized control of the island of Guadalcanal, to the east of New Guinea. Shortly after Guadalcanal was secured, American military intelligence got wind of a Japanese plan for recapturing the island. Admiral Yamamoto's combined fleet was steaming toward the island. In response, the US Navy immediately dispatched the aircraft carrier *Hornet* from Hawaii toward the Solomons. And it ordered the *South Dakota* and the *Washington*, another newly commissioned battleship—along with the antiaircraft cruiser *Juneau* and a host of destroyers—to head toward the Pacific.

THE BATTLE OF SANTA CRUZ

On August 16, 1942, the *South Dakota* began its first war cruise, moving down through Chesapeake Bay to the Atlantic. Heading south along the eastern coast of the United States and Central America to the Panama Canal, the *South Dakota* led the *Washington* across the Western Hemisphere and into the Pacific toward the island of New Caledonia, which lay south of the Solomon Islands.

It was not an auspicious entrance into the Pacific theater. In its haste to rendezvous with the *Hornet* near New Caledonia, Shriver's vessel tore open its belly on a coral reef east of Fiji, damaging the ship's hull and spilling oil into the sea. Rather than rendezvousing with the *Hornet*, the *South Dakota* went north to Pearl Harbor for repairs.

Now early September, the timing was fortunate: It afforded the *South Dakota* the opportunity to be fitted with dozens of the new 40-millimeter antiaircraft guns that had just rolled off foundry assembly lines. An American version of a Swedish-made gun called the Bofors, the new "forties" would prove to be extremely effective in combating Japanese airplane attacks.

Although Capt. Tom Gatch was known to be lax about formal aspects of navy protocol, he was a stickler about keeping his men combat ready, and he drilled his gunners—including Shriver's Eighth Division—endlessly on the operation of the new guns. "No ship more eager to fight ever entered the Pacific" than the *South Dakota*, wrote the naval historian Samuel Eliot Morison in *The Two-Ocean War*. "The skipper, by constant target practice on towed planes, ignoring lapses in spit-and-polish, and exercising a natural gift for leadership, had welded his green crew into a splendid fighting crew. They 'looked like a lot of wild men,' said one of his officers, and they all adored Tom Gatch." "Gatch may not have had much passion for clean fingernails or white-glove inspections," another historian has written, "but he did like a bull's eye. All the way from Pearl Harbor, Gatch had kept his men busy at target practice. Squeegees and buckets lay neglected in *South Dakota's* lockers and the big ship became a slattern . . . she was probably the dirtiest ship in the United States Navy, but also one of the deadliest."

Perhaps surprisingly, Shriver and many of his shipmates describe this time as one of the happiest in their lives. The varying blues of the ocean and the sky, combined with the lush greens of the South Pacific islands, provided a beautiful tableau for them to gaze upon from atop the deck. They were doing something meaningful, fighting for their country and for the ideal of freedom, aboard the pride of the US Navy, a big, gleaming, new battleship. Captain Gatch's leadership—and soon, the shared experience and horror of combat—bonded the men, cementing them together in an intense spirit of camaraderie. "The ship was like your wife and your girlfriend both," recalled one enlisted man years after the war; the men on board were "closer than a lot of brothers."

Even after the anticipation of war gave way to the grisly reality of it, the men of the South Dakota continued to derive a real happiness, or at least an intensity of positive feeling, from life on the ship. In recollecting their time aboard the ship a half century later, many of Shriver's peers would in one breath lament the friends they had lost and the carnage they had witnessed and, in the next breath, say without any sense of contradiction that the years aboard the South Dakota were "the best time of my life."

In the wee hours of October 26, Captain Gatch and his slovenly but well-drilled men steamed with a US naval convoy toward the lower Solomons, passing about 125 miles north of the Santa Cruz islands. Serving as part of the "screen" of gunships meant to provide cover for the USS Enterprise, which was the navy's flagship aircraft carrier, the South Dakota cruised in formation with the heavy cruiser Portland, the antiaircraft cruiser San Juan, and eight destroyers. A few miles to the south and east, the Hornet—one of only three seaworthy carriers remaining in the fleet—cruised northward similarly encircled by a protective screen of gunships.

A buzzing noise portended aerial bombardment, and the South Dakota braced itself for its first combat. Shriver, frantically scanning the sky for a target, saw only low-hanging clouds from the still-dissipating squall. Suddenly, dive-bombing Japanese Vals burst forth from behind the cloud cover just above the South Dakota, bearing down hard from the rear. The South Dakota, with a great roiling of its metal guts and a frenzy of activity on deck, cranked into action—and Shriver, from his position in a turret on the starboard side, ordered his gunners to fire at will.

Bullets from the Japanese Zeros, small, light fighter planes, strafed the deck all around Shriver, ricocheting wildly. Hundred-pound bombs rained from the sky, creating titanic splashes in the water when they missed and fearsome explosions, along with the sounds of rending metal and the cries of wounded men, when they hit. Flying low over the bow of the *South Dakota*, a dive-bomber dropped a 500-pound bomb that landed squarely on the No. 1 turret, the foremost of the battleship's main 16-inch batteries. Captain Gatch stood alongside the turret not 20 yards away, and he didn't duck or flinch as the Japanese plane and its deadly tonnage bore in on him. ("I considered it beneath the dignity of a captain of an American battleship to flop for a Japanese bomb," Gatch would say later.) The turret's armor plating shuddered and bent but held, and the gunners inside continued to load and fire, shaken but unharmed. Captain Gatch, however, received a shoulderful of shrapnel; it looked as though he would bleed to death.

Shriver and his fellow gunners returned fire. "Attack," commanded Gatch, before going down with his wound, whereupon "a hundred muzzles flamed and fell, flamed and fell, like lethal pistons, and a cloud of dark-brown powder smoke drifted off [the ship's] stern."

As the Japanese planes swooped in low over the water, just a few dozen yards away from the *South Dakota*, Shriver tracked them in his sights, much as he had once tracked grouse and pheasant in the Maryland countryside. For a moment, he was able almost to forget where he was and the magnitude of what he was engaged in and to concentrate solely on hitting his targets—as many as thirty at a time swooping in and out of view—as they skimmed above the water like stiff metal birds.

But as the planes flew in closer, aiming to drop their deadly cargo, it was impossible not to think about how the difference between hitting his target and missing it could spell the difference between victory and defeat, and between his own life and death. As the first plane drew in close, Shriver recalled that he could see the Japanese man inside his cockpit, could make out the insignia on his helmet—he could even see his face. Years later, Shriver would swear that he actually locked eyes for a moment with the enemy. Staring at each other for a few seconds, each knowing that in a moment one or the other of them would likely be dead, Shriver imagined that a glimmering of understanding passed between them: Nothing personal, each was thinking, it's just that I've got to kill you before you kill me. This mutual understanding, Shriver believed, almost amounted to a form of respect.

Or maybe that was simply what he needed to think to himself in order to pull the trigger. "Fire," Shriver ordered. His station, operating in tandem, locked onto the target and shot, and bullets ripped into the cockpit and fuselage of the Japanese plane. Through his aiming scope, Shriver saw the pilot's eyes widen and his mouth grimace in a rictus of fear as he realized he had been hit. And then the plane dipped violently downward, plunging into the Pacific not 15 yards from the *South Dakota*, trailing black smoke behind it. He had made his first kill.

Shriver had no time to celebrate or lament this fact, because dozens more planes were circling above, each promising to unleash deadly havoc on the battleship and the other vessels in the convoy if the antiaircraft gunners relaxed even for a moment. So the Eighth Division, along with the other antiaircraft divisions aboard the ship, continued to fire away amid all the noise and smoke and flashes of light—and amid the blood that had begun to trickle across the battleship's deck, and which was now swirling red in the water, a beacon for sharks.

Each time it seemed the American ships had beaten the Japanese planes back, another wave would appear. In front of the *South Dakota*, the *Enterprise* was being bombarded. The carrier's power went out; fires raged on deck; torpedoes rent the hull asunder; for a time, it even seemed as if the men might have to abandon ship. Meanwhile, to the starboard side of the *Enterprise*, a Japanese Kate, a torpedo bomber, had flown directly into the forward gun mount of the *Smith*, an American destroyer, and had turned its bow into a blaze of fire. The *Smith* had to fall behind the *South Dakota* and bury "her flaming nose in the battleship's high foaming wake to put her fires out."

The *South Dakota* had problems of its own. The bomb that wounded Captain Gatch had pitched the ship into chaos, and "for a single, confused minute, *South Dakota* spun out of control and made straight for *Enterprise*." The *Enterprise* quickly granted the battleship right of way, narrowly averting collision. Order was restored aboard the battleship, but other American ships were going down. The *South Dakota* had to break formation to avoid smashing into the sinking *San Juan*. Meanwhile, a few thousand yards to the east, the commander of the *Hornet* gave the order to "abandon ship."

By noon, the Battle of Santa Cruz was effectively over. Less than three hours had elapsed since the first Japanese dive-bombers had appeared. But in that time the US Navy had lost one of its three carriers, the *Hornet*, to the depths of the sea and had seen another, the *Enterprise*, badly damaged. It had also suffered grievous wounds, some of them mortal, to its fleet of carriers and destroyers. Although there was rejoicing in Tokyo at the apparent victory, the Japanese had also suffered significant damage. US bombers from the *Hornet* and *Enterprise* had incapacitated two Japanese cruisers and, more important, the *Shokaku*, a flagship carrier. The battle had also bought American forces on Guadalcanal precious time with which to prepare for the looming fight. Moreover, the battle had cost the Japanese 100 aircraft (and some of their best pilots); after Santa Cruz the role of Japan's carrier-based aircraft in the struggle for Guadalcanal would be insignificant.

The force most directly responsible for the reduction in Japan's carrier-based aircraft were the antiaircraft gunners of the *South Dakota*. As Samuel Eliot Morison was later to recount, the first Japanese air strike at Santa Cruz would have destroyed the *Enterprise* were it not for the "magnificent shooting by the 'wild men' of *South Dakota*. She in this action secured for battlewagons the place of honor that they occupied during the rest of the war—defending carriers from attack." Shriver and his fellow gunners on the battleship shot down thirty-two Japanese planes that day by their own count (the navy officially gave them credit for only twenty-six; in the chaos of battle, no one could credibly claim a precise accounting). Even from the vantage point of a half century later, when the quest for world peace had become one of his most treasured ideals, Shriver could not help swelling a bit with pride at what he and the other men of the *South Dakota* had accomplished that October day in the Pacific.

GUADALCANAL

By October 27, 1942, the *South Dakota* had retreated south to the island of New Caledonia, where it sought refuge in port at Nouméa for damage assessment. Captain Gatch had nearly died: only the quick action of a seaman who stanched his commanding officer's bleeding amid all the pyrotechnic activity on deck had kept Gatch alive. Some of Shriver's fellow American sailors had perished in the battle, but there was little time to mourn the dead.

Guadalcanal's Henderson Field, although it remained tenuously in American hands, was still clearly the principal object of Japanese forays into the Solomon Islands. Retaining control of the airfield was of paramount strategic importance for the US naval effort in the Pacific. The Pacific front had seen an almost unrelenting string of victories for the Japanese: Through the first ten months of 1942, as one historian has put it, "Every confrontation with Japanese warships had been a humiliating defeat." For the Americans to lose Henderson Field now would be devastating; their one land-based airfield in the region would be gone.

After the Battle of Santa Cruz, Shriver was recognized for his courage and calm under enemy fire and for his deadeye accuracy. He was promoted to full lieutenant, senior grade, and placed in charge of his Eighth Division. This was a significant responsibility. It put him in charge of the ship's forward starboard gun emplacements and placed thirty-two enlisted men, as well as a few junior grade lieutenants and ensigns, under his orders.

Two weeks after Santa Cruz, the *South Dakota* was pressed back into action. In the second week of November, American intelligence in the Pacific had learned of a massive convoy of Japanese ships in the vicinity of the Solomon Islands. This likely meant one thing: The Japanese were making another push to seize Guadalcanal. So although the American fleet was not in good condition—on the *South Dakota*, for instance, two big guns in turret 2 were still inoperative from the bomb damage suffered at Santa Cruz—it had no choice but to head northward to guard the island.

Aboard the *South Dakota*, Captain Gatch himself should have been in no condition to see combat again so soon. Having nearly bled to death during Santa Cruz, he had just been released from the infirmary. Shriver recalls that Gatch's mere presence on deck, his arm in a sling and his neck in a bandage, rallied his sailors; they would do anything for their commander. On November 11, *South Dakota* left Nouméa, once again part of a screen for the still-crippled carrier *Enterprise*. On the morning of Friday the 13th, a "Tokyo Express" consisting of eleven transports and a dozen destroyers was sighted heading in a four-column formation toward Guadalcanal. At eight that evening, Admiral Halsey gave the order for the *South Dakota*, the battleship *Washington*, and four destroyers to peel off from the carrier group to head to the battle zone to intercept any enemy bombardment forces coming from the east. Ideally, he would not have risked the navy's two most powerful battleships so close to the island, but Halsey had decided that losing Henderson Field would be even worse than losing the battleships, so he sent the ships forward as a calculated risk.

Late in the evening of November 14, the *South Dakota* came around the western tip of Guadalcanal in a single column behind the battleship *Washington* and the destroyers *Walke, Benham, Preston,* and *Gwin.* The ship had been at General Quarters, or full alert, for twenty-four hours straight. Shriver himself, after a brief respite in the afternoon, came on duty at eight o'clock that night. At 10:15 p.m., as the *South Dakota* followed its destroyer column north into the infamous Iron Bottom Bay, the carcasses of the previously sunken ships that gave the bay its name caused the battleship's magnetic compass needles to twitch and shudder. Up on deck, Shriver and his men gazed onto the calm waters of the bay, illuminated by a clear quarter moon. As the column of ships swept north and west around Savo Island, just above Guadalcanal's northwest corner, they could see Japanese transport ships afire in the distance, bombed into submission by American airplanes from Henderson Field.

At 10:55 p.m., radar picked up a Japanese cruiser a few miles away on the starboard bow. Five minutes later, the command came through Shriver's headphones: "Open fire when you are ready."

Shriver readied his men, but he felt acutely helpless. They were prepared to fire on the enemy, but the Eighth Division's guns were far better suited for shooting down aircraft than for shooting at armored ships. The *South Dakota* and the *Washington* loosed their big guns on the Japanese light cruiser *Sendai.* The shots missed their target, and the *Sendai* doubled back northward. A minute later the *South Dakota* opened fire on the *Shikinami,* and when Captain Gatch announced that they had sunk an enemy ship, a great cheering erupted on deck—prematurely, as it turned out. They had scored a hit but not a fatal one. Both Japanese ships turned in the water and disappeared from Shriver's view.

Still firing at the retreating enemy ships, the *South Dakota* lost electrical power. At 11:30, Shriver's headphones went dead, and most of his division's guns were rendered effectively inoperative. For six agonizing minutes, the great dreadnought drifted impotent and blind, lacking radar and searchlights. "The psychological effect on the officers and crew was most depressing. The absence of this gear gave all hands a feeling of being blindfolded," Captain Gatch wrote in his official report. When the power came on, the ship fired at the first target in sight—which turned out to be the American destroyer *Gwin. Gwin* flashed its lights in a coded pattern to *South Dakota,* and it ceased firing, fortunately without scoring a hit.

Disasters began erupting everywhere. The destroyers leading the American column had run into their Japanese counterparts—with catastrophic results. Japanese torpedoes sped through the waters and slammed into all four of the

American destroyers, and enemy gunfire ripped across their decks. Within minutes, the *Preston* and the *Walke* were sinking, and the *Gwin* and the *Benham* were incapacitated. Still arrayed in a column, the *Washington* and the *South Dakota* steamed through the sinking destroyers' wreckage, "tossing out life rafts to the destroyer sailors as they passed over their ships' graves." The *Washington* passed through the remains of the *Walke* and "was unable to turn away from the survivors and thus ran over them," killing many. The *South Dakota* followed several minutes later. Up ahead, Shriver could see floating piles of steaming wreckage, the remains of the sinking *Preston*. Looking down, Shriver could see hundreds of sailors from the *Preston*, flashlights from their lifejackets dotting the sea below. "We were going close to 30 knots," Shriver recalled,

> which is a high speed for something weighing 45,000 tons. I'll never forget this: The destroyers were sinking, and hundreds of the sailors on those ships were in the water. I was up on the deck and I could see our guys in the water and we cut right through them. We must have killed hundreds of American sailors who were serving on those destroyers. We go right straight through where those guys are. We've got four huge propellers on the stern sufficient to propel this 45,000-ton thing. So the force from this propeller killed scores of them. Admiral [Willis] Lee, the commanding officer of the *Washington*, was not worried about whether we rode over some of our own sailors in the water. He didn't have ten seconds to think about them. Because he focused on winning the battle, rather than the fate of the men in the water, we defeated the Japanese that night, and turned the tide of the war. That was the right thing to do. And yet still, when I think of it now, I feel sick.

Misfortune bred misfortune. When the *South Dakota* accidentally fired on the *Gwin*, the muzzle flash from the battleship's great guns ignited fuel vapors around the two scout planes stationed just behind the *Dakota*'s turrets, and the resulting explosion blew both planes into the sea, igniting fires all over the deck. The fires wreaked further havoc with the ship's electrical system—and, worse, produced brilliant explosions on deck that illuminated the *South Dakota*'s exact location to the Japanese, who responded by bathing the American battleship in searchlights. Five Japanese ships poured salvo after salvo of shells and a slew of torpedoes down on Shriver's ship.

In a period of four minutes, the *South Dakota* was rocked by twenty-seven significant hits. Some of the shells slammed into the battleship's metalwork without exploding. Unexploded shells rolled around the deck sounding, as one of Shriver's shipmates would remark later, like a pack of out-of-control bowling balls. Those shells that did explode made "a loud crash, a rolling explosion," followed by "the sizzling sound that metal fragments make when they crash into cables, guns and the superstructure. All of *South Dakota's* radios and all but one of her radar units were knocked out of commission."

Shriver winced at the noise as the *South Dakota* fired its eight starboard 5-inch guns at the Japanese searchlights, knocking them out quickly. But even with their searchlights doused, the Japanese continued pummeling the American battleship. The foremast was hit. Electrical fires erupted continuously, all around Shriver. Whole gun crews were killed by flying shells. The ship began to slow down, and more Japanese rounds ripped across the deck, killing an officer in the radar plotting room. Three rounds exploded in another battle station, killing a half dozen more men. Steam lines were severed, and the hot, hissing steam scalded numerous sailors. Ladders between decks got knocked out, making putting out fires and attending to the growing scores of wounded much more difficult.

Shriver himself was wounded when metal shrapnel from an explosion lodged itself in his shoulder, a wound for which he was later to be awarded a Purple Heart. He paid little attention, however, because many of those in his division had more dire injuries. (More than half of his division would be killed or wounded before the battle was through.) The scene burned itself into Shriver's memory.

> The sight was terrifying. Screaming projectiles, each weighing a half a ton or more, flew flat and red across the sky, trailing flaming tails of fire. Shells flew in both directions by the dozens. Projectiles as long as a living-room sofa hurtled across the deck, landing with explosive impact. Dozens of my comrades died, some of them not 10 feet away from me. I was goddamned scared, lying flat on the deck, praying to God that the night would end with me alive. I didn't think it would.

In desperation, the *South Dakota* tried to radio the *Washington* for help—in vain, because the *South Dakota's* radio antenna had been shot off, leaving the ship effectively mute. Just after midnight the command center suffered a direct hit that killed several high-ranking officers and rendered many of the gun batteries inop-

erable. One of Shriver's friends was standing several hundred feet away at an officer's posting. Shriver watched in horror as "a shell came through and chopped
this fellow right up to the waist. It severed his body off: his pants, and legs, and
shoes all stayed there, while the top half of his body was whisked away by the
shell." About the same time, one of Shriver's gunners was killed in his gun turret. Another gunner had to climb in and cut out his comrade piece by piece. At
this point, Captain Gatch ordered his engineers to make full speed ahead, in
hopes of pulling out of enemy fire.

For a few minutes, the US naval command in the Pacific feared the *South
Dakota* lost, but by 1:55 a.m. what was left of the ship's crew had finally put out
the last of the fires on deck and a few minutes later had reestablished radio contact with the *Washington*. The two battleships rendezvoused a little before 10:00
a.m. on November 15; together they continued south to Nouméa. As morning
dawned that day, the waters off Guadalcanal ran thick with fuel and blood. The
sun beamed down on burning Japanese transports on the island. The
Americans had lost two cruisers and five destroyers and hundreds of sailors at
least. But they had won the battle. Guadalcanal was saved.

But there was little celebration on the *South Dakota* that morning. Thirty officers and crewmen had already died that night, and sixty more were critically
wounded. Shriver had slept no more than a few hours in the past two days, and
he was bleeding from his shoulder. After the shooting had stopped and the fires
had been doused, Shriver recalled, "I got up and looked around the deck, which
was covered in blood. I helped some of the wounded to the ship's mess hall,
where our doctors had set up an emergency hospital. Filled with bloody
corpses and live bodies undergoing operations to save their lives or their limbs,
that room was an unforgettable picture of the price of victory."

About 6:00 a.m. Shriver went off duty, and he stumbled up two decks to his
bunk on the fifth level. As he recalled,

> I kept slipping on the stairs, which were slick with the blood of my fellow sailors—
> from the dead who had been dragged along there and from the wounded who had
> managed to climb upstairs on their own, dripping blood all the way. Those steps, all
> that blood, were unforgettable. You'd have thought I'd have never been able to sleep,
> with such nightmarish pictures floating before my eyes. But I was so goddamned

exhausted, I could barely stay awake. The terror wipes you out. I collapsed into bed and fell instantly asleep without even changing out of my bloody clothes.

Two hours later, he was back on deck with all the available crew for the funeral service of his fallen comrades. Shriver was struck by how ruthlessly efficient the proceedings were. A chaplain spoke briefly, and then he and some officers gave a brief eulogy for each of the deceased, whose bodies were lined up in bags on a long plank, ready to be dumped into the sea, one after the other. Watching the bodies of the fallen sailors slide down the plank and into the Pacific was one of the most painful experiences Shriver had ever had to endure. He couldn't stop thinking about how devastated all the mothers and wives and children would be to know that the bodies of their loved ones had just been jettisoned into the ocean like, as he put it, "a bag of disposable vegetables."

Shriver helped sift through the body parts, looking for a ring or an ID card or a gold tooth that might identify bloody carcasses destroyed beyond recognition. At one point, he found his friend—or rather, he found the bottom half of him. Pulling the man's wallet from the back pocket of his still-intact pants, Shriver found the man's ID card and, utterly revolted, vomited onto the deck.

"This can have quite a lasting impact on you," Shriver later recalled. "Why wasn't I in one of those bags? Good friends of mine were in those bags. We were proud to have won the battle, but we were distressed that the destroyers and their men had been lost. And I may have been very selfish, but all I could do was keep thanking God for my still being alive."

After Guadalcanal, President Roosevelt announced, "It would seem that the turning-point in this war has at last been reached." And Winston Churchill declared this moment, "the end of the beginning." It would be three years yet before the guns of war would go quiet, but for the first time since Pearl Harbor, it looked as though the Allies might prevail.

The *South Dakota* required significant repair work, so it returned to the East Coast of the United States through the Panama Canal. Although it had been not even a month since Shriver had departed Hawaii for the engagement at Santa Cruz, it seemed like years. He had turned twenty-seven just before the battle of Guadalcanal—but he was a considerably older, sadder man than the twenty-six-year-old who had last walked on American shores, in Hawaii, in mid-October.

On December 18, 1942, the *South Dakota* arrived at the Brooklyn Navy Yard, and the officers and crewmen were granted shore leave while engineers came aboard to repair the ship. The first thing Shriver did when he got ashore was to call his mother. Years later, Shriver could still palpably recall the pleasure this call gave him. "I put a nickel in the phone and said, 'Hi, Mom, how are you?' She damn near dropped dead. For all she knew, I was still in the South Pacific."

Soon, though, he was called back to the *South Dakota*. What followed were eight long, cold months operating in the North Atlantic with the British Home Fleet, patrolling Allied shipping lines to protect them from enemy attack by German submarines. The American battleship made regular forays out into the North Sea and patrolled the European coast. These were some anxious days and nights for the men aboard the *South Dakota*. German submarines had sunk many ships in the area. "Allied ships going to Russia were subjected to a lot of attacks," Shriver recalled. "Our job was to protect them. Our presence up there was to make the Germans reluctant to make trouble." Although they occasionally sighted enemy planes, the *South Dakota* did not see combat during this period. Still, Shriver recalled, "you thanked God every time you returned safely to a friendly port."

THE *SANDLANCE*

Shriver was wearying of life on a battleship. He didn't like getting shot at, for one thing. For another he had always, ever since the Canterbury School, enjoyed being a big fish in a small pond. A battleship is a very big pond. There were more than 2,000 men aboard the battleship, and despite his significant responsibilities as commander of the *South Dakota*'s Eighth Division, he often felt "like a cog in a machine." When his ship had put in at Pearl Harbor after Guadalcanal, he had seen the latest US Navy submarines going out for trial runs, and he was intrigued. The crews were far smaller than a battleship's. Also, he recalled thinking to himself, "being deep under water in one of those steel contraptions looked much more interesting—and safer—than being shot at on the deck of a battleship." So he applied for a transfer to the submarine corps, and in the late summer of 1943, when the *South Dakota* put in at Norfolk, Virginia, he received word that his application to submarine school in New London, Connecticut, had been accepted.

After ninety days of training, Shriver flew with six of his New London classmates out to Mare Island, off San Francisco, to report for his submarine assignment. He was excited about becoming a submariner. Shriver chose the Mare Island assignment strategically: He knew that, as a full lieutenant, he outranked any of the six peers traveling with him from submarine school. He calculated that, once on the West Coast, he would be given important responsibilities, perhaps even partial command of a submarine.

But on the morning that he was supposed to report to the Mare Island base commander, Shriver overslept, arriving in the assignment office at 8:45 a.m. The assignment officer was sitting behind his desk when the young lieutenant walked in. He smiled cheerfully and said, as Shriver recalled it, "Good to see you, Shriver. We've been going over assignments. Your classmates were all in here 45 minutes ago, and they've all been assigned to our new subs heading out to the South Pacific. I'm sending you down to San Diego, to be an officer on the USS *S-40.*"

Shriver's heart sank. S-class submarines were decrepit World War I–era submarines that had been refitted for training. He exploded in anger, demanding an audience with Mare Island's commanding officer.

"Sir," Shriver remembered telling the base commander when granted an interview with him, "I had hoped to rejoin the Pacific fleet."

"We all want that," Shriver recalled the commander replying. "But your classmates who preceded you have all been assigned to those fleet boats and there's no more space. You're going to San Diego."

"I understand that," Shriver persisted. "But with all due respect, I'm a full lieutenant. Doesn't my senior rank entitle me to a Pacific assignment?"

"Relax, Shriver. The war will last a while. Sooner or later there will be plenty of action for everyone. For now, you will report to the USS *S-40.*"

When Shriver continued to protest, the commander erupted. "Shriver!" he yelled. "You have been assigned to San Diego! That is where you will go!"

How ignominious, Shriver thought to himself. While the battle for freedom was being fought in the Pacific, he would be stuck off the coast of San Diego running training expeditions. Walking back to the barracks, it occurred to him once again that someone must have conspired against him. "Someone didn't want to see me back in battle in the South Pacific," he recalled thinking. "And there was only one person that someone might be." Knowing how resourceful his mother could be, Shriver convinced himself that Hilda had, out of concern for her son's welfare, decided to stymie his attempt to return to battle and had called on her family connections to get him relegated to noncombat duty.

In truth, Shriver was likely projecting his own fears about returning to the

Pacific onto his mother; exorcising himself of anxiety in this way made it easier to maintain the brave, even bloodthirsty, swagger that he maintained in front of his fellow officers. He dashed off a withering letter to his mother and was embarrassed, a week or so later, to receive her response. She had played no role, she insisted convincingly, in his assignment to San Diego; moreover, she pointed out archly, he ought to be old enough now to learn to accept things as they came.

Chastened, Shriver reported to S-boat duty in San Diego, still mentally cursing the bad luck that had made him late to report at Mare Island. Within ten months, however, it appeared that his luck had hardly been bad: Each of the submarines to which he had hoped he might be assigned had been sunk. All six of the New London classmates who had traveled with him to San Francisco had been killed. "God must want me to do something I haven't done yet," Shriver recalled thinking at the time.

The longed-for assignment to the Pacific came a year later, in January 1945, when Shriver was assigned to the USS *Sandlance*, a recently commissioned submarine, as a gunnery and torpedo officer. On March 13, 1945, the *Sandlance* cruised from San Francisco to Pearl Harbor, and on April 10 it traveled to the waters off Japan. There, it sank a Japanese freighter and spent nights cruising secretly along the coasts off Honshu and Hokkaido, trying to gather intelligence for what was looking like the increasingly inevitable land invasion of Japan. After dark, the *Sandlance* would surface quietly, 3 or 4 miles off the coast, to refill its oxygen tanks, recharge its electrical batteries, and conduct reconnaissance. Many nights, Shriver would be the senior officer above decks, walking along the top of the submarine with two other crewmen. Gazing off toward land through his binoculars, he could see the lights of mountain villages, and he would watch freight trains chugging up and down the coastal railways in the darkness. Most of Japan was blacked out at night, to make it harder for American bombers to see their targets. It was an eerie, discomfiting experience. Standing in the dark in the vastness of the Pacific, Shriver couldn't help but feel a strange yearning to be ashore in one of those villages, or in the compartment of one of those trains, sharing some tea or sake. He was, he realized, perceiving the humanity of his enemy. Or maybe it was just that the loneliness of the sea induced a craving for warmth wherever he could find it.

On June 6, as the Allies were securing victory in Europe, the *Sandlance* put in at Midway Island and readied itself for what was to be its final war patrol. But just days before the *Sandlance* was to depart again for Japanese waters, the last mail call brought a letter to Shriver that ordered him to report for duty back in New London. Shriver was astonished. He went to the submarine commander, Malcolm Garrison, and demanded to know why he was being transferred. Garrison said he didn't know.

"Well, then, can't you wire the commander of the Pacific Submarine Fleet and ask him why I'm being removed from the sub?" Shriver asked.

"Save your breath," Shriver remembered Garrison telling him. "This is the navy. Submarine skippers don't ask admirals for explanations."

Shriver angrily crated up his gear and shipped it to New London, then caught the next plane to the United States. When the plane made a refueling stopover at Pearl Harbor, he got off the plane and stalked into the personnel office at submarine headquarters. The personnel officer on duty recognized him.

"What the hell are you doing here, Shriver?" he asked. "You're supposed to be at sea!" "That's exactly right," declared Shriver as he threw his orders on the desk. "So explain this."

After looking at Shriver's orders and then rummaging around in the office files, the personnel officer determined what had happened. It turned out that there were in fact *two* Shrivers in the Pacific submarine fleet: Sarge and an officer who had spent the last two years on an escort vessel along the coast of Australia. The orders Sarge received had been meant for the man off Australia. Sarge was told he could rejoin the *Sandlance* next time it docked in Pearl Harbor. So he settled in to wait for his comrades, hoping it wouldn't be too long before he could rejoin them.

THE BOMB

The summer of 1945 wore on. The war in Europe wound down. But although American airplanes were bombarding Tokyo nightly, the Japanese appeared willing to fight to the last man. A land invasion—sure to be as bloody and grueling as anything US soldiers had ever undertaken—looked inevitable. Gen. Douglas MacArthur was predicting that the United States would lose 50,000 soldiers simply establishing the beachhead. Secretary of War Henry Stimson would later write he had been informed that the land invasion of Japan "might be expected to cause over a million casualties to American forces alone."

As the projected invasion became imminent, the navy sent Shriver into training to become a submarine air control officer. The plan was for Shriver to surface in a submarine off the coast of Japan and lead small groups of soldiers ashore by raft at night. These advance soldiers—six or seven men in a group—would then climb to higher ground in the mountainous regions and set up reconnaissance posts, from which they would broadcast intelligence reports: troop movements, what the topography and vegetation looked like, whether there were bombable targets available, and where the effective beachheads for Allied troops were. The goal for these advance teams was to provide as much information to the invading American soldiers as possible, without giving away their own location in the mountains.

The assignment was likely to be, Shriver knew, a suicide mission. "All of us in the submarine corps who were given these orders thought it was a death assignment," he recalled. "We used to talk amongst ourselves that the chances of our coming back alive were about one in a hundred. If they sent twenty teams of four to five guys each at 3-mile intervals along the coast—well, it seemed to me impossible that the Japanese would not be able to find us. I figured this was it. If I didn't get killed, it would be remarkable."

Although no one in Shriver's invasion team looked forward to the assignment, they did feel honored to have been chosen. "Since we couldn't tell anyone outside of the navy," about the top-secret mission, Shriver said, "we made ourselves feel better by talking about what hot rocks we were to be selected to be first onto the islands. We knew we had been chosen for our physical and psychological toughness, and our skills."

For six weeks, Shriver underwent intensive training. He and his fellow team members practiced night landings and knife fighting, learned secret codes for radio transmissions, and ran up and down Hawaiian mountains. In August, as his training moved toward completion and he prepared to head once again to Japan, he endured a recurring nightmare about being captured and tortured by the Japanese.

Thus when Shriver woke up one morning to the news that the first atomic bomb had been dropped on Hiroshima, killing tens of thousands of Japanese, his first emotion was elation. Three days later, when the second atomic bomb devastated Nagasaki, killing many thousands more, he felt the same thing. "All I could do was rejoice," Shriver recalled. "It was a purely selfish reaction." On August 13, the Japanese surrendered.

Shriver and his would-be invasion-force colleagues were overcome with relief. No more bloodletting. No suicide mission. No torture at the hands of the enemy. "I was still in the training camp," Shriver recalled. "You couldn't have had a group of people more excited and relieved than" him and his fellow submarine air control trainees. The barracks and officers' quarters were abuzz with jubilant conversation: When are you going home? Have you talked to your mother and father? Have you called your girlfriend?

Shriver, as a full lieutenant who had seen plenty of combat and been in the armed forces since 1940, was one of the men eligible for earliest release from active duty, and on September 2, 1945, he was detached from the 102nd Submarine Division. Every waking moment he would bask in the feeling of not being at war, of not being about to be killed. He prayed to God and gave thanks for being spared, and he promised to make the most of his remaining years on earth.

For Shriver, who had been raised on the nobility of war—on the justness of the American Revolution, on the tragic grandeur of the Lost Cause in the Civil War, on the heroism of the myriad Shriver soldiers through history—the actual experience of combat had begun to change his view. As his joy at being spared the invasion of Japan receded, it began to be replaced by chagrin at his own rejoicing. The power of atomic weaponry had caused the moral universe to shift on its axis.

Shriver never doubted the justness of the American cause in World War II. But the horror of combat, of seeing carnage up close, solidified his conviction that war was not a noble calling but rather something assiduously to be avoided. The battle for freedom had been won—but the lives of more than 400,000 American servicemen had been lost. "The war had a profound effect on me," Shriver once said. "I gained a greater understanding of what Jesus Christ had done in trying to spare us war."

It had been only about four years since he had left the ivied quadrangles of Yale, but Shriver felt considerably older, wiser, and more humble than he had in the spring of 1941. And although his natural ebullience could not be suppressed for long, the young war hero—now on the cusp of his thirties—returned to civilian life with his tragic sense deepened. His faith, however, remained strong.

PART TWO

The Chicago Years
(1945–1960)

CHAPTER FIVE

Joseph P. Kennedy

Sarge returned to New York in time for Christmas in 1945, moved into the spare bedroom in his mother's place at 151 East Eighty-third Street, and began work at the law firm of Winthrop, Stimson, Putnam & Roberts. He hated it. After serving on a submarine during combat, where every decision could have literal life-or-death consequences, working on minor corporate legal problems as a junior associate seemed absurdly trivial. Shriver would not have chosen to return to war under any circumstances. But the contrast between what he had done between 1941 and 1945, on the one hand, and what he was doing now, on the other, was so stark it left him feeling discombobulated. Many returning servicemen were enduring the same trials; war heroes, thrilled to be victorious, reveling in the very mundanity of everyday life during peacetime, were at the same time confused about who they were and what their postwar role was.

Shriver's natural restlessness compounded the problem. He couldn't abide sitting still for long. He needed action and challenges. And he needed creative energy to be flowing around him. Winthrop, Stimson was one of the most respected firms on Wall Street. But the way to advance at a firm like Winthrop,

Stimson was to keep your nose to the grindstone, working diligently and patiently toward achieving partnership. Shriver was by nature neither quiet nor patient, and he couldn't bear sitting at a desk all day. "I'm bored," he told his mother. Wasn't there more to life than wrestling with tax problems?

Around this time, an assistant editor's position opened up at *Newsweek* magazine. Sarge learned about it from his Yale roommate, Mac Muir, whose father, Malcolm, was now the magazine's publisher. Shriver was well qualified for the job—not only had he edited the *Yale Daily News* but he had also reported articles for *Time* magazine in the late 1930s—so Mac's father hired him. His position was special assistant to Muir himself, and his unofficial role was "idea man," tasked with coming up with story ideas and ways to improve the magazine. But Shriver's fertile mind produced ideas faster than the magazine's institutional structure was equipped to digest them. He was dismayed when his ideas languished on Muir's desk or got bowdlerized in committee meetings.

Shriver exorcised his frustrations by maintaining a vigorous social life. In 1946 the frosty early winds of the cold war had already begun to blow, but for the most part life still felt like one long victory party. "As a decorated veteran," Shriver said, "I could go to the 21 Club and always get a plum table. I'd wear my medals and go from party to party, the Plaza, the St. Regis, the Waldorf-Astoria, dancing late into the evening."

Many unmarried servicemen returned from the war and threw themselves into torrid romances, a sizable number of which resulted in rash, ill-advised marriages. Whether by luck or by discernment, Shriver avoided this fate. Partly it was that he had so many female admirers—why should he limit himself to the company of just one woman when so many of them were clamoring for his attention? But Shriver was also very particular about the qualities he sought in a wife. He wanted her to be beautiful, of course, but more important than that he was looking for someone who was intelligent and driven, someone with a personality strong enough that she wouldn't constantly be shrinking in his considerable presence. And he wanted a wife who was as devoutly Catholic as he was. (Some of Shriver's friends say that he also wanted a wife who had money.) This constellation of qualities was rare enough to prevent him from meeting the unhappy marital fate of many of his peers.

Although Eleanor Hoguet DeGive, Shriver's longtime paramour, was now married, he remained friendly with her and her large extended family, and he regularly attended parties at the lavish Hoguet mansion at 47 East Ninety-second Street. At one of these parties, in 1946, Shriver recalled,

> there was this breathtakingly beautiful woman, surrounded by a bouquet of men, all appearing to clamor for her conversational attention. Her beauty was not an ordinary one; it was starker, more austere. Her dress didn't look as expensive or fashionable as the ones the other girls were wearing. But she conveyed a magnificent sense of complete self-possession. As she held forth on some subject or another, the men and women around her stood rapt. I was intrigued.

Shriver walked over to join the woman's colloquy. "She was talking about politics and foreign affairs and describing her experience at the Court of St. James, in England, where her father had been ambassador during the war," Shriver said. "'Aha,' I thought to myself: 'So *this* is Eunice Kennedy.'"

Eunice Mary Kennedy. Shriver had never met her before, but he had met members of her family over the years, and he certainly knew her family by its growing reputation. He had gone to school with Jack at Canterbury, and he had become well acquainted with Eunice's older sister, the effervescent Kathleen, whose best friend through the 1930s had been Eleanor Hoguet. Jack Kennedy, no longer the sallow little runt Shriver had known at Canterbury, had become a war hero. After the war Jack had gone to San Francisco as a journalist to cover the founding meeting of the United Nations. Now, like Shriver, bored with journalism, he was exploring a career in politics and contemplating a run for Congress in Massachusetts's Eleventh District.

The Kennedy with the most outsized reputation was still the family patriarch, Joseph P. Kennedy. The son of Patrick Kennedy, a Boston barkeep, and the son-in-law of the colorful John Francis Fitzgerald, widely known as "Honey" Fitz, the first native-born Irish Catholic to be elected mayor of Brahmin-dominated Boston, Joe Kennedy had in his way outdone both of them. Rising through the ranks of the Boston banking industry, he went on to make a fortune in finance and the movie industry. During the Depression, when most financial speculators were wiped out, Kennedy shrewdly shorted the market and got richer. This not only solidified his reputation as a shrewd financier and investor, but it also contributed to his reputation as a shady operator. This reputation, in turn, led to FDR's inspired decision to install Kennedy as founding chairman of the Securities and Exchange Commission in 1934: Kennedy, President Roosevelt figured correctly, knew all the illicit speculators' tricks and therefore would be able to spot malfeasance in the markets before anyone else could. After a successful term in that post from 1934 to 1935, Kennedy had been rewarded by being appointed head of the United States Maritime Commission and subsequently with a posting to the Court of St. James, as ambassador to England, where he served from 1937 to 1940.

In England the large Kennedy brood had become darlings of the society pages; their comings and goings were chronicled as though they were American royalty. As the drums of war beat ever louder in Europe, Kennedy had kept his name in the American papers by boldly declaring that the United States should stay out of the war. Kennedy supported Chamberlain's compromise at Munich and argued that the United States should simply make its peace with Germany and let it have the run of Europe. As damning as this position seems in retrospect, Kennedy's motivations were not malignant: Like Shriver, he was familiar with the damage and the death toll that the Great War had wreaked on Europe, and he did not want American soldiers—and particularly his own sons, Joe, Jack, Bobby, and Teddy—getting killed for somebody else's business. Kennedy's stance against the US involvement in the war through 1939 and 1940 had endeared him to Shriver and the founders of America First at Yale.

Eunice Kennedy had an imposing reputation in her own right. Shriver had known of her existence for years—she had gone to the Noroton School of the Sacred Heart just after Eleanor Hoguet and Kathleen Kennedy had left there, and Eunice had followed Eleanor by a few years at Manhattanville College. During the war, she would appear on both British and American society pages with the rest of her family, and she was often seen around New York society on the arms of dukes, industrialists, and celebrities.

Shriver was eager to meet her. "Here I was," he recalled, "a measly assistant editor, a war veteran, sure, but a poor one without money or status to recommend me, especially by Kennedy standards." But he brazenly inserted himself into her conversation. "Never had I met a woman so intelligent, so sure of herself, so well versed on so wide a range of topics," Shriver recalled. "We ranged from domestic politics to world affairs to religion to her experiences abroad to interest in the problems of juvenile delinquency. I was dazzled by her intellect and seriousness. I left the Hoguets in a daze."

A few days later Eunice accepted Sarge's invitation to 5:30 p.m. tea at the Plaza Hotel, followed by a dinner party and dancing. But when he tried to kiss her goodnight she responded diffidently; in a letter to her a few years later, he would recall "that memorable evening outside the Plaza Hotel when I first kissed you only to find you picking morning glories out of the window box behind me." Shriver was smitten, but he tried to deny himself any illusions. He recalled,

Eunice Kennedy had far more on her mind than the affections of some hotshot junior editor. And I don't just mean she had other men. She was too busy working on the problems of the mentally retarded, helping her father with various projects, attending to the germinal political career of her brother Jack, appearing at dozens of society functions each week, and working with the Catholic Church on a host of charitable efforts. In the scope of all she had going on in her life, I was a matter of small concern.

One morning not long after his date with Eunice, the phone rang in Shriver's office at *Newsweek*. He picked up the receiver and heard, as he recalled, "Shriver— This is Joe Kennedy. I'm staying at the Waldorf-Astoria Hotel. Can you meet me here tomorrow morning, at eight o'clock, for breakfast?" Sarge said he could and before he could ask why, Kennedy had hung up. Joe Kennedy! What could he be calling about? Shriver wondered. Have I done something to offend his daughter?

The next morning he reported promptly at eight to Kennedy's suite at the Waldorf-Astoria, where breakfast had already been laid out. Kennedy didn't waste time with small talk. "The force of his personality imposed itself on me immediately," Shriver recalled. "He was not a terribly large man, but he had a very self-confident physical bearing and the strongest blue eyes that had ever looked at me." Kennedy's company, Joseph P. Kennedy Enterprises, was by now a sprawling operation that included interests in the filmmaking, liquor distribution, and real estate industries, among others. He was worth hundreds of millions of dollars. Although he was fifty-eight years old, the Kennedy patriarch looked younger, trim and fit and highly attuned to everything around him. Shriver recalled the conversation as follows.

"Sit down," Kennedy said. Shriver sat. "My daughter tells me you're an editor." Shriver said he was.

"The reason I've brought you here today is I've got these papers." He handed Shriver a manuscript. "These are all by or about my son Joe Jr. Large parts of it are his letters and diaries. It's about what we did when we were over in England, and about what he did" in Spain in 1944, during the civil war there. Shriver riffled through the pages while Kennedy spoke. "Some people have encouraged me to publish these papers as a book. Will you take a hard look at them and give me your honest opinion about whether they should be published?" Kennedy asked. Shriver said he would. "Good," Kennedy said. "Then let's eat."

Shriver had met the Ambassador's son, Joe Kennedy Jr., several times at parties in New York City and at the Long Island estate of Shriver's patron, John Thomas Smith, before the war. When the war was over, Shriver learned that young Joe had died in a crash when test-flying a plane over Belgium in 1944. He also knew through the grapevine that Joe Sr. had been devastated by the loss; the Kennedys were a close-knit family, and the father had clearly had high aspirations for his eldest son.

Shriver was flattered that Mr. Kennedy had selected him to pass judgment on his son's papers. But he was baffled, too. Why, Shriver wondered, had Kennedy chosen *him*? He was an editor, yes, but a relatively junior one. Surely Joe Kennedy, with the connections and the influence he possessed, could have gotten someone more senior and experienced to read the papers. Shriver wondered if Mr. Kennedy was testing him.

Shriver spent the next several days reading Joe Jr.'s papers. "It was clear from reading the papers how much affection the whole Kennedy family had for Joe Jr.," Shriver recalled, "and there were parts of the book that were quite interesting." But the manuscript was not, he concluded, something he thought the public would want to read.

Mr. Kennedy had called and arranged for a second breakfast to discuss his son's work. "Sorry, Mr. Kennedy," Shriver said bravely upon joining Eunice's father again for breakfast at the Waldorf-Astoria, "but in my opinion these are not suitable for publication." Shriver braced himself for a withering tirade.

But Kennedy, after fixing him for a long moment with his piercing blue eyes, broke into a rueful grin and said, "I didn't think so. Thank you for your opinion. Now let's eat." For the next hour and a half, Kennedy asked Shriver questions about his job at *Newsweek*, about what he had done at Winthrop, Stimson, about his experiences in the war. When they were through, Shriver thanked

Kennedy for breakfast and headed for his *Newsweek* office, believing that would be the last he heard from the famous businessman.

But a week later he answered the phone at his office to find Mr. Kennedy on the line again. "Shriver," he remembers Kennedy saying to him. "I'd like to offer you a job at Joseph P. Kennedy Enterprises." Sarge was stunned. "You're young but you're smart," Kennedy continued. "I could use someone like you to help me out." Shriver thanked him for the offer and said he would think about it.

A job offer from the famous—the infamous—Joe Kennedy. What was Shriver to make of this? On the one hand, he was honored: Kennedy was known to be a harsh judge of talent, and to have been deemed worthy of a personal job offer from him seemed to Shriver a mark of some accomplishment. On the other hand, Kennedy had a bad reputation in many circles. Some said Kennedy was brilliant; others, however, said he was unscrupulous.

Shriver called around to people he knew and respected, to get their opinion of Kennedy and their advice on whether he should go to work for the man. One of the first people he spoke to was Eleanor Hoguet's father. Robert Hoguet was still head of the Emigrant Industrial Savings Bank; he was also a shrewd investor in his own right and relatively wealthy. And yet he was an old-line French Catholic of the sort who might be threatened by or resentful of Kennedy's vigorous Irish-Catholic strivings. Hoguet's wisdom would be meaningful. "For Christ's sake, Sarge," Shriver remembers Hoguet telling him, "definitely work for Kennedy. You'd be a fool not to take this opportunity. He's one of the smartest guys ever to operate on Wall Street. You'll learn a lot from him."

But the next person Shriver talked to was Raymond Moley, a Columbia professor and one of FDR's early brain trusters, who had gone on to become a famous political commentator and *Newsweek* editor. Shriver respected him greatly and considered him a staunch ally. Shriver also knew that Moley had been for a time Joe Kennedy's closest friend and source of information inside the Roosevelt administration. His advice would mean as much as Hoguet's. "Joe Kennedy?" Moley said when Sarge inquired about him, "Don't go anywhere near the bastard. Don't you know what a complete son-of-a-bitch the guy is? He'll eat you alive. Don't take that job."

Shriver asked more people their opinions of Mr. Kennedy, hoping to find some kind of consensus. He was disappointed—people's opinions broke down almost evenly along opposing lines. Either they worshiped and admired Joe

Kennedy or they feared and despised him. This was intriguing. How could different people's feelings about one man be so drastically different—and yet always so strong?

By now, Shriver had also run afoul of *Newsweek*'s management by seeking to organize a union, and he was being threatened with a transfer to the magazine's Toledo office. "I went over things in my mind," Shriver recalled. "I'm not getting very far here with *Newsweek*, I thought to myself, and my bosses don't think as highly of my talents as I do. On the other hand, working for Kennedy could be awful." What tipped the balance, according to Shriver, was Eunice. "In the back of my mind I knew that working for Joe would provide me an opportunity to get close to Eunice." It's likely that Joe Kennedy was thinking the same thing in reverse; that is, Kennedy must have known Shriver was seeing his daughter on occasion, so it's possible—given how Kennedy stage-managed his children's lives—that while he was officially offering the young man a job, what he was really doing was inspecting him for the position of son-in-law.

Shriver gave notice at *Newsweek* and went to work as an associate at Joseph P. Kennedy Enterprises. Meanwhile he continued to court the boss's daughter, who remained polite but distracted in returning her suitor's affections.

At the end of 1946, after just a few months at JPK Enterprises in Manhattan, Joe Kennedy made Shriver another offer. "I've just bought this building out in Chicago," Kennedy told him, "and I need someone to go out there and watch out for my interests. I'd like you to be my representative out at that building." Shriver knew that the building to which Kennedy was referring was not just any building—it was the Merchandise Mart, the largest piece of real estate in the world, 4 million square feet, with room for more than 30,000 people to work inside it. Shriver was incredulous.

"Look," Kennedy said, as Shriver recalled. "I know you don't know anything about the real estate business. But I want you to be my eyes and ears out there, keep me abreast of what's going on. And I want you to bring in tenants to the building. Fill her up so I can earn some rental income."

Once again, Shriver canvassed his friends and advisers—and once again got starkly contrasting recommendations. Some businessmen who respected Kennedy thought it was a tremendous opportunity—how many thirty-one-year-olds were given the chance to be second in command at a multimillion-dollar enterprise? Others continued to advise him against it. It's a deal with the devil, they told him. Shriver's law school classmate Bob Stuart had grown up in Chicago. He recalls giving the following advice: "Sarge, I think you'll enjoy Chicago, but remember, when you make a commitment to the Kennedy family you probably are pretty well committed for a long time." Stuart, although he had gotten some money from Joe Kennedy when he founded America First, warned that "the Kennedy family was not particularly highly regarded." A letter from his old headmaster at Canterbury chilled Shriver by implying that in signing on with Joe Kennedy, he had forsaken God for Mammon. "Thanks for your letter," Hume wrote to him in December 1946,

> in which you tell me you have given up your job with News Week and intend to go to Chicago to work for Joe Kennedy. Be sure that I wish you every success. However, I see you go with a certain feeling of disappointment. . . . I am not sure whether, however successful you may be, your success can be measured by any other terms than those of the amount of money you can make. Forgive me for saying this so bluntly, but if my saying so keeps your eye on what really is the main objective and doesn't let other things get in the way of making a right use of the talents and the opportunities that come to you, then it won't matter if the statement is a little blunt, provided you understand it is made in a spirit of great interest in you.

In the end, the lure of working for Kennedy was too attractive to resist. Here was a world-famous financier giving Shriver major responsibility for turning a giant, multimillion-dollar piece of property from a money loser into a profit maker. And, perhaps sensing the financial burden that weighed on a young man responsible for supporting his mother, Kennedy also offered him an apartment to stay in, rent free, in Chicago—Kennedy's own residence in the Ambassador East Hotel.

Two days after accepting the position, Shriver was on the New York Central Express, the overnight train to Chicago. He walked over to the Merchandise Mart, on the north bank of the Chicago River between Wells and Orleans streets. At first glance, the building looked unimpressive. Gazing upward, he could count only eighteen stories, or twenty-five, including its towers. That was nothing compared with New York skyscrapers. But then he began to walk around the building. "Pretty soon," Shriver recalled, "I realized I had walked two blocks and was still in front of the same building. It was enormous, about two-and-a-half football fields long."

The Merchandise Mart had been originally constructed in 1930, at a cost of $30 million, by Marshall Field and Company, to house its offices and a collection of household furnishing wholesalers. It was, the Field company advertised, to be not only the world's largest building but "the Colossus of Market Places." In Chicago, which was known as the Great Central Market, buyers and sellers from around the country could find everything they needed, not just in one city, but in one *building*.

But the building opened for business just as the Depression took hold; for a time, it looked as though the giant building might forever be merely a monument to the grandiose expectations of the late 1920s. The Mart's prospects had improved considerably by the end of the war, but Marshall Field valued the company on its books at only $21 million, $9 million less than the original construction cost. Although selling the building meant Marshall Field would take a loss, more than one-third of the office space was occupied by federal and state government agencies paying low rents, so the company decided it was better to sell the building as a tax write-off than to wait for the building to become profitable.

In 1934, when Joe Kennedy had joined the Roosevelt administration as head of the SEC, he had given up speculative investments. As both a matter of propriety and in the interests of securing his family's future, he had put his money into more cautious, low-yield investments. Beginning in the early 1940s, however, he had begun to branch out into real estate—it was, some said, his attempt to distract himself from the pain of Joe Jr.'s death—and moved quickly in and out of several properties in midtown Manhattan, making enormous profits. The financial pages marveled at his canniness and bravery; using his holding company the Park Agency, he would leverage himself heavily, often borrowing more than 90 percent of the capital he needed. In July 1945, he expanded his sights beyond Manhattan and bought the Socony-Vacuum Oil Company building in Albany, New York, for a reputed $1.8 million.

That was just an appetizer. Two weeks later, in what *Business Week* called a "thumping bargain," Kennedy bought the Merchandise Mart for $13 million, all but $500,000 of it borrowed. Still, when he bought the building, some real estate experts were convinced that Kennedy "had become the owner of the world's largest white elephant." But Kennedy was shrewd. Before closing the sale, he made sure that the low-rent federal tenants would be moving out when their leases expired. Kennedy intended to fill the space left behind by the government agencies with higher-paying private tenants. This was a substantial challenge: The Merchandise Mart had 93 acres of leasing space, with 6.5 *miles* of plate-glass display windows and more than 6 miles of interior corridors. So the new owner launched a big promotional campaign and hired Sargent Shriver to help bring it to fruition.

Upon arrival in Chicago, Shriver found himself part of the triumvirate running the building under the distant but watchful eye of Joe Kennedy. Shriver's office was next to Wallace Ollman's, the Mart's general manager. Ollman was tall and thin, and although he at times seemed reserved, he had a way of speaking that commanded attention. He and Shriver got along well. The third man in the triumvirate was the Mart's advertising director, Tom King. Shriver's job as assistant general manager of the building was partly administrative, but his real strength, as Kennedy had anticipated, proved to be sales, and he found himself soon after his arrival as the de facto vice president in charge of bringing companies into the building. During his twelve years at the Mart, Shriver succeeded in attracting such blue-chip tenants as NBC, Eastern Air Lines, Western Electric, Field Enterprises, and Quaker Oats.

Through Kennedy's prescience, Ollman's managerial acumen, and Shriver's salesmanship—with some help from Chicago's postwar resurgence as an economic epicenter—the Mart was a phenomenally successful investment. By 1955 the annual revenue generated by rental income alone was more than Kennedy's initial $13 million investment. The building became the cornerstone of the Kennedy family fortune: In 1947 Joe Kennedy established a trust dividing ownership of the Mart among family members; more than forty years later the Kennedy family sold the building to a realty company in a deal—partly brokered by Sargent Shriver—that yielded $625 million for the surviving heirs.

Shriver had never been to Chicago before being sent there for his new job, but several Illinois-based friends eagerly absorbed him into their social circles. Bob Stuart, Shriver's old law school classmate and cofounder of America First, was living in the area with his wife and working as a junior executive in his father's company, Quaker Oats. Lloyd Bowers was another old friend from way back; he had gone to elementary school with Shriver at the Browning School in New York. Bowers was on his way to a successful career in business, and his wife, Frances "Faffy" Bowers, hailed from an old Illinois family whose great wealth had been somewhat diminished by the Depression. Through the Bowerses, Shriver became acquainted with Bill Blair, who became one of his best friends in Chicago. William McCormack Blair was a member of the Chicago McCormacks, one of the wealthiest and most prominent families in the city. Blair had been a founding member of the Committee to Defend America by Aiding the Allies, America First's most prominent opposite number. But Blair and Shriver were both bachelors and shared a love of tennis. Because Blair's family had an indoor tennis court on their estate, Shriver ended up spending many weekends at the Blair mansion, engaging in marathon tennis sessions punctuated by vigorous political arguments.

In 1948 this group coalesced around the gubernatorial campaign of Adlai Stevenson, an Illinois Democrat. Blair permanently switched party affiliations to become one of Stevenson's top aides-de-camp. Shriver would have joined Stevenson's staff as a part-time paid staffer if Mr. Kennedy had not snuffed the idea. "My political life is temporarily shattered," Shriver wrote to Eunice in October 1948. "The Democratic candidate for governor, Adlai Stevenson, through his local staff, offered me a job writing speeches and propaganda, but your Dad said nix."

By 1947 Shriver was beginning to establish himself as a man about town. For a few months he had a serious girlfriend, Helena Carter, a beautiful B-movie actress from New York, who briefly edged out Eunice as the primary object of his affections. He had a regular table in the Ambassador East Pump Room—Table 1, which was Joe Kennedy's when he was in town—where Chicago's celebrities came to see and be seen.

"I was having a great time," Shriver recalled. "I was squiring the most beautiful ladies around town. I had season tickets for the White Sox baseball team. I hobnobbed with the Chicago elite at the Pump Room." Life in Chicago began to look as though it held real promise. But just as he was beginning to feel settled in Chicago, he was told to leave.

"Sarge," said Mr. Kennedy, "I need you to go to Washington to help Eunice."

CHAPTER SIX

Eunice

In 1947 Eunice Kennedy was an astonishingly accomplished and well-traveled young woman. The fifth child of Joe and Rose, Eunice had from early childhood set herself apart from her siblings. With the exception of Rosemary, the eldest daughter, who had been born with behavioral and developmental problems and later underwent a partial lobotomy in an attempt to "cure" her, all the Kennedy girls were sharp, worldly, and bright. Kathleen, Eunice, Pat, and Jean were eight years apart from oldest (Kathleen) to youngest (Jean). Amid this tight-knit group, Eunice and Kathleen were distinct, Kathleen as the most socially effervescent, Eunice as the smartest. Eunice also displayed a commitment to religion and to public service that went beyond what the other members of this very public-spirited family showed.

Eunice worshiped her father and inherited from him many of his distinctive traits: an acute intelligence; a savvy political sense; a total lack of patience; an unwillingness to suffer fools gladly; and an almost superhuman willpower that gave her the ability to set goals and achieve them, no matter who or what stood in her way. All these qualities were leavened in her by a devout religiousness that exceeded her father's, and by a physical frailty that often left her incapacitated.

The brother to whom Eunice was closest in both age and friendship— Jack—was also the brother she most resembled in her combination of political intelligence and weak physical health. They both had an uncanny ability to size up a political situation instantly, and they endured the same litany of medical ailments, including back problems, legions of stomach problems, and Addison's disease. Eunice's chronic stomach problems left her consistently underweight, leading her family to call her "Puny Eunie."

As war broke out in Europe in the fall of 1939, Eunice returned to the United States, where she began her undergraduate education at Manhattanville College in New York. She did not particularly enjoy the two years she spent there. One reason for her unhappiness at Manhattanville was the suffering of her older sister Rosemary. By the fall of 1941, Rosie's behavior had begun to seem uncontrollable. She kept escaping from the convent where she was in school. Despite her stunted emotional and intellectual development, Rosemary had grown up to be a physically attractive young woman. Her parents feared she would fall prey to "pregnancy, disease, and disgrace" at the hands of some predatory young man. Meanwhile, magazines were lauding the effects of an experimental new medical technique called "psycho-surgery"—in other words, a partial lobotomy. "The doctors told my father it was a good idea" for Rosemary, Eunice recalled. The operation was not a success. Rosemary "regressed into an infantlike state, mumbling a few words, sitting for hours staring at the walls, only traces left of the young woman she had been, still with those flashes of rage."

Desolate over the fate of her elder sister, Eunice had transferred in January 1942 to Stanford University, in Palo Alto, California, where it was hoped that the temperate climate would warm her soul. It didn't. She studied—and played—with her characteristic intensity, but she did not enjoy herself, especially now that the war was on.

After graduation, Eunice returned east to the family estate at Hyannis Port, on Cape Cod. But any emotional respite was short-lived. On the second Sunday in August 1944, Joe and Rose, along with their children Jack, Bobby, Teddy, Pat, Jean, and Eunice (Kathleen was in England with her husband, and Rosemary was in an institution) learned that Joe Jr. had died in a plane crash. Eunice, now twenty-four, dealt with her grief by throwing herself into unrelenting motion, "as if by sheer will and frenetic activity she could remake the family lives. Tennis. Golf. Touch football. Charades. Game after game. Challenge after challenge. Competition after competition."

She also threw herself into the world of politics and public policy. Through her father's connections, she got a job at the State Department in Washington, where she worked on issues having to do with returning prisoners of war from Germany. And in 1946, after the war was over, she moved with Jean and Pat into the Ritz-Carlton Hotel in Boston, where Jack had just declared his candidacy for Massachusetts's Eleventh Congressional District.

In some ways, Eunice took more naturally to politics than her brother. She loved the intellectual challenge of campaigning, loved the competitiveness of it. Many observers, both inside the family and outside of it, have commented that had she been born a generation later, she (not Jack) would have ultimately been the presidential candidate. As her father memorably put it, "If that girl had been born with balls she would have been one hell of a politician." Jack's friend George Smathers, a congressman from Florida, put it more delicately in 1976: "Of all the kids in the family, Eunice was far and away the strongest minded. Sort of the leader of the clan. Very tough when she wanted to be. Eunice would have loved to be the one the father picked to run in the Eleventh Congressional District in '46. If she'd been a little older, and if it had been today, when a lot of women are running for office, I suspect the history of the Kennedy clan would have been quite different."

On July 18, 1946, Jack Kennedy stunned many observers by winning his Democratic primary and then coasting to victory in November in the heavily Democratic Eleventh District. The astonishing run of Kennedy family electoral success had begun.

Jack moved to a three-story townhouse on Thirty-first Street in Georgetown. Eunice was spending a lot of time in New York, where she was doing social work in the Harlem ghetto. But she wanted to be at the center of the action, and that was in Washington with Jack.

In 1945, as the war ended, the US crime rate soared to record levels and then continued to rise in successive years. By 1947, according to the Justice Department, out of a population of less than 150 million there were 7 million criminals.

And of those 7 million, half were under twenty-one years of age. Confronted with what was becoming known as the "crisis of juvenile delinquency," Harry Truman's attorney general Tom Clark had formed the Attorney General's Panel on the Juvenile Problem. Over the course of 1946, the panel had hosted two large conferences for representatives from community service organizations. Now Clark wanted the panel to become permanent.

Eunice's work on Jack's campaign and in Harlem had attracted some attention, and just after Christmas 1946, Joe Kennedy got a letter in Palm Beach from Clark, asking if Eunice might come to work in the Justice Department, as head of the new Committee on Juvenile Delinquency. It was an enormous responsibility to offer a twenty-five-year-old woman. "I think that someone with her training and background," Attorney General Clark wrote of Eunice, "would do wonders in keeping this worthwhile work" on juvenile delinquency going.

As a result of her work in Harlem, Eunice had grown passionate about the problem of juvenile delinquency, and she accepted Clark's offer. So in January 1947 Eunice joined her brother, his legislative assistant, and their longtime housekeeper Margaret Ambrose in Jack's Georgetown townhouse and began her job as executive secretary for the Committee on Juvenile Delinquency. "Substantial efforts must be made to keep adolescents from quitting school at fourteen or fifteen and to give them a chance to learn a trade or develop special skills," she announced to reporters as she began her job. Strikingly tall and skinny, with the high cheekbones of a film starlet, the new Justice Department employee arrived in Washington "in a burst of publicity surpassing even the attention received by her older brother, who, after all, was merely another new member of the House."

But Eunice was not well organized; the size of her new task soon overwhelmed her, as Jack reported to their father. So Mr. Kennedy sent for his new assistant manager at the Merchandise Mart. "You're a lawyer," Shriver remembers Kennedy telling him. "She's in the Justice Department. Go down and help her."

In 1947 there were two things Shriver particularly wanted: to advance in the world by impressing his boss, and to woo Eunice Kennedy. So when Mr. Kennedy commanded him to "help Eunice," it seemed his stars were aligned— doing his boss's bidding meant spending time with the object of his affections.

The situation posed formidable challenges. In 1947 it could not have been easy for an ambitious young man to have a woman for a superior—especially if the young man hoped to marry her. Although Shriver was now technically an employee of the federal government, there was not yet money in the Justice Department budget to pay his salary. So he earned a nominal government salary of one dollar while Joe Kennedy continued to pay his regular salary. This reinforced the strangeness of Shriver's position: working under Eunice Kennedy, and also courting her, while being paid by her father.

Both Sarge and Eunice were frustrated by the glacial pace of government bureaucracy. Inflamed with enthusiasm for addressing the problems of juvenile delinquency, they formulated grandiose plans for fixing them. But to make anything actually happen proved extremely hard. There were forms to fill out, red tape to negotiate, approvals to seek. For two young strivers accustomed to getting things accomplished fast, this was infuriating.

Charles Bartlett, the political columnist who became a close friend to Jack Kennedy, said it was clear that "Sarge was in love with Eunice" from the day Shriver reported for duty at the Justice Department: "Eunice was not so sure that she was romantically interested in Sarge, but she was not fickle in her demands. She worked with him all day calling out his name again and again—'Sarge . . . Sarge . . . Sarge . . .'—in an overwrought voice that was less a request than a command. . . . She thought nothing of calling his apartment in the middle of the night, considering Sarge the best available cure for her insomnia."

While Eunice lived with her brother in the fancy Georgetown townhouse, Shriver took up residence in much more modest quarters, sharing a bedroom in the bachelor's residence of his college friends Merle Thorpe and Walter Ridder, who had a small house on N Street Northwest. "He and Eunice saw a lot of each other," Ridder recalled some years later, and it was clear to him that Shriver was in love. But her late-night phone calls—which inevitably woke Ridder up, since he shared Sarge's bedroom—suggested the interest was mutual. "She was thinking about him. She wasn't well at the time. She was having trouble sleeping. She'd wake up in the middle of the night, want someone to talk to, and give Sarge a ring. I can remember him jabbering away with her at three or even four o'clock in the morning."

Shriver spent a great deal of time at the Kennedy townhouse. He liked Jack Kennedy and was impressed by his intelligence and charisma—indeed, at times he had a hard time believing that the poised, charming, and self-possessed man who presided over the Georgetown salon was the same person who had seemed so out of his depth at Canterbury School, not much more than ten years earlier. Jack liked Shriver well enough, too, and treated him with respect because he knew how highly his father thought of Sarge. But Jack and his younger brother Bobby had trouble taking Sarge entirely seriously: being Eunice's deputy, as well as her most ardent suitor, made Shriver appear to the Kennedy brothers to be almost an appendage to their sister, rather than an individual in his own right. Pat Kennedy, for her part, initially found Sarge to be an insufferable flirt, incorrigibly charming and unserious in his approach to life. "If you think you can change Sargent Shriver, Eunice," she told her sister, "you must be out of your mind!"

Jack frequently entertained his fellow congressmen, and Shriver enjoyed meeting these politicians from all over the country. He met only one he didn't like. On one evening, Kennedy invited a group of his fellow freshmen congressmen to the house for dinner. It was a large crowd, and some of the guests who couldn't fit at the large dining-room tables spilled over onto small, outlying tables. As Shriver recalled,

> I ended up alone at a table with this freshman Republican from California I'd never met before. It was the oddest experience: I felt like I couldn't get a handle on this guy. I couldn't pin down what his opinions on anything were. He bobbed and weaved, like a cowardly boxer. Half the time, it seemed he was barely paying attention to me. He'd be looking over my shoulder at the other tables, as though he were trying to eavesdrop, trying to figure out what the other congressmen were saying. It's rare that someone makes as strong an impression on you as this guy did on me. But I came away thinking that he was smart, crafty, and a scheming conniver, more interested in establishing his position with Jack and other luminaries than in anything I was saying.

Such was Shriver's first encounter with Richard M. Nixon.

Eunice liked Sarge well enough and appreciated the help he provided at the Justice Department, but she remained for the most part indifferent to his feelings for her. She was too preoccupied with work. Although they did see each other socially, and even, toward the end of their time in Washington, would indulge in an illicit office-hours kiss ("Remember how you would let me," Sarge wrote to Eunice in a letter a year later, "chase you around the Justice Department office, letting me kiss all the lipstick off your face just before you were to see the Attorney General?"), Eunice was more passionate about her job than about Shriver. To him, of course, this only demonstrated how virtuous she was, and therefore how worthy of his affections, and served to fuel his desire. "Government girls should stick at their jobs four years and then get married," Eunice told a newspaper reporter. "As for me, I'm sure all my sisters will be married long before I am!"

On June 19, 1948, after less than a year on the job, Eunice and Shriver jointly resigned from the Committee on Juvenile Delinquency. The official reason for the resignation was, as Eunice told the press, "I finished the job I had to do." Attorney General Clark accepted her resignation with "exceeding regret" and insisted that there was no "story-behind-the-story" to the resignation. And— the sudden death of her sister Kathleen in a plane crash on May 13, 1948, notwithstanding—there wasn't any single precipitating event that caused her to leave. But her pent-up frustration over her inability to have a faster impact on juvenile delinquency had boiled over. She felt restless and wanted to go abroad. She planned in August to sail for England and to travel from there to France, Spain, and Italy. After that she planned to return to the United States to study social work.

Less-driven people might have been quite satisfied with what Kennedy and Shriver accomplished. Building on the attorney general's work, they assembled an impressive continuing committee headed by G. Howland Shaw, a former assistant secretary of state, and including Hubert Humphrey, the liberal young mayor of Minneapolis, among many others. They established an organizational structure and a budget for the committee. And, in convening dozens of local conferences and a few major national ones, they helped establish a constructive approach to reducing juvenile delinquency.

They also developed a model for social action that both of them would employ later in life when they were entrusted with much larger responsibilities. Kernels of ideas that animated the War on Poverty two decades later, for instance, are evident in the prospectus that Shriver and Kennedy wrote for the committee in the summer of 1947. They thought big; unlike traditional bureaucrats, they thought in terms ungoverned by normal institutional constraints. The attack on juvenile delinquency was to be multipronged and "not limited to formal agencies." (Here is evidence of Sarge's lifelong aversion to the strictures of "formal agencies.") "The attack on delinquency cannot be piece-meal," they wrote, but rather must be a coordinated assault that drew together the work of juvenile courts, local police departments, recreation and parks programs, guidance centers, probation officers, social case workers, parents, social scientists, and volunteers. The prospectus stated that the attack on delinquency should be made "by the people themselves, in their own communities, striking at their own local problems." This emphasis on "joint community action" anticipates the core ideas of both the Peace Corps and elements of the War on Poverty, particularly its Community Action Programs. The notion did not originate with Shriver, but his emphasis on local empowerment of impoverished groups constitutes one of his most revolutionary ideas.

The time Shriver spent with Eunice in Washington convinced him that she was the woman he wanted to marry. But while Eunice respected his abilities and was flattered by his attentions, his constant, insistent presence could be cloying. Marry him? She didn't know about that. For the moment she had too many other things to think about. When she left Washington in the early summer of 1948 and then sailed for Europe a few weeks later, Sarge was just one of the many things on her mind.

CHAPTER SEVEN

The Long Courtship

⁓

In the summer of 1948 Shriver returned to Chicago to resume work at the Merchandise Mart. In some ways, it felt liberating to be back, working with businessmen and entrepreneurs rather than bureaucrats and policymakers. As he wrote to Eunice in September, "I was just so happy to be rid of that Washington mess that I've selfishly put the whole thing behind me—a closed chapter."

Many of Shriver's friends from this time remember him as carefree and content, but his letters to Eunice tell a different story. In one he writes, "This weekend it is Bill Blair's place—open & indoor tennis courts, swimming pools, gay young things, Sat. night party, etc. But despite it all, darling, I think only of you & want only you."

In another, from December 1948, he wrote, "In the middle of a dinner party I'm suddenly, horribly, & painfully alone. . . . Last night at the Rendezvous I was alone, on the dance floor even there I'm alone. Tonight it's Sylvia Whitehouse; tomorrow a big dinner party at the St. Regis for Willa & Herbert [Shriver]; tomorrow night back to a party for Kathy MacMahon. And on every one of those nights I laugh and dance and probably flirt & suddenly & piercingly & all over again & all over & through me I'll be alone. Oh! how I would that you loved me!"

But as she traveled through Europe with her sister Jean, Eunice remained frustratingly, if affectionately, aloof. Hardened by the deaths of two siblings and accustomed by the constant presence of her physical ailments to enduring suffering, Eunice had developed a tough inner core that Shriver found profoundly attractive. "You who don't cry," Shriver wrote to her, "you who *never* feel deserted, you who *never need* the devoted love & help of a friend, a lover, a saint—you, adorable one, I want! I want no clinging vine, no flattering helpless creature; for it is your courage & strength, precious, that make you a desirable creature to comfort in an hour of tribulation."

Lending Shriver's peculiar set of circumstances—working for the father, living in the father's apartment, while pining for the daughter—an even stronger Oedipal tinge was the stationery on which Shriver wrote many of his letters to Eunice: Using black pen, he would cross out the "Joseph P. Kennedy" across the top of the letterhead.

THE BOSS'S DAUGHTER

Although Sarge's declarations of love seemed not to have much effect on Eunice, his work at the Merchandise Mart continued to impress her father, an irony that both pleased and frustrated Shriver. "Your Dad has been here for several days," he wrote to Eunice in London, "& I'm proud as punch of the confidence he appears to put in me; I've an awful lot to learn, I know that; but he seems to think I'm worth telling things to. And he even tells me some things he doesn't tell everyone else! For my money that's terrific. Now if you'd do the same, my heaven would already have arrived here on earth!"

By Thanksgiving of 1948, Eunice and Jean had returned to New York from their European travels. When it came to seem a real possibility that Eunice might move permanently to Chicago—might she finally succumb to his constant marriage proposals?—Shriver began to worry more about the relative disparity in family wealth. Shriver felt he could not expect the wealthy Kennedy heiress to accept a marriage proposal unless he could support her on his own. "I should have known," he wrote Eunice, "that our Lord would someday let me meet a girl like you who is worth every penny I've ever earned or could ever earn, & I should have saved my money just to be able to give it all to her." "Incidentally," he wrote in another letter, "did your mother say she waited for your Father because he had no dough, but that consideration did not apply to you and me? I hope she hasn't any illusions on that score! Your Pop hasn't, I'm sure, because I've gone out of my way to see to it he knows the facts."

Shriver was also anxious to establish himself as a man of accomplishment. Middle age was now visible in the distance—he was thirty-three—and he felt he had yet to make his mark on the world. Some of his friends had become men of means, and others were rising through the ranks of their professional universes. Eunice's brother Jack—who was a year younger than Shriver—was already in his second term in Congress. Too much of the previous twelve years, Shriver felt, had been spent in fruitless pursuit of will-o-the-wisps, or in unproductive activities that yielded him no real world advancement. "I'm a way behind time," he wrote Eunice, "in starting to get something done with my life, first because I spent 3 years after college going to law school, 5 more in the Navy, 10 months at Newsweek, & finally $1\frac{1}{2}$ years with you in Washington." Although he didn't necessarily regret any of these things, he said, the time he had spent doing them meant he now "should stick close to my knitting."

Eunice remained consumed by her commitment to public service. She was still interested in the problem of juvenile delinquency, particularly among women, so in 1950 she traveled to Alderson, West Virginia, to live on the grounds of the Federal Penitentiary for Women for two months. Shriver once said, "I used to say that I'm the only guy I know who went and courted a woman at a federal penitentiary."

In 1950 Eunice moved into an apartment at the Ambassador East in Chicago with Jean, just upstairs from Shriver, and took a job as a social worker at the House of the Good Shepherd, where she worked with wayward teenage girls, trying to rehabilitate them and help them return to mainstream society. Meanwhile, she enrolled in the social work program at the University of Chicago. Shriver was naturally thrilled to have her living in the same city—and in the same building—with him. But though they continued to see each other with some regularity, Shriver began to resign himself to the likelihood that she would never consent to marry him. "After going out with her on and off for several years, and wanting to marry her for much of that time, I had pretty much given up hope," Shriver recalled. "I don't think she had anything against me; I just think she was working on so many projects at once, and her family was so consuming, she just didn't have the time to focus on whether she even wanted to marry at some point. But after a while I began to doubt she would ever have the time. So I tried to write off the possibility of ever marrying her." Meanwhile, Eunice was romantically linked to (the soon-to-be-infamous) Senator Joe McCarthy of Wisconsin, but she eventually passed him on to her sister Pat. Eunice also introduced Pat to the actor Peter Lawford, whom Pat eventually married.

During this time when Sarge and Eunice's romance cooled, their intellectual partnership solidified and grew. Shriver toned down the ardent desperation of his letters; their correspondence became less passionate, but more substantive. Eunice wrote to him from the Alderson penitentiary asking him for advice, and he wrote back with ideas for programs she could start there. He wrote letters to church organizations and government agencies on her behalf and put her in contact with relevant Merchandise Mart business connections, with whom he thought the prison might be able to set up arrangements for teaching the inmates job skills. When she moved to Chicago and began work at the House of the Good Shepherd, he regularly accompanied her to the home for wayward girls on Grace Street and gave her ideas for programs. Eunice had already developed a great respect for his intellect and judgment based on their experience in the Justice Department; now, she found she was becoming dependent on him for these qualities.

KENNEDY VERSUS LODGE

One night in the winter of 1952 the phone rang at the Kennedy sisters' apartment in the Ambassador East. It was Jack calling. He had decided to run for the Senate and he wanted their help.

As early as 1949, after he won reelection to his Eleventh District congressional seat, it had been almost a foregone conclusion that Jack Kennedy would run for higher office. Ever since Joe Jr. had been killed seven years earlier, Joe Sr. had placed all his own stymied presidential ambitions—which he had previously reposed on Joe Jr.—onto Jack. Joe Kennedy would not be satisfied until Jack was elected president. And although in 1952 it looked unlikely that this would ever happen—Jack was nothing but a diffident backbencher, one who hardly looked old enough to be in the House of Representatives—Joe Kennedy would not let his son remain content to be a mere congressman.

In 1952 the respected Republican senator Henry Cabot Lodge, who hailed from a Brahmin family that had been prominent for years in New England politics, was up for reelection. Jack coveted the opportunity to run against him—in part because beating Lodge would establish Kennedy as a political player to be reckoned with, but also in part because it would be sweet revenge for the Kennedy family, and indeed for the entire Irish immigrant population: Thirty-six years earlier, in 1916, a time when animosity between Irish Catholics and Anglo-Saxon Protestants ran high, Lodge's grandfather had beaten out Jack's grandfather, Honey Fitz, for the same Senate seat in a bitter campaign. The prospect of historical redress was delicious to the Kennedy family.

Jack sprang into action, beginning to build the "Kennedy machine" that would drive his presidential campaign eight years hence. It included all the Kennedy brothers and sisters (except Rosemary); Bobby Kennedy's Harvard friend Kenny O'Donnell; Larry O'Brien, a local Irishman and Jack's contemporary, who had deep political connections all over the state; and Jim Landis, a twenty-year veteran of the Roosevelt and Truman administrations, a longtime New Dealer, and a friend of Joe's. At the machine's center was not the candidate but rather the candidate's father.

After Joe Kennedy's volatile temper threatened to derail the campaign, Bobby Kennedy reluctantly took on the role of official campaign manager. But Joe remained the engine of the operation, running things with his brain trust from behind the scenes. Kennedy allowed only those people he trusted completely into the brain trust. And along with Landis, O'Brien, and O'Donnell, that brain trust included Sargent Shriver.

In some ways, Shriver was the odd man out among the Kennedy brain trusters. There were the local operatives—like Frank Morrissey, Tony Galluccio, and Joseph DeGuglielmo—who knew the Massachusetts political scene up and down. There was the young Irish crowd, sometimes called (with either affection or derision, depending on who was doing the talking) the "Irish Mafia"—who were closest to Jack. And there were the Jim Landis types, with backgrounds in academia or Democratic presidential administrations.

But if Shriver lacked the combination of qualities that would have placed him neatly in one of these categories, he did have traits that placed him at the center of the campaign: intelligence, energy, and above all the confidence of Mr. Kennedy. So much so, in fact, that when Shriver moved to Boston in the summer of 1952, he took up residence in the Ambassador's apartment at 84 Beacon Street on Beacon Hill, just down the road from the state house and around the corner from Jack's headquarters at 122 Bowdoin Street. The Ambassador and Mrs. Kennedy had separate bedrooms, as was the custom in some Catholic families; Shriver's bedroom lay right in between them. Indeed, living in Mr. Kennedy's apartment in Chicago, and working for him, and living next to him in Boston, Shriver seemed almost to have become the Ambassador's adopted son; for Shriver, whose mother had been widowed a decade earlier, this was like gaining a father.

Of course, Kennedy never granted Shriver pride of place before his biological sons, and there was often something instrumental in the way he used Shriver, demanding that he shelve his own political ambitions in deference to Jack's. But Shriver's adoption of Kennedy as a father figure was instrumental in its way, too. In the late 1940s, Shriver had told the Hoguets he intended to apprentice himself to a top businessman, as a way of advancing himself in the world.

Sharing an apartment with the Ambassador and his wife, Rose, allowed him for the first time to become well-acquainted with Eunice's mother, with whom he soon developed a special relationship. He, like many people, was charmed by her warmth and style. Rose, in turn, sympathized with his plight in courting a woman (Eunice) from a more affluent, higher-status family: Her husband had faced similar circumstances in courting her forty years earlier. This endeared Sarge to her. Also, Rose, along with Eunice, was the most devoutly Catholic member of her family and she recognized a similar devoutness in Sarge.

The odds against a Kennedy victory looked long. Lodge had been a prominent fixture of Massachusetts politics for twenty years and had convincingly beaten three of the state's most popular Irish politicians, including the notorious James Michael Curley, whom he had outpolled by nearly 150,000 votes when Lodge first ran for the Senate at the tender age of thirty-four.

As Shriver studied Lodge's record, he became increasingly worried that it would be hard to make a distinction between the candidates that would play in Jack's favor, especially among liberal voters. When Shriver told the Ambassador this, Joe decided on a two-pronged strategy: Jack would move left on the issues in an effort to secure the liberal vote, while Joe would try to turn conservatives embittered by the scuttling of Ohio senator Robert Taft's presidential candidacy (which the moderate Lodge had helped to derail) against the incumbent. Republicans were scarce enough in the Bay State that Lodge depended on the votes of crossover Democrats to gain electoral victory. The thinking in the Kennedy campaign was that if they could prevail upon the Democratic presidential candidate to campaign for Jack, and to emphasize the young congressman's liberal bona fides, it would be greatly to Jack's advantage.

Here, Shriver's ties to the Democratic presidential nominee, Adlai Stevenson, proved useful. (Shriver's close friend Bill Blair was by now Governor Stevenson's top aide and constant companion, and his friend Newt Minow was serving as Stevenson's campaign manager.) Adlai himself liked Sarge and thought highly of his abilities. Thus when Governor Stevenson was about to pass through Massachusetts on a campaign swing, he called Shriver at Joe Kennedy's apartment and asked him for a list of things he should and should not do while in the Northeast. Shriver responded with a memo suggesting that the Illinois governor point out Jack Kennedy's support for some of the more liberal policies in President Truman's "Fair Deal." He also asked that Stevenson refrain from attacking Joe McCarthy—who had dated both Eunice and Pat and remained a close friend of the Ambassador's—on the logic that the stronger Jack appeared on communism and domestic subversives, the more it would hurt Lodge among the Republicans angry at his dismissal of the staunchly anti-Communist Taft. "Up here this anti-communist business is a good thing to emphasize," Shriver wrote.

Stevenson heeded Shriver's advice, and on the weekend he passed through New England, giving a noontime speech in Springfield, he praised John Kennedy as "my type of guy" and emphasized Kennedy's strong anti-Communist stance. Following a suggestion from Shriver, Stevenson also pointed out that it was Kennedy, and not Eisenhower's running mate Richard Nixon, who had obtained the first citation of a Communist labor leader for perjury. Stevenson's carefully modulated endorsement seemed to have the desired effect: On election day, Kennedy won large swathes of both conservative Taft supporters and liberal Stevenson supporters.

Shriver's role in the campaign, although significant, was probably less determinative than Eunice's. Eunice, Jean, Pat, and their mother, Rose, along with Bobby's young wife, Ethel, hosted teas throughout the state, which turned out female voters in droves. A quip making the rounds of Massachusetts political operatives was that the combined effect of Jack's rakish good looks and the Kennedy women's prosletyzing made every old woman want to be his mother and every young woman dream of being his mistress. Eunice was the most aggressive campaigner. Campaigning at a furious pace several hours a day, she urged Democratic Party regulars "to get out the vote" for her brother. "John F. Kennedy has dedicated his life for the benefit of the people," she said.

In the end, Eisenhower defeated Stevenson in a Republican landslide that reverberated across the country. In Massachusetts, the general outpolled the Illinois governor by 210,000 votes, and the Democratic governor lost to a Republican challenger by more than 14,000. But bucking the day's trends, the young upstart Kennedy won 51 percent of the vote for the Senate seat, beating Lodge by 70,000 votes. "At last," Rose said exuberantly, "the Fitzgeralds have evened the score with the Lodges."

CHAPTER EIGHT

Marriage

In November 1952 Shriver had just turned thirty-seven years old. Although he had contemporaries (Jack Kennedy among them) who, like him, were still bachelors, he was reaching an age at which his unmarried status made him seem, if not quite disreputable, then a bit rakish. Most of his close friends in Chicago were either married or in the priesthood. His older brother, Herbert, was married and living in New York City. As Sarge's mother never tired of reminding him, it was high time for him to marry.

But whom to wed? Shriver was at once a romantic and a pragmatist in his approach to women and marriage; he was also, of course, a Catholic. The romantic in him would not allow him to marry but for love. His parents' relationship loomed as a worthy ideal: a partnership based on mutual affection, admiration, respect, and trust. But the pragmatist in him was attuned to other qualities in women: their wealth, their social status, their willingness to support him in his career. He was no longer truly a young man, but he still thought of himself as a Young Man of Promise. He had large, if not clearly articulated, ambitions for himself; the choice of a wife, he knew, could help or impede those ambitions. Finally, any woman he married would have to be a good Catholic.

Tall, athletic, confident, handsome—he now looked like the movie star William Holden in his prime. Every Catholic mother—or so it seemed—wanted to set Sarge up with her daughter. Among the myriad beauties he went out with, several seemed to be serious wifely prospects. One of these was a young former model who had transplanted herself from New York to Chicago when she was hired by Mr. Kennedy to work at the Merchandise Mart. The circumstances of Shriver's relationship with this woman were somewhat peculiar. As he recalled, "She was blonde, with a tall, curvaceous figure, and she was very sophisticated. She worked part-time at the Merchandise Mart and spent the rest of her time modeling. Mr. Kennedy always had an appreciation for female beauty, and I don't doubt that his decision to hire this woman had something to do with hers."

Several of Shriver's friends from the time say it was clear to them what Mr. Kennedy's gambit was. He wanted this woman to stay in Chicago so that he could visit her when he traveled to the Midwest. But since he spent much of the year elsewhere, he wanted to make sure the woman was kept happily occupied when he was not around. Kennedy introduced Shriver to the young woman and suggested he chaperone her around town. Kennedy calculated—correctly—that Shriver's charm would ensure she had a good time and that his impeccable Catholic morals would preserve her virtue.

But what Kennedy didn't figure on, Shriver's friends say, was the woman's falling in love with Sarge. She made clear to him that she would like to marry him. He replied that he liked her very much but could never marry her because she was not Catholic—a factor which, Shriver's friends say, Joe Kennedy may have counted on as a final safeguard against Shriver's stealing her away.

There were other women that Shriver's friends speculated he might marry (Ann Wharton, a young widow, was one of them; Devon Meade, an attractive young socialite, was another), but the only other woman of any significance in Shriver's life remained, as ever, Eunice. It had been nearly seven years since he had first met her, and two years since he had more or less forced himself to stop hoping she would consent to marry him. His friends believed it more likely he would marry Devon Meade or the model than Eunice.

One night in early 1953, after Sarge and Eunice had been out for dinner together with some friends, Eunice asked him as they parted ways in the lobby of the Ambassador East if she might join him for Mass in the morning. So, as Shriver recalled,

> I met her in the hotel lobby the next morning and we walked to Mass together. We sat through Mass and when it was over she said, "Sarge, will you join me at the side altar over there?" She was pointing over to the left where there was an altar to the Blessed Mother. Eunice has a tremendous devotion to Mary, so I assumed she just wanted to say some special prayers. We walked up to the altar, and knelt down side by side, on the barrier in front of the statue. She said a prayer. Then she turned to me.
>
> "Sargent Shriver," she said, "I think I'd like to marry you."
>
> I nearly fell off the altar rail. After five years of wanting to marry her, and then giving up hope, and then for her, in effect, to propose to me! "Eunice," I said, "that's the best news I've ever had."

That evening, as he recalled, Shriver went to the apartment of the model and told her that he was going to marry Eunice. The next day, she moved back to New York.

Shriver's next order of business was to call Mr. and Mrs. Kennedy: He wanted to obtain their blessing before making the engagement official. This was a project that caused Shriver considerable anxiety, largely because he was sensitive to the fact that he and his family were far less wealthy than the Kennedys. He also knew that even were they to bless the marriage, hitching himself to such a rich and increasingly famous family would raise some eyebrows. As a journalist stated the situation in 1964, Shriver "realized, as he will tell you now, that the day of the Alger-boy hero has gone, that people no longer look with unreserved admiration on the struggling young man who ups and weds the Boss's daughter." This didn't deter him.

Joe and Rose's enthusiasm about the engagement was so strong it got Shriver to wondering if maybe they had been hoping for such an outcome all along. Had his seven years as an employee of JPK Enterprises really been a prolonged audition for son-in-law? A less charitable interpretation, proposed by some of Shriver's old friends from Chicago, is that when it became clear the fashion model Shriver was chaperoning on Kennedy's behalf had fallen in love with Sarge, the Ambassador became irritated. Worrying that Eunice would lose her opportunity to marry Shriver, the Ambassador told his thirty-one-year-old daughter that it was high time she got married. For the family's sake, he said, it was time for her to tie the knot. Joe Kennedy was asked about his role in instigating the marriage many times in the years before his death in 1969, and he always maintained that although he thought highly of Sarge, he had never consciously played matchmaker. Eunice says that her father always made clear his high regard for Sarge, but he never pressured her to marry him. "I don't know what made me decide to marry him" after all that time, she says. "I guess I must have been in love. I did take my time, didn't I? Seven years is a long time."

Several of Shriver's friends have said that Joe Kennedy asked Father Ted Hesburgh, the soon-to-be president of Notre Dame, to impress on Eunice the importance of marrying. But Hesburgh credits Shriver's persistence for breaking down Eunice's resistance to marriage. "He was relentless," Father Hesburgh recalled. "Eventually, Eunice turned away from other attractions—not other men, but all her other activities."

"Sarge is one of the very, very few people who could have married into the Kennedys and survived," Hesburgh says. "The family tends to attract people who are hangers-on or who are looking for shared glory. Sarge kept his independence, which is not easy to do, since they tended to subjugate people."

Some of Sarge's friends were not happy to hear he was marrying into the Kennedy family. They were reluctant to lose Sarge, since he was such a vibrant part of their lives in Chicago, and they felt they would inevitably see less of him once he was engulfed by the Kennedys. "We thought he was sort of giving up a little of himself," says one of these friends. "It was hard for us to see him go. I mean, the Kennedys led a very different life than most of us did. And so we felt that Sarge had sort of given up on himself a little in order to join this." Bob Stuart recalled, "Sarge would have emerged to something very much in the limelight even if he hadn't met the Kennedys. With his family background in Maryland and his pizzazz with people, I think Sarge could have been a political figure in his own right in Maryland or Illinois. There's no question he's extremely happy in his marriage. It's the best marriage in the Kennedy family. But it was a tragedy for Sarge in a lot of ways because of what he had to give up."

The wedding, held Saturday, May 23, 1953, at St. Patrick's Cathedral in New York City, was an extravaganza. Seventeen hundred invited guests attended. Traffic on Fifth Avenue was halted for the length of the ceremony. No mere priest could officiate at such a wedding: Francis Cardinal Spellman, the archbishop of New York, celebrated the Mass assisted by three bishops, four monsignors, and nine priests. The pope himself sent an apostolic blessing from Rome.

The guest list, as the *Boston Globe* reported, was "a directory of Who's Who in the nation," including senators, governors, mayors, bishops, Supreme Court justices, Irish Catholic political operatives, actors and actresses, movie moguls, socialites, foreign diplomats, and the managers of the 21 Club. "Why, everyone's here except Rin Tin Tin," someone remarked at the reception. The New York society pages called it "the $100,000 wedding." The Kennedy family issued a press release describing the affair as "one of the most important and colorful weddings ever held in America."

For the reception, Joe Kennedy had reserved the Starlight Roof Room and the Grand Ballroom at the Waldorf-Astoria, which could accommodate all 1,700 wedding guests plus a few hundred additional revelers who couldn't be crammed into St. Patrick's. It was a lavish affair. The wedding ended in the late morning, and eight hours of dining and dancing to a fifteen-piece orchestra ensued. The eight-tiered wedding cake was taller than Eunice; she had to stand on a chair to cut the first piece.

To some in the Shriver party, the reception was a somewhat controversial affair: They felt there was "too much Kennedy, not enough Shriver" in the event. Part of this was caused by Eunice's Oedipal wedding toast: "I looked all my life for someone like my father, and Sarge came the closest." As toast after toast referred to Eunice and the Kennedy family with nary a mention of Sarge or the Shrivers, Burton Maclean, a Yale classmate of Shriver's who had become a Protestant minister, was finally moved to stand up and say, "Kennedy, Kennedy, Kennedy. Enough already. Let's talk about Sarge!" The Shriver tables cheered and the Kennedy tables laughed. But when somebody decided to sing "Maryland, My Maryland" to honor Sarge's family, the Kennedys interrupted by singing "Marilyn, My Marilyn," referring to Marilyn Monroe, and "the Shrivers were appalled."

Sarge himself, buoyed by champagne and love, was oblivious to all this. He was marrying the woman he loved—his seven-year courtship had been rewarded. To Sarge, it was a glorious thing to be marrying a Kennedy. He knew it would be a wild ride, and he looked forward to a marvelous adventure.

Not that marrying into the Kennedy clan didn't give him occasional misgivings.

Shriver had planned an elaborate month-long honeymoon in Spain, Portugal, and France, so the next evening found the Shrivers in a marine terminal at the edge of Manhattan, boarding the plane that would take them to Europe. "Ten minutes before the plane was scheduled to take off," Shriver recalled, "who should come ambling down the aisle but young Teddy Kennedy." "Goddamn," Shriver thought to himself, "will I ever be able to get away from these Kennedys? Had Joe sent his son to spy on me on my honeymoon?"

Eunice was thrilled to see her little brother, but Sarge was annoyed. "Jesus, Teddy," Shriver recalled saying to him, "what the hell are you doing here?" Teddy told a story about how he had fallen in love with a Portguese-French actress whom he had met at a show in New York. Her troupe was touring Europe and would be performing for a few nights in Lisbon. "And—what a coincidence—he was to be staying at the very same hotel in Portugal we were!" Shriver was dismayed. "'I knew it,' I thought to myself. 'He's spying for Joe.'"

Teddy's story turned out to be true, and once he had reunited with his actress in Lisbon, Sarge and Eunice never heard from him again. But the experience caused Shriver to reflect on what he had just entered into.

> It was an important lesson for me about the Kennedys—they're everywhere. For better or for worse, they were impossible to get away from—and when I married Eunice I was marrying the whole clan. I would always have to share her. Over the years, I've come to count this as a blessing, not a burden, but it took some time to figure out how I could be an independent agent separate from the Kennedy family after working for the father and marrying the daughter.

CHAPTER NINE

Religion and Civil Rights

After the honeymoon, Eunice and Sarge returned to Chicago, and they didn't waste much time before starting a family. At 5:00 p.m. on April 28, 1954, just eleven months after his parents had married, Robert Sargent Shriver III was born. The following year, on November 6, Bobby was joined by a sister, Maria Owings Shriver. Three additional sons—Timothy Perry, Mark Kennedy, and Anthony Paul—would be born over the next ten years.

The Shrivers were a stunning couple, famous for the parties they threw; their comings and goings were regularly chronicled in the city's society page columns. Shriver still made the rounds of parties at the Marshall Fields' estate, tennis at Bill Blair's house, and weekends with the Minows and the Bowers in the northern part of the state. The difference now was that he and Eunice were a unit. Eunice was a formidable presence; she was such a force of nature that Shriver's friends at first assimilated her into their group only partially and reluctantly.

Eunice was never one to trim her sails to fit into a particular milieu. This sometimes had dramatic consequences. One night at a dinner party in the late 1950s, Lloyd Bowers, who was seated at a table with his wife and Marshall and Kay Field, stood up and gave some toasts. In one of them he toasted Sarge, whom he said would be the next governor of Illinois—if only Jack Kennedy weren't running for president. Eunice, seated at another table, angrily launched a full glass of champagne across the room at Lloyd. She missed and drenched Kay Field's green satin dress. The hurled glass would become a staple of Eunice's arsenal: Several years later, when Jack was president, someone had the temerity to predict that Barry Goldwater would win Illinois in 1964; Eunice responded by emptying a glass of water in the prognosticator's face.

Eunice always did things her own way. At parties at their apartment, Eunice would sometimes suddenly vanish from the living room. When the guests moved to the dining room for supper, they would find Eunice sitting by herself, almost done with her dinner of boiled chicken and mashed potatoes. When she was tired, she would go to bed—even if the party had just started. She would simply disappear up to her bedroom, leaving Sarge to entertain the guests until the party wound down. In at least one instance, her guests caught her trying to slip upstairs and importuned her to stay awhile longer. "Okay," Eunice said, "but only if we can play blind man's bluff." (This was not an unusual request—parlor games were standard fare at Shriver events.) "I'll start," Eunice said, and after the guests had shut their eyes, she led them on a Conga line that danced through the apartment. "Open your eyes," Eunice shouted, and everyone did so, just in time to see the elevator doors closing before it would carry them down to the lobby. "Good night," they could hear Eunice saying. "Thanks for coming."

Eunice could be prickly, difficult, even rude, and her relentless competitiveness in everything she did endeared her to some and appalled others. She proved an easy target for the growing chorus of Kennedy bashers. But in a family of public servants, she was the most public minded of them all. After marrying Sarge, Eunice continued to supervise the rehabilitation of delinquent girls at the House of the Good Shepherd, and she would often invite the wayward young women into her home. The presence of these juvenile offenders scandalized some of the neighbors in the Shrivers' Gold Coast apartment building. Sarge, too, was disconcerted by their presence. "Many nights I'd be sitting there reading the paper or poring over work from the office, and the doorbell would ring," he recalled. "I'd go to the door and there would be a woman with a suitcase and a plaintive look on her face. 'Uh-oh,' I'd think, 'another one of Eunice's girls.'"

THE CATHOLIC INTERRACIAL COUNCIL

By the mid-1950s, Shriver was directly involved in many of the burning racial issues of the era: housing discrimination, hospital discrimination, and especially school integration.

One day, Shriver's assistant Mary Ann Orlando was sitting in her office in the Merchandise Mart when a man rushed breathlessly into her office. "You should have known better," the man shouted at her. "You should not have let him come!"

"What are you talking about?" Orlando asked.

The man explained, rather huffily, that Orlando's boss was at that very moment in the act of perpetrating a grave faux pas: He was dining at the Merchants & Manufacturers Club, the Merchandise Mart's exclusive private dining club—with a Negro! "What," the man demanded, "do you propose we do about this?"

Orlando looked back at the man fiercely and asked him, "Do you know who Mr. Shriver's Negro guest *is*?" The man didn't. "It's Ralph Bunche," she told him, the Nobel laureate famous for his diplomatic work with the State Department and the United Nations over the previous decade. This flummoxed the man; it would not reflect well on the M&M Club to throw a Nobel Peace Prize–winner out on his ear. Orlando grinned inwardly, suspecting that Shriver had known taking Bunche to the M&M Club would have a discomfiting effect on the guardians of the club's racial purity—but would leave them helpless to do anything about it.

Until about a half century after the Civil War, racial problems were seen to afflict primarily the South. In 1940, 77 percent of the black population still lived below the Mason-Dixon Line. But over the middle decades of the century more than 6 million African Americans would move from South to North. As the development of mechanized cotton pickers after World War II reduced the number of available sharecropper jobs in the South, stories of a more racially tolerant North trickled down to black families suffering under Jim Crow laws. Together these forces—one pulling, one pushing—produced a thick black

stream flowing northward. And although the stream had tributaries that trickled into Detroit, New York, Cleveland, and other places, it flowed most strongly
to Chicago. As Shriver put it in 1959, "In Chicago . . . there are today approximately 800,000 Negroes, which is almost 25 percent of the population, more
than any southern city. No, there can be no doubt that the Negro is on the
move from the South to the North, both East and West."

Chicago's South Side had become the "capital of black America." Joe Louis,
heavyweight boxing champion and the most famous black man in America, lived
there. So did Mahalia Jackson, the best-known black singer. So did William
Dawson, the only black member of Congress. The South Side featured nationally
known black institutions like the *Defender* newspaper, the Regal Theater, and the
Savoy Ballroom, and it had a sizable population of middle- and lower-middle-class
black residents. But it also had the highest concentration of slums in the city.

The flow of black migrants to Chicago was testament to the opportunities
the city afforded, but the size of the influx—at one point in the 1950s there were
2,200 black people moving there every week—sorely taxed the region's ability
to assimilate them. Samuel Cardinal Stritch, the Catholic archbishop of Chicago,
surveyed the scene at the Illinois Central railroad station, with its hundreds of
new arrivals from the South sitting in the waiting room with all their worldly
belongings beside them, and he could see that "race relations were inevitably
going to become not just an issue but *the* issue in the North."

Although its primary legislative achievements were a decade away, the civil
rights movement was gaining national momentum by the mid-1950s. The landmark Supreme Court decision in *Brown v. Board of Education*, ruling "separate
but equal" schools for different races unconstitutional, was handed down in
1954, and the Montgomery bus boycotts began in 1955. Progressive reformers
in government, and liberal activists and lawyers out of it, labored to reduce segregation and discrimination.

In Chicago, one of the strongest impetuses for improved race relations
came from the Catholic Church. This had not always been the case; nor, by any
means, was it universally the case in the 1950s. Many Catholics drew their identity from the local Catholic parish where they lived and worshiped; when the
arrival of blacks threatened to displace them from their homes, they resisted.
By the 1950s, however, there had grown up a reputable strain of progressivism
within the Church's membership, inspired by Catholic activists like Dorothy

Day, among others. And given that Catholics accounted for fully 40 percent of the Chicago population during these years, and that Cardinal Stritch was himself very progressive on racial issues, allying himself with the left-wing organizer Saul Alinsky's efforts to integrate neighborhoods, the Catholic Church had the potential to have a significant impact on race relations in postwar Chicago.

The institutional Church made little overall contribution to civil rights until late in the 1960s, but an informal network of lay people and activist priests and nuns was in the vanguard of the movement. One of the first prominent Catholics to take an active role in crusading for improved race relations was a Jesuit priest, Father John LaFarge. By 1934 the fifty-four-year-old Father LaFarge, a friend of Hilda and Robert Shriver, had pulled together a mixed-race group of about 800 Catholics in New York City to form the Catholic Interracial Council of New York. Its goals were to foster better race relations within the Church and to effect positive social change outside of it.

In Chicago, Catholic lay activism had been institutionalized under the leadership of a priest named Reymond Hillenbrand, who ran an influential seminary. In 1946 he received approval from Cardinal Stritch to found a Catholic Interracial Council (CIC) modeled after New York's.

Archbishop Stritch officiated at the Holy Name Cathedral, where the Shrivers worshiped. Through his participation in some of the church's social and civic projects, Sarge had become well-acquainted with the cardinal, and through him with the work of the Catholic Interracial Council.

One night in 1952, through some friends from church, Shriver met Lloyd Davis in the Pump Room. Davis, a soft-spoken young African American, had grown up next to a brothel on the South Side, where the neighborhood prostitutes taught him to be a good Christian. Although he had been raised in the African Methodist Church and nurtured in the bosom of South Side black culture (he considered Mahalia Jackson to be almost a second mother), Davis didn't like the way local pastors often used the Methodist Church more as a political foothold than as a place for spreading the word of God. Consequently, he converted to Catholicism during the Korean War, which he spent at a fort in Missouri. Not incidentally, Davis's time in the army coincided with President Truman's executive order integrating the US armed forces; for a young soldier who had spent most of his life comfortably within the all-black confines of his South Side neighborhood, this was the first experience of being a minority. It wasn't pleasant, mainly because some of the whites in his newly integrated regiment were not happy to find themselves serving cheek-by-jowl with Negroes.

While in the military Davis developed close relations with some Catholic chaplains who told him that if he was serious about his religion, he should leave the army when the war was over and join Chicago's Catholic Interracial Council, which was looking for a black director. Davis leapt at the opportunity. He was devout in his faith, had seen the problems of interracial hostility first-hand, and moreover was active politically, having at a young age been initiated, as many young blacks were, into Congressman William Dawson's Democratic submachine.

The overriding mission of the CIC was to eradicate "the sin of racism," beginning by bringing racial justice into the Church itself, "to get it to clean its house up and stop being a perpetrator of racism and segregation and exclusion," Davis recalled. "You could not deal with the larger community if the Church itself was a perpetuator of everything that you wanted to fight. And so the Catholic Interracial Council had as its first responsibility trying to make the Catholic Church embrace interracial justice as a way of life, and trying to get it to accept diversity." The next step was "to reach out to blacks and others and reform the institutions. I mean, blacks were being turned out of schools and neighborhoods, and being refused admittance to hospital emergency rooms."

But it was hard to find devoted Catholics willing to work toward reforming the Church from within. Thus Davis's encounter with Shriver in the Pump Room was fortuitous. The two men talked long into the evening, and Davis had soon persuaded Sarge to accept the chairmanship of the CIC's school committee.

Shriver was so effective as head of the school committee that he was asked to join the CIC board, and in 1955, he was elected CIC president. One of Shriver's main goals as president was to get qualified black students into some of Chicago's stronger Catholic high schools. None of these schools actually forbade the admission of black students in their bylaws or charters, but their high tuition costs effectively made them "whites only" schools. To combat this, Shriver got the CIC to establish a scholarship program that placed dozens of black students in fifteen Catholic high schools. As John McDermott, who succeeded Lloyd Davis as the Chicago CIC's executive director, recalled, "Shriver's scholarship drive had the effect of getting Negroes into schools where there

had never been any before." Catholic secondary schools in Chicago were integrated considerably earlier than their counterparts in most other cities.

THE BOARD OF EDUCATION

Shriver was able to play a particularly significant role in the desegregation of the
Chicago school system because, in addition to being president of the Catholic
Interracial Council, he happened to be the president of the Chicago school board.
He got the school board job, he recalled, by accident. "After I married Eunice, I
felt that by keeping her in the Midwest I was depriving her of all kinds of interest-
ing activities in Washington. So I always had my eye out for opportunities for her.
One day, I picked up the paper and saw there was a vacancy on the Chicago Board
of Education. 'Aha,' I thought to myself, 'Eunice would be perfect for that.'"

So, Shriver recalled, he carefully crafted a letter to Bill Twohey, a Chicago
judge influential in Democratic politics, proposing Eunice for the position. But
he proposed her in a somewhat elliptical way, knowing that "anything put in
writing in the world of Chicago politics was dangerous because everyone
would end up reading it." So Shriver wrote something along the lines of, as he
recalled it, "Bill, you and I both know someone who would be an extraordinarily competent and successful member of the board of education. The
appointment of this individual would be a great credit to the mayor." (In
Chicago, the mayor directly appointed members to the board.) Shriver thought
the letter was "properly circumspect but also very clear."

Two weeks later Shriver got a call from Judge Twohey. "The board of education appointment is all set," Twohey told him, as Shriver recalled. "Kennelly's
going to go ahead with it."

"God, Bill, that's wonderful," Shriver said. "Thank you for making this happen. Eunice will be pleased."

"Well, she should be very proud of you," Tuohy said.

"Well, I'm proud of her. She'll be a great asset to the board," Shriver said.

Twohey seemed confused. "What do you mean?" he asked

Shriver repeated himself, saying that Eunice would be an asset to the board.
"You did get my letter, didn't you?" he asked.

"Of course," Twohey said. "That's why I'm calling. You made a very good case
for yourself. The mayor is going to announce your appointment tomorrow."

"*My* appointment?" Shriver said. "I was proposing my wife."

Twohey burst into laughter. "Well, doggone it, Sarge, you should have said so. You're the nominee now."

So Shriver began what was to be a six-year tenure on the Chicago Board of Education. For someone who was supposed to be a trustee of the public school system, he had surprisingly little experience with public schooling—none at all, in fact, since his entire education had taken place at private or parochial schools, and his own children weren't old enough yet to attend school. But on October 26, 1955, barely a year after being appointed, he was elected president of the school board, making him the senior figure in overseeing the large Chicago school system. The *Chicago American* editorialized, "We think the School Board made a good choice in electing Robert Sargent Shriver president. . . . Shriver has served on the board only since May 1954 but he has demonstrated both a devoted interest in education and an extremely intelligent grasp of the needs of the Chicago schools. He has given special attention to the development of the vocational and special education programs. . . . We congratulate him and the people of Chicago on his election." The *Chicago Sun-Times* echoed these sentiments. This was the beginning of his never-consummated romance with Illinois state politics and his love affair with the city's editorial columnists. "We predict that president of the school board will be only a starting point for him in public service," the *Sun-Times* declared. "He is destined for even bigger things."

"Ideas bubble from Shriver," reported the *Chicago American* in 1957. In 1954, the year before he was elected president, the board had divided Chicago into sixteen districts, each with a regional superintendent. When he stepped into the presidency, Shriver seized on the district arrangement as an opportunity to experiment—just as individual states can serve as laboratories of democracy for the federal system, so the individual districts could serve as laboratories of education for the whole school system. One idea he conceived during these years was a means of dealing with difficult or delinquent youth. Wouldn't it make sense, he asked School Superintendent Benjamin Willis, to use some of the rural or forested land outside of Chicago to build camps for delinquent students, a place where they could go to be separated from their often damaging family lives or crime-ridden cultural environments? In the woods, students could be successfully divorced from their oftentimes dismal urban surroundings, while reaping the physical and emotional benefits of an active outdoor life. Immersed in round-the-clock instruction and activity, delinquent youths might be rehabilitated.

Willis and Shriver tried to implement some small pilot programs along these lines, but they were never able to obtain the legal rights to the grounds they wanted to use. Shriver was frustrated, believing the concept to be a sound one—so he held onto the idea and put a version of it into effect nationwide ten years later as the Job Corps program, one of the cornerstones of the War on Poverty.

At Shriver's insistent prodding, the Illinois legislature also voted a series of pay increases for teachers. When he took over the school board presidency in 1955, fourteen major cities in the nation paid their public school teachers more than Chicago did; by the time he stepped down from the school board, in 1960, Chicago's teachers were the highest paid in the country. In a 1956 speech to the finance committee of the Chicago city council Shriver said, "As a result of the unanimous action of our board of education, Chicago's teachers are now paid as well as or better than those in all cities with a population of 500,000 in the USA. If Chicago is to claim credit for being the first city of our nation in any respect whatsoever, I can think of none better than being America's number one city in terms of teachers' salaries." In 1954, Shriver's first year as a board member, the city spent $171.9 million on public education; by 1960, the year he stepped down, it was spending $261.8 million—yet he continued to be routinely praised by the city's editorialists for the parsimoniousness of his budgets. And in 1956 the president of the American Association of School Administration adjudged Chicago's school program to be "the boldest, most creative and far-reaching in the country"; in my judgment, he said, "no city in the country can top Chicago's school leadership" of Willis and Shriver.

As president of both the school board and the Catholic Interracial Council, Shriver was ideally situated to press for school desegregation, especially after Richard Daley was elected mayor in 1955. (Shriver was a frequent visitor in Mayor Daley's office, and the two men regularly attended White Sox games together.) Some ardent reformers rebelled at Daley's sometimes heavy-handed political and management style. But Shriver felt he could harness Daley's predilection for law and order and make it work toward interracial harmony.

In 1955 Chicago was still among the most racially segregated cities outside of the Deep South. Racial strife—riots, beatings, and active discrimination in jobs, housing, and hospital admissions—was widespread. But the continuing migration of blacks from the South, along with a small but growing black middle class buoyed by the continuing postwar economic prosperity, gave neighborhood demographics a dynamism that continually challenged established racial boundaries. Every week throughout much of the 1950s, three and a half blocks changed from white to Negro, as new black families arriving from the South forced existing black neighborhoods to expand into white ones.

In Chicago, as elsewhere, school systems generally followed residential patterns—children attended the local neighborhood school. Thus, once a single black student enrolled in a white school, it was technically considered "integrated." But in the pre-Daley era, students could file for transfers to public schools outside of their residential area—so the influx of a few black students into one public school often would lead to an exodus of white students, who would transfer to an all-white school nearby. The effect was a kind of rolling segregation: As soon as one school would integrate, many of its students would simply resegregate somewhere else. Shriver prevailed on Mayor Daley to prohibit this practice. "Public high school students in Chicago now go to the high school in their district," Shriver said in 1958; schools that got integrated now stayed integrated.

The problems of segregation and discrimination were as persistent in Chicago housing as they were in the Chicago school system. Trumbull Park, for instance, was a formerly all-white community that the city had forced to absorb twenty-five Negro families in the early 1950s. The black families were taunted, harassed, and physically abused by neighborhood whites; students and teachers at the Trumbull Park Catholic schools made life so miserable for black students that they were forced to withdraw; the community paper, the *Daily Calumet*, called for the removal of the black families, by force if necessary. And some of the local Catholic parishes made it clear to the new residents that blacks were not welcome to worship there. "Racial violence in Trumbull Park has become normal," said one black leader, and retaliation by African Americans became a growing problem: "A white person takes his life in his hands if he walks through the Black Belt on the South Side at certain hours."

At Shriver's insistence, the Catholic Interracial Council devoted hundreds of hours to meeting with local leaders in the Trumbull Park Community and to providing support to the twenty-five black families. Shriver personally involved Cardinal Stritch in the neighborhood, and the council distributed some 25,000 pieces of literature in an attempt to lift the veil of ignorance from bigoted eyes. CIC members personally escorted black families to St. Kevin's Church so they could attend Mass. But recalcitrant whites sought revenge on the CIC, throwing rocks through the council windows with notes attached that said, "Keep your hands off Trumbull Park or else." For several weeks, the CIC offices had to be kept under twenty-four-hour police surveillance.

Another problem Shriver strove to address through the CIC was racial discrimination in Chicago's hospitals, and in particular in Catholic hospitals. The number of black doctors was declining. Worse, there had been many unfortunate incidents of hospitals refusing to admit black patients, even when patients in dire need of medical attention appeared in emergency rooms. In 1955 Shriver had the CIC convene a Catholic Hospitals Conference for hospital administrators, both to alarm them by exposing the extent of discrimination prevalent in their institutions and to educate them about how to rectify the problem.

Perhaps Shriver's greatest coup as CIC director was to get Cardinal Stritch to speak out publicly against racial discrimination in the Church and in the surrounding society. Although Stritch was known within the Church hierarchy to hold relatively progressive views, he had never been outspoken about them in public. But at the Catholic Hospitals Conference on October 24, 1955, Stritch addressed the crowd gathered at the Sheraton Hotel and "called for an end of bias in Catholic hospitals" and said that "he expected them to not only admit persons of color but to hire them for administration, support, and staff medical positions."

A year later, at a meeting of the CIC's board of directors in September 1956, Cardinal Stritch made one of the boldest statements to date by a senior member of the Church hierarchy on the matter of racial discrimination. "Injustices done to Negroes," he said, "are one of the blots in our history. It is no use trying to cover them up. We're pleased that many people are realizing it is a blot, because as we know from our Catholic teaching, we must have admission of sin before contrition." He praised the council for helping blacks "not in a warped spirit of condescension [that goes] slumming to the blacks" but rather that "strives to bring men together in neighborliness."

The fruits of Shriver's work on race and religion reverberated well beyond Chicago and continued to do so into the next decade, as the civil rights movement reached full flower. In August 1958, the Chicago CIC hosted a meeting at Loyola University for the growing number of local Catholic Interracial Councils nationwide. The meeting produced the National Catholic Conference for Interracial Justice (NCCIJ), officially chartered in 1960 under the directorship of Matthew Ahmann, who had worked under Shriver and Davis at the Chicago CIC. Prompted in part by the Loyola meeting, the American bishops made a dramatic statement in November 1958, in a pastoral letter titled "Discrimination and the Christian Conscience." "The heart of the race question," the bishops wrote, "is religious and moral." This was the first time the Catholic hierarchy itself had framed the issue in this manner; earlier it had addressed racism (most notably in a 1943 statement by the Catholic bishops) in only political and economic terms.

Shriver became a board member of the new national group, and in 1963, the NCCIJ was represented as one of the ten co-chairs of the 1963 March on Washington at which Rev. Martin Luther King Jr. made his historic "I Have A Dream" speech. That same year, at an event at Chicago's Orchestra Hall, Shriver presented King with the Chicago CIC's John F. Kennedy Award for improving race relations.

Working always within the context of the Catholic Church, the CIC was never truly an institutional part of the civil rights movement. Still, it can be fairly said that the CIC in the 1950s played a key role in incubating future civil rights activists and in priming the black and Catholic populations of Chicago for the social upheavals that were to come. More important—according to Lloyd Davis and other interested contemporary observers—it took someone like Shriver to influence Cardinal Stritch and the other cardinals not only to integrate the Church itself but also to prepare it for an institutional role in achieving the civil rights victories of Montgomery and Selma, Alabama.

In 1958, as a tribute to his hard work on behalf of improved race relations, the council presented Shriver with the James J. Hoey Award for Interracial

Justice, which each year rewarded "a white or Negro Catholic who has done effective work against ending racial bigotry." In June 1961, after Shriver had moved to Washington to work in the Kennedy administration, Mayor Daley hosted a "Salute to Sargent Shriver" dinner at the Conrad Hilton Hotel to recognize his work on race relations. Thousands of Chicagoans turned out to fete him. Vice President Lyndon Johnson sent a telegram, paying tribute to Shriver's work in race relations. "I congratulate the city of Chicago for paying tribute to him," Johnson said. "Sarge is to Chicago what Jack Kennedy is to Boston."

CHAPTER TEN

Chicago Politics

B y 1955 Shriver had established himself as a man to watch in Illinois politics. Gossip columns called him a "hot prospect" to be the Democratic nominee for governor. In October 1955, the *Chicago American* reported that the thirty-nine-year-old Shriver "looms as a 'dark horse' candidate for governor in the Democratic primary next April," a good "compromise candidate" who might be able to unseat William Stratton, the Republican who had succeeded Adlai Stevenson in Springfield. By 1958 Charles Cleveland, political editor of the *Chicago Daily News*, was reporting that Shriver was a "winter book" favorite to be the Democratic nominee for governor of Illinois in 1960, "unless Mayor Daley should decide to go for the governorship himself." Shriver's friend Harris Wofford would later recall attending a school board dinner in 1959 at which "almost everyone at my table predicted that Shriver would someday be governor. Several who had worked with him closely said he was the most imaginative, effective, and humane executive they had ever known." "To tell you the truth," one of them told Wofford, "he's my real choice for president."

Shriver felt the tug of his political potential keenly. He read the newspaper columns touting his candidacy. He heard the whisperings in the Daley machine casting him as the mayor's favorite. And he listened to his friends urging him to throw his hat into one ring or another. "As I have often told you," Lloyd Bowers wrote to him, "I know of no one that I would more happily support for office." But Shriver was ambivalent, unsure of how the Kennedy family would regard him choosing a political course that was independent of the family's plans for Jack.

THE 1956 CONVENTION

The 1956 Democratic National Convention was to be held in Chicago. As the event approached, there was growing speculation in the newspapers that first-term senator Jack Kennedy was a potential vice presidential nominee. At first, most people—including the senator himself—dismissed this as idle chatter. As August drew nearer, however, Jack found himself seduced by the possibility: He began quietly promoting his candidacy behind the scenes. In July, Shriver sent Jack a telegram quoting a *Chicago Sun-Times* article in which the Democratic front-runner Adlai Stevenson said his current top choices for running mates were Humphrey and Kennedy. The *Sun-Times* editorialized in favor of Kennedy, seeking to allay concerns about his youth and inexperience by recalling that FDR had been a year younger than Kennedy when he was nominated for the vice presidency on the James Cox ticket in 1920.

Because of his close relationship to Adlai Stevenson, Shriver was dispatched to make the case for Kennedy to the former Illinois governor and to gather intelligence regarding the governor's current thinking on the matter of a vice presidential selection. Sitting with Stevenson on a plane going to Chicago from California, where Stevenson had just beaten Estes Kefauver in the decisive primary, Shriver asked him if he had given any thought to a running mate. Stevenson said that he had not yet settled on a short list of candidates. After Shriver outlined what he thought his brother-in-law could bring to the ticket, Stevenson responded by bluntly asking about Kennedy's physical health and about how the Kennedy family would feel about Jack's running. Shriver told him he thought they would be in favor.

Stevenson then brought up Kennedy's Catholicism. Earlier in 1956 Kennedy had dispatched Ted Sorensen to research voting records to see how a Catholic candidate would affect the Democratic ticket's chances against Eisenhower. Sorensen had drawn up a detailed analysis purporting to demonstrate that a Catholic running mate would decidedly help a Protestant presidential candidate. Bristling with statistics, the report argued that enough Catholic immigrant offspring had reached voting age to have a decisive impact in the big states where urban immigrants were concentrated.

Such predictions of demographics and politics, Stevenson said, were at best an "educated guess." "It is not the political advantage of the vice presidential choice that is crucial," he told Shriver, "but the needs of the United States— who [can] best perform the duties of the job." And then he said something that startled Shriver. "I hope the convention will give a good deal of deliberation to the vice-presidential question."

Shriver wondered what that meant. Was Stevenson not planning to pick his own running mate? Stevenson went on to say that "Kennedy, with his clean, 'all-American boy' appearance and TV personality, would be a splendid contrast to Nixon and his heavy, thick looks." Shriver brightened at this, but Stevenson went on to say (as Shriver reported to Joe Kennedy) that perhaps Humphrey could "'give Nixon hell' better." It was a confusing, mixed message.

When Shriver reported back to the Kennedy camp, however, it was enough to keep attention fixed on the possibility of Jack's winning the nomination, and Jack's operatives continued to campaign discreetly among receptive members of Congress, governors, and national party leaders. Later, Stevenson told a journalist that "I had a personal fondness for Jack and I admired him, and I told his father that. Then, of course, Jack's sister Eunice and her husband, Sarge Shriver, are good friends of mine. There was also our concern for the Catholic vote, which we had lost in 1952. Yes, we had thought seriously about Jack as a vice-presidential candidate."

Joe Kennedy, vacationing on the French Riviera, was adamantly opposed to Jack's joining the Democratic ticket. The Ambassador worried that Adlai Stevenson, running as the Democratic presidential nominee for the second time, would be trounced by President Eisenhower and that Jack could see his own reputation tarnished by association with such a defeat. Worse, Joe worried, Stevenson's defeat might be blamed on Kennedy's Catholicism. Joe also implied that Jack had yet to earn his spurs.

In response, Jack asked Shriver to write a memo to his father recounting Sarge's conversation with Stevenson. Governor Stevenson, Shriver wrote to Mr. Kennedy, had been assured that "you were 100 percent behind Jack, that you gave him and his campaign everything you had even if perchance you might disagree with the basic wisdom of the decision Jack might make." In other words: If you appear ambivalent about supporting your son for vice president now, you risk embarrassing both Jack and Stevenson.

By the time the convention opened on August 13, Kefauver appeared to be the clear vice presidential front-runner, with Humphrey the obvious second choice. And if the conservative Southern Democrats wanted a less liberal alternative, there was always Senate majority leader Lyndon Johnson of Texas. Jack Kennedy—only partway through his first Senate term—looked to be a long shot.

Jack and Jacqueline Kennedy (who had been married in 1953, several months after the Shrivers) arrived in Chicago on Sunday, August 12. Jack checked into the Conrad Hilton Hotel, not far from the International Amphitheater where the convention was to be held. Jackie was seven months pregnant, so to keep her distance from the action she moved into the Shrivers' apartment on Lake View Avenue, along with Jean Kennedy and Bobby's wife, Ethel.

Eunice and Adeline Keane, the wife of an alderman from Chicago's Thirty-first Ward, were appointed heads of the convention's Entertainment Committee. "In less than half a decade," the *Chicago Daily News* reported, "Eunice had become so much a part of Chicago life that she could be chosen for such a highly visible task, seeming like a real Chicagoan and not an interloper from the East." Eunice, for her part, was all in favor of her brother joining Stevenson on the Democratic ticket. "We think that public office is a natural field for him and that he'd be terrific as vice president," she told a reporter a week before the convention. When asked about her own husband's political future, she took the official Kennedy family line, which subordinated Sarge's career to Jack's. "I'm perfectly satisfied leaving him remain president of Chicago's Board of Education," she said, making it sound as though Sarge had no choice in the matter.

Stevenson caught everyone by surprise when (as he had suggested to Shriver that he might) he announced that he was throwing the choice of vice presidential nominee to the convention. Apparently, Stevenson personally preferred Humphrey, but he was loathe to alienate Kefauver and other hopefuls, whose help he would need to defeat Eisenhower. The vote would be the next day— meaning candidates had only twelve hours to campaign.

The extended Kennedy family sprang into action, prowling the convention floor trawling for delegates and then, forgoing sleep, going from hotel room to hotel room all night, trying to add to Jack's tally for the next day. Only Jackie remained at the Shrivers' apartment that night. "When I got to Jack's hotel room," Shriver recalled in an interview some years later, "there were Jack and Bobby and Eunice and Jean and Teddy and it looked like a family conference up at the Cape instead of a political meeting, except there were Ted Sorensen and [Connecticut's powerful political boss John] Bailey and a few others. There was Bobby with a yellow pad in his hand, writing down the states and the delegates, and Jack would say, 'I think I can get four or five of those delegates,' or something like that. It was all pretty amateurish."

Amateurish but effective: Kennedy won 304 votes on the first ballot the next day, second only to Kefauver, whose 483 1/2 votes were not enough to secure a majority. On the second ballot, both New York and Texas switched their votes to Kennedy. He needed only 33 1/2 more votes to become the nominee.

But Kefauver held firm on the third ballot, and some of the Southern delegations began drifting back to him from Kennedy. Shriver ran back out onto the convention floor, where it became evident to him that Jack had peaked on the second ballot; momentum had turned against him. Shriver then returned to the Stock Yard Inn in time to find Jack putting on his suit. He put his arm around his brother-in-law and delivered the bad news. Sure enough, when the results of the third ballot were announced on television, Kennedy had not gained. Kennedy turned to Sorensen and Shriver and said, "Let's go."

Kennedy walked to the podium to thunderous applause and made a gracious speech in which he moved that Kefauver be nominated by acclamation. And then he left the convention and two days later flew off to France to recuperate with his father on the Riviera. "Don't feel sorry for young Jack Kennedy," the Boston Herald editorialized. "Despite his defeat . . . he probably rates as the one real victor of the entire convention."

Several weeks later, the Kennedys gathered at Hyannis Port for Thanksgiving. The primary topic of discussion was Jack's political future. Eunice was the most ambitious on behalf of her brother—perhaps even more ambitious than Joe. "Eunice was ambitious as hell, and bright, and dogged," George Smathers recalled. "She encouraged Jack, in my judgment, more than Rose did, I think as much as Joe." There was little question that Jack would run for president in 1960.

THE KENNEDY FOUNDATION

Meanwhile, Eunice was growing worried that while the Kennedy men were all focusing on Jack's career, the philanthropic organization her father had founded in memory of his deceased eldest son was being neglected. She hated to see the public service potential of the Joseph P. Kennedy Jr. Foundation squandered. So she approached her father. "Daddy," she said, "I'd like to do something for the foundation. I'd like to see if I could help get it a kind of focus." He said that sounded fine and asked her what kind of focus she had in mind. "Well, you know I'd like to go out and really find out what the big need is." The Ambassador approved.

Sarge and Eunice traveled around the country for several weeks, calling on everyone they could think of on philanthropic boards and charitable foundations, asking experts what they thought America's most pressing social needs were. They spoke to journalists and academics, social workers and politicians, anyone they thought could provide guidance.

Ultimately, Eunice decided that mental retardation should be the foundation's driving cause. This was not, she has always insisted—legions of Kennedy biographers' assertions to the contrary—because of her sister Rosemary. According to the oft-repeated story, the family's experience with Rosemary had left Eunice with a searing feeling of guilt that she felt driven to assuage by throwing herself into work with the mentally retarded. In truth, although having a "special sister," as Eunice says, may have sensitized her to the plight of the mentally handicapped, the real motivation for her years of toil in this field was her sense that, based on her experiences in various other areas of social work, no one was doing anything significant to help these people—at least 5 million of them in the United States alone in the late 1950s. "I originally wanted to be a sociologist," she says, "and when I did graduate work at the University of Chicago [in the early 1950s], I went to work with the underprivileged and I saw that people who were handicapped were, in my judgment, very badly treated. It was not because of my sister. It was just that I had noticed that in all of my work when I saw people who were 'slow,' no one seemed to be doing anything for them."

To Eunice, this was a travesty, one she thought might be rectified somewhat by the Joseph P. Kennedy Jr. Foundation. Sarge wasn't sure he agreed with her that this was the most burning problem of the time, nor was he convinced that all the money and time in the world could necessarily ease the plight of the retarded or improve their lot in life. At the time, he shared with most Americans the sense that the congenitally retarded were a lost cause, structurally limited in how much they could develop or accomplish in life. But clearly Eunice thought she could accomplish something for the retarded, even if no one else did, and that was enough for Sarge.

Together, the Shrivers crisscrossed the country, interviewing anyone who knew anything about the mentally retarded. Because they had several million dollars a year to dole out for research that the foundation deemed worthy, scientists and university presidents received them eagerly. Eunice and Sarge hired a team of academic consultants and dragged them around the country looking for the best research sites. In the end, they recommended establishing programs at the University of California at Los Angeles, the University of Wisconsin, and Johns Hopkins University. No one knew it at the time, but the Shrivers had just planted the seeds of both Head Start and the Special Olympics.

SHRIVER FOR GOVERNOR?

As the 1960 election cycle approached, Shriver once again saw his name bandied around as a serious gubernatorial prospect. In 1957, after he had traveled to Springfield to lobby for increased funding for the Chicago public schools, the newspapers reported that he had launched himself into contention to succeed Governor Stratton. "In a round of handshaking sessions with lawmakers who comprise the statewide backbone of the Democratic party, Shriver unknowingly set off a favorable chain reaction for himself. . . . Said one Senator, 'This fellow Shriver is a natural, a combination of Jimmy Stewart's handsomeness and suave winning ways and the sincere statesmanship of a finished politician.'" The reporter concluded that Shriver was "being quietly boomed as Democratic gubernatorial candidate in 1960."

Although Shriver never formally declared his intention to run for office, he was turning the possibility over in his mind. He knew he could count on Adlai Stevenson and many of his top aides and political advisers to support him. And his relationship with Mayor Daley, whose power was steadily increasing, put him in good stead with the all-important Cook County Democratic machine. But Shriver knew that Jack Kennedy planned to make a run for the Democratic presidential nomination in 1960; he might therefore be better off lying low until 1964 and running for governor then.

A Kennedy presidential campaign posed at least three potential problems for a Shriver gubernatorial campaign. First, there was the religion question. As Shriver well knew, there had never been a Catholic president or vice president. Although the country manifested considerably more religious tolerance in the late 1950s than it had in the early 1920s, it remained a real question whether a Catholic could be taken seriously as a presidential candidate.

Mayor Daley was also a Catholic—not surprising, since downtown Chicago was still largely Catholic. But the country as a whole—and Illinois as a whole—was not. Thus the possibility of a Catholic candidate for president and a Catholic candidate for governor—especially when there was already a Catholic in the mayor's office—did not excite either the Cook County political machine or the Kennedy organization. Shriver for governor might be one Catholic too many—the rock that would sink the whole Illinois Democratic slate. And with Illinois being such a large electoral state, the sinking of its slate could drag down the national ticket.

The second potential problem was too many Kennedys. The family had nowhere near the ubiquity or celebrity it has possessed since the 1960s, but it was already very much in the news. Jack's political operatives feared that another Kennedy—even a Kennedy in-law—running for political office would not sit well with the voters.

The third potential problem, related to the second, was limited family resources. The way the Kennedys worked was everyone coming together and pressing toward the same goal. This had worked in Jack's campaigns for the House of Representatives and in his two Senate campaigns, and it had almost worked at the 1956 Democratic campaign. If Shriver were to run for governor, it would mean the family would have to divide its financial and political resources, giving full attention to neither Jack nor Sarge.

Although Shriver had little to offer Jack Kennedy in the way of money or a field organization, Kennedy probably needed Shriver more than Shriver needed him, largely because of Sarge's political clout in Illinois. Joe Kennedy did have his own direct conduit to Mayor Daley and the Cook County political machine—a connection that may well have been the decisive factor in the 1960 election—but it couldn't hurt to have Shriver, who had his own relationship to Daley, in the fold as well. Also, the civil rights movement was gaining momentum within the Democratic Party, and Jack had not yet proven his bona fides to the civil rights activists. Someone like Shriver, with his work at the CIC and his connections to prominent African Americans, might help Jack build connections to that wing of the party.

Finally, there was that unique resource: Eunice. No one threw herself more zealously into campaigning than she did. But could she possibly have the time to campaign for both Jack and Sarge?

"I don't have any gnawing compulsion to run for political office," Sarge told an interviewer around that time. "I can be very happy in private life." Still, he felt the call of public service strongly. Politics, in Shriver's eyes, fell not far below the priesthood in the hierarchy of worthy callings. He felt sure he could do some good as governor.

All this was swimming through his mind when he traveled with his family to the Kennedy retreat at Palm Beach for Easter 1959. Shriver's cousin Mollie and her husband, Stuyvie Pierrepont, also had a place in Palm Beach and were visiting that weekend. Mollie recalls coming over to the Kennedys' one day for lunch with Sarge and Eunice. The four of them sat in the garden outside, while the Ambassador sunbathed in his "bullpen," a separate fenced-in area alongside the house at the top of the beach, completely naked but for his wide-brimmed planter's hat, as was his custom. "Mollie?" she remembered him saying, "Is that you? C'mon over here. I want to see you." She went into the bullpen and stood before Mr. Kennedy, feeling uncomfortable as he lay there smeared in cocoa butter, naked but for a small towel perched delicately over his privates, while he looked her up and down.

They talked briefly and then Kennedy asked Mollie to fetch Sarge, which she did.

"Sarge," Kennedy said, "now what's this I hear about you running for governor?" Shriver explained that it was true he had been approached by Illinois political operatives encouraging him to run, and that he had been told by people in the know that he had a good shot at winning if he ran, but that he himself had not made any decision on the matter. "Good," Mr. Kennedy said, "because under no circumstances are you to run for governor next year." He went on to make it clear that 1960 was to be Jack's year and that all the family's political efforts were to be channeled in that one direction. A Shriver campaign, Kennedy continued, would be a drain and a distraction for the family. "Besides," he concluded, "Jack needs your help on the campaign."

CHAPTER ELEVEN

Dawn of the New Frontier

Shriver had no inkling of how signing on to work for his brother-in-law's campaign would dramatically alter the direction of his career. For years after he moved to the East, he would cast nostalgic glances toward the Midwest, hoping someday to resume the life he had left: his business career, his Catholic lay work, his civil rights work, his old friends, and his political prospects. For more than a decade, he kept close tabs on the local Chicago political scene, talking discreetly to his friends among the ward bosses and the newspaper columnists, waiting for the right opportunity to return to his adopted home city. Several times, such opportunities appeared to present themselves. Each time, however, whether because he hesitated too long before taking decisive action or because other demands asserted themselves, the moment would pass.

Some of Sarge's friends, especially those with more jaundiced views of the Kennedy family, hated to see him give anything up on that family's behalf. Even some disinterested observers were puzzled. The political columnist Charlie Bartlett, a friend of Jack's, reflected later, "I'm not so sure I'd drop everything just because my brother-in-law wanted to be elected something or other." Especially since, as Bartlett observed, Shriver's own chances for governor in 1960 or 1964 looked pretty good. Why, in short, when he was so happy in Chicago—and clearly had so much potential as a politician there—would he abandon everything to become merely "a subaltern in his brother-in-law's presidential drive"?

The simple answer was because he had been asked. Jack, Ted Kennedy said several years later, "knew and respected Sargent's abilities and quite naturally expected him to respond to a call for help when he was really needed." Also, Jack's request came with the implicit endorsement of the two people to whom Sarge was least likely to say no: Joe Kennedy and Eunice.

In October 1959 Shriver reluctantly stepped down from the presidencies of the school board and the Catholic Interracial Council. "Chicago's Loss, Kennedy's Gain," declared the headline of an editorial in the *Sun-Times*; "An Unwelcome Resignation," declared the *Chicago American*; "Shriver Did Well," declared the *Daily News*. "He was a public official who did his 'homework' well," one paper editorialized. "He tackled the work with verve and dedication. While he cannot, of course, take sole and personal credit for improvements, it is a fact that during his tenure as president the city school system improved." "Along with many Chicagoans, we regret the resignation of R. Sargent Shriver Jr. as president of the school board," editorialized another. "Shriver has made an outstanding record of the post."

THE PRIMARIES

In 1960 Shriver was considered to be on the liberal edge of the Kennedy clan; Jack, among others, joked good-naturedly that Sarge was the "house Communist." In truth, Shriver was as anti-Communist as anyone in the family—and as befit a protégé of Joe Kennedy, he was friendly to business, as well—but his interest in civil rights and his abiding Christian concern for the poor placed him to the left of the Kennedy wing of the Democratic Party. Shriver hoped he could help Kennedy win the election with a strong complement of liberal support, so that as president he wouldn't be beholden to retrograde Southern—and often segregationist—Democrats. According to Harris Wofford, Shriver

badly wanted Kennedy's nomination to come through liberal support (along with the more natural Irish and Catholic constituency), not through an alliance with

Southern conservatives. Kennedy was saying that himself during this period—at least to liberals. Shriver well knew that there was a tug-of-war within Kennedy and within the family . . . between the liberal and conservative poles. Kennedy spoke disparagingly of those "doctrinaire 'liberals' . . . who are so opposed to me" but said if "professional liberals made him uncomfortable" he "knew too many conservatives with whom I have nothing in common" to identify with their camp. When asked whether he would be a liberal or conservative President, he had replied, "I hope to be responsible." Shriver hoped Kennedy would find himself responding to a convention and a campaign in which the liberal wing gave him decisive support.

This affected how Shriver campaigned. His first campaign assignments were in the crucial Wisconsin and West Virginia primaries. By the spring of 1960 the principal contenders for the Democratic presidential nomination appeared to be Minnesota senator Hubert Humphrey and Kennedy, with Missouri senator Stuart Symington and Senate majority leader Lyndon Johnson waiting to move into the picture if either Humphrey or Kennedy faltered. Meanwhile, Adlai Stevenson, the Democratic candidate from the two previous elections, lurked in the background, hoping in his diffident way to be drafted to run once again. Thus although Kennedy and Humphrey led in Democratic polls going into 1960, each felt he needed to demonstrate strength in key primaries to prove to Democratic party bosses that he was a viable national candidate.

In Wisconsin, Shriver was placed in charge of the First and Second Districts, a region of agriculture and dairy farms (along with some small patches of industry) in the southern part of the state, just over the northwestern border with Illinois. Half of Shriver's job would be easy and half would be hard: The First District was predominantly Catholic, so Kennedy could expect to do well there, but the Second District, centered on the state capital of Madison, was largely Protestant. Consequently, Shriver concentrated his efforts in the Second District. Sarge and Eunice wore out their shoe leather walking the precincts, knocking on doors from early in the morning until late at night.

The Second District would be challenging for Kennedy because, in addition to its Protestantism, Madison was a hotbed of Left-liberalism. The University of Wisconsin was there; so was *Progressive* magazine, founded by Wisconsin liberalism's patron saint Robert La Follette. Jack Kennedy, Shriver knew, lacked

Humphrey's liberal bona fides. Although Wisconsin voters had elected the infamous Joe McCarthy to the Senate some years earlier, the progressives around Madison faulted Senator Kennedy for not being a vocal enough critic of McCarthyism; with a brother who had worked for McCarthy's committee, a father who had made political contributions to McCarthy, and a sister who had dated him, Jack seemed to Madison liberals to be guilty by association.

In order to compete with Humphrey in the Second District, then, Shriver knew he would have to bring in someone from outside the family, a prominent liberal who could speak credibly on Jack's behalf and who could allay concerns about Kennedy's platform being inimical to progressive concerns. The obvious choice, Shriver thought, was Chester Bowles. Bowles, who in his illustrious career in public service had worked for both FDR and Truman and who had, in the 1950s, served as ambassador to India, was now a congressman from Connecticut. Although some suspected that the sixty-year-old Bowles still harbored presidential aspirations himself, he signed on in early 1960 as Kennedy's senior foreign policy adviser, with the understanding that he would become secretary of state if Kennedy were elected. Bowles was known to be a proud arch-liberal, and Kennedy had enlisted him not only for his wisdom but to appease the progressive wing.

If Shriver could get Bowles to campaign in the Second District, it would surely swing some liberal Humphrey supporters to Kennedy. He made a desperate phone call to his friend Harris Wofford. In 1959 Notre Dame president Ted Hesburgh had written to Shriver telling him that Wofford, who was teaching law at Notre Dame, was "exceptionally able" and that he ought to draw on him for his work with the Catholic Interracial Council, even though Wofford was Protestant, because of his strong background in civil rights. So in the autumn of 1959 Shriver went to the Chicago City Club to hear Wofford give a talk on the work of the Civil Rights Commission. Shriver was fascinated to learn of Wofford's deep commitment to civil rights, and in particular to the teachings of Mohandas Gandhi, whom Wofford and his wife had met during a long sojourn in India, an experience they recounted in their book *India Afire*. After Wofford's talk, in which he had referred to Gandhi's concept of "symbolic action," Shriver stood up and asked, "As someone who has studied Gandhi, what would you suggest that the school board of the city of Chicago do—what symbolic action could it take—to help break the vicious circle of race and poverty in our school sys-

tem?" Afterward Shriver introduced himself and asked if Wofford would be willing to reflect further on the question of how symbolic action might help end
racism in Chicago schools. A week later, Shriver wrote to Wofford saying that
"because of de facto segregation in housing, the school system [is] in real trouble," and that if Wofford had any ideas about what to do, please send them along.

A few weeks after that, Wofford recalled, "the phone rang and it was Shriver
in town for a Notre Dame football game, asking me to join him at the stadium.
Off and on for two hours he laid out the Chicago problem and pressed me for
suggestions—all the time following the game. By the fourth quarter, he had
enlisted me to spend some time at the school board in Chicago, reviewing the
facts and brainstorming about solutions."

In the spring of 1960 Wofford was teaching at Notre Dame and at the same
time helping out Ted Sorensen by writing speeches for Senator Kennedy.
Shriver knew that Wofford was close to Chester Bowles, and he pleaded with
him to get Bowles to campaign in Wisconsin.

The problem was, however, that Bowles had signed on with Kennedy on the
condition that he would never have to campaign directly against his friends
Stevenson and Humphrey. This left Shriver in a bind. Kennedy's forthrightly liberal
foreign policy adviser would be conspicuous by his absence in the Wisconsin campaign, particularly around Madison. Needing a replacement, someone who could
speak convincingly of Kennedy's liberal credentials, Shriver asked Wofford if he
might be willing to fill in for Bowles at a campaign rally at the University of
Wisconsin. Wofford was respected by liberals and civil rights activists, even though
he was a young man with none of Bowles's national reputation at that point.
Wofford agreed to stand in for Bowles. Speaking to the liberalism of the region
Wofford said, "I am campaigning here for Kennedy because I know that he has
approximately the same view of the world as Humphrey, Stevenson, and Chester
Bowles. . . . It is the vision of a world community, of a world in revolution, of a
world in unprecedented economic development, of a world waiting for full
American participation, waiting for American leadership to end the cold war and
establish and strengthen the institutions of peace and law." The speech earned
Wofford a handwritten note from his friend Humphrey. "Et tu, Brute" was all it said.

It was a good speech, Shriver thought; it delicately addressed Kennedy's perceived liberal deficiencies. Unfortunately, Wofford lacked Bowles's drawing
power and, as Wofford recalled, "to our dismay, about twenty people were scat-

tered about the good-sized law school lecture hall when I arrived." So Shriver had thousands of copies of the speech printed and distributed around the state.

The Kennedy family charmed the Wisconsin press, which had never seen such a large and glamorous family campaigning together. As the primary drew nigh, predictions ran increasingly in Jack's favor. Some even projected he would sweep all ten districts, effectively ending Humphrey's campaign then and there. But when the primary votes were tallied on April 5, the results were less than decisive. Kennedy had won the state, but in garnering only 56 percent of the total vote, he had failed to score the smashing victory he needed to demonstrate his electoral strength to party leaders. (Of Shriver's districts, Jack won the heavily Catholic First District and lost the heavily Protestant Second.)

"What does it mean?" Eunice asked her brother, as they watched the ambiguous results broadcast on television. "It means," he said, "that we've got to go to West Virginia in the morning and do it all over again."

In retrospect it is easier to see that Humphrey's loss in Wisconsin all but ended his presidential hopes for 1960. If he could not win his neighboring state, one similar in demographic and economic composition to Minnesota, what hope had he farther afield? But Humphrey was convinced that the Wisconsin result had been a fluke—that its 31 percent Catholic population and its open voting rules, which allowed Republicans to cross over to vote in the Democratic primary, had allowed Kennedy to sneak to an unmerited victory. For its part, the Kennedy campaign remained worried: It had failed to make enough of an impression on political observers to drive Symington, Johnson, and Stevenson out of contention.

This made the next primary loom even larger. West Virginia was 96 percent Protestant, and its stricter voting rules limited the Democratic primary to Democrats only. Humphrey salivated at the prospect of defeating Kennedy outside of the Midwest and demonstrating to the party bosses that the young Massachusetts senator had no viability in solidly Protestant areas. For the Kennedys, beating Humphrey in a heavily Democratic, heavily Protestant state would demonstrate that Jack's appeal was more than narrowly parochial. The risk was that losing could destroy Kennedy's chance at the nomination.

Kennedy's early polling in West Virginia in 1959 had shown him leading Humphrey, but that was before his religion had become widely known. By

April 1960 it was clear that the Catholic question would arise in national politics for the first time since Al Smith's last presidential campaign in 1928. When
West Virginia voters learned that Kennedy was Catholic, he plummeted in the
polls, falling 20 points behind Humphrey.

Shriver arrived in West Virginia on April 11, six days after the Wisconsin primary,
to meet with the other Kennedy "area commanders" at the Kanawha Hotel. Larry
O'Brien, Kenny O'Donnell, and Bobby Kennedy doled out the marching orders.
Shriver, one of eight commanders, was sent to the city of Huntington, which lay
in the Ohio River Valley near the intersection of West Virginia, Ohio, and Kentucky,
and placed in charge of Cabell County. The county lay in the southwestern corner
of the state extending eastward to the Kanawha River; parts of it were the poorest, most underdeveloped section of the state. "My first night in West Virginia, I
was taken to a minstrel show, where white guys got dressed up in black face and
mimicked black people. There was lots of fanfare and revelry to accompany it. That
gave me an idea right away of how backward parts of the state were."

Shriver threw himself into campaigning with gusto. Mary Ann Orlando
served as his deputy. Congresswoman Edith Green, from Oregon, who would
later become a Shriver nemesis when he ran the War on Poverty, came to help,
as did Marjorie Lawson, an African American civil rights lawyer from Washington. According to an academic study of the West Virginia primary, Shriver
was a real "ramrod" for the region. He walked the precincts and shook hands
eighteen hours a day.

Because of Shriver's insistence on frugality, the Cabell County headquarters was a store front in Huntington that "should have been condemned years
before." "In the middle of the floor," Mary Ann Orlando recalled, "there was
this hole, and I can't tell you how many times people fell through that hole,
including me. You were in such a rush you'd forget about it and fall in the hole."
Everyone took turns trying to get everyone else to fall in the hole, which contributed to the general hilarity of the enterprise.

At first Kennedy declined to address the religion question head on. But it
quickly became clear that religion was *the* issue for West Virginia voters. "We've
never had a Catholic president and I hope we never do," said one little old lady,
echoing a common refrain. "Our people built this country. If they had wanted a
Catholic to be president, they would have said so in the Constitution." In 1960,
anti-Catholic bigotry was still virulent among West Virginian Protestants. The
counties Shriver was responsible for, he recalled, "were the poorest part of the

state, the most rural part, the most peasantlike [and] also the most anti-Catholic part." Ministers from some mainline churches—Presbyterians, Methodists, Baptists—directly attacked Shriver's brother-in-law, and "not a single Protestant minister rose to Kennedy's defense." "They would distribute flyers saying that the Romans had killed Christ," Mary Ann Orlando recalled, "and that therefore we were Christ killers." Shriver recalls standing at the entrance to a coal mine by the Kanawha River, trying to shake hands with the miners as they came to work, as he had done with factory workers in Wisconsin. In West Virginia, it sometimes seemed as though more men swore at him or slung anti-Catholic epithets than shook his hand. "I remember one day I was standing in front of a coal mine, handing out literature about Kennedy. One of the guys came out and I handed him a pamphlet. He looked at the picture of Kennedy and then he looked at me and spit right in my face."

As the primary drew closer and the religious issue failed to recede, Jack told his advisers he thought he ought to confront his Catholicism head on; most of them disagreed, saying that would torpedo his candidacy. Shriver dissented from these advisers. Kennedy's pollster, Louis Harris, agreed with Shriver and produced data showing that it would be beneficial for Jack to speak to the question directly. Ultimately, Kennedy did so, in a television broadcast to West Virginia voters the weekend before the May 10 primary election, directly addressing Protestant fears that a Catholic president's primary obeisance would be to the pope rather than to the US Constitution. "When any man stands on the steps of the Capitol and takes the oath of office of president," Jack said, "he is swearing to support the separation of church and state." After that Humphrey's lead began to dwindle and then to evaporate completely.

On a raw, rainy primary day, Kennedy won the state, 61 to 39 percent, and shocked the country. At about 1:00 a.m., Humphrey sent a concession telegram to Kennedy headquarters and was soon declaring that he was no longer a candidate for the Democratic presidential nomination. Kennedy had proven himself to the nation.

THE CONVENTION

Shriver now moved his operation to Democratic Party headquarters at 1028 Connecticut Avenue in Washington and established a broad portfolio composed of doing "whatever was necessary" to help Jack get the nomination. At first, his duties consisted mainly of raising money and maintaining communication between the Kennedy campaign field offices and the Democratic National Committee. Later, Shriver was also given responsibility for rounding up convention delegates for many of the states between the Rocky Mountains (Teddy Kennedy's territory) and the East Coast.

But by far Shriver's most important assignment was to create the campaign's civil rights division. Officially, this meant he was responsible for formulating Kennedy's civil rights positions and policies; in practice this meant doing whatever was necessary to win the support of black voters. While in the Senate, Kennedy had not been particularly active on civil rights issues. Kennedy was not opposed to civil rights; it was just that they had yet to arouse his passion, and he saw them at this point more in terms of political strategy than moral cause. By May 1960, right around the time of the West Virginia primary, the Kennedys were realizing that the Negro vote might be a problem for them.

Kennedy knew that Harris Wofford had good connections to civil rights figures. One day Kennedy called him into his office. "Are we in as much trouble with Negroes as it seems?" Jack asked him. Wofford told him he was; Kennedy's reputation among black leaders was poor. Also, Wofford told him, the black advisers Kennedy had consulted were not in the mainstream of the civil rights movement. Kennedy asked Wofford to do what he could to rectify this. Wofford and Shriver in turn set up meetings for Jack with Martin Luther King Jr. and Roy Wilkins, head of the NAACP.

Kennedy failed to impress these black leaders. In early May, Bobby Kennedy summoned Wofford to his office. "We're in trouble with Negroes," Bobby told him. "We really don't know much about this whole thing. We've been dealing outside the field of the main Negro leadership and have to start from scratch." Bobby went on to explain that they were asking Sargent Shriver to supervise the work of attracting the Negro vote because "he knows all these things." "We want you to head up a Civil Rights Section," Bobby told Wofford, "and work through Sarge and do everything you need to do to deliver every Negro delegate going to the convention." Shriver was made director of the section and Wofford the coordinator. To help Wofford, Shriver also recruited his friend Louis Martin, the publisher of the *Chicago Defender*, Chicago's leading black newspaper. "Kennedy knew himself to have only weak support from African Americans," Shriver recalled. But Shriver was close to William Dawson, the congressman (and acolyte of Dick Daley, the Chicago mayor) known to be able to deliver the majority of Chicago's black vote to Democratic candidates of his choosing. He also knew Martin Luther King Jr.: "I introduced him at the Orchestra Hall on Michigan Avenue in Chicago," Shriver has noted, "at what I think was the first speech he ever made north of the Mason-Dixon Line."

The inner circle at Kennedy headquarters considered the Civil Rights Division to be only a marginally important assignment. "I had responsibility for all the African American vote, wherever it was located," Shriver recalled. "This was the part of the campaign nobody else gave a damn about—this wasn't like being given responsibility for the state of New York or California. I got the assignment because Bobby and his advisers said, 'Well, this guy is the brother-in-law of the candidate and he knows the minority community and we need someone to fill the position, so why not give it to Shriver?'"

The Democratic National Convention was to begin on July 11 at the Sports Center in Los Angeles. Shriver arrived two days early to check into the Biltmore Hotel and begin meeting with black delegates from around the country. Based on his careful tallies, it appeared that Kennedy had the support of a majority of the more than 250 black delegates (out of about 4,500 total delegates) and alternates at the convention. Moreover, every leading black Democrat—save for the mercurial congressman from Harlem, Adam Clayton Powell, who had declared himself for LBJ—had come out for Kennedy. "Early each morning, for a couple of hours, our civil rights contingent operated a hospitality suite in the Biltmore," Wofford recalled. "By now this group included Kennedy's early black supporters and civil rights activists in a dozen delegations. Delegates came to talk, to question Kennedy's record, and to ask what they could do to help." To ensure that the black delegates did not get swept up in the movement to draft Adlai Stevenson, Shriver and Wofford repeatedly pointed out that there was nary a black face among the pro-Stevenson demonstrators outside the convention hall.

The convention itself began under beautiful sunny skies that lasted for the duration of the event. The Kennedy campaign nerve center was on the eighth floor of the Biltmore Hotel. Shriver was responsible for several Midwestern delegations, the most important of which was Illinois. Although he had been assured by Mayor Daley, who controlled the delegation, that he could deliver solid support for Kennedy, Shriver was nervous: As momentum for Adlai

Stevenson built, he worried there would be a groundswell of support for the former governor from his home state. On the Sunday afternoon before the opening ceremonies, Shriver fretted outside a hotel conference room while the Illinois delegation caucused in secret within. When Daley emerged, he announced to Shriver's great relief that Illinois would vote 59 1/2 for Kennedy, 5 1/2 for Symington, and only 2 for Stevenson.

Still, Shriver knew from Bill Blair and Newt Minow that Stevenson still coveted the nomination and believed he could win it if the first ballot was not decisive. That night, Blair arrived at a preconvention party thrown by Peter and Pat Lawford at their Santa Monica home and found himself seated between Nat King Cole and Judy Garland. Shriver came over and pulled Blair aside, asking whether there was any way Blair could dissuade Stevenson. Blair said he would see what he could do.

Over the course of the week, Kennedy's momentum waxed and waned. The early signs from the delegate counters were encouraging; it looked as though Jack was on his way to wrapping up the nomination easily. But when Minnesota senator Eugene McCarthy nominated Stevenson in a soaring peroration ("Do not reject this man who has made us all proud to be Democrats. Do not leave this prophet without honor in his own party.") the convention erupted with hosannas for Stevenson. On Tuesday night, a burgeoning revolt in the North Dakota delegation threatened to unravel that state's support for Kennedy. "All through the night," as Theodore White reported in his account of the convention, "brother-in-law Sargent Shriver had worked on the wavering North Dakota delegate whose half-vote carried the necessary majority to invoke the unit rule [which required the state's delegation to vote as a bloc], and North Dakota's eleven votes were safe again." On Wednesday, Shriver's first concern, once again, was Illinois. But after tracking down Dick Daley on the floor, he was assured that the mayor had the situation well in hand. A few minutes later, Daley would tell Stevenson that he didn't have any significant support in the Illinois delegation. The Stevenson threat was extinguished.

On Wednesday night at eight o'clock Los Angeles time, the voting began with Alabama, which went primarily for Johnson. But as the vote proceeded alphabetically through the states, Kennedy rapidly piled up delegates, passing the 100 mark with Illinois. Shriver cruised the floor, counting and recounting delegates and giving encouragement to those who hadn't yet voted. As the votes were tallied, he noted with satisfaction that every black delegate, save for a few who went for favorite sons, had voted for Kennedy. When Wyoming cast all 15 of its votes for Kennedy, lifting him to a total of 763, Jack became the Democratic nominee for president of the United States. (Johnson finished second with 409 votes.)

Jack, who had been watching the vote on television from a friend's house nearby, made his way to the Sports Center, stopping first in his communications center outside the arena. As he came in, he saw Shriver and Bobby Kennedy talking in a corner, with jubilant looks on their faces. On the other side of the room, 30 feet away, stood some of the more powerful members of the party establishment, the kingmakers and wise elders. Averell Harriman. Dick Daley. Carmine de Sapio. Mike DiSalle. John McCormack. John Bailey. Abe Ribicoff. As Jack entered, these political behemoths started instinctively toward the new nominee and then froze. They seemed to shrink, as though in awed deference to what they had created; only Shriver, it seemed, retained his natural presence. Kennedy walked over to him and Shriver congratulated him warmly. "They stood apart," Theodore White recorded, "these older men of long-established power, and watched [Kennedy]. He turned after a few minutes, saw them watching him, and whispered to his brother-in-law. Shriver now crossed the separating space to invite them over. . . . No one could pass the little open distance between him and them uninvited, because there was this thin separation about him, and the knowledge that they were there not as patrons but as clients." Perhaps it was only appropriate that Shriver—who was often kept at arm's length from the campaign's inner circle because he was seen as too liberal, too Catholic, too much of an independent operator—would be the one to bridge this symbolic gap, to bring together the old guard and the new.

From there, Jack went into the arena to greet the cheering convention.

LYNDON BAINES JOHNSON

The next order of business was to pick a running mate. When Jack left the convention that night a little before 2:00 a.m., most campaign insiders thought that his choice would come down to Stuart Symington and Washington senator Henry Jackson. But before Kennedy climbed into bed that night, he read a congratulatory telegram from the defeated Lyndon Johnson, whose effusiveness implied that he might, despite initial evidence to the contrary, be interested in the second spot on the ticket.

In some ways, Johnson seemed an unlikely choice. For one thing, Johnson had always said he would "never, never, *never* trade his senatorial vote for the vice presidential gavel." Moreover, as a Southern Democrat, Johnson would be anathema to many of the Northeastern and Midwestern liberals whose support had helped carry Kennedy to the nomination.

But about 2:30 a.m., the phone rang in the Biltmore Hotel room Shriver and Wofford shared. Shriver answered and Wofford overheard him say, "Lyndon will? All right, I'll get the word to Jack first thing in the morning." Shriver hung up the phone and rolled over to face Wofford's bed to tell him one of Johnson's top aides had called. "Johnson will accept the vice presidential nomination if Jack offers it to him," Shriver said. "We've got to wake up early so I can warn him before any move is made."

At eight the next morning, Shriver was waiting at the eighth-floor head-quarters when the nominee arrived. Buttonholing his brother-in-law, he quietly described to Jack the 2:30 a.m. phone call. Jack raised his eyebrows. He summoned his assistant, Evelyn Lincoln, and asked her to set up a meeting with Johnson for later that morning. Then he instructed Shriver to call around to party leaders and discreetly solicit their opinions of Johnson as a running mate.

Just at that time Bobby Kennedy arrived at the suite. When Jack told him about Shriver's late night chat with the Johnson aide, Bobby grew visibly perturbed, and when Jack said that he planned to meet with the Senate majority leader Bobby became even more upset and pulled his brother into the bedroom, leaving Shriver outside. Disgruntled voices were audible from within. Before long, the suite was filling up with the Kennedy inner circle. When Bobby told O'Donnell that Jack was considering putting Johnson on the ticket, O'Donnell was irate. "I was so furious I could hardly talk," he recounted in his memoir. He had a visceral dislike of Johnson and moreover had promised many liberal supporters that under no circumstances would Johnson be on the ticket. "I felt that we had been double-crossed."

A wound that was to fester for years had been opened. And Shriver—who, as it happened, would later be drawn into close orbit around Johnson, earning the additional enmity of certain Kennedy acolytes—now appeared to be implicated in causing the wound, simply by virtue of having been the messenger from the Johnson camp.

In truth, Shriver, too, was dubious about the wisdom of hitching Johnson to the ticket. Before the convention, the *Washington Post* had run an article reporting that if Kennedy won the presidential nomination, Johnson would be the most likely running mate. Upon reading this, many black delegates were furious. LBJ, although he would later be known for passing landmark civil rights legislation in the 1960s, was best known among blacks for having eviscerated similar legislation in the late 1950s. So Shriver and Wofford had been dispatched to assure them that Kennedy would never pick Johnson. Now, as Kennedy contemplated doing precisely that, Shriver was afraid he would look like a liar. Thus, although Shriver was planning to call some of the party bosses to get their thoughts on Johnson, he now told Wofford specifically to call liberals and civil rights activists to see how they would react to Johnson's being named. "There's still a chance to stop this if there's enough opposition," he told Wofford.

While Jack went to meet with Johnson, the grumblings in the Kennedy suite continued. And when Jack returned to say that Johnson was in fact interested, the grumblings became even louder. Bobby Kennedy, who already instinctively disliked Johnson and would grow to loathe him (a feeling Johnson reciprocated), would later say that Jack had offered him a place on the ticket purely as a pro forma gesture, fully expecting that Johnson would respectfully decline.

In any event, when Jack returned from his meeting with Johnson, all hell broke loose in the Kennedy suite as "key members of their staff and liberal, labor, and civil rights supporters besieged and beseeched them." O'Donnell, in particular, was seething. "This is the worst mistake you ever made. You came here . . . like a knight on a white charger . . . promising to get rid of the old hack politicians. And now, in your first move after you get the nomination, you go against all the people who supported you." Jack explained that he didn't plan to die in office and that Johnson would help him secure a large electoral mandate to govern on.

This momentarily silenced O'Donnell, but other liberals in the Kennedy coalition threatened a convention floor flight to block Johnson's nomination. Voices were raised; Michigan governor Mennen Williams almost came to blows with LBJ supporters, who had by now arrived in the Kennedy suite. Shriver watched all this and remained tight-lipped, on the fence about Johnson himself.

In his memoir, O'Donnell reported that when he talked to Shriver about the LBJ nomination, Shriver told him he "was feeling as terrible as I was."

But Shriver was quietly reconsidering. Wofford recalls,

> During a lull around midday, Shriver took me over to the window and asked, "What do you really think [about Johnson as running mate]? Is it as bad an idea as we're saying it is?" I said I had been arguing back and forth with myself and about an hour ago had decided I was for it. Not only might it mean carrying Texas, it might break the Southern monolith against civil rights and bring the South back into the mainstream of politics. I recalled Roy Wilkins' prediction that Johnson would do more for civil rights than any other politician.
>
> "You bastard!" Shriver said. "That's about the way I come out, but I was keeping it to myself, doing my duty by all our friends and breaking my back to get them all in to see Kennedy and stop it." We laughed, in mutual relief, and agreed that anyway Kennedy needed to hear and deal directly with the opposition.

Even as Shriver was coming around to see the virtues of Johnson for the ticket, Bobby continued to seethe in another corner of the suite. What exactly Bobby did next has been disputed for decades, but it seems he went down to Johnson's suite to tell the Senate majority leader that because a floor fight over his nomination looked inevitable, he would have to settle instead for an appointment to the chairmanship of the Democratic National Committee instead. The Johnson people were appalled, and Philip Graham, publisher of the *Washington Post* and a Johnson supporter, called Jack to complain about Bobby's visit. Don't worry about it, Graham reported Jack had told him. "Bobby's been out of touch and doesn't know what is happening."

The whole truth of what transpired among Jack, Bobby, and LBJ that day may never fully be known, but in his 1997 book *Mutual Contempt* Jeff Shesol pieced together all the documentary evidence and concluded that Jack had dispatched Bobby to Johnson's suite, wanting "only to determine LBJ's state of mind and to make a final choice shortly thereafter; but found, to his discomfort, he had inadvertently committed himself to a running mate he was not certain he wanted, a running mate who might inspire a revolt by liberals and labor. JFK was trapped."

However it happened, the fateful pairing was made, with profound implications for Jack, for Bobby, for Johnson—and for Shriver, who would spend much of the next eight years caught between Bobby and LBJ.

Until the formal announcement of Johnson's selection was made, liberals and labor leaders continued to lobby Shriver to do something to block Johnson. In the end, after Johnson had appeased Northern liberals (and aggrieved some Southern conservatives) by giving his word that he would support the Democrats' strong civil rights plank (which had been drafted by Chester Bowles), Johnson was nominated by acclamation, and the following day Shriver watched with the crowd of 80,000 at the Los Angeles Coliseum as Jack made his acceptance speech, declaring the dawn of a "New Frontier." The New Frontier, Kennedy said, "sums up not what I intend to offer the American people but what I intend to ask of them. It appeals to their pride, not to their pocketbook; it holds out the promise of more sacrifice instead of more security." It conveyed a sense of new hope that would dawn with the sixties—"the old era is ending," he said, "the old ways will not do."

"YOU CAN CRY. YOU'RE A SHRIVER"

Shriver was to play a highly visible and important role—perhaps the key role—in the campaign over the next four months, but from the beginning he was not part of Kennedy's innermost circle. This is interesting for what it says about his distinctive role in the family. The Kennedy siblings were notoriously competitive with one another (if also unfailingly loyal to one another when dealing with the outside world), and this competitiveness extended to in-laws as well. Joan (Teddy's wife), Jacqueline (Jack's wife), and to a lesser extent Ethel (Bobby's wife) were all at various times subjected to genial hazing by Jean, Pat, and Eunice, which, however good-natured, established clearly who were the insiders and who were the outsiders in the family. Similarly, the intense filial bonds linking Jack and Teddy and Bobby were never fully extended to Sarge, Peter Lawford (Pat's husband), or Stephen Smith (Jean's husband).

Where one stood in the family before 1961, particularly as an in-law, had much to do with how one stood with the Ambassador. Jackie, for instance, although intimidated and put off at first by all the loud, brazen Kennedy siblings and by the occasionally domineering patriarch, eventually earned Joe Sr.'s respect and the two became quite close. After that, she was a more integral part of the family. Shriver, of course, had always been well thought of by Mr. Kennedy. From their first meeting, Joe's keen eye had identified in the young navy veteran a talent and intelligence that he thought might be put to good use by JPK Enterprises. That he trusted Shriver not only with his daughter but also with the management of his largest investment holding, the Merchandise Mart, speaks volumes about what he thought about his Chicago-based son-in-law. Moreover, the father's trust in Shriver sent a message to the Kennedy brothers: No matter how much they had laughed at Sarge's lovesick pursuit of their sister, they understood that he was a formidable personality, someone worthy of their trust and respect.

Yet for all the faith in Sarge's abilities that Joe Kennedy had, he also perceived that Shriver lacked the hard-edged ruthlessness that he himself possessed and that his sons, particularly Bobby, were capable of displaying. Shriver was, as Theodore White observed in his account of the 1960 election, the kindest and gentlest of the extended Kennedy family, and over the years that observation and others like it have been made many times by close family observers. (Once, at Hyannis Port, one of Shriver's young sons fell and hurt himself and burst into tears. Looking on, Bobby Kennedy said, "Kennedys don't cry!" Shriver picked up his son and said, "That's okay, you can cry. You're a Shriver.") Within the family, Shriver's gentleness was often taken as weakness.

Shriver genially participated in the family competitions—on the football field, on the tennis court, in sailboats, at the dinner table. For the most part, however, he shunned the mortal-stakes intensity that possessed his wife's family.

While Shriver greatly admired Jack and felt warmly toward Teddy, his relationship with Bobby was respectful but cool—a harbinger of the chilliness that would waft between them when politics got in the way after 1963. But as a devoted husband to Eunice and a dutiful acolyte to Joe, willing to defer his own political ambitions for the good of the family, there was no gainsaying Shriver's family loyalty. In short, he was a Kennedy extended-family member in good standing.

But as Eunice's younger sisters married, bringing new male in-laws into the circle, the family dynamics changed subtly. Joe had qualms about Peter Lawford, both because he was an actor and because he was only a convert to Catholicism, when Pat married him in 1954. Thus Shriver retained pride of place in his father-in-law's eyes. But when Stephen Smith, the wealthy business executive from a distinguished Irish immigrant family, married Jean in 1956, Shriver for the first time had to share his claim to being the favorite son-in-law. Smith, Joe Kennedy recognized, had that hard-boiled inner core, that cutthroat toughness that Shriver lacked. This subtly changed Shriver's position in the family, moving him ever so slightly from the center toward the periphery. According to a pair of Kennedy family biographers, Jack also gravitated to Smith, who was "'cool,' to use one of Jack's favorite words, a study in hard surfaces. Unlike Shriver, he also came from a moneyed background and could afford to behave more independently. He thus became the 'inside brother-in-law,' leaving the 'outside' role to Sarge."

Although it took him farther from the decision-making core, Shriver was content to assume the outside role. It suited him. Whereas Smith was cool and hard-edged, Shriver was warm and gregarious. Smith was more bottom-line minded, good with numbers, and more the calculating strategist; Shriver was good with people, a charismatic public face for the family. In some ways, the two in-laws were like oil and water. But they were both dedicated to the Kennedy family, and they coexisted, for the most part, without rancor within it. The Smiths, the Shrivers, Ted and Joan Kennedy, Jack and Jackie, and the Ambassador and Mrs. Kennedy by now all had houses within five minutes of one another in Hyannis Port, a symbolic geographic bond that established them all, whatever their internal tensions, as part of the same family enterprise.

Shriver's relationship with some of Jack's top advisers also kept him away from the inner circle. "Jack and Bobby had a couple of guys working for them, Ted Sorensen and Mike Feldman," Shriver recalled. "Both of them were very smart. But these guys, you might say, weren't wildly enthusiastic about me." Both Sorensen and Feldman were speechwriters and very close to Jack, and Shriver felt they viewed him as somewhat of a naïf, because both of them had DC political experience and had worked on Capitol Hill, while Shriver—his brief tenure in the Justice Department notwithstanding—had not. They were skeptical of his wanton enthusiasm for everyone and everything, and they had picked up from Bobby Kennedy a concern for Shriver's politics, which seemed at once too liberal (for one thing, he had been a critic of Joe McCarthy, whereas most of the Kennedy family was still firmly in his corner) and too Catholic-inflected. "Bobby always spat on Sarge," said Charlie Peters, who, after working with Bobby during the campaign, went to work for Shriver at the Peace Corps. "His people considered Sarge weak, a nonplayer. . . . That was what he had bought into by marrying Eunice." As noted, when Harris Wofford signed onto the campaign in 1960, Ted Sorensen had told him that Shriver "was viewed by the family as 'the house Communist'—too liberal, unduly idealistic, a Boy Scout."

If Sorensen and Feldman, along with the cerebral former federal investigator Richard Goodwin and an array of Harvard academics like John Kenneth Galbraith and Archibald Cox, stocked Jack Kennedy's intellectual armory, members of the "Irish Mafia" (Kenny O'Donnell and Larry O'Brien, plus Dave Powers and others) supplied his political arsenal. Both of these groups viewed Shriver as a starry-eyed idealist. The Irish Mafia, in particular, found his exuberance grating and his idealism naive. According to Adam Yarmolinsky, a longtime Shriver aide, O'Brien, O'Donnell, and company "interpreted [Shriver's] cheerfulness as weakness and his independence as showboating. They suspected him of too much self-promotion; they didn't think he had supreme loyalty to [Jack], though he did."

None of this covert hostility, according to Ralph Dungan, a top Kennedy aide, "was very significant in terms of how effective Sarge was; I don't think it really impeded him in his work. It may have been annoyance from time to time, but never, I would say, very substantial. Sarge was such an inner-directed guy that none of this ever bothered him. He danced to his own drummer."

THE CIVIL RIGHTS DIVISION

Shriver was given several key responsibilities during the campaign. One of them was being the Illinois campaign chair. Illinois was a crucial state; many political observers predicted that the state could spell the difference in the election. And Shriver's great popularity in and around Chicago, as well as his extensive connections to both civil rights and business leaders in the region, played into his being given the assignment. But in truth he was "in charge" of the Illinois campaign only nominally: Everyone knew that Dick Daley pulled all the political strings in Chicago.

Shriver's assignment to the Civil Rights Division was far more important. As noted, Shriver's work on the "Negro vote" had begun before the convention. But after Lyndon Johnson became the vice presidential nominee, Shriver's work became that much more urgent—the selection of a Southern senator, especially one perceived to be an antiliberal rube, was seen as a betrayal by Northern white liberals and blacks alike.

In 1960 Democratic preoccupation with black voters was a relatively new phenomenon. Persistent Jim Crow laws that made it hard for blacks in the South to get to the polls had tended to make the black vote far less significant electorally than it ought to have been. Moreover, for the first four decades after the Civil War, blacks had voted heavily Republican; the GOP was "the party of Lincoln." Finally, many blacks, victims of segregation into impoverished schools, were illiterate and ill-informed; they didn't know enough to vote or consider it worth their while to do so. Thus for decades the few available black votes seemed hardly worth pursuing—especially in the South, where any position calculated to appeal to blacks would surely alienate a larger number of whites.

Outside of the South, anyway, that had begun to change with the New Deal, which brought jobs, strong unions, social security, public assistance, unemployment insurance, and other aspects of the social safety net to black voters. FDR became a political hero to many of them; the Democratic Party began to look more appealing. More important, the great migration northward during the middle years of the century allowed blacks to throw off the yoke of Jim Crow oppression and freely exercise their right to vote. And as they thronged into industrial cities in the North, they were absorbed by Democratic political machines. In Chicago, for instance, Congressman William Dawson, himself a former Georgia Republican who had switched parties during the New Deal, shepherded thousands of fellow blacks onto the Democratic rolls. After 1948, when Harry Truman squeaked past Thomas Dewey on the strength of less than 50,000 votes in key states like Illinois and Ohio, it was evident to Democratic leaders that the party's electoral success in national elections would depend on the votes from Northern industrial cities, whose demographic coloration was laced heavily with black.

In the twelve years since 1948, as the electoral significance of the Negro vote had become more obvious, black leaders discovered they had newfound political leverage. By threatening to withhold their votes in the North, Negro leaders in the industrial Northeast and Midwest realized, they could exact promises from white Democratic aspirants on behalf of Negroes in the South. White politicians like Jack Kennedy, in turn, had to play a delicate balancing game, promising to deliver civil rights legislation to black leaders without alienating the segregationist white Democrats of the Solid South.

Shriver's responsibility was therefore an awesome one. Since the Kennedys had yet to turn to civil rights as a passionate policy concern, it remained a distinct challenge to assuage the truculent black leaders who accused the Kennedy family of indifference to the Negro plight.

In the Civil Rights Division, Harris Wofford continued as civil rights coordinator, and William Dawson, as head of the Minorities Division of the DNC, was named chairman. Frank Reeves, who was well connected with local chapters of the National Association for the Advancement of Colored People (NAACP) all across the country, was assigned to travel with Kennedy. Marjorie Lawson, the civil rights attorney who had worked with Shriver during the West Virginia primary, was to focus on working with local black Democratic organizations state by state.

Shriver enticed Franklin Williams, a former NAACP lawyer, to leave his job as assistant attorney general of California to spearhead the project of registering black voters. This was a crucial task. Proportionally fewer blacks than whites, by a significant margin, were registered to vote; blacks voted disproportionately Democratic; thus it was unequivocally in Kennedy's interest that as many blacks as possible get registered. The problem was, such registration efforts could be expensive, and the Democratic Party had only limited funds available to spend. Under Williams's direction, the registration drive was set up through black churches. This made the project officially nonpartisan, which in turn meant that it could be financed by tax-exempt contributions from individuals and foundations, rather than from scarce political funds.

After Shriver and Wofford, the most important member of the civil rights team was Louis Martin, the publisher of a chain of black newspapers. Shriver had become acquainted with him through his work on the Catholic Interracial Council. Martin didn't suffer fools, and he could be acerbic. In 1960 he had just returned to the country from a year in Nigeria, where he had been setting up newspapers and radio stations. He refused to come out for Kennedy at the convention in Los Angeles, saying, "I'm just back from Africa and I don't know anything." But Martin felt warmly toward Shriver, and after Kennedy won the nomination he agreed to join the campaign. His first task was to design and place advertising in black publications.

Martin's second order of business, undertaken at Shriver's behest, was to induce the flamboyant Harlem congressman Adam Clayton Powell to support the Kennedy campaign. The iconoclastic Powell had initially supported Lyndon Johnson for the nomination, one of the few Northern blacks to do so, but Martin—with the help of a campaign contribution authorized by Stephen Smith—prevailed upon Powell to campaign for Jack. Powell subsequently barnstormed the country, traveling with an enlarged copy of the deed to Richard Nixon's house, which contained a covenant signed by Nixon prohibiting the sale or lease of the property to Negroes or Jews.

Congressman Dawson was, in his crusty way, as iconoclastic as Powell. He had been born in the backwoods of Georgia and made his way north during the early years of the Great Migration. Dawson was a loyal Democrat and an essential cog in Dick Daley's political machine, and he commanded enormous power and respect among Chicago's black population. But Dawson was no wild-eyed civil rights activist. His first loyalty was to the Cook County machine, which he thought was more important than some abstract cause. Moreover, he still retained ties to his Georgia roots and had cultivated long-standing relationships with powerful Southern party leaders, which he was reluctant to jeopardize. He wanted Kennedy to win and saw the Civil Rights Division's task as simply getting out the black vote on behalf of the Democratic slate—and he didn't see how white interlopers like Shriver would help him do that. Nor, really, did he even see the purpose of giving the division an aggressive name like "civil rights"—couldn't Shriver see that would just antagonize Southern Democrats, whose support Jack sorely needed? "Let's not use words that offend our good Southern friends, like 'civil rights,'" Dawson said at one meeting.

Dawson caused other logistical difficulties as well. Shriver had set up the Civil Rights Division office on a whole floor of a building on K Street in Washington, and he arranged it in an open style, without closed individual offices. This was a practice he had experimented with and found successful at the Merchandise Mart, because it fostered camaraderie and good communication. But when Dawson flew in from Chicago to visit and saw that he would be given no private quarters but only a desk and a phone like everyone else, he balked. It was, Dawson said, "totally impossible" for him to work in the open like that. Shriver failed to convince him otherwise and in the end had to construct a single enclosed office for the congressman, right in the middle of the

open-floor plan. "Uncle Tom's Cabin," some of the blacks in the division deri-
sively called it.

THE CALL TO KING

On Wednesday, October 19, Martin Luther King Jr. led a group of Negro
activists into the Magnolia Room restaurant, located in a giant department
store in Atlanta, Georgia, and demanded to be served lunch. The Magnolia
Room was a segregated facility, as were many other Atlanta restaurants that
were occupied by Negro protesters that day. King refused to leave the restaurant when asked and was arrested with his fellow protesters. Charged with tres-
passing, he declined to post bail. "I'll stay in jail a year, or ten years," King said,
"if it takes that long to desegregate" the restaurant. Over the next few days,
Negro occupations of segregated facilities continued. More arrests were made.
The Ku Klux Klan began marching up and down Atlanta's streets. Tensions in
the city threatened to boil over into widespread civic unrest.

Meanwhile the Southern Christian Leadership Council, the group King
headed, had telegraphed both Kennedy and Nixon, hoping that one or the
other (or both) would make a public statement against the arrests or intervene
in some way. At the Kennedy campaign headquarters in Washington the feeling was that something had better be done soon: The incident was proving an
unwelcome reminder of Southern Democrats' racist past. Shriver feared that
Negro voters, after witnessing this episode—and the persistent racism of the
Georgia Democrats—would turn against the party. But no one in the campaign
seemed to know quite what to do.

Harris Wofford called his friend Morris Abram, a prominent civil rights
lawyer, urging him to get Bill Hartsfield, the Atlanta mayor, to do something.
Mayor Hartsfield reacted strongly by holding a press conference in which he
announced that in response to "the personal intervention" of Senator Kennedy,
he had reached an agreement with Negro leaders and the prisoners would be
released. This infuriated Kennedy's political advisers, who perceived correctly
that this would be seen as an unwarranted intrusion by a federal political candidate into Georgia's affairs. Kenny O'Donnell and the Irish Mafia savaged
Wofford for acting imprudently and sought to control the damage, issuing a
tepid press release giving Kennedy credit only for making inquiries into the

arrest and assuring reporters that the senator had no intention of meddling in Georgia's affairs.

Because Hartsfield had already declared the prisoners' release, members of the Southern Christian Leadership Conference, including King's wife, Coretta Scott King, who was five months pregnant, descended on the jail to celebrate their freeing. But when they arrived at the jail, King was not there.

As it turned out, several months earlier the Kings had driven a white friend of theirs to a hospital in De Kalb County, Georgia, a bastion of the Ku Klux Klan. A policeman saw them driving with a white woman, stopped the car, and, although Martin had his Alabama license, charged him with driving without a Georgia license. As a penalty, King was fined $25 and placed on a year's probation. Now a De Kalb County judge had ruled that the trespassing charge put him in violation of that probation. King was sentenced to six months' hard labor in state prison.

Shriver urged Kennedy to make a public statement criticizing the imprisonment and urging King's release. Wofford went so far as to draft such a statement. But Georgia governor Ernest Vandiver and Kennedy's Georgia campaign manager Griffin Bell said that if Jack were to make a statement like that, he would be guaranteed to lose Georgia to Nixon. After multilateral negotiations, Bell prevailed on Vandiver to get King released as long as Kennedy made no further public statements to embarrass Southern Democrats. Kennedy agreed, and everyone thought that would be the end of it.

But three days later, King was still in jail. Wofford had become good friends with the Kings through his work in the civil rights movement, and on this day he received a call at home in Virginia from Coretta King in Georgia. "They are going to kill him, I know they are going to kill him," she said in a tearful voice, and she expressed her fear that her baby would be born without a father. Wofford told her that the Kennedy campaign was doing what it could, but he knew that "this was not very reassuring to a wife who felt her husband's life was in danger every minute he remained in jail."

That night, Wofford and Louis Martin went out for beers to discuss the situation. (Shriver was traveling through the Midwest with Jack.) "Who cares about public statements?" Wofford recalled saying. "What Kennedy ought to do is something direct and personal, like picking up the phone and calling Coretta. Just giving his sympathy, but doing it himself." "That's it, that's it!" Martin responded. "That would be perfect."

It wasn't until the next morning that Wofford was able to reach Shriver on the phone. "If Jack would just call Mrs. King down in Atlanta," Shriver remembers Wofford saying, "and tell her he's very sorry about what has befallen her husband, that gesture will be incredibly important to Negro voters."

"It's not too late," Shriver responded. "Jack doesn't leave O'Hare [International Airport] for another forty minutes. I'm going to get to him. Give me her number and get me out of jail if I'm arrested for speeding."

Shriver rushed out to the airport motel where Jack was staying, getting there just a few minutes before Jack was to leave. The candidate was getting dressed. But the motel room was filled with his top advisers, who surely would have raised significant objections to Kennedy's getting further involved in the King imbroglio. So Shriver anxiously bided his time, waiting for the right moment to present his message. He was prepared to take Jack forcibly aside if necessary, but he was hoping it wouldn't come to that, since a private audience with the candidate would surely arouse suspicions among his advisers. Ted Sorensen went back to his room to finish a speech. Press secretary Pierre Salinger went off to meet with reporters for a preflight briefing. Only Kenny O'Donnell lingered, eyeing Shriver warily, knowing he wasn't supposed to be there that morning. When O'Donnell stepped into the bathroom, Shriver seized his chance.

As Jack folded his clothes and put them in his suitcase, Shriver explained to him about King's plight and told him about the telephone call Wofford and Martin had proposed. "Jack," he said, "you just need to convey to Mrs. King that you believe what happened to her husband was wrong and that you will do what you can to see the situation rectified and that in general you stand behind him." "At first he seemed distracted," Shriver recalled, "then, as he began to focus, he grew somewhat skeptical, but I pressed forward with my argument." "Negroes don't expect everything will change tomorrow, no matter who's elected. But they do want to know whether you care. If you telephone Mrs. King, they will know you understand and will help. You will reach their hearts and give support to a pregnant woman who is afraid her husband will be killed."

Jack zipped his suitcase and looked up at Shriver. "That's a pretty good idea. How do I get her?" Shriver pulled the telephone number from his breast pocket and handed it to his brother-in-law.

"Dial it for me, will you?" Jack said. "I've got to pack up my papers." He began picking them up and piling them into a briefcase.

As Shriver recalled,

I sat down on Jack's bed and dialed the number. Mrs. King came on the line. I told her who I was and that I was with Jack Kennedy in Chicago who was about to fly to Detroit to do more campaigning but that he wanted to speak with her for a moment before he left. Would that be okay? She said it would be and I handed Jack the phone. He talked to her for only ninety seconds or so, but in that time he managed to convey his warmth and sympathy, and to explain that he would do what he could to see that justice was done. Then he ran out to catch his plane.

Emerging from the bathroom, O'Donnell overheard the tail end of Jack's conversation with Coretta King and intuited the gist of what had happened. "You just lost us the election," he said to Shriver.

Back in Washington, Wofford and Martin got blasted by Bobby Kennedy. On the plane to Detroit, Jack had remarked offhandedly to Salinger that he had called Mrs. King. Salinger had radioed word to Bobby, even before the plane had landed. Bobby erupted. "With his fists tight, his blue eyes cold, [Bobby] turned on us," Wofford recalled. "Do you know that three Southern governors told us that if Jack supported Jimmy Hoffa, Nikita Khruschev, or Martin Luther King, they would throw their states to Nixon?" Bobby said. "Do you know that this election may be razor close and you have probably lost it for us?"

Bobby was right about the razor closeness of the election but wrong about the outcome and the phone call's effect on it. Wofford had by now already received a grateful phone call from Mrs. King, followed by a call from Morris Abram, who reported enthusiastically that he just had had a visit from Coretta and her father-in-law, Martin Luther King Sr., the pastor of the Abyssinian Baptist Church in Atlanta. "Daddy King," as he was known, had been with Coretta when she received the call from Kennedy and, as he told Abram, "if Kennedy has the courage to wipe the tears from Coretta's eyes, [I] will vote for him whatever his religion." Daddy King had voted Republican in the past and had earlier in the year signed a newspaper advertisement for Nixon, on the grounds that he preferred a Protestant president to a Catholic one. But now he had reconsidered.

Daddy King's conversion, Shriver and his colleagues quickly realized, had potentially momentous implications; his influence in the Negro population was enormous. Not only did he have his own large congregation and followers in Atlanta, but he was also at the center of the network of Southern black churches. If word could be got out that Daddy King was strong for Kennedy, the impact could be significant.

The next day, Coretta King was quoted in the Atlanta papers as saying that Kennedy's phone call had made her "feel good." "I have heard nothing from the vice president or anyone on his staff," she added. Nixon and Eisenhower could have done something to intercede on King's behalf at this point, but they stayed mute.

By that afternoon, Bobby had apparently reconsidered his initial reaction to the Shriver-Kennedy phone call and had decided he ought to do what he could to capitalize on it on his brother's behalf. Bobby called the De Kalb sentencing judge directly and made clear that he thought the judge had overstepped his bounds in imposing four months' hard labor on King for a minor traffic violation. If you know what's right, Bobby later recalled telling the judge, you will release King by sundown.

The judge, citing public pressure, released King on $2,000 bail. Upon his release, King made a public statement thanking Jack Kennedy. "I am deeply indebted to Senator Kennedy, who served as a great force in making my release possible. For him to be that courageous shows that he is really acting upon principle and not expediency."

On October 28, nine days after his arrest and only ten days before the presidential election, Martin Luther King Jr. enjoyed a joyous homecoming at Ebenezer Baptist Church in Atlanta. King used his sermon to call for more civil disobedience in the fight against segregation. And he endorsed Kennedy in coded terms. "I never intend to reject a man running for President of the United States, just because he is a Catholic. Religious bigotry is as immoral, undemocratic, un-American and un-Christian as racial bigotry."

The more important statement came that evening, when King's father made a much less restrained pronouncement. "I had expected to vote against Senator Kennedy because of his religion," Daddy King said. "But now he can be my President, Catholic or whatever he is. It took courage to call my daughter-in-law at a time like this. He has the moral courage to stand up for what he knows is right. I've got all my votes and I've got a suitcase and I'm going to take them up there and dump them in his lap."

Martin and Wofford brainstormed, trying to conceive how to reap maximum benefit from Daddy King's conversion to Kennedy. Martin could easily have arranged to have the story published in Negro newspapers, but most of them came out only weekly, and with so little time remaining before the election, they wouldn't be able to disseminate the story widely enough. Martin proposed publishing a pamphlet that could be printed by the hundreds of thousands and distributed through black churches across the country. But Wofford reminded him that after his brother's call to Mrs. King, Bobby Kennedy had proscribed any further such freelancing by the Civil Rights Division. Bobby had specifically warned them not to make any new public statements.

Martin called Shriver in Chicago, hoping he would know what to do, or that he might be willing to try to argue Bobby into allowing the publication of a pamphlet. After listening to Martin explain the situation, Shriver immediately outlined a plan of action. If the pamphlet only reproduced statements made by Daddy King and other Negro leaders and didn't introduce any new editorial statements, Shriver reasoned, then it wouldn't fall within the limits of Bobby's proscription. "You don't need to ask Bobby's permission," Shriver said. "What you're planning is not within his ban. Let's do it. If it works, he'll like it. If we don't do it, and we don't get enough Negro votes, he and Jack wouldn't like that, and we would all be kicking ourselves for a long time."

Within six hours *The Case of Martin Luther King* was being printed. To avoid conflict with the Democratic National Committee, the publication was officially sponsored by two black ministers calling themselves the Freedom Crusade Committee. The pamphlet reproduced the statements of Martin Luther King Jr., his wife and father, and several other black Protestant leaders. "I earnestly and sincerely feel that it is time for all of us to take off our Nixon buttons," declared Ralph Abernathy in one of the statements. "Senator Kennedy did something great and wonderful when he personally called Coretta King. . . . Since Mr. Nixon has been silent through all this, I am going to return his silence when I go to the voting booth."

Shriver authorized the printing of an initial 50,000 copies of what he came to call "the blue bomb" (for its light blue paper), and by October 30 they were being mailed from Washington all across the country. Two days later (one week before election day) Shriver printed another 250,000 in Chicago for distribution throughout every Negro church in Illinois and Wisconsin. More and more calls came into headquarters from local Civil Rights Division workers across the country, and by Sunday, November 6, 2 million copies had been distributed. That day, the last Sunday before the election, Shriver strove to ensure that hand-bills were posted on the wall of as many Negro churches across the country as possible. When it got too late in the week for the postal service to deliver by Sunday, he arranged for printing on local presses. In a few cases, Wofford and Martin piled bundles of pamphlets onto Greyhound buses bound for important cities, where local civil rights workers retrieved and distributed them.

Martin and Shriver also called on their friends to spread the word on foot. Shriver's numerous connections on the Catholic Interracial Council and the school board spread the word of the Kennedy phone call to the farthest reaches of Chicago's South Side and West Side neighborhoods. Martin called Northern Negro Democrats like Raymond Jones, recommending that they send "run-ners" into bars to make sure barroom denizens knew that Kennedy had helped spring King from jail.

"When 'Ray the Fox' reported back that the bars of Harlem were all going our way," Wofford recalled, "and when we got widespread reports of whole congregations of Negro Baptists and Methodists pledging to vote for Kennedy, we sensed that a tide was running for the senator in practically every commu-nity, North and South."

As the results were tallied on election day, exit polls indicated that more than seven out of ten Negro voters had gone for Kennedy, and a higher total proportion of blacks had voted than in any previous election. As Theodore White wrote, "It is difficult to see how Illinois, New Jersey, Michigan, South Carolina or Delaware [with 74 electoral votes among them] could have been won had the Republican-Democratic split of the Negro wards and precincts remained as it was, unchanged from the Eisenhower charm of 1956." If even two of those states had gone Republican, Kennedy would have lost.

Even Kennedy's key electoral victory in Illinois, which is reputed to have been delivered by the aggressive (and perhaps corrupt) vote-gathering tactics of the Cook County political machine, may owe more to the King phone call than to Dick Daley: In a state that Kennedy won by only 9,000 popular votes, some 250,000 blacks went to the polls. James Michener later called the King phone call and its aftermath "the single event which came closest to being the one vital accident of the campaign." "In doing this," Michener wrote, Kennedy "did not lose Georgia or South Carolina or Texas. Instead he won the Negro vote in New York and Chicago and Philadelphia, and thus the Presidency." Eisenhower grumbled that Kennedy's phone call had spelled the difference in the election. Nixon himself later attributed his defeat to the King affair and lamented that if he, too, had made some kind of "grandstanding" action, he might have won the election.

It was not solely the King call that accounted for the margin of victory, of course, even among African American voters. But the inroads Kennedy had made among those voters since he had set up the Civil Rights Division under Shriver were impressive. Before the Democratic convention in July, Kennedy had been less popular among blacks than all the Democratic hopefuls, including even the Southerner Lyndon Johnson. On election day, three months later, he won more than 70 percent of the black vote. The call to Mrs. King was the coup de grâce that solidified the Negro vote for Kennedy and secured him the election.

THE SEEDS OF THE PEACE CORPS

If Shriver's greatest impact on the election of his brother-in-law was through the telephone call placed to Mrs. King from that airport motel, the greatest impact the campaign was ultimately to have on Shriver was through a speech Jack Kennedy gave in Ann Arbor, Michigan, five days before Martin Luther King Jr.'s arrest.

On the evening of October 13, Jack Kennedy flew from New York City, where he had just participated in his final debate with Richard Nixon, to Ann Arbor, where he was scheduled to address some students at the University of Michigan. But his flight was delayed, and he didn't arrive until 2:00 a.m., so when he staggered bleary-eyed off the plane he assumed his speech had been canceled. Upon arrival on campus, however, Kennedy was stunned to find an audience of more than 10,000 waiting for him and chanting his name as he climbed the steps of the student union.

Taken aback by this show of support, the candidate began extemporizing in an attempt to match the students' ardor. Picking up on the theme he had established in his New Frontier speech at the Democratic convention, Kennedy appealed to their youthful idealism, asking them whether they would be willing to serve their country. "How many of you," he challenged them, "would be willing to spend your days working"—as teachers, doctors, and engineers—"in Ghana?" The audience roared its response and Kennedy continued. "On your willingness not merely to serve one or two years in the service, but on your willingness to contribute part of your life to this country, I think will depend the answer whether we as a free society can compete" in the cold war world. The audience was "wildly responsive," and as Kennedy headed off to bed after the speech he told his aide Dave Powers that he thought that "he had hit a winning number."

A few years later, Shriver would write, "No one is sure why Kennedy raised the question in the middle of the night at the University of Michigan." Some of Kennedy's aides later reflected that it was a response to an assertion Nixon had made in the debate earlier in the evening, in which he called Democrats the "war party" (Democrats Woodrow Wilson, Franklin Delano Roosevelt, and Harry Truman had presided, respectively, over the American entry into the two World Wars and the launch of the Korean War), and that this call to international service was an attempt to respond to the charge. Another possibility was that Kennedy had remembered that the university's International Studies Department was where Samuel Hayes taught; Hayes was the author of a report, given to Kennedy a month earlier, that made the case for an American volunteer program in the third world.

Whatever the genesis of Kennedy's inspiration that night, this was one of those times when a man and an idea and a historical moment come into alignment. The idea for an international volunteer service had been floating around for decades, at least since William James had called for a service program that produced for young men "the moral equivalent of war," and there was even a pending bill (sponsored by Hubert Humphrey) in Congress calling for such a thing. But it was at this moment at Ann Arbor that the spirit that animated the Peace Corps truly began to gather and build.

Kennedy's speech got little notice, since it occurred after newspaper reporters had filed their stories, but he could see from the reaction of the students that—in speaking not just to the students' needs but to their aspirations—he was onto something.

The students took what he said seriously. Two weeks after the speech, Kennedy received a letter from a newly formed student group calling itself "Americans Committed to World Responsibility." In their letter, the students requested that Kennedy, if elected, establish an international service program—and they included a petition of a thousand names of people who would sign up.

On November 2, one week before election day, Kennedy developed this idea into a campaign issue and gave it a name. The occasion was a speech at San Francisco's Cow Palace auditorium; the scheduled topic, how to maintain peace and America's global stature through smart foreign policy. Before an audience of 40,000, Kennedy began by criticizing the US foreign service and its "ill-chosen, ill-equipped, and ill-briefed" ambassadors, noting that 70 percent of new foreign service officers could speak no language besides English and that many American diplomats could not communicate with the citizens of the countries to which they were posted. The Soviets, he warned, were doing a better job endearing themselves to the developing world, sending emissaries abroad to teach the world technical skills while also propagandizing about communism. There were now more Soviets providing technical assistance to developing countries in Asia than there were Americans. The same would soon be true of Africa. "We have to do better," Kennedy said. It was a matter of both moral value and cold war necessity.

"There is enough know-how and enough knowledgeable people to help [developing] nations help themselves," Kennedy said. "I therefore propose that our inadequate efforts in this area be supplemented by a 'Peace Corps' of talented young men willing and able to serve their country in this fashion for three years as an alternative to peace-time selective service—well-qualified through vigorous standards; well-trained in the language, skills, and customs they will need to know." This would be a volunteer service, Kennedy said, not a draft, and he concluded that "our young men and women, dedicated to freedom, are fully capable of overcoming the efforts of Mr. Khrushchev's missionaries who are dedicated to undermining that freedom."

The next morning a front-page *New York Times* headline declared, "Kennedy Favors US 'Peace Corps' to Work Abroad." The idea now had a name, and it had become an official part of the Kennedy campaign. It would be a while yet before it would be brought to fruition—and it would change and gain nuance as it developed—but the idea was now a part of the political conversation, and Kennedy himself alluded to it several more times over the next week, including the day before the election. America, he said, "needs 'a Peace Corps' of young men and women who will be willing to spend two or three years of their lives as teachers and nurses, working in different countries . . . spreading the cause of freedom."

Shriver read the newspaper accounts of the Cow Palace speech. It spoke to his own concerns about the Soviets' quest for global Communist domination. It spoke equally strongly to his convictions about the value of cross-cultural exposure for young people. But Shriver was preoccupied with campaigning in the Midwest and getting the word out about the King phone call. For the moment, the man who would midwife the Peace Corps into existence paid it little heed.

When election day, November 8, arrived, the far-flung members of the Kennedy operation returned from their disparate locations, converging on their home base at Hyannis Port. Shriver stopped off in Chicago, to vote at his polling place on 2441 North Clark Street, before flying to Cape Cod. As he watched the early election results on television from Jack's house, he was despondent. "I can still vividly recall the dejection I felt when the early returns from Illinois and other places began to come in," he would say forty years later. "Bobby came in from the lawn, where he had been throwing a football around with Teddy. 'We're being clobbered,' Bobby said, after glancing at the television. He was right; things didn't look good. Oh, God, I thought, we've lost my home state. Jack's lost Illinois, I thought, and it's my fault." Finding the prospect of defeat unbearable, Shriver crept off to bed. He recalled,

> I climbed into bed, glancing at the radio on the bedside table, knowing I should turn it on and listen to the final results but unable to bear doing so. I stretched out on top of the covers, without even taking my clothes off. I couldn't remember a time when I'd been more depressed. I must have drifted off sometime after midnight, because I awoke to an insistent knocking on my door. "What is it?" I yelled. "Sarge," someone yelled back, "you're wanted in Jack's house."
>
> Well, this was it, I thought. Jack had lost. With heavy tread, I made my way across the lawn. A few dozen family members and close aides were watching the television—and cheering! The newscasters were projecting a Kennedy victory! We all clapped each other on the back exuberantly, and drank boisterous toasts.

Thrilled by the victory, Shriver didn't take the time to contemplate the effect his brother-in-law's election would have on his own life.

CHAPTER TWELVE

The Talent Hunt

⟋

After a day of celebration and press appearances, the Kennedy inner circle met at 10:30 a.m. on November 10 at Bobby Kennedy's house to get down to the business of preparing for the presidency. Present were Shriver, Ted Sorensen, Bobby Kennedy, Pierre Salinger, Larry O'Brien, Joe Kennedy, and, of course, the president-elect. When Jack walked in, everyone assembled rose to stand, in instinctive tribute to his newly exalted status.

There were only seventy days until the inauguration in January, hardly enough time, it seemed, to fill seventy-five senior cabinet and executive branch posts, name hundreds of other people to positions in the administration, reshape the Democratic National Committee, develop a legislative agenda, draft a budget, and plan the inauguration itself, among hundreds of other sundry tasks. Thus Jack got right down to the business of assigning interregnum roles to people. He named O'Donnell his aide for administration and appointments, Salinger his chief press aide, and Sorensen his top aide for policy and programs. Clark Clifford, a prominent Washington lawyer and a Stuart Symington supporter who had served as an adviser to Harry Truman, was made special counsel to the president. At this point, no specific role was assigned to Bobby, but it was obvious he would be a central part of interregnum planning.

Kennedy came to Shriver almost last. "Sarge," he said, "I want you to help me put the cabinet together. We've got to find the most dedicated, bright, tough-minded, experienced guys in the country. You know, we have to get somebody to develop the budget right away because we've got hardly two months to come up with a new one for next year. So we need someone to head up the Bureau of the Budget. And then we need to fill in the most important positions: secretary of defense, state, justice, and all the others. I want you to find these people for me."

Why did Kennedy pick Shriver for this important task? Several factors determined Kennedy's decision. First, he had seen Shriver in action on the campaign trail and had been impressed by his unflagging enthusiasm, even in the face of setbacks and hardships. "Though people were sometimes ruffled by Shriver's courtesy and easy amiability into dismissing him as something of a Boy Scout," Arthur Schlesinger has written of Shriver's assignment to this task, "the President-elect had confidence in his energy and imagination—a confidence Shriver had justified in the campaign and justified again now." Second, Jack had come to see why his father respected Shriver's judgment so much: Most of the important decisions Shriver had made during the campaign had worked to Jack's benefit. Third, an important component of Shriver's judgment was evidently his eye for talent. The people he had brought into the campaign, or whom he moved from the periphery of the campaign toward the center—people like Harris Wofford, Adam Yarmolinsky, Marjorie Lawson, Louis Martin, and scores of others—had worked out well and impressed the president-elect. Fourth, although Shriver had at times been kept apart from the campaign's central decision-making process, that had never seemed to bother him—he just went off and did the jobs he was assigned to do. This suggested to Kennedy that Shriver could work on his own initiative and wouldn't require management. Finally, Shriver was "the most outgoing member of the immediate circle, who was thought to have the widest range of acquaintanceship." Who else counted Negro blues singers and Catholic bishops, professional athletes and corporate executives, janitors and Supreme Court justices among his friends?

Walking over to the Ambassador's house after the long meeting at Bobby's house had ended, Shriver started to feel intimidated by his assignment. "I had never worked at the higher levels of federal government. I was not a professor of public administration. I had never made a budget for myself, let alone for the United States government. 'My God!' I said to myself, 'where do I even start if I need to find someone to be in charge of the Bureau of the Budget.' So I called up McGeorge Bundy, an old friend of mine who was a Harvard dean, and asked him to have breakfast with me the very next day at the Ritz-Carlton in Boston." As dean of the College of Arts and Sciences for some ten years at Harvard, Shriver recalled, "Bundy had been running a 'talent hunt' of his own, searching for the most imaginative intellectuals in the world. He knew the names and numbers of all the 'first team' academics everywhere." Shriver asked Bundy to start compiling a list of all the people he knew in academia or public life or business who he thought might be well-suited for a position in the Kennedy administration. The Talent Hunt had begun.

As soon as breakfast was finished, Shriver got on the phone to Harris Wofford and told him it was time to spring into action once more. "If you thought you were going on vacation," Shriver told him, "enjoy it quickly—between now and Sunday. Monday morning we go to work." "Jack has asked me to organize a talent search for the top jobs," he told Wofford. "The cabinet, regulatory agencies, ambassadors, everything. We're going to comb the universities and professions, the civil rights movement, business, labor, foundations, and everywhere, to find the brightest and best people possible."

Telling Wofford to round up Louis Martin and Adam Yarmolinsky—whose cerebral brilliance as head of the campaign's Urban Affairs Section had greatly impressed him—Shriver scheduled a meeting for first thing Monday morning at the Mayflower Hotel in Washington. In the few days before then, they were to learn everything they could about how previous cabinet transitions and recruitments had worked.

Kennedy wanted to avoid the executive breakdowns and partisan rancor that had complicated the transfers of power between Hoover and Roosevelt in 1932 and between Truman and Eisenhower twenty years later. This meant, as he told Shriver, that he wanted to make his major cabinet selections without excessive concern for partisan affiliation—what mattered more than politics was temperament and, especially, talent.

Shriver set himself, Wofford, Martin, and Yarmolinsky and their assistants up in a suite of rooms in the Mayflower, and within a few hours of their initial meeting on November 14, they had begun the work of calling around for recommendations from their network of contacts. As Wofford noted, "Shriver knew the kind of man Kennedy wanted. More accurately, since Kennedy worked well with and respected a wide range of types, Shriver knew the kind *not* wanted: the too ideological, too earnest, too emotional, and too talkative— and the dull." "One of the things we had to keep in the forefront of our minds," Shriver recalled, "was that what we thought of a [candidate] wasn't as impor- tant as what Jack might think of him. Especially where the higher posts were concerned, our chief job was to find men and women we had reason to believe could work harmoniously with the president-to-be." Shriver instructed his staff not to worry about whether a given candidate was actually likely to be avail- able. "I was to go after the best people we could find without regard to avail- ability," Yarmolinsky recalled, "and we would worry about that when we came to it." Shriver told reporters at the time that he didn't even ask candidates their party affiliation. He was more concerned with age, he said, seeking appointees between thirty and fifty years old, "because we are trying to strengthen the country and the party for the long pull, five to fifteen years."

Eventually, the Talent Hunt procured an office, in a corner of the Democratic National Committee headquarters at the corner of Connecticut Avenue and K Street, where Shriver had maintained an office during the cam- paign. Shriver concentrated on combing the business community; Wofford, the academic and political science communities; and Yarmolinsky, the law schools and foundations. They shared an office suite with Larry O'Brien and Ralph Dungan, who were heading up the Political Patronage Section of the executive staffing operation. It was the job of Dungan and O'Brien to see to it that impor- tant campaign workers, contributors, and supporters who sought jobs in the Kennedy administration were rewarded with them. "In a sense," as Arthur Schlesinger put it, "the Shriver group began with the positions and looked for people qualified to fill them, and the O'Brien group began with the people and looked for positions they were qualified to fill." This inevitably led to what the parties involved called "a state of friendly competition."

Generally, Shriver found the people he wanted rather than the other way around. Indeed, it was a guiding principle of the Talent Hunt that Plato had gotten it right in his *Republic*: Those most suited for public office don't seek it. Thus Shriver worked his networks relentlessly—friends, family, business asso- ciates, political connections, civil rights colleagues, college and law school classmates, old professors, navy buddies—and solicited their input and asked them to ask their friends for *their* input. As a *Chicago American* reporter visiting Shriver's office wrote, the atmosphere was less one of political patronage than "that surrounding the choice of a dean for a law school."

Shriver put Louis Martin in charge of recruiting black candidates. During the campaign, Kennedy had made a commitment to hire record numbers of African Americans, so Martin reached far and wide into the Negro community in search of worthy candidates, eventually collecting 750 names. "I had a candidate for almost every job," he later recalled. "I don't give a damn what the job was, I came up with a Negro." Because of who Kennedy's friends and patronage appointments tended to be, the Talent Hunt had to develop a compensatory bias *against* Irish Catholics and Harvard academics, selecting from these groups only when there was "offsetting evidence of spectacular excellence."

Shriver had Yarmolinsky draw up a standard form for rating a job prospect in the key categories he thought important to the president-elect: judgment, integrity, ability to work with others, industry, toughness, and devotion to Kennedy's programs. The last category was in some ways the most problematic, since most of Kennedy's specific policy proposals had yet to be formulated—this made it hard to guarantee that prospects were committed a priori to a "Kennedy program." The "toughness" category provoked the most amusement: When some candidates learned of the "toughness" category, they would phone into the office and declare, "I'm tough."

Neither Wofford nor Martin nor Yarmolinsky had any real experience working in government. At one point, Shriver brought in a consultant from IBM to help systematize procedures, but after a few days the consultant threw up his hands, concluding that the Talent Hunt was not susceptible to normal corporate streamlining procedures.

If he was not quite systematic, Shriver did try to be as comprehensive as possible in his recruitment effort. After he had accumulated a list of dozens or hundreds of names for a position, his staff would begin the process of evaluation. First, they would call people who knew the prospect under consideration and would ask them to evaluate him or her according to Yarmolinsky's standard criteria. The Talent Hunt staff would also explore how well regarded an individual was in his field and seek to assess how much he might add to the status of the administration in that field. All this information was dutifully recorded on

Yarmolinsky's forms and duplicated when a candidate appeared qualified for more than one job or department. When enough files for a position had been amassed, Shriver would go through all of them and send the ones he deemed best to Kennedy. Shriver would have the political team of Dungan and O'Brien vet the candidates for the top positions—those designated "confidential and policy-making positions"—before passing their names on to the president-elect.

After Kennedy had made his selections, it was sometimes up to the Talent Hunt to persuade the chosen individuals to accept some of the lower-level positions in the administration. This could be challenging, given the pay cuts recruits from the private sector were being asked to make. But Shriver proved a master of salesmanship, and when the Talent Hunt had concluded, Yarmolinsky spoke "admiringly of his ability to lure men away from jobs they had every reason to hold onto." The journalist David Halberstam marveled at Shriver's ability to recruit luminaries, likening him to "a big-game hunter."

The most urgent need was for someone to serve as director of the Bureau of the Budget (now called the Office of Management and Budget) because almost every policy and program Kennedy might hope to change or implement in his first year in office must necessarily be determined, or at least guided, by the 1961 federal budget. Following McGeorge Bundy's advice, Shriver met with John Kenneth Galbraith, the towering liberal (both in reputation and actual size; he was 6 feet 8 inches tall) of the Harvard economics department to get ideas. Galbraith in turn recommended his Harvard colleague David Bell, who had worked in Truman's Budget Bureau as a junior economist and had subsequently worked in Pakistan as an economic consultant. Galbraith wasn't sure that Bell, at age forty, had the gravitas and experience to direct the bureau but thought him well suited to serve as associate director. Shriver immediately ordered Yarmolinsky to call around for opinions of Bell, then flew to Boston himself to interview the professor.

After meeting with Bell for several hours, it was evident to Shriver that he was Kennedy's kind of guy and that—his relative youth notwithstanding—he was an ideal candidate to head up Jack's Budget Bureau. Upon returning from Boston Shriver told Wofford and Yarmolinsky that Bell was "low-key, well informed, experienced, unideological, sensitive, quick, somewhat ironic, and good-humored— just the sort Kennedy responds to best." Shriver passed on his recommendation of Bell to the president-elect. As Shriver had predicted, Bell and Kennedy hit it off, and Jack was soon announcing the nomination of his budget director.

For treasury secretary, Kennedy chose Douglas Dillon over the objections of liberal advisers Galbraith and Schlesinger, who were appalled to learn from Shriver that the Republican head of an investment bank was being considered for the position. Dillon had also served as a cabinet under secretary in the Eisenhower administration and had even contributed more than $12,000 to the Nixon campaign. But Shriver had brought Dillon to Kennedy's attention, along with other bank presidents, because he knew the treasury secretary had to be someone with whom the financial community could be comfortable. Schlesinger sought an audience with Kennedy and argued the case against Dillon, recommending instead Averell Harriman, Senator Al Gore, and several congressmen, all of whom favored Keynesian spending to stimulate economic growth. "Oh, I don't care about those things," Kennedy responded. "All I want to know is: is he able? And will he go along with the program?"

According to Shriver, Kennedy picked Dillon not only for his government experience but also for his "judgment, his knowledge, his technical competence, and his nondogmatic politics. In other words, Dillon was not an ideological Republican." After appointing Dillon, however, Kennedy did go on to surround him with Humphreyesque liberal Democrats like Walter Heller, who was named head of the President's Council of Economic Advisers. In the end, this arrangement—a fiscally conservative Republican surrounded by liberal Democrats—seemed to work for Kennedy, and Dillon soon became one of the cabinet members closest to the Kennedy family.

Other positions were filled more straightforwardly. During the campaign, when Shriver had formed the "Business for Kennedy" Section, he had recruited North Carolina governor Luther Hodges, who had been a businessman before turning to politics, to serve as its chair. Hodges was thus a natural choice for secretary of commerce. Minnesota governor Orville Freeman was named secretary of agriculture, reportedly after another candidate had put Kennedy to sleep with his dullness. Stewart Udall, congressman from Arizona, was made secretary of the interior. Arthur Goldberg, a longtime union lawyer and an old, New Deal–era liberal, was named secretary of labor. After turning down an offer to become attorney general—because, as he told Bobby Kennedy, he thought it would be politically problematic for a Jew to be putting Negroes in Protestant schools in the South—Connecticut governor Abe Ribicoff was named secretary of health, education, and welfare.

The appointment that Kennedy seemed to find most important was secretary of state. Shriver's team had amassed information on dozens of candidates, which they dutifully sent down to Palm Beach, but in the end the short list consisted of Adlai Stevenson, Chester Bowles, UN Under Secretary-General Ralph Bunche, McGeorge Bundy, Senator William Fulbright, veteran diplomat David Bruce, Republican banker (and Truman's secretary of defense) Robert Lovett, Chase Manhattan Bank president John McCloy, and Rockefeller Foundation president Dean Rusk. Lovett and McCloy withdrew themselves from consideration, but that still left seven candidates. Kennedy stewed over the decision in Palm Beach.

Personally, Shriver's first choices would have been Stevenson, Bowles, or Bunche, and he conveyed this to Kennedy. But Bunche was not high on Kennedy's list, and though Bowles might have been, Nixon made clear to Jack not long after the election that he thought Bowles was soft on China. If Kennedy were to nominate Bowles, Nixon warned, he would campaign to have his confirmation blocked in Congress. Stevenson, who was being promoted by Eleanor Roosevelt, desperately craved the secretary of state job and had at Kennedy's request written up a report on foreign policy. But ever since the convention, when he had resisted taking himself out of contention for the presidential nomination before the first ballot, Kennedy had considered Stevenson unreliable.

By late November, Kennedy had let Shriver know that Stevenson was no longer a serious candidate but told him not to tell anyone. Still, debates raged within the inner circle about whom Jack should select. At the christening ceremony for the newborn John F. Kennedy Jr. in late November, Shriver watched, bemused, as the priest struggled to silence the arguing long enough to perform the rite. No sooner had everyone quieted down and the ceremony been performed than everyone started up again. Jack and Bobby were arguing with each another, and family friend Bill Walton and political columnists Charlie Bartlett and Joe Alsop were all debating with one another. Walton lobbied for Averell Harriman, whom Bobby dismissed as too old. Bartlett was making the case for Fulbright. Alsop was strongly against both Bowles and Stevenson, whom he considered too liberal, and was promoting David Bruce.

By the second week in December, Kennedy had still not made his selection. His options were thinning and the pressure to make a choice was mounting. According to Bobby Kennedy, the final choice came down to David Bruce and Dean Rusk, the smooth and intelligent Georgian who had been an under secretary of state under Truman. Although the first interview between Rusk and Kennedy did not go well, Jack liked an article Rusk had written for *Foreign Affairs* and found his understated personality appealing. In the end, almost by default, he named Rusk secretary of state. And as he had done at the Treasury Department, Jack followed the Shriver team's advice and surrounded the somewhat cautious and conservative-minded Rusk with liberals: Adlai Stevenson was made UN ambassador; Chester Bowles was made Rusk's under secretary; and Michigan governor Mennen Williams was named under secretary of state for Africa. Rusk deputized Bowles to make most of the top State Department hires and ambassadorial appointments, and Bowles in turn relied directly on Shriver for personnel recommendations. Staffing the rest of the State Department, as Arthur Schlesinger has noted, "involved complicated negotiations among Kennedy, Rusk, Bowles, and the Shriver office."

The Talent Hunt team ended up playing a particularly significant role in the selection of ambassadors. This responsibility redounded directly to Shriver's personal benefit in the coming years, when as Peace Corps director he had a whole crop of new ambassadors around the world who were politically indebted to him.

The most sensitive cabinet appointment, of course, was that of Bobby Kennedy to the Justice Department. Shriver had no inkling that Bobby would be given the position of attorney general when he launched the Talent Hunt, and in fact he had concluded that, of all the cabinet departments, it was most important that the head of the Justice Department not appear to be a political, or partisan, appointment. So Shriver set out to compile a list of the best legal minds in the country, irrespective of party affiliation. Little suspecting at first that Jack's selection would be not political but filial, Shriver did not put Bobby Kennedy on the list. Indeed, as Wofford has written, in no way did Bobby "seem to have the fair and thoughtful cast of mind required of the nation's chief legal officer." When Jack made it known that Bobby was a candidate for attorney general, Shriver was privately appalled, but he kept his thoughts to himself and even argued on Bobby's behalf when confronted with internal opposition within the Talent Hunt. Still, he was hopeful when Jack called one day, requesting Shriver's list of candidates.

The next day, however, when Shriver presented his list, Jack said, "Why are you giving me these? Bobby will be attorney general." Shriver's heart sank. But

Kennedy kept wavering back and forth. Bobby himself was resisting. I've never had a private law practice, Bobby told his brother, and besides, do you really want to appoint your brother to such a sensitive post? That's just inviting criticism. So Kennedy called Shriver and asked for still more names. On December 1, Kennedy called Shriver's friend Bill Blair, the longtime Stevenson adviser, to see if Stevenson would be interested in becoming attorney general. (Stevenson, at this point, had been offered the UN ambassadorship but had yet to accept it.) Stevenson declined.

For this one final time, Joe Kennedy was the final arbiter on a key decision. Although Jack reported "serious reservations" about making his brother attorney general, the Ambassador insisted. "Damn the torpedoes, full speed ahead," Joe is said to have responded when Jack presented his concerns, and after some further deliberations, the decision was made. Jack joked that to avoid the brickbats of political columnists and opponents, he would have to make the announcement in the middle of the night. But he made the announcement in the middle of the day on the steps of his Georgetown home, cracking that he had named his brother to the Justice Department so he could get "a little experience before he goes out to practice law."

Once Bobby was named, one of Shriver's tasks was to help him fill the Justice Department with top-notch talent. Shriver presented him with a thick sheaf of recommendations. Among the more prominent were Archibald Cox as solicitor general and Burke Marshall as assistant attorney general for civil rights. (Bobby had already named Byron White, Shriver's Yale classmate and friend, as his deputy attorney general, and White later became Kennedy's first Supreme Court appointment.)

The recruit Shriver was most proud of was Robert McNamara for secretary of defense. On the day after the election, when Shriver read newspaper accounts reporting that McNamara had just been named head of the Ford Motor Company, he remembered having been impressed, some years before, by a report on McNamara and the other "whiz kids" hired by the Pentagon as management consultants in the 1940s. Thus when Kennedy asked Shriver to head up the Talent Hunt that day in Hyannis Port, McNamara was on his mind, and Shriver asked the president-elect whether he would be interested in considering him for a cabinet position. Kennedy said he would but expressed his doubts about whether McNamara, having just been made head of a major American company, could be lured away from his new job.

Shriver began to investigate and when he interviewed Robert Lovett, who was also under consideration for several cabinet positions, he learned that when Lovett was assistant secretary of war under FDR, he had been the one responsible for hiring McNamara at the Pentagon. When Shriver asked Lovett whether McNamara had been any good, Lovett told him, "the best." When Shriver asked him what cabinet positions Lovett thought McNamara was best suited for, Lovett told him treasury or defense.

McNamara was a Republican, but he had supported Kennedy for some time. Shriver grew more impressed. When he heard that McNamara was reading one of his favorite theological works, *The Phenomenon of Man*, he exclaimed with pleasure, "How many other automobile executives or cabinet members read Teilhard de Chardin?" As Wofford recalled, "With each call made about McNamara, we heard further commendation of his judgment, analytic ability, and administrative efficiency. He emerged as a man who could effectively help a president cope with the military-industrial complex which Eisenhower had warned was difficult and dangerous." Shriver recalled, "We talked with [McNamara's] competitors, with labor leaders, with golf club caddies, with his Ford Automobile Company driver."

Shriver made a strong case to Kennedy that if he could persuade McNamara to join the administration, it would "symbolize the new administration's power to draw top talent, even from the ranks of business." After reading Shriver's files on the new Ford president in early December, Kennedy said, "Let's do it." The newspapers were already saying that Senators Stuart Symington and Henry Jackson were the most likely candidates for secretary of defense, but Kennedy told Shriver he could fly out secretly to Detroit to solicit McNamara's interest in the position.

Shriver knew that getting McNamara to express serious interest was a long shot: He had just become the chief executive of one of the biggest companies in America. Not only would taking a cabinet position mean taking a massive pay cut, but he was also one of the few people in the country for whom a senior cabinet position might be deemed a step down in status. Moreover, he would be a Republican in a Democratic administration, and he might fairly worry that this would constrain his influence.

But when Shriver arrived at the Detroit airport (incognito, because reporters had by now learned that following him around was a good way to figure out who likely cabinet appointments were) he was struck by a brainstorm. Why not expand McNamara's options—and flatter his ego—by offering him the choice of *two* positions, both defense and treasury? (At this point, the treasury position had not yet been offered to Dillon.) Offering him this choice, Shriver reasoned, would signal to McNamara how strongly Kennedy wanted him and would indicate the latitude Kennedy was prepared to offer him should he join the administration. So Shriver called Kennedy from a pay phone and presented the scenario. Good idea, Jack told him. Go ahead and try it.

When Shriver met with McNamara in Dearborn later that day, the new Ford president dismissed the treasury offer out of hand but was impressed enough by the dual offer that he agreed to fly to Washington several days later to discuss defense. When McNamara and Kennedy met, each grilled the other intensely—and both came away favorably impressed. McNamara accepted the nomination to become secretary of defense.

Shriver's intuition about McNamara's compatibility with the incoming president proved accurate. Ted Sorensen said that in his eleven years with Kennedy, he had never seen him take to anyone so quickly as he did to McNamara. Shriver himself, however, jokingly regretted the appointment, at least at first, because McNamara made such extensive use of the Talent Hunt staff in recruiting his Defense Department personnel that they began falling behind in recruiting for any of the other departments. Finally Shriver had to tell him, "It's your shop now, Mr. Secretary. Nobody else is doing the job you are in finding people. We're needed in other places."

Kennedy's cabinet was, as Sorensen commented, "nonpolitical and bipartisan to an extent unusual for Democratic presidents in particular." Out of a dozen members it included only four men who had previously sought public office and only four men—one of them his brother—who had supported Kennedy before the early primaries. Kennedy wanted a "ministry of talent," and his cabinet was decidedly not a patronage reservoir.

The "remarkably high quality" of Kennedy's appointees, Sorensen wrote, was a reflection of the Talent Hunt, whose "vast card file of candidate evaluations was both less systematic and more sensible than some news stories reported."

[Kennedy's] search succeeded. The men he picked were for the most part men who thought his thoughts, spoke his language, and put their country and

Kennedy ahead of any other concern. They were scrupulously honest; not even a suspicion of scandal ever tainted the Kennedy Cabinet. They were, like him, dedicated but unemotional, young but experienced, articulate but soft-spoken. . . . All spoke with the same low-keyed restraint that marked their chief, yet all shared his deep conviction that they could change America's drift.

At a seminar on the JFK legacy held in 1984, Shriver recalled that Kennedy's natural magnetism had made the work of the Talent Hunt much easier. Government was not yet "the enemy" it became under Carter and Reagan, the perceived "capital of an evil empire of bureaucrats and dunces and incompetents." The president-elect's "example and leadership" was a spur to both Republicans and Democrats. "If you believed in America's destiny, the efficiency of democracy, this was truly a glorious time to be alive," Shriver said, reflecting the idealism and the optimism—and not a little of the hubris—of 1960.

By late December, the Talent Hunt began to wind down. J. Edward Day's appointment as postmaster general, on December 17, marked the completion of the cabinet. After filling another 200 or so subcabinet positions, Shriver turned his files over to the White House, where they became the province of John Macy, the incoming chair of the Civil Service Commission, and Ralph Dungan, who continued to draw on the Talent Hunt's research in filling positions over the next three years. But the "casting" of the Kennedy administration, as the newspaper columnist Mary McGrory called the Talent Hunt (with Shriver as "casting director"), was largely complete.

As inauguration day approached, Shriver and Wofford joked that they had done such a good job filling slots there were no good ones remaining in the Kennedy administration for themselves. "One by one the people we most respected, often at our initiative, were being appointed to key posts, and the relatively few jobs that interested either of us were being filled," Wofford recalled.

Wofford, for his part, hoped for a presidential appointment not only for himself, but for Shriver, whom he thought was a good influence on Kennedy. "Shriver was hardly Eleanor Roosevelt," Wofford has written, "but I could see why he was considered the 'house liberal,' or worse, by some of those around Kennedy. He seemed close to the president, if not to some of his aides, and could speak up to him, when necessary; I thought Kennedy would do well to have Shriver near at hand, and hoped he would be appointed to the White

House staff." The Talent Hunt had forced Wofford to spend many long hours with Shriver; often traveling and spending the night with him in hotels, the idealistic young civil rights lawyer had grown increasingly admiring of this Kennedy brother-in-law. Shriver would, Wofford recalled,

> regularly read in his bed long after midnight, turning from the endless memos of the talent search to something philosophical, religious, or literary. Stirred by a passage in Saul Bellow or a verse in a poem, he would read it aloud, and a conversation would spring up until sleep put it out. . . .
>
> Not many outside his family saw this side of Shriver. Superficially he gave the impression that one was not virtuous unless exhausted by work, but those who worked and traveled with him discovered that meditation and philosophical thought were never far from the surface. His pace was too fast, though his enthusiasm and good humor generated energy and excitement in those he didn't wear out. Yet just as you would think he will never stand still and listen, he would ask a penetrating question opening new lines of thought and action. He persistently tested where a course was right or wrong by measures of both principle and practicality.

Shriver, however, had surprisingly little interest in remaining in Washington. Certain positions intrigued Shriver, but he was eager to return to Chicago. He had put his life there on hold, and he wanted to return to thinking about his own political future in Illinois. Also, he was worried about Eunice's health. Although he knew she could not be made to sit still any better than he could, he thought some rest, and some distance from the rest of the Kennedys, might do her some good.

But he underestimated her indomitable will to action, her need to be where things were happening. And he underestimated, too, how strongly he had proven himself in the president-elect's eyes in managing the Talent Hunt. Jack now saw, if he hadn't before, why his father had relied so heavily on Sarge for so many things. And he wasn't about to let him return to private life in Chicago.

PART THREE

The Peace Corps
(1961–1963)

CHAPTER THIRTEEN

The Towering Task

Inauguration day dawned crisp and cold and clear. A winter storm the night before, one of the heaviest in the city's memory, had blanketed the capital in eight inches of snow, making the roads untraversable. Cars were stuck in snowdrifts at every intersection. Only the work of the US Army, which had provided hundreds of truckloads of men with shovels and flamethrowers to labor through the night, ensured that the roads were clear for the inauguration.

Eunice and Sarge Shriver, like the other members of the Kennedy family and its inner circle, had spent the previous day and night going from event to event, concluding the evening at the pre-inaugural concert at the Armory, where Peter Lawford and Frank Sinatra had assembled a parade of celebrity performers. Eunice had recovered from the exhaustion that had landed her in the hospital in mid-November, but earlier in the week she had sprained her ankle rushing to catch a plane and had to rely on a cane to help her limp through all the inaugural events.

Now they stood in the cold on the East Plaza of the Capitol with fourteen other Kennedys, President Eisenhower, former president Truman, Vice President

Nixon, Chief Justice Earl Warren, and a host of other officials, waiting for the mantle of power to pass to Jack. John F. Kennedy was about to become the leader of the free world.

On this day, January 20, 1961, the Peace Corps did not exist. It remained to be seen whether the idea Kennedy had expressed ("We need young men and women to spend two or three years abroad spreading the cause of freedom") in Ann Arbor and San Francisco in the waning days of the campaign would be brought to fruition and turned into a real program, or whether it would be forgotten, a forever-unrealized campaign promise. In all the hours spent helping to fill hundreds of positions, the Talent Hunt group had devoted not a moment's thought to the Peace Corps—this despite the fact that Kennedy "received more letters from people offering to work in, or to volunteer for, the nonexistent Peace Corps than for all the existing programs of the United States government put together." This volume of interest might have suggested that starting a "Peace Corps"—whatever such an entity might turn out to be—was in order, but Kennedy gave Shriver and his associates no indication that he had plans to follow through on this campaign idea anytime soon. Besides, the Talent Hunt people had enough positions to worry about in existing agencies to concern themselves with filling jobs in a merely potential one.

But although the Peace Corps had yet to be given shape or form, the underlying spirit that would animate it was very much present on inauguration day. "Let the word go forth that the torch has been passed to a new generation of Americans," Kennedy's inaugural address began. "Let every nation know, whether it wishes us well or ill, that we shall pay any price, bear any burden, meet any hardship, support any friend, oppose any foe to assure the survival and success of liberty."

"To those peoples in the huts and villages of half the globe struggling to break the bonds of mass misery," he said a few moments later, "we pledge our best efforts to help them help themselves, for whatever period is required—not because the Communists may be doing it, not because we seek their votes, but because it is right." And, building to the most famous words of his oration: "Now the trumpet summons us again—not as a call to bear arms, though arms we need—not a call to battle, though embattled we are—but a call to bear the burden of a long twilight struggle year in and year out. . . . And so, my fellow Americans: Ask not what your country can do for you—ask what you can do for your country."

Kennedy was speaking, of course, not only to Americans but to the world—and especially to Nikita Khrushchev and the Soviet Union, to whom he wished to send the message that the United States would remain an unyielding adversary in the cold war struggle. But in Kennedy's address lay the spirit of sacrifice and willingness to serve that would be the essence of the Peace Corps. President Kennedy may or may not have been thinking explicitly of the Peace Corps when he spoke these words—more likely not—but he captured the spirit of the age when he uttered them, and it was this same spirit that would be so successfully harnessed by the soon-to-be born agency.

Both the Peace Corps and the New Frontier were products of a specific generation. When Kennedy, the youngest man to be elected president, began his address by invoking "a new generation of Americans," he was implicitly bidding farewell to the fustiness, not just of President Eisenhower himself (who at age seventy-one was the oldest elected president) and his administration, but also to the Eisenhower generation, which had presided over the postwar years of the 1950s.

Kennedy's was not just any generation. It was, as the president declaimed in his address, a generation whose identity had been forged in the crucible of war and its aftermath. This generation, which had helped to vanquish the totalitarian and imperialist regimes of Hitler's Germany, Mussolini's Italy, and Tojo's Japan, had also lifted America to global pre-eminence. America now confronted a new enemy in the totalitarian communism of the Soviet Union. But Kennedy's generation shared the conviction—garnered through victory in a hard-fought war—that the world might yield to its efforts. Hard work and the American spirit, this generation concluded, could produce peace and progress. "We were arrogant in a funny kind of way," recalled Bill Haddad, one of Shriver's top aides during the Peace Corps' founding era. "We were guys of the forties who thought there was nothing we, or America, couldn't do."

Part of this optimism sprang from the idealism of youth. The members of Kennedy's generation were in their early forties or younger (Shriver was forty-five)—not yet middle-aged. The energy of the New Frontier was inseparable from its youthfulness. "The difference between the outgoing Eisenhower and the incoming Kennedy," one observer said in 1961, "was the difference between a slow march and a jig. Washington is crackling, rocking, jumping. It is a kite zigging in the breeze." And although the attitudes and beliefs of the Kennedy-Shriver generation were not monolithic, the men of this era shared the common bond of war, which (the social science data suggest) lent them a stronger sense of patriotism, a greater sense of the importance of American values and of the duty to serve these values. It was partly to this sense that Kennedy spoke in his inaugural address. "The 16 million young men who had gone to war in the 1940s were taking over from the generals and the admirals," the political scientist Richard Reeves has written, "and this was their new adventure. They could finish the job of remaking the world in America's image." The men of the Kennedy administration were the "junior officers of the Second World War finally come to power," as the wife of Walt Rostow, one of Kennedy's advisers, described them. A generation of young men who had returned from war only to find themselves adrift (as Shriver had for a time), waiting their turn behind the Eisenhower generation, now rallied behind their compatriot Kennedy, who was promising them an outlet for all their pent-up energy and frustrated idealism.

As a product of the 1960s, the Peace Corps is apt to be associated with starry-eyed hippies and the crunchier aspects of the counterculture. Yet the founding fathers of the Peace Corps, from Kennedy and Shriver on down, were almost all World War II veterans. And to understand the Peace Corps—its animating impulses and its phenomenal early success—one does best to consider it as the product of the camaraderie and values of the World War II generation.

After the inaugural ceremony, following a luncheon at the Mayflower Hotel arranged by Joe Kennedy, some members of the family traveled in a chartered tour bus to the White House, where they were to wait for the formal arrival of the new president. They swarmed through the building, looking at the furniture, marveling at the trappings of power. Eunice went upstairs with Jack's friend Lem Billings to look at the Lincoln Bedroom, where they bounced on the bed and laughed giddily as they photographed each other spread out on the counterpane. At one point, Eunice looked up and said, "You know what this reminds me of? That scene in *Gone with the Wind* where Scarlett's colored servants move into Tara with her after the war. I feel like the old mammy who takes a look around and then says, 'Man, we's rich now.'"

The next day, after the inaugural ball, the Shrivers flew home to Chicago. Sarge had had discussions with Jack and others about positions in the various executive departments, including State, Justice, and Health, Education, and

Welfare, but so far none of them had come to anything. He had also heard his name mentioned as a possible member of the White House staff, but he wasn't interested. He just couldn't see himself fitting in with either the "Irish Mafia" (Ken O'Donnell, Larry O'Brien, Dave Powers) or the "eggheads" (Ted Sorensen, Arthur Schlesinger), who made up the president's inner circle of advisers. Both the O'Donnell and Sorensen groups viewed him, Shriver knew, as too much of an "independent operator."

But the Shrivers had been back in Chicago for only a few hours when the phone rang. It was the president. After talking to Eunice for a few minutes, Jack asked to speak to Sarge. When he got on the phone, Jack asked him if he would head a task force that would study the feasibility of starting a program like the Peace Corps. In the years since then, Shriver has frequently joked that the reason Jack asked him to lead the task force—and later the Peace Corps itself—was that everyone knew the program would be a disaster and that when the day of reckoning arrived "it would be easier to fire a relative than a friend."

During the interregnum and the early days of his administration, Kennedy had set up several task forces for the purpose of exploring various policy initiatives. The Peace Corps seemed tailor-made for such a task force. On the one hand, in the months since his Ann Arbor and Cow Palace speeches, interest in the Peace Corps had grown. Not only had Shriver, in his role as talent hunter, been besieged with inquiries regarding employment at the Peace Corps, but 25,000 people had also written to the president, asking about it. A week after the election, a *Washington Post* editorial urged Kennedy not to allow the Peace Corps to become merely a forgotten campaign promise. A week before the inauguration, a *New York Times* article said that the Peace Corps was "something that is in the spirit of this democratic country, a forward-looking thing, and it is heartening that so many of our young people are responding with vigor and eagerness to it." A Gallup Poll conducted near the time of the inauguration found that 71 percent of Americans were in favor of establishing the Peace Corps.

But despite the breadth of support for the program, resistance was strong in certain quarters. During the campaign, Nixon had attacked the idea as nothing more than a haven for prospective draft dodgers, calling the program "inherently dangerous." Nixon and his supporters took to deriding the Peace Corps as a "kiddie corps." Eisenhower called it "a juvenile experiment." The *Wall Street Journal* editorialized, "Who but the very young themselves can really believe that an Africa aflame with violence will have its fires quenched because some Harvard boy or Vassar girl lives in a mud hut and speaks Swahili?" Conservative members of Congress said they would never appropriate money for such a program.

The strength of this opposition caused Kennedy to want to proceed cautiously. He declined to announce definitively during the interregnum period what he had in mind for a "Peace Corps" and deferred launching even an exploratory task force until after the inauguration. The extent of what he did before calling Shriver was to ask Max Millikan, a professor at the Massachusetts Institute of Technology who had advised Kennedy on economics and the third world, to write a report on how such a program might work. "Have Max take on the responsibility of working up a Peace Corps idea into something I could implement," Kennedy wrote to Walt Rostow in the weeks after the election. But he also told Rostow that what he had in mind was something small and experimental, nothing that might cause young Americans to get involved in some sensitive foreign policy area overseas that would result in his looking like a naive young president.

Rostow contacted his MIT colleague Millikan, and Millikan wrote a long memorandum called "An International Youth Service," in which he supported the idea of a "youth service," but only very tentatively. "We simply do not know a great deal about how to make a program of this kind work," Millikan wrote. On January 9 Kennedy released Millikan's report to the public and proposed the creation of an International Youth Service Agency "on a limited pilot basis." The agency would fall under the auspices of US foreign assistance and would be strictly "experimental." No more than a few hundred young people would participate for the first few years, and "there should be no pressure to achieve greater volume until there is sufficient evidence and background study to give some confidence that expanded numbers can be wisely used."

The truth was, Kennedy didn't seem to know what he wanted out of a Peace Corps. He could see that it spoke to the burgeoning youthful idealism of the time, and it resonated with his own concerns about America's place in the cold war world—but he was also sensitive to the impression in certain circles that he was a callow neophyte in world affairs, and he was anxious not to embarrass himself with a half-cocked program fueled more by idealism than by hard-headed good sense. Thus, although he had Millikan's report in hand, he called for a task force to explore the idea.

Why Shriver to head it? Kennedy had good reasons for selecting his brother-in-law. The president by now had had ample opportunity to see Shriver at work, and he was a strong admirer of Sarge's abilities. Joe Kennedy, of course, had always spoken approvingly of Shriver's skill and judgment, but Jack had watched Shriver for the last eight years himself. Kennedy had been impressed by Sarge's efforts in the 1952 Senate campaign and by his work on the Civil Rights Section of his presidential campaign and on the Talent Hunt. Shriver was someone to whom Kennedy could give minimal instructions and yet who would return later with maximal results.

Kennedy also knew that the Peace Corps spoke especially to Shriver's interests and strengths. And he knew that Chester Bowles, a strong supporter of the idea, and Shriver saw eye-to-eye on foreign policy. Moreover, the president was aware from his conversations with his brother-in-law that Shriver's worldview had been significantly shaped by his experiences as a teenager in the Experiment in International Living, whose motivating principle of cross-cultural learning and exchange would necessarily be shared by any successful Peace Corps program.

Public relations would also be important: The American people already seemed to be largely sold on the idea but their interest would have to be maintained, and the US Congress (who would legislate the program) and foreign countries (where Peace Corps volunteers would be sent) still needed to be convinced of its virtues. Kennedy knew that Shriver would be a good salesman for the program.

Finally, he had to put Shriver somewhere, since Jack knew that Eunice wouldn't be content to remain in the Midwest when all the action was in Washington. The Peace Corps task force was one of the few options that was left.

Jack didn't articulate any of these considerations when he called his brother-in-law on January 21. He just told Shriver that he wanted a Peace Corps task force and asked him if he would head it. Shriver demurred, arguing that someone with State Department experience, or with an academic background in foreign policy, would be better suited to the position. (He also pointed out that his appointment would invite charges of nepotism.) But Jack persisted and Shriver acquiesced; it was hard to say no to the president of the United States on his first day in office. Shriver assumed, however, that once the task force's job—"to report how the Peace Corps could be organized and then to organize it"—was complete, he could return to Chicago to prepare for a Senate run in 1962.

The first step was to form the task force, so before returning to Washington, Shriver called Harris Wofford. "You thought you were going to have a vacation?" Shriver said. "The president just asked me to set up a task force to see whether the Peace Corps idea really makes sense. When shall we have our first meeting?" Wofford was the natural first person for Shriver to call: Not only had they become close and effective colleagues during the election and Talent Hunt, but Wofford also had a particular interest in the Peace Corps idea. Some ten years earlier he had been a founder of the Student World Federalists, who proposed a "peace force" of volunteers for development projects in communities abroad; in the 1950s he had consulted with American unions about a large-scale American volunteer service in developing countries; and he had been directly involved in launching the International Development Placement Association, which placed American students overseas.

Shriver and Wofford reconvened at the Mayflower Hotel, where they had spent so many hours during the Talent Hunt, and picked up where they had left off, calling people across the country who might fruitfully contribute to the Peace Corps task force. They began by rounding up the usual suspects: Louis Martin and Adam Yarmolinsky from the Talent Hunt soon joined them. Notre Dame University president Father Theodore Hesburgh—Shriver's friend and Wofford's former boss—came to the Mayflower. So did George Carter, a civil rights campaign worker, and Albert Sims, who ran an organization called the Institute of International Education and who, the year before, had helped Shriver with a student airlift from Kenya subsidized by the Kennedy Foundation. Shriver took special pleasure in recruiting Gordon Boyce, who had succeeded Donald Watt as head of the Experiment in International Living, to the team.

Early in 1960, some months before Jack Kennedy first invoked the Peace Corps in campaign speeches, Hubert Humphrey and the Wisconsin congressman Henry S. Reuss (whose wife was also a graduate of the Experiment in International Living program) had sponsored legislation calling for research into the viability of Peace Corps–type programs. Humphrey's bill, which included the first known use of the name "Peace Corps" to describe such a program, called for "young men to assist the peoples of the underdeveloped areas of the world to combat poverty, disease, illiteracy, and hunger." Humphrey and Reuss stopped by the Mayflower in early February to take part in the discussions, along with dozens of other people.

As during the Talent Hunt, according to the historian Gerald Rice, "one name soon led to another. During the last week of January and the first week of February, scores of people from academic, business, and religious circles passed through the lobby of the makeshift Peace Corps headquarters in the Mayflower Hotel. It was an informal setup, more like a group of friends gathering together to discuss a pet subject than an official committee establishing a governmental organization." Even if he had wanted to, Shriver wouldn't have known how to make the arrangements more formal. He had no experience working in federal government and didn't know how to procure an office or financial resources, or how to pay his staff. And as he didn't feel he had time to worry about such things, he just counted on being able to telephone people and have them show up quickly, motivated by Shriver's enthusiasm and their own public-spiritedness. "My style," he has said, "was to get bright, informative, creative people and then pick their brains." What little administrative wherewithal he had for his task force was initially provided by Mary Ann Orlando, his assistant from the Merchandise Mart, who had only just returned home to Chicago after the inauguration before getting a phone call from Shriver saying, "Get yourself back here. We need you."

Even before Shriver's task force began formal deliberations, reports and recommendations had begun streaming in from all quarters, many of them contradictory in their advice. The International Cooperation Administration (ICA), a federal government agency, sent along a study called *The National Peace Corps,* which recommended that volunteers be paid $3,000 per year and that the whole project be subsumed in existing government assistance programs. Samuel P. Hayes, the University of Michigan professor whose report had helped inspire Kennedy's impromptu campaign speech in Ann Arbor, which had generated the initial momentum for the Peace Corps, sent along a supplemental report recommending coordination with the United Nations. Researchers at Colorado State University—who were funded with $10,000 provided by Congressman Reuss's "Point Four Youth Corps" bill—sent in a paper called *A Youth Corps Service Abroad,* recommending that the Peace Corps submit control of its country programs to existing governmental foreign policy agencies. And Shriver already had the Millikan report, which recommended much the same thing.

Hundreds of other reports flowed into the Mayflower—from universities (Harvard, Yale, Stanford, and dozens more), foundations (Rockefeller, Brookings, and the National Council of Churches, among others), and individuals (from the expert to the insane)—but "the only point of unanimity among all the reports," as Gerald Rice put it, "was that the Peace Corps should begin cautiously and on a small scale." Although this cut against the grain of Shriver's nature—which gravitated to the bold and the large-scale—he had to concede that the argument made a certain amount of sense.

The task force began meeting informally in January, just days after the inauguration. After the first few sessions, Shriver was worried: No real consensus was emerging on the scale or scope of the program, or even on what the program's basic goals should be. The task force couldn't seem to arrive at any kind of collective sense of what the Peace Corps was supposed to be. Kennedy ratcheted up the pressure on the task force on January 30 when, in his first State of the Union address, he mentioned that the "formation of a National Peace Corps, enlisting the services of all those with the desire and capability to help foreign lands meet their urgent needs for trained personnel" was under way. The task force could no longer be considered merely an exercise. In early February, when the president called him at home to ask for a report by the end of the month, Shriver really began to feel anxious. "I needed help badly," Shriver recalled. "Kennedy wanted to know what was taking us so long. . . . I replied weakly that no one had ever tried to put a Peace Corps together before."

Help was on its way. It came, on the face of it, from an unlikely source. Shriver knew, based on Kennedy's remarks at the Cow Palace and elsewhere, that the president did not have an especially high regard for how things were done at the existing foreign service institutions (like the ICA) of the federal government. Thus, Shriver had consciously gone outside the conventional foreign policy agencies in seeking advice on how to start the Peace Corps.

Yet when the inspiration that finally fired Shriver's imagination arrived, it came from deep within the bowels of the foreign service bureaucracy. For the Peace Corps—an agency that would soon develop a reputation as a maverick, antibureaucratic institution—to have had its spark of creation emanate from within the heart of the bureaucracy was ironic. But it also made a certain sense. Who knew better how to vanquish the bureaucratic beast than those lodged within its belly? And who better than practiced veterans of the federal bureaucracy to steer the creative energies of Shriver's band of brilliant amateurs into the formation of a viable government organization?

In 1961 Warren Wiggins and William Josephson were mired deep in the federal government's foreign policy bureaucracy, but neither of them, it is fair to say, had a bureaucrat's mentality. The thirty-four-year-old Wiggins had already helped oversee the Marshall Plan in Western Europe, served as a US economic adviser in the Philippines, and directed America's aid program in Bolivia. At the time of Kennedy's inauguration, he was serving as deputy director of Far Eastern operations for the ICA. Bill Josephson had just turned twenty-six, but as counsel for the ICA's Far East section, he had earned a reputation as one of the agency's toughest and most brilliant lawyers.

The spirit of idealism and renewal surrounding the Kennedy campaign had impressed both Wiggins and Josephson, and they noted with interest Kennedy's comments about the ossification of the foreign service. Wiggins, based on his own experiences overseas, was appalled by US foreign assistance programs, which had American diplomats living in "golden ghettoes," apparently oblivious or indifferent to the third world squalor that surrounded them. Kennedy's critical comments in his Cow Palace speech about the average age of foreign service officials, and about how few of them spoke the native language of the countries in which they were stationed, resonated strongly with Wiggins.

When Kennedy won the election, Wiggins saw an opportunity to effect change within the foreign aid bureaucracy, and he and Josephson joined some of their ICA colleagues to write a series of papers on important issues—on the situation in Laos, for instance, which was struggling with communism, and on the reorganization of the foreign aid program—to which they hoped to draw the incoming president's attention. At first, they didn't give much thought to the Peace Corps; they initially thought it a "silly" idea.

But as newspapers continued to editorialize in its favor and popular sentiment for it remained strong, it unavoidably became a topic of regular discussion in foreign aid circles. People kept asking Wiggins what he thought of it; it seemed likely that Kennedy would even make it a reality. Moreover, the other papers Wiggins and Josephson had been releasing had met with condescending responses—or no response at all—from the Kennedy people, who didn't want to take advice from those they perceived as bureaucrats, people "on the inside." So shortly before Christmas of 1960, Wiggins told Josephson that he thought the Peace Corps might be just the opportunity they were looking for. "We've got to have a vehicle [for reforming US foreign aid programs], you know, and if this has to be the vehicle, it has to be the vehicle, so let's write a paper on the Peace Corps."

Josephson remained somewhat skeptical, concerned that the worst fears of the Peace Corps' critics would be realized: ill-informed kids running off to foreign countries, disrupting American foreign aid policies. But Wiggins kept after him and Josephson soon relented. So Josephson and Wiggins, along with several other staff people from the Far East section, got together and produced a series of drafts that spelled out their ideas for what the Peace Corps should be. "Josephson and I decided that if they didn't want to hear what we were writing about, we'd have to write about something they wanted to hear," Wiggins recalled. "Which seemed at the time to be the Peace Corps. We could see, too, that it had the promise of becoming something quite important if done right, and that is the level at which we made our connection. We started writing [our report] in December 1960, and we sent it over to Shriver in early February of 1961." "Frankly," Josephson recalled, "we didn't think much of the whole [Peace Corps] idea when we began writing, but we went ahead with it in order to gain attention." Josephson did most of the initial writing, but Wiggins did the final rewrite over a weekend and that version became the product they tried to deliver to Shriver's task force.

Calling their paper *The Towering Task,* after a remark Kennedy had made in his State of the Union address on January 30 ("The problems [of third world development] are towering and unprecedented—and the response must be towering and unprecedented as well"), Josephson and Wiggins argued that, contrary to the counsel of all the academic and political experts, the Peace Corps needed to be launched on a big, bold scale. A "small, cautious Peace Corps may be worse than no Peace Corps at all," they wrote. "It may not receive the attention and talent it will require even for preventing trouble." The reports from Millikan and others had urged small, pilot programs with only a few hundred volunteers over the first few years, but *The Towering Task* called for "a *quantum* jump in the thinking and programming concerning the National Peace Corps," suggesting that there be "several thousand Americans participating in the first 12 to 18 months" and tens or even hundreds of thousands of volunteers once the program was fully up and running. The smaller the Peace Corps, they reasoned, the greater the likelihood that "an anticipated bold 'new frontier' may fall into disrespect rather rapidly."

Proposing that the Peace Corps begin with a large program of English instruction in the Philippines and then be extended to such countries as Nigeria, Pakistan, India, and Mexico, *The Towering Task* concluded that the Peace Corps should be launched within the next twelve months at a level sufficiently large to ensure maximum chance of success: "an immediate program which would look toward the utilization of, say, 5,000 to 10,000 youths in the next 12 to 18 months." The paper also provided a rough outline of how the Peace Corps might be set up administratively and from where it might draw its funding.

Now that their report was written, Wiggins and Josephson had to figure out how to get it read by the right people. All the earlier papers they had sent to Kennedy's State Department had been sent back by someone in Under Secretary George Ball's office with comments to the effect that "we're not interested in the ideas of ICA insiders." So they figured they had to get this to Shriver and his task force directly. In order to maximize the chances of Shriver's actually seeing their report, they sent copies via multiple routes. They sent one copy to the official ICA working group on the Peace Corps. They sent a copy to Dick Goodwin, on the White House staff, who they heard had helped write the Peace Corps section of the Cow Palace speech. They sent a copy to Harris Wofford, whom Josephson had met when he had brought some of his earlier policy papers over to the Talent Hunt operation. And they had a copy delivered to Shriver's hotel room at the Mayflower.

There are varying accounts of what happened next, but the one that has worked its way into the standard mythology of the Peace Corps' founding— and has therefore acquired a status that might be said to be deeper than truth— is the "Midnight Ride of Warren Wiggins." By this account, Shriver received one of the copies of *The Towering Task* on Sunday, February 5, and read it in his hotel room late that night. He was so taken by its contents, by the boldness of vision that spoke to his own convictions, that he tracked down Wiggins's address and telegrammed him at home in suburban Virginia at 3:00 a.m., telling him to report to the following morning's task force meeting in the Mayflower just seven hours hence.

The reality may have been less dramatic—Wiggins remembers no telegram— but its substance was the same: He was present at the Monday morning task force meeting by virtue of his having talked his way in as an interested ICA expert. But upon arrival at the meeting, he was stunned to see "mimeographed copies of *The Towering Task* set out neatly at every task force member's place." And he was flabbergasted when Shriver opened the meeting by asking for Wiggins, introducing him to the group, and saying, "Now I've never met this man before this morning. But before we begin today's meeting, I want you all to read his report because it comes the closest to representing what I think should happen."

Shriver had indeed been struck by the boldness of *The Towering Task*'s proposed approach. "If you want to succeed with an idea that may fail," Wiggins said later, "you have to do something big enough and bold enough to overcome the critics." This was what Shriver had been waiting to hear. He immediately proceeded, in effect, to throw all the previous academic reports out the window. Shriver liked Wiggins's comparison of the Peace Corps to the Marshall Plan, which he said might have failed if it had not been "started on a scale sufficiently large to enable the United States and the European countries to 'handle it' right." Moreover, having earlier conceded the logic of a small, experimental approach, Shriver now saw the greater wisdom of Wiggins's argument that if the Peace Corps started too small, it would never gain the institutional constituency necessary to propel it to success. And Shriver agreed as well with Wiggins's argument that if the Peace Corps were to be a truly *national* project, worthy of Kennedy's New Frontier and strong enough to survive in the harsh world of cold war geopolitics, it needed to be big.

As he had no experience in getting new federal agencies started and funded, Shriver had had little idea about how to get the Peace Corps off the ground. He knew that eventually Congress would probably have to pass legislation for it—and appropriate the necessary money for it—but he hadn't yet figured out how to actually bring the Peace Corps into existence. Fortunately, buried inconspicuously in *The Towering Task*'s paragraph on administration, was an idea. Wiggins and Josephson had written that the president could put the Peace Corps concept into action "with a major presidential statement or speech" that came "in advance of legislation and formal administrative structure," and that a director and a staff could be hired, and their activities funded, by "a Presidential Determination, utilizing Mutual Security funds through the exemption route . . . of the Mutual Security Act."

Translated from the government bureaucratese, this was a simple proposal: The Peace Corps could be launched, and initially funded, by an executive order from the president. This was Josephson's most significant contribution to *The Towering Task*. When Shriver asked Josephson to elaborate after the February 6 meeting, the young lawyer explained that since congressional wrangling on a Peace Corps bill might take months and dilute popular enthusiasm for the program, the president would be better off signing the Peace Corps into existence with an executive order, thereby avoiding—at least temporarily—the need for congressional approval. If they were to wait the six months or more that it would take to get legislation passed, Josephson warned, the Peace Corps would be too late to get volunteer recruits from the graduating college classes of 1961—meaning that the program might not get up and running until late 1962 or 1963. Josephson told Shriver that, based on his research, Kennedy could release up to $12 million to start the program. Responding to the speed and directness inherent in Josephson's executive order proposal, Shriver resolved to make it one of the centerpieces of his report to President Kennedy.

After Shriver asked him to help him prepare his report to the president, Wiggins left his job at the ICA the next day to work for the task force, despite the fact that Shriver told him he didn't even know how to put anyone on a federal payroll so that they might be compensated. Several days later Josephson got dispensation from Henry Labouisse, Kennedy's newly appointed ICA director, to be detailed to the task force as a legal adviser.

The Towering Task had provided a viable model for the Peace Corps as well as the legal means for bringing it into existence. But Shriver still had only the barest outline of what the scope and cost of the program might be. Hundreds of important decisions still had to be made—not to mention an executive order to be drafted. And by the time Josephson—whom Shriver assigned to write the executive order—came on board it was already February 9. The president had said he wanted the task force's report sent to his office by the end of the month. That left less than three weeks to write up a detailed proposal on how to start a brand-new, multimillion-dollar government program.

For the next twenty days, no one on the task force rested. Days began early and ended late. Fierce shouting debates were common, as each task force member sought to have his own ideas included in the report. Shriver encouraged as much argument as possible, having learned from watching Joe Kennedy that

the best way to reach a smart decision was to listen to each point of view articulated by its most ardent proponent—if possible in open debate with that point
of view's most ardent opponent—and then weigh in his mind the pros and cons
of each. "My theory of why the task force was successful," Shriver has said,
"was its wonderful, rousing fights. From those meetings came the structure
of the Peace Corps. My ability was the ability to listen to all the arguments and
then say, 'Okay, here's what we're going to do.'"

Probably the most fundamental disagreement during the writing of the
report was between Wiggins and Gordon Boyce. Boyce, speaking from his perspective as head of the Experiment in International Living, argued that the
Peace Corps should be primarily an administrative and grant-issuing organization, leaving the actual running of the in-country programs to universities
and private agencies that already had personnel and expertise there. Wiggins
strenuously disagreed, pointing out that this would reduce the new agency to
being merely a "Peace Corps Foundation" that would dole out money but not
play any substantive assistance role itself. Wiggins argued that, to be successful, the Peace Corps should retain direct control over all its programs.

Through all these debates, Shriver managed to strike the right balance
between argumentativeness and concord among the different factions. Many
veterans of his employ have observed that he was a master at this practice—
although it was not for the weak-willed or the faint of heart. He would let
debate rage until it seemed about to become hostile, and then he would rein
it back in and make his decision, leaving no doubt that the final authority to
resolve all the important questions rested ultimately with him.

The questions that remained to be resolved were many and important, but
Shriver didn't have the luxury of time for leisurely contemplation of them. He
had promised his brother-in-law that the report would be delivered before the
end of the month—and at times the president seemed impatient even with that
deadline, calling Shriver twice more to ask him how the task force was pro-
gressing and publicly stating on February 21 that he hoped the Peace Corps
would soon become a reality. Thus, even as the members of Shriver's team continued to debate key issues, they were already beginning to draft and redraft
the report that they hoped would become the Peace Corps' blueprint.

As the end of February approached, the already frenzied pace of the task
force accelerated. Tempers grew short. Shriver was incredibly demanding of his

team's time and energy, but every time it seemed on the verge of collapse, he would spur the group on with an inspiring peroration. As the report neared completion, the scene in Shriver's Mayflower suite was one of barely controlled chaos. Charles Nelson, an ICA veteran, sat in one room writing the original copy for the report. In the adjacent room, Josephson sat revising it, making sure all its technical and legal assertions were accurate. In a third room sat Harris Wofford, injecting his own ideas and turning the drafts into polished final copy. Wiggins ran frantically back and forth among all three rooms, delivering pieces of paper along the chain. Overseeing the whole enterprise with a stern but cheerful eye was Shriver. Chaotic though it may have appeared, the process worked: Shriver delivered the report to the White House on the morning of Friday, February 24.

The report bore Shriver's characteristically bold stamp. "Having studied at your request the problems of establishing a Peace Corps," it began, "I recommend its *immediate* establishment." "If the world situation were moving at a snail's pace," the report said, a Peace Corps that was "timidly conceived and administered could keep in step." But, the report continued, the "world situation" was highly dynamic in the early 1960s. Nations were winning their independence from colonial powers in Africa; the post–Korean War situation in East Asia was constantly changing; and the cold war often appeared liable to go hot. If you authorize the program, Shriver challenged Kennedy, "we can be in business Monday morning."

This was not the report's most audacious recommendation. The report's most daring assertion was that the Peace Corps should have institutional independence from the existing foreign aid establishment. It should be not a tool for the ICA but an autonomous agency unto itself. "This new wine should not be poured into the ICA bottle," the report said. Granting that the new organization would have to reside in the State Department (to draw on the experience of the professional diplomats there), Shriver wrote that the Peace Corps should be "a small, new, alive agency operating as one component in our whole overseas operation."

Moreover, the report continued, as an independent agency the Peace Corps must have "great flexibility to experiment." "No one," it said, "wants to see a large centralized new bureaucracy grow up. . . . This must be a cooperative venture of the whole American people—not the program of some alphabetical agency in Washington." The palpable animosity toward the hidebound ICA was ironic, given that two of the principal authors of the report had just emerged from that agency. But Wiggins and Josephson (and Wofford, too) shared Shriver's allergy to bureaucracy and conformist thinking, and the report's boldness picked up right where *The Towering Task* had left off. If Kennedy were to launch the program immediately, the report said, the Peace Corps could have 2,000 volunteers in the field within nine months.

The report, a document of some twenty pages, went into considerable detail about how the Peace Corps would actually work. It proposed a term of service between one and three years for volunteers, who, it said, could be of any age and either gender. A college degree would not be required. A volunteer could *defer* a military draft call-up but could not *avoid* it outright: The corps was resolutely not to be seen as "a haven for draft dodgers." The report also proposed some initial guidelines for selection of volunteers. Written and oral tests would be required of Peace Corps applicants as they would be of any foreign service applicant.

The report proposed some of the development projects on which Peace Corps volunteers might work: teaching; public health projects, such as fighting malaria; agricultural and rural development programs; large-scale construction and industrial projects; and government administration and urban development. The need for development assistance in all these areas is sorely needed in the third world, Shriver wrote; academic studies had demonstrated this fact. "If the shortage of able personnel is not made up from outside, some development programs will grind to a halt—or fail to progress fast enough to satisfy the newly aroused and volatile expectations of people of these lands. The Peace Corps can make a significant contribution to this problem."

The report concluded by arguing that not only could Peace Corps volunteers contribute significantly to economic development in third world countries abroad, but that their exposure to foreign cultures would also benefit America and lead to more harmonious international relations.

> With thousands of young Americans going to work in developing areas, millions of Americans will become more directly involved in the world than ever. . . . The letters home, the talks later given by returning members of the Peace Corps, the influence on the lives of those who spend one or two or three years in hard work abroad—all this may combine to provide the first substantial popular base for

responsible American policies toward the world. And this is meeting the world's need, too, since what the world most needs from this country is better understanding of and more responsibility toward the world.

At first, the task force report was not terribly well received. "This looks interesting," Ted Sorensen told Shriver, "but it's not at all what we had in mind." Kennedy's political and foreign policy advisers had hoped for something inexpensive and small that could be folded into existing foreign aid programs. They were expecting something that would be more a tool and a public relations ornament for the ICA—which, as the result of another Kennedy task force, was now in the process of being reconstituted as the Agency for International Development (AID)—than a full-blown program in its own right. Moreover, Josephson's idea of starting the Peace Corps via executive order made the political advisers nervous: Kennedy's popularity was still very high, but they were reluctant to have him squander precious political capital by unilaterally appropriating money for a new program that had yet to receive congressional approval.

Thus Shriver and his team spent the last week of February arguing their case with the White House. Kennedy's staff argued that rushing so many young people abroad quickly could lead to diplomatic catastrophe. The potential for a foreign policy embarrassment—and subsequent congressional vengeance—was high. But Shriver argued that the moment was ripe for capitalizing on enthusiasm for Kennedy's New Frontier. Delay would only sap the Peace Corps' momentum.

Josephson, rooting around for historical precedent that might justify launching the Peace Corps expeditiously, pointed out that President Franklin Roosevelt had launched the Emergency Conservation Corps via executive order in 1933. He acknowledged that the times were different then, but he argued that, politically anyway, the Peace Corps was similarly a "special case" that merited such a bypassing of Congress. Besides, he and Wiggins repeatedly told Shriver, if the Peace Corps were not launched immediately, it might never be launched: Presidential leeway for inaugurating bold and experimental programs, so strong in the first months of a new administration, dissipated progressively as time passed.

Shriver pressed the case avidly with the president and his aides. Despite their wariness of him, the president's advisers yielded to Shriver's arguments. Their acquiescence probably owed something to Shriver's personal relationship with the president; Eunice gave Sarge access to the president that other federal officials lacked. Although Shriver was reluctant to take advantage of this access for Peace Corps purposes, the knowledge that the access was there may have cowed presidential aides who might otherwise have been inclined to take issue with the executive order approach. The task force's arguments won the day and, according to Arthur Schlesinger, the Peace Corps became the only agency in the Kennedy administration to be given the status of an "emergency agency."

On March 1, 1961—three weeks after *The Towering Task* had found its way into Shriver's hands—President Kennedy signed Executive Order 10924, giving the Peace Corps its official existence. The president also sent a message to Congress, asking them to prepare to pass Peace Corps legislation. In his message to Congress, Kennedy said, "Our own freedom and the future of freedom around the world depends, in a very real sense, on the underdeveloped countries' ability to build growing and independent nations where men can live in dignity, liberated from the bonds of hunger, ignorance, and poverty." His new program would help these newly independent nations—and these nations, in turn, would be contributing indirectly to the United States. "Our own young men and women," he said, seizing on an aspect of the program that Shriver had strongly recommended he tout, "will return better able to assume the responsibilities of American citizenship and with greater understanding of our global responsibilities." Newspapers across the country put coverage of Kennedy's announcement on their front pages, and many editorials waxed enthusiastic about the new program.

Shriver and his fellow task force members were thrilled: Kennedy had—despite considerable political risk to himself—taken their report to heart and rushed the program into administrative existence. Moreover, the favorable initial public response seemed to have borne out their advice to him. The Peace Corps could now begin to take concrete form.

CHAPTER FOURTEEN

Shriver's Socratic Seminar

B ut who was to run the Peace Corps? In the task force report, Shriver had recommended several academics who had had experience placing students in programs in developing countries. The president rejected all of them on the grounds that an ivory tower academic would not project the adventurous image he wanted the Peace Corps to have. Shriver himself, in contrast, would project that image. According to Gerald Rice's history of the program,

> Kennedy knew that Shriver was young enough to endow the Peace Corps with the vital image which he hoped it might project. He was also bright, handsome and, in the terminology of the New Frontier, "vigorous." Moreover, he was a respected figure in the world of education, business, and civil liberties, and his family ties to Kennedy would give the Peace Corps a much-needed visibility; the appointment of his brother-in-law as Director would also indicate the President's personal interest in the undertaking. These factors, as well as Shriver's sterling work as head of the Task Force, made him an appealing choice.

Shriver, however, strenuously resisted. He had already turned down Abraham Ribicoff—who had asked him to be a cabinet under secretary at the Department of Health, Education, and Welfare—because he thought it would invite charges of nepotism. Being appointed to an executive agency, Shriver thought, would invite even stronger criticism. Top-level cabinet appointments, after all, at least required Senate approval, ensuring that those positions had the congressional imprimatur; the Peace Corps, however, as an executive agency, would not require Senate approval for its director. This, Shriver worried, would make Congress that much hungrier to assert its prerogatives when the time came to pass Peace Corps legislation or to appropriate money for it. "It would be a serious mistake," Shriver wrote to his brother-in-law, "in my judgment, to appoint me as director of the Peace Corps . . . and then make me the only agency head in the government *not* approved by the Senate. This is not good for the agency, the people in it, or for me. When I do have to face Congress . . . they'll be tougher then—and they will have no responsibility for having okayed me now." Why don't you, Shriver advised, pick "another person to head the Peace Corps, which is now well-organized, well-manned, and aimed in the right direction?" But when the president persisted, Shriver acquiesced, on the condition that Kennedy would seek Senate confirmation for the position.

On March 4, Kennedy announced Shriver's appointment as first director of the Peace Corps. A day later, Shriver announced to reporters that the Peace Corps would "take the world by surprise" and that it would amaze people who "think America has gone soft." He appeared before the Senate Foreign Relations Committee in late March and was confirmed as director by the Senate on May 21.

Having been named director, Shriver now had to form the agency. Although he had the task force report as a blueprint, many of the important details had yet to be addressed and none of them had been finalized. No one had spoken to heads of state in developing countries to see if they actually would receive volunteers. Shriver himself had no experience with the federal government. He had no idea how one went about securing arrangements with foreign countries. He didn't know how to prepare legislation. He didn't know how to procure office space or how to put people on the federal payroll. He didn't even know how to find the people who *did* know how to do these things.

In retrospect, Shriver's lack of knowledge may have been one of his greatest assets in starting the Peace Corps. It meant, for one thing, that he didn't know what *couldn't* be done. He wasn't constrained by the bureaucrat's understanding of institutional limitations; he didn't have the elected politician's blinkered view of what was allowable. His boundless energy and optimism were not trammeled by any knowledge of bureaucratic limitations. This expanded the horizons of what was possible.

Shriver's energy and optimism—and his ignorance of proper bureaucratic protocol—infected his task force, as well as the core of staff he began rapidly to recruit after Kennedy had ordered the Peace Corps into existence. The culture of the new agency in its first months—and indeed in its first five years and beyond—was one of cheerful amateurism. Shriver was, of course, able to draw from the beginning on the bureaucratic legerdemain of Josephson and Wiggins, as well as on the administrative resourcefulness of Mary Ann Orlando; as the months passed, a Peace Corps bureaucracy was inevitably formed. But the agency under Shriver's direction never lost the anything-is-possible creative anarchy—a mixture of idealism, naivete, and brilliance—that had characterized it from the beginning.

The early Peace Corps didn't cut red tape so much as shred it. "You guys had a good day today," read a memo from the administrative consultant brought over from the National Aeronautics and Space Administration (NASA). "You broke fourteen laws." By March 15, the agency had carried out at least twenty-two illegal actions. With the signing of the executive order came an initial $1.5 million to spend, as well as three offices on the sixth floor of the ICA's building at 806 Connecticut Avenue. Known as the Maiatico Building, 806 Connecticut was just a few hundred yards from the White House, across Lafayette Park, and it had earlier served as the headquarters for the Marshall Plan. But there was not enough space to accommodate all the new support staff, so Shriver, having no idea how to requisition office space, rented space in the nearby Rochembeau Hotel. Since he didn't know how to procure the money to pay for this space, he paid for these rooms—as well as for supplies, transportation, and other miscellaneous costs—with his Merchandise Mart credit cards and accounts.

The new offices had hardly any furniture. Through the first days of the Peace Corps' existence, its employees were standing, sharing desks, squatting on floors. Albert Sims and Gordon Boyce had only a single desk and chair between them. When one of them had someone in for an appointment, the other would have to go sit on the floor in an adjoining room. Furniture ordered from the federal government, Shriver learned, could take weeks to arrive. Fortunately, Mary Ann Orlando discovered some unused furniture on an upper floor and simply hauled it all downstairs on the elevator. "That's what we did when we started the Peace Corps," Orlando recalled. "We just did what we had to do and filled in the gaps later." Padraic Kennedy, one of the first persons hired by the Peace Corps, recalled "midnight requisitioning" trips, "which meant raiding the AID [formerly ICA] offices in the same building in the middle of the night. It wasn't difficult. The AID people always left at 5:00 p.m., whereas we were working half the night."

The task force was allowed no rest. "We had been prepared to wait a few days, possibly longer" for the announcement of the executive order, Wiggins recalled. "Shriver, of course, knew Kennedy was prepared to go the executive order route, but no one guessed it would happen so fast." Wiggins went to work planning and developing overseas programs. Josephson began working on the legislation for Congress. Boyce began contacting private voluntary agencies that might be given grants to run Peace Corps programs overseas. Al Sims reached out to universities to develop relationships with them for both the administration of overseas programs and the domestic training of volunteers.

In recruiting staff from beyond the ranks of the task force, Shriver was as creative and relentless as he had been in the Talent Hunt during the interregnum. Often, Shriver would make job candidates read Max Millikan's MIT report that had proposed a cautious start to the Peace Corps—and anyone who spoke approvingly of its caution would be promptly rejected. "Shriver didn't want anyone around who was going to be too cautious," one successful applicant recalled.

Peace Corps lore abounds with stories of men yanked abruptly from jobs and personal lives all across the country, summoned by Shriver's insistent voice on the other end of a phone line. "Shriver couldn't wait three months for a guy," Wiggins said. "He had to come at once. So, the first priority was talent and the second was availability. If he found somebody he thought had unusual talent, he'd think of a job for him to do, or let the person create one if there wasn't something on the organization chart that suggested itself." Shriver's recruitment methods stood in stark contrast to normal government hiring procedures. Suddenly, as Wiggins recalled in Coates Redmon's Peace Corps history *Come as You Are*, "Sarge flings open the doors and starts hiring at incredible speed and with great flamboyance a whole slew of people, some of whom came running to us and a few of whom Sarge had to pry out of budding, even spectacular, careers in law, medicine, academia, journalism. Shriver made no pretense that this was an orderly or predictable affair. He was grabbing at talent, period. . . . It really didn't matter what you were—a lawyer, a fisherman, a preacher, a government bureaucrat."

People from diverse professions all over the country heeded Shriver's call. When Kennedy aides Fred Dutton and Pierre Salinger spoke highly of a reporter at the *San Francisco Chronicle* named Tom Matthews, Shriver reached him at a bar in Utah, where Matthews was on a ski vacation. Matthews arrived at Peace Corps headquarters the next day, still wearing his mittens and ski boots. Matthews, in turn, recommended a *Chronicle* colleague, Donovan McClure. When McClure met Shriver he was spellbound. "He was just enormously impressive. All the clichés fit: tall, dark, and handsome. Fit as a college athlete at forty-five. He was warm and friendly and funny—was interested in everything, full of anecdotes. He knew as much about sports as he did about politics and as much about the civil rights movement as he did about theology." McClure soon joined Matthews in the Peace Corps' public affairs office.

Franklin Williams, who would become the Peace Corps' first black executive, had worked with Shriver in the Civil Rights Section of the 1960 campaign. When he came to Washington in 1961 seeking opportunities in the Kennedy administration, Williams dropped in on Shriver at Louis Martin's suggestion. Shriver "began pounding his desk and saying, '*This* is where the action is,'" Williams recalled. "He made it sound so damn exciting." When Shriver asked him to start work right away, Williams explained that he couldn't leave his job in the California attorney general's office. "Yes, you can," Shriver said, and as Williams looked on in wonder, Shriver called the California attorney general and negotiated Williams's instant release from employment there.

Seeking an expert psychologist to establish the standards for selecting volunteers, Shriver called Nicholas Hobbs, the provost of Vanderbilt University in Tennessee who at the time was working on a multimillion-dollar research project. "How much time do I have to decide?" Hobbs asked when Shriver got him on the phone. "Twenty minutes," Shriver said. Hobbs hung up and booked a flight to Washington.

Shriver's recruitment efforts attracted a broad array of talent. Morris Abram, the prominent Georgia attorney who had been one of Shriver's conduits to Martin Luther King Jr. during the campaign, became the Peace Corps' first general counsel. Thomas Quimby, chairman of the Michigan chapter of the Democratic National Committee, helped run volunteer recruitment. Bill Haddad, the Pulitzer Prize–winning *New York Post* reporter who had worked on the Kennedy campaign, signed on as a top aide to Shriver and went on to head up the famous Peace Corps evaluation division. Bill Kelly, who had worked as an administrator for NASA, took charge of logistics and administration.

Charlie Peters, a West Virginia state legislator who had worked on Kennedy's primary campaign in 1960, thought he would "just come up for about three months to share in the exciting task of getting the New Frontier started"—and ended up working in the Peace Corps' evaluation division for five years. Shriver's gravitational force, it seemed, was just stronger than other people's; once you found yourself in his orbit, it was hard to leave, no matter how hard you were working or what the damage to your personal life. "Wives of staff men," Wofford said, "tended to be jealous because Shriver harnessed their husbands' energies and loyalties—and weekends."

Charlie Peters, like many of Shriver's recruits, found the camaraderie and idealism of the Peace Corps staff and volunteers enormously appealing. "In my life, I had met many people I liked but comparatively few who shared my feelings and values," Peters wrote in his memoir, *Tilting at Windmills*. "At the Peace Corps it seemed as if I found someone like that every day. . . . It was exciting to work for the United States government in the early sixties. We walked to the office each morning alive with the sense that we had important business to attend to, serving a country and a president we believed in." Jack Kennedy, Peters wrote, "was an inspiring leader, and I was proud to serve him." Peters felt the same way about Jack's brother-in-law. "Shriver had the kind of charisma that makes men charge the barricades. He inspired enormous effort on the part of those who worked at the Peace Corps."

Perhaps the most significant addition to the new agency was Bill Moyers, who found his own way to the Peace Corps. Moyers was only twenty-six years old in 1961, but he was already something of a legend. Born in Oklahoma, he had grown up to become a Baptist minister in Texas, where he went to work as an aide to Lyndon Johnson, who was then Senate majority leader. Moyers soon distinguished himself as the star on Johnson's staff. He was idealistic but also politically astute; he could be a ruthless Machiavellian operator when he needed to be. He was famous for being one of the few people who could withstand the notorious Johnson barrages—both the unctuously heavy-handed "treatment" the vice president would lavish on people he wanted to impress and the volcanic torrents of profanity he would unleash when he was in one of his fearsome rages. "Johnson would just come in and stand over you and try to overpower you with his physical presence," Shriver recalled. "And he'd do that to Moyers. And Moyers was just a kid, maybe less than 125 pounds. Johnson would yell at him, tell him what to do. And then I'd see Moyers stick his head back, and his jaw would clench and he'd grit his teeth—and say 'No.'" Moyers also had an enormous capacity for hard work under high pressure, although at the expense of painful ulcers that occasionally incapacitated him. By the time Johnson took office as vice president, Moyers was Johnson's top aide.

The job of chief aide to the vice president of the United States was a heady one for a twenty-six-year-old, but Moyers had become intrigued by the Peace Corps. Kennedy's New Frontier resonated with Moyers's idealistic side, and he saw the Peace Corps as its most vivid expression. "In my Baptist church," Moyers later said, "there was a continuing emphasis upon the importance of service, upon the value of commitment, upon expressing your faith in practical, realistic ways." Shriver drew on the same emphases in his Catholicism and was infusing the Peace Corps with them. Moyers didn't know Shriver, but he saw that his organization grew out of this religious motivation as well as out of "the barn building myth . . . [the idea of] America as a social enterprise . . . of caring and cooperative people." So he let it be known that if the new agency had a suitable position available, he would be interested in it. (Moyers, Johnson later recalled, "cajoled and begged and pleaded and connived and threatened and politicked to leave me to go to work for the Peace Corps.") But when Shriver made a move to hire Moyers, Kenny O'Donnell objected angrily. "He's the only one on Johnson's staff we trust," O'Donnell told Harris Wofford, who was by then serving as special assistant to the president. "The president's going to tell him to stay there, and you can tell Sarge to keep his cotton-picking hands off Moyers."

Moyers went directly to President Kennedy, who was so impressed with the strength of Moyers's interest in the Peace Corps that he told him he could go if Shriver wanted him. On March 14 Moyers left Johnson's staff and joined the Peace Corps as a "special consultant." Within two years he would be made the agency's deputy director—the youngest person in history to fill such a high-ranking position in the federal government. Nevertheless, Moyers carried out his most historically significant role in the first few months of the Peace Corps' existence, when he served as the organization's congressional liaison and as an invaluable conduit to the White House. But Kennedy's advisers were not happy with what they saw as the pillaging of the White House staff by the Peace Corps; thenceforward, the Peace Corps had to combat a reputation as a personnel pirate, stealing talent from elsewhere in the federal government.

When Shriver said he intended to have fifty people on the Peace Corps staff within thirty days, the experts at the Bureau of the Budget rolled their eyes; he's crazy, they said. But, as Wofford recalled, "the government's usual lethargic pace was broken and Shriver got his staff." When a General Services Administration budget manager was hired to maintain standard regulations, he found his efforts futile. "Briefly he tried sending around memorandums saying, 'There will be no more overtime unless it is authorized at least three days in advance.' At a time when almost everyone was working overtime, that rule did not last."

No one had ever seen a government agency like this before. Shriver was accomplishing more, faster, and with less, than anyone thought possible—a fact that cheered Peace Corps supporters and worried its detractors. Harris Wofford says that the early Peace Corps days were "an intoxicating and illuminating experience." Working with Shriver, Wofford wrote in *Of Kennedys and Kings*, "was the closest to decision-making through a Socratic seminar that I have ever experienced in government. Except that after listening and questioning, proposing and prodding, Shriver would decide on a course of action, usually with a strong consensus behind him but sometimes in the face of strong opposition."

Another Greek model comes to mind: Alexander was said to have imagined at night, while drunk, but to have decided in the sober light of dawn. There was not much drinking at the Peace Corps, but sometimes the night would end in a free-for-all, in which a new idea would take flight in Shriver's mind and he or his close associates would "shriverize" it. Used behind his back, that verb meant to esca-late, to enlarge, to speed up, to apply greater imagination. Then a second Shriver would preside critically and thoughtfully at the next morning's staff meeting.

Shriver's energy was the fuel the Peace Corps ran on; his optimism was the oxy-gen it breathed. This was powerful stuff: In retrospect, the speed with which he established the Peace Corps as a going entity is astonishing. Today, when the Peace Corps is an established part of the government landscape, it is easy to forget that Shriver, in effect, made something from nothing. "In 1961, President Kennedy had not even given me a bill," Shriver recalled. "Rather I'd had only four or five sentences from a campaign speech in California to go on. It was like seeing a picture of a cake and then told to bake one—there were no ingredi-ents, no measurements, no idea even of what kinds of substances it should include." As Peter Braestrup, one of the reporters who first covered the Peace Corps for the *New York Times*, later reflected, "To get an agency going takes oth-ers two or more years. Shriver did it in six weeks." Warren Wiggins concurred, saying that the speed with which Shriver got the Peace Corps running was "a record for a government agency. Something like a year or two is usually the case. But he got it together [in weeks]; he created its laws, its principles, and he staffed it up."

CHAPTER FIFTEEN

The Battle for Independence

⌒

Disaster nearly struck the new Peace Corps in May. From the earliest days of the task force, Shriver had insisted strenuously that the Peace Corps remain separate from the ICA. Drawing on his own instinctive dislike for entrenched bureaucracy, as well as on what Wiggins and Josephson had told him about the hidebound ways in which the ICA approached foreign aid, he felt that in order to succeed, the Peace Corps had to establish its own identity and not get absorbed into the ICA's way of doing things. If the ICA were to absorb his program, Shriver worried, it would be tantamount to strangling the Peace Corps before it was fully born.

Part of President Kennedy's motivation, after all, in conceiving the idea was the fustiness of the traditional foreign service. In 1958 Eugene Burdick and William Lederer had published a novel called *The Ugly American,* which, although fictional, contained a lacerating attack on US foreign service professionals, whom the authors criticized as hypocritical, incompetent, and cynical. The typical American diplomat in the novel didn't speak the language of the country to which he was posted; lived exclusively in the hermetically sealed world of embassy cocktail parties, limousines, and private clubs; and had little connection with the denizens of the country. Many believed that *The Ugly American* was, at least partially, the inspiration for Kennedy's Ann Arbor and Cow Palace speeches; Kennedy had mentioned the book, saying that it made him "shudder" when he read it.

Although many good people worked at the ICA, the agency represented exactly what Kennedy was reacting against by proposing a Peace Corps. It wouldn't do, Shriver believed, to start this bold new Peace Corps program only to see it folded into the agency it had defined itself against. Wiggins and Josephson, as veterans of the ICA, felt particularly strongly about this, and they egged Shriver on in his campaign for independence. Congress, Josephson had warned him in February, sees the traditional foreign policy establishment as a series of "boondoggles"; developing countries, moreover, perceived that establishment as "imperialist."

Shriver took Josephson's admonitions to heart, and in his report to the president stated that "beginning the Peace Corps as another ICA operation runs the risk of losing its new appeal." Secretary of State Dean Rusk was an ardent supporter of the Peace Corps, so Shriver went to him, telling him that it was important that the Peace Corps not be seen as merely an ICA tool, just "another foreign aid resource like development loans or Food for Peace." Kennedy's vision for the Peace Corps, Shriver reminded Rusk, required "an identifiable, visible body of people, a corps in the fullest sense of the word with an esprit de corps all its own." Only in this way would the new program be seen as distinctively Kennedy's. Rusk concurred, as did his under secretary Chester Bowles, who told Kennedy that there "was wide agreement on the necessity and importance of the Peace Corps maintaining its own separate identity."

Elsewhere, however, there was vehement resistance to an independent Peace Corps. For one thing, under Kennedy's own proposal to reorganize the ICA as the Agency for International Development, the entire US foreign assistance apparatus—with all its constituent components—was to be placed under a single bureaucratic roof. If this proposal, announced in March just days after the launching of the Peace Corps, were to be carried out, then all the federal government's foreign development initiatives would be housed in one place. Why should the Peace Corps be exempt?

Naturally, too, members of the foreign policy establishment resented the

Peace Corps' implicit criticism of their traditional way of doing things—and at the same time, they wanted to make use of what the Peace Corps could provide. As Bill Moyers pointed out, "The old-line employees of State and AID coveted the Peace Corps greedily. It was natural instinct; established bureaucracies do not like competition from new people." And then there was of course the concern that Eisenhower and others had raised: Did the United States really want a bunch of untrained youths running around in alien countries, raising a ruckus and causing trouble for America's "real" foreign policy? If we must have a Peace Corps, the foreign policy traditionalists argued, place it under the direct control of the new AID—that way, at least, an experienced hand can rein in these kids.

If this argument had initially been waged directly between the old-guard foreign policy types on the one hand and Shriver's gang of eager neophytes on the other, the old guard very likely would have prevailed, and the Peace Corps would have been absorbed immediately into AID. But because the president himself had taken such a keen interest in the Peace Corps, and because his brother-in-law was its director, the foreign policy establishment was reluctant to argue too strenuously before it knew what the president wanted. And for the moment, Kennedy was being cryptic; no one knew what he wanted.

A tense bureaucratic standoff began. In late March, when Shriver saw an early draft of Kennedy's message to Congress on the reorganization of foreign aid, he was dismayed to see that the president was planning to situate the Peace Corps in the new AID after all. A few days later, Shriver steamed as he sat through a meeting at the White House in which he was shown AID's organizational chart: The Peace Corps was in a little box on the far right in a section called "resources." As he had feared, his program was being reduced to one among many items in the AID tool kit. He argued his case but to little avail and returned from the meeting angry and uncharacteristically disconsolate. "There are about twenty people in Washington who have our concept of an autonomous Peace Corps," he seethed to his staff at 806 Connecticut Avenue, "and 20 million public administration experts who want a tidy organization chart."

Eunice was at this point in the hospital in Boston with one of her periodic bouts of illness brought on by Addison's disease, and in the midst of all the Peace Corps politicking, Sarge went up from Washington to be with her. As the date of Kennedy's message to Congress approached, Josephson and Wiggins flew up to Boston for a final briefing with Shriver. They met in the basement of the Ritz Carlton to compose a memo to the president, reiterating once more the argument for Peace Corps independence. Shriver also continued to argue by phone with Ralph Dungan, who was heading the AID task force, and with Ted Sorensen and Dick Goodwin, all three of whom thought the Peace Corps should logically reside under AID control. The Peace Corps director's vote should have carried more weight than Dungan's, Sorensen's, or Goodwin's, but as Bill Haddad observed, "in those days the Kennedy people didn't have the respect for Sarge that later developed."

Shriver's emergency memo to Kennedy won the Peace Corps at least a temporary reprieve. In his March 22 message to Congress on foreign aid, the president hedged, saying neither that the program would be located within AID nor outside of it—only that it would retain its "distinctive identity" (this was a nod to Shriver) and be a "flexible tool" (this was a nod to Dungan and the AID crowd) of the foreign aid program. The Peace Corps team regarded the president's ambiguous statement as "a signal to keep pushing," and they did.

But the president's aides remained intransigent, and a week later Kennedy announced that Henry Labouisse, who had been head of the ICA, would coordinate a task force charged with incorporating the disparate foreign assistance programs—including the Peace Corps—into AID. Sensing Shriver's recalcitrance, the president sent him a sternly worded memo saying that he expected Shriver to give Labouisse his full cooperation.

Shriver immediately set about pressing his case with Labouisse, Dungan, and Sorensen, once again making the argument that for both political and practical policy reasons, the Peace Corps would be better off as an independent entity. In a memo he sent to Dungan and Labouisse on April 11, Shriver said that it would destroy the Peace Corps to have it subsumed in the larger foreign aid bureaucracy.

> The Peace Corps . . . embodies a broader concept than foreign aid. In historical terms, the Peace Corps is a new effort in the long history of American initiative in assisting other less fortunate people around the world. . . . Integration of the Peace Corps with the new foreign aid program, however, would jeopardize its ability to win the full support of the kind of individuals and groups who historically have played most important roles in this kind of endeavor. . . .
>
> Politically, the public image of the Peace Corps at home and abroad must

be clear and unfettered. Its obedience to the policies of the State Department and the new aid administrator must not be obvious. It must accomplish its mission under a new banner.

Had the president at San Francisco [in the Cow Palace speech] merely proposed an extension and expansion of ICA . . . the political response would have been negligible. It would not have kindled the dormant idealism of young Americans and certainly not won the praise of Congress.

In the eyes of those abroad particularly, clear connection with foreign aid programs may hurt the Peace Corps. . . . The disadvantages of tying the Peace Corps completely to the foreign aid program and thus to the month-to-month twists of, and reactions to, United States foreign policy are clear.

As White House staff refused to relent, Shriver grew desperate. The clock was running out. The meeting at which the Peace Corps' fate would be decided had been scheduled (purposely, Shriver thought) for April 26, four days after he was to begin a tour of developing countries to try to solicit their interest in receiving Peace Corps volunteers. Dungan and company, Shriver felt sure, would take advantage of his absence to allow AID to devour the Peace Corps. "I don't want to go gallivanting around the world, if, while I'm gone, all of the most fundamental decisions about the Peace Corps' 'bureaucratic stance' are being taken," Shriver wrote to Labouisse.

Thus he ratcheted up the pressure: I don't want to have to do this, he told Dungan and Labouisse, but if I must I will go directly to the president and press my case with him. Labouisse took umbrage at this threat, saying that Shriver's trading on his familial relationship with the president would amount to foul play. Shriver in turn responded with an angry memo to Labouisse, which he copied to the president. "I agree," he wrote, "that we should avoid troubling the president at this time" but—and this was intended to ensure that Kennedy paid attention—"these issues about the future place and role of the Peace Corps are of such fundamental importance that he ought to participate in their resolution. His espousal of the Peace Corps notion in the course of his campaign was an important political commitment, and he has a genuine interest in the success of the Peace Corps as well." It would be a grave mistake, Shriver wrote, to allow "organizational neatness" to take precedence over political wisdom.

An early high noon for the Peace Corps was at hand. Shriver would have liked to stay to press his case at the April 26 meeting himself, but he had told the president he would make this trip. Hoping that the president's own interest in seeing the Peace Corps succeed would carry the day, Shriver left it to Wiggins and Josephson to represent the Peace Corps on April 26, and on April 22 he took off from Idlewild Airport in New York for East Africa, accompanied by Wofford, Franklin Williams, and Ed Bayley, the Peace Corps director of information. The trip was to take them from Ghana to Nigeria, India, Pakistan, Burma, Thailand, Malaya, and the Philippines.

A dark pall dulled the excitement that should have surrounded Shriver's trip. The pall was cast by two sources. First, there was the impending April 26 meeting. Shriver tried to retain his normal optimism, but Wiggins—who had had several encounters with Dungan in which Dungan hinted that the president was on AID's side in the debate—had told him that the situation did not look good.

Second, the American-sponsored invasion of Cuba had ended just a week earlier with the Bay of Pigs disaster. On April 17, in a plan hatched by the CIA under Eisenhower but approved by Kennedy, a group of several hundred Cuban exiles went ashore at Cochinos Bay, hoping to lead a revolt that would bring down the Communist regime of Fidel Castro. The invasion was a dismal failure, and by April 20, two days before Shriver took off from Idlewild, all the invading forces had been captured or killed. This brought Kennedy's popularity, both at home and abroad, to its lowest ebb so far and greatly increased skepticism among developing countries about the benevolence of American intentions. The winds of the cold war blew chillier. All this would make Shriver's job of selling the Peace Corps to the international community that much more challenging. In addition, Kennedy was now being subjected to criticism that said he was a ham-handed executive of foreign policy; this could only, Shriver feared, make the president less open to a more independent role for the Peace Corps. Finally, dealing with the political fallout from the Bay of Pigs debacle was taking most of the president's available time, so he wouldn't be able to attend the foreign aid meeting in person. Instead, he deputized Ralph Dungan to chair the meeting and represent the White House.

This was horrible news. Wiggins and Josephson knew that Dungan, as head of the AID task force, was staunchly opposed to giving the Peace Corps its independence. Sure enough, at the meeting on April 26, while Wiggins and Josephson made the case once again for keeping their program out of the traditional foreign aid establishment, both Labouisse and Bureau of the Budget director Dave Bell argued for folding it into AID. Dungan, chairing the meeting on the president's behalf, made the decision to incorporate the Peace Corps into AID, saying that, as Josephson recorded it in a memo immediately afterward, "the Peace Corps could not be favored or given extraordinary treatment at the expense of overall government considerations."

Shriver was sweltering in his New Delhi hotel room in the 110-degree heat when a telegram from Wiggins arrived. "PEACE CORPS NOT REPEAT NOT TO HAVE AUTONOMY" it said. "DUNGAN DESCRIBES HIMSELF AS ACTING ON BEHALF OF THE PRES-IDENT." "We had lost," Shriver recalled. "The White House had decided to put the Corps in AID. I remember just sitting there for some time, half-way around the world from Washington, holding the bad news in my hand and feeling help-less. I was convinced . . . that the Peace Corps was about to die a-borning."

Shriver paced back and forth in his hotel room, trying desperately to think of how he might save the program. Casting his mind back over the past few weeks, he recalled a discussion he had had with Bill Moyers and Lyndon Johnson, after Moyers had joined Shriver's staff. "Boys," the vice president had said in his inim-itable patois, "this town is full of folks who believe the only way to do something is their way. That's especially true in diplomacy and things like that, because they work with foreign governments and protocol is oh-so-mighty important to them, with guidebooks and rulebooks and 'dos' and 'don'ts' to keep you from offending someone. You put the Peace Corps into the Foreign Service and they'll put striped pants on your people when all you'll want them to have is a knapsack and a tool kit and a lot of imagination. And they'll give you a hundred and one reasons why it won't work every time you want to do something different." Johnson concluded, "If you want the Peace Corps to work, friends, you'll keep it away from the folks downtown who want it to be just another box in an organizational chart."

This articulated Shriver's fears precisely, and at the time of the conversation it had caused him to think that Johnson was smarter and more formidable than some of Kennedy's people seemed to believe. Thinking back on the conversa-tion now, it dawned on Shriver that the vice president might be his only hope. LBJ was "the lone ace up my sleeve," he recalled. He cabled Wiggins and Moyers and told them, "Talk to Lyndon!"

Moyers went to Johnson and, playing on the vice president's sympathy for the Peace Corps' plight, asked him to intercede with Kennedy. Johnson agreed and set up a meeting for May 1. On that day, Kennedy and Johnson met in the Oval Office. Johnson pointed out that the foreign aid general program's unpopularity in Congress would make it hard for the Peace Corps to get funding and that if the new program were to succeed it needed to have a "special identity," distinct from AID's. As Josephson later reported, Johnson "badgered" Kennedy ceaselessly until the president relented. When Johnson finished making the case, Kennedy said, "All right, Lyndon, since its being independent is so all-fired important to you and Sarge, let it be independent."

Wiggins relayed the good news back to Shriver by telegram. Shriver was exuberant. Disaster had been averted. Vice President Johnson had saved the day. Shriver's regard for LBJ reached new heights, and from that point forward he took to calling the vice president "a founding father of the Peace Corps."

The Peace Corps had won its independence. But Dungan, Labouisse, and Bell seethed, especially when a front-page New York Times headline on May 4 blared, "Peace Corps Wins Fight for Autonomy." Kennedy's aides chastised the Peace Corps crew for allowing the story to leak; they suspected Bill Haddad of leaking the story, since he was a friend of Times reporter Peter Braestrup. (Haddad denied being the leak.) Dungan agreed to abide by the president's decision to allow the Peace Corps its independence, but he let it be understood that he was not happy about it. Certain members of Kennedy's staff had always felt cool toward the Peace Corps in general and to Shriver in particular. Now they made it clear that they not only disagreed with Peace Corps independence as a matter of policy but also that they were, as Gerald Rice put it, "extremely annoyed at the unusual methods which Shriver and his team had used to achieve their objectives. Deploying Vice President Johnson was considered particularly sharp practice." So was Shriver's trading on his status as presidential brother-in-law.

"Dungan was highly irritated about these hotshots in the Peace Corps," Josephson recalled. "Ralph called me up and said we were on our own. I said, 'Would you like to come over and talk about this? We're going to be working together for a long time.' And he said, 'Absolutely not. You are on your own. Don't ever come here asking for help.'" If the Peace Corps wasn't going to play by the rules established by the White House staff or by AID, then it shouldn't expect to get any assistance or sympathy from those quarters. Now that the Peace Corps had its independence, it would have to sink or swim on its own.

CHAPTER SIXTEEN

"The Trip"

W ith the specter of absorption in AID no longer haunting the Peace
Corps, Shriver could concentrate on the matter at hand: convincing
leaders of developing countries that they could use Peace Corps assistance. This
promised to be a formidable challenge. Shriver's report to the president had
emphasized that the Peace Corps would go only to the countries that had
invited it—yet to this point, only a single country had seen fit to do so. No one
in the US government had had time to make initial inquiries with foreign leaders until the beginning of April. And now, with the Bay of Pigs fiasco darken-
ing the foreign relations horizon, there was some question whether the Peace
Corps would ever be welcomed anywhere at all.

The first suggestion that there might be a request for volunteers had come
some eight weeks earlier from Tanganyika, an East African nation that was in
the process of gaining its independence. Chester Bowles, the former ambassador to India and now an under secretary of state, had good relations with Julius
Nyere, the Tanganyikan prime minister. An ardent Peace Corps supporter,
Bowles told Nyere about the new program, and the prime minister said he was

at least provisionally interested; the country was about to embark on a national road-building project, and it needed surveyors, geologists, and engineers, among other technical assistance. Nyere inquired whether the Peace Corps might be able to provide that help with the project.

Shriver immediately determined to send a Peace Corps representative to investigate the situation in Tanganyika. He wanted someone who could discern the country's needs and make sure the country was suitable for American involvement—and someone who could get a commitment from the prime minister before he changed his mind about the Peace Corps. But who could do this?

Lee St. Lawrence was a former program officer from the ICA who joined the Peace Corps as one of its first employees in early March. During the 1950s he had worked as a program officer in Laos, Vietnam, and the Belgian Congo. He was "shrewd, learned, utterly unafraid, an almost legendary taker of risks," and he spoke several languages fluently; with his rascally attitude and long-shoreman's profanity he reminded some people of a soldier of fortune. "He was swashbuckling, courageously foolish—or foolishly courageous," Josephson recalled. In the Congo, he twice was beaten up by rebelling Congolese soldiers and once was nearly hanged. St. Lawrence, in short, was just the sort of buccaneering adventurer Shriver admired.

When St. Lawrence volunteered to go to Tanganyika in early March, Shriver eagerly assented. The next day St. Lawrence got on a plane—and vanished. "Didn't hear a word from him for weeks," Josephson said. When St. Lawrence finally returned a month later, Franklin Williams recalled that Shriver turned "phosphorescent" with pleasure at the stories the conquering adventurer told. St. Lawrence told of "bushwhacking the country from end to end in order to see the exact conditions under which volunteers would live and work, all this glamorous stuff about trudging through the high grass, seeing giraffes and Masai warriors, talking politics with the prime minister." Shriver was impressed—and he was, of course, thrilled to hear that Nyere had formally proffered an invitation to the Peace Corps. The audacious success of St. Lawrence's trip set a high standard for Peace Corps excursions; St. Lawrence had made it seem that "with enough determination and imagination . . . anything was possible."

But one country was not nearly enough. Even with Tanganyika enlisted, Shriver felt that the pressure on him to make this trip succeed was enormous.

The first challenge was to get countries to invite him to come and present the case for the Peace Corps. As Wofford recalled, "We were not supposed to fish for invitations, obviously," but Shriver had to "prime the pump of foreign interest." Wofford's own best connections were in India, and when he heard that the Indian ambassador to the United States had expressed an interest in the program, he immediately invited the ambassador to his house for dinner with Shriver. At dinner, Shriver enthusiastically regaled Ambassador B. K. Nehru— a cousin of Jawaharlal Nehru, the Indian prime minister—with his plans for the Peace Corps, explaining how he thought young American volunteers could provide valuable assistance on the subcontinent. Through it all, however, the ambassador remained impassive, apparently impervious to Shriver's charm and energy. The evening seemed destined to end in disappointment: If India, the world's largest democracy and the leader of the "neutral bloc" of countries officially aligned with neither the United States nor the Soviet Union, was not interested in Peace Corps volunteers, what country would be?

But as Ambassador Nehru walked out the door of Wofford's house, he looked over his shoulder and addressed Shriver: "Am I correct, Mr. Shriver, in thinking that you would not be averse to an invitation from our prime minister to visit India and talk about your program?" Shriver's heart rose. Several days later, an invitation from Prime Minister Nehru arrived via the State Department.

Once word leaked out—and Shriver made sure that it did—that India had invited him to discuss the Peace Corps, invitations from other countries soon followed, and an eight-country itinerary was rapidly thrown together.

Shriver and his team took off from New York on April 22. The first overnight stay on the itinerary was Accra, the capital of Ghana, on the west coast of Africa. Upon arrival in Ghana, Shriver found himself stricken with laryngitis—perhaps a result of his having stayed up all night on the flight from New York, playing cards and drinking gin martinis with Thurgood Marshall, soon to be named to the federal bench by President Kennedy, and who happened to be on the same plane. At his press conference at the airport Shriver rasped, "Sorry, I've lost my voice. But that's all right. The Peace Corps' purpose in Ghana is to listen and learn." In Shriver's meeting with the Ghanaian president, Kwame Nkrumah, Nkrumah told him that he didn't want Peace Corps volunteers "indoctrinating our young people. So don't come as social science teachers. . . . You should come to teach science and mathematics. We don't want you to *affect* them; we just want you to *teach* them. Agreed?" Although Peace Corps volunteers would in the course of events profoundly "affect" their students, Shriver agreed. "Fine," Nkrumah said. "We will invite a small number of Peace Corps teachers. . . . Can you get them here by August?" One country down, seven to go.

Next on the itinerary was Nigeria, which just months earlier had gained its independence from the British. The country, although rich in oil resources, lacked the skilled workforce necessary to take advantage of oil development. The key to building such a workforce was education, but there was a shortage of Nigerian teachers: Only 14,000 classroom slots were available for the more than 2 million school-age children.

Shriver perceived a golden opportunity for the Peace Corps and hoped that Nigeria's leaders would recognize how his program could help the country. They did. Both President Nnamdi Azikiwe and Prime Minister Tafawa Balewa greeted him warmly, expressing their wish that Peace Corps volunteers might help them staff Nigerian classrooms and teach English.

Because Nigeria comprised a loose federation of independent states, Shriver had been advised that if he wanted to get Peace Corps volunteers into the country, he would need to gain the support not just of the national leaders Balewa and Azikiwe but also of regional heads of government and various cabinet ministers. So over a frenetic three days, Shriver and company crisscrossed the country by car and airplane, visiting seven of Nigeria's largest cities and towns to consult with government officials.

The next stop was India. India, Wofford later wrote, "was the hardest and most critical test of the trip—and with its half billion people and leading role in the Third World, it was our chief objective." But the Indians, already wary about what seemed to them America's imperial designs on the developing world, had been further alarmed by President Kennedy's ill-fated invasion of Cuba. Fortunately, Chester Bowles, who had been the American ambassador there during Truman's second term, was still a highly popular figure in India. He made sure Prime Minister Nehru, as well as his daughter Indira, received Shriver's team openly. Still, Shriver and company had to work hard to convince their Indian hosts that any Peace Corps projects would not be undertaken in a "neocolonial spirit." It was possible, Shriver insisted, to teach poultry production without pre-

suming to "teach democracy to a nation that since 1948 had been regularly holding the world's largest free elections." The grandiosity of what Shriver thought
the United States could accomplish in the world was considerable—but his
humility about what the United States still needed to learn was genuine. He
emphasized that Peace Corps volunteers would seek not merely to teach technical skills to Indians but also to learn from them about democracy.

This argument seems to be what won Nehru over. During his meeting with
Shriver, Nehru reclined deep in his chair and appeared to sleep as the Peace
Corps director described how the program might be beneficial to India. But
Nehru roused himself and said, "I am sure young Americans would learn a
good deal in this country and it could be an important experience for them."
Saying he would be happy to receive a small number of volunteers, Nehru then
warned Shriver not to expect too much. "I hope you and [the volunteers] will
not be too disappointed if the Punjab, when they leave, is more or less the same
as it was before they came."

This was not exactly a rousing endorsement of the Peace Corps' prospects,
but that hardly mattered. The mere fact that Nehru would allow volunteers
into India would signal to other developing countries that the Peace Corps
should be welcomed. John Kenneth Galbraith, President Kennedy's ambassador to India, had predicted that Nehru's diffidence would make him unrecep-
tive to Shriver's entreaties and had advised Shriver not to ask for too much. But
after watching the meeting between Nehru and Shriver, Galbraith wrote in his
diary that he left the prime minister's office "a little dazed and with my reputation as a strategist in poor condition." "The Peace Corps had to succeed so
as to prove that idealism was still worthwhile—to disprove the case of those
who considered kindness to be subversive," Galbraith wrote. "Then Sarge took
over and made an eloquent and moving plea on behalf of his enterprise. The
effect was just right—natural, uncontrived, and sincere."

Once India had agreed to receive volunteers, Pakistan, Thailand, Malaya
(now Malaysia), and the Philippines all followed suit readily. In Rangoon,
Burma, U Nu and his government received the Peace Corps team warmly and
gave them an elaborate reception at Nu's residence. At one point, Nu took
Shriver off to the side and said, "Mr. Shriver, do you believe that there are young
Americans who would volunteer to work in the jungles of north Burma with
the same zeal for democracy as young Chinese Communists are doing for their

cause?" "I told him yes, absolutely," Shriver recalled, but "my reply was based on faith rather than knowledge. At that time I had never so much as laid eyes on a Peace Corps volunteer."

The trip was a triumph: all eight countries that Shriver formally visited had invited Peace Corps volunteers. Within days of their return to the United States, Wofford, putting on his hat as special assistant to the president, was moved to send a memo to Kennedy singing the Peace Corps director's praises. "Shriver is a born diplomat," Wofford wrote.

> I have never been witness to so successful an international operation. His meetings with government officials, newsmen, and private citizens all produced good results for the Peace Corps and US relations. Our ambassador and other overseas officers in every country expressed to me and others their admiration at how much was accomplished in such a short time, and their increased hopes for the Peace Corps in their respective countries.

Despite these successes, Shriver's traveling companions at times found the experience trying. For Franklin Williams and Peace Corps public relations official Ed Bayley, this was their first prolonged exposure to Shriver. They marveled at him. The first thing Williams noted was that his boss was "absolutely indefatigable." In "twenty-six days, in and out of eleven countries, if you count all the detours and airports, [Shriver] never got tired," Williams said. "I found it irritating."

Williams also noted the devoutness of Shriver's Catholicism. "He kept a Bible with him. He often consulted it. He got up at 5:00 a.m. to go to mass in any city, town, or village, in any country, where there was an available Catholic church that held early mass." Finally, Williams was both impressed and annoyed at the needless hardships Shriver would endure "to avoid the appearance of being on a 'junket'—the idea of a government official taking his ease on an alleged 'fact-finding tour' at the taxpayer's expense." "Why," Ed Bayley wondered, "does Sarge insist in running the Peace Corps as if it was the last stage of a presidential campaign?"

Shriver returned to Washington a conquering hero. Not only had the Peace Corps' independence been secured—through the intervention of LBJ—but there were also now eight countries to which a total of 3,000 volunteers could be sent. Once word spread of the eight invitations, more flooded into the office at 806 Connecticut Avenue unsolicited. Within a week of Shriver's return on May 17, President Kennedy announced that there had been more than two dozen formal requests for volunteers. By early July, the first six Peace Corps projects—in Tanganyika, Ghana, the Philippines, Columbia, Chile, and St. Lucia—had been officially announced.

Shriver came back from his trip with "a lot of important scalps on his belt," recalled Charlie Peters. "He had negotiated with some of the most fabled and powerful third world leaders during a period when the third world was not anti-American per se, but was certainly suspicious about any kind of neocolonial approaches and which was by and large burning up with independence fever. Sarge had no previous training or experience in international diplomacy nor any experience in the federal bureaucracy, and yet, while he was accomplishing the former he was also pulling off the latter, forcing the issue of bureaucratic independence at a remove of 10,000 miles. Having accomplished all of this in less than thirty days, he came back home *more* than the brother-in-law of the president."

CHAPTER SEVENTEEN

Storming Capitol Hill

When President Kennedy brought the Peace Corps into existence with his executive order on March 1, he made clear that its funding—which came for the time being from his executive branch discretionary funds—was temporary. Only Congress could appropriate money for it on an ongoing basis. This meant that Shriver's next task was to persuade Congress, and in particular the skeptical Southern conservatives, to pass Peace Corps legislation. Despite the program's general popularity, this would not be easy. Congress was notoriously hostile to foreign assistance programs in general (in early March, for instance, the very week Kennedy signed the Peace Corps executive order, the House Appropriations Committee refused to authorize a single dollar of the $150 million in foreign policy emergency funds the president had asked for) and was feeling particularly ornery about the Peace Corps. Members of Congress felt that the president had usurped their prerogatives by launching the program via executive order. The White House received letters from aggrieved senators and representatives.

Shriver initially assumed that he would have significant assistance from the White House in selling the Peace Corps on Capitol Hill. After all, the president had reaped considerable political benefit from his support of the program, and it was closely identified with the New Frontier. Moreover, a majority of Americans seemed to be in favor of the Peace Corps. *Time* magazine had recently reported that "the Peace Corps had captured the public imagination as had no other single act of the Kennedy Administration." It seemed Kennedy would have little to lose by deploying White House aides to help in crafting political strategy.

But Kennedy's aides had other ideas. When Ralph Dungan had told Bill Josephson that the Peace Corps was on its own now, he had meant it: If Shriver and company weren't going to play along with AID, then they could damn well craft their own legislative strategy. According to Josephson, Dungan and Larry O'Brien derided the Peace Corps people as "empire builders." As Wofford recalled, "When we returned home [from the trip to Africa and Asia] at the end of May, we found there was a price to pay for the Peace Corps' newfound freedom. It took Shriver a few weeks to realize what was happening: O'Brien and the White House congressional staff were doing nothing whatsoever to promote the Peace Corps Act."

When the White House staff's recalcitrance became apparent to Shriver, he initially assumed that the president himself was unaware of it. Flying to Cape Cod one weekend, he mentioned this to Eunice. That weekend in Hyannis Port, she mentioned the situation to her brother. "If Sarge hadn't demanded that it be separate," Jack replied (as Eunice later reported it to her husband), "I would have only had to ask for a congressman's support once and we could have got AID and the Peace Corps together. But now I left it out there by itself at their request—they wanted it that way, they didn't want me to have it in AID where I wanted it—so let them go ahead and put the son of a bitch through." Getting the AID bill through was going to be "goddamn difficult," Jack told his sister, and he didn't want to then have to turn around and worry about getting the Peace Corps through, too.

Eunice went back to Sarge and told him: "Jack feels that you and Lyndon demanded that the Peace Corps be separate and that therefore you ought to get your damn bill through Congress by yourselves." "The business of trading favors," Wofford wrote in *Of Kennedys and Kings*, "was bad enough among politicians, but it seemed even worse to him among brothers-in-law. Because of that family relationship, [Shriver] says, he 'never spoke one more word to President Kennedy asking him or anybody in the White House ever to do anything for the Peace Corps—ever again.'"

Shriver later recalled his reaction to Jack's response.

In wanting to have the Peace Corps have a separate identity . . . I then found myself saddled, you might say, with *all* of the responsibility, because I had made that request. So I said, "Okay, if it's my baby, I will never ask anyone for help again." And I never did. . . . I just took the bull by the horns and said, "Okay, it's the Peace Corps against everybody else." If it had to be done entirely by ourselves, I was damned well sure it was going to be done successfully.

From the moment Eunice conveyed the president's go-it-alone dictum for the Peace Corps, Shriver said, "I really went to work." Shriver approached Hubert Humphrey and Henry Reuss, who, as sponsors of previous legislation relating to the Peace Corps, were natural choices to be floor managers for the bill in the Senate and the House. Humphrey's assistance was crucial. As Senate majority whip, Humphrey had considerable influence over his fellow Democrats; and with a seat on the Foreign Relations Committee, he was well positioned to help shepherd the bill from committee to the Senate floor. In anticipation of having to help a Peace Corps bill through Congress, Shriver had on March 5 paid a call on the most powerful man in the House of Representatives, Lyndon Johnson's old congressional colleague Sam Rayburn, the Speaker of the House, seeking his advice and support.

In late March he had placed Bill Moyers—who despite his youth had had plenty of legislative experience from working as LBJ's deputy when Johnson was Senate majority leader—in charge of establishing a congressional liaison office for the program, modeled on the White House operation run by Larry O'Brien. On March 22, the office had begun planning its congressional strategy. Josephson took the lead in drafting the bill, with the assistance of Moyers, Wiggins, Morris Abram, and Roger Kuhn, a lawyer who had drafted legislation for the ICA. Kuhn and Abram argued that ultimate authority for the Peace Corps should reside in the program's director, in order to signal its independence. Josephson disagreed, arguing that authority should in the end reside with the president, so that if the Peace Corps were to come under bureaucratic assault at some point in the future, it would have the president's protection. The sacrifice of some autonomy, he argued, would be well worth the insurance this would provide. Josephson also suggested that the Peace Corps ask for only a year's appropriation at a time. If the program had to approach Congress every year, Josephson reasoned, it would assuage congressional anxiety about the Peace Corps' becoming "a renegade, uncontrollable organization."

The drafting of the bill was completed on May 11, and it was submitted for review to the Bureau of the Budget, the State Department, and the White House. At this point, Shriver and Moyers cranked into action, storming Capitol Hill. Hubert Humphrey had told Shriver, "Forget about talking to women's clubs in Detroit." Shriver had been making speeches to various groups across the country in the hopes of building and sustaining popular support for his program. "They don't get your bill passed. We in the Congress do. Don't sit down to another meal between now and the time your Peace Corps bill comes up for a vote unless there is a senator or a congressman sitting by your elbow. . . . Make each senator feel like you care about his views. Massage our egos." Moyers also sought advice from LBJ, who like Humphrey advised that Shriver and Moyers call on as many individual congressional members as possible. "You've got a great asset in Shriver," Johnson told Moyers. "No member of Congress will turn you down because it is the president's brother-in-law and they will know that that will give them cachet as well as access" to the White House.

Peace Corps legend has it that between them Moyers and Shriver personally called on every single member of Congress. As one of Humphrey's aides later commented, "Shriver and Moyers carried on the greatest romance act with the Congress since Romeo and Juliet, and they literally saw over 400 House members and senators."

Shriver and Moyers launched each day with a breakfast on Capitol Hill with several congressmen. Following breakfast they would wander the congressional office buildings, going from appointment to appointment, preaching the gospel of the Peace Corps. Moyers would brief Shriver before each meeting, telling him the congressman's background and interests and recommending how Shriver should couch his description of the program. Sometimes, once all their scheduled appointments for the day were through, Shriver and Moyers would patrol the congressional hallways from door to door, looking for offices with lights on, trying to find more people to talk to.

"You know why I really voted for the Peace Corps?" one House member later asked. "One night I was leaving about seven-thirty and there was Shriver walking up and down the halls, looking into the doors. He came in and talked to me. I still didn't like the program but I was sold on Shriver—I voted for him." This scenario, or variations on it, recurred over and over. One night, Shriver and Moyers were walking the halls and came upon the office of Barry Goldwater, the notoriously conservative senator from Arizona. As Shriver recalled, he turned to Moyers and said, "I think I'll just go in and ask him whether or not he would vote for the Peace Corps." Moyers told him not to bother, that they had no chance of winning over Goldwater. Shriver recalls, "I said, 'Well, I'm sure that we're not going to get him if we never even ask him.' So we rapped on the door and went in, and fortuitously he was there and willing to talk to us. We talked for an hour, after which he said, 'That sounds like a great idea. I'll vote for it.'"

All through the spring and summer of 1961, Shriver and Moyers kept up their barrage on Congress—"saturation bombing," they called it. Shriver was eager not to appear partisan, and he pursued Republicans and Democrats with equal vigor. But he concentrated on the program's most ardent and public doubters, like Goldwater, Southern conservatives, and Congresswoman Frances Bolton of Ohio, who said she thought the Peace Corps to be a "terrifying scheme" and that it gave her "the shivers to think of ill-prepared American youths getting into all kinds of trouble in remote foreign lands." One by one, he brought the doubters into the Peace Corps camp. Marguerite Stitt Church, a Republican on the House Foreign Affairs Committee, later said she could think of no one who had "made such an effort to bring his story personally to members of Congress."

On June 1, Hubert Humphrey introduced the Peace Corps bill in the Senate, asking for $40 million in appropriations for the first year. Later that month, Shriver appeared before the Senate Committee on Foreign Relations. He dazzled the committee, not only with his charisma, but with his detailed knowledge of Peace Corps spending plans. He knew how much everything would cost—from jeeps to administration overhead—and repeatedly assured the committee that the program would be cheap and efficient.

With the vote looming sometime in the late summer or early fall, Moyers and Humphrey calculated that the Peace Corps bill would likely pass. It helped the bill's cause that the Peace Corps selection committee had seen fit to recruit and announce volunteers from the districts of the doubting congressmen, adding to the pressure for a yea vote. By midsummer, it seemed conceivable that the Peace Corps might send volunteers into the field before the bill was voted. There was a danger in the Peace Corps' appearing to outrun its mandate—thereby further antagonizing Congress—but Shriver thought the chances for legislation would improve if volunteers were already in action.

The process of volunteer selection and training had been under way throughout the summer. Soon, however, it became apparent that recruiting and selecting volunteers would be harder than had been expected. During the task force planning phase, Shriver had anticipated there would be 15,000 serious applicants within the first few months of the program. But by the time Shriver embarked on his tour of Southeast Asia and West Africa in late April, the flow of applications had slowed to a few hundred per week.

Shriver took pleasure in telling Congress that it would be hard to become a Peace Corps volunteer and that selection standards would be rigorous. Every applicant had to provide six references and then submit to a battery of tests—one of which was a six-hour general exam—established by psychologist Nicholas Hobbs, the Peace Corps' first chief of selection, who had helped screen Air Force personnel during the Second World War. This winnowing process meant that only one out of every five applicants made it through to training, with additional cuts being made during the training period. Although this process did ensure a higher caliber of volunteer (and it did assuage Congress), it also made Shriver's projections about the number of volunteers who would be in the field before 1962 that much harder to reach. In May, Warren Wiggins sent Shriver a telegram in Africa warning that if the number of applicants didn't rise soon, the program would be in trouble. Newspaper reporters were starting to ask, "Where are all those aspiring volunteers Shriver has been braying about?"

At Wiggins's urging, Shriver refocused his attention on recruitment and assigned Bill Moyers to spearhead those efforts. Shriver assured reporters that the recruitment process was going well and that if the quantity was somewhat lower than anticipated, well, the quality was even higher than he could have hoped. Privately, however, he was "in a sweat," worried that he would not be able to deliver on the promises that he had made to foreign heads of state and that this would enrage Congress.

Consequently, he threw himself into recruiting, personally approaching CEOs (whom he asked to grant leaves of absences to volunteers) and college presidents (whom he asked to promote the program among their student bodies). Meanwhile, he authorized a substantial public relations and advertising effort: Peace Corps advertisements appeared in subways and on television; a Peace Corps information booth was set up in the middle of Times Square. Shriver and his public affairs staff fed Peace Corps stories to newspaper reporters and magazine journalists, to great effect: the Peace Corps had astonishingly good press coverage from the moment of its launch.

Shriver had a knack for publicity and formulated the Peace Corps' image in such a way that would attract attention. Sometimes his apparent predilection for gloss over substance surprised even his public relations staff. Once, a staff member brought him a detailed, generally positive piece that had just appeared on the front page of the *New York Times*. Shriver read it, said, "That's nice," and then casually put it aside. A few minutes later, when he was handed a Chicago gossip column that described him changing from his business suit into a tuxedo as he sped in a taxicab from the airport to the White House for a dinner, he lit up with pleasure. "This is how to score," he scrawled across the clipping. "Let's have more of this kind of thing."

"The Peace Corps," CBS commentator Eric Sevareid said archly, "is pure intentions supported by pure publicity." But although there is no doubt that Shriver had a showman's desire to entertain, these antics were driven by a serious purpose: Shriver calculated that by giving the program an aura of dash and color to go along with its natural reputation for adventurous hardship in the field, he could keep the American people interested in the Peace Corps.

The publicity assault paid off. By June the Peace Corps had received enough applications to yield a good number of qualified volunteers, and Shriver was once again able to concentrate on his member-by-member sales job on Capitol Hill and on his wooing of foreign leaders.

In June he flew to West Africa to meet with Sekou Toure, the president of Guinea. Guinea had become an independent state only in 1958, and Toure was a strong leader, a fierce nationalist who was in the process of turning the country into the first overtly Marxist state in Africa. Both Red China and the Soviet Union were already providing manpower and technical assistance. The

Kennedy administration was eager to keep Guinea from turning to the Soviet Union for further succor or financial support. Providing Peace Corps assistance might be one way of doing this. Although Toure would in fact soon make Guinea into a quasi-client state of the Soviet Union, Shriver did succeed in getting the Peace Corps into Guinea, and the program's presence in a Communist-inflected country gave it considerable international credibility.

Shriver returned from Guinea to find the Peace Corps legislation still hanging in the balance. Some members of Congress, still fuming that the executive order appeared to have bypassed their right to advise and consent, were threatening to exact their revenge by delaying a vote on the bill indefinitely. Unwilling to approach Kennedy or his staff for assistance—and unlikely to receive it at this point, even if he had—Shriver turned once again to the man he was coming to recognize as a political genius, Lyndon Johnson. Johnson, Shriver knew, was as shrewd a congressional tactician as ever graced the Capitol. So he wrote to the vice president in July, explaining that further delay in passage of Peace Corps legislation would "seriously damage" the program and "embarrass the president and the administration politically." Johnson responded right away, and he met personally with key senators to press the case for the bill.

Still, the bill continued to languish. As August approached it became apparent that the biggest obstacle to its passage in the Senate was not, for the moment, Republicans hostile to foreign assistance but rather the indifference of Arkansas senator William Fulbright, who chaired the all-important Foreign Relations Committee. Fulbright was a Democrat and for the most part friendly to the administration, but he was highly skeptical about the Peace Corps' potential effectiveness. He worried that it would have a hard time attracting high-quality volunteers and that it would alienate the developing world by being only a one-way—not a reciprocal—program; inflicting ill-trained youth on developing countries as a way of "helping" them could only appear patronizing. More selfishly, Fulbright also worried that the Peace Corps might prove an unwelcome competitor for his own Fulbright Fellowship program, which provided funding for educational exchange. Although it seemed unlikely that Fulbright would decline to release the bill from his committee and thereby prevent a full Senate vote, Shriver feared that the Arkansas senator would recommend shrinking the program before voting on it.

Sure enough, on August 3 the *New York Times* quoted Fulbright as recommending decreased funding for the Peace Corps. In the draft of the bill circulating on the Hill, Shriver had requested $40 million for fiscal year 1962; Fulbright was intimating that he wanted the figure cut to only $10 million. Such funding cuts, the *Times* reported, would "cripple the Peace Corps, embarrass the President abroad, and encourage the more conservative House [of Representatives] to make even deeper cuts."

Infuriated, Shriver lobbied everyone he could think of, requesting that they apply whatever pressure they could on Fulbright and the Senate Foreign Relations Committee. "Peace Corps appropriation serious danger being cut in half," Shriver cabled to Ambassador Galbraith in New Delhi, in a typical plea. "Respectfully suggest telephone call from you to chairman Senate Foreign Relations Committee expressing your evaluation and support for our program. Your opinion highly regarded by the chairman who is today our principal stumbling block. . . . Our request $40,000,000. Urgent it not slip below $35,000,000."

Shriver was concerned enough that he even violated his pledge never to ask anything of the president or his staff. On August 3, he asked Larry O'Brien, the White House congressional liaison, to support the Peace Corps cause with Democratic members of the Foreign Relations Committee. It would be "good to point out to them the political importance of that committee's reporting out $40,000,000. Unless the Senate committee reports out that much, we will be cut substantially in the House. . . . I hesitate to bother you when you are so busy on other matters, but I believe very firmly that the Peace Corps is essential to the political image of President Kennedy."

Shriver had gleaned from Moyers numerous lessons about how Congress worked, one of which was that momentum was crucial. His greatest fear, as he intimated in his memo to O'Brien, was that if the liberal-leaning Senate began trimming funding for the Peace Corps, the more conservative House members would take this as a cue to slash even more deeply. Thus he had, on August 2, sent a frustrated memo to the president, asking that he make more active use of his bully pulpit in promoting the program. "Unless we can build a climate of opinion in which the Peace Corps is considered 'must' legislation," Shriver wrote, "we are in trouble—regardless of the general goodwill that surrounds this proposal." The White House, Shriver continued, must provide sufficient leadership and pressure so that there will be no doubt in the minds of Congress that the president feels the bill must be passed this session. Unless the White House supplies this leadership, the lateness of the session alone"—it would be ending in the fall— "may doom the chances for Peace Corps legislation and appropriations this session." After the Senate Foreign Relations Committee voted, the whole Senate would have to vote; then the House would have to vote on its bill; then the two bills would have to go to a House-Senate conference to be reconciled. The congressional session might end, Shriver worried, before a bill was sent to Kennedy for his signature. "Bill Moyers and I have been living on the Hill," Shriver told Kennedy. But "at this point the Peace Corps itself has done all it can on the Hill." It was time for the White House to do its part.

On August 4, Shriver testified in the House, and he was grilled by hostile Republicans. "Throughout the two hours of verbal bombs in the chilly atmosphere," the *Washington Post* reported, "Shriver rarely showed any sign of discomfort. He did bite his lip, and clenched his fist a time or two. But he remained composed and answered every question politely and in detail." When he left the House floor, an aide took him aside to give him some exciting news: While he was testifying in the House, Fulbright's Foreign Relations Committee had unanimously (14–0) approved legislation to authorize the Peace Corps—and the entire $40 million to finance it. The full Senate and House still had to vote, but a major obstacle had been surmounted.

Now Kennedy brought his presidential weight to bear on the issue. "The Peace Corps," he said in a press conference on August 10, "has had a most promising beginning, and we have an opportunity if the amount requested by the Peace Corps is approved by Congress, of having 2,700 volunteers serving the cause of peace in fiscal year 1962."

The debate over the bill began on the full Senate floor on August 24. Hubert Humphrey and Senate majority leader Mike Mansfield took the lead in arguing against an amendment proposed by Iowa Republican Bourke Hickenlooper that would have "cut $15 million out of the unnecessary fat" in the Peace Corps appropriations request. Fulbright said he still had "misgivings" and voted, along with seven other Democrats, in favor of the funding reduction, but the Hickenlooper amendment was defeated. On August 25 the Peace Corps Act passed the Senate.

Shriver's attention now turned to the House. He knew the House was generally more likely than the Senate to slash his funding, but he was particularly concerned about the House Subcommittee on Appropriations, headed by the fearsome Louisiana Democrat Otto Passman, who was as conservative as anyone in Congress on fiscal matters. He loathed public spending; he abhorred foreign aid. He would not, needless to say, be inclined to grant Shriver's funding request.

Shriver and Moyers and their aides had paid multiple visits to Passman, where they had been treated to his florid denunciations of the Peace Corps. Oddly enough, in all the time he spent cultivating the colorful, flinty Southerner, Shriver had grown to like and respect him. That feeling was reciprocated. In his memo to Kennedy of August 2, Shriver had noted that he and Moyers "may even have laid the foundation for at least the beginnings of a good working relationship with Congressman Passman."

This didn't mean that Passman would make life any easier politically for Shriver. "You know, Ah lahk you Saahge," Passman would drawl, "but the Peace Corps is a terrible idea and I'm not going to vote for its full appropriation." In conversations in his House office, Passman was ever the courtly gentleman, but he warned that he would savage Shriver and his team during congressional testimony. "Nothin pehsonal, Saahge," Passman would say before grilling him relentlessly on the House floor.

The day before the House vote, opponents of the bill were trying to delay action on the bill until 1962, or to slash its funding in half. Shriver, wanting to leave as little as possible to chance, continued to lobby individual congressmen, spending all his free time on Capitol Hill. This effort paid off in an unexpected way. As Shriver recalled, "When the Peace Corps legislation was on the floor of the House, I still did not have an office of my own [in the Capitol], and so I was sitting in a cubbyhole off a corridor in the House Office Building making frantic phone calls to my political strategists. Old Judge Howard Smith, a Virginia representative and the apotheosis of conservatism, walked by and shouted, 'Hey, Shriver! What are you doing there?' I explained my predicament. And this courtly curmudgeon—who might never in his life agree with anything I stood for—took me into his office, sat me in his chair, and instructed his secretary to give me the run of the place and the use of his phone."

This was a significant gesture. Congressman Smith was, as Shriver noted, a hard-core conservative and a likely opponent of the Peace Corps bill. Smith was also chairman of the House Rules Committee, in which position he had the power to prevent bills he didn't like from even getting to the House floor.

By September, Shriver had personally called on Smith four or five times; as a consequence, the two men had struck up a cheerfully adversarial friendship.

Smith seemed to develop a strong respect for Shriver. Still, Smith wasn't about to use personal affection as a justification for voting in favor of a bill that his conservative constituency loathed. He couldn't vote for the Peace Corps legislation. So he absented himself from the Capitol on the day the vote was to take place, claiming pressing business elsewhere. This meant that although he wouldn't be casting a vote in favor of the Peace Corps, he could at least avoid having to cast a vote against it.

Better yet, Smith allowed Shriver the continued use of his office while the congressman was away from the Capitol. This was not just a matter of convenience. As Rules Committee chairman, Smith had an office directly off the House floor. The congressman was sending a powerful message to his colleagues: I may not be here to vote on this bill, Smith seemed to be saying to his congressional peers, but you can all see that I've given its principal advocate the use of my office and you can infer my thoughts on this matter from that. "I had the chairman's goddamned office," Shriver recalled. "And anybody who had any doubt in his mind about the bill was on my side right away. It was not that they were voting for the Peace Corps; these guys were voting because they wanted to maintain a nice relationship with the Rules chairman."

With Smith's tacit support, the bill sailed through: On September 14, the House passed the Peace Corps bill by a margin of 288 to 97. After a House-Senate conference reconciling their two bills, President Kennedy signed the Peace Corps Act on September 22, establishing the Peace Corps on a permanent basis.

Of all the bills Kennedy sent to Congress, only the uncontroversial disarmament agency bill had passed by a larger margin in the House than the Peace Corps bill. Much of this was attributable to the cultural climate: The pent-up idealism of the 1950s was ready for expression, and the Peace Corps was its outlet. Public support for the idea had been strong ever since Kennedy had first raised it on the campaign trail. Moreover, despite the Bay of Pigs fiasco, Kennedy was still enjoying his honeymoon period with Congress. With the president and the public so strongly behind the Peace Corps, Congress felt considerable pressure to fall in line behind it as well.

Even so, Shriver's personal role in getting the legislation passed was remarkable. The speed with which he conceived and threw together a new organization, the success he had in coaxing invitations from wary developing nations, the remarkable two-man assault he and Moyers staged on Capitol Hill—all this helped give even some diffident members of Congress great confidence in the Peace Corps director. ("If we had ten Sargent Shrivers we could conquer the world," said Wyoming senator Gale McGee.) Many of them, in fact, later said that even though they disliked the Peace Corps, they had voted for the bill because they thought so highly of Shriver. President Kennedy paid tribute to this notion when, as he signed the bill on September 22, he turned to his right, grinned, and said, "Also, I want to express my esteem for the most effective lobbyist on the Washington scene, Mr. Sargent Shriver."

As the *New York Times* reported a few months later, the passage of the Peace Corps legislation "erased the impression long held in some Washington circles that Shriver is merely another Kennedy-in-law, a glamorous Yale dilettante who espouses liberal causes . . . and married the boss's daughter Eunice. Now, he suddenly begins to look like one of those rare animals in Washington: the fellow who can get things done."

CHAPTER EIGHTEEN

Shriverizing

Ralph Waldo Emerson once observed that an institution is the lengthened
shadow of one man—and to a remarkable degree, the Peace Corps was a
direct reflection of the man who first led it; in some sense, the Peace Corps *was*
Sargent Shriver. Bradley Patterson, the Peace Corps' first executive secretary,
recalled that Shriver "[projected] himself onto his staff and everybody who
worked for or had relations with the Peace Corps." "Stylistically," according
to Albert Meisel, one of the Peace Corps' first training officers, the program
"was 100 percent Shriver—kind of an eagle-scout-on-the-make style." The president was saying, "Let's get this country moving again . . . and there we were,
most of us about thirty [years old], in a huddle with the president's brother-
in-law, *making things happen!* I think that the Peace Corps was probably even
more exciting, innovative, and daredevil than anything in the New Deal."
Journalists and historians have made similar observations. As Gerald Rice put
it in *The Bold Experiment*, "No organization chart could possibly convey Shriver's
all-pervading influence. Since everything important went through him, the
image of the Peace Corps and Sargent Shriver became virtually a single entity."

Or as Robert Liston wrote in 1964, the Peace Corps "is one hundred per cent Shriver, a uniquely personal and unorthodox operation, any appraisal of which is in essence an appraisal of Shriver himself. . . . Every thought, deed or document associated with the organization must bear the stamp of his personality."

The new agency reflected Shriver's distinctive strengths and weaknesses alike. Perhaps his greatest strength was his powerful idealism, which—drawing on the ambient hopefulness of the time—saturated the entire program, making Peace Corps staff and volunteers feel as though they were part of a crusade, or a higher cause.

Another of Shriver's strengths was his intellectual flexibility. Peace Corps meetings were famously free-for-all, with ideas and arguments flying around the room. Almost no idea was too beyond the pale to get a hearing; no person was too low level, or too far outside of the director's inner circle, to have his or her ideas taken seriously. Shriver himself was a maelstrom of creativity— but not always productively so. "Shriver's mind churned out thousands of these ideas a week," Albert Meisel recalled. "He would pop them on anyone at anytime. You might get a call at midnight or at 7:00 a.m. He might collar you in the men's room. . . . He was crazy about these ideas, and many of these ideas were, in fact, crazy."

Shriver's openness to new experiences and cultures made him an ideal evangelist for the Peace Corps overseas. His easy embrace of all that was exotic in other countries—the food, the language, the customs—conveyed an enthusiasm for learning about their cultures that was entirely sincere. Indeed, it was in large part this openness, as it trickled down and saturated the agency's institutional culture, that made the Peace Corps such a public relations success internationally. It may be that only a program that sought not merely to assist developing countries but also genuinely to learn from them could have so successfully overcome the doubts of those who suspected all American foreign aid projects of harboring neocolonialist ambitions. Shriver's almost childlike wonder at all that was new—new people, new cultures—was completely unfeigned. In some ways, infusing the Peace Corps with his natural openness, curiosity, and wonder was the most important thing he did.

If the agency's institutional culture benefited from his strengths, it also suffered from his weaknesses. Sometimes his strengths *were* his weaknesses. "Shriver's most serious fault was also his greatest virtue," Charlie Peters has written. "He set goals that goaded the organization to action but the pressure to meet those goals sometimes caused his subordinates to err."

Many have observed that Shriver's capacity for hard work was superhuman; the frenzied work ethic that permeated the Peace Corps inspired some people to paroxysms of effort they otherwise never could have achieved. "When you come to work at this place," one Peace Corps staffer said in the mid-1960s, "you must be prepared to run a 100-yard sprint for 10 miles every day." But Shriver couldn't understand why everyone couldn't always work as hard as he did, and he pushed his staff to the point of collapse. Some who couldn't keep up dropped out. Others suffered ill health. Others saw their marriages fall apart. ("Family men abandoned family for the greater glory of saving the world," as Coates Redmon put it.) "When you join the Shriver team," one Peace Corps veteran recalled, "you put yourself in line for an ulcer, a heart attack, or a nervous breakdown. I held on until I was forced to quit by all three."

A representative mechanism was the "buzzer bomb." As the Peace Corps staff expanded and began to fill up several floors at 806 Connecticut, Shriver grew frustrated at not having all his top aides within shouting distance at all times. Thus he had a primitive intercom system installed that allowed him to buzz his staff offices. Significantly, the intercom worked only one way; Shriver's aides could not buzz him back. Staff members learned that the sudden eruption of dissonant buzzing in one of their offices meant the director was summoning them—and that they had better hustle quickly to Shriver's office. "The secretaries were just terrified of the thing," Donovan McClure, of the public affairs office, recalled. "They knew it was Shriver in person, that he wanted something impossible. . . . So, when it went off, they'd jump up and come screaming after us."

"A job on the Peace Corps staff," Gerald Rice wrote, "was not for the timid or stuffy. The atmosphere was one of bedlam, the hours were late, the rivalries were fierce and, of course, everyone was playing to Shriver." Staff meetings, where policy was made, could be "bloody affairs." Grown men were known to burst into tears when caught underprepared. As Brent Ashabranner, the first Peace Corps representative in Nigeria and later the agency's deputy director, recalled, "Shriver's style of management was to encourage fierce competition and debate among his key staff and to make policy by being the arbiter of who had come out best in the competition." Although Ashabranner remembered

Shriver as an "exciting leader" who always kept morale high, "there was always a winner and a loser in the staff clashes; many wounds were licked and tension was an everyday ingredient of Peace Corps life in Washington."

Shriver also had the habit—which he had picked up from Joe Kennedy—of assigning multiple people to do the same task independently, often without telling them; Shriver would then take the best final product and discard all the others. At times, this tactic produced brilliant results. At other times, however, the forced competition bred resentment, suspicion, and feelings of redundancy.

Another Shriverian trait that could be a strength as well as a weakness was his allergy to bureaucracy. He wanted at all times to retain maximum flexibility for his organization, often to the point of doing away with all bureaucratic protocol. One early staff member recalled that whenever anyone proposed doing something according to an established bureaucratic precedent, Shriver would reject the proposal as a matter of principle. "The worst possible argument that could be made [to Shriver] was that the Department of State did it that way. The second weakest argument was that it had been done that way before. The strongest argument was that it had never been done before and let's try it." Or as Shriver put it in a memo to his staff in December 1961, "There will be little tolerance of a 'tomorrow' philosophy or an 'it can't be done because it hasn't been done before' attitude."

Shriver deprecated rules and violated existing ones with glee. To him, picayune regulations were not important; the spirit of the place was what mattered. "Working with the Peace Corps," he wrote in a memo to his staff, "should not be like working with another government agency. We have a special mission which can only be accomplished if everyone believes in it and works for it in a manner consistent with the ideals of service and volunteerism."

Shriver's ad hoc approach to establishing policy often put him at odds with officials from other government departments. Once, when someone from the Bureau of the Budget asked Shriver for a long-term budget projection, Shriver burst out laughing. "Look," he said, "it's a very legitimate question, but how in the hell do I know where we're going to be in five years?"

Shriver, aware of his own administrative untidiness, brought in better-disciplined minds—like those of Wiggins, Josephson, Moyers, and Bill Kelly, the director of the Division of Contracts and Logistics—who could rein in his tendency toward chaos. These men could also, when necessary, temper his great idealism and openness, two other great Shriver virtues that could at times become faults.

Even hemmed in by his tough-minded deputies, Shriver managed to imprint himself on every aspect of the Peace Corps. Everything was, as his staff put it, "Shriverized." He made not only all the large decisions; he had a hand in most of the small ones as well. It sometimes seemed as though he wanted to analyze every overseas program, interview every prospective employee, personally approve every training site, review every press release, and formulate all office policies himself.

His relentless energy ground people down and wore them out. And his soaring idealism and his concern for humanity could sometimes seem purely abstract. "He can be indifferent to the point of callous about the problems of the bloke working beside him," complained one Peace Corps staffer.

Yet despite all the hardships he imposed, Shriver remained much beloved by the Peace Corps staff. The journalist Robert Liston, writing in 1964, concluded that "hardly anyone on his staff dislikes him. The same is true of those he has dismissed or who have left his employ, beaten down by the pressures or disgusted by the unending righteousness." As one staff member put it,

> There's no getting around it. The man is hypnotic. You can be sitting at your desk, seething at all the work he's piled on you. Seething because you know you've got to do it fast and well and that if you don't, he'll chew you out in that gentle, soft-spoken, devastating way of his. But let him summon you to his office. Just spend a few minutes with him there, and you leave the place walking on air, convinced he's the greatest guy in the world and that anyone who doesn't work for the Peace Corps, or who does and is thinking of quitting, is a first-class stinker.

Life at the Peace Corps was fun. Frank Mankiewicz was the first Peace Corps head of Latin American operations and went on to run presidential campaigns for Bobby Kennedy and George McGovern. He recalls, "The thing about the Peace Corps was that—more than anything else I've done—it was fun all the time. It was serious business but there wasn't a day went by that you couldn't laugh about something." Again, this was a clear reflection of the director; Shriver himself was clearly having so much fun that his staff couldn't help having fun, too. Important staff meetings, for all their seriousness and competitive tension, were often broken up by torrents of hilarity. Bill Haddad has observed that the early days of the Peace Corps were like a war movie without horror: all camaraderie and joking and desperate situations and narrow escapes and high hopes. At times, the Peace Corps was less like a war movie than a series of scenes from a Frank Capra film, or a screwball romantic comedy from the 1940s: full of comic high jinks, madcap antics, and boisterous repartee. This helped mitigate what some outside the organization found to be the agency's insufferable earnestness about the righteousness of the Peace Corps cause.

THE DROPPED POSTCARD

The emphatic passage of the Peace Corps Act by Congress had been a great triumph for Shriver and his new program. But now, having been given the money, the Peace Corps had to deliver the goods. Conservative opponents continued to skewer the agency, mocking its jejune idealism and warning that disaster awaited. Some liberals, too, were worried. Eleanor Roosevelt met with Shriver and expressed her fears about women being sent off alone into the jungles of Africa.

Privately, Shriver himself worried. If anything went wrong, all the goodwill he had generated over eight months could vanish instantly. The critics were watching for any misstep. All it would take was a dead volunteer or an angry host country, and all the hard work he had done getting the program legislated could unravel.

Also, Shriver felt at some level directly responsible for the well-being of each and every volunteer in the Corps. If something—tropical disease; wild animal attack; suicidal depression brought on by acute culture shock; Communist co-optation; assault by an anti-American mob; rape; a hiking or boating or climbing accident—were to befall one of them, it would be on his conscience. As he later wrote, "I used to wake up in the middle of the night with the question tearing at me: How are we ever going to protect the health of the Peace Corps volunteers? Could we go to the parents of this nation and say to them, yes, we want your sons and daughters, and admit at the same time that for two years they would be overseas—many of them in primitive and remote towns and villages—with no medical assistance?" Shriver knew that in the event of the inevitable Peace Corps death or disaster, it would be up to him to face the victim's parents and tell them what had happened.

Shriver didn't have to wait long for his first crisis involving a volunteer. Margery Michelmore, a recent honors graduate of Smith College, was one of the first thirty-seven volunteers sent to Nigeria, arriving in Lagos on September 26, 1961. From Lagos, her cohort traveled to the University College of Ibadan, in the country's western region, where they were to complete their Peace Corps training in-country before beginning their work.

Twenty-three years old at the time, Michelmore was by all accounts smart, poised, and mature. But she had grown up in a wealthy manufacturing family in Massachusetts and when, after her seven-week training program at Harvard, she arrived in the city of Ibadan, she was stunned by the poverty and squalor that confronted her there. She wrote a postcard to her boyfriend in the United States that recounted her dismay—but also her fascination—at what was to be her home for the next two years. "Dear Bobbo," she wrote,

> I wanted you to see the incredible and fascinating city we were in. With all the training we had, we really were not prepared for the squalor and absolutely prim-itive living conditions rampant both in the city and in the bush. We had no idea what "underdeveloped" meant. It really is a revelation and after we got over the initial horrified shock, a very rewarding experience. Everyone except us lives in the streets, cooks in the streets, sells in the streets, and even goes to the bathroom in the streets.

Her note (with its description of Ibadan as "incredible and fascinating" and of her living there "a very rewarding experience") was not by any means wholly negative. But she dropped it on the way to the post office, and to the Nigerian students at the University of Ibadan who found it, Michelmore's postcard was offensive. "No one likes to be called primitive," the Nigerian ambassador to the United States subsequently explained.

Within a few hours, Nigerian students had distributed thousands of copies of the postcard's text, and small riots were erupting in the men's dormitory where the male Peace Corps trainees were lodged. Peace Corps volunteers were banned from the student union. By the next day students had organized a large demonstration against the United States, in which volunteers were labeled "agents of imperialism" and members "of an international spy ring." The dropped postcard became front-page news in all the Nigerian papers for weeks. Editorial comment was "bitter." There were angry denunciations of the Peace Corps and calls for its banishment from the country.

Wire services picked up the story, and when it was published in the United States the gloating by Peace Corps critics was palpable. The incident had proved their argument that "immature young Americans would do nothing but get the U.S. in trouble" and "[provide] glorious ammunition for Moscow and Peking." American newspapers published critical articles, arguing that "the Peace Corps idea had now been exposed for what it was: a dangerous, unworkable exercise in do-goodism." Former president Eisenhower, speaking at a Republican Party fund-raiser, noted that there was now "postcard evidence" that the Peace Corps was unworkable. Why don't we send volunteers to the moon? Ike joked. It's underdeveloped, but the volunteers can't cause trouble there.

It seemed to some in Shriver's inner circle that this could be the beginning of the end. Congress had just passed legislation with trumpets and fanfare— and now the Peace Corps was falling on its face. There was great pressure to pull the entire volunteer contingent out of Nigeria. "The Peace Corps could be thrown out at any moment," Wiggins recalled the staff at 806 Connecticut thinking. "It could be the domino theory—first we're kicked out of Nigeria, then out of Ghana, and so on."

But Shriver did not panic. He met with President Kennedy—who was aggrieved at the bad publicity the situation was generating for his administration—and assured his brother-in-law that he could bring the situation under control quickly without terminating Peace Corp relations with Nigeria. After cabling back and forth frantically with Sam Proctor, the Peace Corps representative in Nigeria, Shriver decided that Michelmore should be brought home to the United States but that the other volunteers would stay.

Margery Michelmore, meanwhile, to escape all the vitriol being poured on her in Ibadan, had gone to Lagos to stay with the American family of a deputy at the American embassy, and she had written an open letter of apology to Nigerians in which she offered to resign from the Peace Corps. This was mimeographed and posted on the campus at Ibadan. She expressed to Peace Corps administrators in Nigeria her desire to go home and her belief that she would no longer be able to volunteer effectively.

But Shriver was concerned not to appear that he was abandoning a Peace Corps volunteer, or forcing her out of the program, at the first sign of trouble.

So he conceived the idea of having the president "invite" Margery back to the United States to work at 806 Connecticut in the Division of Volunteer Support. Michelmore flew home to New England for a rest and then began working at Peace Corps headquarters. She stayed there for a few months—long enough not to embarrass either Shriver or the president—before moving back home.

Coverage of the incident continued in both the Nigerian and the American press for several weeks, but the intensity of the criticism rapidly diminished. Although Michelmore remained for many years the most infamous Peace Corps volunteer, the furor over her dropped postcard soon abated, to the great relief of Shriver and his staff.

A consensus soon developed at 806 Connecticut that the postcard incident had been a blessing. "It was like a vaccination," Wiggins said. "The greatest thing that could have happened to the Peace Corps in the beginning was a postcard from a volunteer mentioning that people pee in the streets in Nigeria." Everyone knew that the Peace Corps would eventually "get sick," Wiggins said, but no one knew how or from what. "Well, it was Margery—a very, very minor bug in the system. But boy, did it take. Since then, the Peace Corps has had rape, manslaughter, bigamy, disappearances, volunteers going insane, meddling in local politics, being eaten by crocodiles, but never again did it get a bad play in national news." "In the long run," Wofford wrote, "Michelmore's debacle added significantly to the Peace Corps' sensitivity and success."

After the Michelmore incident, Shriver had a new section added to *The Peace Corps Handbook*. "Like the proverbial goldfish," the *Handbook* said, "the Peace Corps volunteer will be 'in view' constantly. . . . Your every action will be watched, weighed, and considered representative of the entire Peace Corps. . . . You must learn—and respect—the local customs, manners, taboos, religions and traditions, remembering always that the slightest 'goof' will quickly be seen and talked of by many persons."

The Peace Corps stayed on in Nigeria. On November 28, just six weeks after the incident, Prime Minster Balewa issued a warm welcome to the second contingent of volunteers to his country; by the end of 1961, the first two contingents of volunteers had been joined by a third. By the time the first volunteers left, two years later, Nigerian students were lamenting, "No amount of praise showered on [the volunteers] for their work is too much. . . . To our Peace Corps friends about to leave us, we say: We are indeed sorry to see you go. We shall miss you and your services." It was said that the Nigerians had become much more favorably disposed to the Peace Corps when a volunteer saved a drowning Nigerian. Shriver didn't buy that. "Dramatic incidents, even symbolic acts," he said, "do not count as much as the quiet work, the daily drudgery of volunteers on the job."

THE CONSCIENCE OF THE PEACE CORPS

The postcard incident reinforced for Shriver the importance of identifying and addressing problems early, before the press got wind of them. Shriver was already wary of the institutionalized blindness that regular bureaucracies naturally fostered in their executives: each person in a corporate hierarchy, he believed, had a vested interest in telling the person above him only what that higher person wanted to hear. With bad news getting filtered out on its way up the ladder, leaders would hear only good news. Shriver believed this could be crippling to an organization. A sign that hung prominently in his office declared: "Bring me only bad news. Good news weakens me."

Establishing this principle via platitude, however, was not enough. Shriver wanted it inscribed into the very administrative structure of the Peace Corps. Hence, in the spring of 1961, as the earliest selected volunteers began entering training programs at sites across the country and in Puerto Rico, Shriver and Bill Haddad conceived the idea of sending observers from outside the regular organizational hierarchy to evaluate the training programs. Haddad, a longtime newspaperman, believed deeply in the value of investigative reporting. By sending Peace Corps–employed investigators to report directly to the Washington office the truth of what they saw in the field, Haddad advised, Shriver would have a much fuller knowledge of how things were actually working than if he had relied only on the usual organizational channels. Moreover—and the postcard incident brought this home powerfully—if investigative reporters working for the Peace Corps could discover scandal or incompetence before investigative reporters working for the press did, this would serve (to use Warren Wiggins's analogy) as a potent inoculation against bad publicity. The idea, as Shriver put it, was "to get the *Time* magazine story before *Time* magazine did."

Bill Haddad became the Peace Corps' associate director for the Division of Planning and Evaluation. Haddad in turn hired Charlie Peters, who had worked on the Kennedy campaign in West Virginia, as the Peace Corps' first chief of evaluation. Originally sent over to the Peace Corps as a patronage hire—which did not immediately endear him to Shriver, who believed patronage placements were generally of inferior quality—Peters soon impressed the Peace Corps director with his ability to cut through red tape, which he did while negotiating for Peace Corps training sites in Puerto Rico in May 1961.

Peters was sent initially to the University of California at Berkeley to observe the first group of volunteers being trained for a tour of duty in Ghana and then to Texas Western College in El Paso, where volunteers were being trained to do surveying in Tanganyika. As the first Peace Corps "evaluator," Peters was not a popular figure among the organization's rank and file. But he was invaluable to Shriver. "The advantage of the evaluation process began to emerge," Peters recalled. "I was reporting problems that Shriver had not heard through the regular chain of command. This was good for Shriver but did not bring instant delight to the chain of command. The bureaucrats, who were not aware of the problems I was reporting or, if they were, had chosen to conceal them, counterattacked, guns blazing, accusing me of being a spy and being completely unqualified to evaluate what they were doing."

Peters had planned to work for the Peace Corps for only a few months before returning to his West Virginia law practice, where he hoped to begin plotting his path to the governor's mansion. The assaults on him by the "chain of command" only made him more eager to return home. But Haddad prevailed on him to stay longer; Haddad also persuaded Shriver to ignore the angry squawking from the subjects of Peters's evaluations: the fact that these people were angry and disliked Peters, Haddad said, only proved that Peters was doing his job. At first Shriver was uncertain—he could see how the process of evaluation was threatening to people in the ranks—but after the Margery Michelmore affair he became convinced of the necessity of the evaluation process. He and Haddad pressed Peters to stay on, and in February 1962 Peters became the founding chief of the Peace Corps' Evaluation Division.

In this position, Peters remained unavoidably unpopular with many at Peace Corps headquarters, as well as among the Peace Corps representatives—the administrators charged with running programs and overseeing the volunteers in foreign countries—whose work Shriver had ordered him to evaluate with merciless objectivity. Many times, under assault by various Peace Corps representatives and higher-ups from within the Washington headquarters, Peters thought he was about to get fired; other times, beleaguered and harassed, he felt he ought to quit. "It got to the point," Peters recalled, "where I knew that even though it was clear that some of the [people in Wiggins's Planning, Development, and Operations Division (PDO)] respected me and even kind of liked me on a social level, they wanted me out, and the sooner the better. I was feeling harassed and scared of their hostility to the point that I'd avoid them . . . when I saw them coming down the hall. I'd duck into the men's room or slip into someone else's office."

But Shriver had become so convinced of the value of the Evaluation Division that he almost always publicly backed his evaluation chief against the complaints of the bureaucracy, and Peters stayed on for seven years. By the time he left, Peters had been respectfully dubbed "the conscience of the Peace Corps" by his admiring peers.

At first, Peters alone constituted the whole of the Evaluation Division. The first reports Peters and his staff sent back from the field were merely brief outlines of how they thought various training programs were working. Over time, however, the evaluations became much longer and more complex. Whole teams of evaluators would go overseas for weeks or months at a time to examine a country's program. Shriver began enthusiastically recruiting high-profile journalists, academics, and ex-government officials to serve as evaluators. Richard Rovere, Calvin Trillin, James Michener, Renata Adler, John McPhee, and others wrote evaluations. This raised the Peace Corps' glamour quotient, but it also made the evaluation reports themselves more colorful and readable. Shriver also pointed out that hiring these famous writers to do evaluations would also have the collateral effect of turning influential opinion-makers into Peace Corps advocates.

Nothing, Shriver decreed, was to be off limits. "As an evaluator," Peters wrote, "you have a duty to raise hell." This hell-raising contributed to the already considerable feelings of tension that permeated the organization. In Pakistan, the entire overseas administrative staff was fired as a result of an evaluation. Although evaluations were marked "Eyes Only" and submitted straight to the director's office, they were shown to the subjects of the evaluations, who often took umbrage at them. Harris Wofford, who in 1962 would become the Peace Corps representative in Ethiopia, carried on a long correspondence with his friend

Shriver, denying the accuracy of the Ethiopian evaluations. The Peace Corps representative in Liberia once wrote a twenty-page rebuttal to an evaluation.

Shriver himself would at times question whether the Evaluation Division was worth the trouble it caused, but he valued having the intelligence it provided. Without the Evaluation Division, Shriver would never have had as complete a picture of his organization as he did. As Brent Ashabranner observed in 1971, "I doubt that any federal agency has ever taken as completely honest a look at itself as the Peace Corps did through its evaluation division." Equally important, Shriver valued anything that kept members of his growing staff on their toes. His abiding fear was that the Peace Corps would ossify into an entrenched bureaucracy, which might cause it to lose its creativity, flexibility, and crusading spirit. Peters's Evaluation Division, if nothing else, was a guard against complacency.

CHAPTER NINETEEN

Timberlawn

Despite his peripatetic travel schedule, by the late autumn of 1961 Shriver was finally beginning to settle into life in Washington. Through his friend Merle Thorpe, he found a picturesque 30-acre estate in Rockville, Maryland, just northwest of Bethesda. The estate was known as Timberlawn, and the owner was looking for a new tenant.

When Shriver had first visited the house in July, he had fallen in love with the property, and in particular its spacious backyard: more than 25 acres of the most beautiful lawn he had ever seen rolling down from the house into a valley. At the end of the lawn, where the property ended, was a fence and a road and then another 250 acres of hills and woods and farmland. Looking at it, he was reminded of the old Shriver homestead in Union Mills. When the realtor told him that his family could have access not only to the 25 acres of lawn but also to much of the acreage that lay beyond it, Shriver decided on the spot that this was where his family would live. By the time Eunice arrived from Chicago over Labor Day, bringing with her seven-year-old Bobby, five-year-old Maria, and two-year-old Timothy, the new Shriver home was ready for them.

Timberlawn became a bustling bucolic outpost of the New Frontier. An epicenter of social life among the nation's governing elite, Timberlawn's parties were known for the eclectic array of guests they attracted: senators, representatives, and the president and his staff; high-powered lawyers, judges, and Supreme Court justices; business executives and millionaire financiers; labor leaders and community organizers; famous professors and best-selling authors; professional football, baseball, and tennis players; foreign ambassadors and heads of state; and of course cardinals, bishops, and priests. The parties the Shrivers threw at Timberlawn were like the parties they had thrown in Chicago, only on a far grander scale—interesting, unpredictable, full of political chatter. John F. Kennedy's White House was known for its youth and vitality, and for the constant stream of interesting and talented people who passed through its orbit. Timberlawn was like that, but with a joie de vivre distinctively its own.

Timberlawn also became the weekend headquarters of the Peace Corps. At the Peace Corps there weren't weekends as such. Edgar May, who worked briefly at the Peace Corps before becoming inspector general for the Office of Economic Opportunity, recalled an illustrative episode. "One time it was eleven o'clock on Friday night and someone walked by and asked my secretary what day it was and she said, 'Friday—only two more working days.'"

Shriver realized he had to make some concession to family life—his own if not his employees'. Once ensconced at Timberlawn, he realized that family time and work time could be combined for the Peace Corps upper management. Thus most weekends would find Shriver and his deputies bivouacked around a table inside the house while their wives and children frolicked on the grounds. It was like a giant summer camp for everyone: There would be round-robin tennis tournaments on the Timberlawn court; relay races in the pool; ongoing games of hide-and-seek, cops-and-robbers, kickball, and football on the lawn. There was a stable full of horses, offering rides to the children. The Shrivers' dogs—as many as sixteen of them at one point—would run among the guests. Late in the afternoon, Shriver would open the bar. The day would usually end with the families reuniting at the house from the far corners of the estate, ready for the evening barbecue and predinner swim.

The spirit of these Timberlawn weekends was much like the spirit of the Peace Corps generally: constant motion and barely controlled chaos, all hell breaking loose, with Shriver presiding and infecting the proceedings with his energetic good cheer.

CAMP SHRIVER

Meanwhile, Eunice remained obsessed with the plight of the mentally retarded. "I have seen sights that will haunt me my whole life," Eunice would write in 1964, referring to her early visits to institutions for the retarded. "If I had not seen them myself, I would never have believed that such conditions could exist in modern America . . . adults and children . . . in barrack-like wards, their unwashed clothes and blankets in rags."

During the chaotic first months of the Peace Corps' existence, Sarge somehow found the time to help Eunice continue to expand the Kennedy Foundation's involvement in the field of mental retardation. "Behind all Eunice's efforts," one author has observed,

> stood Sarge, an omnipresent advisor, sitting in on meetings, making phone calls on his wife's behalf, providing an emotional ballast to his often overwrought wife. As a political couple, the Shrivers were sometimes compared with Eleanor and Franklin Roosevelt. Unlike the Roosevelts with their separate agendas and constituencies, the Shrivers were ideologically and politically bonded, and had an emotional closeness that the Roosevelts had lost early in their marriage.

Earlier, on November 9, 1959, while meeting with a team of researchers in Baltimore who were hoping to receive Kennedy Foundation money to start a mental retardation program at Johns Hopkins University, the Shrivers were introduced to Robert Cooke, a forty-year-old professor of pediatrics at the university. "Of all the academics who clustered about the Shrivers," the medical historian Edwin Shorter has written, "Cooke has perhaps been most their match in terms of force of personality and style. A man of movie-star looks and dean's-corridor grooming, he projected the Kennedy image of fast-lane dynamism. As someone with first-class intelligence and strong moral convictions, he could hold his own in any after-dinner debate at Timberlawn."

What interested the Shrivers about Cooke, however, was not his "Kennedy style" but his expertise in the field of mental retardation. Cooke and his wife were the parents of two severely retarded children, and as a result in 1956 Cooke had turned his research attentions toward the subject. By the time of his meeting with the Shrivers in 1959, he was established as a leading expert in the field. Sarge and Eunice were greatly impressed by him, and they brought Cooke onto a scientific advisory council the foundation was establishing; before long he had become the family's most trusted adviser on all health-related matters. This led to multiple responsibilities within the Kennedy family: Eunice dispatched him to give health care ideas to her brother during his presidential campaign; after the 1960 election, Cooke became a member of the president-elect's health care transition team. He also became the Shriver family's pediatrician. After 1964 Cooke would also be integrally involved in many of the programs started by Shriver's Office of Economic Opportunity, playing a key role in the founding of Head Start. From 1960 Cooke was Eunice's right-hand man on mental retardation issues.

In 1961, as her brother ascended to the highest office in the land, Eunice saw a singular opportunity: As the sister of the president, she would have his ear. She made a conscious decision to use this access to help advance her chosen cause. Eunice urged her brother to start a new institute exclusively dedicated to research into children's health issues, with a special focus on mental retardation. According to Shorter, "Eunice, needling her brother for the new institute . . . sliced through normally fearsome bureaucratic opposition. She quickly acquired the authority to give orders to White House adviser Mike Feldman, who in turn gave orders to Wilbur Cohen," who was the assistant cabinet secretary in the Department of Health, Education, and Welfare charged with attending to the department's youth-related policies. "Let's give Eunice whatever she wants so I can get her off the phone and get on with the business of the government," the president would say jokingly to Bobby Kennedy. Her persistence paid off; legislation providing funding for the institute was passed and then signed into law by the president.

But Eunice wasn't done. Even as she was lobbying for the establishment of the Institute for Child Health and Human Development, Eunice and Bob Cooke were also pressing the White House to hold a national conference on the mentally retarded, to generate publicity for the issue. On October 11, 1961, two weeks after he signed the Peace Corps Act, President Kennedy announced the formation of a national panel to study mental retardation. "We as a nation," he said, "have for too long postponed an intensive search for solutions to the problems of the mentally retarded. That failure should be corrected."

Officially listed as only a consultant to the panel, Eunice was in reality its de facto leader and driving force, "the prime mover" as one panel member observed. Leonard Mayo, the panel's official director, once had a phone conversation with Sarge in which he explained, "Well, Mr. Shriver, I want you to know one thing. . . . [Eunice] may be a consultant on paper, but as far as I'm concerned, she's the chairman of the board."

"Well," Sarge replied. "I see I don't have to draw any pictures for you."

Eunice persuaded Jack to appoint Dr. Stafford Warren, a vice chancellor for health services at UCLA, as special assistant to the president for programs in mental retardation. "In theory," Shorter wrote, "Warren and his staff were responsible for jockeying the panel's many recommendations through the federal government. In practice, it was the Shrivers who retained the oversight and gave Warren and his people their marching orders."

In effect, Sarge and Eunice Shriver had put themselves in charge of a small section of the federal bureaucracy—but without having any official authority vesting them with the power to do so. "In retrospect," Shorter said, "it is actually quite breathtaking to see a major agency of the federal government captured in this manner by outsiders. . . . It was as though the Department of Defense had been captured by Jimmy Carter's brother Billy." Even more than Sarge, Eunice tended to blind herself to the obstacles standing between her and her public interest goals. Red tape, conventional protocol, historical precedent—none of these could be allowed to stand in the way of helping the mentally retarded. She would not allow a little thing such as not having an official position in the federal government stop her from running a government agency. She would give orders to Mike Feldman at the White House; Feldman would give orders to Wilbur Cohen at HEW; and Cohen would execute them.

Once, when Cohen walked into the Oval Office, the president greeted him by saying, "Hello, Wilbur. Has my sister been giving you trouble again?"

"How did you know?" asked the stunned Cohen.

"I know my sister," Kennedy said.

If Eunice "hadn't nagged the hell out of Sarge Shriver and her brother," Cohen recalled, "there wouldn't be a mental retardation program." If Eunice ever wanted something, the president would say, "For God's sake, Wilbur and everybody else, do it! Get her off my back!"

While the panel on mental retardation was still doing its work during 1961 and 1962, Eunice told Leonard Mayo that she would like to contribute to the panel's research and recommendations on physical education. From the start, Eunice had wanted the panel to make recommendations that would be of immediate practical use to the parents of the mentally retarded. She wasn't aware of any research on, or opportunities for, physical activity for the retarded. Eunice herself had been an athlete all her life—and, like all the Kennedys, a hypercompetitive one—and felt she had derived enjoyment and health from her participation in sports. But she knew from her experience with the mentally retarded that they tended to be physically unfit, often overweight. Was this physical unfitness directly related to their disability—or was it simply a result of no one's providing opportunities for exercise to the mentally disabled? Eunice didn't know. She did recall, however, that her sister Rosemary, despite her mental infirmities, was able to "swim, sail, and play ball" and that Rosemary's ability to participate in sports kept her from feeling isolated from the family.

Eunice began to research the issue for the panel. She consulted with Sarge and then started phoning the roster of experts they had met with over the preceding three years, asking them what they knew about programs to promote (or research that had studied) physical activity by the mentally retarded. To her dismay, there was almost nothing. "It was really pitiful, the lack of programs," she recalled later.

She decided to take matters into her own hands. In the spring of 1962, she inaugurated "Camp Shriver." If Timberlawn had been a scene of joyful chaos before, Camp Shriver ratcheted the chaos to a new level. Scores of mentally handicapped children were bused in from local institutions. Dozens of inmates from a local prison—most of them African American—would be bused in to serve as counselors. Teenagers from local Catholic high schools descended on the estate as volunteers. And then all of them—the mentally retarded, the prisoners, the teenage volunteers, plus the Shriver children and their friends— would frolic around the grounds.

Coming home from work, Sarge would find bedlam—Timberlawn overrun by mentally retarded children and their camp counselors. There were retarded children in the pool getting swimming lessons. Children on trampolines. Children by the stable getting horseback-riding lessons. Children in the woods learning how to climb a rope. Children on the court, learning to play tennis. Children on the "confidence course," a series of exercise stations that Eunice had persuaded the District of Columbia's Recreation Department to set up on the Timberlawn grounds. Children in one corner of the lawn learning soccer from a volunteer recruited from the British Embassy. Children in another corner of the lawn learning South Asian dance from a volunteer recruited from the Philippine Embassy. Some children were even being induced to compete against one another, in swimming and running races. In the middle of everything, usually right in the center of the fray, would be Eunice. "When I'd come home from the office, there's my wife in the pool, holding this mentally retarded child in the water to see if it's possible for that child to swim." This was craziness, Sarge thought. Everyone knew that the most humane thing to do with the mentally retarded was to send them to an institution where they would be cared for and kept out of the way of normal society. Shriver had learned a lot in his travels around the country on behalf of the Kennedy Foundation, but nothing he had seen had suggested to him that having a bunch of mentally retarded kids running loose around your home was a good thing for anyone involved. Shriver's skepticism increased when he came home one night to discover that camp counselors had raided his liquor cabinet, denuding it of thousands of dollars worth of imported wine.

The notion that the mentally retarded might actually engage profitably in athletic competition had theretofore been unimaginable. But there they all were, Sarge saw, running around and obviously having a good time. His own children would be playing among them "as if it were the most normal thing in the world." Slowly, his skepticism lifted.

It helped that he trusted his wife's judgment implicitly, because although Eunice hired some experts early on—for instance, she hired Sandy Eiler, a former Olympic swimmer from Canada, to run the camp—many employees of Camp Shriver were novices. Most of these counselors had never met a mentally retarded person. "We had no idea of what it would be like," said one. "To tell the truth, all of us were a little afraid."

In 1962 mental retardation still carried a powerful social stigma. Retarded children were kept hidden by their parents or sent quietly away to dismal institutions that were often little more than warehouses for the disabled. Having a retarded child was shameful. Even the Kennedys themselves had kept Rosemary's situation a secret—she was still being cared for by nuns in Wisconsin. (Eunice would go public with the secret later that year.) Most healthy people had had little or no contact with the retarded. A businessman who visited the camp asked Eunice, "Aren't you afraid to work around the retarded? Won't they go berserk?"

To the extent that the shame of retardation has now been lifted, this is to an astonishing degree the result of the work of one woman and the camps she started at Timberlawn in the spring of 1962. After 1962 Eunice used the example of Camp Shriver—which continued to be held every summer—to proselytize about the value of physical activity and competition for the retarded, and she used the Kennedy Foundation's money to subsidize similar camps for the retarded in other venues. In 1963 the Kennedy Foundation supported eleven day camps for the mentally retarded in several locations around the country; by 1969, when the program gave way to the Special Olympics, the foundation was supporting thirty-two camps—serving 10,000 children—across the country.

"COMPLETE AND TOTAL ANARCHY"

With Camp Shriver during the week, all-day Peace Corps meetings on weekends, and parties all the time, the scene at Timberlawn was one of wild and unrelenting activity. "It was chaos, really," Bobby Shriver recalled. "Complete and total anarchy."

"There were at least a hundred people at our house every weekend," Maria Shriver says. "Baseball games, barbecues, relay races, touch football games, and meetings, lots of meetings. The house was always full of people with ideas. And Daddy was kind of the hub of all of that."

All the Shriver family projects tended to blend together in joyful chaos at Timberlawn. As Maria Shriver recalls, "You would have retarded people running around with White House people who are running around with Peace Corps volunteers who are running around with Head Start people who are running around with political people."

The three eldest Shriver children all vividly recall a large retarded girl named Moofa, who always wore a football helmet to keep her from hurting herself when she would bang her head violently against walls and trees. Bobby, Maria, and Timothy were all afraid of her. "My mother, in her wisdom, never really explained to any of us what all this was about," Maria recalled. "Her whole thing was 'Everybody's normal, everybody's the same.' So you would wake up in the morning and people would be banging their heads into the trees and running around and screaming, and nobody really bothered to tell us children what was going on. You had to figure it out on your own."

"Half the time," Maria recalled, Timberlawn would be filled with "the most brilliant minds of the country. And then the other half of the time it would be filled by people banging their heads into the trees. There would be a hundred Peace Corps volunteers and a hundred retarded children there at the same time. Or you would have Bob McNamara and Lyndon Johnson and Moofa, all there together! I look back at it sometimes and I think to myself, 'I can't believe I survived that.'"

The unifying strand tying these disparate groups together, Maria says, was the idealism and hopefulness. "Almost everyone who visited Timberlawn in the 1960s," she recalled, "believed they were helping to change the world."

CHAPTER TWENTY

Bigger, Better, Faster

By early 1962 the Peace Corps was well into its honeymoon period. Shriver and Moyers had conquered Congress. The organization had weathered the dropped-postcard incident. Favorable press coverage of volunteers in the field had begun appearing regularly in daily newspapers and in weekly and monthly magazines. The Peace Corps had taken on a lustrous glow. For President Kennedy, it was a political bonanza: He needed to attend to it little if at all, yet it was generating political capital for him domestically as well as goodwill toward his administration abroad.

At this point it might have seemed prudent to slow the pace of growth, to allow time for Peace Corps headquarters to catch up administratively, and to permit more careful evaluation of the overseas volunteer programs that were already under way. But it was not in Shriver's nature to slow down. *Bigger, faster, better* were his watchwords. This meant getting more and more volunteers into more and more countries as soon as possible. He gave a hint of the scale of his ambition for his program when, at a meeting with the Bureau of the Budget in the spring of 1962, he said he wanted to get 10,000 volunteers in the field as quickly as possible—because from that level he would be better able to evaluate whether the Peace Corps could get to 50,000 or 100,000 volunteers working around the world by 1964.

Growth generated more growth. As countries welcomed volunteers and began to sing the Peace Corps' praises, other countries decided that they, too, would like to invite volunteers. Shriver was now a national celebrity; fawning articles about him were appearing regularly in magazines and newspapers. When he spoke at the University of California at Berkeley he was greeted by a five-minute standing ovation and with the announcement that Berkeley would be offering its students a "Peace Corps Minor," a special program meant to prepare them for volunteer service abroad. Overall, 1962 was a year of "wild and uncontrolled growth" for the Peace Corps—the number of countries hosting volunteers expanded from nine to thirty-seven.

But "bigger" and "faster" were not always consonant with "better." Some Peace Corps executives thought it was growing too fast. "There is no doubt that [the rapid speed of its launch] contributed to the troubles of the early programs and the volunteers who comprised them," Brent Ashabranner, who succeeded Bill Moyers as deputy director of the Peace Corps, has written. "Officials of receiving countries frequently did not understand who volunteers really were or what they were to do. Usually there was not time to see if the number of volunteers requested in any way matched the number of jobs—or in fact if real jobs existed." Shriver's May 8 meeting with the Bureau of the Budget was a harbinger. The budget department staff kept asking Shriver for more accurate projections, and Shriver kept saying such projections were difficult if not impossible. The budget officials persisted until finally, in exasperation, Shriver explained that the Peace Corps staff was so busy running its program that it didn't really have the staff to do long-range planning.

POLITICS AND THE PEACE CORPS

In 1962 many American politicians shared an almost religious conviction: Communism must be, if not conquered, then contained. Congress, the president, and just about everyone involved in American government viewed all global politics and international relations through the prism of the cold war; their counterparts on the Soviet side of the iron curtain did the same. Thus it was inevitable that, as the Peace Corps spread into neutral and even Soviet-backed countries, Communists would view it with great suspicion. And it was also inevitable that some in the US foreign policy establishment would seek to use the Peace Corps for strategic cold war purposes.

The Soviet Union denounced the Peace Corps as a tool of capitalist imperialism; so did Maoist China and Fidel Castro's Cuba. Other leftist governments, many of them Soviet-supported, declared that the Peace Corps was simply a front for espionage operations. In March 1961, Radio Moscow reported that the Peace Corps would be engaging in "the collection of espionage information for Allen Dulles's agency," the CIA. In many countries the Peace Corps entered, the local Communist newspaper or Communist Party cell published attacks on the volunteers as "agents of imperialist domination." In Peruvian shantytowns where volunteers were working in community development, some local children developed stomach upsets from the richer milk provided by the Peace Corps. Communists in the area distributed leaflets accusing the Peace Corps of "poisoning" Latin American children with "Yankee insects"—"Death to the Yankees," Communist radio broadcasts demanded. In Somalia, one Communist newspaper alleged, female Peace Corps volunteers were seeking to corrupt and brainwash Somali nationals by teaching them the salacious movements of "the Twist." Shriver was, to his amusement, called "a bloodthirsty Chicago butcher and sausage-maker." And in a bit of propaganda that Shriver took great delight in repeating, Radio Moscow in 1962 broadcast that "Director of the Peace Corps, Shriver, is an old employee of the CIA."

In fact, Shriver had been at great pains to establish an impenetrable firewall between the Peace Corps and the CIA. With the colonial era in Africa only just ending, and with the whole world highly sensitized to the reverberations of cold war actions, the Peace Corps was bound to be regarded suspiciously by many in developing countries. It would certainly have made some strategic sense for the Peace Corps to be a tool of the Pentagon or of American espionage operations. (AID missions were already known to be rife with CIA operatives.) Aware that this sort of suspicion already floated freely through developing countries, especially in neutral-bloc and Communist countries, Shriver believed it absolutely essential that there be not the slightest hint of imperial or espionage designs associated with the Peace Corps. Even the *appearance* of being an intelligence-gathering operation or a US propaganda machine, Shriver thought, could do irrevocable damage to the Peace Corps' international image, perhaps even undermining its whole reason for being. Thus he needed at all costs to keep the CIA—which in the early 1960s was just beginning to become known as somewhat of a rogue institution within the US government—away from the Peace Corps.

One problem with monitoring the CIA was that its operations were by their nature cloaked in secrecy. Even within the United States, few people beyond those at the upper reaches of the government (and sometimes not even those people) knew much about what the CIA was doing at any given time. Shriver was aware that even if he declined to allow the spy agency to have any public or official association with the Peace Corps, he would have no way of knowing if agency operatives were infiltrating the program by posing as volunteers. The temptation to do this, Shriver understood, must be considerable. A CIA agent undercover as a volunteer in Latin America or Africa or Asia would have an easy, on-the-ground vantage point from which to do intelligence gathering.

In order to prevent this, Shriver not only publicly made clear that such activities would be intolerable to him but also approached his brother-in-law privately and demanded assurances that the CIA not use the Peace Corps for espionage purposes. The president agreed, and he passed Shriver's wishes directly on to Allen Dulles and, later, to John McCone, who succeeded Dulles as CIA director. This agreement became known around the Peace Corps as "the Treaty."

The Peace Corps' official policy on intelligence was released on September 6, 1961. "We do not want the Peace Corps publicly identified in any way with intelligence work," the official directive stated, "and we do not want the Peace Corps used as a vehicle for intelligence work." The directive stated that no one who had worked in intelligence in any capacity within the previous ten years— and no one who had ever worked for the CIA or who was married to an intelligence operative—was eligible to join the Peace Corps as a staff member or volunteer. Even secretaries who had once done typing for the CIA were not allowed to work for the Peace Corps. Furthermore, according to the arrangement that Shriver worked out privately with President Kennedy, the CIA was not allowed to hire Peace Corps volunteers until ten years had elapsed since their term of service—and even then they could not be deployed as operatives in the countries where they had volunteered.

In 1963 Shriver heard rumors that CIA operatives were exploring making use of the Peace Corps. He called the president immediately. "I'm getting rather suspicious over here that . . . despite your instructions . . . some of our friends over in the Central Intelligence Agency might think they're smarter than anybody else and that they're trying to stick fellows in the Peace Corps." Call Richard Helms, Jack responded, the CIA's deputy director, and tell him "that I don't want anybody in there. . . . And if they are there, let's get them out now."

The Treaty seems to have held. "All available evidence," Gerald Rice wrote in 1985, "indicates that the Peace Corps and the CIA had a perfect relationship: they stayed as far away from each other as possible."

Distancing the Peace Corps from covert intelligence operations was one thing; distancing it from overt politics was another. As Shriver had indicated to the president upon his return from Guinea in the spring of 1961, the Peace Corps' success as a political enterprise was in fact contingent on its appearing *not* to be a political enterprise. This apparent paradox lay at the heart of the Peace Corps' place in cold war geopolitics.

Jack Kennedy had planted the idea for the Peace Corps in a seedbed of idealism. The off-the-cuff remarks he made to University of Michigan students in October 1960 were aimed to appeal to youthful optimism, to the hopeful sense that the world could be made a better place for its inhabitants if Americans were willing to dedicate a few years of their lives helping developing nations. But these remarks were also unavoidably issued and interpreted in the context of the cold war struggle for influence over the nonaligned countries of the developing world. Kennedy's subsequent comments on the Peace Corps—in which he referred to the threat posed by Communists providing technical assistance in developing countries—made this reality clear: If the United States did not send volunteers to such countries, the Soviet Union would—and that, in turn, might tip the global ideological balance toward communism.

One of the guiding ideas of the Peace Corps, then, was that by providing "nonpolitical" help (in the form of no-strings-attached humanitarian and development assistance) it would be helping to accomplish an important political goal—the rollback of global communism. And precisely by being nonpolitical, by claiming idealistic and humanitarian motivations, the Peace Corps could demonstrate the power of the American ideals of freedom and democracy. The idea was that when people in the developing world got to know Americans, and to see how pure their motivations to provide aid were, they would feel compelled to learn more about the American political system. Eventually, it was hoped, foreign nationals would come to understand and appreciate the American system more. And this, of course, would be an important step in the battle against communism.

In aiming to be simultaneously political and nonpolitical, the Peace Corps was perhaps peculiarly American. Europeans, with their longer-marinated sense of history and more sophisticated Continental conceptions of political theory, would likely have had a harder time allowing that any state-sponsored policy could be purely nonpolitical. Americans, however, with their distinctive mix of canniness and naiveté, were equipped to carry off this balancing act with sincere enthusiasm.

Shriver himself possessed the perfect combination of genuine idealism and strategic savvy to lead this endeavor with aplomb. He had no trouble living with the contradiction inherent in using an explicitly nonpolitical program for political ends—because to him this was no contradiction. "It is important that the Peace Corps be advanced not as an arm of the cold war but as a contribution to the world community," Shriver had written to the president in March 1961. "The Peace Corps is not a diplomatic or propaganda venture but a genuine experiment in international partnership." And if this international partnership helped drive communism from the developing world, well, that was only as it should be; Peace Corps volunteers couldn't help but spread democracy and freedom—and this, Shriver would explain, wasn't a political endeavor that served the United States, but a moral one. "The Peace Corps," the historian Elizabeth Cobbs Hoffman has written, "used culture-to-culture diplomacy to make friends in nations that had little inherent power but that could without warning become theaters of the cold war. . . . The Peace Corps was a countermove against the Soviets and a gesture of friendship toward the third world." Through the Peace Corps, President Kennedy became very popular—much more popular than Eisenhower—in much of the recently decolonized world. In Africa and Latin America, he became known as "the great one" and "the good man" and "the friend of the colored man everywhere."

THE ROMANCE WITH CONGRESS CONTINUES

Shriver's love affair with Congress continued, to a degree that confounded the Peace Corps' critics. Although a few individuals in Congress—most notably

Otto Passman of Louisiana—continued to attack it, the Peace Corps enjoyed remarkably cordial relations with the legislative branch after 1961. As the program rapidly grew, Shriver asked for more money, and Congress freely granted it. Part of its willingness to dispense money was a result of Shriver's practice, all but unprecedented in the annals of government, of bringing the Peace Corps in under budget—and of actually returning unused funds, "with well-publicized flourishes," to Congress at the end of the fiscal year. The press took to describing Shriver's relationship with the Eighty-seventh and Eighty-eighth Congresses as a "love affair." The relationship was cast in romantic terms even in the Peace Corps' internal memos. As debate began on the budget reauthorization in March 1962, Shriver was able to write to the president, "Our House Foreign Affairs hearing last Thursday was a love-feast."

In the House, where support for the Peace Corps had been weakest in 1961, passage of the full authorization—$64 million—seemed very likely. In the seven months since the original September vote, the Peace Corps had become so popular in Congress that even the archconservative Judge Smith of Virginia was able to come out comfortably in support of reauthorization. So unlikely was the support of Congressman Smith that Senator Fulbright, when he heard of it, raised his eyebrows and said "Shriver, I'm getting suspicious about you." But "best of all," Shriver told the president, "Smith permitted the Rules Committee to vote unanimously in open session for the Corps—something the House Parliamentarians tell me is almost unprecedented." In 1961 the Peace Corps bill had barely escaped from the Rules Committee; it was allowed to the floor by only a slim 8–7 margin. What a difference a year made: In 1962 the Peace Corps bill passed unanimously out of the Rules Committee.

Shriver's handling of Congress was so skillful that Hubert Humphrey wrote him a letter to express his admiration and offer assistance after watching some of Shriver's congressional testimony in late March.

> You are setting a wonderful example for other administrators, and as long as you follow the standards that you have set for yourself, you will have no trouble here on Capitol Hill. If something goes wrong with the program, come tell the committee. If you need some changes in the law, don't try to get a legal interpretation that ignores the intent of Congress, instead, just ask Congress to change the

law. You can get what you want from this Congress simply because what you are asking for you can justify.

At an appropriations hearing in April, Otto Passman accused the Peace Corps of causing a teacher shortage in the United States by stealing all the best teachers and sending them abroad. Shriver withstood the grilling with his usual panache, producing survey statistics indicating that most Peace Corps teachers would not be in the profession if they had not joined the Peace Corps. Before April was out, the House had passed the Peace Corps legislation by a staggering 317–70 vote; in the Senate, support for the bill was so strong that no more than a voice vote was needed to pass it.

Almost as gratifying as the size of the vote was a letter Shriver received from Georgia Delano, the wife of the Peace Corps' general counsel William Delano. "Dear Mr. Shriver," she wrote,

> As . . . I sat in the Senate gallery today listening to your verbal bouquets from the Senators, I thought it was about time you received a bouquet from a Peace Corps wife.
>
> On one of the nights Bill was away, some non–Peace Corps guests from New York, after much talk about the Peace Corps itself, asked "What is it like to be a Peace Corps wife?" There was a short silence and then I said it was like being married to a dedicated doctor. It is rare and beautiful when interest, concern, hope, and one's bread-and-butter combine in one job to be done. The chance to be part of a job like this for one period of life is a wonderful gift and I want you to know that I appreciate it for Bill.

But the congressional victory rapidly became bittersweet. On April 22, 1962, Lawrence Radley and David Crozier became the first Peace Corps volunteers to die on the job, killed when their plane crashed into a mountain in Colombia. Shriver knew that eventually, given the number of volunteers he was sending abroad, deaths during Peace Corps service were inevitable. That didn't make the loss, or his feeling of responsibility for their demise, any easier to bear. In June he traveled to Puerto Rico with the deceased volunteers' parents, to dedicate the new Peace Corps field training center there in honor of the two volunteers.

While there, Crozier's parents shared with Shriver some of the letters their son had written home to them from Colombia, where he had been working in community development. "Should it come to it, I would rather give my life trying to help someone than to have to give my life looking down a gun barrel at them," Crozier wrote in one letter. "It is better to live humbly for a cause than to die nobly for one," he wrote in another.

The unfortunate deaths of Crozier and Radley did not cause the crises of bad publicity that some had feared. Part of the reason was that their demise had come not, as doomsayers had predicted, at the hands of murderous natives or a rare tropical disease but rather as a result of a simple accident, a commercial airplane crash that also killed many Colombians. More important, however, was the outpouring of sympathy from both the American and Colombian people that the volunteers' deaths elicited. "I render homage with admiration, gratitude and love to the members of the Peace Corps who died in the terrible airplane crash," Colombian president Guillermo León Valencia said in his inaugural address that August. "They came . . . to understand us, to help us . . . to suffer our misfortunes and dangers." Their dying alongside Colombians represented "the cornerstones of a new American understanding" of the developing world. David Crozier's parents wrote to Shriver, thanking him for giving their son the opportunity to serve in Colombia. "We are not sorry he went," they said. Elena Radley and Gordon Radley, Larry Radley's younger sister and brother, both joined the Peace Corps to finish what their older brother had started.

CHAPTER TWENTY-ONE

Psychiatrists and Astrologers

$\smile\!\!\!\!\sim$

During the 1950s a rash of books by prominent social scientists appeared, lamenting the drab, conformist, consumerist culture of the Eisenhower era. The first and most famous, David Riesman's book *The Lonely Crowd* (1950), observed that Americans were becoming more conformist (or "other-directed," as Riesman put it) and less individualistic ("inner-directed"). Other books, like C. Wright Mills's *White Collar* (1951) and William Whyte's *Organization Man* (1956), followed, combining with dozens of magazine articles on the subject to raise alarm about the increasing dullness, weakness, and moral softness of American life. Although some argued that America's conformist, collectivist mentality was what was driving its tremendous postwar economic growth, by 1960 the general consensus among thoughtful Americans was that their country had gone soft in the belly.

Indeed, it was in large part as a reaction to this consensus that Jack Kennedy conceived the Peace Corps; the calls to "sacrifice" and to "idealism" that suffused his campaign rhetoric and inaugural address were designed to wake Americans from their self-perceived torpor. And many of Shriver's early public statements on the Peace Corps consciously made reference to the hardship that volunteers would be willingly subjecting themselves to; this was supposed to demonstrate, as Shriver often said, that Americans were not as "soft" as they were thought to be.

The vogue for "generational" studies in the 1950s and early 1960s brought together the disparate realms of politics, pop psychology, and research psychiatry. In the summer of 1962, one young clinical associate at the National Institute for Mental Health (NIMH) found himself charting a new course across all three of these realms.

That July, Joseph English was wrapping up his third year of psychiatric residency at NIMH. English had been in college when the generation just ahead of him returned from wartime service. As a college student he had been struck by how different the formative experiences were between his own generation and the veterans getting reassimilated into "normal" American life. The veterans, only a few years older than he was, seemed eons more mature. The experience of war had clearly transformed them, made them grow; English's own generation had no shared experience like that to bond them together or to forge their individual and collective identities so distinctly.

Not that life was easy for the veterans, English learned. As he began studying psychiatry in medical school, he read studies about what a difficult time some combat veterans had adjusting to life after the war. The contrast between peace and war was so stark that many veterans were suffering what amounted to severe culture shock. Even though life was safer and easier for veterans during peacetime, it had lost some of its moral clarity. During the war, these men had been fighting for freedom from tyranny; their enemies—Nazism, fascism, Japanese imperialism—were clear. Now, although the cold war had restored some clarity (Soviet communism was now the enemy), daily life, in all its golden-era material abundance, felt disorienting.

For English, these observations presented an interesting empirical question: Was there something intrinsic in the nature of 1950s youth, or in their upbringing, that made them seem at once self-centered and conformist? Or was this self-centeredness rather a function of the times in which they lived—a function of there being, in other words, no great mobilizing idea or war or experience to inspire them? Most social scientists believed (along with Kennedy and Shriver) that it was the latter. The times—the 1950s of Truman and Eisenhower—were simply not conducive to inspiration and idealism.

As a concept, the Peace Corps had piqued English's interest because it had created an outlet for youthful idealism. He also wondered about the psychological adjustments volunteers would have to make as they moved into and later out of foreign cultures. But English was trying to build a psychiatric career; the Peace Corps wasn't his concern.

At 806 Connecticut Avenue, however, it was becoming apparent that there were a growing number of problems overseas. Some of these problems had to do with the political problems of the host countries. But most seemed to stem from one of two related general causes: The first was poorly administered, insufficiently structured overseas programs; the second was unhappy volunteers. The evaluation reports of Charlie Peters's staff made clear that many programs were ineffectual and that many volunteers were frustrated and angry.

The volunteers were, as Shriver constantly emphasized, the lifeblood of the Peace Corps. Fundamentally, if the volunteers were unhappy, then the program was in a very important sense a failure. Shriver and his staff read and discussed some of the more unfavorable program evaluations. In some cases, the causes were clear and the problems easily resolved: Some jeeps might be sent to this country (where the volunteers had trouble getting to their work sites), or the Peace Corps representative might be replaced in that one (where administrative mismanagement was clearly the problem). But in many places, finding the source of the problem was trickier. If volunteers felt feckless and unhappy, was that an indictment of the host country (in which case countries needed to be better chosen)? Of the overseas management and program design (in which case the Peace Corps needed to design its programs more carefully and hire better administrative personnel)? Of the volunteer selection and distribution process (in which case screening needed to be refined)? Or was it, in fact, simply the nature of the beast? That is, if you sent people from an affluent society to a developing society for a long period of time, was it inevitable that they would suffer periods of culture shock or depression? And, if so, how should the volunteers—and the Peace Corps as an organization—cope with that?

Shriver's reaction to all these questions was, in May 1962, to hire a team of Peace Corps psychiatrists to evaluate the situation and then to help the agency craft solutions. This was a controversial decision. First, the practice of psychoanalysis had become relatively widespread in the United States after World War

II (in part because many important psychoanalysts had fled as refugees from Europe to the United States before and during the war), but many people not familiar with the field still thought of it as quackery. And outside of science research institutes and espionage agencies (where psychiatrists studied propaganda techniques and the like), one wasn't likely to find many psychiatrists on the federal payroll. Yet here was Shriver, proposing to make them an integral part of the Peace Corps operation.

Shriver's rationale for hiring psychiatrists was rooted, in part, in his experiences with the Kennedy Foundation. When he and Eunice canvassed the country's universities, they found that many of the few people working in mental retardation research were in departments of psychology or psychiatry. Shriver, English later wrote, "knew far more than most men in government about psychiatry. He recognized that Peace Corps volunteers would be more vulnerable to psychological stress than to amoeba." Shriver was also motivated by desperation. He needed answers fast; psychiatry might provide them.

Peace Corps psychiatrists, as Shriver discussed with his medical staff at a meeting in June 1962, could help the program in at least several ways. First, they could help the Medical Division during volunteer training to select out the medically unfit. Second, they could help to "select in" those individuals psychologically equipped to cope with stressful situations abroad. Third, they could meet one-on-one with volunteers-in-training to help provide forewarning of culture shock: a process of "strengthening the healthy" for their service abroad. And, finally, the psychiatrists could be made available to travel to host countries to meet with volunteers on an as-needed consulting basis.

Through a byzantine series of connections, Shriver got Joe English's name and brought him in for an interview at 806 Connecticut. "Look," Shriver told him, "despite our best efforts we may have a volunteer who succeeds in assassinating a foreign minister of government. And then I'm going to find myself up in front of some hostile congressional committee, getting grilled by Otto Passman. And they're going to ask me how I could have let anyone into the Peace Corps who would do something like this. In that situation, I have to have somebody to punt to—and that's going to be the psychiatrist."

When English returned to NIMH after a few days' vacation, he was summoned to the office of the institute's director, who told him he had been requested by the Peace Corps to serve as chief of psychiatry and that he was to report to 806 Connecticut immediately. On English's second day of work, a Tuesday in August, a secretary tracked him down and said that Shriver was on the phone and wanted to speak to him. "Be at the airport Thursday morning," Shriver told him. "And make sure you've got your passport and have had your shots. We're going to the Far East."

This was only the second conversation Shriver had had with English, and he was telling him to get ready—in forty-eight hours—for a trip to the Far East. Why him? When he asked some of his new colleagues they said, "Well, you're a doctor aren't you? You'll probably be responsible for ensuring Shriver doesn't get stricken by some horrible tropical disease—and for curing him if he does."

English reported dutifully to the airport Thursday morning and met his travel companions: Shriver; Bill Kelly, the Peace Corps' director of contracts and logistics; Dick Graham, the deputy associate director for public affairs; and Douglas Kiker, the new director of public information. Shriver's goal for this trip was to visit existing Peace Corps programs in Laos and the Philippines, where there had been widespread volunteer discontent, and to talk to heads of state about bringing programs to Indonesia and Singapore.

Larry Fuchs, the Peace Corps representative in the Philippines, greeted the Shriver team at the airport in Manila. Shriver's traveling companions were exhausted. "All we wanted was to go to our hotel and lie down in a bed, a real bed, and go to sleep," English recalled. "But what does Shriver insist we do first? Go to a gym to work out."

That night, English awoke in his hotel room at 3:00 a.m. with piercing stomach pains. He immediately suspected what was wrong: appendicitis. He took a cab to the local hospital, San Juan de Dios, and promptly got wheeled in for emergency surgery. Before he was put under general anesthesia, English asked to be anointed with the last rites of the Catholic Church. When he awoke the next morning to the sight of a giant lizard that had crawled into his room, English thought at first that he had died and gone to hell.

Meanwhile, Shriver's first full day of meetings with volunteers had not been pleasant. The volunteers complained that they were poorly managed; they had no clear direction from the Peace Corps staff, they said, and found the Peace Corps' Manila office unresponsive to their needs. The staff in Manila, in turn, was surly and defensive. Everyone was unhappy. And now, Shriver learned, the man he had brought along with him specifically to deal with this situation, a psychiatrist trained in such matters, was incapacitated with appendicitis.

But as word got around that the Peace Corps' director of psychiatry was lying in San Juan de Dios Hospital, recovering from an appendectomy, a group of curious volunteers decided to pay him a visit. "I was lying on my back with my sutures still in," English recalled, "and was not in that position the most intimidating figure."

This was fortuitous. English's vulnerability humanized him to the volunteers. Immediately, much of their suspicion of and hostility toward the Washington staff dissipated. Had he appeared in his white doctor's coat, looking official, the volunteers might indeed have suspected English of being there merely to "brainwash" them. Instead, they came in, sat on chairs in his hospital room, and began what English calls "some of the most remarkable conversations of my life." "They told me what the problems with the Philippine Peace Corps program was," he recalled, and he began to formulate ideas for how to help them cope psychologically with the stresses of culture shock.

When Shriver returned to Manila after several days flying around the far-flung Philippine islands visiting Peace Corps sites—200 volunteers scattered over 4,000 miles—he stopped by the hospital. After talking to many of the Philippine volunteers and to all of the Peace Corps staff in Manila, Shriver felt reassured that the situation was perhaps not as dire as it seemed. The first group of volunteers to arrive in the country had experienced the greatest difficulties; subsequent arrivals, although they still experienced many frustrations, were on the whole happier than the first group had been at the same stage. This was simply because, as Shriver explained to the Washington staff when he returned, the first group had been settling in at the same time as the administrative staff. Many of the logistical problems had been ironed out. And Shriver was in the main quite impressed with Larry Fuchs and his staff.

Shriver was even more impressed with some of the volunteers. He spoke with particular admiration of a twenty-two-year-old woman who had grown up on Fifth Avenue in Manhattan and attended Vassar—and who was now rising every morning to walk 3 miles, then paddle a boat 2 miles across a bay, then climb a 1,500-foot mountain to get to the school where she was teaching.

Shriver had also come to understand better some of the frustrations inherent in the volunteers' situation. Many constantly fought feelings of torpor and uselessness. This, Shriver learned, was the reality of the Philippine barrio, the phenomenon of *bahala na*. The underlying meaning of *bahala na* ("it doesn't matter, never mind") was that the fundamental conditions of barrio life, with all its hardship and squalor, could not be changed. This was what the Filipino people believed—and it was what the volunteers were having to contend with, and they found it deeply discouraging.

Many volunteers also expressed resentment of the Washington headquarters. It seemed to them that the staff at 806 Connecticut was more concerned with Congress than with the volunteers in the field. And they resented all the glowing publicity the Peace Corps was getting (and which they were reading in the weekly news publications that Shriver had mailed to them each month). "It seemed we were being lionized before we had done anything, and I resented references to our courage and sacrifice," a female volunteer complained to Fuchs. Many other volunteers also commented on the gap between the glowing accounts of what the Peace Corps was supposedly accomplishing and the anemic bits of productive work they were actually able to get done.

Most of all, the volunteers explained, they hadn't anticipated the feelings of loneliness and cultural isolation they would feel. Many in the first group of volunteers, Larry Fuchs later wrote, were "emotionally exhausted" after a few months. During a few "tense, frightening weeks" as many as half of the first group of 128 volunteers had said they would resign if they could do so honorably. By the time Shriver arrived in mid-August 1962, the acuteness of this feeling had abated, but the loneliness and isolation persisted. This reinforced Shriver's conviction that psychiatric evaluation and, especially, preventive counseling were essential to the Peace Corps' continued success.

On August 16, Shriver, Kiker, Graham, and Kelly departed Manila for Bangkok, Thailand. (English stayed behind for a few days, waiting for his sutures to be removed.) After four days in Thailand, Shriver flew to Malaya, where he met for half an hour with the Malayan prime minister, Abdul Rahman, who was so enamored of the Peace Corps that he told Shriver he would like to produce and appear in a movie that would "explain the purposes and successes of the Peace Corps."

After stopping in Singapore, which, it was determined, did not need volunteers, Shriver traveled to the rugged lands of Borneo. Shriver had planned to visit newly arrived volunteers in rural villages in the north, but when he arrived at the American Embassy, officials advised him not to go. Fierce tropical storms could make the going difficult and could flood the rivers along the way, making travel impossible. Shriver laughed off these admonitions and, to the alarm of Graham, Kiker, and Kelly, dragged his team with him off into the wilds. They arrived in the north before heavy rains fell but then remained trapped by monsoons in North Borneo for several days. When English, just released from the hospital in Manila, arrived at the embassy, the staff there was growing worried. They had not heard from Shriver and his team, who were now several days late in returning.

English joined a search party that headed upcountry to rescue Shriver. When they found him, he hardly seemed in need of rescuing. He and his colleagues were drenched from the days of rain and from crossing swollen rivers on a homemade raft, but Shriver was clearly enjoying every moment of his adventure. Reunited with English, the Peace Corps team returned to civilization.

Shriver's original itinerary had called for him to return home from Borneo. But a day before he was scheduled to return, he was contacted by the government of Indonesia, which lay just south of Borneo across the Java Sea. Indonesia was one of the largest developing countries in the world, and the Peace Corps staff in Washington had long thought it would be a good place to send volunteers because of the many needs of its large and impoverished population. Some of the standard political motivations obtained as well. Indonesia had won official independence from the Netherlands in 1949 and had, since the end of World War II, been seeking to distance itself from its former colonial patrons. But President Sukarno, the leader of the independence movement, had through the 1950s actively allowed Communist representation in the government to increase significantly. By the early 1960s, the Indonesian Communist Party was a force of considerable influence; the government was importing military hardware from the Soviet Union; and Sukarno himself had become something of a despot.

Thus President Kennedy and the State Department applied the usual pressures on Shriver to bring the Peace Corps to Indonesia, as a means of importing a model of democracy to that region of the Far East. Shriver, however, could not send volunteers where they had not been invited—and Indonesia had yet to invite the Peace Corps in for even a conversation. Anti-American sentiment had run high in the country since 1958, when the CIA had supported a coup against Sukarno. But in

August 1962, while Shriver was elsewhere in the Far East, President Kennedy had helped Sukarno resolve (if only temporarily) a territorial dispute with the Dutch over West New Guinea, at the far eastern edge of Indonesia. Now Shriver and company returned from their journey across the waters of Borneo and Sarawak to find that relations between Washington and the Indonesian capital, Jakarta, had momentarily thawed. When the Peace Corps director found a personal invitation from Sukarno waiting for him at the American Embassy in Pontianak, he accepted.

As usual, Shriver horrified the American Embassy staff in Jakarta by insisting on visiting, unannounced, a slum on the outskirts of the city. "The embassy types were aghast," Joe English recalled. "The area, they claimed, was 'heavily communist.' They insisted the visit was politically volatile and physically dangerous."

Ignoring the importunings of embassy officials, Shriver and his small entourage went to the slum. English later wrote an account of the visit.

As we walked along the intricate pathways we saw, through the open doorways, pictures of John F. Kennedy as well as of President Sukarno. Finally, Shriver stopped beside one neat, little dirt-floored home. Through an interpreter, he asked the woman in the doorway if he might enter. She stood there, uncertain and awed, but finally nodded. Then, Shriver stepped forward, bent down, took off his shoes, and walked inside.

It was all there, in that simple gesture, the giving of respect without the loss of dignity. And so they stood there, that tiny Indonesian woman and the towering American. They talked of her neighbors and of his brother-in-law, the American President. And, as they talked, first ten, then fifteen, then fifty, and soon more than a hundred children crowded around the doorway.

When we left, the children gathered about Shriver. With a few words from his interpreter, he tried to talk with them. They laughed and answered and followed us back towards the city. We left that "dangerous, communist-ridden" slum with the shouts and laughter of some 150 children ringing in our ears.

Shriver had little notion of what to expect from his audience with Sukarno. The chargé d'affaires at the embassy said he didn't think anything of substance would be accomplished. Shriver asked Joe English to accompany him to the presidential palace for the meeting. "Why me," English asked, "and not an expert on Indonesia, or a Peace Corps programmer?" "Because," Shriver explained, "Sukarno is known to often consult with astrologers. I don't have any astrologers. But I do have a psychiatrist." Sukarno, as it turned out, "was delighted with the notion" that psychiatrists were the American equivalent of Indonesian astrologers. Sukarno brought in all his astrologers to meet with English and compare notes on their methods.

As English conversed with the presidential astrologers, he noted that Shriver and Sukarno seemed to be hitting it off quite well. The conversation they were having, however, seemed quite puzzling. Shriver kept trying to steer the conversation toward matters of political substance—and Sukarno kept peppering him with questions about Hollywood. "Do you know this actor?" the Indonesian president would ask him, referring to a Hollywood celebrity. "How about that one?" Shriver answered as best he could, but he couldn't understand why Sukarno was continually steering the conversation back to the entertainment business.

"Sarge," English hissed. "I think he thinks you're Peter Lawford!" Shriver considered this for a moment and then laughed. English was right. Sukarno knew that President Kennedy had a brother-in-law who was a movie star; and he knew that President Kennedy had a brother-in-law who ran the Peace Corps—he just didn't know that the two men were not the *same* brother-in-law.

Unsure how to correct the Indonesian leader's misimpression without embarrassing him, Shriver decided to live for the moment with his mistaken identity. "The actress, Marilyn Monroe," Sukarno said. "What really happened to her? How did she die?" As English recalled, Shriver looked momentarily alarmed. "Well, gee, it's hard to say and there's a lot of speculation," he stammered. Then, recovering his composure, Shriver said, "But Dr. English is a psychiatrist. *He* can tell you."

English was beginning to try to explain that Monroe's death was most likely a suicide, but that it was hard to say for sure, when Sukarno cut in. "No, it was not suicide," Sukarno said. Both Shriver and English were taken aback. "It wasn't?" English said. "No," Sukarno said. "Let me tell you what happened." And the Indonesian president proceeded to explain patiently to Shriver and English that what surely had happened was that Monroe had taken her sleeping pills, fallen asleep, and then been awakened by a phone call. Forgetting that she had already taken her sleeping medication, the actress took a second dose, this time overdosing. "Which is very common, isn't that right, doctor?" Sukarno said to the astonished English.

As the conversation veered from psychiatry and astrology to Marilyn Monroe, Shriver tried to steer the conversation in a more serious direction, but Sukarno merely brushed him off and called for more refreshments. Just as Shriver was beginning to despair of accomplishing anything with his visit, he thought he overheard Sukarno saying, "And when the Peace Corps comes to Indonesia. . . ." Shriver wasn't even sure he had heard right, but he forged directly ahead. "When the Peace Corps comes to Indonesia," Shriver said, "where would you like the volunteers to go?" Sukarno responded with a list of towns and villages where he was already making arrangements to accommodate volunteers. As easy as that, the Peace Corps was on its way to Indonesia. Shriver, after a short trip to Bali, was on his way back home in time for Labor Day 1962.

CHAPTER TWENTY-TWO

Growing Pains

S hriver returned to 806 Connecticut that fall to find a new crisis on his hands: The simmering conflict between Warren Wiggins's Planning, Development, and Operations Division and Charlie Peters's Evaluation Division had erupted into full-blown warfare. Many on the Wiggins team had long resented and disliked Peters, whose job—or so it seemed to them—was simply to criticize them and make their jobs harder. Now they were openly angling for his head.

In March 1962 Peters had gone on an extended tour of Peace Corps sites in Africa, the Middle East, and the Far East and had found the programs riddled with problems. The people in charge of the Pakistan programs, where less than a quarter of the volunteers had productive jobs, Peters told Shriver, "ought to be fired for lunatic stupidity." After reading Peters's report, Shriver agreed; he fired the heads of the Pakistan program. This did not endear Peters to the PDO Division. Now "the PDO people *really* hated me, were out to get me," Peters recalled. "Sarge had taken my word over theirs. They were livid."

By late summer 1962, as Shriver was touring the Far East, Bill Haddad was warning Peters, "You are an inch away from being fired." Haddad was Peters's boss, and probably his biggest supporter in the organization, but he recognized that the situation had become untenable. So many people were clamoring for Peters's dismissal that it was clear Shriver would have to do something: either come out with a public statement in support of Peters or fire him. So Peters sat down and wrote a long memo to Shriver explaining his view of everything he had found wrong with various Peace Corps programs. Peters concluded the memo by saying, in effect, "I realize there is disagreement as to what the truth about the Peace Corps is. But only you can decide what is right. I believe that you should go out almost immediately and have a look at our field operations. Observe closely; talk to the volunteers, who are themselves the truth, and then come back to this memo and compare what the Division of Evaluation says to what the PDO says, and decide which is right."

Shriver did as Peters suggested. In late October 1962, Shriver stuffed all of Peters's evaluation memos in his suitcase and set off for Africa. This took a certain boldness on Shriver's part. The Peace Corps, after all, was receiving highly positive press attention. Congress loved him. It would have been tempting simply to bask in the adoring glow, especially since almost the entire PDO Division was claiming that Peters's evaluations lacked merit. But Shriver wanted to know the truth.

The timing of Shriver's trip reflected another kind of boldness, or perhaps an otherworldly sense of optimism, as well. On Monday, October 22, President Kennedy had announced to the American people that the Soviets were building nuclear missile launching sites in Cuba. Kennedy was evacuating troops from Guantanamo Bay and was blockading Cuba with American warships. He also served notice on the Soviet Union that the launch of missiles from Cuba would be tantamount to a declaration of nuclear war—and that the United States would respond to such a declaration in kind. The nation stood closer to open (and nuclear) conflict with the Soviets than at any time since the dawn of the cold war. The world held its breath.

Yet at 7:30 in the morning on Thursday, October 25, Donovan McClure, the Peace Corps' director of public affairs, got a telephone call from Mary Ann Orlando, telling him to get over to the hospital for inoculations immediately, since he would be leaving for East Africa that night. "In my shock and panic at this message," McClure recalled, "I formed the brief but totally insane notion that with the Russian missiles pointed at us, Shriver, always resourceful, was aiming to set up a government-in-exile." On the plane from Idlewild that evening, after Shriver had fallen asleep, McClure talked with his colleagues Joe Colmen and Joe Kaufman, who were also accompanying Shriver on this trip. All of them wondered why, when the world teetered on the nuclear brink, this trip to Africa was so urgent. Couldn't it be delayed? While his deputies twisted uncomfortably in their seats, Shriver slept peacefully *under* his seat, as was his custom—a practice that was described in a *New Yorker* Talk of the Town piece after skeptical newsmen denied that such a thing was possible. He was evidently unconcerned by momentous world events unfolding around them.

After landing in the city of Asmara, Shriver set about trying to see as many of the 275 volunteers in Ethiopia as possible. "He was racing around in a jeep from sunup to sunset, shattering the poise of countless volunteers by suddenly appearing in their classrooms or at the doors of their houses, hand extended: 'Hi! I'm Sarge Shriver." On Shriver's last day in Ethiopia, he was unexpectedly invited to the imperial palace for a formal dinner with Emperor Haile Selassie. Although Shriver had been hoping to meet with Selassie, he had not anticipated such an official audience and had not packed any formal attire. Fortunately, an aide to Arthur Richards, the US ambassador to Ethiopia, was on hand to lend Shriver a tuxedo; unfortunately, the aide was half a foot shorter than Shriver. The pants were too short and, as Donovan McClure recalled, "if worn normally, the cuffs missed the shoe tops by six inches. If he tugged the pants down to meet his shoes, the trousers left a wide expanse beneath the vest." What to do?

Shriver realized that if he pulled the trousers down to his shoes and walked hunched over, no gap between his vest and his pants would be apparent. Shriver's back began to hurt, but he dared not straighten up for fear of exposing his belly. This absurd situation proved fortuitous. It was later reported to Shriver that Emperor Selassie had been "much impressed" with Shriver's deferential manner, and with the lengths to which he had gone to disguise the significant height difference between himself and the tiny emperor.

After dinner with the emperor, Shriver, still hunched over, was taken on a tour of the palace grounds that included a visit to the outer garden where Emperor Selassie kept his pet lion, Tojo. When Shriver asked if he could pet Tojo, Joe Colmen turned to Joe Kaufman and asked, "What is the line of succession at the Peace Corps, anyway?"

After leaving Ethiopia, Shriver and company spent five days visiting volunteers, by jeep, in Tanganyika. From Tanganyika it was off on a decrepit DC-3 to Somalia, which Charlie Peters had reported as being one of the most problematic locations in the Peace Corps. The visit was not a good one. The Somalia program was a disaster. The Peace Corps representative there seemed to resent the volunteers' lack of toughness, and he treated their adjustment problems with disdain. The volunteers, in turn, felt frustrated, homesick, directionless. Shriver initially was personally impressed by the Somalia representative, who had the swashbuckling, charismatic style he found irresistible. But after meeting with many of the volunteers he reluctantly decided that the representative needed to be replaced. He cabled back to headquarters in Washington. "Tell Peters his reports are right," it said. The cable quickly circulated throughout 806 Connecticut. Peters's job was clearly safe, and his stature in the organization instantly elevated. He had weathered the storm.

The Peace Corps continued to grow quickly—too quickly, by some estimations. Charlie Peters, for instance, believed that many of the problems in the field were caused by a rate of growth that produced more volunteers than were needed or could be supervised. Nine new countries received the Peace Corps in early 1963, bringing the total from thirty-seven to forty-six, and the size of the program's budget appropriation doubled. Volunteers were being sent to places that weren't yet equipped to accommodate them. Despite the clear evidence from the Evaluation Division that such rapid growth was taking its toll on both morale and effectiveness, Shriver still led a "manic drive" to put more volunteers in the field.

The Peace Corps, in Shriver's mind, could never be too big. If anything, he believed, the program needed to get even bigger, even faster. "Our country and our times have had plenty of experience with programs that were too little, too late," he wrote in 1963. Besides, he argued, more pressure was put on the Peace Corps to grow by developing countries demanding volunteers than by people within the organization itself.

The rapid rate of growth continued to produce botched programs, including some—like those in Somalia, Pakistan, and parts of Bangladesh—that were complete failures. Under great time pressure, program planners in Washington had drawn up completely unrealistic program outlines. On balance, however, given how rapidly the organization was growing, most Peace Corps programs were remarkably successful.

THE FIVE-YEAR FLUSH

Even as the program grew, Shriver managed to preserve the distinctively non-bureaucratic character of the organization. Partly he did that by keeping the staff small. But he also did it by insisting that the Peace Corps remain a service, or a tour of duty, not a career. This was unprecedented in the annals of the federal government, where lifetime appointments and comfortable sinecures were the norm. Shriver codified this in a policy, sketched out in a 1963 memo by Franklin Williams titled "In, Up, and Out," which came to be known in the Peace Corps as the "Five-Year Flush": Terms of service in the agency's administration would be limited to five years. No one, not a director or a secretary, would be able to stay longer.

This caused some consternation both among more-experienced government executives and among the organization's congressional liaisons, who worried that the constant turnover would cause disruption or that it would lead to "administration by rookies." As the *Wall Street Journal* reported, "This transient turnover, antithesis of the orderly promotion and tenure procedures espoused by the Civil Service Commission, has been institutionalized at the Peace Corps. Over the objections of the Civil Service chief John Macy, Mr. Shriver persuaded the just-adjourned Congress to clamp a five-year service ceiling on Peace Corps official-dom." Shriver, the *Journal* reported, "seems not to recognize a requirement for a permanent cadre of civil servants to manage major Federal activities; in his view, the inspired amateurs can quickly acquire the necessary, though bothersome, bureaucratic competence. Lest initiative and imagination be stifled, the ... Peace Corps shun[s] organizational stability and job security. Most of all, the Shriver system of ... staffing calls for constant tension, turmoil and turnover to infuse freshness and force into the federal bureaucracy."

Critics scoffed, and the Civil Service protested fiercely. "Shriver's Peace Corps policy is ridiculous," lamented one critic. "If you've got a good running organization, why routinely force out a large proportion of the staff each year?" But Shriver was adamant. He appointed Bill Moyers, whom he had made his deputy director in February 1963, the head of a task force whose mandate was embodied in the title of a memo—"To Keep the Peace Corps Flexible." Shriver and Moyers felt strongly enough about keeping careerists out of the Peace Corps that they endeavored to have the Five-Year Flush written into federal law. White House aides and the Civil Service Commission blanched. "This approach is so fundamentally in conflict with the idea of the career service," the commission chairman told Shriver, "that I believe, even under the special circumstances of the Peace Corps, that this limitation would constitute inappropriate public policy." Moyers wrote a memo to the White House that tried to make the case. "Sarge is also concerned to . . . assure that the Peace Corps will retain its fresh, critical, and spirited approach to business. A five-year limitation on employment will guarantee constant injection into the Peace Corps of new ideas and energies." It took two years, but the Five-Year Flush was written into law in October 1965.

"THEY PADDLED THEIR OWN CANOE"

The Peace Corps' breakneck growth continued. Over the summer of 1963, the first volunteers arrived in Guinea, Indonesia, and Uruguay. Meanwhile, countries that already had Peace Corps programs in place were preparing to bid good-bye to their first round of volunteers and welcome their second. In almost every country the number of volunteers requested was holding steady or growing; almost nowhere was it shrinking.

This led to a problem. Although the Peace Corps did not publicly admit this, it was beginning to face a serious shortage of volunteers. In the initial flush of enthusiasm following Kennedy's election and inauguration, Shriver and his small staff received more volunteer applications than they could handle. The deluge of applications continued to flood 806 Connecticut as the early publicity for the program made it sound patriotic and exciting. The Peace Corps became in some way the repository for the hopes and dreams of the (mostly young) Americans touched by the hopefulness of the New Frontier.

Now, however, the rate of applications had declined somewhat, even as the need for volunteers was growing; the demand for qualified volunteers abroad was threatening to outstrip the supply. At a staff meeting Shriver announced,

> We're almost at the point where the requests for volunteers will outnumber our
> supply. We didn't expect this to happen so quickly, since we started out on open-

ing day with over 20,000 banging on our doors and we didn't even have a single request from overseas. . . . But by this time next year I predict we'll be in fifty countries and the ones we're in already are asking for as many as triple the number they now have. So we've got to be much more aggressive about the way we recruit. Much more imaginative.

Because Shriver would not countenance discussion of lowering selection standards, this meant the Peace Corps would have to launch a more aggressive recruitment program. The recruitment drive began in the spring in the Midwest and then moved on to California, which had proved the most fertile ground during the first two years of the program, producing 14 percent of all the volunteers. There was a debate at 806 Connecticut over how big and how public the recruitment campaign should be. Everyone recognized the need to generate more applications, but some of Shriver's deputies feared that a campaign that was too aggressive would make the Peace Corps seem desperate; they thought it inappropriate to resort to a Madison Avenue–style advertising pitch to draw volunteers. Shriver disagreed: The bigger and louder the campaign was, he believed, the more effective it would be.

Thus the first week of October 1963 saw the Peace Corps descend on the Golden State en masse. "Blitz recruiting," the Peace Corps called it: Fifty staff members, led by Shriver himself, marched across the state, making speeches and setting up recruiting stations at forty-four colleges. Shriver gave eight convocation addresses at universities, and four speeches to civic associations, in four days. The assault yielded more than 2,500 applications and ultimately an estimated 1,000 volunteers, helping it climb toward its goal of 13,000 by the beginning of 1964.

This rapid expansion made some Republican lawmakers nervous. Congressman Passman snarled angrily in the Peace Corps' direction. As a November vote on a $102 million Peace Corps appropriation neared, several other members of Congress made a joint statement accusing the program of being "a burgeoning bureaucracy." Pointing out that the Peace Corps budget had nearly doubled in a year, the representatives argued for a more modest growth rate and warned against its becoming "perverted" into an "enthusiastic crusade." Shriver, confident that the president would use his bully pulpit to back up the appropriation if necessary, cheerfully responded that of course it was an enthusiastic crusade and that the additional money was necessary if the program were to expand deeper into Africa and Latin America, where it was sorely needed.

As long as President Kennedy was still popular, it would be hard for Passman and others to get much political traction from trying to bring down the Peace Corps. In November 1963, as the recruitment drive continued, no one had any reason to think that Shriver would not continue to enjoy Kennedy's indefinite support for the remainder of his first term and for what looked highly likely to be a second term as well.

Shriver often joked that it would be easier for Kennedy to fire a family member than a political friend, but the truth was that Shriver's relationship with the president made him and his program in some sense untouchable. Both Kennedy and Shriver knew this. After the Peace Corps was up and running, Kennedy did whatever Shriver asked: made public appearances with volunteers, wrote letters, lobbied Congress. Shriver, in turn, cultivated the relationship, not by playing the in-law card (since that had backfired in the fight over independence from AID), but through a nonstop public relations campaign directed at the White House. Every week, Shriver would send Kennedy at least one official memo summarizing Peace Corps activities, and many times he would supplement it with one or more personal letters. Although there was clearly an element of self-promotion in this stream of material Shriver sent to Kennedy, his main goal was to deepen Kennedy's relationship with the program itself and to keep him from having to worry about it. Evidently the strategy worked. "Sarge is really on the ball," the president told an aide after reading one of Shriver's memos.

The situation was ideal, from Kennedy's perspective. The Peace Corps was, as Harris Wofford put it, the president's "special baby, and in a sense the first offspring of the New Frontier." Yet (to extend the metaphor) Kennedy never had to worry about childcare. "How are Sarge's kids doing?" the president would ask Ken Galbraith, the US ambassador to India, whenever Galbraith visited Washington. "They paddled their own canoe," McGeorge Bundy, Kennedy's national security adviser, said of Peace Corps management. This left Kennedy free to focus on the crisis of the moment, whether in Havana, Moscow, or Berlin.

Shriver's privileged access to the president was not without its anxieties. He had learned in 1961 the folly of trying to use Eunice to get to her brother. And Shriver could be sensitive about his relationship to the Kennedy family. Once, when a reporter asked Shriver whether he had benefited unduly from this relationship,

Shriver bristled. "[Being brother-in-law to the president is] a fact of life, why think about it at all? I'm perfectly capable of looking after myself." But on balance, as Peter Braestrup, who covered the Peace Corps for the *New York Times*, later recalled, Shriver's relationship to Kennedy was "essential" to the start of the Peace Corps. Because Shriver was the president's brother-in-law, members of Congress and federal government administrators "couldn't lean on him as if he had just been another guy"; Shriver "scared" the bureaucrats. Fred Dutton, a presidential adviser, said that people in the federal bureaucracy were always aware that the Peace Corps was Kennedy's "favorite child." For better and for worse, behind Shriver always loomed the shadow of the president. Shriver took this for granted and assumed that as long as he headed the Peace Corps, it would always be the case.

The success of the California recruiting blitz was followed in late November by a more modest recruiting trip to colleges in Pittsburgh. Shriver flew into the city on Wednesday, November 20, and over the next two days he made speeches at three universities, gave radio and television interviews, and held a press conference. The mayor officially declared it "Peace Corps Week in Pittsburgh." Reporters from radio station KDKA, which Shriver had first heard when it broadcast balloting results from the 1924 Democratic Convention into his Maryland living room, followed him around.

Flying home to Washington on the morning of November 22, 1963, Shriver had every reason to think about how lucky he was. The recruiting drive was going well. The Peace Corps was more successful than anyone could have imagined two years earlier; it had grown faster than any peacetime agency in history; and it was the program President Kennedy felt proudest of. It was also the program with which people, both at home and abroad, most identified Kennedy. Several months earlier, in July, *Time* had put Shriver on its cover under the headline, "The Peace Corps: A US Ideal Abroad." The Peace Corps, the article said, is "the single greatest success the Kennedy Administration has produced." In March the *New York Times* columnist James Reston had written, "Of all the agencies of the federal government, only the Peace Corps has surpassed the hopes and claims of the Kennedy Administration." The Peace Corps, Reston continued, "stands above the rest as the only thing new and vigorous that has managed to avoid the pessimism of intractable problems." Shriver, it seemed, had found his calling. "I have the best damned job in Government," he told *Time*.

CHAPTER TWENTY-THREE

Tragedy

That same day—Friday, November 22—Eunice Shriver, who was six months pregnant, had an appointment with her obstetrician. Afterward, on a whim, she decided to bring her four-year-old son, Timmy, to Peace Corps headquarters to see if her husband, who had just flown in from Pittsburgh that morning, might have time for lunch. The three Shrivers were sitting quietly in the dining room of the Hotel Lafayette when an urgent call came through for Sarge from his assistant, Mary Ann Orlando. Sarge excused himself and took the call, assuming a problem had come up at the office.

"I'm sorry to tell you this way," Orlando said, "but the president has been shot; they don't know whether he is alive."

Returning to the table, he told Eunice, "Something's happened to Jack."

"What?" she asked.

"He's been shot," Sarge said.

"Will he be all right?" she asked.

"We don't know," Sarge said.

Eunice closed her eyes for a moment, then said, "There have been so many crises in his life; he'll pull through."

They ordered lunch. Eunice was just finishing her soup when a second telephone call came through: Jack was in critical condition.

Shriver's first concern was for his pregnant wife (how would she endure the death of a third sibling?), and he thought perhaps he should escort her home to Maryland. Outside the restaurant, Sarge recalled, Eunice quavered for a moment and he held out his arm to steady her. Then she set her jaw—she was visibly struggling to contain her emotions. "But nothing can overcome Eunice," Shriver would say later, because of the depth of her religious faith. Within a minute she was barking orders, telling her husband that he was needed at the Peace Corps and that she felt she ought to get to the White House soon, to meet with Bobby Kennedy.

Sarge and Eunice hurried across Lafayette Park to Shriver's office, where Eunice called Bobby for an update. "It doesn't look good," Bobby told her. A Peace Corps staffer brought in a wire flash, saying that the president was dead. Sarge embraced Eunice and proposed that all present say a prayer for Jack's soul. Sarge and Eunice, along with Joe English and a Peace Corps public affairs officer, knelt around Sarge's desk, and over and over again they intoned in unison "Hail Mary, full of grace" until they were interrupted by a knock on the door—someone from the press office bringing another sheaf of wire reports from Dallas.

Standing up after they had all finished praying, Shriver resumed worrying about what effect the shock of the news would have on his wife and unborn son. English, who was a doctor, had the same concern. "Now, listen, Eunice," English said, "we're all going to have responsibilities here but you've got the biggest one of all—responsibility for two. My suggestion is that we should get you out of here and send you up to be with your mother in Hyannis Port." Shriver agreed and pressed Eunice to go to the Cape. She reluctantly agreed but insisted on going to the White House first, to consult with Bobby. Worried about their children, the Shrivers sent Timmy home in the care of Mary Ann Orlando, who was instructed to pick Bobby and Maria up at their schools on the way.

Shriver called a brief meeting of the senior Peace Corps staff. About a dozen people gathered in his office, many of them in tears, everyone looking ill. Shriver declared that the Peace Corps would continue to run as normally as possible. He also decided that his office would send out a wire bulletin to all

Peace Corps representatives and volunteers in the field, reporting what had just happened in Dallas and reassuring everyone that the program would not be affected. "We didn't want Americans in the field hearing about the death of the president from unreliable sources," Shriver recalled. "We also didn't want volunteers to worry that the Peace Corps had died with the president."

Out in the streets, bedlam had erupted. The bells of St. John's Church, just north of Lafayette Park, were tolling incessantly. Motorists, as William Manchester reported in *Death of a President*, were "going berserk," ignoring traffic laws and swerving as though drunk from lane to lane, sometimes abandoning their cars in the middle of the road. But the Shrivers and English, in a White House car procured by Mary Ann Orlando, managed to navigate around Lafayette Park to the White House. In his urgency to get there, Shriver insisted that the driver head for the nearest gate, on the northwest side of the White House, by driving the wrong way down West Executive Avenue. As the secret serviceman on duty at the northwest gate, his nerves already on edge, saw a car careening toward him the wrong way down the avenue, he drew his machine gun and prepared to open fire. (For all he knew, this was step two of a coup attempt in which step one had been the assassination in Dallas.) As everyone else in the car took cover, Shriver leaned his head out of the car and waved. English thought Shriver would be shot dead. But at the last minute the guard recognized him and waved the driver through. They parked on the south grounds of the White House.

Once inside, the Shrivers found not Bobby but Teddy Kennedy, who had been elected a first-term senator the previous fall. The Shrivers conferred with Ted and all three agreed that he would take Eunice to Hyannis Port, so that she could be there to console her mother. It was also decided that Ted would break the news of the president's death to Joe Kennedy, who had suffered a debilitating stroke several years earlier. English, meanwhile, still concerned for Eunice and the baby she was carrying, went to the White House medical office to get some mild sedatives. He gave Ted the pills in an envelope and explained that he should give them to his sister on the plane, to keep her from getting hysterical. Three days later, at President Kennedy's funeral, Ted would return the envelope to English with the pills still in it. "Right medicine, Doc," Ted would say then. "Wrong girl."

Before leaving for Cape Cod, Eunice talked to Bobby, making plans and establishing a new chain of command within the family: She was the eldest surviving child, but Bobby, the eldest male, would call the shots. The three Kennedys—Bobby, Ted, and Eunice—divided up the family responsibilities. Bobby would officially represent the Kennedy family and would meet and escort the president's widow, Jackie, over the next few days. Ted and Eunice would fly to Hyannis Port to be with their parents. And Shriver was to stay at the White House and begin to make all the funeral arrangements. "I'll get Jackie back to the White House," Bobby told Shriver. "But you take it from there." As Shriver would later recall, Jackie Kennedy also independently conveyed through a phone call to the White House that she wanted him in charge of funeral planning and of management of the press. "Twenty minutes after walking into the White House, I was in charge of everything."

Why did Jackie pick Shriver to run the funeral? Partly it was a straightforward matter of running down the line of Kennedy family succession: Jack was dead; Bobby would be taking care of Jackie; Ted was going to Hyannis Port; and Joe, the patriarch, was at home on Cape Cod, incapacitated by a stroke. Among the in-laws, Shriver had the virtue of already being physically present in the White House.

But if this helps explain why Bobby and Ted were willing to put Shriver in charge, it doesn't fully explain Jackie's explicit request that Shriver take responsibility for the arrangements, rather than, say, a close family friend like Lem Billings or Bill Walton, or an aide like Ted Sorensen, Dick Reardon, or Kenny O'Donnell. Shriver, some thirty years after the event, reflected that Jackie had several reasons for entrusting matters to him. First, everyone associated with the Kennedy administration knew that Shriver was an effective leader; his performance during the 1960 campaign, and especially as director of the Peace Corps, had demonstrated that clearly. And his obvious skill at handling Congress and the press suggested that he was good at managing public relations, something that was important to Jackie even in her shock-stricken condition; she cared deeply about how Jack's memory would be preserved by history, and she felt it important that the proper image of his administration be conveyed by the funeral.

But Jackie Kennedy and Sarge Shriver also shared the experience of being in-laws in the Kennedy family—and the two of them, more than any of the other in-laws, had a knack for striking a balance between independence from and submersion in the Kennedy family. Jackie and Sarge, numerous observers have noted, were two of the kindest and warmest people in the extended Kennedy clan. They were also the two Kennedy family members with the greatest sense of style, and they preserved their distinctive styles even amid the powerful Kennedy culture, which dictated a style of its own. (Both were descended, too, from aristocratic Continental Catholic families of the sort that historically had seen Irish Catholics like the Kennedys as socially inferior.) And yet each of the two, for whatever independence they maintained, was clearly loyal to the Kennedy family. Shriver, Jackie instinctively would have recognized, would know how to strike the right tone in the memorial planning—how to make it a Kennedy family funeral without its being *exclusively* a Kennedy funeral. Jack, his wife believed, belonged also to God and to the American voters who had elected him. Shriver was independent enough to recognize this, while also being deeply enough connected to the family to make sure their concerns were properly honored. He may have been the only person capable of doing all this adroitly, without faltering under the pressure.

At 2:40 p.m., the television networks confirmed for America that President Kennedy was dead. Twenty minutes later, after seeing Ted and Eunice off from the helicopter pad, Shriver began walking back up the lawn to the White House. As he did so Jack McNally, one of Kennedy's staff assistants, walked up to Shriver and suggested he come over to McNally's office where some former Kennedy aides had gathered to discuss what to do next. Shriver declined. Bobby Kennedy had deputized him to be the Kennedy family's representative at the White House until the slain president's body arrived. This responsibility, Shriver felt, demanded that he set up his own command post. "I'll use Ralph's office," he said, referring to Kennedy's special assistant Ralph Dungan. Shriver may also have sensed the ineffectuality of the East Wing gathering in McNally's office. Incapacitated by shock and grief, many of Kennedy's aides stood mutely gaping at the television. Anyone could see that they wouldn't be able to accomplish anything.

So Shriver took charge. He commandeered Dungan's office, and over the next few hours he issued commands like a drill sergeant, making arrangements for much of what would take place in the time between Friday afternoon and Monday, when the president would be memorialized and buried. European observers at the funeral on Monday marveled: How could such an elaborate state funeral have been put together so quickly? The duke of Norfolk, who had worked on Winston's Churchill's funeral, was in awe: "Three days—*how?*" The answer, as William Manchester wrote, "lay partly in America's national temperament, partly in the fiber of the men who gathered around Shriver and Ralph Dungan that Friday afternoon."

> Dungan brooded behind his desk, sucking on an unlit pipe; Sarge sat in front on a straight-backed chair. Between them they reached the first funeral decisions during the next two hours. They were never alone. One of their fellow planners described the meeting—which was to continue nonstop through three successive nights—as "Jack's last campaign." It was a lot like a campaign; a man almost had to be a political veteran to function in it.

Dungan's office was almost always teeming: McGeorge Bundy, Everett Dirksen, Angier "Angie" Biddle Duke, Joe English, John Kenneth Galbraith, Dick Goodwin, Katherine Graham, Averell Harriman, Jack McNally, Ted Reardon, Arthur Schlesinger, Ted Sorensen, Adlai Stevenson, Bill Walton, and dozens of others—including a large complement of priests and policemen—came and went frequently.

Everyone seemed in a daze—except Shriver, who seemed almost to gain clarity as others lost it. This lent force to his authority; as he gave everyone their assignments, no one questioned his orders. He quickly sized up who was in a condition to handle which tasks—who might benefit from having something important to do, who might buckle under the strain. He sent one group of aides to compile a list of President Kennedy's friends, divided into appropriate categories, so the process of figuring out whom to invite to the funeral (and where they should be seated) could begin. Shriver consulted with Adlai Stevenson and Angie Duke, who had been the president's social secretary, about protocol for presidential funerals and funeral processions. At 3:42 p.m., Shriver was informed that the president's body would soon be on its way to Andrews Air Force Base. He quickly assigned aides to meet the plane there, to be accompanied by a protocol officer from Angie Duke's staff.

Shriver then turned his attention to the burial and began consultation with Lt. Col. Paul C. Miller, who was the federal government's official ceremonies officer. What, Shriver asked him, does a formal state burial entail? Miller explained that presidents and five-star generals and admirals were supposed to lie in state. Where the president would lie in state depended on where the burial was to take place. If the president were to be buried somewhere in Washington, Miller suggested, his body might lie in state either in the East Room of the White House or in the great Rotunda of the Capitol. Miller wasn't sure what to do if the president were to be buried in the family plot outside Boston, but he had begun to make arrangements to have the body delivered there, either by train, airplane, or naval destroyer.

Most of those thinking about the issue believed that the president should be buried in the Kennedy family plot in Brookline, Massachusetts, but Shriver believed that as a navy veteran and the commander in chief of the US armed forces, Jack should be buried at Arlington National Cemetery. So he called Arlington and spoke to its superintendent, John Metzler. Shriver's first question was whether there was any rule prohibiting a Catholic burial in a national cemetery. "Negative," Metzler responded. "We have Catholic ceremonies almost every day." Shriver also asked whether children could be buried at Arlington. They could be, Metzler told him. Jack's children Caroline and John could be buried alongside him. Discussion about the burial site would continue within the Kennedy inner circle, but for Shriver the issue was settled. No ordinary cemetery would do. The president belonged to the country as much as to the Kennedy family. Jack must be buried at Arlington.

The next issue Shriver had to worry about was more grisly: What would happen to the president's body once it was returned to Washington? Who should receive the body? Should an autopsy be performed? And who would prepare the body for burial? These were matters of grim protocol that no one had contemplated. It was determined that the president's body would be delivered to Bethesda Naval Hospital, in Maryland, where it would be autopsied and embalmed.

While Ralph Dungan, Ted Sorensen, and other aides flew by helicopter to Andrews Air Force Base to receive the president's remains, Shriver, Dick Goodwin, and Bill Walton stayed behind in Dungan's office with Colonel Miller to begin planning the funeral parade. The president's aircraft—carrying Lyndon Johnson, Lady Bird Johnson, Jacqueline Kennedy, and President Kennedy's remains, as well as aides and secret service agents who had been in Texas with them—arrived at Andrews about 6:00 p.m. Jackie Kennedy and Bobby Kennedy went from there to Bethesda with the late president's remains, while President Johnson headed for the White House with some of Kennedy's old aides.

Once at the White House, Johnson went to Ralph Dungan's office to offer Shriver his condolences. Shriver accepted them briskly before fielding the first of a series of calls from Bobby Kennedy, who was relaying requests from Jackie at the hospital. Shriver took Bobby's call in Dungan's reception room and stepped back inside the office with the new orders. After Shriver got off the phone, his first words to the assembled crowd in Dungan's office were that Mrs. Kennedy wanted the president's burial to be "as distinguished a tribute as possible." One specific request involved the question of where the president's body would lie in state. Jackie remembered that on page 39 of the White House guidebook for tourists there was an engraving of Abraham Lincoln's body lying in state on its catafalque, in the East Room of the White House. The East Room, Jackie decided, was where she wanted her husband to lie. Furthermore, she conveyed to Shriver, "While my husband is there, I should like the room to look as much as possible as it did when Lincoln was there."

Shriver, of course, knew little about how the East Room had looked after Lincoln's assassination. So he asked the Kennedy administration's resident historian, Arthur Schlesinger Jr., to research the Lincoln funeral. Schlesinger, in turn, made an emergency call to the Library of Congress, which sent archivists scurrying through the stacks with flashlights, looking for accounts of the ceremonies that followed Lincoln's assassination. The most detailed accounts were delivered to Goodwin, who laid out two that included sketches—*Frank Leslie's Illustrated Newspaper* and a May 6, 1865, issue of *Harper's Weekly*—for Bill Walton to pore over.

The sketches depicted the East Room draped in heavy black crepe, and Lincoln's casket covered in a canopy. Reproducing these effects, Walton and Shriver concluded, would look ridiculous to modern eyes. Besides, exactly duplicating the East Room's appearance would have involved removing huge chandeliers that had been installed sometime since 1865. Shriver and Walton agreed that it would be best to try to capture the spirit of the Lincoln sketches without trying to copy them exactly. Walton set to work doing that. (Several years later, William Manchester would write that "the two most impressive men" in the White House that evening were Shriver and Walton.)

Shriver had to juggle multiple tasks while always keeping one eye on the clock, since he wanted to have an honor guard ready in time to receive the president's body when it arrived at the White House. The best estimates of what time the president's body would leave the morgue kept getting later. Originally, Shriver was told it would be 11:00 p.m. Then it was midnight. Finally Shriver was told to expect the body about 4:00 a.m. Shriver borrowed Colonel Miller's copy of *State, Official and Special Military Funeral Policies and Plans* and tried quickly to glean what he needed to know. He also initiated a series of conversations with Richard Cardinal Cushing, a Kennedy family friend, about what the funeral Mass should include.

This was not a simple issue to resolve—there had never before been a Roman Catholic funeral for an American president. About midnight, Angie Duke suggested that perhaps a secular funeral would be more appropriate, especially given the lengths to which President Kennedy had gone to maintain the proper separation of church and state. A nondenominational funeral, Duke went on, would be on safer constitutional grounds, especially if it were to be held at the White House. Shriver listened to Duke for as long as he could bear before cutting the protocol chief off curtly. "The family will not permit a non-religious funeral," Shriver said.

A priest who was present suggested to Shriver that the funeral be a pontifical Mass—or High Mass—of requiem. According to David Pearson, a young Peace Corps aide who was present, Shriver shook his head. He glanced at Joe English, who understood exactly what his boss was thinking. "Let's take the low road, Sarge," he said. When the priest looked dismayed, Shriver said, "Look, [the president] made it a point to attend Low Mass himself every Sunday. Why should we force a High Mass on him now?"

Telephone calls flowed into the White House all day and night. All "idea" calls were routed to Shriver by the switchboard operator, who prioritized them and delegated volunteers to attend to the best and most urgent of the ideas. As soon as each call had been dealt with, Shriver would return to presiding over the compiling of lists. Which foreign leaders should be invited to the funeral? Which governors? The whole Supreme Court? The Reverend Billy Graham? Kennedy's comrades from PT-109? There were always more people to remember. At one point, after a phone conversation with Cardinal Cushing, Shriver clapped his hand to his forehead and exclaimed, "My God! We forgot to invite Truman, Ike, and Hoover"—the three living former presidents.

John Bailey, the Connecticut political operative who had been instrumental in securing the Democratic nomination for Kennedy in 1960, kept rattling
off names of politicians who he thought should be invited. Shriver rejected
most of them. When Bailey persisted in rattling off more such names, wasting
valuable time, Shriver glared at him and interrupted. "John," he said curtly, "we
are not trying to return political favors here tonight. We are trying to ask only
those people who we know were personal friends of the president."

Then another gruesome question: Should the president's casket be open or
closed for the funeral? Jackie, Shriver surmised, would want the casket closed.
But Lyndon Johnson had conveyed his desire that the casket be open. He feared
a closed casket would fuel conspiracy theories—for instance, about the casket
being empty, or containing a body other than Kennedy's—that would somehow cast doubts on the legitimacy of Johnson's presidency. Ultimately, the decision was an easy one. Once the president's body arrived, Joe English and Bill
Walton looked at it to see if it was fit for viewing. "The embalmers had done
as good a job as possible," English recalled, "but it was still clear that the back
of his head had been blown off. So that settled that."

As the hour of the dead president's arrival drew near, Shriver headed downstairs to check on the progress of the decorations in the East Room. As he
walked through the curved corridor on the White House's main floor, Shriver
swore he could hear Jack's voice. For a moment he thought he might be going
mad or hearing a ghost. But rounding a corner he came upon a small office,
vacant but for a television set showing his brother-in-law addressing the
German people in West Berlin. Hearing his brother-in-law intone "Ich bin ein
Berliner!" in his idiosyncratic New England twang, Shriver walked into the
office and sank into a chair in front of the television to watch. He sat several
minutes riveted to the television screen. No one dared speak to him.

As the German crowd roared its approval of the American president on the
screen, Shriver stood up and continued toward the East Room, where there was
a great deal still to be done. Bill Walton was commanding a large crew of volunteers—including everyone from Arthur Schlesinger and Dick Goodwin to
the president's dog handler and the official White House upholsterer—who
were engaged in a frenzy of draping black crepe over everything. The East
Room was the biggest room in the mansion, and Shriver feared it would not be
done before Jackie Kennedy saw it. So he rolled up his sleeves, clenched some

carpet tacks between his teeth, and began hammering black cloth onto the walls and doors. The motley crew of decorators spoke little as they went somberly about their work. Whenever a question arose, everyone deferred instinctively to the judgment of Walton and Shriver.

The East Room was finally beginning to look as Walton and Shriver imagined Jackie Kennedy would want it to look: stately without being pompous; somber without being crushingly so; and capturing the essence of how it had looked when Lincoln had lain there in state, but without violating modern standards of taste. Walton began attending to important details, such as whether a crucifix—a statue of Christ nailed to the cross—should be placed atop the president's coffin. A gold and silver crucifix was delivered from the Shrine of the Immaculate Conception, but when Walton saw it he deemed it too gaudy for Jackie's taste. After a few others were brought in and deemed wanting, Walton began to wonder whether a crucifix was even necessary. But when he again consulted the 1865 engravings, a crucifix was plainly evident at the foot of Lincoln's bier. President Kennedy would have to have one.

Doesn't anyone have one that would fit?" Walton asked, beginning to panic.

"I'll get mine," Shriver said, thinking of the simple black cross, hand-sculpted by Benedictine monks in Minnesota, that hung on the wall of his Timberlawn bedroom. More than twenty years earlier, on a vacation in the Bahamas while at Yale, Shriver had struck up a close friendship with a priest there, the pastor of the church in Nassau, who had sent him the cross as a wedding gift. Shriver had carried the cross with him from place to place ever since; it had hung on his bedroom wall in every apartment and home in which he had lived. He immediately sent a White House car to Timberlawn, with instructions to have Mary Ann Orlando—who was helping the Shriver family nurse-maid take care of the three Shriver children while Eunice was in Hyannis and Sarge was at the White House—pull the cross from the wall in his bedroom.

When the driver returned with Shriver's cross, Walton looked it over. "Perfect," he declared. "It could have been ordered for the occasion."

Shriver walked out to the north portico, the White House's front entrance. Although it was after three in the morning, thousands of people were walking aimlessly around Pennsylvania Avenue in a state of collective shock, waiting for the president's body to arrive, perhaps feeling somehow that their presence outside the gate that night would honor him. Seeing these people, it occurred to

Shriver that something more was needed to make the setting equal to the occasion. In 1963 the White House was not illuminated from outside; at night, the mansion had a cold, foreboding aspect. He recalled some of the White House parties he had attended, at which Jackie had arranged to have the grounds illuminated by low-slung, flaming pots. Perhaps something of that nature, he thought, would provide the touch of grace and warmth the moment called for.

He summoned all the military officers present and announced, "This funeral for a president is going to vary a little bit from the manual. I know he isn't really coming home, but I want it to look that way." To that end, he explained, he would like the road from the gate to the north portico to be lit. Could the officers retrieve some lights? There were none available, he was told. "*None?*" Shriver asked, incredulous. "Not even flashlights?" The military men looked at one another helplessly. What if we beamed a searchlight down from a helicopter, one of them suggested tentatively. "Ridiculous," Shriver replied, deciding he had better take the matter into his own hands. Remembering that he had occasionally seen low-slung, hand-lit torches on the highways at night, to warn drivers of construction work ahead, he went inside and called the Washington Highway Department to see if they had any such torches available. They didn't—the highway department had recently converted to electric lights and all the old equipment had been thrown out. Shriver hung up in despair—only to be informed a short time later that the department had tracked down some of the flambeaux in an old warehouse. They would be delivered by 3:30 a.m.

By 4:00 a.m., in William Manchester's account, Walton and Shriver "had created a scene of indescribable drama: the flame-lit drive, the deep black against the white columns, the catafalque ready to receive the coffin." As Robert Liston would write in *True* magazine several months after the assassination,

> This scene, and those brutally emotional ones which pinned the world to its television sets for the next three days came more out of Shriver than out of anyone else. Mrs. Kennedy's wishes were dominant, but it was he who translated them into the multiplicity of details which lent majesty to the national tragedy and moved a nation to tears.
>
>   He was, at times, the dynamic executive, forgetting personal feelings to get a tough job done well—and going without sleep and food in the process. He was the man of seemingly endless energy, still running strong when younger men

were ready to drop. He was the aesthetic man of taste and sensitivity, the proper greeter of dignitaries at the White House and the family man in step behind Jacqueline Kennedy on her mournful march to her husband's funeral.

Playing these interlocking roles perceptively was characteristic of Shriver, and he emerged from them all with stature greatly enhanced.

Now all that remained was to prepare to receive the president's remains. Shriver looked around, hoping to see the military personnel who could form an honor guard to grace John Kennedy's arrival. "All right," he said to Taz Shepard, who had been Kennedy's naval aide, "where are they?"

Shepard indicated he didn't know. Shriver looked at him icily.

"The president of the United States is going to be here any minute," Shriver said, "and there's nobody to meet him. Goddamn it, Taz, we want some soldiers or sailors who will walk slowly and escort him to the door, reflecting the solemnity of the occasion."

Dean Markham, who had been the head of JFK's narcotics commission, remembered that there was a Marine Corps barracks on the corner of Eighth and I streets, southeast of the Capitol. Shepard called the barracks duty officer while Colonel Miller ordered a bus to deliver them. Within seventeen minutes, the drill team had gone from lying in their bunks to standing at arms on the south portico of the White House. They marched double time through the Diplomatic Reception Room to arrive, just in time, on the north portico.

"They made it," Shriver whispered to Joe English, as the Marines aligned themselves in rows.

The late president and his entourage arrived at the White House at 4:30 a.m. Shriver was ready to greet them at the northwest gate with his casket team. Bobby Kennedy and Jackie Kennedy emerged from the ambulance first. As Shriver recalled, "The ambulance doors opened at the back, and Bobby and Jackie climbed out on the arms of two soldiers who helped them down. Then the soldiers slid the casket out into the night. Jackie walked up to me. I kissed her, and whispered condolences." It required an effort not to gasp at Jackie's appearance; she was spattered with blood, still clad in the outfit she had worn that morning in Dallas. Shriver clasped Bobby by the hands.

Seven soldiers carried President Kennedy up the steps of the north portico into the White House, across the marble hall into the East Room, where they laid his coffin on the catafalque. A priest said a short prayer and Jackie Kennedy knelt, pressing her face into an American flag. Then she climbed the stairs to her living quarters.

Shriver spent the next few hours greeting Kennedy relatives who had been arriving throughout the night and helping them to figure out where in the White House they would be sleeping. At about 6:00 a.m., he and Eunice's sister Jean Smith knelt together in the East Room, their heads bowed near Kennedy's coffin, to pray.

As the sun, oblivious to events on earth, rose stubbornly through the fog in the east, Shriver drove home to Timberlawn to take a shower and check on his children. Climbing the stairs to his bedroom that morning, Shriver felt more tired than he had in thirty years—since the night in 1942 when he had wearily climbed another set of stairs, aboard the USS *South Dakota*, slipping on blood shed by his fellow sailors at the Battle of Guadalcanal. On this night, as on that earlier one, he had performed heroically. His calm under pressure, his natural assumption of leadership, and his steady command once he had assumed it had kept the White House from devolving into dysfunction.

After changing clothes, Shriver drove back to the White House. The inner circle gathered for morning Mass in the family dining room, just across the hall from the formal State Dining Room. A makeshift altar had been set up, and people crowded around it, one's proximity to the altar a rough signifier of how close one had been to Jack's family: As the Kennedy siblings and cousins who were present all crammed into the front row, Sarge was relegated to the second row with his fellow in-laws Ethel Kennedy (Bobby's wife) and Joan Kennedy (Ted's wife); friends and aides were arrayed behind them.

After Mass, the parade of visitors began. Shriver stood with Angie Duke, greeting diplomats, legislators, and dignitaries as they passed through. It was deemed appropriate that the first person to visit President Kennedy after his family should be his successor, Lyndon Johnson. This should have been an uncontroversial matter. It wasn't.

In Dallas, conflicts between the bereft Kennedy aides and the shell-shocked LBJ hardened long-simmering resentments. Johnson, eager to provide the appearance of stability for a shaken nation, pressed for a rapid swearing-in ceremony on Air Force One before returning to the Capitol, so that the reins of the presidency might not lie slack for too long. Many of Kennedy's closest aides, who already could barely conceal their dislike for LBJ, were offended by how eager Johnson seemed to be to seize the mantle of power from their fallen leader.

Johnson felt as strong a distaste for many of Kennedy's advisers as they did for him. He knew they looked down on him, despite his vastly greater political savvy and experience. But after the president's death, Johnson knew he needed them—for advice and support, but also for the appearance of continuity. The American people would be profoundly shaken by the loss of their president, who had symbolized the promise of the New Frontier. Johnson knew it would be necessary to preserve as many as possible of the policies, personnel, and symbolic trappings of the Kennedy administration. So Johnson importuned the Kennedy advisers for assistance.

And some of them rejected him. Not outright, but everything in their tone and gestures signified their disgust for him. In their shock and grief, they could not get past the fact that Johnson was not Jack Kennedy and never would be. Some mouthed empty words of support; others simply turned their backs. (Some JFK aides, it should be said, pressed on valiantly in service to the new president, despite their grief. "It is hard to write for a new man," Ted Sorensen was overhead to say of the challenge of composing speeches for LBJ.)

President Kennedy's death had an enormous and direct impact on the United States, and everything that transpired the weekend after his death was of enormous symbolic significance for all the country's citizens. But for Sarge Shriver in particular, that weekend established the context of much that would follow over the next decade. The death of Jack Kennedy thrust Shriver into a peculiar new role—a lonely and uncomfortable position between Lyndon Johnson and the Kennedy family inner circle.

Shriver had grown to greatly admire and respect the former Senate majority leader. Johnson's important interventions on behalf of the Peace Corps had solidified a bond between the two men. Shriver also now saw it as his civic duty to regard Johnson as the legitimate president of the United States and to view him with the respect that position accorded him. William Manchester divided the principal players that weekend into "loyalists" (most notably Arthur Schlesinger, Ted Sorensen, Ken O'Donnell, and, above all, Bobby Kennedy), whose first priority was proper respect to the slaughtered president, and the "realists" (most notably McGeorge Bundy, who kept exhorting everyone that "the show must go on"), whose first priority was the national interest. Shriver tried harder than any other individual to bridge the gap between the two groups. At one point on Saturday he walked over to the loyalists' offices in the West Wing to offer his assistance in ensuring an orderly transition of government. To his surprise, the offer was not accepted; in fact, as he later recalled, he received "a lot of flak." As Drew Pearson and Jack Anderson would later put it in their political column, "After the assassination, when Bobby's bitterness boiled toward the new president, Shriver tried to act as a peacemaker. He failed. 'I found it was a buzz saw,' he told a friend, 'and since then I have stayed out.'" The very act of offering to help ease the Johnson regime's assumption of power was seen by the loyalists almost as an act of betrayal. In the loyalists' minds, Shriver was signaling that he was more in the realist camp than in theirs.

Johnson recognized this. He genuinely like Shriver, and he admired what Sarge had done with the Peace Corps. But he also realized what a political asset Shriver could be: He was part of the Kennedy clan but not blindly loyal to it. Publicly associated with the Kennedys, Shriver often stood in the shadows of Jack and Bobby. But he was also clearly his own man. Out of a mixture of genuine admiration and political calculation, Johnson reached out to Shriver on the weekend of Kennedy's death.

On Saturday afternoon at 2:30 p.m., while JFK still lay in state in the East Room, Lyndon Johnson presided over his first cabinet meeting as president of the United States. He began with a prayer and then asked each cabinet secretary to submit recommendations to him on Monday about what he should do. Bobby Kennedy, as attorney general, was a member of the cabinet and was accustomed to attending such meetings when they were presided over by his brother. On this day, however, preoccupied by funeral arrangements and his own grief, he planned not to attend. Only at the insistence of McGeorge Bundy did he consent to participate. But he arrived late, walking in and sitting down in the middle of Johnson's remarks. Johnson interpreted this as a conscious attempt to humiliate him.

After the meeting, Johnson expressed his resentment at Bobby's behavior but otherwise remained sensitive to the feelings of the Kennedy family. He discussed with another cabinet member when he should make his first address to Congress. The cabinet member suggested it should be as soon as possible, to lend the new administration legitimacy quickly. Johnson agreed but worried that addressing Congress too soon "might be resented by the family."

While the cabinet meeting was in session, Shriver walked over to Johnson's office in the Executive Office Building, adjacent to the White House, hoping to find Bill Moyers, who had suddenly become perhaps the most powerful man in the US government after the president. Moyers was still officially working for Shriver as deputy director of the Peace Corps, but he had traveled to Texas with his mentor LBJ as an advance man for the presidential entourage. (Having grown up in Oklahoma, he knew the region far better than Kennedy did, so he was brought along to help the president with speeches and other matters there.) On Friday morning Moyers had been having lunch in Austin with state Democratic Party leaders when he was told that the president had been shot and that Vice President Johnson wanted to see him in Dallas immediately. He had chartered a private plane as quickly as he could and boarded Air Force One in Dallas. When Johnson entered his stateroom from his private bedroom a few minutes later, a note was on the desk. "Mr. President," it said, "I am here if I can be of any help—Bill Moyers."

Moyers's demonstration of loyalty and support contrasted starkly with the behavior of other Kennedy aides on the flight back to Washington. Twice during the flight, Johnson sent Moyers back to ask Ken O'Donnell to come join him in his stateroom to discuss crucial matters of the transition. Twice O'Donnell refused, choosing instead to stay with Jackie Kennedy by her husband's coffin. Kennedy's aides likely saw Johnson's very invitation as an affront to the slain president and to his grieving wife. Johnson saw their decline of his invitation as a direct rejection of him and of his presidency. In response to these sleights, Johnson drew the aides he could count on, like Moyers and Walter Jenkins, even closer around him. After this, LBJ would not allow Moyers to continue at the Peace Corps; the hard-driving young Baptist would henceforth be working in the White House, always within shouting distance of the president.

This would be a loss for the Peace Corps. Moyers worked well with Shriver, and his blend of idealism, organization, and political smarts was a good fit for the agency. And Moyers at some level regretted leaving the Peace Corps; it had been, after all, his dream job. But Moyers was dutiful (and ambitious) enough that he would never have considered turning LBJ down.

Moyers's presence in Johnson's inner circle should also have been a great political boon for Shriver—and in some ways it was. During the Kennedy administration Shriver had derived considerable political capital from being the president's brother-in-law, but he didn't have a strong champion in the West Wing of the White House. With Moyers soon to be installed there, however, he would. The problem for Shriver was that the more tightly connected to Johnson's inner circle he appeared to be, the more he alienated Bobby Kennedy and other JFK loyalists, who would come to seem over the ensuing months almost like a government-in-exile. Although it would be some years yet before all these heated sentiments would develop and harden into full-blown, ill-concealed enmity, they were present in clear if incipient form in the emotional hours between the assassination and the funeral.

Shriver found Moyers in the foyer of Johnson's suite. Johnson was inside his office, conferring privately with a member of his cabinet about what he believed were RFK's attempts to humiliate him. Shriver and Moyers talked quietly until the cabinet member left. Moyers then ushered Shriver into LBJ's office. Johnson slathered him with unctuous flattery.

"Well, Sarge, it's a terrible thing," Johnson said. "I'm completely overwhelmed, but I do want to say that I've always had a very high regard for you. It hasn't been possible for me to do anything about it until now, but I intend to." Shriver wondered what Johnson meant by this, but for the moment he focused on the challenges of the moment.

"Is there anything I can do?" Shriver inquired.

There were two things, Johnson told him. He was wrestling with difficult decisions. One was the question, which he had already discussed with several cabinet members, of when to make a televised address to a joint session of Congress. Bobby Kennedy and other family members and former Kennedy advisers, Johnson knew, would want him to delay the address as long as possible, to allow time for public recognition and mourning of JFK without the distraction of a new president moving into the limelight. But Johnson said there was also "pressure" on him to make the address as soon as possible—ideally Tuesday, the day after the funeral. Several members of the cabinet had, indeed, pressed for an address as soon as possible, as Moyers did again now, but it was clear to Shriver that much of the pressure to make the address sooner rather than later came from Johnson's own anxiety about his legitimacy. Still, Shriver agreed. A shaken American public needed to be reassured that the previous day's tragedy would not prevent an orderly transition of government. Based on his extensive Peace Corps travels in politically unstable countries, Shriver knew that many people in Africa, South America, and central Asia would conclude from the political logic of their own experience that "whoever had killed President Kennedy would now be president." Thus, in order to broadcast the durability of constitutional democracy, he believed, it was essential to show that there would be continuity of government. The address to Congress would have to be soon, Shriver agreed.

An unspoken question hung in the air. Who would tell the attorney general? Shriver broke the silence. "I'll tell Bobby," he said.

Johnson had another, similar conundrum, equally vexing. When should he leave his vice presidential office in the Executive Office Building to take up residence in the Oval Office of the White House? Secretary of State Rusk and National Security Adviser Bundy were urging him to set up shop somewhere in the White House's West Wing right away—if not in the Oval Office itself, then somewhere nearby. All the president's important communications equipment was there, including the hotline to the Kremlin and the apparatus that gave the chief executive control over America's nuclear arsenal. For symbolic reasons, too, it seemed important for Johnson to base himself in the White House soon; it would signal that he held the levers of power firmly in his grasp.

But there would be objections. After Abraham Lincoln was assassinated, his successor, Andrew Johnson, had waited eight weeks before moving to the White House, working in the interim out of the Treasury building. And with Jack's personal effects yet to be removed, and with his body hardly cold, RFK and the Kennedy advisers would perceive a quick occupation of the Oval Office to be grossly insensitive.

Shriver was genuinely conflicted. On the one hand, the president was telling him that Bundy had justified a quick move by explaining that the Oval Office belonged to the office of the presidency, not to an individual person; as president, LBJ should be in there, hurt feelings be damned. But Shriver also knew from his discussions with Bobby and others that they felt the office was still Jack's—that it should be preserved, at least for a time, as a shrine to him. "I'd been in the navy," Shriver later recalled, "and I was inclined to agree with Bundy; you don't leave a command post empty because the commander has fallen." Yet "it seemed unseemly . . . to move into that office before Jack was

out of the White House. Jack's body, after all, was still lying in the East Room."
He made clear his ambivalence to LBJ, who decided that if Shriver, the most
kindly disposed to him of all the Kennedy family, was not convinced that he
should move right into the Oval Office, then he was better off waiting.

Shriver set off to carry out the unwelcome task of consulting Bobby about
a Tuesday address to Congress. The task was more difficult than he knew.
Unbeknownst to Shriver, Johnson had already dispatched Bundy to carry out
the same mission—and Bundy had failed. Evidently, the new president thought
a Kennedy in-law would have more success than the national security adviser.
He was wrong.

Shriver walked back over to the White House, and when he found Bobby he
relayed Johnson's desire to make the congressional address on Tuesday. Bobby,
having already told Bundy clearly that he thought Johnson's address could wait
until at least Wednesday, erupted in anger. "Why does he tell you to ask me?"
Bobby said, as William Manchester reported. "Now he's hacking at you. He
knows I want him to wait until Wednesday." There was clearly no point in arguing, so Shriver retraced his steps back to the Executive Office Building, where
he again found Moyers, who took him into the president's office. "Bob prefers
you wait a day, unless there are overriding reasons for having the address earlier,"
Shriver told LBJ. As president of the United States, it was officially Johnson's prerogative—not Bobby Kennedy's—to decide when to make the address. But
Johnson said nothing in response to Shriver's report; instead, as Moyers and
Shriver watched, he picked up the phone, dialed, and said curtly, "It will be on
Wednesday." Shriver trekked across the White House lawn to the West Wing yet
again and told Bobby the news. Although the scheduling of the address was
resolved without the public knowing about the tug-of-war between RFK and LBJ
that had gone on behind the scenes, Shriver recalled that it was clear from the
conflict that "there was a condition that was exacerbating."

Despite growing tension with Bobby, Johnson thought it important that he
preserve as much of the Kennedy team intact as possible, as a sign of continuity with Kennedy's New Frontier. He needed, he said, to retain the "aura of
Kennedy." And he seemed, in the first few days of his presidency, to believe that
he could do this. But Schlesinger had already begun drafting his resignation letter, and Sorensen's first meetings with Johnson made it obvious that the two
men could never work together effectively. Others from Kennedy's "Irish

Mafia" had already made plain their dislike for the new president, to the point that it seemed at times they blamed him for Jack's death. (If Jack hadn't had to shore up weak Democratic senators in Johnson's home state, the president would never have been in Texas.) Johnson soon realized he would have to make do with his own staff.

But he still felt he needed some publicly obvious link to the Kennedy administration. Johnson concluded that Shriver, as not only a Kennedy in-law but also the head of the New Frontier's signature program, the Peace Corps, was a natural link. From this point forward, almost anything Shriver did—or didn't do—for Johnson would become fraught with symbolic weight. In staying on as a prominent member of the Johnson administration, Shriver inevitably became, for good and for ill, "the Kennedy in the Johnson administration." As Johnson had hoped, this did lend continuity to the functioning of the executive branch; indeed, Shriver's presence was integral to the expansion of Kennedy's New Frontier into Johnson's Great Society. But Shriver also became, almost but perhaps not wholly against his will, a crucial pawn (a "hostage," as some said) in the high-stakes political chess match between Johnson and Bobby Kennedy. This role—as the symbolic bridge and the symbolic wedge between Johnson and the Kennedys—was one that would in many ways define Shriver's political existence for the next five years. In some ways it would define him for the rest of his public life.

On this day, however, although Shriver could dimly sense the growing animosity between RFK and LBJ, he was still completely consumed with the funeral planning.

Once again, he took up residence in Ralph Dungan's office. Many other people were there making decisions along with him, such as Angie Duke, Dungan, Taz Shepard, and Colonel Miller, but Shriver was—as Dungan put it— the "one iron man." "Except for occasional brief absences he sat hour after hour in front of the desk with a yellow pad in his lap, making meticulous notes and firing off orders."

Jacqueline Kennedy had requested that for the funeral procession on Monday, the streets be lined with soldiers from the US armed forces, saluting their slain commander. So at one point during the day, Shriver gathered high-ranking military officers in Dungan's office and began telling them what they needed to do to ensure that the funeral procession was as Jackie wanted it.

Most of these men were more accustomed to giving orders than receiving them and were clearly not happy to be ordered around. At least several of them, not knowing who Shriver was, wondered where a mere "sergeant" got the temerity to be issuing commands to admirals and generals.

Shriver explained that there was to be a large military presence, with soldiers lining the streets and air force planes flying overhead. The officers objected: planes would scare the military horses that will be on the ground, they said. Shriver continued, saying he wanted a force of several thousand officers and enlisted men on the ground along the procession route, to give the event a real martial atmosphere. Again, the generals objected, saying that marshaling so many soldiers for a purely ceremonial function was impractical; besides, the generals said, it wasn't clear there were that many nondeployed soldiers even available. The meeting went on like this, with Shriver making requests and the officers rejecting them or offering weak compromise proposals.

Earlier in the day, Moyers had asked to be informed any time Shriver ran into any problems or resistance in his funeral planning. Joe English, watching Shriver grow frustrated at being repeatedly stymied by the military men, decided this was one of those times. He quietly slipped out of Dungan's office and retrieved Moyers from a meeting with cabinet members in the West Wing. After English explained the situation, Moyers went back into the meeting and whispered in Robert McNamara's ear. The defense secretary nodded, stood up, and then walked down the hall to Dungan's office.

Seeing McNamara, the generals fell silent. Shriver was sitting in Dungan's chair, facing the military men across the desk. McNamara sat down on the arm of Shriver's chair, and put his arm around the man who had brought him into the Kennedy administration. "I hear there's some difficulty here," he said to the generals. One of them responded, describing Shriver's requests and explaining why they were impractical. McNamara said: "If this man says he wants 500 soldiers, you get 500 soldiers. If he says he wants 5,000 soldiers, you *get* 5,000 soldiers. And if he says he wants 50,000 soldiers, then you call out the reserves and you get 50,000." When it was clear that McNamara's order of absolute obeisance to Shriver's commands had been fully understood, the secretary of defense went back down the hall to rejoin his meeting.

After another brief night's sleep and a quick visit with his children, Shriver was back in Dungan's office early Sunday morning, joined now by Cardinal

Cushing and Bishop Philip Hannan, frantically trying to finalize details for the next two days. After a break for morning Mass, Shriver returned to Dungan's office to resume planning. Several minutes later, the phone rang. As Dick Goodwin recalled, Shriver picked up the receiver, listened for a moment, and then said, "Somebody just shot Oswald." All over America, the reaction to this news was pandemonium. In Dungan's office, no one said anything. As Goodwin recalled, "We went on with our business."

Scarcely an hour later, it was time for the president's casket to be transferred to the Capitol Rotunda for the afternoon ceremony there. Official protocol required two rows of a military honor guard to stand along the steps on the east side of the Capitol, to salute the coffin as it passed by. Shriver introduced a variation on this tradition. He replaced uniformed soldiers with the thirty-six presidential aides who had been closest to the president, "a muster of New Frontiersmen."

On Sunday afternoon Rose Kennedy, along with Ted, Eunice, and others from Hyannis Port, arrived at the White House. Rose appeared stoic and composed as she was led upstairs to embrace Jackie. But when Shriver escorted Rose to the Lincoln Bedroom where she was to sleep, she broke down. Only three years earlier, Eunice had been jumping up and down on the bed, giddy at her family's political good fortune. Now, seeing that same Lincoln bed, Rose burst into tears and fell crying into the arms of her son-in-law. "It just seems so incredible," she sobbed, "Jack being struck down at the peak of his career and my husband Joe in a wheelchair."

"Grandma, you've had the book thrown at you," Shriver said. "Rosemary, young Joe, Kick, Mr. Kennedy—and now this."

"But think of Jackie!" Rose said. "I had my nine children. She's so young, and now she doesn't even have a home."

Shriver responded that he was amazed at how well both Rose and Jackie were holding up.

"What do people expect you to do?" Rose said. "You can't just weep in a corner."

When Eunice and her sisters arrived in the Lincoln Bedroom, Shriver left them to attend to the next matter: finalizing the details of the funeral Mass. A meeting was scheduled that evening with Cardinal Cushing at the home of Archbishop Patrick O'Boyle, on Warren Street, north of Georgetown near American University. Shriver drove over with Ted Sorensen.

Shriver and Sorensen had a common goal: to get the cardinal and the archbishop to sign on to the Kennedys' plans for the funeral the next day. "Your Eminence," Shriver said to Cushing, "this is how the family would like it done," and he gestured to Sorensen to make his presentation. Sorensen made several proposals—such as secular music and Kennedy quotes sprinkled throughout the service—that violated Church rules for Mass. Shriver suspected that the suggestions would be unacceptable, but he was for the moment too tired to interrupt.

When Sorensen finished speaking, there was a long silence. Then Cushing said, "I'll do anything in the world for Jacqueline Kennedy, but I can't change the text of that Mass. I have to read it exactly as it is in that book on the altar."

Here Shriver spoke up. "Jackie wants a Low Mass," he said.

Cushing said that was fine. Sorensen said that Jackie wanted the service to be as simple as possible. Cushing said that they would bury Jack "like a Jesuit" (meaning with a Low Mass) but again insisted "we have to do it according to the book."

This bargaining continued back and forth for two hours or so, with Sorensen and Shriver negotiating each element of the service with the cardinal. Sorensen sought as many concessions to the family's wishes as the Church officials would grant; Shriver, too, wanted to see Jackie's demands met, but his fundamental feeling of obeisance to the Church hierarchy complicated his negotiating position. Outwardly, he always sought the maximum the Church would grant; inwardly, he felt conflicted about imposing demands on a cardinal, whose authority he had always been taught to respect. At one point during the evening's negotiations the phone rang. It was Ethel, calling to say that Bobby wanted Communion offered at the service. Shriver was in favor of this, but the prelates were hesitant: With thousands expected to be in attendance, Communion could take all day. Shriver agreed to a compromise in which only the extended Kennedy family would take Communion. Finally, sometime after midnight, it seemed that all the important issues had been resolved. Shriver and Sorensen drove back to the White House to make sure that all the final arrangements were in order.

Monday morning, after a third consecutive night of scarcely an hour's rest at home, Shriver was back at the White House, serving as host to all the many heads of state who had flown in from around the world. As Peace Corps director, he was already friendly with many, particularly those from developing countries in Africa and South America. Haile Selassie, the emperor of Ethiopia, remarked to all those within hearing that Ethiopia had no need to build a physical monument to the memory of Kennedy; the American president would always be remembered through the work of the Peace Corps in East Africa. This set off a torrent of praise for the Peace Corps, as each leader of a country hosting Peace Corps volunteers strove to outdo the last in his effusiveness for the program.

The day's plan—dictated by Jackie—called for a procession on foot from the Capitol Rotunda to St. Matthew's Church, near Dupont Circle, a distance of several miles. Almost everyone had advised Jackie against the march: It would be a logistical nightmare, they said, as well as a security hazard; also, infirm heads of state would have a hard time on foot. But Jackie was adamant; others could drive if they chose, but she insisted on walking. Which meant of course that her family—and President Johnson, who could hardly choose the safety of an armored limousine if the Kennedy family had not—would have to walk, too.

As the hour of the march from the Capitol approached, the Secret Service, the FBI, and various foreign intelligence agencies were all growing increasingly anxious. There was still concern that some kind of conspiracy or coup attempt against the government was in the works. Behind the scenes, the FBI director urged Shriver to call off the march. Shriver erupted. "That's just ridiculous," he said. "We're *all* concerned. You don't have to be the Director of the FBI to know it's going to be dangerous—even the White House doorman knows that." He went on, accusing the FBI director of simply trying to cover himself, so that in case something did actually happen, he could say, "I told you so."

At the Capitol Rotunda, Jackie, Bobby, and Ted Kennedy knelt together in prayer by the dead president's casket. About eleven o'clock the procession set off for St. Matthew's. Jackie led the way. At first Bobby held her hand but she soon broke away and pulled ahead of him, the whole legion of Kennedys following behind. Shriver walked directly behind her, alongside Stephen Smith. Behind them were Lyndon and Lady Bird Johnson, followed by a car carrying young Caroline and John Kennedy. And then came the ranks of foreign leaders who had begun by walking in orderly rows but who had soon broken apart into a formless mass, as taller dignitaries walked faster than shorter ones, and younger ones faster than older ones. They overtook and then surrounded all Jack's sisters, including Eunice, who was clad in a formal black maternity dress.

The television networks all covered the funeral procession live. Some of Shriver's friends later remarked to him that the TV cameras rarely picked him up, although he was directly behind Jackie. His friends asked him if he had consciously sought to stay out of the spotlight. "No, I don't think so," he responded. "It just happened that way, and it was perfectly proper. After all I wasn't there to be seen. I was there to do whatever I could to help the family." But newspaper photographers captured him well, still standing tall and upright despite three long days of sleeplessness and sadness. He looks grim-faced yet handsome and well coiffed despite all the frantic preparations he had commanded.

Monday, the day of the funeral, was also John F. Kennedy Jr.'s third birthday, and a small party had been planned for 7:00 p.m. at the White House. But Eunice was exhausted, and Shriver was concerned that she had been through more stress and activity than was healthy for a woman in the sixth month of a pregnancy. He felt near collapse himself. Besides, Sarge and Eunice had seen their own children for no more than an hour or two since the assassination. They stumbled out of the White House about 6:00 p.m. and headed home to Timberlawn. Shriver took the crucifix that had lain on Jack's casket and, with great sadness, returned it to its place on the wall above his bed.

PART FOUR

The War on Poverty (1964–1968)

CHAPTER TWENTY-FOUR

Shriver for Vice President

There was no time for mourning. At noon on the day after the funeral, Shriver gathered his executive staff at 806 Connecticut Avenue for their regular meeting and with heavy heart tried to reassure them that Lyndon Johnson would be as avid a supporter of the Peace Corps as President Kennedy had been. He told the story of how Lyndon Johnson, through Bill Moyers's intervention, had preserved the program's independence, keeping it from being absorbed into AID. Without Johnson's intervention, Shriver explained, there would have been no Peace Corps. Trying to lift people's spirits, Shriver closed the meeting by saying, "I just don't see any cloud on the horizon as far as the Peace Corps is concerned. Let's double our efforts to make the Peace Corps twice as good as before."

In the following days Shriver was preoccupied with steadying the shaken staff and volunteers of the Peace Corps; many felt as though they had lost a family member and wanted to return home. Newspaper articles in the weeks after JFK's death said that Shriver was considering running for governor of Illinois and reported speculation that the Peace Corps would die if its director left. Shriver sent a series of cables out to Peace Corps representatives around the world, asking them to reassure the volunteers that the program would continue to operate as before and that their work was now more important than ever. Johnson asked Shriver to convey a direct message to the volunteers. "I know these days have been especially hard for those like you who are far away and separated from your countrymen," Johnson said. "In one respect, however, you are very fortunate. Across the length of our nation people are asking, 'What can I do?' You have already chosen to strive in an enterprise that was as close as any I know to President Kennedy's heart."

Shriver refused to allow Peace Corps recruitment efforts to slacken, and he traveled to New York, Puerto Rico, and the American Southwest to recruit Spanish-speaking students for programs in Latin America. Some students were struck by how much Shriver resembled the late president in his mannerisms and spirit. "For a while there I forgot it was someone else talking about Kennedy's programs and thought it was the president himself," one Columbia University student told the *New York Herald Tribune*. "You feel a little better after an experience like that."

For many young Americans, Shriver and the Peace Corps became for a time the bearers of the New Frontier torch. The Peace Corps was seen as the essence of JFK, and Shriver did what he could to make the program's image reflect that perception. After a brief recruiting trip to New York City in early December, where Shriver gave eleven convocation addresses in three days, the Peace Corps received a record number of applications. Meanwhile, former congressional opponents of the Peace Corps spoke out eloquently about how they had changed their minds and become heartfelt supporters of it. The agency's 1964 appropriations request cruised easily through the Senate.

Even as Shriver poured his energy into steadying and enlarging the Peace Corps in the tense weeks after the assassination, he wondered what Lyndon Johnson had in mind for him. He remembered that conversation in the Executive Office Building on the day after the assassination, when the new president had told him that he was now in a position to do something that would reflect the high regard he had for Shriver. And in a letter of December 2, Johnson had written, "I need you—and I need the services of the splendid group that was knitted together under your leadership—even more than they were needed by the man whom I have succeeded." Shriver knew that Johnson was transmitting similar sentiments to many former Kennedy advisers, but he believed Johnson to be sincere. He let Johnson know again that he was available to help him in any way he could. And to try to smooth relations between the Kennedys and LBJ—as well as to make sure it was understood that he was not blindly loyal to the Kennedy family—Shriver gave the new president a full briefing on all the complaints Bobby Kennedy had made about Lyndon Johnson's behavior in the hours and days after the assassination: for instance, that Johnson had made Jackie Kennedy wait on the ground in Air Force One in Texas while he got sworn in as president, and that he had been too eager to move Jack's possessions out of the Oval Office.

In the days leading up to the assassination in November, Shriver had been finalizing his plans for a Peace Corps trip to the Middle East and central Asia. After November 22 those plans had been put on hold. But as affairs slowly returned to normal in late December, Shriver submitted his itinerary to the president for approval, as protocol demanded. Johnson signed off on the trip, but not before asking Shriver to deliver personal messages to the foreign leaders he would be meeting, assuring them that policies begun under President Kennedy would be continued under President Johnson.

Over Christmas, while the Shriver family was visiting Eunice's parents at the Kennedy estate in Palm Beach, President Johnson called from his Texas ranch. "I hear you're going to Israel," the president said when Shriver got on the phone. Shriver said he was. Johnson told him that Pope Paul VI was planning a visit to that country at the same time, making a three-day visit to Christian shrines there. "I haven't had the chance to meet him," Johnson said, "and I want you to take along a personal letter from me."

So it was that on January 3, 1964, Shriver departed Washington, bearing messages for the shah of Iran; the prime minister of Turkey; the kings of Afghanistan, Jordan, Nepal, and Thailand; the presidents of India and Pakistan; and Pope Paul VI. Shriver was accompanied on this trip by Dick Goodwin, who would become one of the few Kennedy aides to remain for an extended period under Johnson, and by his old Yale friend Walter Ridder, the newspaper publisher. Shriver also brought along with him the crucifix from his bedroom wall, the one that had lain atop President Kennedy's casket in the East Room.

The trip was welcome therapy after the dark times in Washington. Shriver was greeted warmly by all the foreign leaders he met. And everywhere he went he felt with great poignancy the "almost miraculous" impact of the life and personality of Jack Kennedy. It wasn't just the Peace Corps volunteers who said they had been inspired by the late president; it was also the people of the countries he visited. Peasants in Nepal, who had never laid eyes on even a picture of Jack Kennedy, Shriver recalled, had gotten their idea of America through the Peace Corps and through their image of Kennedy.

For Shriver, the highlight of the trip was the meeting with the pope. It turned out that on the same day Shriver was to deliver his personal message from LBJ to the pope in Jerusalem, the pope was scheduled to meet with Athenagoras, the patriarch of Constantinople, who was the head of the Eastern wing of the Catholic Church. This was an epochal event in the history of Christianity.

For 1,400 years, the Roman Catholic Church and the Eastern Orthodox Church had jostled theologically and politically, as each wing wrestled for supremacy over all Christendom. On July 16, 1054, with neither side able to gain undisputed supremacy over the Christian religion, the leader of each wing of the Church had declared the other a heretic. With these mutual excommunications, the Church of the East and the Church of the West were irrevocably rent apart. The divide grew larger and more violent in the eleventh and twelfth centuries, and the sack of Constantinople by the Fourth Crusade in 1204 engendered centuries of enmity between the Greek and Latin churches. Over the ensuing 800 years, the violence and bloodshed had subsided and the two wings of the Church had fallen into an uneasy coexistence. But leaving aside a failed attempt at reconciliation between Pope Eugenius IV and Patriarch Joseph II in 1431, there had not been a single meeting between the heads of the two churches in all that time. Until now. The meeting between Pope Paul and Patriarch Athenagoras was, as Shriver would recall, "an event of ecumenical significance such as the world had not witnessed in a thousand years."

Shriver and company arrived in Israel on January 4 and the next morning went to the Church of Nazareth, where the pope was saying Mass. That evening, the Shriver party proceeded to the large, yellowish stone Apostolic Delegation building on the Mount of Olives, where the pope was holding his historic meeting with the seventy-eight-year-old Patriarch Athenagoras.

At about 10:00 p.m., Shriver, Goodwin, Ridder, and Paul Conklin, a Peace Corps photographer, were ushered into a second-floor anteroom to wait for the pope to conclude his meeting with the patriarch. "Suddenly the door swung open and in walked the pope," Shriver recalled. "Just like that. I had expected someone to formally escort me to his presence in another more private room. And here he was, bursting in on us. . . . I had been sitting on a sofa, and I jumped up, but he motioned me to sit down, and seated himself next to me." Goodwin, Conklin, and Ridder tactfully excused themselves. Pope Paul, "leaning forward slightly, in a very direct, personal way," asked Shriver if he spoke French. Shriver said he did and, as Shriver recalled, "We started talking . . . very easily at once." The pope complimented the Kennedys on their dignity and composure in the aftermath of President Kennedy's death, and Shriver said that the Kennedy family had asked him to convey their respects to the pope. He handed the pope LBJ's letter and watched as he read it. When the pope was finished, he looked up and said he would be delighted to meet with LBJ.

After a few minutes of conversation, Shriver brought out the crucifix that ordinarily hung on the wall of his bedroom. This cross, he explained, had been a gift of a Bahamian priest and had recently lain on the bier of John F. Kennedy. It is my most precious possession. Would you bless it for me? Pope John obliged. Six days later, Shriver would meet with Patriarch Athenagoras in Istanbul and ask him to bless the cross as well. "How many crucifixes in the world," Shriver would later ask, "have been blessed by the heads of both the Eastern and Western wings of the Catholic Church?" For years, it continued to hang above his bed—not only a sad reminder of Jack's death but also a talisman of luck and a tribute to God.

At almost precisely the same time, events in Washington were altering the course of Shriver's life. On the evening of Monday, January 6, as Shriver and the pope traveled through Israel, Lyndon Johnson was hosting the annual reception for the White House staff. Some 1,200 guests were present to enjoy cold cuts and cocktails in the Blue Room, followed by the Marine Band playing calypso in the East Room. The president himself was an hour late to the event, delayed by a cabinet meeting. But he lingered past the 7:30 departure time listed on his official schedule and then surprised everyone, including the ten or so reporters who were present, by holding an impromptu press conference.

Standing in front of the still-decorated Christmas tree in the Blue Room, Johnson talked briefly about a few pressing topics and then talked longer about the pope's pilgrimage to Jerusalem, explaining that he had arranged for a personal emissary, Sargent Shriver, to deliver a message to the pope. Johnson ended his remarks by explaining why he had asked Shriver, in particular, to deliver his message. "I regard Sargent Shriver," Johnson said, "as one of the most brilliant, most able, and most competent officials in the government. I regard him as my real confidant."

Lyndon Johnson may have been the most political creature ever to stalk Capitol Hill. In private he was capable of genuine warmth and wayward enthusiasms, but in public he rarely said anything that was not politically calculated. Thus he knew that his statement in the Blue Room would have an instant effect on those who heard it.

The speculation began immediately. Was the president preparing the public for the announcement that Shriver would be his running mate in 1964?

The proposition made a certain amount of sense. When President Kennedy had been killed, the Constitution stipulated that Vice President Johnson instantly become president. But there was no automatic mechanism for filling the vice presidency that LBJ had left behind. For the moment, there was no vice president.

Vice presidents play at least two crucial roles. One is to serve as the president's understudy, the person who can assume command in an emergency. Shriver had clearly demonstrated at least several of the key qualities of a successful president: charisma, leadership, and—especially—the ability to get along with Congress. One Peace Corps colleague marveled to *New York Times* columnist Anthony Lewis how completely Shriver had wooed Congress; Shriver is, Lewis wrote, "a grand politician in the sense that his brother-in-law [President Kennedy] was." Shriver also had the advantage of already enjoying good personal relationships with many of the executive branch aides and cabinet secretaries—he had personally recruited many of them during the Talent Hunt. He had better rapport with many foreign leaders than most vice presidents historically had upon taking office. Finally, there was his inescapable Kennedy connection: If Shriver were to become vice president and then for whatever reason were to succeed Johnson, it would have represented to many Americans the proper restoration of Kennedy's Camelot. Shriver wasn't a Kennedy by blood, but he was one by marriage—and in looks and spirit and public record he was everything that the New Frontier was supposed to be.

From Johnson's perspective, however, a potential running mate's fitness to serve as president was a necessary but not sufficient condition for selection, subordinate to the more important considerations of what political benefits the running mate brought to the ticket. In thinking about Shriver, in particular, as a vice president, Johnson's calculations were doubly political. Political in the electoral sense—what additional votes would Shriver be likely to bring to the national Democratic ticket and what votes might he be likely to repel? But also political in a more psychological and Machiavellian sense—he could use Shriver to keep Bobby Kennedy *off* the ticket and as a kind of vaccine to immunize himself against attacks from Bobby's wing of the Democratic Party.

Shriver could bring more-conventional political capital to the ticket as well. From LBJ's perspective, one of Shriver's greatest assets was his continued popularity in Illinois. The state had been crucial to JFK's victory over Nixon in 1960—and he had won it by only the thinnest of margins. Johnson, as a Southerner, figured Illinois would be even more crucial to his election chances than they had been for Kennedy. As one Democratic leader from Illinois, speculating in 1964 about Shriver's joining the Johnson ticket, put it, "Johnson's going to need Illinois in 1964 and personally I think Shriver could carry it for him. Don't forget that in 1960 Shriver did as much, if not more, than any other single individual to get [that state] for President Kennedy."

But Shriver could bring more than merely regional appeal to the ticket. As head of the Peace Corps, poll data showed, he was the most popular figure in the federal government (after President Kennedy himself) among young voters. He would bring the nation's Catholic voters to the ticket. And, because of the connections built up through running the Catholic Interracial Council and his experience heading the Civil Rights Section of the Kennedy campaign, he was as assured as any Democrat of wooing to the ticket black voters skeptical of President Johnson. And because Shriver had generated so many elite business contacts through his job at the Merchandise Mart, the business community would not fear him as it might other candidates as liberal as he was on civil rights. "He hasn't made enemies," one Democratic political insider explained in 1964. "Even Southern Democrats like him, whereas Bobby Kennedy and Senator [Hubert] Humphrey . . . are anathema below the Mason and Dixon line."

In the end, of course, Shriver's biggest political asset was his connection to the Kennedy family. As an in-law, he didn't have the Kennedy name and was therefore less politically potent than Bobby or Ted would have been, but he was seen in 1964 by most outside observers as a better alternative than either of Jack's brothers. Ted, one Democratic political operative said at the time, "was too young and inexperienced." Bobby, even leaving aside his grief and his combustible relationship with Johnson, had "made too many enemies as a hatchet man for the late president" to be a good candidate. That left Shriver. And Johnson loved the idea that selecting Shriver could inoculate him against political attacks by Bobby.

As was so often the case, however, the Kennedy connection had a paradoxical effect. Although it would have made Shriver in some ways the ideal vice presidential candidate, it also served ultimately to prevent Johnson from selecting him. For one thing, there was the concern that because Shriver had never held elective office in his own right, putting him on the ticket would create the perception that a Kennedy dynasty had somehow inappropriately taken control of the federal government. A housewife told Anthony Lewis that Shriver "has never been elected to anything. He's the brother-in-law of a president. That's just not the way it ought to be." Even Chicago's Mayor Daley, a longtime Shriver friend and supporter, was reported to have scoffed when he heard that Johnson was considering Shriver for the ticket. Daley had seen how Shriver had been forced to submerge his interests to the Kennedy family in 1960, putting his own political prospects in Illinois aside to work for Jack's national campaign; Daley knew that the Kennedy family would never allow a close associate to jump the line of succession in front of Bobby or Ted. A Johnson-Shriver ticket that won in 1964 might win again in 1968. That would make Shriver the natural Democratic candidate for 1972—meaning that Bobby and Teddy would be blocked from the presidency until possibly 1980. And the Kennedy family would never stand for that.

CHAPTER TWENTY-FIVE

Origins of the War on Poverty

Some 7,000 miles away, Shriver was for the moment oblivious to all this talk. Traveling through the Middle East, he had no idea that Johnson's calculated invocation of his name had set the wheels of Washington political gossip churning. Nor, of course, was he aware that President Johnson's Blue Room encomium to him would ultimately have less effect on him than what Johnson would say two evenings later, as part of his first State of the Union address to a joint session of Congress.

"This administration today here and now declares unconditional war on poverty in America," Johnson said to a prime-time television audience on January 8, "and I urge this Congress and all Americans to join with me in this effort." He continued, "It will not be a short or easy struggle—no single weapon or strategy will suffice—but we shall not rest until that war is won. The richest nation on earth can afford to win it. We cannot afford to lose it." With 20 percent of American families not able to meet even their basic needs, he explained, poverty was a national problem and a coordinated federal-local effort would be required to address it. He wanted, he said, to ensure that "more

Americans—especially young Americans—escape from squalor and misery."
And he couched this call to arms in the rhetoric that would characterize much
of what would come to be known as his Great Society projects (such as
Medicare, the Secondary and Elementary Education Act, and the Civil Rights
Act of 1964). The cause of poverty, he said, lies "in our failure to give our fellow citizens a fair chance to develop their own capacities—in a lack of education and training, in a lack of medical care and housing, in a lack of decent
communities in which to live and bring up their children."

In his address, Johnson took care to emphasize points of continuity with
the Kennedy administration. In his post-funeral address to Congress, on
November 27, he had purposely echoed the words "Let us begin" from
Kennedy's inaugural address by saying, with emphasis, "Let us continue."
Johnson pressed Congress to pass Kennedy administration legislation (primarily a tax cut to help the economy and a civil rights bill) that had stalled in 1963.
But, as he told his speechwriters, he also wanted to present something that had
a distinctive Johnsonian imprint. Something that emanated from the Kennedy
administration but that he could make his own. Something bold.

But an "unconditional war on poverty"? Many people—and especially many
liberals, who believed Johnson's true colors to be a conservative Southern
Democrat's—were surprised by this, not only by the boldness of the rhetoric but
by the mere acknowledgment of poverty as a national problem. Since World War
II, America's economy had grown steadily. Through the 1950s, sociologists and
cultural commentators had focused more on rising affluence as a problem—its
effect on morals and social conformity—than on poverty. In the early 1960s only
a very few Americans—such as the social worker Dorothy Day, the liberal economist John Kenneth Galbraith, and the Illinois senator Paul Douglas—were making any kind of effort to make poverty a national issue. The Kennedy administration had never made any significant statement about poverty. In fact, before
1964, the word *poverty* had not appeared even in the index of either the
Congressional Record or the *Public Papers of the Presidents*. So how did it happen,
people wondered, that Johnson had seized upon this issue with such gusto?

In truth, the seeds of the War on Poverty were planted by the Kennedy
administration. By background, President Kennedy himself, born into affluence, was an unlikely champion for the poor. But he had become attuned to
the problems of poverty in the spring of 1960, during the West Virginia primary

race against Hubert Humphrey. Campaigning in the hollows of Appalachia, Kennedy had been struck by the terrible destitution he saw there: illiterate families living in shacks, children in rags, adults with no teeth. Many families in the region had lived in poverty for generations—and appeared to have no means of escaping it in the future. Some places in West Virginia seemed like a third world country, and Kennedy's experience there seems to have moved the problem of poverty more toward the center of his consciousness. That August, speaking at an event celebrating the twenty-fifth anniversary of the Social Security program, Kennedy spoke of this New Deal–era program as being part of a "war on poverty." At his inauguration the following January, he referred several times to poverty, something no American president since FDR had done. "If the free society cannot help the many who are poor," Kennedy said, "it cannot save the few who are rich."

But for the first two years of his administration, Kennedy's legislative priorities lay mainly elsewhere. "The notion of declaring a war on poverty in 1960 just wouldn't have grabbed people," Kennedy is reported to have said. Insofar as he addressed poverty at all in the first months of his administration, it was through dealing with a longtime concern of his sister's: juvenile delinquency. In the spare moments when she wasn't pressing her brother to have the federal government do more for the mentally retarded, Eunice was urging him to have the federal government do more for juvenile delinquents.

President Kennedy assigned his brother, the attorney general, to set up a program in the Justice Department. Modeled on the commission that Eunice and Sarge had headed under Truman, Bobby began working on the President's Committee on Juvenile Delinquency (PCJD) in the first months after the inauguration in 1961. To direct the PCJD, Bobby hired David Hackett, a prep school classmate.

Although the PCJD itself never became a major federal program, it was a crucial intermediate step on the road to Johnson's Great Society. Hackett knew nothing about juvenile delinquency, so he began traveling the country and talking to experts who did. On March 16 he met Lloyd Ohlin, a professor at Columbia University who, with his colleague Richard Cloward, was studying urban gangs and delinquency. Ohlin argued that juvenile delinquency was attributable primarily not to individual moral failings but rather to the "social systems" in which these individuals lived. The proposed solution was to fix the problems of the delinquents' communities. Hackett hired Ohlin as the PCJD's technical director. (About this same time, the Ford Foundation launched its "Grey Areas Project," which similarly explained urban poverty as a result of *community* rather than *individual* pathologies. Ford gave funds directly to cities in desperate need, charging them, as Ohlin put it, to "change the institutional life of poor communities.")

Between 1961 and 1963, Hackett disbursed money to seventeen communities across the country so that they could develop "comprehensive" plans for combating juvenile delinquency. The PCJD was still a small program in the scheme of the federal budget, but it became the only government agency that dealt directly with the urban ghetto.

At first Bobby Kennedy was head of the program in name only; he left operational decisions to Hackett. Over time, however, as he accompanied Hackett on his trips to Harlem ghettos, Kennedy grew increasingly attuned to the "bottom-up" approach to urban problems advocated by academics like Ohlin. He believed that the residents of poor communities should decide for themselves how to use the federal aid given to them. The process of making these decisions would "empower" poor citizens.

The government program that provided the closest analogue to what Ohlin and Hackett were advocating could be found in the Peace Corps, where many volunteers in Latin America had been assigned to practice what had come to be called "community development." Frank Mankiewicz, the Peace Corps representative in Peru and later the director of Peace Corps operations for all of Latin America, was the staunchest advocate of this revolutionary tactic. "The ultimate aim of community development," he wrote, "is nothing less than complete change, reversal—or a revolution if you wish—in the social and economic patterns to which we are accredited." The basic idea was to combat apathy: to get villagers involved in decision making and help them grasp the power of collective action to solve problems.

Through the first two years of the Kennedy administration, even the most ardent practitioners of Ohlin's "opportunity theory" approach could never have imagined that their work would soon become the centerpiece of an ambitious federal initiative. A series of events beginning under Kennedy in 1962 helped produce this unlikely outcome.

The first event was the publication, in March 1962, of Michael Harrington's book *The Other America*. Harrington had grown up as a conventional, upper-middle-class Midwestern Catholic, attending Holy Cross College and Yale Law School. But Harrington's opposition to the Korean War and to Joe McCarthy's anti-Communist witch hunts had radicalized him. Living in Greenwich Village during the 1950s, he joined Dorothy Day's Catholic Worker movement and became a socialist, a labor organizer, and a left-wing social critic. In 1958 Harrington accepted an assignment from *Commentary* magazine, which at the time was a liberal publication, to write about the persistence of poverty in the United States.

In his article for *Commentary*, Harrington looked at data from the Federal Reserve Board and the Commerce Department and concluded that between 40 million and 60 million Americans (out of a total population of 180 million) lived in poverty. The idea that the rate of poverty was declining, Harrington wrote, was a "myth." "As many as 50 million Americans continue to live below those standards which we have been taught to regard as the decent minimums for food, clothing, and health." More striking than the sheer number of people in poverty, however, was poverty's persistence from generation to generation. Poverty existed, Harrington wrote, as a "separate culture, another nation, with its own way of life." The idea of a "culture of poverty" is commonplace today, but in 1958 only a few sociologists and anthropologists had advanced the concept, and it was not understood by middle-class America. "The poor are not like everyone else," Harrington wrote. "They think and feel differently; they look upon a different America than the middle class looks upon." It was not enough simply to lift incomes or provide jobs, Harrington wrote; the whole "slum psychology" needed to be changed.

Harrington began expanding his writings on poverty into a book not long after Kennedy was elected, in the hope that he could impress on the American people the scope of poverty and suffering in their midst. *The Other America* was respectfully reviewed in the *New York Times* and other mainstream press outlets, but it sold only modestly in the first months after publication and did not seem to have any impact on the thinking of government policymakers nor, certainly, on the general public. Several months later, however, the *New Yorker* commissioned the influential critic Dwight Macdonald to review Harrington's book. The piece Macdonald wrote, "Our Invisible Poor," turned out to be the longest (at fifty pages) and possibly the most influential review the magazine had ever published. Macdonald called *The Other America* a "most important" book and concluded that it made a convincing case for a direct federal approach to reducing American poverty. "The extent of our poverty," Macdonald wrote, "has suddenly become visible." Harrington's book sales jumped from fewer than 10,000 to more than 100,000; *The Other America* became, in the words of one historian, "a minor American classic of the stature of *Uncle Tom's Cabin.*"

President Kennedy's adviser Ted Sorensen was one of those who read and was affected by Macdonald's article; Walter Heller, the chair of Kennedy's Council of Economic Advisers (CEA) was another. Both men passed copies of the *New Yorker* article, which appeared in January 1963, to President Kennedy, who was clearly struck by it. He was also struck by a series of articles by the reporter Homer Bigart that appeared in the *New York Times* about this same time, describing the dismal lives of rural coal miners in eastern Kentucky. What Upton Sinclair's book *The Jungle* had been to Theodore Roosevelt's presidency, provoking him to create the Food and Drug Administration, these articles were now to John F. Kennedy's, leading him to consider making poverty a major priority of his administration in 1964.

Kennedy began by asking Heller to look more deeply into the problem. Was what Harrington was saying true? To help explore the question, Heller hired Robert Lampman, an economist at the University of Wisconsin. Lampman had been a protégé of Heller's at Wisconsin; he had also conducted statistical studies of poverty at the behest of Senator Paul Douglas several years earlier. Heller now asked him to condense and update his study on the president's behalf. Lampman did so—and the results, forwarded to the president on May 1, 1963, were distressing.

Heller discovered a "drastic slowdown in the rate at which the economy is taking people out of poverty." This was a disturbing finding, given how rapidly the gross domestic product had grown during the postwar period. In 1963 Kennedy was trying to push a tax cut through Congress. The hope was that by cutting taxes the government could help the economy grow and reduce the unemployment rate, putting more of the Americans who had lost their jobs in the recession of 1960–1961 back to work. But the tax cut, as Kennedy and his advisers understood it, would increase the jobs available for primarily middle-class workers. If 50 million Americans were not only poor but mired in a culture of poverty (as Harrington argued), and if the economic growth since

1957 had been pulling fewer and fewer people out of poverty (as Lampman's statistics showed), then there was a real question of how far a tax cut could go in reducing the number of American poor. A tax cut might create jobs, in other words, but it wouldn't prepare chronically poor people to fill them. Kennedy began to think differently about poverty: Maybe, rather than merely investing in industry and tinkering with macroeconomics through a tax cut, he should be investing in "public services and human beings."

Kennedy asked Heller to explore further and Heller pressed onward, convening what came to be known as "the Saturday group." On Saturday afternoons during the spring and summer of 1963, representatives from various cabinet departments would gather in a small conference room in the Executive Office Building, hoping to come up with a program or programs that might fruitfully complement the president's tax cut.

At first, the meetings were not terribly productive. The economists and the sociologists fought with one another. (The economists argued that poverty could be reduced easily; the sociologists were more pessimistic.) When some of Kennedy's political advisers were brought into the meetings, they were appalled at how diffuse the discussion was. Late in the summer Sorensen told Heller that he needed to focus and come up with a few simple antipoverty proposals that the president might be able to make part of his reelection campaign in 1964.

Lampman, convinced that no real program could emerge from these meetings, returned to Wisconsin for the fall semester. Heller replaced him with a CEA staff economist named William Capron, who had taught at the University of Illinois and worked for the Rand Corporation. In October Capron delivered a list of the 150 different proposals the various cabinet agencies had put forward. The list was a mess. "Go back and do some more homework," Sorensen told the task force.

Capron and Heller were now beginning to panic, "badly in need of the public-policy equivalent of the cavalry riding to their rescue." The cavalry arrived in the form of Bobby Kennedy's juvenile delinquency committee. Bill Cannon, who was representing the Bureau of the Budget on the interagency task force, was a friend of Dave Hackett, and he had kept Hackett abreast of the turmoil in the task force, urging him to get Bobby Kennedy to alert the White House that plans for a comprehensive poverty program were failing to come together. In early November, Cannon persuaded Heller to meet with Dave Hackett and his colleague Dick Boone, who had come to PCJD from the Ford Foundation.

"Community action appealed to me immediately," Heller recalled. He could see that the origins of juvenile delinquency and the origins of poverty were more or less the same—and a "comprehensive neighborhood approach," as Hackett put it, might help to reduce both. By the end of the meeting, Heller had decided to make PCJD's concept of Community Action the "organizing principle" for a more full-blown antipoverty program.

On the evening of November 19, three days before Kennedy's fateful Dallas trip, Heller had an audience with the president. "Yes, Walter," Kennedy told him as two-year-old JFK Jr. scampered around the Oval Office. "I am definitely going to have something in the line of an attack on poverty in my program. I don't know what yet. But yes, keep your boys at work, and come back to me in a couple of weeks."

The evidence suggests that Kennedy was serious about attacking poverty. During his last cabinet meeting, on October 29, the president had scribbled the word "poverty" half a dozen times on his yellow pad, circling and underlining the word amid the soybean prices and the picture of sailboats he had sketched on the pad. And in a conversation with Arthur Schlesinger in November about January's upcoming State of the Union address, Kennedy had said, "The time has come to organize a national assault on the causes of poverty, a comprehensive program, across the board."

The day after his meeting with the president, Heller flew with six other cabinet members to a meeting in Japan. On the way back, they learned that the president had been shot. For the remainder of the long flight across the Pacific, as the cabinet members tried to deal with their shock, they speculated about what kind of a president Lyndon Johnson would be. Kennedy's antipoverty program was not actively discussed, but it surely occurred to everyone that under President Johnson—who was generally thought to be more conservative than his predecessor—any plans for an aggressive attack on poverty would be left to wither on the vine.

Back in Washington on Saturday night, November 23, as Shriver and others scurried around the city preparing for Monday's funeral, Heller was summoned for his first audience with the new president at 7:40 p.m. At the meeting, which lasted about forty minutes, Heller briefed Johnson on what the Council of Economic Advisers had been working on recently—in particular the Kennedy tax cut proposal and research on a poverty program. As Heller recalled, "I told him very early in our conversation that the very last substantive conversation that I had had with Kennedy was about a poverty program." "That's my kind of program," Johnson said. "I'll find money for it one way or another. If I have to, I'll take money away from things to get money for people."

Heller was surprised by the evidently sincere enthusiasm Johnson expressed. Then Johnson went further. Heller recorded what happened next in his notes of the meeting. As Heller opened the door to leave, Johnson pushed it gently shut and pulled the CEA chairman back into his office. "Now, I want to say something about all this talk that I'm a conservative who is likely to go back to the Eisenhower ways or give in to the economy bloc in Congress," Johnson said. "It's not so, and I want you to tell your friends—Arthur Schlesinger, Galbraith, and other liberals—that it is not so. . . . If you looked at my record, you would know that I am a Roosevelt New Dealer. As a matter of fact, to tell the truth, John F. Kennedy was a little too conservative to suit my taste."

Thus began a competition between LBJ and the associates of the late President Kennedy to claim the "more liberal" mantle. In the coming days, Schlesinger and other Kennedy advisers began trumpeting their late boss's support for a bold "national assault on poverty." Even Sorensen, who had recently expressed his ambivalence about the idea of an antipoverty program, now joined the chorus of support for it. It was as though the "Kennedy liberals" were laying down a gauntlet: You may claim to be liberal, Lyndon Johnson, but you're not as liberal as John Kennedy was. The Kennedy people, the journalist Nick Lemann has observed, changed the stakes of the poverty program after Kennedy died. "The question, instead of being whether Johnson could take over what had been a small, stagnating Kennedy idea and make it his first major initiative without appearing to be one-upping the dead President, became whether Johnson could possibly be as fully committed to fighting poverty as Kennedy had been." Johnson feared that if he appeared to waver in his support for an aggressive antipoverty program, he would bring down on himself "another hail of sophisticated liberal contempt."

Johnson's political strategists warned him that launching a poverty program might be a political time bomb, blowing up his support among the lower middle class in particular. But Johnson's "powerful conviction that an attack was right and necessary blotted out any fears that this program was a political landmine," he later wrote. Also, he was terrified of being attacked from the left by the Kennedy faithful. At a press conference in December, he announced that a poverty bill would be "high on the agenda of priority" in his requests to Congress for 1964.

Despite Johnson's bold public pronouncements about an antipoverty program, there was still no consensus—not even a general idea—of what a poverty bill would contain, or how much it might cost. Johnson himself provided little direction. Remembering his own work during the Depression on FDR's National Youth Administration, LBJ seemed vaguely to imagine that a poverty program might involve, as Heller recalled, young people working outside. "Bulldozers. Tractors. People operating heavy machinery." The Kennedy liberals associated with the PCJD, meanwhile, ardently supported making Community Action the centerpiece of a Johnson antipoverty program. As a project overseen by Bobby Kennedy's Justice Department, it seemed the surest way to impose a Kennedy imprint on the program.

On December 20 Heller outlined his conception of the poverty program in a memo to the White House. In his memo, Heller wrote that Community Action should be a significant component of any antipoverty legislation, and he agreed with Dave Hackett that Community Action programs should start with small "demonstration" projects in maybe ten cities. But to satisfy Johnson's desire for boldness, Heller proposed that the program's overall budget be $500 million per year, and that the Department of Health, Education, and Welfare (HEW) be given much of that money to administer another dozen or so antipoverty miniprograms under its auspices.

It was unclear, as yet, whether there would be a new poverty agency that would run antipoverty programs or if the existing cabinet departments would simply add antipoverty programs to the programs they were already administering. The fights were intense. Community Action advocates wanted a new agency; the Labor Department and HEW were strongly opposed. Labor secretary Willard Wirtz stormed out of a meeting on December 20, muttering that there was no need for "any more damn new agencies." Bill Capron, who was advocating a new agency, suggested in a memo that either Abe Fortas, a prominent Washington lawyer, or Sarge Shriver might be an effective salesman for an antipoverty bill in Congress.

Over the Christmas holidays, while Shriver prepared to leave for the Middle

East, Heller and Gordon flew to LBJ's ranch in the hill country outside Austin, where they outlined their proposal. As Johnson recalled,

> I walked from the main ranch house to a little green frame house we call the "guest house," a distance of about 200 yards. Inside, seated around a small kitchen table, were Walter Heller, Budget Director Kermit Gordon, Bill Moyers, and Jack Valenti. The table was littered with papers, coffee cups, and one ashtray brimming over with cigarettes and torn strips of paper. Just a few feet away from the window several of my white-face Hereford [cows] were grazing placidly and a little noisily. It was an incongruous setting for Gordon and Heller, those two urbane scholars. I sat down at the table to talk about the program they were preparing.

According to LBJ, Heller and Gordon presented their plan for a limited number of "demonstration projects" that would employ the principles of Community Action and measure whether they could be effective. Johnson's first response was that the program, to attract the national following necessary to propel a bill through Congress, couldn't be a mere demonstration. "It had to be big and bold and hit the whole nation with real impact." In his memoir, Johnson said that although Community Action was presented to him as something "new and radical," it struck him as being based on a traditional American principle—local self-determination. The idea of Community Action, Johnson wrote, also resonated strongly with him because of his experience in the 1930s as a schoolteacher in Cotulla, Texas, where he had formed a parent-teacher association that was not unlike a Community Action agency. Johnson also recalled, from his time as a regional director of the National Youth Administration, that programs that the poor were involved in designing were more successful than those designed by bureaucratic fiat.

According to others who were present at the meeting, Johnson's acceptance of Community Action was not so immediate. He wasn't happy that it was just a demonstration program. Nor could he see how it would create jobs—the stuff of political capital—quickly. And the political implications of giving up so much federal and state-level control to local authorities scared him. He flat out rejected Community Action at first, and it took at least a full day of persuading before he seemed to reconsider. As Heller recalled, Johnson kept throwing their proposals back at them, saying "Look, I've earmarked half a billion dollars to get this program started, but I'll withdraw that unless you fellows come through with something that's workable." Johnson kept going on about the National Youth Administration and how it had "hard, bedrock content" to it. Also, LBJ initially rejected Community Action because he saw it as a Bobby Kennedy project. Instinctively, to prevent the late president's brother from accruing any additional political capital, he would have wanted to kill any proposal that Bobby put forth. The problem, however, was that Sorensen, Schlesinger, Bobby, and company had now attached themselves to Community Action—and if Johnson failed to adopt it he would be accused of betraying the Kennedy legacy. As one of his aides recalled, "If he'd said no to it, people would've said, 'Oh, he's not really sincere, he's just a Southern racist.'"

In early January the *Economic Report of the President* for 1964 was published, with a full chapter on poverty, most of it drawn directly from the study Robert Lampman had written the previous summer. Echoing Michael Harrington, the report declared that 20 percent of American families were poor. Written with unusual passion for an economic report, it laid out a broadly based strategy for attacking poverty. The list of weapons to be deployed included the tax cut, civil rights legislation, improvements in health care, area development plans, adult education, and Medicare. But in order to stop "poverty from breeding poverty," the report concluded, the central antipoverty assault would have to be carried out by Community Action programs.

CHAPTER TWENTY-SIX

"Mr. Poverty"

"Pity the poor soul who gets charged with running *this.*" This was Shriver's thought as he read accounts of Johnson's declaration of war on poverty.

When Johnson delivered his first State of the Union address, on January 8, 1964, Shriver was halfway around the world, sweltering in the heat of Pakistan. He didn't give the president's declaration of an "unconditional war on poverty" a second thought. He missed his family, whom he had barely seen in the days since President Kennedy had died. He was looking forward to going home.

But when he stopped over in Hawaii on his way back to the East Coast several weeks later, Shriver was surprised to see Bill Josephson waiting for him at the bottom of the steps of the airplane. Ordinarily he would have been pleased to see Josephson, but he worried that his general counsel's presence in Hawaii signaled some crisis with the Peace Corps. When Shriver got to the bottom of the stairs, Josephson handed him two enormous black briefing books. Shriver asked what they were about, and Josephson explained that several days earlier he had been called into a meeting with Bureau of the Budget director Kermit Gordon, Bill Moyers, and the president. Gordon and Moyers had explained to Josephson what the president had in mind for his poverty program. Johnson then said that he had decided whom he wanted to run his War on Poverty: Sargent Shriver. Johnson knew that Shriver was somewhere in the Far East, but he was impatient to get started. So he handed the briefing books to Josephson and said, "Find Shriver."

On Friday, January 31, flying home from Hawaii to Washington, Shriver tried but failed to focus on the contents of the briefing books. He had little interest in their contents. He was chagrined to find a White House car waiting for him at the airport in Washington. The president wanted to see him right away.

Johnson received Shriver warmly in the Oval Office. The Peace Corps director launched into an enthusiastic travelog, regaling the president with the story of how he had witnessed the reconciliation of the pope and the patriarch. Then he began reporting on the status of the Peace Corps in the various countries he had visited. "That's great, Sarge, that's really wonderful," Johnson said, cutting Shriver off. "Let's go for a walk."

He took Shriver by the arm and led him out through the Rose Garden to the driveway on the White House's South Lawn. It was a crisp January day, and the trees on the edge of the lawn were laced with snow. Johnson asked Shriver what he had thought of his State of the Union address. Shriver said politely that he liked what he had read in newspaper accounts. He tried to steer the conversation back to the Peace Corps, but Johnson wasn't interested. Instead, as the two men walked up and down the driveway, Johnson talked about his fierce desire to get his poverty program going. It was appalling, the president said, that in a prosperous and democratic nation, 35 million people should have insufficient opportunity to lead a decent life. As a young man in Texas he had seen poverty, he told Shriver, but he had always thought of it as a rare and isolated phenomenon that was disappearing as the economy grew. Now, the president continued, we are learning that the poor inhabit a nation within the nation, locked into a cycle of despair by lack of skills, poor health, and inadequate education.

"Now you know we're getting this War on Poverty started, Sarge," the president said. "I'd like you to think about that, because I'd like you to run that program for us." Back in the Oval Office, Johnson handed him a sheaf of documents and sent him on his way.

The next day, Saturday, was to have been Shriver's first free day with his family in a month. But just after lunch, as he was outside playing with Bobby and Maria, he was summoned inside to take a phone call from the president.

"Sarge," Johnson said, as his Oval Office taping device secretly recorded the conversation. "I'm gonna announce your appointment at that press conference."

"What press conference?" Shriver asked, clearly confused and a little peeved.

"This afternoon," Johnson said.

Shriver was shocked. A press conference? To announce his appointment to lead the War on Poverty? That couldn't be. He had had no time to prepare. He wasn't an expert on poverty. He hadn't told his executive staff at the Peace Corps; that agency would be thrown into turmoil if it were suddenly announced, he was leaving.

"God," Shriver said, "I think it would be advisable, if you don't mind, if I could have this week and sit down with a couple of people and see what we could get in the way of some sort of plan." If you announce me before I know what the hell I'm doing, Shriver told him, I'll be forced to contend with questions from reporters that I'll have no idea how to answer.

"Just don't talk to them," Johnson told him. Go into seclusion and figure out what you're doing before you talk to the press. And you can "work out your Peace Corps" any way you want. Keep running the Peace Corps through your deputies.

Johnson was keen to move ahead quickly. For one thing, he didn't want to give Shriver time to back out. For another, he knew that it was politically important to seize the moment. Kennedy's death had rendered Congress especially receptive to Johnson—especially toward anything that he could present as continuing the Kennedy legacy. But Congress's eagerness to please would not last, Johnson knew, and he felt also that it was important to generate visible movement on the poverty program while the well-received words of his State of the Union address were still ringing in people's ears.

"I want to announce this and get it behind me, so I'll quit getting all these other pressures," Johnson told him. "You've got to do it. You just can't let me down. So the quicker we get this behind us, the better. Don't make me wait until next week."

Of course, the biggest pressure on Johnson came from Bobby Kennedy. The president's concerns were several. One was that he knew Bobby had come to feel strongly about doing something to alleviate poverty. Johnson didn't want Bobby staking a claim to the antipoverty program, and he thought he could preempt such a claim by appointing Shriver. Johnson had to walk a fine line here: Walter Heller had presented the poverty program to him as a Kennedy initiative, and Johnson had himself been promoting it as such. But he wanted very much to make the poverty program his own—a "Johnson program." Making Bobby director would certainly have demonstrated the poverty program's connection to the Kennedy family—but it would also surely have weakened Johnson's own imprint on it.

Shriver responded. "Number one: I'm not going to let anybody down, least of all you. You've been terrific to me." But he continued to try to buy some time. "Second, I would like to have a chance to prepare the [Peace] Corps."

"But that'll leak out over forty places," Johnson said. "Why don't I tell them you are not severing your connection with the Corps?"

Shriver agreed that was better but he still thought a more cautious announcement, one that didn't commit him to anything long term, would be best. "Could you just say that you've asked me to study this?" he asked.

"Hell no!" Johnson said. "They've studied and studied. They want to know who in the hell is going to do this. . . . I want to say that you're going to be Special Assistant to the President and executive in charge of the poverty program."

"The problem with that is that it'll knock the crap out of the Peace Corps," Shriver said.

"Not if you tell them you're not severing your identification with the Peace Corps," Johnson retorted.

Shriver was still concerned, though. "I think it would be better if you would say that I'm going to continue as director of the Peace Corps." The Peace Corps was his baby, it was running well, and he worried that if he were to leave it in someone else's hands so soon after Kennedy's death, its long-term survival would be endangered.

To Johnson, however, the Peace Corps was clearly of secondary importance here. "I'm going to make it clear that you're Mr. Poverty, at home and abroad, if you want it to be. And I don't care who you have running the Peace Corps. You can run it? Wonderful. If you can't, get Oshgosh from Chicago and I'll name him. . . . I want you to get rid of poverty, though. The Sunday papers are going to say that you're Mr. Poverty, unless you've got real compelling reasons which I haven't heard."

Shriver protested feebly that based on what he had read about the poverty plan, the program would be best administered out of HEW, rather than as a new, wholly independent agency. Soon he would be arguing fiercely against this very proposition, but now he was grasping for anything that would enable him to escape the responsibility Johnson was trying to saddle him with. Johnson dismissed Shriver's HEW proposal. And when Shriver continued to express concern about the impact the announcement would have on the Peace Corps, the president questioned Shriver's energy. This is a promotion, Johnson yelled. "You've got the responsibility, you've got the authority, you've got the power, you've got the money. Now you may not have the glands."

"The glands?" Shriver didn't know whether the president was referring to his manliness or making an unfortunate reference to the Addison's disease that had afflicted both Eunice and Jack Kennedy, preventing their adrenal glands from functioning normally. Either way, it was insulting. "I've got plenty of glands," he said.

"I'd like to have your glands then," Johnson said. Trying to defuse Shriver's anger, he joked that he would have the White House doctor inject him with some goat glands.

But Shriver was still annoyed. "I would have much preferred to have had forty-eight hours" to prepare myself, he said.

How could you not have been prepared? Johnson asked him. Many newspaper reports had been published speculating that Shriver would be appointed.

"I didn't know beans about it, because I've been overseas," Shriver explained.

"Well, you don't need to know much. . . . You'll have an international Peace Corps—one abroad and one at home."

Shriver asked if he could at least have Bill Moyers back to help him. (Moyers had by now gone back to Johnson's staff, full time.) Johnson explained that the White House needed Moyers: "I need him more than anybody in the world. . . . He's good for Shriver here." Shriver asked if he could have Mike Feldman, who was deputy special counsel to Johnson, and with whom both Eunice and Sarge had good working relationships. "Now don't go raiding the White House," Johnson yelled. "Go on and get your own damn talent."

"For Christ's sake," the president continued, "if your wife—if the Kennedys had—they wouldn't have this fortune if they had as many baby-sitters as you've got in the Peace Corps. You've got 10,000 people and you've got 1,100 administrators. There's not a Kennedy compound that's got a baby-sitter for ten. And you've got it in the Peace Corps around the world. All right, I'll see you later, and good luck to you. And happy landing!"

Happy landings indeed, Shriver thought bitterly.

He hung up the phone and told Eunice about the conversation. "I don't really want to run this thing," he told her. She responded that he should be honored that the president wanted him to run his new program. But if you really don't want to do it, she told him, you should make that clear.

At 2:25, just a half hour before Johnson's scheduled press conference, Shriver called the White House and was put through to the president in the Cabinet Room, where he was meeting with aides. Shriver again protested that it was a bad time for him to be abandoning the Peace Corps. I've just traveled the world trying to get volunteers charged up, Shriver said. What kind of message will it send if I leave now?

The president spoke softly, so others in the Cabinet Room wouldn't hear. "You can stay in the Peace Corps and do this other thing at the same time. . . . You've got the Peace Corps under control. And this new thing, there's nothing to run yet. We just want you to put it together and get it through Congress. That's all I'm asking you to do."

Shriver again asked for just "a few more days" to prepare himself. "I want to do it successfully for you and I just feel that if I get stuck out there today in a position where I am completely exposed—"

The president cut him off. "Why don't you let me leave it where we were? Now I'm here with all this staff trying to get ready for the three o'clock meeting. . . . I need it for very personal reasons."

Shriver immediately called Warren Wiggins at Peace Corps headquarters and broke the news. Shriver explained that he didn't want the appointment Johnson was giving him—but "I don't seem to be able to stop him." Shriver had Wiggins compose a cable to be sent to all Peace Corps countries, announcing his appointment and explaining clearly that he would not be leaving the agency. "Explain that this is just a study group" Shriver told Wiggins. Still unable to believe that Johnson would really make the announcement so soon, Shriver told Wiggins to hold off on sending the cable until Johnson actually made a formal announcement. "If he announces [my appointment], send the telegram. If he doesn't, tear it up," Shriver said.

A few minutes later, Shriver watched the president's press conference on television. Johnson declared how happy he was that Sargent Shriver would be heading the War on Poverty. Shriver felt, he recalled later, like Homer's Ulysses:

finally home after twenty years of wandering but now having to strap on his armor to depart for another Troy.

When the press conference ended, Shriver called the White House again, got Bill Moyers on the line, and began expressing his displeasure at the assignment. He wouldn't mind being made secretary of HEW, he said, "or this vice president thing." But he didn't want Johnson to send him "screwing around doing one job after another" that wasn't going to lead anywhere. "I don't know whether I maybe ought to go out to Illinois and run for governor."

Just then, the president got on the line. LBJ explained that he hadn't been able to speak freely earlier, because of all the advisers and cabinet members milling about. None of these people, Johnson implied, thought Shriver was the right man to launch the poverty program. "Now I don't want to make you feel bad, because you're too successful and I'm too proud of you to ever pour cold water on you," Johnson said patronizingly. "But up to one minute before I appeared [on television], I was meeting violent protest to naming you. Now I couldn't let that grow and continue." Hence the precipitous timing of the press conference.

Johnson did not let up. He told Shriver that high-ranking insiders, "about as powerful people as we have in this government," had backed other candidates for the poverty post—implying that Bobby Kennedy had not only personally opposed but actively campaigned against Shriver's appointment. "They all think that you're a wonderful man," the president granted, "*but* one of them said this morning, 'He's never had anything to do with anything like this. As a *public relations expert*, he's the best.'" Johnson emphasized "public relations expert," knowing that this moniker had dogged Shriver for several years—and hoping that it would fuel Shriver's ire against whoever had said it. The president continued. "But I think that as an administrator and as a *candidate* that you have great potentialities."

Johnson's intention here seemed clear: to create a polar opposition between Bobby's team and Lyndon's team. Bobby's team (Johnson was saying) thinks you're a mere public relations guy, not up to the task of running a new program. Lyndon's team thinks you're not only a good administrator but also a potential vice presidential candidate. Pick my team.

Promising Shriver another job if the poverty program ever failed—perhaps secretary of defense, if McNamara ever were to step down—Johnson concluded by saying, "Now don't go trying to figure out who opposed you." This was a clearly disingenuous message: Human nature dictated that trying to figure out who had opposed him was precisely what Shriver would do.

Two hours later, evidently concerned that he had been too harsh on Shriver earlier, the president called back and read him some of the positive press his appointment had been receiving. However, Johnson still tried to stoke Shriver's animosity toward the Kennedy camp by mentioning that "incidentally," Ted Sorensen continued to think it was a terrible idea for Shriver to continue on at the Peace Corps while taking charge of the antipoverty program. When Shriver failed to take the bait, the president launched into one of his classic perorations.

> Now you've got to see how in the hell you're going to administer this thing. Then, you're going to have to get that bill and that message together. And you got to get on that television and start explaining it. Let's find out any dollar that's appropriated, how we can use it for poverty. . . . And you'll have more influence in this administration than any man in it. You'll have a billion dollars to pass out. So you just call up the pope and tell him you might not be in time every morning for church on time, but you're going to be working for the good of humanity.
>
> The sky's the limit. You just make this thing work, period. I don't give a damn about the details. And anybody you want us to meet with, we'll do it on our spare time, when we get a night off. Because this is number one on the domestic front. Next to peace in the world, this is the most important. Get all the damn publicity you can, get on all the televisions you can, as soon as you know enough to talk about it.

And then another quick shift, another turn to flattery. Did Shriver know that Moyers had been lobbying on his behalf, urging LBJ to select him as running mate for 1964? Shriver, in turn, asked the president if *he* had seen a recent Associated Press report. ("I'm not running for anything," Shriver had told the AP, adding that Bobby Kennedy would be a "terrific" vice president.) "Yeah, I saw that you eliminated yourself from the race completely," Johnson said wryly. "We'll get you back in it, though."

"That's all right," Shriver said.

"Yeah, that's all right," Johnson said. "I think that a man runs for vice president is a very foolish man. Man runs away from it's very wise. I wish I had run farther away from it than I did. And I never was a candidate for it, I'll tell you that. And don't you ever be a candidate, and don't let anybody else be a candidate." Bobby Kennedy's name floated unspoken in the air here. "Tell them anybody ever runs for it never gets it."

"I'm with you till the end," Johnson continued, with Bobby Kennedy still the unnamed presence hanging over the conversation. "Death do us part. We're not going to let anybody divide us, so just bear that in mind. And when everybody else has quit you and gone and through with you, I'll still be standing there by your side."

In appointing Shriver head of the poverty program, Johnson had carried out a brilliant coup. Although all the Community Action proponents were based in Bobby Kennedy's Justice Department, they would now be answering ultimately to Shriver. With Shriver at the helm, the general public would perceive the poverty program to be an "official" Kennedy project—meaning that it would be hard for Bobby, or any of his close associates, to criticize it publicly. Meanwhile Johnson was calculating (wrongly, for the most part) that Shriver resented being treated as a hired hand of the Kennedy family and that he resented implications that he lacked Kennedy "toughness." "Believe me," Bobby's aide Adam Walinsky said, "Sarge was not a close pal brother-in-law and he wasn't giving Robert Kennedy any extra breaks."

In one fell swoop, Johnson had satisfied the public's demand for a Kennedy imprimatur on the poverty program; inoculated the program against public criticism from the Kennedy camp; solidified the connection between the Oval Office and the one person in the Kennedy family he felt he could trust; and deepened the wedge between the two brothers-in-law. And by installing Shriver on turf that Bobby perceived to be rightfully his, Johnson was angering Bobby, who was powerless to do anything about it.

Of course, Johnson had nobler reasons for appointing Shriver, as well. He liked Shriver's ability to think unashamedly in the big, sometimes grandiose terms that he did. Shriver also had demonstrated that he was capable of starting a new program from scratch. More important, he had shown he could get legislation through Congress. "I think he forced the job on me," Shriver said, "because he thought it was going to be difficult to get it through Congress and he thought I could help get it through."

Shriver's ability to work with Congress was important, because Johnson wanted the program legislated and operational extremely fast. Johnson had a certain amount of carte blanche to carry out Kennedy's ostensible policy priorities, but it would not last forever. He needed to push the program through Congress in the next session. Shriver had gotten the Peace Corps up and running in no time at all—now Johnson wanted him to do the same with the War on Poverty. "The president had asked for immediate action," Shriver recalled. Thus he went to bed that night knowing that "the next day, Sunday, was to be my first working day in the War on Poverty."

CHAPTER TWENTY-SEVEN

A Beautiful Hysteria

Shriver didn't have much to work with—a rough draft of the antipoverty statute that Walter Heller and Kermit Gordon had hastily drawn up at the LBJ ranch in December and a rough draft of the message to Congress, written by Ken Galbraith, that would accompany LBJ's presentation of a poverty bill to Congress. That was it; that was all there was to the president's unconditional War on Poverty. Shriver had not even had forty-eight hours to think about the problem—and now he was expected to conceive, design, administer, and push through Congress a brand-new, billion-dollar program. And the president had indicated he wanted all of this done within two months.

Shriver's only consolation was that he had once before done as much with even less. At its inception, the Peace Corps had a far less concrete mandate than the War on Poverty now did. In 1961 President Kennedy had not even given him a draft bill; all Shriver had had to go on were a few sentences from a couple of campaign speeches.

But the stakes were higher now—ten times higher in budgetary terms. And incalculably higher in political terms. President Kennedy had launched the

Peace Corps almost as an afterthought; he needed to demonstrate he was following through on a throwaway campaign promise that had garnered him unexpected plaudits. It had started small and paid off big. But the poverty program, relatively speaking, was starting off big. Moreover, it was not to be some ancillary program but rather the core of President Johnson's legislative agenda, and of his election campaign, for 1964. And the whole enterprise was vexed by the political tensions between Johnson and the Kennedy old guard, led by RFK. Shriver would have to lead any antipoverty army he could recruit through a dangerous minefield.

On Sunday, Shriver read through the sparse materials he had been given and called a meeting at his Peace Corps office with the most brilliant advisers he could recruit on short notice. Johnson wouldn't let him take Moyers, so Shriver turned to Adam Yarmolinsky instead. Yarmolinsky had demonstrated his brains and effectiveness working in the Civil Rights Section and during the Talent Hunt; in those days, his sharp organizational skills had helped balance the sometimes dilettantish enthusiasms of Shriver and Harris Wofford. Yarmolinsky had since gone to work as a special assistant to Robert McNamara at the Pentagon, where he had developed a reputation as "one of the most brilliant of all the brilliant young men in the Kennedy administration—someone who worked ceaselessly and got things done." Yarmolinsky was also known for his prickly, even caustic relations with people whose judgment he found wanting—he would "demolish people with sarcasm," one colleague recalled—and Shriver was aware that conservatives had on occasion attacked Yarmolinsky for his allegedly left-wing background. But if Yarmolinsky had passed muster at the security-conscious Defense Department, then surely it wouldn't be a problem for him to work in a domestic policy agency. Yarmolinsky became Shriver's top deputy.

Shriver also turned to Frank Mankiewicz, his Peace Corps representative in Peru. Serendipitously, Mankiewicz had just arrived in town to testify before the House Foreign Affairs Committee about what the Peace Corps was doing in Latin America. On Sunday morning, just as Mankiewicz was reading the *Washington Post*'s article about Shriver's appointment as head of the poverty program, the phone rang. It was Shriver, asking if he knew anything about poverty. As it happened, Mankiewicz was a friend of Michael Harrington's and had read a fair amount about poverty. He was also, of course, a champion of community development work in Peru and elsewhere. The two men talked for a while. Later that afternoon, as Mankiewicz was working on his congressional testimony, Mary Ann Orlando called and told him Shriver wanted him to attend a six o'clock meeting.

That Sunday evening, in a conference room on the fifth floor of the Peace Corps building, Walter Heller, Kermit Gordon, and members of their staffs briefed Shriver, Yarmolinsky, Mankiewicz, Mike Feldman, Warren Wiggins, and some Peace Corps assistants on all the work the Budget Bureau and the Council of Economic Advisers had done so far. Charles Schultze, assistant director of the Bureau of the Budget, described the Community Action concept and explained that both the CEA and the Budget Bureau believed that Community Action should form the basis of the War on Poverty. The program, Schultze explained, should be designed to get at the "root causes" of poverty, not simply to mitigate its effects. This would not be an income-transfer program but, rather, one that sought to improve education and family living environments, so that residents of poor neighborhoods would develop the skills and self-assurance to lift themselves out of poverty. The pioneering experiments conducted by the PCJD and the Ford Foundation were cited as examples of how Community Action would work. The Heller-Gordon team proposed that President Johnson's entire budget for the poverty program ($500 million) be spent on building a nationwide network of Community Action agencies.

Shriver and his team listened politely to the presentation. Shriver already had a good understanding of how Community Action worked; it was, after all, what many Peace Corps volunteers were already engaged in, especially in Latin America. He recalled later, "Community action—which the people in Community Action thought was so revolutionary—was something we had been running in the Peace Corps for four years before it ever got into the War on Poverty. So I thought Community Action was absolutely sort of normal." He appreciated how effective the Community Action concept could be in empowering the poor to work for their own civic and material improvement. And he strongly agreed that making Community Action part of the War on Poverty could be effective, both as politics and as policy. Politically, it would allow program administrators to emphasize two important facts that would play well even in the conservative South. First, it emphasized local control rather than central planning; this was not creeping socialism but a way of giving control to local communities. Second, Community Action wasn't just "hand-outs" or a perpetuation of public assistance; its goal was to induce individual initiative.

But when Shriver and Yarmolinsky ran into each other in the men's room during a break in the presentation, they just looked at each other and shook their heads. "It'll never fly," Shriver said. "From the day it was handed to me," Shriver said later, "I knew damn well that Community Action could not be the sole thing in the War on Poverty." In his view, there were several related problems with making Community Action the exclusive focus of the poverty program. First, it wasn't broad enough. Community Action was designed for urban communities; it might not work effectively in rural areas. Second, Community Action couldn't by itself generate jobs—and what good was a program that prepared poor people for jobs that didn't exist? The antipoverty legislation, Shriver felt, needed to have some kind of jobs component. Third, and most important, the president needed the War on Poverty to produce results fast: Community Action wouldn't do that.

The Heller-Gordon team thought that Shriver simply wasn't hearing what they had to say. "Sarge's focus that night was . . . to repeat the political success of the Peace Corps," Bill Cannon recalled. "He wanted something glamorous, something easily understood, apparent in its workings, and which you could succeed at. . . . He was just not listening to us, as hard as we kept trying to sell him."

In the days and weeks after this initial briefing, there was talk of deploying Bobby Kennedy to convince his brother-in-law of Community Action's virtues. There were even rumors of a conversation in which Bobby had managed—by force of logic or by threat—to bring Shriver around to support Community Action. Shriver emphatically denied that such a conversation ever took place. "That's just false," he said. "The reason why it's false is that, with all due respect to the people who were interested in Community Action, I think I knew more about Community Action than they did. . . . We'd been running community development in the Peace Corps for three years before it ever started . . . in the War on Poverty. My wife and I had started the program on juvenile delinquency in the Department of Justice [in 1947]. So there wasn't anything new that anyone had to sell to me." Shriver believed the hard-core Community Action supporters were being politically obtuse. "I did play down the idea that Community Action could be the totality of the War on Poverty. . . . I still think that decision was correct, to make Community Action an essential part but not the whole of the War on Poverty."

In the days of the Peace Corps task force, Shriver had made his suite at the Mayflower Hotel into an ongoing seminar whose purpose was to generate as many good ideas from as many brilliant minds as possible. If chaotic brainstorming had worked for the Peace Corps, then why not for the War on Poverty? To begin generating ideas on how to broaden the assault on poverty, Shriver called for a series of meetings at Timberlawn. The meetings commenced on Tuesday, February 4, just two days after Shriver's initial briefing, and continued more or less continuously for twelve days.

A great deal of intellectual firepower was present at these meetings. Shriver, Yarmolinsky, and Mankiewicz were joined by Daniel Patrick Moynihan, a rising star in the Labor Department; most of the gang from the PCJD (Dave Hackett, Dick Boone, Lloyd Ohlin); Michael Harrington, the *Other America* author; Paul Jacobs, another writer, who had recently traveled the country pretending to be a derelict, to understand better how the poor lived; Walter Heller; William Capron, a member of LBJ's Council of Economic Advisers; Lane Kirkland, second in command at the AFL-CIO; Charlie Schultze; Paul Ylvisaker from the Ford Foundation; Louis Martin; Harris Wofford; John Kenneth Galbraith; Secretary of Labor Willard Wirtz; Under Secretary of HEW Wilbur Cohen; Donald Petrie, the CEO of Avis Rent-a-Car; Richard Goodwin; and dozens of other cabinet secretaries and under secretaries, academics, foundation officers, business executives, college presidents, and mayors.

As the task force members surveyed the world around them, it seemed that the prospects for liberal social change were, if anything, greater than they had been at the dawn of the New Frontier, greater in fact than at any time since the New Deal. The Democrats had controlled Congress for years. Eisenhower's eight-year Republican presidency seemed to have been merely a brief interregnum in a period of solid liberal consensus. The New Deal was an accepted part of the political and policy landscape. The economy was strong, making social beneficence more affordable than in the past. And for Shriver and his generation, which had seen the federal government end the Depression, defeat Nazism, and help produce an era of great American prosperity, it was an article of faith that government could solve big social problems. Now they had been offered a golden opportunity to solve one of the most persistent problems themselves. "For the proponents of social legislation," Yarmolinsky recalled, "this was our Camelot."

Almost all of the current knowledge about American poverty was gathered in that room—and it still wasn't very much. Robert Lampman had provided a complete bibliography of every worthwhile book or article on poverty; it was less then two pages long. Even the presence of Michael Harrington, the person most responsible for putting poverty on the political map, didn't help much. Harrington was more radical, and more pessimistic, than most of the other meeting participants; his view was that Johnson's proposed budget for the poverty program, large though it may have seemed in political terms, was way too small to even begin to dent poverty. You're not going to end poverty by spending "nickels and dimes," he told Shriver. "Oh, really, Mr. Harrington," Shriver replied. "I don't know about you but this is the first time I've spent a billion dollars."

Shriver knew he didn't have much time; Johnson had told him he wanted a comprehensive plan as soon as possible, so that both houses of Congress would have time to pass legislation before their adjournment and the campaign season in the fall. The only clear piece of direction Johnson gave him came through Moyers. "You tell Shriver, 'No doles,'" LBJ said. But despite the time constraints, Shriver made a determined commitment to trawl widely for new ideas. He recalled, "I decided that in the brief time we had, we would read *everything* that had been written about poverty; listen to *anyone* who had anything to say; accept advice from *any* source."

He recruited anyone he thought might have something to contribute. Edgar May was a reporter for the *Buffalo Evening News* who had recently written a series of articles on poverty and welfare that had won him a Pulitzer Prize and who had just published a book called *The Wasted Americans*. May was working late one Friday night when Shriver, whom he had never met, called him on the phone. "My name is Sargent Shriver, and I'm down here in Washington with the Peace Corps, and we're trying to put together a task force to do something about poverty," he said. "I read your book last night, and I just want to know, how long are you going to criticize this stuff, and when are you going to *do* something about it." Several hours later, May was on a flight to Washington. He would work by Shriver's side for the next ten years.

What May saw when he joined the task force was "vintage Shriver": a "diverse and sometimes exotic group of people, most of whom had done something that had made a headline, whether they were Davis Cup tennis players or downhill skiers or left-handed pool shooters or Pulitzer Prize winners," all of them woven together by the magical "chemistry" that Shriver's collaboratives rarely failed to generate.

Shriver gathered together people who otherwise would likely have had no occasion to meet. Shriver was always eager to get the perspective of the business community, because he believed they were often better "problem solvers" than academics or government bureaucrats. As one task force participant recalled, "There were all kinds of millionaires popping in and out for a day at a time." Radicals like Harrington, Paul Jacobs, and Saul Alinsky sat alongside businessmen and industrialists.

Shriver's method of operation was the same as it had been when he ran the Peace Corps task force. He would encourage debate and "wild brainstorming." Yarmolinsky recalled the meetings as being like "a college seminar." Hyman Bookbinder was a labor lobbyist who joined the task force and who later became an associate director of the OEO. He recalled, "Shriver would bring down people. He'd sit them on one side of a conference table and . . . would say, 'The president has given me an assignment to eliminate poverty in this country. What would you do if you had to eliminate poverty in this country? Where would you start? Give me some ideas.'"

Those who hadn't known Shriver before were struck by what seemed to be the apparently naive simplicity of this method. Jim Sundquist, the deputy under secretary of agriculture who had been dispatched by the Agriculture Department to participate in the task force meetings, told the journalist Murray Kempton, "I've never known anyone as open to ideas as Shriver is. If a man came in with an idea, he would seem to accept it right away, and if you objected, Sarge would say, 'What's wrong with it?' and the burden of proof would be on the one who objected instead of the one who suggested the idea." Others were less charitable: Shriver was, one observer said, "a dilettante with a propensity for schoolgirl enthusiasms."

There was truth to acid comments like these, but Shriver knew how his own mind worked. That's why he tapped Yarmolinsky to be his deputy. He had used men like Moyers and Wiggins to rein him in at the Peace Corps; now he used

Yarmolinsky as a check on his enthusiasms on the poverty task force. Yarmolinsky was not always popular among the task force members, but his aggressiveness was necessary to "thin the ranks of both antipoverty warriors and their nostrums."

Shriver was also more discerning than he let on. As Sundquist observed, "Nothing ever seemed very systematic, but there may have been more system in it than appeared on the surface." Shriver initially kept the floodgates wide open to make sure he captured every possible proposal, and plenty of bad ideas were injected into the mix. But the ideas that ultimately made it into the poverty program were for the most part smart ones, both as politics and as policy—and almost every one of those ideas emerged, in concept if not in name, within the first several days of his freewheeling brainstorming sessions.

Shriver was better versed in the ways of the federal government than he had been when launching the Peace Corps three years earlier, but his seat-of-the-pants management style still prevailed. For the first few weeks after Shriver's appointment, the poverty task force operated exclusively out of his Maryland living room and his fifth floor Peace Corps offices at 806 Connecticut Avenue. He borrowed staff from the Peace Corps and elsewhere in the government, and he held meetings late at night, sometimes at midnight, because so many of the task force participants had other jobs. When the swell of people grew too large for the fifth floor to accommodate, they expanded into vacant offices on the twelfth floor. When the burgeoning program outgrew its space in the Maiatico Building, staff members spilled out into "three or four nooks and crannies around Washington, most of them within walking distance of the Peace Corps."

The poverty program spent its first months of existence migrating from place to place. First, there was the beautiful old Court of Claims building, originally constructed as an art gallery and later used as a barracks by Union soldiers during the Civil War before being adapted for use as a courthouse and then abandoned. Alas, this building turned out to be structurally unsound: When construction began on a nearby site, 200-pound chunks of the court's ceiling started falling from 30 feet above. Engineers determined the building was near collapse and everyone was forced to evacuate on two hours' notice, carrying all their files and possessions with them. The task force split up and moved into two spaces: a temporary office in the basement morgue of a condemned hospital and an old, abandoned hotel that in an earlier incarnation had been a "second-class whorehouse." Poverty agency officials claimed old hotel rooms as their offices. Secretaries worked out of adjoining bathrooms. Bathtubs served as file cabinets. There were far more toilets than desks.

The logistical challenges were enormous. Every time the staff moved, everyone would be assigned new telephone numbers, so no one ever knew how to reach anyone else. The otherwise simple task of requisitioning paper clips or stationery became almost impossible. Eventually, task force administrators learned to do what the early Peace Corps employees had done: make guerrilla raids on other agencies to steal their supplies. Movers were constantly losing boxes of files, or delivering them to the wrong place. Sometimes, important working papers went missing for weeks.

Bill Kelly, the former NASA official who had helped bring administrative order to the Peace Corps, was called in to do the same for the poverty task force. At first, he couldn't even figure out how many people Shriver was employing in the task force because they were scattered all over town, "squatting" in other people's office space. No money had yet been appropriated for a poverty program; all Shriver's task force had was $30,000 from the president's contingency fund. In effect, lack of money made the poverty planners—as one of them would later put it—"warriors without guns."

Despite these challenges and the generally frenzied environment, the task force enjoyed "excellent esprit de corps," according to Kelly and many others. The atmosphere, Robert Lampman noted, was like being in the hotel lobby of a national political convention: fun, full of energy and excitement, a sense of high stakes, with people running back and forth and yelling at one another at all hours of the day and night. Another participant described the task force period as a "beautiful hysteria."

Even Lyndon Johnson was affected. In his memoir, the president discussed the "contagious" excitement generated by Shriver's task force. "I followed closely the work of those men over the next few weeks [in February and March]. They went at it with a fervor and created a ferment unknown since the days of the New Deal, when lights burned through the night as men worked to restructure society."

"MAXIMUM FEASIBLE PARTICIPATION"

The creative ferment LBJ and others observed was in some ways remarkably productive—from this hopeful chaos the contours of an antipoverty program began to emerge, and many enduring social programs were born in an aston-ishingly short time. Yet as one task force participant reported to the *New York Times,* the in-fighting was so bitter "sometimes the walls dripped with blood as the empire builders clashed with the empire wreckers." In the early months of the Peace Corps, too, there had often been "blood on the floor." But at the Peace Corps most of the early wounds quickly healed; this time many did not, and the political damage they caused was substantial.

Beginning at the initial briefing meeting on February 2, there were disputes over Community Action. Community Action had lobbyists in two separate camps. The first was Bobby Kennedy's gang from the PCJD—the "Guerrillas," they called themselves. The second were the economists in the Bureau of the Budget who had become convinced that Community Action was the most eco-nomical way to wage war against poverty.

But even without having had time to study the matter, Shriver instinctively felt that the poverty program would be a political failure if Community Action were the sum total of what it offered. So although Community Action was not completely taken off the table at the first all-day brainstorming session on February 4, Shriver presented it as merely one component of what the poverty program would become.

This did not sit well with some of the Community Action advocates, espe-cially because they believed that Shriver was diminishing their idea. Community Action's academic supporters had an opposite concern—that the War on Poverty was irresponsibly inflating the concept, transforming it from a small-scale, demonstration project in a limited number of areas into a large-scale, nationwide program. Better to take it slow, the academics advised, to spend the time to see if Community Action works before deploying it nationally.

Won't work, Shriver said. An "unconditional war," he said, could not be fought on a demonstration basis. Not only must the War on Poverty be more than just Community Action, he insisted—Community Action itself had to be bigger and bolder than the cautious academics imagined it. When Paul Ylvisaker was asked to draw up a proposed budget for Community Action and came up with a figure of $30 million, Shriver told him to add another zero.

The concept of Community Action, at this point, seemed to mean differ-ent things to different people. To practical-minded people in the Bureau of the Budget and the Council of Economic Advisers, it was merely a planning and coordinating mechanism, a way of bringing together all the disparate institutions—such as the federal government, the state government, the city government, the school system, and neighborhood organizations—involved in dealing with the poor. For the academics and foundation executives, it was a way to encourage social experiments—a "way of attempting to test out a variety of solutions to the poverty program," as Adam Yarmolinsky put it. For Bobby Kennedy's PCJD Guerrillas, Community Action was a hybrid of political mobilization and "social therapy."

At times, competing factions within Shiver's task force would both be talking about Community Action but meaning completely different things. Rather than settling on a single, narrow definition at this point—which might have pushed disagreements over its meaning to the breaking point—the task force left Community Action's meaning fuzzy, allowing it to withstand a broad range of interpretations. This worked well in the short term, but it prevented the task force from ever thinking clearly about Community Action's political explosiveness.

A few early conversations did hint at political explosions to come. The most significant was over the question of exactly how involved the poor should be in planning and administering their own Community Action programs. One point that just about everyone in the task force agreed upon was that the "board ladies" and "bureaucrats" who populated the current welfare-services delivery system were hidebound and ineffective. The antibureaucratic spirit of the Peace Corps task force, which had bridled at the notion of being absorbed into the old-line foreign aid bureaucracy, carried through now into the poverty task force. The "old-line" welfare system didn't work—so Community Action would work around it, by going outside of the usual bureaucratic chain to give money to locally based organizations. This, it was thought, would have the salutary effect of compelling the old welfare services operations to reform themselves.

But how much control was it necessary to give the poor in order to give them "ownership" of their program? There was general consensus that the poor had to have *some* input in the planning and *some* direct involvement with administration in order for the assault on the old-line bureaucracy to work. But there was little agreement about exactly how much control and how much input. Some thought the involvement should be minimal, at the level of having one or two poor people on the boards of local Community Action agencies, to ensure that the voice of the poor was being heard. "My conception of what it meant was that you involved poor people in the process, not that you put them in charge." Adam Yarmolinsky recalled. Bobby's Guerrillas at the PCJD thought the poor should have much more active control and involvement. The phrase that came to represent this latter viewpoint was "maximum feasible participation" of the poor.

Dick Boone, Dave Hackett's deputy at the PCDJ, seems to have been the first person to use it. At the first meeting at Shriver's house, Boone repeatedly insisted that Community Action had to have the "maximum feasible participation" of the poor. Finally, Yarmolinsky turned to him and said, "You have used that phrase four or five times now."

"Yes, I know," Boone replied. "How many more times do I have to use it before it becomes part of the program?"

"Oh, a couple of times more," Yarmolinsky said. Boone did—and "the maximum feasible participation" of the poor was written into the requirements for Community Action.

One of the biggest supporters of Community Action—and of "maximum feasible participation"—was presumed to be Bobby Kennedy. Yet he was conspicuously absent from the task force meetings. As a champion of Community Action, Bobby might have been expected to attend these meetings. But he was still consumed with grief. More to the point, perhaps, he was bitter that the president had made Shriver head of the task force. Bobby felt that by rights *he* should be running the poverty program; he was a *real* Kennedy, and therefore better suited to carrying the Kennedys' antipoverty torch. Shriver, in Bobby's mind, had inappropriate dual loyalties—to the Kennedys *and* to LBJ.

Shriver was aware that Bobby and some of his associates perceived anything he did for LBJ to be a betrayal of the Kennedy family. "The disgust of Bobby and his people was blatantly visible," Shriver recalled. "I'd get reports from various people or criticism from various people for doing this or that. But that didn't matter to me. I had been given responsibility by the US president to develop the best possible programs for the poor people. I didn't care whether these programs had originated with John Kennedy's followers or Bobby Kennedy's followers or Lyndon Johnson's followers."

"I never heard anything directly from Bobby," Shriver continued. "He never uttered a word to me. But I knew that Bobby and those friendly to Bobby were complaining about the way I was organizing the poverty program. Bobby thought that everything done in the poverty program should be credited to Jack. But my opinion was that Lyndon Johnson's administration was putting up the money; I never thought that he was trying to steal credit. Also, I didn't think that just because Johnson got credit that Jack Kennedy lost credit. To me, it didn't matter whether Lyndon Johnson or John Kennedy or Joe Smith had thought of it. My job was to get the poverty program started."

"I never heard anything from Eunice, either," Shriver added. "If people bitched to her, she never said anything to me." Former JFK advisers, Eunice recalled, "were upset about *anybody* working for President Johnson. Sarge felt a real loyalty to the programs. I agreed with him. What was the alternative? I think Sarge has terrific talent and great concern for people who are underdogs. That's not something he came upon when he married me or when he went to work for the Johnson administration. It was part of the very core of his being. If you take that out of somebody's life because you think he's being 'disloyal' to a man who is dead, well, I just didn't think it made sense."

Although Bobby did not attend the Timberlawn meetings, his presence was palpable. "What would Bobby do?" was the question that governed the thinking of many of the participants at Shriver's meetings. At least once, Shriver and some associates made pilgrimages to Bobby, to seek his blessing on the evolving poverty program. "We went to see him early on," Frank Mankiewicz recalled. "Sarge and I, maybe Harrington, Moynihan, Dave Hackett, and Dick Boone. He looked awful. He just sort of sat there. He was still in shock. He asked if what we were doing was what President Kennedy had in mind, and Hackett and Boone assured him it was. He said, 'Fine.'"

TURF WARS

The fights over bureaucratic turf were even more heated than the arguments about Community Action. The main instigator in these fights was Willard Wirtz, the secretary of labor, whom Shriver had recruited for Kennedy's cabinet from Adlai Stevenson's law firm in Chicago. Wirtz, like Shriver, felt there had to be more to the poverty program than Community Action. At the first all-day meeting at Timberlawn he strongly advocated making a jobs program the centerpiece of the War on Poverty.

Both Shriver and Lyndon Johnson agreed with Wirtz instinctively: A jobs program could be a valuable complement to Community Action programs that provided training and neighborhood services. But Wirtz angrily dismissed the idea of anything *but* jobs programs. When Walter Heller released the first CEA report recommending Community Action, Wirtz "violently attacked" it and tried to suppress its publication.

Shriver was prepared to give Wirtz a receptive hearing. He, too, believed that a jobs program must be an integral part of any War on Poverty. But Wirtz sabotaged himself by proposing a massive jobs program that would cost between $3 billion and $5 billion per year. As policy, this may have been a good idea. But as politics it was absurd—President Johnson had already said he would be asking for a *total* of only $1 billion for *all* antipoverty measures. Moreover, Wirtz made his argument seem completely self-serving and therefore non-credible by arguing that this multibillion-dollar program be run under his auspices at the Labor Department. "If Wirtz had had his way," Shriver recalled, "the War on Poverty bill would simply have been a vehicle via which long dormant or suspended programs would get pushed through Congress. Once we had fought the legislation into law, the individual programs would be peeled off and handed to the bureaucrats in Labor, HEW, or (eventually) the new Department of Housing and Urban Development (HUD). The new poverty agency would have become just a hollow shell without money or authority to run anything."

Shriver had another, more personal reason for wanting to retain control of a jobs program. Long before he was tasked with starting the War on Poverty, Shriver had given serious thought to a distinctive kind of jobs program. In the 1950s, when he was president of Chicago's Board of Education, he had been forced to contend with the problem of large numbers of underachieving youth. What do you do with the students who graduate as unemployable? At the time Shriver had thought, "What we ought to have is a big institution that takes those kids—they've already quit the school system because they are permitted to do so when they're 16, but we will take them, and not force them, but we will try to get them to volunteer to join an institution, which we'll have right here in the city, which will train them for jobs." But Shriver was not able to implement this plan before being pulled to Washington by Jack Kennedy. Now, as director of the poverty task force, Shriver had the opportunity to implement the concept on a national scale. There was also clear public-relations value to a jobs program: The image of previously unemployed youths doing tangible work would be political gold.

Once it became clear that Shriver was going to make the big jobs program his own, Wirtz basically withdrew from the task force, delegating responsibility for representing the Labor Department to his ambitious young deputy, Daniel Patrick Moynihan. Moynihan, who had a knack for igniting political controversy, was seen as smart but ineffectual by Shriver and his closest associates, "an impractical intellectual" and "a water-carrier for Wirtz." Wirtz, for his part, believed Moynihan had been co-opted by Shriver's people and made into a convert to the cause of Community Action. Playing both sides against the middle, Moynihan got in trouble with everyone. Wirtz blamed Moynihan for losing Labor Department control of the jobs program; Shriver's people blamed Moynihan, who helped draft the presidential message to Congress that accompanied the poverty bill, for diminishing Community Action in order to exaggerate the role of the jobs program. Several years later, in response to all this criticism, as well as to the general political problems that by 1968 were besetting the War on Poverty, Moynihan would publish a caustic history of the War on Poverty's launch, titled *Maximum Feasible Misunderstanding*. In the book (parts of which might be described as creatively revisionist), Moynihan casts himself as a lone prophet, warning against the perils of Community Action in 1964.

DRAFTING A BILL

The poverty bill came together with astonishing speed. Within three weeks of the February 2 meeting, a complete bill had been drafted—and most of what went into it had been introduced at least tangentially by February 4. The concepts that would come to fruition as Community Action, Job Corps, Neighborhood Youth Corps, Upward Bound, and VISTA (Volunteers in Service to America) had all been discussed by the end of the second brainstorming session at Timberlawn. The seeds that would blossom a year later as Head Start and Legal Services for the Poor had also been planted.

After a task force meeting on February 23, Norbert Schlei, who was an assistant attorney general, composed a first draft of the poverty bill. The draft included a section on Community Action, along with the language that Dick Boone had lobbied for: A "Community Action Organization" would be one "which is developed and conducted with the maximum feasible participation of the residents" where the organization was based. Jim Sundquist later noted that "the clause . . . relating to participation of the poor was inserted with virtually no discussion in the task force and none at all on Capitol Hill." No one was aware then of its implications. "It just seemed . . . like an idea that nobody could quarrel with."

The draft bill had six parts. Title I contained the Job Corps, the Neighborhood Youth Corps, and a work-study program. The Job Corps was aimed at youths between the ages of sixteen and twenty-one who had finished school but could not find a place in the labor market. The bill called for two types of Job Corps programs. The first would be rural camps, modeled on FDR's Civilian Conservation Corps, where participants would receive basic skills training and do conservation work on public lands. The second (Shriver's most cherished part of the whole poverty program) would be urban boarding schools, where kids would receive food, clothes, and medical care, along with basic education and work skills.

The Neighborhood Youth Program was aimed at the same demographic group but did not include a boarding component. In this program, state and local agencies would employ poor youths to do low-skill work. The idea was to give young people an income while instilling a work ethic and teaching them basic job skills. The work-study program, a project that Francis Keppel, the US commissioner of education, had been trying for some time to get legislated without much success, would pay schools or nonprofit organizations to employ low-income students in part-time jobs.

Title II established Community Action. Reflecting the task force's vague definition of Community Action, the establishing language was quite broad. Community Action would, according to the bill, mobilize public and private resources to reduce poverty; provide services to the poor; draw on the "maximum feasible participation" of the poor themselves; and be administered by a local agency that fairly represented its surrounding community. As the bill's principal drafter, Norb Schlei, said, "The Community Action program can take on anything and everything." Community action agencies could develop projects on housing, health care, education, job training, child care, juvenile delinquency, and "other fields."

Title III, inserted at the insistence of Jim Sundquist and Secretary of Agriculture Orville Freeman, called for the establishment of loans and grants to poor farmers, to help them upgrade their technology and improve their efficiency. Title IV established a program of small-business loans to be administered by the Small Business Administration. Title V called for a work-experience program to provide job training to unemployed heads of family receiving public assistance; HEW would administer it.

Title VI established VISTA, under which volunteers would work in cooperation with state and local agencies to reduce poverty. It was expected that VISTA volunteers would work to further the objectives of Title I and Title II.

The bill, called the Economic Opportunity Act, also called for the formation of a new agency called the Office of Economic Opportunity (OEO). Task force members agreed on the need to create a wholly new umbrella agency; without one, there would be no chance of achieving their stated goal of working around the established welfare bureaucracy. But there remained considerable disagreement over the function of the new agency. Would it merely coordinate the different programs, serving as a liaison among the different cabinet departments? Or would it have actual operating responsibility, directly administering programs itself?

Shriver was of the strong opinion that the OEO should have operating authority. A new kind of war called for a new kind of army with a wholly new command structure. The cabinet secretaries disagreed. President Johnson intervened to effect a compromise. In the end, the Labor Department got control over the Neighborhood Youth Corps, and HEW took charge of health and training programs, but OEO got complete coordinating authority along with operating authority over VISTA and the two major components of the poverty program—Community Action and the Job Corps.

CHAPTER TWENTY-EIGHT

Mobilizing for War

T he frenetic days of February blurred into the even more frenetic days of early March. Yarmolinsky continued to serve as task force commander, but now the individual programs were beginning to get their own field commanders.

One day in February, Vernon Alden, the president of Ohio University, was lying on the beach in Hawaii when a resort employee told him that the president of the United States was on the line. When the bewildered Alden went inside and picked up the phone, President Johnson told him he needed to get on a flight to Washington right away. Alden asked why. "I'd like to have Sargent Shriver explain that," the president said. Shriver spoke up. "We want to talk to you about being part of an exciting new program we're developing." Alden explained he was on vacation and that he could come to Washington in a week. "What do you mean, next week?" Shriver said. "We expect you tomorrow."

Meeting with Shriver and LBJ at the White House, Alden found Shriver's offer—to chair the group planning the jobs component of the poverty program—compelling. Shriver explained that he wanted this part of the program to have the imprimatur of American higher education; a college president could provide not only the latest educational thinking but also prestige. ("In those days," Alden says, "people were much more in awe of university presidents than they are today.") Shriver particularly wanted Alden because he had gone to Harvard Business School and served on numerous corporate boards—Alden, in other words, was not some ivory-tower philosopher but a real manager. The jobs program needed that.

On March 25 Shriver announced Alden's appointment as chair of the task force subgroup on jobs, and Alden began spending several days each week in Washington, working on a jobs program. Alden would get up at five in the morning, fly to Washington, work all day long, "talk with Shriver until well into the evening," and then work all the next day before flying back to Ohio late at night.

Several controversies arose. Having worked in the Defense Department, Yarmolinsky knew that the armed forces had two things the Job Corps needed: logistics capability and unused bases. Why not have the military provide retired bases to the poverty program for use as camps? And why not allow the military to put its skill at housing, feeding, and clothing people to good use as part of a domestic social program? Shriver loved the idea when Yarmolinsky proposed it. The Civilian Conservation Corps—which was one of the models for the Job Corps—had relied on military assistance to grow quickly. And Shriver liked the notion of the American war machine being deployed for peaceful domestic purposes. Defense Secretary McNamara also liked the idea, so by the second week of February, memos were circulating that explained what the Defense Department's role would be.

But the proposed role for the military at these camps provoked "the anguished cries of the knee-jerk liberals," as Yarmolinsky put it. "We didn't want the military to get their dirty paws on it," one liberal poverty planner recalled.

Sure enough, a week later a column by Rowland Evans and Robert Novak in the *Washington Post* reported the internal debates over how much operational control of the Job Corps should be given to the Defense Department. When "a proposal to put the US Army on the front lines of President Johnson's War on Poverty . . . became known," Evans and Novak wrote, "blood vessels began popping in official Washington." As Evans and Novak subsequently reported,

Senator Hubert Humphrey of Minnesota (a rival of Shriver's for the vice presidency) protested personally to the president. Johnson heard more of the same the next day at one of the liveliest cabinet meetings since the New Deal. The military camp plan was attacked in quick order by Willard Wirtz, secretary of labor; Anthony Celebrezze, secretary of health, education, and welfare; and Orville Freeman, secretary of agriculture. All charged Shriver with adding too many military trappings to the war against poverty. According to one official present, LBJ, playing peacemaker, then told Shriver, "Sarge, we shouldn't give this thing too much of a military flavor."

Shriver was forced to agree to scale back the military's role significantly.

Liberals also objected to the role Shriver proposed for private corporations in administering the Job Corps camps. But here Shriver prevailed. He instructed Alden to reach out to the business community to recruit a business advisory board and to find companies that would be interested in running the camps as modest, for-profit enterprises. Shriver was himself a liberal on many issues (it was not for nothing the Kennedys called him their "house Communist") but because of his own background at the Merchandise Mart he was always much more willing than many liberals to recognize that businessmen offered strengths that academics and government workers lacked.

To help make corporations an integral part of the Job Corps, Shriver hired John Rubel, who had previously served as assistant secretary of defense and was now a vice president at Litton Industries, one of the first large business conglomerates. Rubel's task force colleagues didn't quite know what to make of him. His conversations "often left others either bedazzled with the breadth of his knowledge, or uncertain as to what on earth he was trying to say."

Rubel pointed out that the position of the poverty program in 1964 was analogous to that of the US space program in 1969, when Kennedy vowed to put a man on the moon. Manned space flight was an enormously complex undertaking, so the Defense Department and NASA had turned for help to private companies that not only had more "systems capability" than government bureaucracies but also had a broader range of knowledge and technical skill.

The Job Corps, Rubel observed, was in its way as complex as space flight. No one person knew the best way to recruit unemployed dropouts and mold them into productive, employed taxpayers. Private companies would surely have more "systems design and management capability" than the federal government did. Why not ask corporations to bid to run Job Corps centers?

Shriver was enthusiastic; this was "exactly the kind of innovation that appealed to him." For one thing, bidding out contracts to private companies would allow him to work around the government bureaucracy, avoiding "the stodgy professionalism he abhorred." Also, involving private corporations directly in the program could help get its graduates jobs: "If industry did the training, industry could hardly refuse to hire the products."

The reaction to this idea among the business community was favorable. Within the ranks of his own task force, however, it provoked dissension. Offering business the opportunity to make *profits* from the poor? Appalling, some said. This didn't deter Shriver, however. He knew a winning idea when he saw one, and three days later he had an extended conversation with Rubel to hammer out the details of how the Job Corps should be structured. In essence, Rubel and Shriver decided that they would experiment with different ways to run centers. Federal employees would run some; universities would run some; and private companies would run some—and over time, the most effective way of running Job Corps centers would become apparent.

"YOU'RE JUST ASKING FOR IT, SARGE"

Just a few days before he was to submit the Economic Opportunity Act to the president for his approval, Shriver visited the Oval Office to brief Johnson on what he could expect. He began by describing the legislation point by point, beginning with Title I. As Shriver outlined the Job Corps and the Neighborhood Youth Corps, it seemed to him that the president's thoughts were "focused inward." Shriver imagined Johnson was thinking about the poverty-stricken children he had taught in Cotulla, or about the National Youth Administration programs he'd headed in the 1930s.

But when Shriver began describing Community Action, with its emphasis on "maximum feasible participation." the president seemed to snap to attention. "He swiveled in his chair, his face darkened, and slapped his hand on the desk," Shriver recalled. "It was like a storm sweeping across a Texas prairie."

"No," Shriver remembered Johnson saying. "You can't do it! You can't give federal dollars to private agencies. It won't work." The president's sensitive political radar sensed danger. Let private citizens administer taxpayer money? Unthinkable. "You're going to be in terrible trouble," he continued. "You'll have a helluva thing on your hands. And so will I. It's going to be just awful. The people will steal the money. The governors and mayors will hate it. You're just asking for it, Sarge."

Shriver was shaken by this outburst, but he felt the planning for Community Action was too far along to be turned back now. He explained to the president that the War on Poverty needed to have new weapons to rally Americans' excitement about it. How could poor people be enlisted in the war if they weren't provided such a weapon?

Johnson remained unconvinced—his political instincts cried out against this. Shriver worried for a moment that Johnson was about to scuttle the whole thing. In the end, though, he didn't. The president's heart and conscience—which told him that reducing poverty in America required unusual methods—overrode his political instincts. Just promise me one thing, Johnson reportedly told Shriver. "I just want you to make sure that no crooks, communists, or cocksuckers get into the program." Community Action stayed. Several days later, on March 16, 1964— less than six weeks since Shriver had convened the first task force meeting—LBJ sent the $962.5 million Economic Opportunity Act to Congress.

Ultimately, Johnson's political fears about Community Action would prove well founded. But at this moment, Shriver recalled, "All of us who had worked so hard, learned so much so fast, and assembled so many experimental concepts were convinced that the Economic Opportunity Act would work." It seemed to him—and to others, as well—that the civil rights movement of the 1950s and the impulse toward economic justice that had its source in the New Deal of the 1930s had now coalesced into one propitious moment. To some, it seemed that the torch of John F. Kennedy had been passed.

"HALF A KENNEDY"

Bobby Kennedy did not agree. In his view, which was shared by some of his aides and former aides to President Kennedy, only he could pick up the New Frontier torch. Anyone who claimed otherwise was blind to the usurpation Lyndon Johnson was perpetrating. Johnson had taken a Kennedy program and made it into a Johnson program; he was stealing the glory that rightfully belonged to Jack Kennedy. And Shriver, in accepting command of the poverty program, had become an accomplice in that theft.

In Bobby's view, Shriver was now compounding the issue by not removing himself from consideration for the vice presidency. Bill Moyers had earlier written a memo to LBJ making the case that Shriver would be an ideal running mate. Johnson said he agreed, and he ordered Moyers to leak the memo to the press. For a Kennedy in-law even to contemplate joining LBJ's ticket in 1964, Bobby believed, constituted a betrayal of the Kennedy family and of him personally. An emissary from Bobby's camp went so far as to send word to Johnson that if he selected Shriver it would tear the Kennedy family apart. And Moyers got word that "if you are going to take a Kennedy, it's got to be a *real* Kennedy"—not "a half a Kennedy." (Actually, LBJ sometimes worried that Shriver *was* a real Kennedy. "Just remember," Johnson told Moyers, evidently forgetting that Shriver was a Kennedy only by marriage, "blood is thicker than water.")

Bobby's antipathy to a Shriver vice presidency was on some level understandable. Bobby had never intended to go into elective politics; he was shy and intospective, and he had based his political career up to 1964 around helping other public figures. But when he emerged from a deep depression following his brother's assassination and saw the reception he got at public appearances, he realized that the hopes JFK had aroused in people were now focused on him. He felt he had a legacy to fulfill. At the same time, he found it difficult to accept that LBJ was now in the White House, setting a course and an agenda slightly different from Jack's.

Shriver, in contrast, was in some ways a born candidate; he was good at the backslapping and handshaking that Bobby hated. Moreover, his successes in Illinois had made him the perfect candidate for office in that state—an honest patrician serving the people in the mold of Adlai Stevenson and Paul Douglas. And before Jack had tapped him to run the Peace Corps, after all, Shriver had set a course for elective office in that state.

But given Bobby's background, the idea of a member of his family pursuing a political career that was independent of the family was difficult to swallow—especially if that family member was from the same party he was, appealed to constituencies similar to those he did, and held similar views on public issues to his own.

This competition, indirectly created by an assassin's bullet, was—as always happens—exaggerated by the chatter of aides and the exaggerations of the press. But it formed the environment in which Shriver and RFK had to co-exist, and it fueled Bobby's grief-driven discontent.

Naturally, Shriver was aware that his name was being promoted for the 1964 ticket, and he knew, too, that Johnson was using him as a defense against, and provocation of, Bobby. One day Ken O'Donnell was meeting the president in the Oval Office when Moyers's voice came over the intercom on LBJ's desk. Moyers reported that Shriver would be willing to join the 1964 ticket and that Bobby would not object. "The hell he wouldn't!" O'Donnell exclaimed.

Shortly after this incident, according to a *New York Times* report some years later, "Robert Kennedy sat in icy silence aboard the Kennedy plane on the way to Hyannis Port, deliberately ostracizing his brother-in-law." Even Eunice would later say, in a 1972 interview with *Life* magazine, "At the beginning, I was for Bobby. I thought he should have it over Sarge because of his experience." "I think maybe there were some difficulties," she said of the strife the vice presidency question caused within the family, "but Sarge handled that." (Today, Eunice says she doesn't recall ever saying that it was "Bobby's turn," or that she favored her brother over her husband for the position.)

The door on the vice presidency wouldn't publicly slam shut until midsummer, when LBJ officially eliminated people already serving in his administration from vice presidential contention. But from Shriver's perspective, it was effectively slammed shut one spring weekend at the Kennedy compound in Hyannis Port. Earlier in the week, yet another newspaper columnist reported that the president had been singing Shriver's praises and that the Peace Corps director sat atop the list of likely vice presidential candidates. At a family gathering that weekend, Bobby told Shriver he wanted to speak to him alone. The brothers-in-law walked outside to the lawn. In the background, Atlantic waves crashed onto the beach nearby. "Did you plant that story in the paper?" Bobby asked. Shriver replied that he hadn't and added that he had not even had any real conversations with anyone in the Johnson administration about the vice presidency. But Bobby, still fueled by grief at Jack's death, moved in close so that his face was nearly touching Shriver's. "Let me make something clear," Bobby growled. "There's not going to be a Kennedy on this ticket. And if there were, it would be me."

Above: Sarge spent his childhood summers at the Shriver family homestead in Union Mills, Maryland, where the air was still thick with the unresolved animosities of the Civil War.
SHRIVER FAMILY COLLECTION

Left: When some of his parents' friends first saw Sargent Shriver after his birth on November 9, 1915, they deemed him "fat as a pig." SHRIVER FAMILY COLLECTION, JOHN F. KENNEDY LIBRARY

Above: From childhood, Shriver was a leader in nearly everything he did, including serving as captain (he's wearing the captain's *C*) of his baseball team at the Canterbury School, where he was briefly a classmate of young John F. Kennedy. SHRIVER FAMILY COLLECTION, JOHN F. KENNEDY LIBRARY

Right: James Cardinal Gibbons, the Catholic archbishop of Baltimore, alongside Sarge's older brother, Herbert Shriver *(on step),* and an unidentified boy. A classmate of Sarge's grandfather at seminary, the cardinal spent his summers in the Shriver home in Union Mills and exerted a powerful influence on Sarge's budding religious sensibility. SHRIVER FAMILY COLLECTION

Top: Shriver (second row, second from left) with the crew of his submarine, the USS *Sandlance,* during a change of command at Midway Island, in June 1945. SHRIVER FAMILY COLLECTION, JOHN F. KENNEDY LIBRARY

Above, right: After seven years of courtship, Sarge married Eunice Kennedy on May 23, 1953. CORBIS

Left: Naval lieutenant Shriver walks the streets of Manhattan in the early 1940s. SHRIVER FAMILY COLLECTION, JOHN F. KENNEDY LIBRARY

Opposite, above: Through his work with the Chicago Catholic Interracial Council in the 1950s, Shriver became friendly with Martin Luther King Jr. and other leading figures of the civil rights movement. In 1960 Shriver was instrumental in arranging JFK's phone call to Coretta Scott King, which some believe was what enabled Kennedy to eke out his victory over Richard Nixon. CORBIS

Opposite, below: By marrying Eunice, Shriver hitched his fate to that of a large, powerful clan. Seated, left to right: Eunice Kennedy Shriver, Rose Kennedy, Joseph P. Kennedy, Jacqueline Bouvier Kennedy, Edward "Ted" Kennedy. Standing, left to right: Ethel Skakel Kennedy, Stephen Smith, Jean Kennedy Smith, John F. Kennedy, Robert Kennedy, Patricia Kennedy Lawford, Sargent Shriver, Joan Bennett Kennedy, and Peter Lawford. CORBIS

Left, above: At a 1960 parade for Democratic presidential nominee John F. Kennedy, Shriver sits alongside Chicago mayor Richard Daley, while Eunice peers around from behind her brother. ASSOCIATED PRESS

Left, below: Shriver and his brother-in-law at the White House, not long after Kennedy's election. SHRIVER FAMILY COLLECTION

Above, left: Shriver at a White House press conference with Bill Moyers, who left LBJ's staff to become deputy director of the Peace Corps. After JFK's death, Moyers returned to LBJ's staff, where he remained a crucial Shriver ally. SHRIVER FAMILY COLLECTION, JOHN F. KENNEDY LIBRARY

Above, right: President Kennedy hands Shriver a pen used to sign the Peace Corps Act, on September 22, 1961, giving the organization permanent status. Standing next to the president, Senator Hubert Humphrey—the future vice president and 1968 Democratic presidential nominee—looks on happily. CORBIS

Right: Shriver at work with Charlie Peters, the "conscience of the Peace Corps." Peters, a young veteran of the 1960 Kennedy campaign, joined the Peace Corps staff in 1961 and led the famed Evaluation Division that helped make the organization so distinctive. CHARLIE PETERS

Top: Shriver, on a trip to the Middle East in 1964, attracted a following among the children of Jordan.
PAUL CONKLIN

Above, right: Shriver first graced the cover of a major newsmagazine in the summer of 1963. By this point, the Peace Corps was widely seen to be the New Frontier's signature program.

Left: Shriver navigates a donkey—carrying himself and his Peace Corps colleagues—through the dusty roads of Nepal. PAUL CONKLIN

Opposite, above: Shriver and Peace Corps colleagues stop at a mill alongside the Khyber Pass in Afghanistan, en route to Pakistan in 1964. PAUL CONKLIN

Opposite, below: Shriver greets schoolchildren taught by a Peace Corps volunteer in Turkey. PAUL CONKLIN

Above: Tragedy—Shriver stands at the North Portico of the White House with Lyndon Johnson, Jacqueline Kennedy, Robert Kennedy, Caroline Kennedy, John F. Kennedy Jr., and an honor guard as they prepare to leave for a memorial service for JFK at Arlington National Cemetery on November 24, 1963. CORBIS

Left: After President Kennedy's death, LBJ dispatched Shriver to deliver a personal message to Pope Paul, whom Shriver met in Jerusalem on January 5, 1964. PAUL CONKLIN

Opposite: Several days after meeting Pope Paul, Shriver had an audience with Patriarch Athenagoras, the head of the Eastern Orthodox Church. Together, Shriver and the patriarch gazed upon an image of JFK.
PAUL CONKLIN

Above: The Shriver family in the late 1960s, right to left: Sarge, Mark, Maria, Timmy, Anthony, Eunice, and Bobby.
SHRIVER FAMILY COLLECTION

Left: Despite occasional political tensions between Sargent Shriver and Robert Kennedy, their families got along well. Here Sarge, Eunice, Ethel Kennedy, and various Shriver and Kennedy children sail off the coast of Hyannis Port. THE ESTATE OF STANLEY TRETICK

The War on Poverty

Sargent Shriver
at Camp Kilmer

SEPTEMBER 13, 1965   35c

Newsweek

Opposite: Maria, Bobby, and Timmy Shriver with President Johnson in the White House at the swearing-in of their father as director of the War on Poverty. THOMAS PLANT

Above: A memorial service for John F. Kennedy, a year after the president's death. Right to left: Robert, Ethel, and Bobby Kennedy Jr. and Sargent, Maria, and Eunice Shriver, with other Kennedy and Shriver children. CORBIS

Left: Shriver's second newsweekly cover, in September 1965, as the War on Poverty celebrated its early successes—and endured its many early problems.

MAY 13, 1966

CROSSFIRE IN THE WAR ON POVERTY

TIME

VOL. 87 NO. 19

Opposite, above: When Shriver was named director of the War on Poverty, LBJ gave him full cabinet status. But for the most part Shriver attended the cabinet meetings only in the early months of the program; after that, he was rarely invited. CORBIS

Opposite, below: At this cabinet meeting, Shriver hands out cigars to the president and cabinet members (including Franklin Delano Roosevelt Jr., brother-in-law Robert Kennedy, and Dean Rusk) to celebrate the birth of his fourth child, Mark Shriver, on March 17, 1964. UPI

Above: Shriver with members of the Job Corps at Camp Kilmer in New Jersey. Despite highly publicized violent incidents at some Job Corps camps, many of the Job Corpsmen revered Shriver, and the program survives today. MORTON R. ENGELBERG

Left: Shriver's third newsweekly cover. In contrast to the bright tones of the earlier covers, this one had the darker, almost sinister tones of the late 1960s, when the War on Poverty—and much else in American society—seemed to be falling apart.

Above: Between 1964 and 1968, Shriver and President Johnson frequently tussled over funding for the War on Poverty—funding that increasingly was diverted to the war in Vietnam. Here, Johnson subjects Shriver to one of his aggressive charm assaults. CORBIS

Right: Shriver arrived in Paris just as the Paris Peace Talks on Vietnam were to begin. Here Shriver appears alongside the chief US negotiators in those talks, Cyrus Vance (left) and Averell Harriman. SHRIVER FAMILY COLLECTION

Opposite: After being appointed US ambassador to France in 1968, Shriver went toe-to-toe with President Charles de Gaulle—and completely charmed him, helping to thaw Franco-American relations at a crucial moment in history. SHRIVER FAMILY COLLECTION

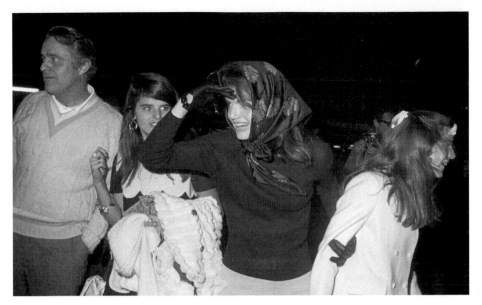

Opposite, above: The Shrivers and the de Gaulles became friends and often socialized together. Here Shriver shoots pheasant with de Gaulle. "A present for you, Monsieur le President," Shriver reportedly said as a pheasant he had shot landed a yard from de Gaulle's feet. SHRIVER FAMILY COLLECTION, JOHN F. KENNEDY LIBRARY

Opposite, below: Shriver was an avid tennis player during his time in France. Arthur Ashe was Sarge's doubles partner regularly and a frequent guest at the residence. SHRIVER FAMILY COLLECTION, JOHN F. KENNEDY LIBRARY

Above: Shriver and Jacqueline Kennedy shared an understanding of the challenges that accompanied life as a Kennedy in-law. They remained close long after President Kennedy's death, and Maria Shriver (left, next to Sarge) spent several summers with her cousin Caroline Kennedy (right, next to Jackie). CORBIS

Left: The Shrivers' Paris home was likely the only ambassadorial residence to have tires strewn about the halls—obstacle races challenged not only the Shriver children but also the mentally retarded French children that Eunice brought in. PARIS MATCH

Opposite, above: "The Lucky Seventh"— After Missouri senator Thomas Eagleton was dropped from the 1972 Democratic ticket, George McGovern (right) was turned down by five other prospective running mates before successfully recruiting Shriver. CORBIS

Opposite, below: Timberlawn, the sprawling Shriver estate in Rockville, Maryland, served as a bustling, bucolic epicenter of the New Frontier and the Great Society through the 1960s. The site hosted a Neil Diamond concert to benefit the McGovern-Shriver ticket in 1972. SHRIVER FAMILY COLLECTION

Above: At a Democratic presidential debate in November 1975, Shriver sits alongside Washington senator Henry "Scoop" Jackson and Georgia governor Jimmy Carter. Carter was the one candidate, Shriver said at the time, that he was sure he could beat. CORBIS

Left: A highlight of Shriver's time in Paris was the Midnight Mass at Sainte Chappelle that he put together for Christmas 1969—the first Midnight Mass there since Louis XIV had decamped for Versailles. SHRIVER FAMILY COLLECTION, JOHN F. KENNEDY LIBRARY

Opposite: Shriver walks alongside Coretta Scott King and Atlanta mayor Maynard Jackson during a march from Martin Luther King's crypt to the Georgia capitol, for a rally celebrating the slain civil rights leader's birthday in January 1980. CORBIS

Above: Although the three brothers-in-law co-existed peacefully within the extended Kennedy clan, at times Ted Kennedy (center) and Steve Smith (left) found themselves politically at odds with Sarge Shriver—often in ways that impeded Shriver's political career. MELODY MILLER / FRANK TETI COLLECTION

Left: Shriver with President Bill Clinton, who awarded him the Presidential Medal of Freedom in 1994. SHRIVER FAMILY COLLECTION

The Shriver kids, from left: Timothy, Bobby, Maria, Anthony, and Mark, at a ball to benefit Best Buddies (the charity Anthony founded) in the fall of 2000. SHRIVER FAMILY COLLECTION

Shriver, age eighty-eight, embraces his son-in-law Arnold Schwarzenegger after Schwarzenegger was elected governor of California in the fall of 2003. Each man strove in his own way to remain loyal to the large and powerful family into which he had married, but without giving up a certain maverick sensibility and style. CORBIS

CHAPTER TWENTY-NINE

Wooing Congress

For the five-month period that began on March 17, Shriver's consuming occupation was to get the Economic Opportunity Act passed by Congress. "In no uncertain terms the president said this morning that he wants a report every night from you on the congressmen you saw and talked to each day," Bill Moyers wrote to Shriver in June. "In a memorandum such as this I dare not repeat the language in which this statement was requested. I cannot possibly emphasize the forcefulness with which the request was verbally delivered. He expects this report by 7:30 every night. . . . The only thing he is asking you to do is to live in the House until the poverty bill is passed."

Shriver had no illusions about how hard it would be to get the bill passed. The Economic Opportunity Act had as many built-in enemies as any piece of legislation of the 1960s. The Republicans had decided to make a partisan issue of the bill. Many members of Congress, on both sides of the aisle, thought the whole antipoverty adventure was nothing more than an election-year gambit cooked up by LBJ: Johnson's executive branch would get a lot of money, hand it out in the right places, and get reelected in the fall. "I know the Republicans thought this to a man," Shriver said. Getting the bill through the House would pose a special challenge. To succeed, said Larry O'Brien, the JFK political aide who stayed on in the Johnson administration as White House liaison to Congress, OEO's supporters in the House and the Senate would need to "pull a magnificent rabbit out of a hat."

House members from the South, Shriver knew, would be especially ardent in their opposition. They were already traumatized by the 1964 Civil Rights Act, which would be signed into law in July—and they were convinced that the antipoverty legislation was another civil rights bill in disguise. Shriver's fear was that Southern Democrats—seeing the Economic Opportunity Act as a civil rights bill—would gravitate toward conservative Republicans in the region and vote as a solid bloc against the program. So he decided to concentrate his lobbying efforts on the most challenging but still-winnable groups: Southern Democrats and liberal Republicans.

Shriver went after these groups several ways. First, he ensured that there would be new Community Action agencies in a majority of congressional districts in the country; this meant federal dollars for members' districts, something they would have a hard time voting against. Second, he sought to downplay any overt racial element in the bill. Although most of the poor people in urban ghettos were black, the popular image of the American poor in 1964 remained the rag-clad white families of rural Appalachia. The task force relentlessly repeated to the press that the bulk of the American poor were to be found in rural and even suburban areas—the coded message this transmitted was that the War on Poverty would primarily benefit white people, not black ones.

Shriver and his team tried, when talking to Southern members of Congress, to obscure the fact that the OEO would be giving money directly to black communities. These efforts were not always successful. When Jim Sundquist tried to sell Texas congressman W. R. Poage, an old-school conservative, on the bill, he used vague words like "opportunity" and technical jargon like "coordinated service delivery" to obfuscate what the act would do: give money and services to African Americans. Poage looked at Sundquist blankly for a moment before the light dawned. "Oh, I see! You're talking about the niggers!" When Christopher Weeks, an early Job Corps administrator, presented an outline of the OEO to Wilbur Mills, chairman of the House Ways and Means Committee, Mills crumpled the paper and threw it across the room, issuing "a few choice words about how he was not going to be involved in any program to help a bunch of niggers."

Shriver's political masterstroke was persuading Rep. Phil Landrum, a conservative Democrat from Georgia, to serve as the Economic Opportunity Act's sponsor in the House of Representatives. Landrum's conservative credentials were impeccable. He was from the South. He had sparred with Shriver over the Peace Corps. Organized labor saw him as an "ogre." No one could mistake Landrum for a liberal. In fact, he was just about the unlikeliest supporter for the poverty bill one could find. Yet Shriver and the White House congressional liaison Larry O'Brien both had good personal relationships with him. And to their "utter surprise" they found him receptive to the poverty bill. There was poverty in Landrum's own district, and he perceived that the legislation in the Economic Opportunity Act could help address it. Recognizing the enormous political advantage that bringing Landrum aboard would give them, Shriver and O'Brien talked him into sponsoring the act. His support of the bill, they knew, would convey to other Southern conservatives that it was acceptable for them to support it. "Landrum coming aboard in the leadership role was a real blockbuster," O'Brien recalled.

Another of Landrum's assets was his seat on the House Education and Labor Committee. Because the poverty bill had so many different parts, it contained elements of interest to practically every jurisdiction in the House and could have gone first to just about any committee. But the composition of the Education and Labor Committee was such that, especially with Landrum's backing, Shriver could be confident of getting the bill reported out with unified Democratic support. Democratic members such as Jimmy Roosevelt, "Topper" Thompson, and Roman Pucinski were all either reliably liberal or close allies of the Johnson administration, or both. Adam Clayton Powell, the Harlem congressman, was the committee chair; he would later become a Shriver nemesis, but early on he was a staunch supporter of the poverty bill, and he willingly stepped aside to let Landrum sponsor the bill. Once Landrum, the most powerful Southern congressman on the committee, had lent his support, "there was not going to be any Democratic opposition to it," and other Democratic conservatives like Carl Perkins of Kentucky would have to fall in line behind it. All the opposition to the bill then came only from the Republican side.

After Landrum and Powell, the most important member of the Education and Labor Committee was Edith Green, a Democrat from Oregon. Like Powell, she would later become a painful thorn in OEO's side. But as a former schoolteacher, she was an early supporter of the bill, and she was so smart and intimidating that she could scare opponents of the bill into supporting it. Once, when a GOP committee member asked an ill-informed question, Green tore him apart so brutally that he never asked another. Powell watched this eruption with a bemused smile. "Edith," he said, "you're the only woman I know who's been going through menopause for forty years."

In the first month of hearings, Shriver, Wirtz, Bobby Kennedy, and Secretary of Defense McNamara all testified on behalf of the bill, along with numerous Democratic mayors and governors, union leaders, and farmers' advocates. Shriver charmed the committee. "I didn't know Shriver really," recalled the Wisconsin economist Robert Lampman, who accompanied him to the opening hearing. "I was impressed by how he easily went to the Republican side of the table and apparently had been at Yale Law School with half of them, I guess." Lampman was also impressed by "how well he seemed to get along with Adam Clayton Powell and the other side of things."

The bill came out of the committee on a party line vote (nineteen Democrats versus eleven Republicans) on May 26. So far, so good.

In the Senate, meanwhile, the process began straightforwardly. Shriver and O'Brien picked Michigan Democrat Pat McNamara to sponsor the bill there, with the idea that McNamara's Midwestern liberalism would balance Landrum's Southern conservatism and thereby demonstrate the bill's breadth of support. Shriver and others testified before the Senate's Labor and Public Welfare Committee in mid-June, and the bill was voted out of committee 13–2 on July 7.

THE STATES' RIGHTS PROBLEM

At this point, difficult substantive issues began to arise. Southerners began objecting that giving federal money directly to local groups was a clear violation of states' rights. Richard Russell, a Georgia Democrat who was a giant of the Senate, was threatening to oppose the bill based purely on its trampling of states' rights. It should be the prerogative of state and local governments, Russell and others said, not the federal bureaucracy, to decide where and how money should be spent on the local level. On some level, Shriver recognized, this was surely true; federal grants to local agencies *were* a violation of the states' rights doctrine. States' rights had been an "absolute cardinal principle" of the Democratic Party in Maryland when Shriver was growing up. Still, the whole point of Community Action was to *go around* the state and local government agencies (and around the old-line welfare bureaucracy) that were doing such a wretched job of helping the poor. Also, Shriver knew from the ongoing battles over the civil rights bill that for white Southerners, states' rights was often just diplomatic cover for racism— a way to block federal money from going to blacks.

What to do? The solution came to him one day on Capitol Hill, while talking to Georgia's other senator, Herman Talmadge. "Look, this is the problem, Senator," Shriver recalled saying to Talmadge. "We can't allow all this money to become bogged down in the state and local government apparatus, and we cannot allow a system to be established whereby the purposes of the legislation can be frustrated totally by the clique that might be hanging around a particular governor. How in the name of God can we get around that problem" and get Senator Russell to support the bill?

Talmadge looked at Shriver, thought for a minute, and then flipped ashes from the big cigar he always had with him into the spittoon he kept by his desk. "Well, Sargent, have you ever considered a veto by the governor?" Shriver said he hadn't. Talmadge suggested that Shriver write into the bill a provision that would allow a governor to veto any program in his state if he disapproved of it. "Now, first of all," Talmadge explained, "they're not going to disapprove of many programs, because the governors all want to have the money come into their states. Secondly, the governor politically doesn't want to be in the position of being the person who is preventing a certain program from taking place in his state." So there were likely to be very few vetoes. "But if you put it in the legislation that the governor has the veto, then Senator Russell will be able to say that the principle of states' rights, states' authority, has been maintained."

Shriver went back to his office and discussed the veto with his deputies and consulted with Larry O'Brien and Bill Moyers at the White House. Ideally, they all agreed, there would be no veto provision. But as a political accommodation to win Russell's support and get the bill through the Senate, it seemed necessary. Landrum introduced the amendment in the House and, in the end, the bill the Senate voted on included the right of governors to veto most poverty program grants within thirty days.

THE EXECUTION OF ADAM YARMOLINSKY

Through all of July, Shriver stalked the halls of Congress, having breakfast, lunch, and dinner there. After adjourning while the Republicans held their national convention, nominating Barry Goldwater, the Senate resumed deliberations on the poverty bill.

The bill rolled along. The Senate passed the Economic Opportunity Act on a roll call vote, 61–34, on July 23. There were some anxious moments in the House, where the Virginia Democrat Howard "Judge" Smith—who had saved the day on the original Peace Corps legislation—bottled the legislation up in the Rules Committee, alleging that the bill would allow funding of "nudist" colonies.

Shriver paid a call to Smith. Much of President Kennedy's New Frontier legislation had languished in the Rules Committee, stymied by Smith and his conservative colleagues. Recognizing the rather narrow limits of Smith's social philosophy, Shriver tried to frame his description of the bill in terms the congressman could support: The War on Poverty, Shriver explained, issuing the program's mantra, would be a "hand-up, not a handout." Smith had no objection to Title I; jobs for juveniles sounded good to him. But when Shriver explained Community Action, Smith stopped him. "Sarge," he said. "You know I have great respect for you. But I've been in this Congress for thirty-six years and this is the worst piece of legislation that's ever been introduced." Smith explained that Title II's broad mandate was anathema to a congressman—not only would it give the federal government more power than the states, but in effect it would also give OEO appointees more power to allocate a district's poverty funds than the local congressman had. No amount of arguing by Shriver could convince Smith otherwise.

But then Smith turned to Shriver and said, "I trust you." I think this bill is wrong, Smith continued, and if it comes to the floor I'll oppose it all the way. But out of our mutual friendship, I won't use procedural tactics to keep it bottled up in my committee. On July 28, the Rules Committee narrowly (by an 8–7 margin, with all the Republicans plus Smith voting against) allowed the bill to go to the House floor.

Only one big hurdle remained: the House vote, where the important question was how the 100 Southern Democrats would vote. Whether the Economic Opportunity Act became law or not depended on how many followed Phil Landrum in supporting the bill and how many joined the Republicans in opposing it. Shriver and O'Brien counted and recounted votes, lobbying wavering Democrats incessantly. As the vote loomed, the margin seemed razor thin.

On Wednesday, August 5, the floor debate began. It immediately took on a bitter, partisan tone. Over the course of that day, Republicans tried to arouse every prejudice in the minds of those most susceptible to them—primarily the Southern Democrats. States' rights. Integration. Separation of church and state. Birth control. City Hall jealousies. Landrum was compelled to accept many amendments to the bill, but nothing that compromised its essence. The vote was scheduled for the next day, and it remained anyone's guess whether the bill would pass.

On Thursday, before the vote could begin, Harold Cooley, a Democratic representative from North Carolina, led the entire delegation from his state up to the podium on the House floor. North Carolina, at this point, had more Democratic votes still uncommitted than any other state. Shriver wondered what Cooley would say. Which way would North Carolina go? Cooley began a lengthy harangue against, of all people, Adam Yarmolinsky. If that "dangerous radical" has any role in the new agency, Cooley declared, then the North Carolina delegation would vote against the bill. Shriver was horrified. If North Carolina's support was lost, then the votes he had spent so much time assembling from the rest of the Democratic South might begin to evaporate. The entire Southern bloc might disappear. The vote would be lost.

How had this happened?

Several days earlier, on Monday, Shriver had found himself in the House office of Porter Hardy, a conservative Republican from Virginia, who was a strong critic of the Johnson administration. He and Shriver agreed on very little politically, but they enjoyed each other's company. "Sarge," Hardy had said to him, "what's this about some fellow in your organization with a Russian-sounding name who is some sort of a way-out liberal or socialist?" Shriver replied that he had no idea what Hardy was talking about. "You know," Hardy persisted, "some wild-eyed radical with a Russian sounding name."

"You don't mean Adam Yarmolinsky, do you?" Shriver said.

"That's the guy," Hardy said.

"Porter," Shriver said. "Let's get this straightened out right now. Adam is operating as deputy director of this task force. He's been McNamara's top assistant at the Pentagon. I myself brought him into the Kennedy administration and I have the highest personal and professional regard for him."

Shriver had gotten to know Yarmolinsky during the Kennedy campaign and Talent Hunt and had found him to be not only brilliant but also a highly effective administrator. Shriver and Yarmolinsky were an unlikely pair: the Catholic, patrician, New Frontiersman and the Jewish, intense, cerebral policy wonk. Yet Shriver thought as highly of Yarmolinsky as he did of anyone he had ever worked with. Thus when Robert McNamara had been looking for people of high caliber to help him at the Pentagon, Shriver had recommended Yarmolinsky, and McNamara had hired him as a special assistant.

In origin and appearance, McNamara and Yarmolinsky were about as far apart as could be. McNamara looked the part of the cold, calculating CEO, his slicked-back hair parted at the center. Yarmolinsky was short, even runty, with fierce eyes, his hair arrayed in uncoiffed spikes around his head. If Robert McNamara was a Soviet cartoonist's stereotype of the American corporation man, Yarmolinsky was a reactionary's caricature of a wild-eyed Bolshevik. A friend of his in Congress observed that "Adam looks like he's got a bomb in his back pocket, ready to throw."

Back in 1961, when McNamara told Shriver he wanted to hire Adam, Shriver told him to check his file first; there were some things about Yarmolinsky's family background that the defense secretary would want to know before some Republican congressman confronted him with them. McNamara called FBI director J. Edgar Hoover and asked him to send the file over. When it arrived, McNamara was alarmed to see that it was "as thick as a Manhattan phonebook." But when he read through it, he saw nothing that suggested Yarmolinsky was unfit, disloyal, or anything other than a man of great sympathy and conscience. He did see, however, that his new assistant's background could invite criticism from political opponents. So he had Roswell Gilpatric, his deputy defense secretary, read the file to make sure he concurred that there was no cause for alarm (Gilpatric agreed there wasn't) and then warned Gilpatric that he would have to be prepared to serve as de facto Pentagon defense counsel when questions about Yarmolinsky's background arose.

In truth, there was nothing sinister in that background. Yarmolinsky's father, Avram, had for decades been in charge of the Russian collection at the New York Public Library, and he had translated all the works of Tolstoy and Dostoyevsky for the Modern Library series. His mother was a poet of minor repute and an espouser of liberal causes. In short, they were typical liberal, Russian-Jewish New York intellectuals. Adam himself, while a Harvard undergraduate, had been an early supporter of American intervention in World War II, and he had been a leader in the fight to wrest the Harvard student government from the control of doctrinaire Soviet sympathizers. After the war, he had graduated from Yale Law School, clerked for Stanley Reed on the Supreme Court, worked in the law firm of George Ball (now Johnson's under secretary of state), and served as a consultant to major New York publishing houses and foundations.

But Yarmolinsky did rub many people the wrong way. He could behave with a peremptory nastiness toward those he considered stupid; he became known at the Pentagon for his brazen interruptions of presentations by top military brass. "Stop rambling and get to the point," he would demand. This made some people, even colleagues and political allies, dislike him intensely. But even those who disliked his style admired his intellect and competence.

Once installed at the Defense Department, where he received a full security clearance, Yarmolinsky was indispensable in helping McNamara achieve firm civilian control over the military. He also was instrumental in forcing several military bases—in North Carolina, as it happened—to become racially integrated. Naturally, this did not endear him to certain individuals in the military. Soon, rumors began percolating in the Senate Armed Services Committee about the background of the man who had put them under a civilian yoke and who had accelerated the integration of the armed services. In 1962, during hearings of an armed services subcommittee, Gen. Edwin Walker testified that "Communists had bored into the heart of our defense establishment." Without saying directly that Yarmolinsky was himself a Communist, General Walker implied that he had Communist connections. This was preposterous. Just a few years earlier, Communist publications had been attacking Yarmolinsky as a "Red-baiter" for trying to purge the American Veterans Committee of Soviet sympathizers.

Sensible people dismissed Walker's charges as the ravings of a paranoid military officer who felt his prerogatives had been threatened by civilian authority. The House Committee on Un-American Activities, a legacy of the

McCarthy era, researched Yarmolinsky's background and found nothing to suggest he was anything other than a loyal American. But among right-wing circles the rumors lingered. The Un-American Activities Committee received so many requests for information on Yarmolinsky from conservative members of Congress that the committee's staff director eventually printed up a form letter, which he sent out in response to all requests. "A search of our files has disclosed no information showing Adam Yarmolinsky to have been a member or sponsor of any organization or entity which has been cited as subversive by this committee or any other Federal authority. Moreover, there is no reference to his name in any of the public hearings and reports of this committee." Yet fringe conservatives clung obsessively to the idea of him as a subversive. "Since the New Frontier did not produce a legitimate Alger Hiss or even a facsimile," the political columnists Evans and Novak wrote, "the Far Right designated Yarmolinsky as a substitute."

Shriver's conversation with Representative Hardy on Monday had alarmed him, but only mildly. After all, the rumors about Yarmolinsky were old—and thoroughly discredited—and Hardy himself, as a Republican, would not have been expected to vote for the poverty bill anyway. But at breakfast on Wednesday with Democratic members of the North Carolina delegation, Shriver's alarm grew when they demanded that Yarmolinsky be excluded from the OEO. Shriver tactfully offered what seemed to be a compromise: He promised that Yarmolinsky would not be head of the Job Corps, a position that would have put him directly in charge of thousands of unemployed youths—ripe fodder for anyone wanting to agitate subversive activity. The congressmen asked if Yarmolinsky might end up with a position higher than Job Corps director. Shriver tried to leave that ambiguous, explaining that he did not have the authority to make hiring decisions for the OEO itself.

Shriver had thought the matter settled. Yet on Thursday the North Carolina delegation was declaring it would vote against the bill if Yarmolinsky was associated with it.

Sensing a crisis, Speaker of the House John W. McCormack called for a meeting in his office, just off the House floor. As debate over the bill continued on the floor, Shriver, Cooley, and Mendel Rivers, a South Carolina congressman, joined McCormack, who took up his customary position in a high-backed leather rocking chair behind his desk. Twenty Democratic deputy whips, the regional vote counters, looked on. Please be reasonable, McCormack implored the Carolinians in his rich, South Boston brogue.

Cooley said the matter was simple: If Yarmolinsky were to be associated with the program, the North Carolina delegation would oppose the bill. Rivers concurred; the South Carolinians would also vote against it unless Yarmolinsky were jettisoned.

"Now, Mr. Chairman," Shriver said calmly, addressing Cooley, who was the chair of the House Agriculture Committee. "I can't say who the president will appoint [as deputy director]. I can't even say whether he will appoint me [as director]."

"That's not what you told three of my colleagues at breakfast yesterday," Cooley shouted. "You told them Yarmolinsky is going to be one of the presidential appointees. That's what you told them."

"Oh, no," Shriver objected. "I can't speak for the president."

McCormack spoke up. "Well, now, Harold," he said. "Doesn't that satisfy you?"

"No," Cooley yelled. "That's not what he told my colleagues at breakfast yesterday. Whom do you believe? Your colleagues in Congress or Shriver?"

The argument continued in this vein, steadily escalating. Cooley kept trying to get Shriver to commit to axing Yarmolinsky; Shriver kept refusing.

The Democratic whips looked on in astonishment. At one point, Massachusetts congressman Torby Macdonald turned to a colleague and said, "It looks like a kangaroo court." Hale Boggs, the House majority whip, who as a Louisiana congressman was himself a Southern Democrat, tried to explain that repeated checks of background files had never uncovered anything improper about Yarmolinsky. Cooley erupted in rage.

There was silence for a moment; there seemed no way around the impasse. Finally, McCormack said, "Harold, would you be satisfied if Sarge gave assurances that he would not recommend Yarmolinsky for a high post in the program?" Before Cooley could answer, Shriver interjected again that the recommendation was not his to make—the president had not vested him with the authority to staff the program. Well then, Cooley suggested, why don't we get the president on the telephone?

Shriver and McCormack retired to a small anteroom off McCormack's office. The Speaker placed the call and explained the situation to President

Johnson: The entire North Carolina delegation wanted a guarantee that Adam Yarmolinsky would not have a job with the OEO; without that guarantee, both Carolina delegations would bolt, take many wavering Southerners with them, and imperil passage of the poverty bill.

"Who the hell is Adam Yarmolinsky?" Johnson thundered. He asked McCormack to put Shriver on the line. Whose decision is it whether Yarmolinsky is made deputy director? the president asked. "That's your responsibility, Mr. President," Shriver said. "I think Adam Yarmolinsky is eminently qualified to be deputy director of the program. But I'm not proposing people for jobs."

"What's the situation over there?" the president asked.

Shriver explained that the debate—both in the Speaker's office and on the House floor—was becoming acrimonious. The vote count was desperately close. In Shriver's estimation, which was corroborated by the Democratic vote counters, if the Carolina delegations defected, the bill would not pass. It seemed to come down to this: Sacrifice Yarmolinsky in order to pass the Economic Opportunity Act and follow through on LBJ's national commitment to eliminating poverty. Or stand on principle—and refuse to submit to extortion—and risk seeing the War on Poverty go up in smoke.

In later years, Shriver thought about what he could have said to the president but did not: "Mr. President, this is a moral issue. If you back down on Yarmolinsky I will quit right now and go home." "I would have been morally justified in saying that," Shriver reflected in the 1990s. "But I didn't feel I had the right to. At that moment, my belief was that the bill would never pass unless the president settled the issue right then and there, while the North Carolina delegation stood in the Speaker's office. I believe the president felt the same way." Not standing up for Yarmolinsky at the moment was, Shriver says, "the hardest decision I ever made in my life," but it is one he would have repeated if put in the same situation again.

The president authorized Shriver to tell the North Carolinians that he would not appoint anyone to the poverty program that Congress did not think was qualified. Shriver went back into the Speaker's office, where he delivered the news to Cooley. The sacrifice of Adam Yarmolinsky had been consummated. Shriver felt, he recalled, "like an executioner," or "like a general who, in order to win a battle, must sacrifice a division under the command of his best friend."

The next day, Friday, August 7, Ohio Republican William Ayres, an opponent of the poverty program, read aloud on the House floor a memo Yarmolinsky had written. Ayres implied that Defense Department funds were already being used to build Job Corps centers, before the bill had been passed. Phil Landrum stood up and said, "First . . . so far as I am concerned, this gentleman, Mr. Yarmolinsky, will have absolutely nothing to do with the program. And second, I wish to state that I have been told on the highest authority that not only will he not be appointed, but that he will not be considered if he is recommended for a place in this agency."

Another Democratic congressman asked, "What is the 'highest authority'?"

"The president," Landrum said.

As Job Corps deputy director Christopher Weeks would later write, "the Southern Democrats had asked for and gotten their pound of flesh—assurance that the abrasive, intellectual Jew of Russian extraction who had roughed up the military rank and file in the Defense Department . . . would be barred from any job in Johnson's poverty agency."

The next afternoon, the House voted on the Economic Opportunity Act. Most of the North Carolina delegation voted in favor. The bill passed, 226–184, a larger margin than expected. That evening, more than a hundred members of the poverty task force celebrated late into the night at a victory party in Georgetown.

On August 20, 1964, Lyndon Johnson signed the act, and the War on Poverty became law. "Today is the first time in all the history of the human race a great nation is able to make and is willing to make a commitment to eradicate poverty among its people," Johnson said.

This was a political triumph for the president and a great accomplishment for Shriver. For the second time in three years, he had created a large new federal agency from scratch and changed Americans' attitudes about a social issue. The War on Poverty was, as Jim Sundquist has observed, "the boldest national objective ever declared by Congress—to do what no people had ever done, what the Bible says cannot be done—to *eliminate* poverty from the land."

Yet sacrificing Yarmolinsky had wounded Shriver deeply. It was, he said, "the most unpleasant experience I ever had in the government of the United States." He felt "as if I ought to just go out and vomit, it was such a despicable proceeding."

On Thursday evening, after the colloquy in the Speaker's office, Shriver had immediately sought out his deputy. As Yarmolinsky recalled it, Shriver came into his office and said, "Well, we've just thrown you to the wolves. This is the worst day of my life." Shriver could see that Yarmolinsky was badly hurt by the news. Not only was he being publicly slandered but the project to which he had dedicated body and soul for the last eight months was being yanked away from him. But Yarmolinsky kept his composure and said, as Shriver recalled it. "Under the circumstances, Sarge, you did what you had to in order to save the program." Shriver hoped Yarmolinsky believed his own words.

Shriver went back to his own office and put his head down on his desk and wept. According to several close colleagues, it was the only time anyone has ever seen him cry.

Was the sacrifice of Yarmolinsky necessary? It's impossible to say. The margin of victory in the House was bigger than expected—big enough that the bill would have passed even without any of the Carolina votes in its favor. In the eyes of many liberals, Shriver had sold out. Even some of his colleagues were surprised and disappointed. Although it was President Johnson who had wielded the axe, people tended to blame Shriver for the execution. "There was a lot of feeling on many people's part that Shriver stood for certain ideals, and political execution was something that Shriver would not tolerate," Christopher Weeks said. "Yet I think it was pretty clear that in this case Shriver certainly didn't come out with any laurels on his head."

Still, the Democratic vote counters had told Shriver that if he lost the North Carolina delegation, he might lose the entire Southern bloc. In this case, the final margin of victory does not accurately reflect what would have happened if Yarmolinsky's role had been preserved. Don Baker, who was working as a Senate staffer on poverty when the vote took place and later became OEO general counsel, says that any criticism of Shriver in this regard was unfair. Shriver, he says, was just doing his duty by the president. "I came as close to Sarge as anybody on the real tough issues. And one of the things that was always remarkable to me is that in this sort of thing in which the White House was involved, he never complained. Whatever the press was saying, he never said, 'The White House told me to do this,' or 'Somebody told me to do that.' He always took the responsibility . . . like a good loyal soldier."

After getting banned from the poverty program, Yarmolinsky returned to working for McNamara in the Defense Department. Nobody objected, demonstrating beyond a doubt that he had been an ideological target, rather than a real security concern for the Southerners, a fact that some of them acknowledged explicitly later.

Whether sacrificing Yarmolinsky was necessary or not, there is no question that losing him was devastating to the War on Poverty. It was, according to one OEO veteran, "the most unfortunate thing that ever happened to the poverty program." Yarmolinsky and Shriver had enjoyed an excellent working relationship; they were perfect complements. As Baker observed, "Sarge was the outside and Yarmolinsky was the inside guy. Yarmolinsky ran a very taut ship, and he made most of the inside decisions. . . . Sarge was free to go ahead and deal with the legislature and the outside groups and whatnot, and Adam did the housekeeping for him." When Adam left, Norb Schlei recalled, "I felt that the whole operation began slowly to unravel." According to Schlei, the problem was that "Sarge is not a good methodical administrator. He works in bursts of tremendous creativity and energy, and then he has to regroup and do his thinking and so on. When he had Adam, the whole operation kept right on going, because Adam administered it and made it all happen and went around picking up the pieces."

Over the next several years, after Shriver formally took charge of the OEO, he would hire numerous top deputies—Jack Conway, Bernard Boutin, Bertrand Harding—but he never again found that single person in whom he could repose his complete trust, no one to whom he would give full operating authority. This was doubly unfortunate. Not only did the OEO lack a top administrator of Yarmolinsky's talents, but Shriver was now stretched far too thin, trying at the same time to be the program's outside salesman, its inside administrator, its principal idea man—*and* to run the Peace Corps. This was far too much, even for someone with his energy. Within a year of beginning operation, the OEO had legions of critics. Shriver had to deal with attacks from Congress, the White House, newspaper columnists—even from within his own agency. All of this "just kept him so busy he couldn't possibly" attend to all the operational issues he should have been addressing, Don Baker said. "And I really think if Yarmolinsky had been there, it would have been a much better program."

Soured by the Yarmolinsky episode, Shriver told LBJ he did not want to serve as OEO director. "As soon as the legislation was passed," Christopher

Weeks recalled, Shriver "expected that somebody else would be selected to head the program, and that would be it." He was "still very much wrapped up in the operation of the Peace Corps. He still loved the Peace Corps. . . . He really did not see himself as being head of the poverty program and didn't seek it, and I don't think he wanted it."

Shriver provided the president with a list of a half dozen alternative candidates, which Johnson summarily rejected. Ultimately, Shriver agreed to take the position, for several reasons. First, he recognized that continuity would be very important in the opening months of the program—especially now that Yarmolinsky was gone. It would help to maintain the same commander at the top. Second, although he had been drafted into the task force against his will, in the six months he had worked on it he had become emotionally and intellectually committed to the War on Poverty. Most important, though, Shriver recognized that if he turned down the position, it would likely signal the end of his formal service to his country, at least for a while.

CHAPTER THIRTY

The Law of the Jungle

A s of October 16, 1964, his first official day as director, Shriver shifted his attention from legislation and budget authorization to setting up the OEO's operations. Every Monday, Wednesday, and Friday, he would begin the official workday by chairing an executive meeting in the "crowded and dilapidated room in the even more dilapidated third-class hotel" where the OEO staff was now concentrated. He ran these discussions as he had run similar ones at the Peace Corps. As at the Peace Corps, these gatherings were not for the thin skinned or weak spirited. Christopher Weeks writes, "To the slow-thinking, the inarticulate, the overly visionary, the diehard but impractical idealist or even just the plain average administrator, no mercy was shown."

Each meeting would begin with operational summaries from various program heads, who would conclude by proposing action plans for moving ahead. Then Shriver would encourage everyone assembled to "attack these plans . . . add to them, or even completely destroy them" in an effort to subject the plans of his top staff to "the roughest tests of imaginativeness, feasibility, efficiency, practicality, and political salability" that anyone could devise. Shriver calibrated the pitch of these meetings just so: anarchic, sometimes vicious, but usually couched within a prevailing spirit of camaraderie.

After the November election, which Johnson won in a landslide, the OEO began operations quickly. By November 25, after a meeting with the president, Shriver was able to announce that his office had already authorized 119 separate grants for antipoverty projects in thirty-three states. Shriver continued to announce new OEO grants and programs at a rapid clip through all of December. On December 17 President Johnson announced 162 separate new War on Poverty projects, including the first three urban Job Corps centers, worth a total of $82.6 million. On January 18, 1965, Johnson announced the launch of another round of projects, totaling more than $100 million. "In the first 101 days of this unique national war effort," he said, "we have brought nearly 400 transfusions of new opportunity to disadvantaged Americans in every part of this land."

But the Office of Economic Opportunity was under assault from the moment it began spending money in November 1964. The main targets of attack were the two cornerstones of the War on Poverty: the Job Corps and Community Action.

On January 15 the first thirty Job Corpsmen arrived with fanfare at Camp Catoctin, a former Civilian Conservation Corps site located not far from Camp David, the presidential retreat that Dwight Eisenhower had established in rural Maryland. Other camps soon followed. The early press attention was positive. For a brief time, the OEO's "overworked, undermanned" staff in Washington basked in "a kind of euphoria." This wouldn't last.

The Job Corps was supposed to be simple: a straightforward, easy-to-understand program that would take poor youths off the streets and prepare them for the workforce. Unlike Community Action, Shriver thought, which would take several years to affect the cycle of poverty, the Job Corps would have an immediate and observable impact on poor communities throughout the country. He hoped that establishing Job Corps centers—where newspaper photographers could capture images of poor youths learning skills, doing conservation work, or sitting in classes—would help buy the time necessary to build political support for Community Action. But for its first year of operation, the Job Corps program generated terrible public relations for Shriver.

During the spring of 1964, Shriver had talked about how the Job Corps, like FDR's Civilian Conservation Corps, would have a momentous impact fast; in June 1964, Shriver promised there would be 40,000 Job Corpsmen within a year. But over the course of the year, as administrative logjams accumulated, he had to downsize expectations—first to 30,000, then to 20,000, and ultimately, as the first Job Corps centers finally began to open in the winter of 1965, to 10,000.

For a while it looked as though even that goal was unrealistic. By the end of April, only 2,000 students had enlisted; by the end of May, only 5,000. "Operation 10,000," as it came to be called, went into high gear. Shriver demanded that the planners do whatever was necessary, working center by center, to attain his declared goal.

"Operation 10,000" worked. During the last few days of June, 4,000 new Job Corpsmen signed up. At ten minutes before midnight on the final day of June, the 10,000th person was registered for the Job Corps. Shriver, who had gone home to bed, was awakened by a telephone call from OEO headquarters: the entire Job Corps Washington staff raucously singing "Happy 10,000 to You!"

But when the first corpsmen arrived at their assigned campsites and urban boarding schools, as Christopher Weeks recalled, "they found a center still half-finished, an overworked and harassed staff, many of whom were just as new to the Job Corps as the recruits. . . . They also found out—very quickly—that group living with other Job Corpsmen was no tea party; it was a rough, tough society in which raw power tended to set the pecking order despite the presence of resident workers and counselors in the dormitories." Job Corps staff, who had generally arrived at the site only three or four days before the recruits, "didn't know what on earth they were supposed to do," Weeks said. "They didn't have the books. They didn't have the materials. They didn't have the equipment. They didn't have the beds, the blankets, the sheets, the towels, the washing machines, any of the things that are needed to get things off the ground."

Reporters pounced. Even before the 10,000th Corpsman had been recruited, Newsweek and the New York Times were reporting that many of the people (nearly 18 percent by Newsweek's reckoning) who had signed up for the Job Corps as part of the first wave in January were dropping out. This was not the sort of article that would make the Job Corps the popular anchor for the War on Poverty Shriver hoped it would be.

Dramatic problems at some centers generated more bad press. The most severe incident took place at Camp Breckinridge, in Morganfield, Kentucky. The center, run by Southern Illinois University, had administrative and discipline problems from the beginning. Fistfights and hazing incidents were common. Life in the barracks there ran "according to corpsman law—and that was the law of the jungle." A group of corpsmen formed an extortion racket, terrorizing other enrollees. In early August a brawl broke out in the cafeteria. The arrival of a fire truck, summoned by camp administrators, instigated a riot that badly injured thirteen people. Fully half the camp took part in the rioting; many of the corpsmen who didn't participate fled the center to hide in nearby towns. It took the arrival not only of state policemen but also of FBI agents and US marshals to finally settle the disturbance.

Local politicians called Shriver, enraged. "I had the telephone switchboard light up continuously, calling on me to 'get the goddamned Job Corps the hell out of Kentucky!'" Shriver recalled. "The governor called me up. 'This is creating a goddamned mess out here; the kids in that Job Corps are derelict sons of bitches now they're getting out of the Job Corps precincts and they're going downtown and fucking women and everything.'"

Two months later, the Job Corps again made the front pages when a few dozen corpsmen at the Custer Job Corps center in Battle Creek, Michigan, got into a brawl with local teenagers that required antiriot police to quell. This was particularly embarrassing for the OEO because Shriver himself had spoken at Custer earlier in the day at the ceremony for the center's official dedication. Additional smaller incidents occurred at Job Corps centers in California, Idaho, Indiana, Montana, and elsewhere.

It soon came to light that some of the troublemaking corpsmen had prison records. This, Shriver would say, was largely the point of the program: to take delinquents from the culture of poverty and transform them into productive citizens.

George Foreman, the former world heavyweight boxing champion, credits the Job Corps with having done just that in his own case: It saved him from a life of drugs and crime. Growing up in abject poverty in Houston, Texas, Foreman recalls, "the streets were my life." Foreman's father had left his mother when George was very little. Teachers wrote him—and the whole deprived culture he came from—off.

You'd go into class and there would be some kids you could tell who had both a mom and dad. And the teachers would automatically gravitate toward them and they would learn. And there would be some of us who would come in and you could tell, you know, there wouldn't be any socks under the shoes or the pants wouldn't match or you could see they were hand-me-downs and they saw we were treated like that. I would try to trick the teachers and I would be really friendly with those kids who had families and it looked like sometimes the teachers, before they found me out, would try to act like they were interested in me, but not much. So you go through the whole school system like that where a lot of the teachers are looking at you like, What are you doing here? And I had to experience, I think it must have been in sixth grade, [when] the teacher gave us a speech because we were going to the secondary school or called a junior high then. And the teacher looked at some of us who'd been kept back so long and because of our age we were just shipped to another school and she said, You know, some of you are not going to make it, you've got to understand that. I don't know what's going to become of you. And she looked me right in the eye.

So Foreman, like many others in his predicament, turned to crime.

A friend of ours showed us how to mug people. It was real easy. You'd watch these guys coming out of beer joints at night. You'd wait until you'd see one stagger a little bit and then we'd roll these guys and take their wallets and run. We'd drink cheap wine to get ourselves in the mood. Just around this time dope was coming onto the streets. The Job Corps saved me before I got into that. And I always think that if I had graduated into the deeper robbing and armed robbing, it would eventually have moved to dope and I would have spent the rest of the days in prison.

One day in 1965 Foreman heard a public service radio announcement in which the football star Jim Brown advertised the Job Corps, explaining that it would teach youths a vocation and help them escape the streets. (Shriver had deliberately sought ways to get word about the Job Corps directly to its potential beneficiaries, and to that end he enlisted as many sports stars, radio disk jockeys, and rock stars as he could to promote the program on radio and television shows.) Foreman "signed up instantly" and was assigned to a Job Corps center in Grant's Pass, Oregon.

Foreman says the Job Corps was a radical, transformative experience for him—beginning from the very moment he began his trip from Texas to Oregon. "I had never been on an airplane. We didn't know airports existed. The world really changed before my face, as I got on that airplane, with the stewardesses looking after us. When I got to Oregon, they gave us new clothes—some for working, some for exercising, and a blazer and slacks for dressing up. I'd never had that many clothes in my life. But most important to me were the three meals a day. I'd never had that before."

At the Job Corps center, Foreman and his peers acquired vocational skills and self-respect. They also, Foreman says, developed a civic sense and learned what it was to be an American. "Before I joined the Job Corps, I thought Lyndon Johnson was the president of Texas. That's how ignorant I was." Being in the Job Corps "changed my life. It gave me pride, made me proud to be an American. At the Job Corps, it was the first time I thought to myself, 'Hey, you're somebody now.' The Job Corps teachers—even though I didn't have a father, even though I didn't have clothes—they embraced me like I was a rich guy. They taught me how to read. They taught me how to build fences. They taught me how to construct a radio. I was so proud of that."

Years later, after Foreman had become a boxing champion and international celebrity, he and Shriver became close personal friends. Foreman helped on Shriver's political campaigns and, later, as a spokesman for the Special Olympics; Shriver helped negotiate contracts for some of Foreman's biggest heavyweight championship fights. But even before he had ever met Shriver personally, Foreman says, the OEO director was a "celestial figure" to members of the Job Corps.

> There was something called *The Corpsmen's Call*, a weekly newspaper given to all Job Corps members nationwide that would tell about Job Corps graduates and how well they were doing. And every week there was a section, a statement, by Sarge Shriver. This man to us was the most beautiful fellow in the world. You could see there was a glow to him. There was something special about him, his hair tucked to the side of his head real neatly, and dressed very fancy. Every time he visited a Job Corps center it was like a parade. He was like an in-house hero to us. We used him as a threat when our friends were misbehaving: "If you do this, we'll tell Sarge Shriver." All the boys felt that way about Sarge Shriver.

Politicians and the press, however, did not feel that way about him. "You'd think that if we took some felons in and could turn them around, we ought to get the Croix de Guerre with five palms, because that not only saves a life but saves society," Shriver recalled. Instead, the Job Corps was heaped with opprobrium, because the middle-class taxpayers who made up the bulk of the voting public felt the program was using their tax dollars to subsidize the wild behavior of a (predominantly black) class of delinquents.

With numerous incidents—arson, rape, and more brawls—gracing the nation's newspapers through the summer and fall of 1965, members of Congress began complaining that the OEO seemed to have no control over the Job Corps centers. Even Mike Mansfield, the Senate majority leader, who was ordinarily favorably disposed toward Shriver's programs, was troubled. "I do not like admonishing the Job Corps," Mansfield wrote after a Job Corps recruit shot at a policeman at a bar in the senator's home state of Montana, "but it seems to me that there is something wrong." By the middle of 1965, the Job Corps' survival seemed very much in doubt.

Shriver reacted by terminating contracts with the administrative bodies—usually universities—at poorly run centers and replacing them with corporate contractors, who tended to run the camps more efficiently. Although this elicited an angry reaction from liberals, who objected to what they considered "poverty profiteering," the change was effective: By the following autumn, there were 30,000 Job Corps members, three times as many as the year before, yet through the summer and fall of 1966 there were no riots or other significant incidents at Job Corps centers.

When the congressional hearings on the OEO's reauthorization began in the spring of 1966, the Job Corps was still on politically shaky ground—and hardly the gold mine of political capital Shriver had hoped it would be. But for the moment, it had survived.

CHAPTER THIRTY-ONE

"Political Pornography"

⌒

The problems of the Job Corps were small compared with those that confronted Community Action. The important idea behind the Community
Action concept, repeated endlessly in the OEO literature, was that the *community*, rather than the state or federal government, was supposed to determine
the best use for antipoverty funds. The federal government, through the OEO,
would provide 90 percent of the funding and impose some guidelines. But local
groups—existing organizations like YMCAs, educational institutions, or nonprofit agencies formed expressly for the purpose—would choose how to spend
the money, and they would be charged with administering the program. Funds
could be spent on education, housing, health care, job training, delinquency
programs, child care—anything the designated Community Action agency
(CAA) deemed appropriate in fighting poverty.

The problem was, as soon as new federal funds were offered up for grabs,
Community Action inevitably became inextricably bound up with local politics. The OEO founders were surprised by the intensity of the political squab-
bling Community Action produced. As Shriver recalled,

We weren't quite prepared for the bitterness and the antagonism and the violence that accompanied an effort to alleviate poverty. There were an awful lot of people, both white and black, who had generations of pent-up feelings. I believe that when you take the cork out of a bottle like that, it's likely to burst forth because of a long period of compression. As result, when we went into communities or when we took youngsters out of communities, like for the Job Corps, there was a lot of acrimony and wild activity, such that the placid life of most middle-class Americans was stunned, shocked, by all this social explosion. There was a lot of animosity revealed in the explosion, and then a lot of fear came into the hearts and minds of a lot of middle-class people—not only fear, but then real hostility.

Applications for CAAs had begun arriving at OEO headquarters in the fall of 1964, usually from groups of local civic leaders led by a mayor. Community Action director Jack Conway, Shriver, and the small Community Action staff would invite these groups to Washington and interrogate them about how involved the poor had been in putting together the grant proposal. Usually the answer was, "Well, not very much but about as much as was feasible." Eager to get CAAs into existence fast, the OEO would generally approve these applications but with the condition that these "mayor's committees" expand the involvement of the poor as they moved ahead to set up the agencies. "It was a wild sort of operation in those early days, making the first grants," Don Baker recalled. "We didn't have any guidelines and didn't have the time really to draft them to start out." The program applications would be taken "en masse to Sarge, who sat around with the program people, and he explored and tested the decisions that were made."

As early as November 1964, "an avalanche of telegrams of protest" from local chapters of civil rights groups like the National Association for the Advancement of Colored People and the Urban League began to arrive on Shriver's desk, arguing that the residents of the area had not been consulted by the mayors, as Title II of the Economic Opportunity Act required. Protests from these moderate civil rights organizations were often soon followed by more strident objections from radicals and militants in the community, often associated with black churches, accusing the mayor's committees of being too "establishment oriented." Sometimes the militants would organize themselves into a group that would submit its own CAA application to compete with the mayor's.

Hoping to avoid divisive public debate, the OEO would invite all the local factions (the mayor's committee, the moderate civil rights groups, and the anti-establishment radicals) to the negotiating table in Washington, in an effort to bring them to some kind of consensus. This was usually a mixed success. The mayor would invite the leading protestors to join his committee, and a new application reflecting a broader base of community support would be submitted to the OEO—but elements further out on the anti-establishment fringe would form a *new* protesting committee that would accuse the protestors that had joined the mayor's group of having "sold out." In most cases, a CAA grant would eventually be made, but the process of achieving consensus would take months. During this time, the local newspapers would be filled with headlines about "delays" at OEO headquarters and about the political "mess" in the community. And any group that felt it had been left out of the process would go to the press and to local members of Congress to complain, creating more flak both for the OEO and for local politicians.

The mayors began to fight back. On January 20, 1965, President Johnson received a confidential letter from the mayor of Baltimore, Theodore McKeldin, complaining that "your plans are being hindered at the federal level by individuals who insist on unrealistic requirements"—the "maximum feasible participation" of the poor—"and who do not understand the problems and requirements of local government." McKeldin said the mayors of St. Louis, Cleveland, and Philadelphia shared his complaints.

Richard Daley of Chicago was by far the most powerful Democratic mayor in the country. He considered himself, with some justification, personally responsible for having made possible the New Frontier and the Great Society. As Johnson's aide Joseph Califano recalled, "Daley was critical to the success of the Great Society. A call to Daley was all that was necessary to deliver the fourteen voters of the Illinois congressional delegation. Johnson and others of us had made many calls to the mayor and Daley had always come through." Thus Daley was not someone President Johnson was keen to anger. But when Daley submitted a grant proposal for a comprehensive CAA in 1965, it lacked *any* involvement of local residents or the poor; in effect, it was a grant request for the Daley machine operation. The Budget Bureau's Bill Cannon was dispatched to Chicago to explain to the mayor the "maximum feasible participation" provision. The meeting was a disaster. "It was clear that there would be no poverty program [in Chicago] without Daley running it," Cannon recalled.

When the OEO continued pressuring Daley to open up the program beyond his patronage machine, Daley went directly to the president to complain. Bill Moyers remembered a call he got from Daley. "What in the hell are you people doing?" Daley demanded. "Does the president know he's putting M-O-N-E-Y in the hands of subversives?" According to Moyers, the president's conversations with Daley soured him on Community Action. "The clearest picture Johnson got of the bad image of OEO was from Daley," Moyers recalled. Daley "really began to rage at Johnson. That began to form a dark cloud in Johnson's mind."

By the late spring of 1965, more and more mayors were adding their complaints to the chorus of those already coming from Chicago and Baltimore. Governors, senators, and members of Congress from both parties were beginning to write angry letters to the president. Vice President Hubert Humphrey, dispatched by Johnson to serve as intermediary between Shriver and the mayors, warned the president in March that "there are numerous problems . . . developing."

In May 1965, at the annual meeting of the US Conference of Mayors, Los Angeles mayor Samuel Yorty and San Francisco mayor John Shelley—both Democrats—drafted a resolution attacking the OEO. The OEO, and the "maximum feasible participation" provision of Community Action in particular, created needless "tensions" at the local level. "Maximum feasible participation," Yorty and Shelley argued, failed "to recognize the legal and moral responsibilities of local officials who are accountable to the taxpayer for expenditures of local funds." "Mayors all over the United States," Yorty said, "are being harassed by agitation promoted by Sargent Shriver's speeches urging those he calls 'poor' to insist upon control of local poverty programs."

If the mayors' draft resolution had been adopted by the conference, it might have spelled the end of the War on Poverty. Shriver could no longer have denied that there was direct, open conflict between two entities—the OEO and city governments—where at least the appearance of cooperation was essential for success. Recognizing this, President Johnson dispatched Vice President Humphrey to the mayor's conference to head off disaster. Humphrey persuaded the mayors to shelve the resolution by assuring them that he would represent their point of view to Johnson and Shriver. "I can tell you now that your important role is assured in this program," Humphrey said. "I'm your built-in Special Agent to make sure that you are represented in this program twenty-four hours a day, 365 days a year. I've been hired for you."

Shriver dealt with the growing controversy over Community Action grants by demanding that every grant application be subjected to careful internal scrutiny by several OEO departments and that no grant be disbursed until he had personally approved it. Each application that survived a preliminary screening process would be presented at a meeting by an OEO field representative. Then, with Shriver presiding over the often rambunctious proceedings, the OEO's legal division, its civil rights staff, and its Office of Inspection would take turns criticizing the application, forcing the field representative to make the best possible case for it. If the application was deemed to pass muster by all the various staffs, Shriver would give his approval. One OEO staffer compared the "minute attention" given to each grant to "woodcarving."

This process was time consuming, but the rigorous cross-examination tended to produce improvements in the CAA programs. As one OEO staffer recalled, "Shriver's sensitive political antennae—his awareness that at any minute his phone might ring, with some congressman or senator or mayor or county commissioner or civil rights leader complaining about a particular program—corrected many deficiencies that might have been embarrassing later."

Still, programs that turned into major, near-fatal embarrassments did slip through the filtering process. One of the most damaging Community Action grants went to the Syracuse Community Development Association (SCDA), in Syracuse, New York.

The Syracuse grant revealed Community Action's built-in conundrum: How far should the federal government go in helping local poor residents fight their own elected officials in city hall? Early in 1965 the OEO had awarded a $315,000 grant to SCDA for the purpose of training community organizers. The idea, as the planners at OEO headquarters imagined it, was to teach the poor how to become engaged in their communities and to help them figure out what civic issues (sanitation, for example, or day care) needed attention and how to get those issues addressed.

It didn't take long for the political conflicts this invited to emerge. One reason the conflicts emerged so acutely in Syracuse was the presence of the radical political organizer Saul Alinsky, whom SCDA had retained as a consultant. Shriver was friendly with Alinsky from their work together on civil rights in Chicago. More recently, however, Alinsky had taken to issuing rhetorical broadsides at the War on Poverty, accusing it at various times of being underfunded, politically cowardly, and a pork-barrel operation in liege to local political machines.

Under Alinsky's direction, SCDA employees from Syracuse University were mobilizing the local poor for direct social action: Syracuse residents began demanding improved garbage collection, lower rents, protection from unjustified evictions by landlords, and better recreational facilities for poor kids. These demands did not make the Syracuse municipal government happy; they could only be construed as an implicit criticism of how that government was functioning.

Worse, though, than the implicit criticism was the explicit mobilization of political forces against the local Syracuse government. The SCDA was organizing sit-ins and protest marches against the Syracuse mayor, William Walsh, and had launched an effective voter registration drive. In some sense the SCDA was doing exactly what it was supposed to do: energizing the poor to affect their community and infusing them with a feeling of civic empowerment. But Mayor Walsh, a Republican, watching as the voter registration drive boosted Democratic Party enrollments in poor neighborhoods, saw this as a partisan operation—one funded by the federal government. Walsh complained to reporters that Alinsky's people "go into a housing project and talk about setting up a 'democratic' organization—small 'd'—but it sounds just the same as Democratic—big 'D.' In a close election it could be decisive."

On April 12 the commissioner of the Syracuse Housing Authority wrote to President Johnson. The OEO's grant to SCDA, he alleged, was financing "activities which do no good and will ultimately cause serious trouble in our community if allowed to continue." When the New York Times reported this story, James Rowe, a prominent Washington lawyer and New Deal veteran who was a staunch Johnson ally, wrote to LBJ warning him that it seemed to him that "high minded . . . innocents" at OEO headquarters were funding political training for militant black radicals. "The political implications of using public funds," Rowe wrote to Johnson, "to instruct people how to protest are quite obvious." This clearly worried the president: He forwarded Rowe's letter to Bill

Moyers with a note that said, "Bill—for God's sake get on top of this and just put a stop to it at once."

In Syracuse the mayor and several other city officials joined forces with the city's old-line welfare agencies to form the Syracuse Crusade for Opportunity, which applied for and was granted a Community Action grant through the OEO. The two conceptions of Community Action represented by SCDA and the Crusade for Opportunity were diametrically opposed. Whereas the Crusade envisioned the local government as the mechanism for delivering social justice to the poor, the SCDA sought to fight against the local government to achieve justice for the poor.

On November 30, 1965, the OEO announced that all of SCDA's future funding requests would have to be made through the Syracuse Crusade for Opportunity, which the OEO was now designating the "umbrella" CAA for Syracuse. The leaders of SCDA erupted in anger and forced a meeting with Shriver on December 8. They accused him of allowing the local government machine to co-opt the local War on Poverty—the very thing that Community Action was supposed to guard against. Alinsky called the War on Poverty "the greatest boondoggle and feeding trough that's come along for the welfare industry for years."

In the battle between city government and community activists, the city government had won. This was a victory for Lyndon Johnson—it helped temporarily to get the mayors off his back—and it enhanced the OEO's political viability. But it was a blow to some of the harder-core advocates of Community Action on the OEO staff, and it contributed to the defection later in the year of Dick Boone, Jack Conway, and others from the War on Poverty.

ROBERT KENNEDY AND THE FORCES OF HISTORY

Although part of the problem with Community Action lay in its ill-defined nature, and in grants that should never have been awarded, the bigger problem may have been timing. The summer of 1965 was when history turned on a dime; no one knew it then, but July saw the cresting of the Great Society. At the time, President Johnson called the last week of that month "the most productive and historic legislative week during this century." The Voting Rights Act was in conference between the House and Senate, on its way to passage; Medicare and Medicaid had been passed into law; Social Security benefits had just been increased by 7 percent;

and the Housing and Urban Development Act, which would create a new cabinet department, was on its way to becoming law. Tom Wicker wrote in his *New York Times* column that "the list of [LBJ's] achievements is so long that it reads better than the legislative accomplishments of most two-term presidents." Senate majority leader Mike Mansfield even went so far as to tell the presidential historian William Leuchtenberg that "Johnson has outstripped Roosevelt, no doubt about that. He has done more than FDR ever did or thought of doing."

Yet in this same week Johnson was planting the seeds of his own undoing by committing 100,000 more American troops to Vietnam. (He had committed the first ground troops there in April.) In August a police incident in the Watts section of Los Angeles ignited five days of rioting that killed thirty-four people and injured thousands. The net effect, ultimately, was to destroy "the mood of triumphant liberal comity" on which the Great Society had been built. "At a stroke," the historian Gareth Davies has written, "the fragility of President Johnson's cherished consensus became apparent," as its ideals were attacked from both left and right. Conservatives now argued that the Watts riots demonstrated that the poor "did not deserve the War on Poverty's largesse"; liberals argued that the riots demonstrated that the poor needed far more. This left the OEO, as one poverty planner recalled, "attempting to reach community consensus at a time when race, politics, and poverty were pulling the community and the nation apart."

Complicating matters still further for the poverty program, Shriver found himself directly caught up in the Shakespearean conflict between Lyndon Johnson and Robert Kennedy. As the tectonic plates of history shifted beneath him, LBJ became increasingly obsessed with "the Bobby problem." He believed that Kennedy—who had won election to the Senate from New York the previous November—was planning to run for president in 1968. For Johnson, the notion that his presidency might turn out to be nothing more than a five-year interregnum between Kennedy administrations became a consuming preoccupation.

In the summer of 1965, Johnson's hatred of Robert Kennedy was becoming such a major distraction that one of his aides wrote him a memo asking him to stop opposing productive pieces of legislation just because RFK happened to support them. The aide added, too, as tactfully as he could, that the president should not spend so much time worrying about whether various cabinet members were more loyal to him or to RFK. Although Shriver remained unwaveringly loyal to the poverty program, that wasn't enough for the president. As Joe Califano observed, even as Johnson continued to use Shriver as a Kennedy family hostage, the president "couldn't look at Shriver without trying to see whether Robert Kennedy was in the shadows behind his brother-in-law."

Shriver still believed Community Action could work—but only if it were given enough time and if it were supplemented by other, more ambitious approaches. At a meeting at the LBJ ranch in mid-summer of 1965, Shriver suggested boosting OEO funding from the proposed $1.75 billion for fiscal year 1966 to $10 billion within several years, with the bulk of that additional money going to fund an income-maintenance program. Shriver was convinced that this plan, in conjunction with an expansion of some other OEO programs, could all but completely eliminate poverty. When LBJ responded that there was no way he could commit that kind of money, Shriver persisted. "If you want to wage war on poverty," he said, "this is how to do it." Johnson responded, as Shriver recalled, "Congressional elections are coming up. After that we'll be out of this Vietnam thing, and I'll give you the money."

But more than Vietnam and fiscal caution lay beyond Johnson's stalling. The president's paranoia about RFK led him to see Shriver's grandiose proposal to eliminate poverty as part of a Kennedy plot. When Shriver sent a follow-up memo to Johnson on October 20, outlining a plan "to end poverty in the United States, as we know it today, within a generation," the president worried that Shriver planned to leak it to the press, to demonstrate that Shriver and the rest of the Kennedy family were willing to commit more resources to fighting poverty than Johnson was. In reality, Shriver had no such intention. The OEO director's loyalties lay more strongly with the cause of fighting poverty than with either party in the LBJ-RFK feud.

SHRIVER VERSUS THE WHITE HOUSE

By the end of 1965, as an early OEO staff member recalled, every

> mayor had a gripe [about Community Action]; congressmen were plagued by visiting delegations from two, three, even four local factions; governors were irri-

tated at mayors; social workers and many other professionals resented intrusions both from the politicians and from the poor; liberals who wanted local programs to shake up the established politicians were upset at the amount of accommodation the OEO required; and established politicians wished they could run their own anti-poverty programs, with their own trusted friends among the poor, rather than negotiating compromises with more vocal and militant local groups and individuals.

In short, by the end of 1965 every conceivable Community Action constituency— including the poor themselves—felt somehow alienated by the program.

The heat on President Johnson to do something about Community Action was rising. But he still held out hope that the War on Poverty could be the signature achievement of his presidency. At a cabinet meeting in July 1965, Johnson is reported to have said to each cabinet head in turn, "You save money on your programs" and then, "You-all give it to him," pointing to Shriver.

But LBJ's support for the OEO became increasingly erratic. That fall even as he continued to publicly avow his support for Shriver and for Community Action, Johnson secretly authorized efforts by his White House staff to rein in the OEO. Charlie Schultze, who had replaced Kermit Gordon as White House Budget Bureau director, wrote a memorandum to Johnson lamenting all the strife Community Action was producing among Democratic mayors. *"We ought not to be in the business of organizing the poor politically,"* Schultze wrote with italicized urgency. If the OEO continued to antagonize local political officials by establishing Community Action agencies that threatened their authority, Schultze warned, the administration may lose the support of local Democratic machines for the midterm elections in 1966. When Johnson read Schultze's memo, he scrawled a note across the bottom of it: "O.K. I agree. L."

Schultze took Johnson's note as authorization for changing the OEO's policy on Community Action. On November 5, the *New York Times* reported that, according to a "high government source," the Bureau of the Budget had instructed the OEO to place less emphasis on policy planning by the poor themselves. The *Times*'s anonymous source—which turned out to be Schultze—also said that the Budget Bureau had "suggested" that the OEO reduce its direct funding of Community Action projects by $35 million. But when Shriver, visiting CAAs on Indian reservations in Arizona, was asked by a reporter about this shift away from Community Action, he vehemently disagreed, and in a speech that day he emphatically disputed any assertions about a changing conception of the role of the poor in Community Action. "No such change in OEO's policy has been directed or ordered by anyone in the administration. Our policy is today and will remain exactly what it has been from the very beginning."

"It is a serious misunderstanding of fact and policy to conclude that there has been or will be a decreased emphasis on maximum feasible participation of the poor," Shriver continued. "There will be no retreat from our earlier policies and no slackening in our effort to press for vigorous and creative compliance with that requirement." Shriver was declaring in no uncertain terms that in the battle between elected politicians and local CAAs he stood with the CAAs. As Shriver recalled, "I didn't bother to clear my statement with anyone. I was simply not going to be kicked around. If the White House had intended to order a retreat, this bugle call to advance would head it off." The dispute between the OEO director and the budget director ended up being reported on the front page of the *New York Times*.

Johnson was furious to see this internal squabble end up as front-page news, and he dispatched his domestic policy aide Joseph Califano to tell both Shriver and Schultze to cease and desist. Each, in turn, responded by writing heated memos to the president. In his memo Schultze accused Shriver of trying to gain unfair advantage in an internal policy debate by deliberately leaking stories to the *New York Times* in order to arouse the ire of the OEO's liberal supporters and its growing grassroots constituency among the poor. Shriver accused Schultze of leaking stories to undermine the OEO, and he insinuated that the president himself was seeking to undercut him. "It was overwhelmingly clear," Shriver wrote to the president, "that serious harm would be done to your War against Poverty unless a forceful clarification was issued." Shriver had made his public statement to the press, he continued, because the original *New York Times* story had "seriously impinged upon, even threatened, important features of the programs for which I am responsible. [Since] I had had no personal indication of any dissatisfaction from you or anyone else close to you . . . I can only conclude that a large part of this gossip is malicious and intended to injure your programs. Those programs needed an explicit defense."

According to Califano, there was solid basis for Shriver's accusation of Schultze's leaking—but LBJ himself may have egged Schultze on. Johnson recognized that the OEO's continued practice of mobilizing the poor against local politicians threatened the president's support among rank-and-file Democratic officials—and LBJ viewed Democratic victory in the midterm elections of 1966 as essential to further consolidating the liberal consensus that his landslide victory over Goldwater in 1964 had established.

Grafted onto LBJ's legitimate concerns about the political impact of Community Action was his knowledge that some of Community Action's most ardent partisans (Dick Boone, Dave Hackett, and Frank Mankiewicz) within the OEO were "Bobby's people." Johnson suspected that Shriver planned to turn the OEO into a de facto election apparatus for Robert Kennedy in 1968, an organizational base within the executive branch from which the New York senator could mount a campaign to unseat the president.

On its face, this suspicion was preposterous. Despite the hardships LBJ was imposing on him, Shriver remained loyal to Johnson—in fact, Shriver's manifest loyalty to the president remained a sore spot with Bobby and his associates. The problem was that as the president's distrust of RFK metastasized, the premium he placed on loyalty within the executive branch grew. To Johnson, everyone was a potential mole—especially anybody with ties to the Kennedy family. Johnson's anxiety about Robert Kennedy fed his ambivalence about the OEO.

Although Shriver and Robert Kennedy rarely spoke outside of family gatherings and Senate hearings, they shared a belief in the power of Community Action as a tool of public policy and social justice—and in LBJ's mind this amounted to the two brothers-in-law making common cause against him. In December 1965 Johnson's fear that the OEO would become a clandestine Kennedy political vehicle in 1968 led him to ask Califano to explore the possibility of disbanding the OEO and distributing its constituent parts among the various cabinet departments. The plan must be drawn up "in strictest confidence" and must require no legislative action, the president explained, in order to avoid a "bloodbath on Capitol Hill."

Califano sent plans for a proposed reorganization of the OEO to the president on December 18; Califano had consulted with Nicholas Katzenbach (Kennedy's replacement as attorney general), who concluded that the dissolution of the OEO could be accomplished without legislative action. Califano's plan called for Shriver to delegate all OEO programs and functions to the cabinet departments. Supervision of the Community Action programs, for instance, could be given to the secretary of the new Department of Housing and Urban Development. As a political face-saving measure for Shriver, Califano proposed that the president name Shriver the founding secretary of HUD. Califano advised Johnson that the "reorganization of the War on Poverty" made "good organizational sense," but he warned that it could end up being "the most politically explosive act the administration could take."

Johnson had the Justice Department draw up all the necessary papers for dissolving the OEO—but in the end he declined to take final action to do so. Terminating the OEO might have made some Democratic mayors happy, but it would have led to politically damaging fights within his administration. Johnson felt that to maintain a broad coalition of support for his social programs, he needed to keep the Left under the Great Society's tent. Moreover, the president did not want to give Kennedy and his liberal allies more grounds than they already possessed for saying that he was sacrificing the needs of the American poor on the altar of the Vietnam War. Oddly, however, given his fears about a Shriver–Bobby Kennedy axis, Johnson's decision to spare the OEO seems motivated as much by his desire to retain Shriver as a bulwark against RFK as by his appreciation for Shriver's loyalty. Johnson told Shriver that he was "pretty disgusted at" his cabinet officers for circling like vultures looking for the OEO carrion to prey on. "Sarge," Johnson said, "you're the only one that's not letting me down. The rest of them are just fighting—the party, the programs, the senators and everybody—I'm just glad somebody is looking out for what they believe in."

Some who worked closely with Shriver at the OEO were struck by the irony of Johnson's occasional doubts about his loyalty. It was plain to them how actively Shriver tried to maintain his loyalty to the president, and at what cost to his personal standing within the Kennedy family. "Shriver," one former aide recalled, "was trying to be extremely careful not to be viewed as disloyal or being part of a Kennedy plan." Although Shriver had started life in the Johnson administration as merely "the token Kennedy member," he eventually "came to have a genuine commitment [to the Johnson administration], and a personally tortured commitment, because he understood that he was going to be using up all of his personal and political capital." But Shriver stayed on. For better or for worse he felt duty bound to keep himself lashed to the OEO ship, even if at times it seemed sure to sink. Shriver's "stubborn idealism," as the newspaper columnist Charles Bartlett described it, won out over his own self-interest.

When colleagues—watching him get pulled in so many different directions, attacked from without and undermined from within—would ask him why he didn't simply leave, he would reply that it was out of loyalty to the War on Poverty. "Somebody has got to hang in there," he would say, "and I can't figure out anybody who's got more credibility with Congress and more political capital and who would be willing to go to bat to keep this program alive in Congress, because it's so controversial."

CHAPTER THIRTY-TWO

Head Start

~~~~

A s Shriver tried to navigate the OEO through its turbulent first year of operation, he was helped tremendously by the development of two programs
that had not been mentioned in the Economic Opportunity Act of 1964.
Neither Head Start nor Legal Services for the Poor was part of the original
poverty bill—because they weren't even conceived until after the OEO was
operational—but they were the two most politically successful and enduring
programs the War on Poverty produced. Without Head Start, it's unlikely that
the OEO would have survived through 1966.

In the late fall of 1964 the Bureau of the Budget produced some pie charts
that Shriver had requested earlier in the year, breaking down all of America's
poor into demographic categories. They showed, for instance, what proportion of the poor lived in rural areas versus urban areas, what proportion of
poor families were headed by single mothers, what proportion of the poor
were elderly. The idea was that this information would allow the OEO to craft
programs for the demographic groups that most needed help.

When he looked at these charts, what struck Shriver was how many of the poor were children. "My God, look at that," Shriver remembers saying to himself. *"Fifty percent* of all the poor people are children." Seventeen percent of the nation's poor children—about 6 million of them—were under the age of six. That 6 million young children lived in poverty in a prosperous society seemed to Shriver to be an appalling moral failure on the part of the American people and the federal government. He quickly concluded that the OEO needed to be doing more for young children.

But how? In 1964 Shriver had been working closely with Eunice at the Kennedy Foundation for nearly a decade, traveling the country to talk to researchers about the mentally retarded and providing Kennedy Foundation funding to those projects deemed most worthy of pursuit. One of those grants had gone to Susan Gray, a psychologist at the George Peabody Teacher's College (now part of Vanderbilt University) in Tennessee. In 1962 Gray and her colleagues had used the grant to conduct a study of mentally retarded children living in poor areas around Nashville, to see if intensive intervention at an early age could in any way "cure"—or at least diminish—retardation. To the surprise of many, the Gray study found that changing the social and intellectual environments of retarded children under the age of six could actually raise their IQ scores.

Eunice followed Gray's research with interest. One day in 1964, as Eunice recalled, while the Shrivers were sitting in their living room at Timberlawn, she described Gray's work to Sarge. He was intrigued but skeptical, so she proposed that Sarge go to Tennessee to see the results for himself. "So we flew down to Gray's research institute," Eunice remembered, "and we visited retarded children at three different sites. Gray and her team had elevated the childrens' IQ so much that some of them were now able to participate in regular classes at their schools." As Eunice had predicted, Sarge was impressed; his skepticism dissipated.

"I was dumbfounded," Sarge recalled. "Like most Americans, I thought that one was born with a certain IQ, as one might be born with black or red hair, and that in fact it was impossible to change the genetic make-up that determined IQ." But Gray's study showed convincingly that the IQ scores of even congenitally retarded children were not immutable. Furthermore, Gray showed that it wasn't just analytical intelligence that could be increased by early intervention; social development could be improved, too.

Eunice now reminded her husband of another Kennedy Foundation–funded study, by Philip Dodge, who was the chair of pediatrics at Washington University Medical School, in St. Louis, which had researched the effects of nutrition on mental development. Dodge and his collaborators found that poor nutrition could in fact lead to lower IQ scores, as well as to arrested social and emotion development.

"On the airplane on the way back to Washington, Sarge turned to me and said, 'If they can do this for the retarded, then maybe we can do it for other poor kids.'" Eunice seized her opportunity, telling him, as she recalls, "Sarge, if you do start an early intervention program for poor kids, make sure you set aside some of that money for the mentally retarded." In retrospect, Eunice says, this was only fair. "If it hadn't been for the mentally retarded, there never would have been a Head Start. The mentally retarded sparked the idea."

For his part Sarge remembered that he was driving home to Timberlawn one evening, thinking about the Gray and Dodge studies, when everything suddenly clicked into place in his mind: "If we, through the Kennedy Foundation, could effectively change the IQ of retarded children by early-childhood intervention, could early intervention have a beneficial effect on the children of poor people?"

"It was not primarily an IQ idea," Shriver recalled. "It was an idea of intervening early in their lives to . . . help them become more capable of going to school, which is normally the first hurdle outside the home a person faces." Shriver began asking doctors and psychologists whether they thought an early-intervention program for poor children would do any good. Dr. Robert Cooke, the Johns Hopkins physician who had worked extensively with both Sarge and Eunice at the Kennedy Foundation, told Shriver he thought an early-intervention program was a fine idea. So did Dr. Joseph English, the child psychiatrist who was serving as Peace Corps medical director.

After discussing this idea informally with these and other doctors, Shriver came to the conclusion that "a lot of poor kids arrive at the first grade beaten or at least handicapped before they start. To use an analogy from sports, they stand 10, 20, and 30 feet back from the starting line; other people are way ahead of them. They don't get a fair, equal start with everybody else when they come to school at age six." Attacking the cycle of poverty before first grade would require overcoming the many handicaps that plagued poor children: poor housing, poor nutrition, poor access to books and other educational materials, not to mention absent or abusive or alcoholic or illiterate parents. So Shriver began to ask: "What can we do to help these youngsters? How can we help them to arrive at the starting line even with other children?"

For a program like this to work, Shriver realized, it would have to reach kids before poverty had damaged them significantly; this meant getting them at an early age—before age five, certainly, and if possible at age three or before. The more people he talked to, the more he became convinced that an early-intervention program geared toward preparing poor children for school would be smart policy. Smart policy is not always smart politics—but Shriver suspected that this was an instance where it could be.

He decided to test this hypothesis by bringing it up at noon one December day in the Hay-Adams Hotel in Washington, where he was having lunch with Eunice and Joseph Alsop, the newspaper correspondent for the *New York Herald-Tribune*. Alsop's reaction would be a useful gauge of the general political reception, because, Shriver figured, "if anybody would be skeptical and caustic about it, perhaps even cynical, it would be Joe Alsop." Alsop was, as Shriver put it, "incorrigibly negativist." "From Joe," Shriver recalled, "I would find out immediately what kind of negative reaction we could expect if we came out with the idea" as part of the War on Poverty. To Shriver's surprise, Alsop responded with enthusiasm. "If Joe's not knocking this idea," Shriver thought to himself, "it's not likely to be knocked."

Alsop's reaction helped Shriver realize some of the other political advantages of a program aimed specifically at children. Taxpaying voters were naturally reluctant to have their tax money subsidize programs for poor adults. In the South, especially, the idea carried a racial tinge: The white working class didn't want tax money going to unemployed black people. But there was, Shriver recognized, a natural bias in favor of helping children—and this bias cut across racial lines. Even in regions of the Deep South where Jim Crow had been the strongest and the racial hatred the most bitter, there was among white segregationists a prejudice (albeit patronizing) in favor of little black children. Shriver realized that "it wasn't until blacks grew up that white people began to feel animosity or show actual violence toward them." His hope was that building a program for young children into the OEO would help to neutralize some of the race-based antagonism against the agency in the South.

After meeting with Alsop, Shriver hurried back to his office and said to Dick Boone and others, "Look, we've got to get a program going, and this is the theory behind it. The theory is that we'll intervene early; we'll help IQ problems and the malnutrition problem; we'll get these kids ready for school." Shriver knew from his experience on the Board of Education in Chicago that many poor six-year-olds arrived at school utterly unprepared. So, Shriver said, "let's get these youngsters *ahead* of time, bring them into school, and 'culturally' prepare them for school: for the buildings and teachers, desks, pencils and chalk, discipline, food etc. At the same time, we'll give them the books ahead of time, show them what they are like, and what you do with books. . . . We'll find out if they need shots"—since most poor children had not had their proper vaccinations—"and get their eyes checked." In short, Shriver said (although the program name had not yet been coined) this will be something to give poor kids a "head start."

One of the key questions that remained to be resolved was how big the program should be. In December 1964, Shriver discussed the question with Jerome Bruner, a child development expert at Harvard. Bruner was in favor of a program like the one Shriver had in mind, but he thought it would be foolish to attempt anything on other than a very small, experimental scale. Bruner told him that he might be able be find enough qualified teachers to deal with 2,500 students in the first year of the program, but not more than that. Shriver responded that he thought it would be nearly pointless to try to reach only 2,500 kids when there were known to be 6 million under age six in poverty. "We had to devise programs that could have mass application, mass effectiveness," Shriver said. "I remember being very discouraged after talking to Dr. Bruner."

He didn't remain discouraged for long, though, because he had an idea for how to get around the shortage of available teachers. If the program could be put together quickly, in time for summer vacation, then there would be lots of teachers available for the program's first three months. With schools out of session, there would be empty classrooms and underemployed teachers available for most of June, July, and August. If the program could be launched quickly enough to take advantage of this, Shriver believed that they could enroll up to 25,000 children in the first summer. That was ten times as many as Bruner thought prudent—and one-eighth as many as Shriver would be urging just a few weeks later.

Shriver asked Dick Boone to recruit all the most knowledgeable people on the topic of child poverty, from both inside and outside government, in order to begin putting the program together. One of the first people Boone called was

Jules Sugarman, who was head of the Children's Bureau at HEW. Sugarman became the administrator for this research task force. Shriver then recommended that Boone and Sugarman contact Dr. Cooke. Sugarman and Cooke together took charge of the effort to compose an OEO advisory board on child poverty.

Meeting with Cooke in his Baltimore office, Sugarman and Dr. Edward Davens, deputy director of health for the state of Maryland, came up with a list of experts who might serve on the early childhood education committee, eventually narrowing the list to ten additional names, most of whom were doctors or psychologists, not educators. "We deliberately tried to make it an interdisciplinary effort," Sugarman recalled, "and I suppose that had a very profound effect on the kind of program Head Start eventually became."

These thirteen people—in effect, the steering committee for Head Start—met several times a week throughout January and February 1965 in an effort to hammer out a program design that Shriver would find satisfactory. (They were urged on, as one committee member put it, by "the usually helpful pressure of Sargent Shriver.") On February 19, the committee presented Shriver with what came to be known as the Cooke Report, a seven-page memo outlining all the basic elements of an early-intervention pre-kindergarten program for four- and five-year-olds.

"No sooner had it hit [Shriver's] desk," Sugarman recalled, "than we were told, 'Okay, let's get it operational.' " Shriver said, "I want, by this afternoon, a budget and a program." A day or two later, Shriver presided over a six-hour brainstorming session to come up with a name for the program. Names like the Kiddy Corps and the Preschool Intervention Program were proposed and rejected. Finally, about two in the morning, Judah Drob, a veteran Labor Department staffer who had been working with the OEO, said, "How about 'Head Start'?" The enthusiasm was unanimous.

There was still some dispute within the committee about what the initial scale of the program should be, however. Some members were arguing, as Jerome Bruner had, that it was important to try the idea out on a small scale. Shriver responded that there was no time for such caution. As one committee member recalled, Shriver "said he respected us as experts in our fields, but that we were not political realists. If we were to go ahead with the kind of small-scale program we were talking about, it would no doubt be excellent and serve a small number of families very well. But few would know about it, and it could have no lasting effect. 'We're going to write Head Start across the face of this nation so that no Congress and no president can ever destroy it,' he said."

After "soul-searching" discussions about the risks involved in launching the program on such a grandiose scale, the committee agreed to recommend an eight-week summer program that would serve 100,000 children in 300 communities across the country. Shriver was thrilled. Bruised by the mounting assaults on Community Action and the Job Corps, Shriver was desperate for the OEO to have a political triumph. Head Start seemed to fit the bill. After all, who could be against helping children?

Within a day of receiving the Cooke Report, Shriver presented it to President Johnson. Johnson shared his enthusiasm—and upped the ante. When Shriver described the Head Start concept, explaining that the Cooke committee had recommended limiting the original summer program to 100,000 kids, Johnson replied: "That's such a magnificent idea. Triple it." This was music to Shriver's ears.

Edgar May recalled a meeting held not long after that in the bridal suite of the New Colonial Hotel.

> All these child-rearing experts were sitting around. Shriver tilted back in his chair and said, "How many children do you think we can have in Head Start by this summer?" "Well, Mr. Shriver, if everything goes according to plan and our studies are completed and we can put all of this together and there aren't too many glitches we can probably have 50,000 children in Head Start this summer." Sarge leaned back and there was a palpably long silence. And then his voice went down about two octaves. You knew there was trouble in River City whenever his voice went down an octave or two. And he said, "Gentlemen, I appreciate everything you've done on this project and I would like you to go back and come back here in two weeks and give me a plan for how we're going to have half a million kids in the program by the summer."

Now Shriver needed someone to direct the program. In his work for the Kennedy Foundation, Shriver had come across the research of Dr. Julius Richmond, who was chair of the Department of Pediatrics at the State College of New York in Syracuse. Richmond and his colleague Bettye Caldwell had been exploring ways to arrest "developmental decline" in low-income children. They had found that poor children developed normally for the first year of life but after that began declining intellectually relative to other children. By intervening to provide an environment more conducive to learning than these youngsters ordinarily experienced in their impoverished homes, Richmond and Caldwell discovered that they could in fact prevent the usual developmental decline.

Shriver decided he had to have Richmond as his Head Start director. So, as Richmond recalled, "in characteristic fashion, he wanted me to drop everything that day and get down there immediately." When Shriver laid out the large scope of what he had in mind, Richmond suggested that the program might be better served by someone with more managerial experience. "Well, if I had wanted a bureaucrat, I would have looked for one," Shriver responded. Within a few days Richmond was installed at OEO headquarters.

Before Richmond could become the founding director of Head Start, the program needed an official launch. Ever attuned to the vicissitudes of public relations, Shriver realized that a program like Head Start, which catered to children, might derive particular political support from women. Thus rather than launch the program in a conventional way, with a presidential announcement, why not announce the program in a more "feminine" way? This might help Head Start get coverage, not only in the political pages of the Washington newspapers and the *New York Times,* but also in the society pages of newspapers across the country. Shriver proposed this idea to the president, who liked it—and knew that his wife, Lady Bird, would share his enthusiasm. "The Head Start idea has such *hope* and challenge," the first lady had written in her diary, after a January meeting with Shriver. "Maybe I could help focus public attention in a favorable way on some aspects of Lyndon's poverty program. Anyway, Sargent Shriver is a superb salesman."

So it was that the official announcement of Head Start was made at a White House tea hosted by Lady Bird Johnson. On February 12, 1965, some 400 luminaries, most of them women, stood in the White House East Room to hear Mrs. Johnson lead a discussion of the program. As Shriver had anticipated, the story was covered on society pages and gossip columns in most places. It was a public relations coup. As Jules Sugarman observed, while the Job Corps and Community Action were "being bloodied every day on the front page, Head Start was receiving glowing tributes in the society and community-news pages from local establishment leaders."

Still, when Richmond began as director of the project in early February 1965, many of his professional contacts were telling him there was no way he could get Head Start running on the proposed scale by summertime. "It's already too late," they told him. "You'll never carry it off." Even many people within the OEO were skeptical that anything could be done by July. Communities didn't even know about the program yet—so how could they apply in time for summer? How could all the applications be processed in time? When—and where—would all the teachers be trained?

In early March, Shriver mailed letters to every school superintendent, nearly every community health official, and nearly every welfare director in the country, informing them about Head Start and telling them to send in a response postcard if they were interested in applying for a Head Start center in their community. Soon the OEO headquarters was inundated with response cards, requesting applications.

This flood was a mixed blessing. The OEO staff had only six weeks to process all the applications, disburse the funding, and open the first centers. But whenever Richmond and his deputies wavered in their confidence, Shriver would insist that they simply could not afford to fail.

Head Start applications continued to flow in through May and June. The early popularity of the program surprised everyone. "It was like wildcatting for oil in your own backyard and suddenly hitting a gusher," Shriver recalled. "Every two or three weeks, it seemed to me, [Richmond and Sugarman would] come to me and say, 'Look, Sarge, this thing is just exploding and we certainly can't begin to finance this" with the money initially set aside for it. So he kept increasing its funding from the OEO budget. When money in the Community Action budget began to run short, Shriver moved money from the Job Corps and other programs into Head Start. Julius Richmond recalled that every time he went back to Shriver for more money—to pay for more students, or more teachers—Shriver would say, "Let me talk to the president." Then a day later he would come back with the money.

When Richmond took charge of Head Start in early February, it had a staff of ten. Within two months, the full-time staff had grown to 400, supplemented by interns and volunteers from other government departments. Once, a courier who appeared at the office to deliver a package was asked if he knew how to type; when he said he did, he was put to work immediately and never delivered the rest of his packages. So relentless was the flow of applications that Sugarman and Richmond resorted to setting up factory-like assembly lines. One observer of this system remarked that he had not seen anything like it since World War II.

In March, while the applications were being processed, Head Start sent out a telegram to hundreds of universities, inviting them to set up training programs—and to the pleasant surprise of the Head Start planners, more than 200 universities agreed to offer six-day training sessions in June, preparing some 44,000 people to work at Head Start centers.

On May 18 LBJ held a press conference with Shriver to announce that at least 2,000 communities would open Head Start programs during the summer. By early July, the OEO had received 3,000 completed applications to serve 560,000 children—nearly half a million more children than the original budget had covered. By the end of the summer of 1965, 580,000 children had spent time in Head Start centers, getting not only preschool instruction but also medical checkups, eye exams, and two nutritious meals a day. The program proved so popular and effective that although it had been conceived as a summer program, it was made into a year-round proposition. One study found that Head Start students saw their IQ scores rise 10 points over the course of the six weeks of the program in the summer of 1965.

Today, Head Start remains the most comprehensive program ever mounted to serve the nation's economically disadvantaged children and their families. Despite what Head Start advocates say is the chronic underfunding of the program (today it reaches only about 40 percent of the children who are eligible), Head Start has enrolled nearly 20 million children since 1965. Kay Mills, a journalist who has covered social policy for four decades, argues that Head Start—"the major remaining battalion" from the War on Poverty—is "the best investment America has ever made in its youngest citizens."

But from the time the program was launched, there was debate about whether the measurable gains that Head Start provided would persist as the children advanced through school. From the beginning, Shriver was very concerned to follow up with Head Start alumni, to measure whether their IQ gains and other intellectual improvements would be sustained several years down the road. Discouragingly, the evidence tended to suggest that these gains eroded over time. This led Shriver to create a supplemental program, called Head Start Follow-Through, whose aim was to provide older poor students with the nurturing intellectual and social environment they had gotten through Head Start.

Although the debates persist today about whether Head Start–induced gains in cognitive development can be sustained as children move through elementary and secondary school, the program retains broad political support, in large part because Shriver and his team always emphasized that the program was about more than just raising IQ. Head Start would prepare poor kids for school, of course, but it also provided their first medical evaluations, eye exams, and in some cases their first nutritious meals. Equally important, it drew the children's parents into their education and in many cases drew whole families into the larger Community Action network, giving poor people access to a range of health care, job training, and other services never before available to them.

Head Start may be, after the Peace Corps, the most quintessentially Shriverian creation. Partly this was the effect of the culture in which it was hatched. The offices, in the basement of the old Colonial Hotel, were shabby and dilapidated. The pace of work was feverishly intense. The hours were long and draining. Shriver pushed people harder than they had ever been pushed; the seventeen-hour workday was standard throughout the OEO. (Within a year, Julius Richmond would end up in the hospital with tuberculosis, the result of overwork.) The staff was brilliant and opinionated. "OEO has attracted more bright and more individualistically thinking people than almost any federal program that I've ever seen," Jules Sugarman said. "But the result of that was, nobody was willing to accept the authority of anybody else to make a decision. Every issue had to be fought out time and time again." And, as at the Peace Corps, Shriver's sense of organization—or lack thereof—drove his employees to fits. "He's a guy that you admired and couldn't stand at the same time," one of his associates said. "Some of his administrative practices made a lot of hair stand on end on a lot of scalps."

Yet despite this frenzy, the prevailing spirit was one of hopefulness, camaraderie—and fun. Head Start epitomized the continuation of the New Frontier under the Great Society banner. Presiding over this glorious chaos was Shriver. "A program as complex as Head Start requires great flexibility to be successful," Julius Richmond said. "The person who made such flexibility possible was . . . Sargent Shriver. He helped us keep our eyes on the fundamental goal: a better life for poor young children and their families. Any decision was always measured in terms of whether it took us further down the road to achieve that goal. He helped us avoid rigid, bureaucratic constraints that might inhibit the development of the program."

Even those who initially didn't like Shriver came to be swayed by his invincible enthusiasm. "When I first came to OEO," Jules Sugarman said, "I was not an admirer of Mr. Shriver. But as I worked with him over a period of time and watched him in operation, I became convinced that he was one of the real geniuses of America. I've never to this day seen anyone with the capacity to continually innovate, to continually push for development, that he has. And I've never seen anyone who was any better at analyzing the potentials and the problems and situations, not always knowing what the answers were, but at picking out the weak points in arguments."

Shriver modulated the cultural tone at Head Start (and at the OEO generally) like a maestro. He would play people off against one another to the point where friendships appeared on the brink of rupture—but would then restore comity all around. ("I've never been in such stimulating staff meetings," recalled William Phillips, who served for a time as the OEO's assistant director for congressional relations. "No one ever went to sleep, because you were always guarding your flank against somebody else.") "Ultimately, what Shriver's strongest point was, was just demanding results," says one early poverty planner. "He was tired of the bullshit."

Head Start was enormously popular, but it was not immune to the political problems that beset the Community Action program more generally. Indeed, the single contract that would end up causing the OEO the most trouble over the course of Shriver's tenure was made on May 18, 1965, with an organization calling itself the Child Development Group of Mississippi (CDGM), which was to operate Head Start centers for 6,000 children. The problems with the CDGM developed slowly, unfolding for several years before building to a crisis that threatened the OEO's very existence. But as early as June 1965, the CDGM was a major political headache for Shriver.

The OEO originally made a $1.5 million grant to Mary Holmes Junior College, in West Point, Mississippi, for the purpose of starting a CAA in the region. Mary Holmes, in turn, subcontracted to the CDGM to operate the eighty-five Head Start preschool programs in twenty-four Mississippi counties. The CDGM grant looked at first to be an auspicious one: It was the largest Head Start grant yet made for the crucial first summer of that program's operation. The poor children of Mississippi were precisely the kind of people that Head Start was aiming to reach.

But on June 3, 1965, Shriver received a telegram from Mississippi senator John Stennis, a conservative Democrat and an influential member of the Senate Appropriations Committee, expressing concern about the location of the CDGM's headquarters. Mount Beulah, Mississippi, where the CDGM was based, was a hotbed of civil rights activism and the home base of the Mississippi Freedom Democratic Party, an all-black political organization. And the CDGM was run almost exclusively by African Americans. In this regard, the CDGM was an anomaly among Southern Head Start programs, many of which were all white or mostly white.

Stennis suspected that OEO monies granted to the CDGM for Head Start centers were being funneled into civil rights work. Not satisfied with OEO investigations into the matter, on June 29 Stennis announced that the Senate Appropriations Committee would be sending its own investigative team to Mississippi. Both the Senate team and the OEO team found all kinds of fiscal malfeasance and general mismanagement at the CDGM. So, on August 1 and 2, Shriver sent deputies to Mississippi to demand that the CDGM move its headquarters out of Mount Beulah. CDGM staffers refused to move, declaring they would sooner resign en masse.

Arrayed here in microcosm were the myriad political forces that threatened to destroy Community Action: Southern white politicians, carrying the banner of states' rights, trying to resist racial integration being imposed on them by the federal government; civil rights activists trying inappropriately to use OEO programs as political tools; conflicts between OEO headquarters in Washington and the CAAs in the field; and conflicts among different factions within OEO headquarters. Head Start officials in Washington tended to side with the CDGM. To give in to the demands of someone like Stennis was to defeat Community Action's entire purpose. Moreover, the Head Start staff argued, to withdraw the CDGM's grant, or even to force it to relocate, would disrupt the functioning of the Head Start centers that had already been set up. This would be an affront to the families of the thousands of children already enrolled in these programs.

Battles raged at OEO headquarters. One faction was led by Bill Haddad, the fire-breathing idealist who ran the OEO's Office of Inspection. (Shriver had brought Haddad over from a similar position at the Peace Corps.) Haddad was a strong believer in the "maximum feasible participation" of the poor. Although he conceded that the CDGM's finances needed to be cleaned up, Haddad (and his allies) felt that it was important to stand on principle and allow the local civil rights activists to have their way, at least to a point. Members of the OEO general counsel's office, along with the OEO's congressional liaison office, argued, in contrast, that the CDGM's misuse of funds constituted a clear violation of the grant's conditions and that the program should therefore be terminated. The CDGM had become " a tool of the black militants," OEO general counsel Don Baker recalled. "Some of those [Head Start] centers were feeding SNCC [Student Nonviolent Coordinating Committee] workers three meals a day out of food that was being purchased to feed Head Start kids." Why risk the entire OEO appropriations package, which was controlled by John Stennis, over this one troublesome program?

By the middle of August, the CDGM and OEO headquarters seemed to have reached a compromise. The CDGM could remain for the time being at Mount Beulah but would have to move elsewhere within the year. On August 13 Shriver wrote to Stennis explaining that "the headquarters of the project will continue to operate out of [Mount Beulah] because it has been determined that any relocation, at this time, would have a damaging effect upon the program and it is just not feasible." Stennis found this unacceptable and, after sending a second team of Senate investigators to Mount Beulah in October, declared that the site remained "a center of civil rights activities . . . and a hotbed of racial zealots." Shriver responded that although he could not control what the thousands of Head Start employees did in their nonworking hours, he had "made clear that civil rights work—or political activity of any kind—would not be tolerated during working hours." He also advised the Appropriations Committee that "rightful concern for frugal use of the taxpayers' money . . . should not becloud our vision so completely that we lose sight of the fact that nearly 6,000 Mississippi children received preschool training, physical examinations and medical care, two warm meals a day, and a Head Start for the future."

Because Head Start was such a popular program, Shriver's plea fell on receptive ears in the Appropriations Committee. Stennis admonished the OEO to strictly supervise the CDGM's administration and to ensure that more whites be included in the program. Basically, however, the CDGM was allowed to continue its operations as before. At the time, this seemed like a definitive victory for the OEO. As it would turn out, however, the battle had just been deferred to another day.

CHAPTER THIRTY-THREE

A Revolution in Poverty Law

~

The bad press swirling around Community Action made communities reluctant to open CAAs. But midway through the poverty program's first fiscal year, Shriver found he still had money left to spend on Community Action. So he conceived the idea of what he called "National Emphasis programs," service programs designed and funded by the OEO in Washington but administered through CAAs at the local level. Although the core concept of Community Action was that programs would be designed *locally*, Shriver thought he might be able to design some politically unthreatening programs at the national level and then provide federal funding to the local community leaders who would run the programs at the neighborhood level. The arrangement between the OEO and community leaders would resemble the relationship between a national restaurant company and the local owners of its franchise outlets: The basic rules and administration are established at national headquarters, but the individual restaurants can tailor the design and structure to the needs of the particular neighborhood. The first National Emphasis program was Head Start.

The other major National Emphasis program that Shriver began planning in 1965 was Legal Services for the Poor. That program, more than Head Start, embodied the basic ideological contradictions inherent in the Community Action model: Was the idea to provide services to the poor that would help lift them into the middle class? Or was the idea to use institutional reform to catalyze the political empowerment of the poor?

Before the 1960s, poor Americans seeking legal redress for their problems had little or no recourse for doing so. In fact, for the first hundred years of American history, there were no concrete means for low-income citizens to get legal assistance. The first legal aid organizations—privately funded charitable groups that would provide legal assistance to indigent people—weren't formed until the 1870s and 1880s, and it wasn't until 1923, when a Harvard Law School graduate named Reginald Heber Smith published a book called *Justice and the Poor*, that there was any serious talk of a national network of legal aid organizations. Under Smith's direction the National Association of Legal Aid Organizations was founded—later to be renamed the National Legal Aid and Defender Association—and the number of local legal aid societies grew rapidly throughout the Depression. Even so, by the mid-1960s the amount of legal help available to the poor was far less than the need: By one reckoning, there was only the equivalent of 400 full-time lawyers for 50 million poor Americans, or one lawyer for every 120,000 people—as opposed to one lawyer for every 560 people for the rest of the population. Moreover, legal aid lawyers were reluctant to pursue institutional reform on behalf of the poor: Over the eighty-nine years that legal aid had existed in the United States prior to 1965, not one legal aid lawyer took a case that made it to the Supreme Court.

In most Western European democracies, the government was bound to provide lawyers to those who couldn't pay for them. In the United States, every discussion of federally funded legal aid had run aground on the objections of the American Bar Association, which argued that if the government subsidized legal assistance for poor people, it would erode market rates for lawyers. Any attempt to provide free legal assistance was criticized as "the socialization of the legal profession."

Shriver had initially declined to include a separate section on "legal justice" in the Economic Opportunity Act because he believed that Title II, the Community Action section, was broad enough to include a wide variety of approaches to fighting poverty, including the provision of free legal assistance.

As the War on Poverty got off the ground, however, it became increasingly clear how strong the need was for some kind of federal legal assistance program. Legal aid societies were not numerous enough to contend with all the legal problems the poor experienced—harassment by landlords, cheating by private businesses, unconstitutional treatment by government agencies—and what few legal aid offices there were tended to be located in downtown business districts, not in rural areas or in urban ghettos where the poor lived.

In early 1961, while the Peace Corps task force had been struggling, Shriver's vision for that program had been instantly crystallized by a paper—*The Towering Task*, by Warren Wiggins and Bill Josephson—that he had happened to read late one night at the Mayflower Hotel. In early 1964, while the War on Poverty task force struggled over various issues, a similar epiphany occurred: In April 1964 Shriver received a paper by a husband-and-wife team, Edgar and Jean Cahn, that was soon to be published in the *Yale Law Journal*. Shriver was powerfully struck by "The War on Poverty: A Civilian Perspective": "It was like Columbus discovering America, an exciting thing for me to discover . . . something that captured my mind and imagination. That's the genesis of Legal Services—it's really pretty simple."

In writing the article, the Cahns had drawn heavily on their experience working in the Ford Foundation's "Gray Area" program in New Haven. In November 1962, they had been part of a group of community leaders and social scientists invited to meet with the Ford Foundation's Paul Ylvisaker, to discuss his idea of experimenting with neighborhood centers as a means of reducing urban poverty. Ylvisaker had proposed that one service that might be offered would be legal assistance, and on January 2, 1963, Jean Cahn and another lawyer had opened an office in the building housing Community Progress, Inc., in New Haven, to "diagnose, refer, and coordinate" the legal problems of the poor. Cahn and her colleague worked on some civil cases, but their role became controversial after they undertook to defend a local black man accused of raping a white woman. When Cahn argued that the woman had willingly consented to sexual intercourse, white New Haven erupted in anger. The Ford Foundation was pressured into rescinding its funding; within weeks of opening, New Haven's neighborhood law offices had closed down.

Jean Cahn took away from this experience not only a strong belief in the value of legal assistance for the poor but also the knowledge that for such assistance to be meaningful, it had to have a power base independent of funders within the local community. In "The War on Poverty: A Civilian Perspective," the Cahns argued that Community Action agencies in liege to local political interests would be impotent to help the poor improve their social environment. Thus a "civilian perspective"—that is, a point of view that was not tied to existing welfare bureaucracies or local political machines but that, rather, served the interests of local residents directly—needed to be built into the OEO's Community Action program.

Who could embody that "civilian perspective"? Lawyers, of course. Not only would lawyers be bound by the canons of the profession to serve the interests of their clients (in this case, the poor), but lawyers also would be empowered to use the American court system to seek redress from institutions, including the CAAs themselves, that failed to act in a just or constitutional manner toward the poor. Thus the Cahns recommended that federal funding for neighborhood law offices be written into the poverty bill.

The Cahns' article struck a chord with Shriver, and after the original OEO legislation was passed in the late summer of 1964 he set up a special task force—led by the Cahns—to explore how lawyers might be able to contribute to the War on Poverty. Although the group reached a general consensus about basic principles—free legal assistance needed to be included among the array of services provided to the poor through the Community Action program—they disagreed about how a legal services program should be structured.

To what degree (if at all) should the OEO Legal Services program rely on existing legal aid societies and local bar associations? Some OEO staffers and Justice Department aides argued that in order for the Legal Services program to be an integral part of Community Action, and to be clearly identified with Shriver's poverty program, there should be little or no effort made to involve either the American Bar Association (ABA) or the National Legal Aid and Defender Association (NLADA). These advocates saw the Legal Services program not as a "law" program per se but as another tool with which to generate changes in the social and institutional habitat of the poor. Gary Bellow, a public defender in Washington, DC, and Robert Kennedy's aide Adam Walinsky pointed out that if the OEO involved the local bar associations, it would be "watering down the legal services organizations with conservative lawyers." What Southern bar association, they asked, could ever be persuaded to take on a civil rights case?

But an opposing faction within the task force, led by the Cahns and Abe Chayes, a widely respected State Department lawyer, argued that the program would fail without the support of the local bar associations. Chayes observed that if bar associations were not enlisted, local lawyers and judges would feel as though their turf were being threatened and would consequently make life harder for OEO lawyers. Jean Cahn agreed; personal experience had taught her that CAAs would not always stand up for OEO lawyers when they took controversial cases. But, she argued, the bar associations would. Eventually, the Cahns' argument prevailed: Enlisting the support of local bar associations would be an integral part of the OEO program.

For the moment, the focus of the Legal Services planners was on *local* bar associations. But about this time Lowell Beck, the assistant director of the ABA's Washington office, read a *Washington Post* article about Edgar Cahn. Beck arranged for Cahn—now installed as a speechwriter and "idea man" at the OEO—to have lunch with him and other ABA staff members. At lunch, Cahn shared his vision of a national network of neighborhood law offices in poor areas. Beck said he thought it possible the ABA would endorse the idea.

When Cahn reported this information at an OEO executive staff meeting in late October of 1964, Shriver recognized that the endorsement of a national organization like the ABA would provide a public relations bonanza for the Legal Services program, and he assigned Cahn to arrange a meeting between President Johnson and the leaders of the ABA. Meanwhile, at an ABA conference in mid-November, Edgar Cahn gave a presentation on the OEO's plans for a national Legal Services program. During the question-and-answer session following his remarks, Cahn was attacked by legal aid lawyers, who demanded to know why OEO didn't plan to make use of existing legal aid societies. It was an insult, they said, that OEO would plan a Legal Services program without so much as consulting any of the network of 246 legal aid societies nationwide. Speaking up to defend Cahn, two Community Action advocates angered the legal aid lawyers further by explaining that the reason the OEO was trying to start something new was "because of hostile attitudes and rigidities in established services." Without meaning to, Cahn and company had earned the opposition of the legal aid community. In December NLADA's executive committee passed a resolution declaring its opposition to an OEO Legal Services program. An OEO Legal Services program, NLADA argued, would end up competing with existing legal aid societies, possibly causing their funding to dry up.

NLADA's opposition to a Legal Services program made winning the support of the ABA all the more important, but Shriver made that task harder with a speech he gave in Chicago on November 17. He announced the launch of a national network of "supermarkets of social service" for the urban poor. Neighborhood centers administered by local CAAs, Shriver explained, would provide a host of services, including "homework aides, recreation aides, health aides, and legal advocates for the poor." These services, Shriver continued, need not be provided by professionals.

When the text of Shriver's speech was printed in newspapers across the country the next day, the reaction by lawyers was immediate and hostile. As Edgar Cahn put it, "the idea of putting lawyers in shopping carts really turned [them] off." Also, the prospect of the practice of law by nonlawyers constituted a direct threat to the very existence of the profession. If nonlawyers could practice law for the poor, and for less money, then the middle class would start demanding cheap, nonlawyer legal assistance, too. ABA president Lewis Powell (later a Supreme Court justice) was deluged with angry letters demanding that he take a stand against the travesty Shriver was proposing.

But Powell recognized that the OEO's program offered probably the best opportunity the ABA would have to become more productively involved in legal aid. Moreover, the OEO was likely to move forward with its plans whether or not the ABA supported it. On January 12 the Cahns met with leading lawyers at the ABA's Chicago headquarters and, over the course of a heated eight-hour session of negotiations, hammered out an agreement whereby the ABA would constitute a large part of a permanent advisory committee that would help the OEO establish its Legal Services policies. Over the next week, Lewis Powell and his associates lobbied the ABA membership, and on February 7, 1965, the ABA's House of Delegates voted unanimously to support the OEO. Shriver immediately sent a telegram to Powell to express his gratitude.

But just as relations between the OEO and the ABA seemed to have gotten on track, internal disputes within the OEO threatened to derail the Legal Services program. Jean Cahn was insisting that the OEO create a wholly separate office for legal services, outside of the Community Action umbrella. Otherwise, she said, OEO lawyers would end up serving the interests of the CAAs, rather than the poor directly.

The directors of Community Action staunchly resisted Cahn's plea for an independent lawyer corps. CAAs were supposed to be umbrella organizations; as many services as possible—education, health care, job training, and legal assistance—were to be coordinated under Community Action's auspices. It made no sense to create an entirely separate bureaucracy for legal services.

Shriver had his own reasons for wanting to keep the Legal Services program contained within Community Action's administrative structure. For one thing, he wasn't sure he had the authority to create a legal services program outside of Title II of the Economic Opportunity Act; all the leeway Congress had given him lay within the Community Action section of the bill. More important, with mayors mounting their attacks on CAAs, Shriver needed the additional National Emphasis program to supplement Head Start. A National Emphasis legal services program would give Shriver something concrete he could show to Congress and to the mayors—something that wasn't simply aimed at organizing the poor against City Hall, as local politicians believed CAAs were. Of course, this meant that when he made the case publicly for a National Emphasis legal services program, he had to gloss over its radical, anti-establishment potential: Clearly, it would be best not to mention that the planners of the program imagined OEO lawyers suing City Hall, or even suing the OEO itself. Several years later, Lewis Powell said that "if ABA members had visualized the extent to which OEO funded legal services would be used to challenge government at state and local and federal levels, there would have been a far more vigorous opposition" to ABA endorsement of the Legal Services for the Poor program.

When Community Action's directors (with Shriver's backing) declined to grant the Legal Services program a separate administrative existence, Jean Cahn dug in her heels. In March, she told Shriver that if the Legal Services program couldn't exist outside of Community Action, then at the very least she (as opposed to Community Action administrators) had to be vested with the final decision-making authority regarding Legal Services grants. If she wasn't given that authority by April 1, she said, she would resign from the OEO in protest. When April 1 came and went and Shriver did not grant Cahn the independent authority she wanted, she carried out her threat and quit.

Shriver had gambled that, despite Jean Cahn's instrumental role in bringing the ABA into partnership with the OEO, the ABA's leadership would not be fazed by her resignation, especially as she had expressed such skepticism toward that organization all along. He was right: According to Earl Johnson, ABA lawyers "did not perceive Mrs. Cahn as the director of the Legal Services program but rather as Mr. Shriver's personal assistant whom he was free to retain or discharge." (At one point after she had quit, Jean Cahn attacked Shriver publicly at an ABA meeting; Shriver, somewhat mischievously, assigned Edgar Cahn to write the official OEO response. Newspapers reported the event as "Cahn Attacks Cahn as 'Bureaucrat.'" "There should have been a divorce," Jean recalled several decades later. "There's no question that we should never have stayed married after that." They did stay married, however, and went on to set up Antioch Law School, in Washington, DC, together, where they served as co-deans for a number of years.)

For several months, the Legal Services program was in disarray, trying to move forward without a permanent director, moving from crisis to crisis as a series of temporary appointees occupied the top job. After the first successor to Jean Cahn, William Downs, lasted less than a month, Shriver transferred control of Legal Services to Bruce Terris, who was a lawyer in the OEO's general counsel's office. Community Action director Ted Berry objected to Terris's leadership, claiming that running the program out of the general counsel's office represented a major conflict of interest. Although Berry's real fear was that Community Action was losing control of Legal Services, his allegation of a conflict of interest had merit: after all, how could Legal Services be expected to properly represent its clients (the poor)—bringing suits, if the clients chose, against the OEO—if the program were housed in the department (the general counsel's office) assigned to *defend* the OEO against such suits? Shriver agreed and placed the Legal Services program's grant-making authority under Berry's jurisdiction.

Without a permanent director in place, the Legal Services program drifted aimlessly through the early summer of 1965. Part of the problem was that Berry and Shriver had different ideas about what kind of director they wanted. Berry wanted a middle manager who would defer to him. Shriver wanted someone with charisma, someone who could lend luster—and credibility with the legal profession—to the program. Berry proposed several directors; Shriver (with the concurrence of the ABA) rejected them all as being of insufficient standing in the profession.

The summer dragged on. Head Start was a smashing success, CAAs were up and running all over the country, and thousands of young people were enrolled at Job Corps centers—yet the Legal Services program still had barely any law offices in the field. For Shriver, the situation had become a personal embarrassment. Several months earlier he had agreed to give the keynote address at the ABA's upcoming annual convention in Miami on August 11; his plan had been to use the occasion to sing the Legal Services program's praises, recount its early accomplishments, and celebrate the OEO-ABA partnership. Instead, he was reduced to apologizing for the lack of progress. Although Community Action now had "a health services unit, an education unit, a labor market unit, and others," he said, "we have been delinquent in establishing a legal services unit. And we have paid a heavy price. A price in misconceptions, in lack of continuity, and of consistency, and of close cooperation with the Bar."

Sensitized to the concerns of the profession by its angry reaction to his "supermarket of social services" speech the previous November, Shriver took the opportunity to assuage some of their worries about the OEO and to signal a spirit of cooperation. "We are not trying to take paying customers away from the private practitioner . . . by taking revenue-producing cases." Nor, he said, are we "trying to replace lawyers with social workers or laymen!"

Several weeks later, the ABA sent Shriver a list of recommended candidates to direct Legal Services: Ken Pye, who was an associate dean at Georgetown Law School and a founder of the Washington-area legal aid program; Jerry Shestack, a partner at a white-shoe Philadelphia law firm, who had done a lot of desegregation litigation in the South; and Clinton Bamberger, a young, Baltimore-based lawyer who had recently been named the chair of the Maryland State Bar Committee on Legal Services. After both Pye and Shestack declined to consider the job, Shriver was desperate; he couldn't afford to have Bamberger decline as well, especially because Bamberger had the kind of flair Shriver was looking for. As one ABA board member described him, Bamberger "was establishment. He was a nut. He looked like a Scandinavian Boy Scout. . . . And he was young, and apparently, restless." So Shriver invited Bamberger to OEO headquarters on September 6, determined not to let him leave until he had accepted the director's position. Bamberger says he never actually agreed to take the job—yet somehow, at the end of the day, Shriver was publicly announcing that Bamberger would be Legal Services director.

What followed, Earl Johnson has written, was "the excitement of participating in possibly the greatest adventure in the history of the legal profession."
(Johnson himself was part of that excitement: Bamberger hired him away from
his position as deputy director of the Neighborhood Legal Services Project to
become Bamberger's chief deputy at OEO. When Bamberger left in April 1966
to run for attorney general of Maryland, Johnson became the director.) Over
the next several months, Shriver, Bamberger, and the small Legal Services staff
embarked on a national "sales campaign" to persuade local bar associations and
existing legal aid societies to apply for federal grants through the OEO and
become a part of the Legal Services program. In a tour de force performance
at the NLADA conference in Arizona in November, Bamberger managed to
bring the previously hostile legal aid community around to supporting the
OEO's new program.

In the eighteen months beginning in January 1966, Legal Services opened
neighborhood law offices in 250 cities and towns across the country. In April
1966 alone, the OEO disbursed $6 million in grants to thirty-four Community
Action agencies for neighborhood law offices; that was more money than was
being spent by all the existing legal aid societies in the country. Over the following year, 300 more neighborhood law offices opened, and the Legal Services
program budget for 1967 was $40 million.

THE QUEST FOR EQUAL JUSTICE

Now that neighborhood law offices were finally opening all over the country,
how could they most effectively contribute to reducing poverty? The basic question for Legal Services remained: Was the proper role for a poverty program to
provide *services* to the poor or to *reform the institutions* that trapped people in
their indigence?

More or less by default, the Legal Services program began by providing
services (helping the poor with their legal problems) and then made a calculated strategic adjustment to concentrate on legal reform (trying "test cases"
and engaging in legal advocacy to actually change laws and institutions). In the
summer of 1966, when the OEO's Office of Inspection made its first reports on
neighborhood law offices, it found a standard pattern. Within a few months of
opening, Legal Services "offices and attorneys were swamped by more needy

clients than they could properly represent." As Earl Johnson recalled, "The entire Legal Services program was drifting steadily toward complete preoccupation with the 'processing' of caseloads."

Shriver, who always wanted his programs to have "maximum impact," soon recognized that without increasing the funding for Legal Services a hundredfold, there was no hope of addressing the individual legal problems of the poor in any kind of comprehensive way. Thus he quickly signed on to the growing consensus among Earl Johnson and his team that the Legal Services program's top priority should henceforth be legal reform. "Equal justice cannot be accomplished by solving the problems of the poor on a case-by-case basis," Shriver declared. "There are too many problems, too few attorneys, and too many cases in which there is no solution given the present structure of the law." Legal Services would try to help the poor by challenging the repressive policies of the police, the court system, or the welfare bureaucracy—and on March 17, 1967, law reform was made the first priority of the program.

From that point forward, the Legal Services program focused on test cases and appeals that would help establish new interpretations of existing laws or that would render unconstitutional those laws that violated citizens' rights. During the nine years of the official existence of Legal Services as a federal program, between 1965 and 1974, 119 Legal Services–sponsored cases were argued before the Supreme Court. Legal Services also engaged in advocacy against consumer fraud and slumlord exploitation and embarked on litigation and negotiation with government bureaucracies.

Mickey Kantor, an early Legal Services lawyer who later served as US trade representative and secretary of commerce under President Bill Clinton, recalled that Legal Services

> caused a lot of trouble because clients were pursuing their legal rights using lawyers who at the end of the chain were paid for by the federal government. Members of Congress were very upset about that, because local officials and state officials were being sued, Legal Services lawyers were winning, and it was upsetting the Establishment apple cart in many communities. I think one of Sarge's signature moments was when a member of Congress wrote to him, complaining bitterly about this and raising the question of whether federal funds should be paying for lawsuits against not only state and local governments but also fed-

eral government agencies. Well, Sarge wrote back and said, "My proudest moment will be when Legal Services lawyers sue *me*." And he didn't have to wait long before this happened.

During the 1960s, the elements of the War on Poverty that attracted the most political attention were the Job Corps and Community Action; today, Head Start is widely seen as the most successful legacy of the War on Poverty. Yet a case can be made that Legal Services for the Poor had the most far-reaching effects on American society. In 1969 the OEO general counsel Don Baker said that "legal aid is maybe the most important thing that we are doing. Legal aid will have more impact on . . . our social, economic, and political structures than anything else that OEO and perhaps even the federal government has done on the domestic scene in our lifetime."

In its first six months of existence, the Legal Services program handled 93,000 clients and won nearly 75 percent of its cases. According to one legal historian, "The LSP . . . did seem to increase feelings of political efficacy among the poor. Armed with a tool of government—lawyers—the poor began to believe that they could fight city hall. The lawyers' translation of the poor's problems into legal issues engendered beliefs in 'rights' rather than pleas for charity."

Legal Services also changed how American society thought about legal aid. Legal Services "changed whole bodies of law," Edgar Cahn would recall thirty years later. "It changed the legal profession. It changed the code of professional responsibility. It changed legal education. And it changed legal scholarship." At the 1967 NLADA convention, following the OEO's example, the legal aid societies for the first time adopted appellate advocacy as a formal part of their mandate. They also passed resolutions endorsing the reform of the welfare system through test litigation and suits against federal, state, and local governmental agencies. For better or for worse, this represented a radical change in the profession's approach to poor law.

Legal Services also changed how ambitious young lawyers thought about their profession. "Before the OEO program," Earl Johnson wrote, "it was almost unheard of for a high-ranking graduate of a major law school to accept employment with a legal aid society." But by the late 1960s, according to Mickey Kantor, "the top people in each law school class—Georgetown, Yale, Harvard—

did not want to go clerk, did not want to go to Wall Street. They wanted to go into Legal Services, or into civil rights law. We wanted desperately to get into Legal Services." Legal Services, Kantor says, "inspired a whole generation of young lawyers to engage in public service."

It also politicized that generation. "We saw ourselves," Kantor recalled, "as part of this larger, almost revolutionary movement in America. Real change was happening: the women's movement, the civil rights movement, dealing with the issues of poverty and deprivation. It was a terrific time, an inspiring time, and Sarge Shriver was the epitome of where America was going."

Kantor recalls that Donald Rumsfeld, who headed the OEO under Nixon in the early 1970s and would later serve as George W. Bush's secretary of defense, lamented half-jokingly that Legal Services was cultivating the future leaders of the Democratic Party. Rumsfeld was right: Hillary Clinton, Bill Clinton, Kantor himself, and other leaders of today's Democratic Party either worked in or were inspired by the Legal Services program. At one point during the Clinton administration, the secretary of transportation (Federico Pena), the secretary of commerce (Kantor), the governor of Maine, and the governor of South Dakota were all former recipients of the Reginald Heber Smith Fellowship, which was awarded by Legal Services to the most promising young poverty lawyers each year.

With Legal Services, Edgar Cahn recalled, Shriver "bought into a whole mess of trouble. And he stood by it. He was putting his personal capital on the line. And all the credibility he had built up with the Peace Corps and his own reputation from the private sector." Yet despite all the attacks Legal Services invited—most notably from California governor Ronald Reagan, who wanted to know why the federal government was funding the "left-wing" lawyers who kept suing California's government agencies—Shriver stuck with it. "He was very clear that this had to be one of the National Emphasis programs, that this had to stand out along with Head Start as one of the major thrusts of the War on Poverty," Cahn said. "He was a fighter. He never backed away."

Shriver once reflected that of all the programs he started at the OEO, he was "fondest of Head Start because I was in a sense its father," but he was "proudest of Legal Services because I recognized that it had the greatest potential for changing the system under which people's lives were being exploited. I was proud of the young lawyers who turned down fat, corporate practices to work for the poor, and proudest of them when they dared to challenge state and federal procedures and win."

NEIGHBORHOOD HEALTH SERVICES

A small but important part of the War on Poverty was the Neighborhood Health Services program. By the 1960s, many studies had demonstrated that poverty and illness were mutually reinforcing: Sick people tended to be poor; poor people tended to get sick more often. So in the spring of 1965 Shriver put together a small staff in Community Action's Office of Program Planning and asked them to explore what kind of health care program the OEO might set up under the research and demonstration component of Community Action. Lisbeth Bamberger, the OEO's acting chief of health services, who had been active in LBJ's fight for Medicare legislation, and Sanford Kravitz, who ran the OEO's Research and Demonstrations Division, recruited doctors, experts, and consultants from elsewhere in the government and across the country. Julius Richmond, because he was already working on health care through the Head Start program, was an integral part of the early planning. So was Dr. Joe English, the medical director of the Peace Corps.

As English recalled it, the OEO's Neighborhood Health Services program was hatched on Bastille Day, 1965, at a fancy French restaurant called Le Bistro, where Shriver had invited English and Richmond to lunch. "We've got to go into health," Shriver said over a bottle of expensive champagne. "We're going to go into health in a big way. And I want you guys to do it." As Shriver recalled, he and English and Richmond "talked about the relationship of health and poverty. The statistics were terrifying—three times more disabling heart disease, twice as much infant mortality, five times more mental illness, retardation, and nervous disorders, four times the chance of dying before age thirty-five."

Out of that luncheon came the idea of the neighborhood health center: walk-in clinics that, following the model of the neighborhood legal services office, would be located in inner-city neighborhoods, where poor people could have easy access to them. Many poor people had never been to a physician's office. The Neighborhood Health Center program aimed to change poor people's attitude toward the medical profession. English recalled, "We wanted to make the centers an entry point into the health care industry—an industry that we knew was going to grow like crazy because it was apparent that President Johnson was going to pass Medicare and Medicaid legislation, providing lots of public money."

Bringing the burgeoning health care industry into poor regions was a way not only of improving the health of poor citizens but of providing them new employment opportunities. "There was no better way to solve the problem of poverty than to give people jobs," English said. "So we would take neighborhood people, we would get them a high school equivalency degree, then get them trained as registered nurses, and so within five years we had some of these people scrubbing up to help with open heart surgery. And some went to medical school."

Shriver and company decided to research two kinds of programs: rural and urban. In June 1965 the OEO issued a health care demonstration grant to fund one of each. The rural demonstration took place in North Bolivar County in Mississippi; the urban one, at the Columbia Point housing project in Boston. Within a few months, it was apparent that both programs were successfully providing medical care to the indigent. By the end of the year, Shriver had authorized seven additional demonstration grants, and by the end of 1966 twenty-five Neighborhood Health Centers were in operation across the country. (Today, there are more than a thousand.) In April 1966 Shriver established the OEO Office for Health Affairs, naming Richmond as its director and English as his deputy.

There was a problem, though. The OEO's authorizing legislation had provided no explicit funding for community health centers. With the OEO budget being squeezed by the war in Vietnam, and most of its individual components already underfunded, there was nothing left over for this new initiative. So Shriver and English decided to use one of their allies in the Senate: Ted Kennedy. In August 1966 English persuaded Kennedy to tour the demonstration program at Columbia Point in Boston. The senator spent three hours at the facility, talking to the doctors and OEO staffers who ran it. "What impressed him most," according to his biographer Adam Clymer, "was seeing women in the waiting room in rocking chairs, where they could look after their children or nurse their babies. He thought that recognized the patients' dignity."

"What happened after Kennedy's visit could not happen today," Clymer writes. "It probably could not have happened in any year after 1966. But

Democrats still had overwhelming control of both houses of Congress. The budget deficit was . . . not a big worry. Most of all, the New Deal idea that government could solve problems had been revived. So within a couple of months, Kennedy got money for a program of community health centers through Congress." According to Clymer, Kennedy's visit to the Columbia Point facility was also the experience that pointed him to the cause—health care—that would ultimately distinguish him in the Senate.

Kennedy's amendment to the 1966 OEO bill authorized an additional $100 million in the poverty program budget to create fifty more centers across the country. The amendment was enthusiastically adopted by the rest of the Senate and then accepted (although reduced to $50 million) by the House-Senate conference. By June 1967, the OEO had established forty-one Comprehensive Health Services Programs—or Neighborhood Health Centers, as they became colloquially known—across the country.

As with the Legal Services program, there was some wrangling with the national professional association—the American Medical Association (AMA)—which worried about maintaining health standards and about threats to its doctors' fees. In fact, the AMA had on principle opposed every federal health initiative before 1965. So Sarge, with the help of Eunice, Joe English, and Ted Kennedy, set out to bring that organization around. At one point, Sarge invited Dr. Charles Hudson, the president of the AMA, out to Timberlawn for breakfast. When Hudson arrived, he discovered that Ted Kennedy and some of his staff were also present. Partway through breakfast, Eunice made a choreographed entrance. "Dr. Hudson," she said. "Very nice to see you. And I am so delighted that you are here, because I think the American Medical Association ought to be helping on developing good health care for the poor. And I have to warn you that if you don't, my brothers will, and they don't know anything about it." Evidently, the ploy worked. Hudson came out in support of the program, and, in general, doctors proved more immediately amenable to the OEO's plans than the lawyers in the ABA had initially been.

CHAPTER THIRTY-FOUR

"Double Commander-in-Chief"

⌒

From February 1964 until March 1, 1966, the fifth anniversary of his official first day at the Peace Corps, Shriver served as director of both the Peace Corps and the OEO. Through these two years Shriver endured a grueling schedule. By all accounts, he *averaged* an eighteen- to twenty-hour workday between 1964 and 1968, when he stepped down as the OEO director. His family rarely saw him. "When I look back now," says Sarge's eldest son, Bobby, "I think to myself, 'Wow, I never saw my father for the whole 1960s.'"

During the week, Shriver carried five briefcases (two for the OEO, two for the Peace Corps, and one for the Kennedy Foundation and other matters) everywhere he went, and whenever Richard Ragsdale, the Shriver family driver and jack-of-all-trades, would drive him from Timberlawn to the Peace Corps, or from the Peace Corps to the OEO, or from the OEO to Capitol Hill, Shriver would open one of his briefcases, take out some work, and begin reading and writing. Colleagues marveled that he rarely seemed tired. Shriver recalled:

As the War on Poverty moved into high gear, I began the schizophrenic routine I would follow for the next year. Monday, Wednesday, Friday, and Sunday on OEO business. Tuesday and Thursday and Saturday at the Peace Corps. When I complained to the president about my double responsibility, he said, "If you can't handle a little $100 million program over there in addition to the OEO, I've overestimated you and so has Bob McNamara." He went on to explain that as secretary of defense, McNamara had dozens of individual $100 million programs within his massive department. If he was capable of managing them all, why couldn't I? I tried to tell him why operating two distinctly separate agencies was different, but he was totally convinced he was right and generously autographed a picture of the two of us, "To My Double Commander-in-Chief."

But the two jobs stretched Shriver too thin; this was obvious to colleagues at both the Peace Corps and the OEO. Stretching Shriver thin may have been LBJ's intention. In February 1965 LBJ's aide Marvin Watson wrote to the president, "Sen. Joe Tydings has a campaign under way to entice Sargent Shriver to run as the Democratic nominee for governor in next year's Maryland election. While my immediate reaction is that no good can come to us from this, I don't think we either could or should attempt to take any action other than maybe keeping Shriver so busy on the Poverty and Peace Corps projects that he has little time to think about anything else." By 1965 Harris Wofford observed, "the chief problem for the Peace Corps was Shriver's consuming new anti-poverty assignment, which should have taken, and almost did take, all his time. Johnson overestimated even Shriver's executive abilities and energy."

For at least the first six months that Shriver was running the War on Poverty, it was obvious that his heart remained with the Peace Corps; he had been pried away from it unwillingly by LBJ. The week after President Johnson announced his nomination to head the poverty task force in February 1964, Shriver had addressed 450 employees at Peace Corps headquarters. "One of the things I am most interested in making clear," he said, "is the fact that I am still very much in love with the Peace Corps, and that I do not want anything on the Poverty Program to interrupt my allegiance to or interest in the Peace Corps both here in Washington and around the world. I have always felt that way about the Peace Corps, but right now I am especially captivated by it."

Slowly, however, he was drawn heart and soul into the War on Poverty, despite its many difficulties. Edgar May worked part time for both the Peace Corps and the poverty program after being summoned to Washington by Shriver in February 1964. "It was fascinating to me in those early days," May recalled. "Sarge loved the Peace Corps as much as he loved his mother. The Peace Corps was everything. He used to give what we called the 'flip-card' speech: Half of it would be about the Peace Corps and the other half would be about the poverty program. In the early days, you could hear his voice change when he got to the poverty program. That fire would go out. It was clear to me, since I wrote both parts of the speech, that there was a change in commitment."

"But then," May recalled, "we started to travel. We went to some of the real ghettos in this country. He already knew about West Virginia. (*Every* Kennedy knew about West Virginia.) But we went to Harlem, we went to the South Side of Chicago, we went to slums in small cities. And once he absorbed all that in his pores and his cranium, the issue had reached him and, one day, there was no longer any difference in emphasis, in tone, in fire, in commitment, between the two halves of the flip-card speech. It was an interesting metamorphosis. And at the end, the Peace Corps was merely an add-on."

President Johnson continued to give his strong support to the Peace Corps. Early in 1965, he asked Vice President Hubert Humphrey to convene a conference of returned Peace Corps volunteers in March 1965, so that they could meet with American leaders and discuss the volunteers' "role in national life." Over three days in March, more than 1,000 returned volunteers met with 250 leaders of American society to discuss national issues. To Harris Wofford, this was a "high-water mark of the Peace Corps," as well as "the last large occasion I know about when the spirit of Kennedy's New Frontier seemed alive and strong, despite the assassination." The moment was, Wofford wrote, "the last time the spirit of the Kennedy era would be joined with Johnson's call to a Great Society, a call that still in the spring of 1965 seemed full of promise."

The conference's opening event was a buffet held in the diplomatic reception rooms of the State Department. The event was quintessentially Peace Corps: "the most informal as well as the liveliest gathering ever to have taken place in the ungainly pile of concrete in the heart of Foggy Bottom," as Richard Rovere wrote in the *New Yorker*. The volunteers impressed everyone. They were "sharp, independent, and confident critics of American society," Rovere wrote, and "most of the observers went away persuaded that the Peace Corps' impact on American life may be an immense one."

The day built to a magnificent crescendo, ending in a packed State Department auditorium where Shriver, Humphrey, Chief Justice Earl Warren, Secretary of State Dean Rusk, Secretary of Defense Robert McNamara, and Harry Belafonte all linked arms onstage and belted out a stirring rendition of "We Shall Overcome."

Shriver was not shy about telling the president when he felt the Peace Corps' basic principles were threatened. Several months after a coup in the Dominican Republican had produced a crisis over whether to the evacuate Peace Corps volunteers (they stayed), India and Pakistan declared war on each other over perennially contested land in Kashmir. At the moment war broke out, the Peace Corps had been about to send 176 volunteers to India, the first of what was supposed to be a wave of 1,500. But President Johnson declared that all US aid to both India and Pakistan would be suspended until hostilities ceased, so the volunteers were dispatched instead for "additional training" on Guam and subsequently on an Israeli kibbutz. In September 1965 the UN brokered a cease-fire and Chester Bowles, who had replaced Ken Galbraith as US ambassador to India, told Shriver to send the volunteers as soon as possible.

But President Johnson refused to let him, saying that he would not restore the flow of US aid to India until that country renounced its claim on Kashmir. As the weeks passed, the volunteers got increasingly antsy; among other things, they were forgetting the Hindi they had learned. Bowles repeated his calls for volunteers, pointing out that if they were not sent soon, the Peace Corps would gain a reputation as "a tool for political blackmail." Still, the president refused to yield.

Warren Wiggins, fearing damage to the Peace Corps' reputation, approached McGeorge Bundy and asked him to explain to the president why the volunteers must be dispatched. "Warren," Bundy said, "If you knew the mood the president was in you wouldn't ask me to do that." Bill Moyers concurred: LBJ had made it clear he didn't want any more advice from "Hindu-lovers" like Bundy and Moyers and that he wouldn't release volunteers to India until Prime Minister Nehru kissed his boot.

In response, Shriver sent a blistering memorandum to the president, reminding him of the role Johnson himself had played in 1961 in keeping the Peace

Corps "independent" of foreign aid and not "tied into" the operations of the State Department. ("Without your intervention," Shriver wrote, "President Kennedy might well have decided to make the Peace Corps a part of the regular AID program.") Johnson's petulance toward India threatened to undermine everything. "The independence of the Peace Corps has been the strongest single thing going for us in the rest of the world." Shriver wrote. "The fact that we are not an instrument of diplomacy has contributed immeasurably to the trust and confidence placed in us around the world. It would indeed be unfortunate if other countries get the notion that we now are treating the Peace Corps the same way we treat military assistance and foreign aid." Shriver argued that in foreign policy crises, the Peace Corps' nonpolitical nature had been a useful "talking point," through which to demonstrate the benign attitudes of Americans toward foreign peoples.

"Time is of the essence," Shriver continued. The excuse that the volunteers needed "further training" before being sent was becoming "threadbare." "Communications from India indicate clearly that there is a growing suspicion that the United States might, in fact, be using the Peace Corps as another tactical weapon. If foreign nations get the idea that the Peace Corps is the same as everything else—the Department of State—the foreign aid program—then its mission will surely be jeopardized." Shriver warned that if Johnson continued to use the Peace Corps as blackmail, he would be giving credence to Soviet allegations that the Peace Corps was merely a political tool rather than "people-to-people" assistance.

Evidently convinced, Johnson relented. The volunteers went to India.

On November 2, 1965, the Peace Corps threw a massive anniversary party at the Cow Palace in San Francisco, where John F. Kennedy had first spelled out his vision for this novel foreign aid program five years earlier. Four years into the program's existence, there were 10,200 volunteers serving overseas, 2,100 in training to go abroad, and 6,500 returned volunteers back in the United States. The political problems that were dogging Shriver in his role as OEO director seemed not to carry over to his role as Peace Corps director. A Louis Harris Poll completed in December 1965 found that 77 percent of Americans believed the Peace Corps to be a "useful" or "very useful" instrument of US foreign policy, while only 2 percent of those polled believed the program did more harm than good. At times, Shriver wished he could simply erase the OEO experience and return full time to the Peace Corps, where his legend remained untainted.

CHAPTER THIRTY-FIVE

The OEO in Trouble

For the Great Society, the year 1966 began on a delusional note: President Johnson's "Guns and Butter" speech to the American people. The United States, LBJ declared in his State of the Union address on January 12, "was strong enough to pursue our goals in the rest of the world"—in other words, Vietnam—"while still building a Great Society at home." But within just a few months it would become apparent that Johnson had not spoken the truth. Guns would increasingly displace butter, and limits on domestic spending growth would greatly constrain the OEO.

Shriver had begun to apprehend the new budgetary realities as early as the summer of 1965. Although LBJ had decided not to implement Califano's plan to dissolve the OEO, the president concluded that he would need to hold the line on domestic spending in order to prosecute the war in Vietnam. In discussions with Johnson over the summer, Shriver argued that a tenfold increase in the OEO budget could substantially reduce poverty within a decade. When Johnson told him this was politically unrealistic, Shriver submitted a more modest budget request of $2.5 billion, not quite double the original year's funding. Even that was too high for the president's liking; just before Christmas, 1965, the *Washington Post* reported that "informed sources" were saying that the Bureau of the Budget planned to cut the OEO request to $1.5 billion. It looked as though the War on Poverty would be the first domestic casualty of the war in Vietnam.

Frustrated, Shriver demanded an audience with the president. As Shriver recalled:

> We sat in his office face to face for the first time in months. I was reminded of the last time I had been with him, discussing Community Action, and he had told me we were in for it. Now he was deadly serious, drained, drawn. He told me about his troubles in Vietnam. We had to live up to our obligations. We couldn't lose there. It would take American boys and arms to turn it around. Looking at him, feeling some measure of his burden, I hated to ask him for anything more. I felt I had already been responsible for causing him grief, but I had to tell him what would happen if he did not demonstrate his faith and continuing support of the War on Poverty by increasing his budget request even by as little as a quarter of a billion dollars. That would give us some room to grow. If we didn't grow, the poor would justifiably lose all hope. That would only hurt him, and the country. Finally, he sighed and said he'd change the request to $1.75 billion dollars. We would all save face that way. I'd been with him about twenty-five minutes, and as I left he said, "Sarge, you can tell your children it cost the president $10 million a minute to talk to you."

Shriver had won a small victory—but by the spring of 1966 the OEO was already spending money at an unsustainable rate. Programs would surely have to be cut. This was a blow to Shriver's aspirations for the agency. Political logic demanded that a new initiative like the War on Poverty sustain momentum. But Shriver's only option was to try to do more with less for as long as possible and to hope that more funds would be forthcoming in the future. The Vietnam War would not last forever, Johnson told him; when it ended, the fiscal floodgates would open. In the meantime, however, Shriver and company had somehow to defuse the inevitable frustration that would well up when OEO services that had been promised to communities, based on the expectation of a larger budget, failed to materialize.

AN "ABSENCE OF LOYALTY"

On top of this, Shriver had to deal with an exodus among his top staff people.

Otis Singletary, who had replaced Vern Alden as head of the Job Corps, returned to North Carolina, where he was a university president. Ted Berry, director of Community Action, fell ill and went on leave. Gillis Long, who had headed the OEO's Congressional Relations Department, went back to Louisiana and ran for Congress. Holmes Brown, a top public affairs officer, returned to the private sector. Sanford Kravitz, who had been the first head of Community Action research, returned to academe. Bill Haddad, the head of the OEO Office of Inspection, who had been by Shriver's side since the early days of the Peace Corps, returned to New York City to work in journalism and politics.

Most damaging of all were the departures in late 1965 of Jack Conway and Dick Boone. By late 1965, both Conway and Boone felt that the original conception of Community Action was in danger of being lost; in accommodating the demands of local politicians, the needs of the poor were being forgotten. Boone decided that what Community Action needed was an outside advocacy group, an entity that could, by serving as a mouthpiece for the poor, help counterbalance the pressure to place Community Action under the control of City Hall. So Boone joined forces with Walter Reuther of the AFL-CIO to found the Citizens Crusade against Poverty, with money coming from organized labor and from the Ford Foundation. Conway, who went back to a job with the AFL-CIO, also became a leader of the Citizens Crusade.

"I was perplexed and somewhat hurt by the absence of loyalty I had experienced in the Peace Corps," Shriver recalled of this dark period at OEO.

> At the Peace Corps, we could have the most violent arguments about what we should be doing and where we should be doing it—but once our positions were argued out within the organization and the director had made the decision, the whole organization swung behind him and made it work. The intellectual exchange would often be loud and bloody, but the wounds were never mortal. Everyone recognized this was a form of natural selection, in which the best ideas were the ones that survived. At OEO, too, we could have a knock-down, drag-out fight about some issue leading to a decision on the part of the director—but instead of regrouping behind his decision, the losers would leave the meeting outraged, take their story to the press, and generally either ignore the decision completely or do their best to subvert it. Having lived a sheltered life in the Peace Corps, I was not used to this kind of treatment.

The rapid turnover in the OEO's upper ranks invited scrutiny not only by the press and by Congress but also by the president. In the fall of 1965 LBJ appointed a team of investigators, headed by Bertrand Harding, deputy director of the Internal Revenue Service, to look into problems with the OEO administration. Harding had a reputation as a top-notch administrator, and by the spring he had produced a 200-page secret report, with hundreds of recommendations for improving management. Harding was rewarded—"a verb that may not be well chosen," as one OEO colleague observed—with the deputy directorship of the OEO in June 1966, and in 1968 he succeeded Shriver as director. (Sandwiched between Conway and Harding was Bernard Boutin, who served as Shriver's deputy for eight months; Shriver and Boutin did not get along well, and Boutin soon moved on to head the Small Business Administration.)

Although Harding's investigation ultimately gave Shriver himself a relatively good accounting, the damage was done. The perception of administrative chaos under Shriver produced a series of major newspaper articles recounting power struggles and back-stabbing at the OEO. As Herb Kramer, Shriver's top speechwriter and public affairs officer reported, "from the very beginning, with Mr. Shriver dividing his time for two years with the Peace Corps—spending three days a weeks [at the OEO], two days a week at the Peace Corps, trying to run both operations and without a strong deputy of his own choosing—the program suffered greatly. Internecine warfare was permitted to be carried out—assassinations in the middle of the night, cloak-and-dagger activities—and [there was] a general failure, I think, really to subject programs and procedures to hard evaluative judgments." Another high-ranking staff member suggested that "'Maladministration' may be too harsh a phrase" to describe what plagued the OEO during this time. It was more the case that "Shriver just wasn't interested in administration."

Shriver had had to contend with the occasional negative article while at the Peace Corps and during the OEO's first year, and he was accustomed to political attacks from his opponents. But this was the first time in his life he was forced to endure a protracted run of bad publicity. Shriver recalled that during this period, "driving to work in the morning, reading the paper, I felt as if I were on my way to a perpetual court-martial."

Suddenly, too, his touch with Congress seemed to desert him. When the House Labor and Welfare Committee hearings on the poverty program began in March 1966, the criticisms of him and his program were much harsher—and more bipartisan—than before. Shriver had to compromise from the outset of the negotiations, agreeing to impose stricter federal controls on CAAs and to limit their "administrative" costs.

Even formerly supportive Democrats on the Education and Labor Committee believed that for the 1967 bill to be passed, Shriver would have to agree to accept significant restrictions on his administration of the OEO, and in particular of Community Action. The Democrats caucused secretly to come up with a plan, with one of them telling the *New York Times* that something had to be done because the "participation of the poor" had led to "ugly problems of the political establishment." When the bill was reported out of committee in mid-May, the budgetary authorization was the same as what the president had requested—$1.75 billion—but the revised bill placed rigorous specifications on how the OEO's Community Action funds could be spent. The wide latitude that Shriver had enjoyed in budgetary administration was clearly diminishing.

In the Senate, Robert Kennedy was the staunchest supporter of increasing the OEO's funding. In April 1966 Kennedy declared that OEO's meager appropriation for 1967 was "unfortunate" and "disturbing"; in September he proposed that the Senate raise the government's debt ceiling, so that the president could spend more money on antipoverty programs. Shriver welcomed Kennedy's support of the OEO. Kennedy had become progressively more liberal on many issues, and he now believed strongly that more needed to be done to help the poor. Kennedy also perceived that because the president remained distracted by Vietnam—and because he was increasingly giving only cursory attention to his erstwhile pet program, the War on Poverty—LBJ was vulnerable to political attack from the Left. Coming out strongly in support of the OEO was a way for Kennedy to establish that his position on poverty was more liberal than Johnson's—thereby confirming what Johnson had been trying for two years to disavow: that the Kennedy wing of the Democratic Party was more liberal than he was.

This tactical alliance between Kennedy and Shriver, albeit undertaken without any coordination between the brothers-in-law, fed Johnson's paranoia about the poverty program, which he increasingly perceived as a stomping ground for his liberal enemies. He told HEW secretary Wilbur Cohen that he distrusted everyone from the OEO, and that he wouldn't bring anyone who had worked there into the White House. He started pretending that he couldn't remember the OEO's name, calling it only "Shriver's group." Once, after reading a newspaper clipping that praised Kennedy and Shriver for their liberal stance on poverty, Johnson sent a note to his political aide Marvin Watson. "Marvin: Start keeping a file on these two."

But despite Johnson's waning support for the OEO, Shriver remained loyal to him, espically since by 1967 the political dynamics within the Kennedy family were changing. As Harris Wofford has noted:

> Robert Kennedy was passing Sargent Shriver on the left, as the director of the War on Poverty staunchly defended the soundness of the programs he had started and the senator from New York sharply questioned their adequacy. For Shriver, who had endured the slings and arrows of his young pro-McCarthy brother-in-law during the fifties, when Robert and his friends considered Eunice's husband too liberal ("the house Communist"), the switch in positions was difficult to take.

Meanwhile, the attacks on the OEO continued. In mid-April, Walter Reuther, Jack Conway, and Dick Boone organized a national convention at the International Inn in Washington for their newly formed Citizens Crusade against Poverty. On the first day of the convention, a woman named Unita Blackwell, who hailed from a poor region of the Mississippi Delta, spoke angrily about the false expectations of empowerment the OEO had raised. In Mississippi, she said, the local CAAs were under the control of the police and the mayors, who would beat African American citizens and deprive them of their civil rights.

Shriver was the keynote speaker at the luncheon the next day. When he said, "Negroes are now on the boards of Community Action programs working with white people," a hail of boos and catcalls rained down upon him from the audience. "Where?" they demanded. A group of poor people in the audience crowded toward him, and it seemed for a moment that he might be in physical danger. He tried to continue his speech, but his voice was drowned out by shouts of "You're lying!" and "Stop listening to him." He finished his prepared remarks looking "strained and upset" and declined to take questions afterward. "I will not participate in a riot," he said as he made a quick exit, visibly shaken.

Shriver had never before endured anything like this. For a man who had dedicated the last five years to trying to help the poor, this was a hurtful blow to absorb.

What had caused this disaster? According to Bayard Rustin, the socialist civil rights leader who was also a speaker at the conference, it was the disjuncture between the sunny picture of the War on Poverty that Shriver presented and the reality of life as most of the assembled poor still lived it—untouched (at least in any measurably positive way) by any OEO program—that had caused them to erupt in anger.

Shriver refused to believe that the attack had been spontaneous. The shouting, he argued later, was led by a group of "anti-establishment" militants who viewed the OEO as part of the "establishment." But Jack Conway told the press that Shriver was partly to blame for the eruption. "Shriver was trying to overwhelm them with success statistics," Conway said. "They released their anger and deepest frustrations at not seeing results."

This was a key moment in the history of the OEO. The event signaled that the group that should have been the OEO's strongest constituency—the poor themselves—could be as antagonistic to the program as the most cantankerous urban mayor or the most racist Southern politician. It also demonstrated the growing rift on the Left: a burgeoning New Left, angry and militant, had splintered off from the liberal alliance of civil rights spokesmen and labor leaders, portending the dissolution of LBJ's liberal consensus. And it was the first time that Shriver's vaunted charm and ebullience had failed him in a public forum—and not just failed him but was flung back in his face. From this point forward, fighting for the OEO in Congress, never an easy task, would be much more difficult.

Deliberations on the House bill stalled over the summer, as a power struggle erupted between Shriver and House Education and Labor Committee chairman Adam Clayton Powell. (Angry that a pet project had had its OEO funding rescinded, Powell demanded that Shriver resign as head of the poverty program.) When the bill finally arrived for debate on the House floor, the Republicans smelled blood. They attacked Shriver in scathing terms and introduced more than twenty-five amendments designed to restrict the

OEO's operating authority or to eviscerate it altogether. Democrats aligned with the Johnson administration were able to muster the votes to defeat the most crippling amendments—such as those that would have given Head Start and Upward Bound to HEW, or the Job Corps to the Labor Department—but they were unable to block an amendment by Minnesota Republican Albert Quie that officially codified, for the first time, what "maximum feasible participation" meant. According to the Quie Amendment, one-third of each CAA board had to be composed of representatives of the poor, chosen by the poor themselves. This rule of one-third was already serving as an informal guideline for Community Action administrators, but the Quie Amendment made it a statutory requirement, thereby depriving the OEO of flexibility to adapt programs as it saw fit. The White House was chagrined, recognizing that the GOP had scored a potent hit: LBJ and the Budget Bureau had wanted to de-emphasize the administrative involvement of the poor, since they were getting so much grief from local politicians about it. Quie, with his amendment, was ensuring that local politicians would remain antagonistic toward the White House.

With the Quie Amendment now part of the bill, Democrats were able to push the legislation through the House by a narrow margin. The final bill passed by the Senate gave the OEO $1.75 billion, the same as the House bill, and it included the provision that at least 36 percent of all Community Action funds be put toward Head Start. After the joint House-Senate bill was accepted on October 18, appropriations hearings reduced the OEO authorization by $100 million. The OEO's 1967 budget would be less than one-tenth of what it optimally would have been, nearly one-third smaller than what Shriver had formally requested from the president—and $138 million smaller than what the OEO administrators had deemed the "irreducible minimum" to keep the agency functioning.

The bill was signed into law on November 8, 1966. Two weeks later, Shriver held a press conference. His usual ebullience was absent. "A triple blow has been struck at our ability to extend the War on Poverty to the poor of urban and rural America," he stated. If the OEO had been granted the $3.5 billion he had requested, it could have continued to mobilize its coordinated assault on poverty. At $1.6 billion, however, the OEO would have to go into retreat. Eight thousand men and women would have to be dropped from the Job Corps.

Summer programs for urban youth would have to be cancelled. Legal Services for the Poor would stall. "In summary," Shriver said, "congressional action has curtailed the War on Poverty in 1,000 communities of America for fiscal 1967. And hundreds of additional communities, especially in rural America, will be unable to join the battle."

Frustrated, Shriver contemplated quitting. "The word is out that I am a political liability to President Johnson," Shriver told the *St. Louis Democrat* on November 18. "There have been reports of my resignation ever since I took this job. They have not been true in the past but I am not saying that my resignation couldn't now come about." When this article was brought to the president's attention, he dispatched Bill Moyers to dissuade Shriver from quitting.

Moyers was able to soothe Shriver, but only temporarily. The budget news from the White House kept getting worse; the Vietnam War was crowding out the War on Poverty. In early December, OEO research director Joe Kershaw was called to the White House for a briefing on the budget. What he heard there, as Shriver later recalled, "was shocking and incredible beyond belief. Decisions had been made to expand Vietnam far beyond anyone's expectations. The budget deficit was going far over projections. The War against Poverty would become a casualty—not dead, but in deep shock." To pay for the Vietnam War, the president was proposing to decrease funding for the OEO in 1968. Driving back in the cab from the White House, Bureau of the Budget director Charlie Schultze told a shaken Kershaw that the president meant it this time. "That son of a bitch Shriver isn't going to get anything out of me," Schultze reported LBJ had said.

Shriver had had enough. Friends had for months been telling him to "get out now." Robert Kennedy had made it clear that the family would be happier if Shriver were out of the Johnson administration. And politicians in both Illinois and Maryland were inviting him to run for office in those states. In mid-December of 1966, Shriver told Moyers he planned to quit. Moyers told him to wait and "think it over."

But on December 19, 1966, Joe Califano delivered a handwritten note from Shriver to the president at his ranch. Shriver was resigning. In his explanation to Moyers, Shriver said his reasons for quitting were as follows:

1. President's interest and OEO's in having a new face and new image. 2. Others may think differently, but I have exhausted my bargaining power in the Congress.

I am out of IOUs up there. I do not believe I can be as effective on the fourth go-round as I was on the first three. 3. Having been in this job for three years, I believe it is time for a change. There are certain jobs in which your capital is eroded faster than in others; this is one of them. Someone needs to come in with different friends and different enemies than I have.

As Moyers wrote to the president in a memo, Shriver "said he hopes that his resignation can be handled in a way that does not give the appearance of bad blood between him and the White House. I raised several times the desirability of holding off again for some further thought, but he said he believed this was the time to act."

Vice President Humphrey could see what was happening. He understood the political headaches the OEO was causing for the president. But he liked Shriver personally, and he believed that the War on Poverty would work if it were given sufficient funding. "During the past ten days I have given a good deal of time to some of the problems with the OEO—Shriver—and the difficulties centering around the funds for the poverty program," Humphrey wrote to LBJ on December 17.

I know that the war on poverty is a subject of considerable controversy, but I do know now that the mayors of our cities are for it. A year ago the mayors of our cities were strongly opposed to the Community Action Programs. Now they strongly support them. The mayors are pouring into Congress their complaints over the cuts and asking that funds be restored. This is true, Mr. President, not only of the United States Conference of Mayors, which represents the big cities, but also the National League of Cities, which represents cities of all sizes. . . . You will be asking for a supplemental appropriation in order to cover the needs for the war in Vietnam. It would appear to me to be both morally right and politically wise to ask for at least $100 million to cover some of the minimum needs of the War on Poverty. Even then you would be below your budget request for fiscal 1967. . . . It would be a powerful psychological shot in the arm for those who are waging the war on poverty and clearly put to rest any feeling that we are letting down in our efforts. . . . It would tell the whole country that we are in fact willing and able to fight both wars: the war in Vietnam and the war on poverty at home. And finally, Mr. President, it will make the mayors and the county officials much happier with the Administration. These local officials are desperately afraid of what is going to happen this summer. . . . I have given this memo a great deal of thought. I have had mixed emotions, as you know, about what to do. But I sincerely believe now, after the most careful examination of all the circumstances and facts, that it would be highly desirable in every way if you could see fit to recommend a supplemental appropriation for OEO of around $100 million.

In response to Humphrey's memo, the president agreed to meet with Shriver, and Shriver agreed to stay on at the OEO, with the understanding that domestic purse strings would soon loosen. But no further money was forthcoming.

"SAY IT ISN'T SO, SARGENT SHRIVER"

Another reason Shriver had wanted to quit was that, after a period of relative calm, the CDGM, the Head Start program in Mississippi, had erupted into controversy once again. The tensions over the CDGM had begun to build in early 1966, when the OEO authorized an additional $5.6 million grant to the Mississippi program on February 22. Senator John Stennis said the grant would fund "extremists."

On July 7, when the CDGM submitted an application for a $41 million grant to put an additional 30,000 children through a year of Head Start, the OEO rejected it. Head Start associate director Jules Sugarman traveled to Mississippi to explain to the CDGM's leaders that their grant request was far too large and that, moreover, the OEO's Office of Inspection had uncovered continuing irregularities in the administration of the CDGM. He gave the CDGM fourteen days to answer a series of questions about, for example, how it was spending its money and why the program still excluded white people (as both staff and clients). The CDGM's answers, sent to the OEO on August 8, were deemed unsatisfactory. On September 26, after many furious internal debates, the OEO Legal Department concluded that the CDGM could not lawfully be refinanced without a complete overhaul of its operations.

Shriver was reluctant to shut off a Head Start program serving thousands of children. Also, although he couldn't say this publicly, he liked the fact that the CDGM served mainly African Americans: To him, that was a strike against

Jim Crow. Elsewhere in the South, members of the Ku Klux Klan and other racist groups were preventing black children from enrolling in Head Start. But with the OEO's 1967 appropriation hanging in the balance—and indeed the OEO's very existence at stake—he couldn't afford to have one program in Mississippi attracting too much negative political attention.

On October 1 the OEO mailed a fourteen-page report to the CDGM board, explaining the decision not to continue its funding. The array of problems was substantial. Many tens of thousands of dollars were completely unaccounted for. Thousands more had been spent on ill-advised or unauthorized expenses. Salaries had been paid to people who hadn't shown up for work. The program, the report alleged, "has been increasingly oriented toward the economic needs of adults rather than the educational and development needs of children." The report concluded, "Further funding of CDGM would not be in the best interest of a strong, well-managed Head Start program, of the type which OEO intends to see continued in Mississippi."

A week later, Shriver announced that the OEO would be awarding new Head Start grants to several colleges and Community Action agencies in the state. In response, more than 3,000 African Americans came together the next day for an anti-OEO rally at the campus of Jackson State University in the state capital. The chairman of the CDGM, Rev. James McCree, declared that he would fight against Shriver's "political tricks and manipulations" until the group's funding was restored. McCree brandished telegrams of support from numerous individuals and groups, including Martin Luther King Jr. and the Citizens Crusade against Poverty.

Shriver wrote back to the Citizens Crusade on October 10, reasserting the OEO's position and highlighting the CDGM's failure to run a racially integrated program. "We see every reason in morality and public policy to encourage racially integrated groups in Mississippi," he wrote. "We intend to encourage such groups in Head Start and other programs. . . . Further procrastination, after weeks of discussion and review, could only deny vitally needed Head Start services to children in Mississippi." The next day Shriver announced another large grant, to Mississippi Action for Progress (MAP), for running a full-year Head Start program for 5,000 children. MAP's board was racially integrated and included many prominent Southerners, including Aaron Henry, the regional NAACP director, and Hodding Carter III, the editor of the *Greenville Delta Democrat Times*.

On October 15 dozens of clergymen picketed OEO headquarters in Washington, accusing the agency of "throwing road-blocks in the way of maximum feasible participation of the poor in antipoverty programs." Shriver met with the protesters and denied that he had bowed to political pressure in cutting off the CDGM's funding. He reiterated that the program had been cut off because of management and racial problems; if those problems could be rectified he would consider renewing the CDGM's funding.

Evidently, his argument was not persuasive. When Shriver opened the *New York Times* on October 19 he was confronted with an alarming full-page advertisement. "Say It Isn't So, Sargent Shriver," screamed the large-point type across the top of the page. Paid for by a group calling itself the National Citizens Committee for the Child Development Program in Mississippi, and signed by dozens of prominent ministers, civil rights leaders, and others, the text of the ad read, in part:

> Awesome political pressures have made Poverty Chief Shriver abandon a Head Start program considered "the best in the country." 12,000 Mississippi children, and their parents, are praying he'll change his mind.
>
> Of all the battles Sargent Shriver has fought to keep politics out of the poverty program, none is more crucial than the campaign to save the Child Development Group of Mississippi.
>
> At the moment it looks as if Sargent Shriver has given up.

Although the CDGM was "what Sargent Shriver and his poverty warriors have been battling for all along," the advertisement charged that political leaders feared "the prospect of a self-emancipated Negro community" and so had pressured Shriver to drop the CDGM in favor of MAP, whose board was more acceptable to the Mississippi establishment. The advertisement deeply upset Shriver. "I'd never really seen him as moved and angry," Jules Sugarman recalled. "It was a terrible reflection on his personal integrity."

Shriver fired back in a letter to the *Times*. "The *Times* prints a message entitled 'Say It Isn't So, Sargent Shriver,' dealing with the Head Start grants in Mississippi. For over two weeks I have been saying that it isn't so, that it hasn't been so, and that it will not be so. But some people are unwilling to listen. It is shocking to me that any Americans, and especially members of the clergy, should rush into public print impugning the motives of a public official before ascertaining the facts." Shriver went on to provide a lengthy history of the OEO's involvement with the CDGM. He explained that he still took "great pride" in the CDGM's past work and that he had hope for what it might accomplish in the future. "There is no group of individuals in the country which has sought and prayed for CDGM's success more than we have at OEO," he wrote. He recounted how the previous February he had given the CDGM one of the largest Head Start grants in the country, "despite problems and loud protests." But "we could not in clear conscience and under the law ignore findings of payroll padding, nepotism, conflict of interest, and misuse of property. I reject and resent charges that forces outside my agency made that decision—or that I knuckled under to any pressures. I did not." He also explained that he had not written off the CDGM and would be meeting with its board a few days later.

Years later, Shriver would recall that

during that period of turmoil . . . I became the bad guy in the picture. What my zealous critics really did not understand—and some of them, I presume, still don't—was that if we had continued financing CDGM in its original form, not only would CDGM have been stopped but the whole War on Poverty might have been stopped. There is no question about that. I was trying to defend CDGM. But those people were so zealous, so religiously dedicated to what they were doing—and not without good cause—on behalf of the black people in Mississippi, that that was all they could see. I was accused of being a political opportunist, of simply trying to curry favor with Congress. My critics thought I was not sufficiently interested in blacks, or in CDGM. They thought I did not understand the situation, or that I was gutless and couldn't take the political pressure.

In fact, Shriver says, he knew exactly what he was doing. Yes, he was concerned about what Congress would think, but he was always thinking also about the racial politics on the ground in Mississippi, something many of his critics failed to understand.

Under pressure from the White House to resolve the situation, Shriver flew to Atlanta to meet with the CDGM board on October 24. Negotiations continued into November, when Shriver was presented with a difficult decision. During this time, the OEO was continuing to issue new Head Start grants on a piece-meal basis to various groups in Mississippi. One of these grants, to a CAA called the Southwest Mississippi Opportunity, Inc., was vetoed by Mississippi governor Paul Johnson, who argued that the group had been infiltrated by former CDGM employees. Under the compromise wording that had been written into the original poverty program legislation, Governor Johnson was within his rights to veto any OEO program in his state—but Shriver, as the OEO director, had the right to override that veto. Up to this time he had rarely invoked this right, in part because few governors ever vetoed federal dollars coming to their states and in part because, when they did, Shriver did not want to antagonize them politically. Sizing up the situation, he determined that there was no reason a new Head Start program shouldn't be allowed to hire employees from an old one; he also recognized that if he wanted negotiations with the CDGM and its supporters to succeed, here was a perfect opportunity to demonstrate his fealty. He overrode the governor's veto.

This seemed to have the desired effect. On December 16, Shriver declared that an "agreement in principle" had been reached between the OEO and the CDGM. The CDGM agreed to bring at least six white people onto its board; to turn responsibility for financial administration over to Mary Holmes College; and to prohibit employees from participating in any political activities during working hours.

On January 30, 1967, the OEO made a $5 million grant to the CDGM, to enroll 6,000 children in Head Start centers in fourteen counties. The crisis was over. Head Start in Mississippi had survived.

But the damage had been done. Shriver had been attacked by Congress, undermined by the White House, and assaulted by the poor. As 1966 drew to a close, Shriver's political standing was the lowest it had ever been.

At Timberlawn over Christmas, Shriver tried to relax with family and friends. But on the night of December 22, the Shrivers were entertaining Randolph Churchill, the British prime minister's son, and his daughter when suddenly the sound of Christmas carols rang out in the still, crisp night. "We listened for a moment, smiling, to this lovely reminder of the season," Shriver later wrote. "Then we realized the words were unfamiliar, harsh, mocking." As Bobby and Maria Shriver looked on wide-eyed, their father went to the door and found a group of forty or fifty angry members of a group called the

Washington Underground, who were upset by the cutbacks in OEO programs. "They had decided to dramatize their discontent by picketing my home," Shriver recalled. "Waving signs that read 'Shriver go to Hell; you too LBJ,' they sang their mocking carols."

Oh Come! All you poor folk
>Soulful and together
Come ye, Oh come ye to Shriver's house
>Come and behold him—politician's puppet
Oh Come and let us move him
>Come and sock it to him
And send him on his way
>To LBJ

CHAPTER THIRTY-SIX

King of the Hill

A s 1967 dawned, Shriver had little reason to be hopeful about the new year. For the OEO, in fact, it looked as if it would be even worse than the year before. The agency would have to function with insufficient money to operate its programs properly and would have to close some programs down. And because the legislative and appropriations process had dragged on for so long in 1966, Shriver had no time to rest before beginning his assault on Congress once again, for fiscal year 1968.

His five-year love affair with Congress seemed finally to have ended. The congressional hearings of the previous year had been more rancorous by far than anything he had experienced in the past—and the animosity generated in 1966 was sure to be amplified in 1967. Worse, 1966 had been a disaster for Johnson and the Democrats at the voting booth: The Democrats had lost fifty seats in the House and three in the Senate. Seen as a referendum on Johnson's Great Society, the 1966 election results could only be interpreted as a repudiation. For Shriver, this meant that getting the 1967 OEO bill passed would be harder than ever. The combination of weaker Democrats, more aggressive

Republicans, and unmet expectations had created a political nightmare for the poverty program.

The support of the president that had been so crucial to the OEO's launch in 1964 was now scarcely in evidence—and in any event, that support would now be of questionable value. Johnson was chastened by the 1966 election results. His approval ratings were in decline. The Vietnam War, far from nearing resolution as he had hoped, had become a quagmire. Riots had raised questions about the president's ability to maintain social comity and order. He looked as if he had aged ten years in the last two.

LBJ's State of the Union address on January 10, 1967, augured poorly for the OEO. Johnson did speak about the poverty program, although not in any way resembling the forceful, positive manner he had in previous years. He called for more programs and more money—but the tone of these requests was subdued, almost desultory. He now stressed the *difficulties* in fighting poverty, rather than the *possibilities*, comparing the War on Poverty to the war in Vietnam. The fight against poverty was "not a simple one. The enemy was difficult to perceive, to isolate, to destroy." There would be as many setbacks as advances; weapons that didn't work would need to be discarded. All in all, it was hardly an enthusiastic endorsement of the OEO's efforts. Indeed, it seemed as though LBJ were capable of viewing domestic programs only through the prism of Vietnam.

The president's support seemed so tepid that rumors began to circulate that he planned to defer to Republican criticism and dismantle the OEO, moving control of Head Start to HEW. On February 16 Joseph Califano held a press conference to rebut these charges. Califano said that the president planned to "fight for [OEO] with everything he's got." Califano added, "I might say that the stuff in the newspapers over the last several months about the president not fighting for the poverty program is just a lot of hogwash and trash. It's just not true. I think he spent as much time working with Sarge on putting together this program as he did on any program that's going up there [to Capitol Hill] this year." This statement temporarily dispelled the rumors about the OEO's impending demise—but coming from Califano, who barely more than a year earlier had himself proposed the effective dissolution of the OEO, it hardly reassured Shriver.

Shriver and his colleagues began preparing for the political battle of their lives. He gathered his most loyal men and women around him. As he recalled,

"Cutting through the agency's organization chart, I brought together a group of people I knew were loyal to me, devoted to the program, and thoroughly able to handle themselves in the clinches of a tough, rough and tumble fight. For an entire year of our struggle with Congress, this group was to meet in my office at nine o'clock each morning. The nature of our strategy was 'us against them.'"

These meetings, which many of the participants have described as the most stimulating experience of their life, would begin with the OEO inspector general Edgar May talking about trouble spots. Then Herb Kramer would describe press coverage. Hyman Bookbinder would report on private organizations. George McCarthy would report on the vagaries of Congress. "In that room," Shriver recalled, "we discussed ideas, strategies, and personalities in terms that could have had us jailed, committed, or fired. But not one leak—not one betrayal of a confidence—ever emerged from those sessions. Phil Hardberger [the OEO executive secretary] would produce action lists, and things would get done."

Early in the House committee hearings, Shriver threw down the gauntlet, declaring that the "single basic issue" before them was whether the OEO would be allowed to continue as "the central command post of the war on poverty." Now that the first two years of the program had put poverty on the national agenda and raised the hopes of the poor, Shriver asked, was Congress prepared "to tear out the engine which powered the progress?"

The general thrust of the bill the White House submitted to Congress was to temper the OEO's ability to innovate and to create new programs. The president requested $2.06 billion for the OEO, a 25 percent increase over what Congress had authorized the previous year. Most of the OEO's existing programs were to receive only slight funding increases or none at all.

Worn down by three years of attacks by mayors and political machines and weakened by the 1966 elections, the White House decided to grant ample concessions to local political establishments. Henceforth, the 1968 draft bill decreed, CAAs would be required to give key administrative roles to local elected officials—in other words, "maximum feasible participation of local politicians."

Supporters of Community Action attacked the administration's bill. The president, they argued, was caving in to mayors who viewed CAAs as independent power bases that threatened City Hall, and to legislators who feared that CAAs would produce rivals for their congressional seats. The net result, critics alleged, was to shift Community Action's emphasis away from its core principle: the participation and empowerment of the poor. If the administration's bill passed, the *New Republic* editorialized, Community Action could be pronounced dead.

Carl Perkins, the laconic Kentucky Democrat who had replaced Adam Clayton Powell as chair of the House Education and Labor Committee, introduced the administration's poverty bill in the House on April 10. Four days later, Pennsylvania Democrat Joseph Clark introduced an equivalent bill in the Senate. The Senate bill got a boost in June when a four-month investigation chaired by Clark concluded that the OEO, although it continued to have administrative problems, was proving on balance to be effective. "Great expectations have been aroused in America for the poverty program, and those great expectations have largely been aroused by the work of the OEO and its dynamic director, Mr. Shriver," Clark said. "The poor are participating in their own programs, sometimes clumsily, sometimes ineffectively, but these expectations have been aroused, and in my judgment they will not be satisfied until many more significant victories have been won than have been won so far."

But on June 8 Albert Quie of Minnesota and Charlie Goodell of New York introduced a bill in the House of Representatives proposing a Republican alternative to the OEO, called "the Opportunity Crusade," which would have transferred all of Community Action, along with other programs, into HEW. Although the Opportunity Crusade actually proposed to *increase* both antipoverty funding and the participation of the poor, its primary goal was to terminate the OEO and call off the War on Poverty.

Congressional hearings on the OEO dragged on endlessly through the summer. Altogether, there were seventy days of hearings, with more than 500 witnesses testifying. Shriver himself spent a staggering amount of time on Capitol Hill. "Like the poor," one congressman joked, "we have Shriver always with us." He spent forty-one hours testifying before the House Committee on Education and Welfare and the Senate Subcommittee on Employment, Manpower, and Poverty.

For a brief period in July, Shriver saw a glimmer of hope. The outpouring of public support for his agency was turning out to be much greater than anyone had anticipated. Testifying before a House Committee that month, he said, "The question at which you have taken a long, hard look is this: Should there be an OEO? Of the ninety-seven public witnesses who have appeared before you, sixty-four have addressed themselves to this question in their testimony. Of these, only one has called for the elimination of OEO."

Beyond the Capitol Hill hearing rooms, deeper historical forces were rumbling: The civil rights movement and Community Action had uncorked years of repressed frustration. In Newark, New Jersey, on the evening of July 12, 1967, the arrest and alleged beating of a taxi driver triggered a week of rioting. Over the following month, 164 violent riots erupted in twenty-seven cities across the country, killing dozens of people, injuring hundreds, and causing hundreds of millions of dollars of property damage. At times, the country seemed on the brink of a full-scale race war. The social fabric, it appeared, was coming undone.

For the OEO, the riots were a catastrophic development. Politicians and reporters accused antipoverty programs of fomenting the riots. Hugh Addonizio, the mayor of Newark, said that riots in his city had been "fueled by the rash of wild and extremist statements and behavior of the past ten or twelve weeks" by antipoverty workers at local CAAs. Politicians from Texas, Illinois, and elsewhere similarly alleged that OEO programs had helped cause the riots.

These allegations were not entirely baseless. In some cases, the OEO clearly had given money to black militants. For instance, the Black Panther Party, the most famous black nationalist group, was founded in the Oakland CAA where Bobby Seale held an administrative job. (Hired to teach black history, Seale was introduced to several of his future Black Panther associates through the poverty program. "I was able to meet a lot of the young cats who would later become lumpen proletarians," Seale later wrote.)

Shriver immediately took action, instructing Edgar May's Office of Inspection to launch a thorough investigation of every single riot or disturbance in a city where the OEO had a program. On July 20, after the first week of rioting, Shriver sent a message to all his regional directors, declaring that OEO funds would immediately be withheld from any program deemed to have tolerated behavior that contributed to civil disorder. On July 31 he appeared once again before the House Committee to explain the OEO's official policy on the uprisings. In his testimony, Shriver struck a balance between a call for law and order and an understanding that the root causes of the violence lay in the impoverished conditions of urban ghettos. "After the riots began," he said, "voices of reason and order swiftly announced: 'We will not tolerate violence. We will not permit lawlessness.' And they are right. But there are voices that say, 'We cannot, as a nation, tolerate the conditions that produce violence and lawlessness.' And they are right, too." The uprisings, he continued, were a result of the "explosive store of discontent" that lay beneath the surface of the American ghetto, "waiting for a random spark to ignite it."

Shriver disclaimed any OEO responsibility for the riots and decried "attempts to create doubt and fear about the role of the War on Poverty" as smear tactics by the poverty program's opponents. In truth, it is hard to measure what kind of contribution Community Action made to the spirit of revolt that seized the nation in the late sixties. Undoubtedly the "maximum feasible participation" of the poor politicized—and indeed radicalized—many formerly docile ghetto residents. And it is also surely the case that the high expectations that the War on Poverty generated and then failed to meet contributed to the frustration felt by ghetto denizens.

Yet after examining the results of Edgar May's investigations, Shriver could truthfully say that "in almost every one of the 1,050 communities where Community Action exists, there is ample evidence that the CAA is calming fears and frustrations, bridging the communications gap between the poor and the rest of the community." Shriver was able to produce testimony from dozens of mayors, police chiefs, and other local officials to the effect that antipoverty workers had done a great job of calming communities down in the aftermath of the riots, helping police and firemen, providing food and shelter, and cleaning up the rubble.

The Senate agreed with Shriver. In the House, however, longtime critics of Community Action seized on the allegations of links between antipoverty workers and rioters. Oregon Democrat Edith Green said that she had grave misgivings about a federal program that financed political disturbances. Green stated ominously that Congress would be scrutinizing the new OEO bill very carefully that year.

The riots continued throughout the summer. It seemed as though every one of the OEO's nine o'clock meetings began with Shriver asking, "Ed May, where do you anticipate next week's riots are going to be?" Shriver hoped that by expanding programs on an emergency basis in areas where riots seemed imminent, the OEO might be able to prevent unrest before it happened. To a degree, this plan seems to have worked. But the policy generated controversy on Shriver's staff: The fear was that once people figured out that to get more emergency federal money all they had to do was prepare to riot, they would manufacture unrest where there would otherwise have been none.

May's office continued its inspections through mid-September, at which point it released a more thorough report, surveying mayors and police chiefs in sixty-four cities. The message these officials sent was clear: They wanted to keep the OEO administration and programs in place.

But this favorable accounting seemed at first to have no effect on Congress. A series of amendments proposed by Republicans would have cut the OEO's budget by nearly 50 percent. Then, on October 11, the House delivered its most stinging blow by adding an amendment to the federal pay raise bill, declaring that the OEO would be the only agency in the government whose employees would not be given pay raises.

Meanwhile, the OEO had run out of money to administer its programs. The previous fiscal year had expired on June 30, and the next year's appropriation still hung in the balance. This in itself was not unusual. In its three years of existence, the OEO had never yet gotten its new appropriation authorization before its previous one had run out; this was true of many other federal programs, as well. Ordinarily, it would not be a problem; Congress could just pass interim "continuing resolutions" for agencies that had run out of funds, so they could keep operating normally. This year, however, Congress dragged its feet in passing continuing resolutions that would have extended the OEO's spending authority. The OEO seemed to have been placed last on Congress's list; every other agency and bureau would be attended to first.

The agency was able to pay its employees through August. But when summer ended without the passage of an authorizing bill or continuing resolution, the situation became dire. The Treasury Department cut off the OEO's credit line. Travel expenses were denied. No new employees could be hired. The agency was barred from ordering supplies or entering into contracts with other government bureaus. By November 9, 1967, Shriver no longer had a single spare dollar to spend on his programs: as a result, three Job Corps contracts lapsed and sev-

eral CAAs were forced to shut down for lack of funds. It looked as though the
OEO would die of fiscal starvation before Congress voted on the new bill.

As he had a year earlier, Shriver threatened to quit over the decreased funding. In an interview with CBS reporter Daniel Schorr on November 6, he said,
"I think it would be a gross deception to delude the American people that
something substantial is being done about problems here at home such as lack
of education, lack of health, lack of justice, lack of housing, lack of opportunity, to delude them that something is being done about it when you appropriate so little money that you can't do anything substantial about it." When
Schorr asked him if he would continue as the OEO director if he were not
given sufficient funds to run the War on Poverty effectively, Shriver said, "No.
I've just said that I think it would be a delusion of the poor. It will be a deception to the general public and therefore I don't think it would be advisable to
continue a fraud."

But at precisely this moment, when it seemed the War on Poverty was sput-
tering to an ignominious demise, a groundswell of support for the program
welled up from the grassroots. When the OEO stopped being able to fund local
CAAs, other entities—state and municipal governments, foundations, and even
wealthy individuals—stepped in with the money to keep them afloat. When
people saw communities working together to keep the OEO's programs functioning—there were stories, for instance, of local VISTA workers being put up
in county jails by local sheriffs so they wouldn't have to pay for housing, and
of CAA employees working for nothing—they expressed a new public sympathy for the War on Poverty. Middle-class voters were outraged when the OEO,
alone among government agencies, was denied the right to issue pay raises.
The OEO, it seemed, had had a strong, if latent, constituency after all—and not
just among the poor. Congress was flooded with letters from prominent
Americans—especially businessmen and industrialists, whom Shriver had personally rallied—and ordinary citizens, demanding that the OEO be funded.
Shriver and his inner circle also successfully launched what they called
"Operation Republican Mayor," in which they got twenty-one Republican mayors to sign a strongly worded letter in support of the OEO. "The programs are
a positive force in lessening social tensions in our cities," the mayors declared.
"All of us are confident that they will continue to improve and are so meaningful as to give our less fortunate citizens a new hope in life."

Succumbing to public pressure, Congress authorized a temporary spending resolution on November 28. The OEO was back in business.

This allowed the OEO to resume normal operations, but only temporarily; the authorizing bill for 1968 still hung in the balance. Indeed, while the OEO had been struggling to stay afloat, Shriver had been mired in debates in the House, where Republican representatives were doing everything they could to prevent the reauthorization of the program. Both Shriver and LBJ knew that if the OEO bill were to have any chance of passage, it would have to include significant concessions to the program's critics. So the Johnson administration's bill included a new requirement that, in each locality, the highest-ranking elected official (normally the mayor) automatically be given a role on every CAA board. Some people, Shriver conceded, would perceive this new stipulation as a "sellout to the establishment." But "the truth is that in nearly all cases locally elected officials already have representation." Community Action worked best, he explained, where the poor and the local public officials worked together—not in opposition.

There is no question that as Community Action evolved, it moved away from the vision that task force members like Dick Boone and Frank Mankiewicz had initially conceived: empowering the poor to agitate *against* the local political structure for institutional reform. This tempering of the program's radicalism is evident, too, in Shriver's changing rhetoric about Community Action; in the context, some tempering of the more radical original premise of Community Action was politically necessary. In truth, though, Shriver's view of Community Action never changed much—and it certainly changed far less than many of his colleagues' views did. From the very beginning, he had viewed Community Action to be more a collaborative project than an antagonistic one. Like Boone and Hackett and others, he wanted to agitate the poor into political consciousness. But such was the nature of Shriver's optimism that he always believed that however "agitated" the poor might become, they would still be working in concert with—rather than in opposition to—local government. His optimism in this regard was not groundless: In the Peace Corps, volunteers raised poor citizens' political consciousness and taught them about civic engagement but also provided various services in conjunction with the local ruling authority; these activities were not mutually exclusive.

It is a measure of how acutely controversial the program had become that when Shriver presented the administration's bill it was attacked harshly from two opposite directions. Community Action's original supporters attacked it as " a sellout" to the establishment; members of Congress attacked it for still having "too much Alinsky in it." Oregon representative Edith Green was the most relentless attacker from the latter camp. "The original legislation did not intend to create a new governmental structure of powerful political bodies with the luxury of millions of federal dollars to spend and none of the responsibilities of raising any of that money," she said. To rectify this, she proposed an amendment that would require the ruling authority for any CAA to be the state or local government. This, Green said, would ensure that although CAAs would still operate under "broad federal direction," their immediate administrators would be locally elected "commanders" who would provide "home rule." Also, the preceding year's legislation had included the stipulation that one-third of the CAA board be drawn from the ranks of the poor; Green's new amendment would require that one-third of the board be elected public officials and one-third be representatives of business or civic groups.

The ensuing debate over Green's proposed amendment lasted for more than two full days. Some of Green's Democratic colleagues strenuously objected to the new stipulation. The OEO issued a statement saying that the Green Amendment, if adopted, would result in a "drastic revision" of Community Action's original mandate to encourage the "maximum feasible participation" of the poor. But just before midnight on October 18, the Education and Labor Committee voted to approve the Green Amendment.

In its official statements, the OEO continued to object vigorously to the Green Amendment, arguing that it would destroy the essence of Community Action if it were not removed from the final bill. Privately, however, Shriver and his colleagues were grateful for the amendment—in fact, the OEO's congressional liaison George McCarthy even helped Green to draft it. The amendment provided the OEO with the necessary political cover to get the bill approved by those critics—the states' rights Southern Democrats, city mayors, and congressional representatives from urban districts—who felt threatened by their local CAAs. (For this reason, Republicans attacked Green's proposal as the "bosses and boll weevil amendment," in reference to the groups it would appease.) With the Green Amendment now giving them effective control over the CAAs' activities, politicians could hardly object to the federal money the agencies brought in.

There was another problem though: the strong pressure, not only in Congress but within the executive branch, to spin the War on Poverty's constituent parts off into other cabinet departments, as a means of dissolving the OEO. LBJ's adviser Harry McPherson proposed junking Community Action altogether—or at the very least "saving what is worth saving and renouncing the rest." Other Johnson advisers were more emphatic than McPherson and proposed moving all of the OEO into the Department of Health, Education, and Welfare under Secretary John Gardner. As always, Southern Democrats and conservative Republicans in Congress were eager to spin off Head Start and the Job Corps in particular, as this would effectively castrate the OEO. Shriver knew that once the War on Poverty's most popular programs were spun off, all that would be left would be Community Action—in other words, "nothing but trouble."

The OEO's congressional lobbyists responded with a deft bit of political jujitsu, asking Southern Democrats if they really wanted to see Head Start under the control of Office of Education director Harold Howe—who was anathema to Southerners because he kept trying to force the integration of their schools— or if they wanted to see the Job Corps under the control of the Labor Department, which was enforcing antisegregation policies in the workplace.

George McCarthy, the OEO congressional liaison, recalled going to Mississippi senator James Eastland about the proposed amendment to spin off Head Start.

"Senator," McCarthy said. "There's going to be an amendment coming up."

"An amendment on OEO!" Eastland said. "You know I can't help you on that OEO business. I can't support that program."

"I know that, Senator." McCarthy said. "I'm not asking you to vote for OEO. What I'm doing is asking you to stop a part of the program from being administered by Doc Howe. . . . They want to transfer a good portion of the program over to Howe's administration."

"George," Eastland said. "I wouldn't vote to give a red turd to Doc Howe. . . . When that amendment is coming up, you call me, because I want to be on the floor to vote against that amendment, and I'm going to get all my Southern friends to vote with me."

Conversations like this were repeated numerous times between Shriver, his deputies, and Southern Democrats, with the result that support grew among the Southern bloc for keeping all the War on Poverty's programs under the OEO. The coup de grâce, however, may have been delivered when Bill Kelly and several other Shriver deputies wrote a speech for Louisiana congressman Joseph Waggoner, which Waggoner delivered on the House floor. "I don't want OEO broken up," Waggoner declaimed. "I want to keep that trash in one pile." Because Waggoner was known to be opposed to the poverty program, this speech had the effect of consolidating the Southern Democrats in defense of keeping the OEO intact. And once Republicans lost the support of these Southerners, the GOP drive to kill off the OEO by amendment fizzled.

From a legislative perspective, the OEO's tactics worked. Satisfied that their major concerns had been addressed and struck by the recent outpouring of support for the War on Poverty, Southerners and big-city Democrats came around to support the OEO bill. Republican members of Congress fought bitterly to the end, and they added many other amendments restricting CAAs, but the end result was astonishing.

According to Don Baker, the OEO's general counsel, "The fact of the matter is, nobody with any responsibility or knowledge . . . in the House of Representatives expected the '67 bill to pass. [Speaker of the House] Carl Albert told Sarge Shriver and me a week before the bill went to the floor that he just didn't see the votes; and when we showed him a list of our canvass, he just went down the list, ticking off the ones that he doubted." Just a few days before the vote, Albert was still saying "We can't possibly pass that bill" and suggesting that the Democrats strike a deal with Congressmen Goodell and Quie to pass a modified version of their "Opportunity Crusade" bill. Even Phil Landrum, the OEO's original sponsor in Congress in 1964, had lost faith in the OEO; he declared that "the legislative program being proposed is doomed to failure."

Yet the final bill that was voted on actually placed *less* overall restriction on the OEO and gave it *more* flexibility in how it spent its money than the original bill drafted by the White House. Moreover, the bill provided a two-year authorization, rather than just one, meaning that for the first time since the agency's founding, the OEO's top staff could focus on policy and planning rather than on battles with Congress. The amount of money ($1.78 billion) Congress ultimately authorized was, Shriver said, the absolute minimum the OEO needed to carry out its operations, but it was an increase over the previous year. The final bill, passed just before the winter holidays, was like an early

Christmas present for Shriver: Against all expectations, it passed by a larger margin in both houses than any previous OEO bill. Given that for most of the year the OEO had seemed on the verge of extinction, this seemed almost miraculous—a political triumph of the highest order. Working Congress as hard as he ever had, Shriver had overcome all the obstacles thrown in his way to once again prove himself king of Capitol Hill.

CHAPTER THIRTY-SEVEN

What Next?

E arly 1968 should have been a time of celebration for Shriver. He had accomplished what many informed observers had said was impossible. Not only had he managed to get a hostile Congress to reauthorize the poverty program but he also had persuaded the legislature to increase the OEO's budget above what President Johnson had proposed for it. The newspapers hailed Shriver's triumph as a masterpiece of congressional salesmanship; subsequent historians have called the OEO reauthorization President Johnson's most significant legislative victory of 1967. Shriver's political star, which had been dimmed to near-darkness only a year before, was flickering brightly once again over Washington.

But the shower of political accolades obscured the fact that the OEO was still not on a healthy fiscal footing. Funding was still well short of what was needed to deliver promised services and programs. The grandiose projections Shriver and Johnson had made about substantially eliminating poverty by 1976 were hollow in light of the insufficient funding the OEO was receiving. Shriver knew this. His staff at the OEO knew it. President Johnson knew it. And although Shriver remained committed to preserving and expanding the programs he had created, he could no longer muster the conviction required to run an "unconditional War on Poverty." He simply did not have the resources to wage such a war. And he could no longer convince himself that such resources would be forthcoming anytime soon.

President Johnson, once the OEO bill of 1967 was passed, gave rote avowals of support for the poverty program, but it was clear he no longer placed much hope in it, either as a vote-getter or as a policy tool; his mind was elsewhere, on Vietnam and the 1968 election. In previous years, LBJ had signed the OEO bills with great fanfare; in 1967 he signed the bill with no fanfare at all. In fact he signed it, appropriately enough, while on a flight to Vietnam.

Johnson, watching Bobby Kennedy's camp with anxiety for signs of a Democratic primary challenge in the spring, was as suspicious of Shriver as ever and seemed to resent the rising of his political star. The OEO itself had become an emblem of shame for Johnson, a symbol of expectations raised but not met by his Great Society. As more and more Democrats opposed LBJ's Vietnam policy, and more and more liberals attacked him, the OEO was like an albatross around his neck, reminding him constantly that, after all his protestations to the contrary, he had done just what the liberals had always said he would: failed to build on the domestic aspirations of President Kennedy. Never mind that this charge was unfair, that the enactment of the Civil Rights Act, the Voting Rights Act, the Elementary and Secondary Education Act, not to mention the establishment of Medicare and Medicaid—all achieved before the Great Society's oxygen was sucked up by Vietnam—had made Johnson a more accomplished domestic president than Kennedy had been. Liberals, angry at Johnson over the war in Vietnam and over the fiscal starvation of his domestic programs, perceived the charge to be true—and Johnson, with his radar-like ability to detect slights, felt their perception acutely.

This unhappy context framed the discussions Shriver and Johnson had about the OEO budget in early 1968. Shortly after New Year's Day, Shriver flew down to the LBJ ranch to meet with the president. The president told him that in his State of the Union address, on January 17, he would be announcing a large new job-creation initiative and an emergency riot-prevention program for summer. The plan sounded like a good one to Shriver until the president told him where the money for the new initiative would come from: the OEO budget. Shriver protested that this would be extremely damaging; the OEO was already having to scale back some of its badly underfunded programs. Additional cuts now would be devastating. The president explained that he needed to start these programs and that, with the budget squeeze caused by the war, there was nowhere else he could turn.

Shriver flew home and wrote a memo to Johnson, saying that he was beginning to cut back OEO programs as instructed. He also said, however, that he wanted to be sure the president fully understood the impact of the cuts he was demanding. Some 13,000 children would have to be dumped immediately from Head Start. Some 170,000 teenagers would have to be dropped from the Neighborhood Youth Corps. Legal Services would have to try 60,000 fewer cases per year. Sixteen Job Corps centers would close. Ghetto residents who had been employed by these programs would have to be let go. Shriver's question for Johnson was all but explicit: Are you sure this is what you want? There was no response from the White House.

In his State of the Union address a few days later, Johnson barely mentioned the poverty program but spoke at length about his new, three-year job creation program. After that, the bitterness at the OEO began seeping out into the press. On February 1, 1968, an OEO source told United Press International that Johnson's proposed cutbacks could lead to a "mass resignation of top officials" in the poverty program. "I would not be surprised at all to see most of our top people leave if things continue in this way. You can bet that if Sarge were to leave tomorrow, a lot of us would walk out with him."

The president was furious when he read this, and he forwarded a copy of it with a memo to Joe Califano on February 4. "Tell Shriver to trace this leak and accept the resignation of this man and any others responsible for it so he will not agonize any further. I consider [Shriver] head of this organization and therefore responsible for it." Yet the very next day an even more damaging report appeared in the *Washington Post*. The article, by J. W. Anderson, included a description of Shriver's angry memo to Johnson about the effects of the OEO cutbacks. Anderson took the memo and the budget cuts as evidence of a larger phenomenon: "The real impact of this budget lies in the drastic cuts in presidential hopes and purposes," Anderson wrote.

Each of President Johnson's historic new social and educational bills was originally designed to operate on a far larger scale than it ever achieved. All over the country there are mayors, city councilmen, and school boards full of wrath because the Federal end of the partnership did not live up to its expansive promises. . . . The cumulative effect of this repeated cycle of Great Society promise and default has been a growing

distrust of the Federal Government. This new distrust is most marked among precisely those people who, five years ago, put the greatest faith in the idea of large new
Federal social programs: those people who are, or were, the urban liberals.

It was becoming clear that Shriver could not profitably stay much longer at the
OEO. Johnson seemed not to trust him any more; no matter what Shriver did
to demonstrate his loyalty, the president always thought he could see the
Kennedys standing behind Shriver's shoulder. The agency, having survived its
birth and tumultuous infancy, was ready for a less unorthodox administrative
hand. Shriver himself, bruised by the political battles of the previous two years,
was tired of the fight. He was ready for a new challenge.

The whispering that Shriver was about to resign to run for office in Illinois
became audible nationwide as early as Christmas of 1967. Otto Kerner, the
Democratic governor of Illinois, was no longer popular with voters and had
fallen out of favor with Democratic kingmaker Dick Daley, who was looking
for someone to replace him. Shriver's Illinois friends and Washington supporters kept throwing his name into the mix.

But the situation in Illinois was complex, because Republican senator Everett
Dirksen was also up for reelection in 1968. Dick Daley, naturally, wanted to find a
Democratic candidate to unseat Dirksen. The complicating factor was that in early
1968, Dirksen was one of the staunchest supporters of Lyndon Johnson's Vietnam
policy in the increasingly unfriendly Senate—so it wasn't entirely clear that it was
in Johnson's best interest that this particular Republican be unseated.

Still, the race with Richard Nixon—who looked likely to become the
Republican nominee—would assuredly be much closer than Johnson's 1964
landslide victory over Goldwater had been. Some experts were predicting the
race would be as close as in 1960, when Jack Kennedy's slender margin of victory in Illinois (7,700 votes) had been the difference between the presidency and
defeat. Illinois, in other words, would be crucial to Johnson's reelection chances.
This meant that running a strong Democratic slate in that state was essential.

As the Democratic Cook County Central Committee prepared for its first
meeting of 1968, the talk among the committee members was whether
President Johnson would pressure Daley to run Shriver against Dirksen. There
were at least two reasons why Johnson might choose to do this. First, a Shriver
candidacy might help neutralize Robert Kennedy; putting Shriver on the Illinois
slate along with LBJ might have the effect of "locking in" RFK behind the pres-

ident. It would be awkward for Bobby to be criticizing the president's record from New York while his brother-in-law was running on that same record in Illinois. Second, it would surely help the whole Democratic slate in Illinois, including LBJ, if the Kennedys came out to campaign for Shriver.

Ever since Joe Kennedy had forced him to abort his 1959 run for governor in Illinois, Shriver had made no secret of his desire to hold elective office there. But what Shriver really coveted was not a Senate seat but the state house in Springfield. Shriver knew that as a maverick who liked to call his own shots, he might have a hard time in the Senate. As governor, however, he felt he might be effective. But he needed Daley's blessing before he could make any move in Illinois. After clashing with Daley so many times over Community Action, he didn't expect this blessing to come anytime soon.

Then, unexpectedly, it did. Daley secretly dispatched Rep. Dan Rostenkowski, the leader of the Illinois Democratic congressional delegation, to sound out both Shriver and LBJ about the possibility of Shriver's running against Dirksen. Johnson gave his blessing and Shriver told Rostenkowski he would be interested in running.

No sooner had Rostenkowski extended feelers to Shriver, however, than President Johnson appeared to get nervous about the idea. The prospect of having to contend with three Kennedys in the Senate (or two-and-a-half Kennedys, if you counted the way Kenny O'Donnell did) for a whole four-year term—all of them likely attacking him from the Left on both Vietnam and the poverty program—was not appealing. Suddenly, Shriver's name started cropping up in conjunction with vacant ambassadorships as far away as Australia.

Daley, too, was having his doubts—but his were about how the president's fading popularity would affect Illinois Democrats. Shriver met with Daley and his committee of slatemakers at the Sheraton Hotel in Chicago. The mayor was worried enough about the top of the Democratic ticket to consider bringing Shriver onto the slate to generate some pizzazz. By the end of January, newspapers were reporting that the Cook County Central Committee was leaning heavily toward running Shriver for the Senate, with Mayor Daley's strong support. Shriver began talking to old friends and Merchandise Mart colleagues about setting up a political organization and beginning to raise money. Meanwhile, he and some close associates commissioned a secret poll to see where he stood among other possible Democratic candidates and to see how he stacked up against Dirksen. (The poll found him doing better than any other prospective Democrat against Dirksen, but still losing by a significant margin.)

In early February, Governor Kerner announced that he would not be seeking reelection. The leading Democratic candidate to replace Kerner was Adlai Stevenson III, who had been serving as state treasurer. Shriver for senator and Stevenson for governor became the Democrats' "dream ticket," the one that would carry the whole Democratic slate to victory in the state.

But if he won election to the Senate, Shriver knew, he would be consigned to live in the shadow of his two brothers-in-law. Regardless of whether or not Johnson beat Nixon in November, it was presumed by many that Robert Kennedy would be the Democratic presidential nominee in 1972. That meant that Bobby would spend the next four years angling for position—and that would mean, in turn, that "anything Shriver did in the Senate, any vote that he cast or speech that he made, would somehow be related by his colleagues and the press to the presidential aspirations of his brother-in-law." So Shriver let Daley know that he would prefer to be slated for governor. Since LBJ preferred not to have Shriver in the Senate anyway, where he might reopen the battles over the OEO's budget, Daley began preparing to switch his original plan, running Stevenson for senator, Shriver for governor. Shriver was thrilled.

But in late February, Stevenson declared his opposition to the Vietnam War, saying that if elected to the Senate he would feel morally obligated to oppose LBJ's foreign policy. Stevenson was immediately removed from consideration for the Senate race: it would never do for Daley to run a candidate (Stevenson) who opposed LBJ's Vietnam policy against an incumbent (Dirksen) who supported it. Just like that, Shriver's name was taken out of consideration for the governor's race and put back in consideration for the Senate. Disheartened, Shriver declined to show up for a Cook County Central Committee "candidate selection board" to which he'd been invited over the last weekend in February, signaling his lack of enthusiasm for taking on Dirksen. The *Washington Post* headline was: "Daley's 'Dream Ticket' Fading, Democrats Dismayed."

Several weeks earlier, not long after the OEO budget imbroglio, Shriver had met with the president, who had offered to appoint him ambassador to France. At the time, still hoping for a chance to contend for the Illinois state house, Shriver had said he needed time to think about it. He was more interested in going to Springfield than to Paris. But now that it looked as if his only chance for political office in Illinois was the Dirksen Senate seat, he began to give more serious consideration to Johnson's offer.

Two events strongly influenced Shriver's decision. The first occurred one warm Saturday in early March, when Shriver's mother-in-law, Rose Kennedy, went to Timberlawn for the day to visit with her grandchildren. After lunch she said, "Sarge, I'd like to take a walk with you." Shriver and Mrs. Kennedy, as he always called her, were extremely fond of one another. Mrs. Kennedy knew how highly her husband thought of Sarge, and she seemed to see that he shared many of her husband's best qualities. Rose was closer to Shriver than she was to any of the other Kennedy in-laws, and he treasured that favored status.

Shriver's relationship with Mrs. Kennedy made him give anything she told him serious weight. As they strolled the Timberlawn grounds together on this day, with dogs scampering around their heels and Maria visible on her pony in the distance, he listened intently to what she had to say. "I understand the president has asked you to be the ambassador to France," Mrs. Kennedy said. Shriver said that was true, but that he had not yet told LBJ whether he wanted it. Why not? she wanted to know. Shriver explained that he still had hopes that something would materialize for him in Illinois or, if not, that he could be of greater service to the country by staying in Washington. "I want to tell you something, Sarge," he recalled her saying to him. "Getting offered the opportunity to be ambassador is the best thing that could happen to you and your family. When Joe became ambassador to Great Britain, it was marvelous for our children. You've got an opportunity here to do for your family what Joe was able to do for ours."

They kept walking, and Mrs. Kennedy continued. "It's a tremendous compliment that the president has asked you to fill this position." Shriver replied that he knew that. "Well, Sarge," Rose said, "then why haven't you told him you're ready to go?"

Meanwhile, Robert Kennedy had begun contemplating something rash: jumping into contention for the Democratic presidential nomination against Johnson and Eugene McCarthy. For almost two years, Kennedy's opposition to LBJ's Vietnam War policy had been growing—and his contempt for Johnson personally had not waned. For the most part Johnson and Kennedy had maintained something of an outward truce; it served neither of their interests, nor those of the Democratic Party, for them to be sparring publicly. In 1964 Johnson had even campaigned with Kennedy in New York. Still, their intense dislike for one another was no secret. Thus, even as Kennedy's conviction grew that the continuing escalation of war in Vietnam was morally wrong, he felt inhibited from publicly attacking the president. Such an attack, he feared, would not only create a damaging rift within the Democratic Party but also risked being written off as motivated more by personal animosity than by moral conviction.

But by the summer of 1966 it had become clear to Kennedy that force of logic would never be sufficient to sway LBJ on Vietnam. Johnson, Kennedy and his advisers felt, was "wholly impervious to argument. The only thing he understood was political opposition." So Kennedy—along with Dick Goodwin, Arthur Schlesinger, Ken Galbraith, and others—took their arguments public. Although still trying to avoid direct conflict with the president, they voiced their arguments in books and articles and (in Kennedy's case) Senate debates, trying to influence public opinion. The strategy partly worked, although not in the expected manner. Johnson seemed unmoved by any shift in public opinion, and his Vietnam policy did not change; but by late in 1966, Kennedy had become the clear focal point for Democratic opposition to LBJ, not only among the disaffected Kennedy administration alumni but among rank-and-file party members who opposed the war in Vietnam. When Gallup Polls asked Democratic voters whom they favored in 1968, more of them said Kennedy than Johnson. Kennedy's "rise in political appeal," Gallup concluded, had been "spectacular."

Kennedy continued to avoid a public break with Johnson. Early in 1967 prominent Democrats had warned him that if he were to venture an assault on Johnson in the primaries the following year, he would be as good as handing the presidency to the Republicans. But by the fall, US involvement in Vietnam had increased to more than half a million troops—and some polls had Kennedy leading Johnson by as many as twenty percentage points. Minnesota senator Eugene McCarthy, moreover, declared on November 30, 1967, that he would be running against Johnson as an antiwar candidate in the Democratic primaries. If Kennedy were to enter the race now he could be accused of cowardice in waiting to follow McCarthy, but at least he couldn't be blamed for initiating the split in the Democratic Party.

On January 31, 1968, the Tet Offensive destroyed any remaining credibility LBJ had with liberal Democrats and lost him the support of the American people generally. After months of Johnson's insisting that the war in Vietnam was soon to turn in the United States' favor, 67,000 North Vietnamese troops had penetrated deep into South Vietnamese territory. Suddenly, the imminent American victory that Johnson had promised seemed very distant, even impossible. Eugene McCarthy's anemic campaign got a sudden boost of energy, as he became the repository for Democratic hopes for ending the war. To Shriver, it seemed quite likely that Bobby would enter the race. This made him hope more ardently that the way would be cleared for him to run for governor in Illinois. Being in Springfield would take him out of the fray of national politics in a way that being in the Senate would not. The problems posed by a potential Senate campaign would be magnified if Bobby were campaigning for the presidency: Would Shriver run on his record in the Johnson administration (which Bobby would be attacking) or would he run as a Kennedy candidate (thereby inviting attack from Johnson)? The situation would be untenable.

As Shriver debated whether to go to Paris, Kennedy debated whether to oppose Johnson. Most of his Senate staff believed he should run; most of the old hands from Jack Kennedy's White House, along with Ted Kennedy, believed he should not. Shriver monitored the situation closely. The moment Kennedy entered the Democratic race against Johnson—if he in fact chose to do so— Shriver would immediately find himself in the position of being a Kennedy family member in the camp of the declared enemy. As early as 1965, Bobby had already conveyed to Shriver that he looked askance on his staying on in the Johnson administration. But as long as there was the veneer of a truce between LBJ and RFK, Shriver could stay on with impunity. Once that truce was broken and Kennedy was openly vying with Johnson for the presidency, Shriver would be seen by the Kennedys as sleeping with the enemy.

By the fall of 1967, Shriver had become convinced that Bobby would run. Shriver's own loyalties remained divided. He had always supported the Kennedy family's political aspirations, even though he never felt as favorably toward Bobby as he had toward Jack. But he was still working for Johnson and believed it was his patriotic duty to serve the president's interests, and so he continued to serve as the administration's resident expert on what Bobby was thinking. On December 8, 1967, Califano wrote a memo to LBJ: "Bill Moyers called to tell me . . . that Shriver believed Bobby Kennedy was getting ready to run against you in 1968."

Shriver was in a no-win situation. Neither Johnson nor Kennedy fully trusted him, as each suspected him of being an agent of the other. So Shriver was stuck with a dilemma. Should he abandon the president to help Kennedy? Or stick with Johnson and risk further alienating his brother-in-law?

Johnson stepped up the pressure on Shriver to accept the Paris appointment. It was bad enough for Johnson that a Kennedy who had once served in his administration was now running against him; he didn't want another Kennedy, one who was still serving in his administration, to join the enemy campaign. He wanted Shriver out of the country—and out of RFK's orbit.

In the second week of March, Shriver told Johnson he would accept the Paris appointment, pending the approval of the French government. Then he left with Eunice for a vacation in Spain. Just a few days later, on March 16, LBJ's worst fear was realized: Robert Kennedy announced that he would contend for the Democratic presidential nomination. On Friday, March 22, Secretary of State Dean Rusk called Shriver in Madrid to tell him that the French government was amenable to his appointment as ambassador. But Rusk wanted to make certain: Are you sure you still want the president to submit your name to the Senate for confirmation? Rusk and Johnson were worried that RFK's announcement would cause Shriver to reconsider going to Paris. But Shriver didn't hesitate. He said he had made up his mind; he would go to Paris.

Johnson was delighted. According to Califano, "LBJ was tickled that he could hold a Kennedy brother-in-law out of the race; to him the appointment of Shriver as ambassador to France was made in political heaven." Johnson gleefully advertised to the press that Shriver had accepted the nomination, despite being given an opportunity to back out after Bobby had declared his presidential candidacy. People close to the family wondered how Eunice, the most politically competitive of all the Kennedys, could bear to move to Paris, so far away from the action of her brother's campaign.

When the Shrivers returned from Spain, the situation got more complicated. Bobby's advisers recognized that Shriver's participation in the campaign would strongly boost Kennedy's chances against Johnson. Emissaries from the Kennedy campaign approached Shriver and asked him if he would help organize Citizens-for-Kennedy, as he had done for Jack in 1960, or if he would be willing to help organize the Kennedy effort in the Indiana primary on May 7. The request put Shriver in an awkward position: In withdrawing from the French ambassadorship and campaigning against the administration, Shriver would be striking a double blow at President Johnson. Also, he wondered why, if Bobby really wanted his assistance, he didn't just pick up the telephone himself and ask him for it. That's what Shriver himself would have done in Bobby's position. After all, Shriver was forever calling up people—even people he had never met before—

and asking them to come and work for him. But that's not how Bobby operated, particularly in relation to his brother-in-law. He always felt more comfortable working through intermediaries, perhaps because his fear of being rejected was mitigated that way. Shriver took this as a mild affront, or at least as a statement about where he stood in his brother-in-law's eyes. Thus he responded noncommittally to these initial tentative overtures from the Kennedy campaign.

Donald Dell, a former professional tennis player and captain of the US Davis Cup tennis team, was a lawyer who had worked as Shriver's right-hand man for a year at the OEO before stepping down to campaign for Robert Kennedy. In the spring of 1968, Dell was coordinating advance work for the Kennedy campaign in some primary states. On Sunday, March 31, Dell went to church and played tennis with Bobby's family at Kennedy's Hickory Hill estate in Virginia before getting on an airplane with Bobby and Ethel in the evening to fly to New York.

When the plane landed, Dell went up to the front of the plane to clear away any press so that Ethel, who was six months pregnant, could disembark without being photographed. But when Dell got to the front of the plane, "a guy comes barging through and I block the aisle, don't let him through, while we're waiting for Ethel to come out of the bathroom." But the man refused to be deterred. "Look, I'm the State Democratic Chairman," he said. "I've got to talk to the senator. Lyndon Johnson just announced he's withdrawing, he's on television, there's 20,000 people outside." (It was true; that evening, while Senator Kennedy's plane was in the air, Lyndon Johnson had gone on television and declared: "I shall not seek, and I will not accept, the nomination of my party for another term as your President.") Dell recalled, "So I turned around and I looked at Bobby and he just stared up at me with those steel-blue eyes and he just sort of smiled, and I said, 'This is for real, Senator.' And he says, 'Yeah, I know.'"

Johnson's withdrawal from the presidential race stunned the nation. It also instantly changed the political calculus of Shriver's going to Paris. Although LBJ's vice president, Hubert Humphrey, would soon announce his own candidacy and pick up the dropped Johnson mantle, Shriver's loyalty to the current president no longer impeded him so strongly from joining the Kennedy campaign. Recognizing this fact, Bobby's people tried once again to reach out to Shriver. The campaign dispatched Dell to do the recruiting.

In early April, Dell flew from the West Coast to Washington, to have dinner with the Shrivers. Before dinner, he joined Shriver at Timberlawn for cocktails. Sitting in a room overlooking the expansive back lawn, Dell said, "Look,

Sarge, I've been asked by Bobby's group, would you change your mind about going to Paris and stay here in Washington and play a major role in Bobby's campaign? You could run Citizens-for-Kennedy from here in Washington and you could help us tremendously." As Dell recalled, "Sarge and I talked about it for maybe ten minutes. And there was some real interest on his part. . . . He was certainly willing to listen about it."

And then, as Dell recalled: "Out of the blue, in walks Eunice. And she says, 'We got to go to dinner, darling. What are you two talking about?' She could tell we were having some kind of conversation of seriousness. And I said, 'Well, you know Bobby and everybody—John Nolan, Joe Dolan [two of Bobby's advisers]— they all asked me to come out and talk to you and Sarge about Sarge having a major role in Bobby's campaign.'" Dell explained what Shriver might do to contribute to the campaign, and how valuable his participation would be. Eunice fixed Dell in her gaze and said, "We're going to Paris as the ambassadors." She turned to her husband. "Sarge, you accepted that with Lyndon, right?" Sarge said he had. "Well, that's where we're going then, to Paris," she said. "Now let's go have dinner!" "I'm not saying Eunice made the decision for him," Dell said. "But it was clear that she was really looking forward to going to France."

"I know there were feelings that we should not have gone," Eunice would tell *Life* magazine in 1972. "But I had this understanding with Bobby and it was very clear and very frank. He never said anything to me about being disappointed that we did not stay." In the end Shriver did not stay on, Eunice said, because he did not feel especially needed. "Sarge was not what you'd call an inner man on Bobby's campaign. He was never a close friend of Bobby's and I don't think he ever felt, quite honestly, that it really made a difference to Bobby. . . . When Sarge is told he can make a difference, he doesn't hesitate twenty seconds."

Neither Sarge nor Eunice intended their decision to go to France to be an insult to Bobby, or a repudiation of his campaign. Far from it. Eunice, in fact, would end up staying in the United States for a week after Sarge had departed for Paris so that she could campaign for her brother. But Sarge believed that since he had already told Lyndon Johnson that he would accept the appointment—and since the French government was expecting him—it would be a dereliction of his patriotic duty to back out now.

"There was a lot of emotional feeling between Bobby and Sarge," according to someone who was close to both men. "That feeling was not necessarily negative—it wasn't—but it was competitive. They were both national public figures. Bobby despised the war, and despised Lyndon Johnson. Sarge had run two programs for Lyndon Johnson since Jack was assassinated and he was running them well. So all that created a certain chemistry and a certain atmosphere between them."

Although Shriver accepted the Paris nomination without malign intent, some of the people in RFK's inner circle saw it as a slap at their candidate. For instance, one person who worked with Shriver at both the Peace Corps and the OEO before going to work for Kennedy calls the decision to go to Paris one of Shriver's lowest moments in public life, right up there with the sacrifice of Adam Yarmolinsky. Among some members of the Kennedy family and their intimates, Shriver's refusal to go to work for Bobby constituted a sort of violation of the family code. For years afterward, when all the Kennedy cousins were gathered at the family compound in Hyannis Port, RFK's children would mischievously taunt the younger Shriver boys during touch football games or other games: "*Your* Daddy didn't come back from France to campaign for *our* Daddy." A few of Kennedy's associates, perhaps absorbing some of their man's Manichean sense of injustice, never forgave Shriver for what they saw as his betrayal.

With rare exceptions, Shriver brushed aside such pettiness, mainly because to him the idea that he was somehow "betraying" Bobby Kennedy by becoming ambassador to France was absurd. It was an important job he had been given, and a good opportunity for his family, and he didn't want to turn it down. It didn't mean he had anything against Bobby's candidacy, or that he wouldn't lend him whatever support he could.

Just how much support he could give, however, turned out to be a complicated question. On April 18, when Shriver appeared before the Senate Foreign Relations Committee (which had to approve his nomination to the ambassadorship before it became official), senators grilled him about whether he would be unduly influenced by foreign policy positions taken by his brother-in-law in his presidential campaign. What will you do, a South Dakota senator asked, if you find yourself caught between conflicting loyalties? "One is toward your brother-in-law, who has a concept of foreign policy that is diametrically different from the man who has appointed you," President Johnson. Shriver replied: "Our ambassador supports the positions of the administration and the government of the United States. It is his duty to explain and support the policies of the government of the United States."

From the Senate's perspective, that was the correct answer. He could have answered no other way and expect to be approved. But it was a response that helped seal for Shriver the animosity of the RFK camp, to whom simply doing his ambassadorial duty would constitute an acceptance of Johnson's pro-Vietnam policy, and a rejection of Kennedy's anti-Vietnam policy.

Shriver was also asked, "If your wife suggests that you come out and help her brother, what are you going to do then?" Caught between State Department rules and his wife's prerogatives, Shriver hedged: "That's an iffy question," he said. "It depends on what happens—what she feels, what the department feels, what I think." A few days later the Senate confirmed his appointment.

Eunice avidly campaigned for Bobby while continuing to stand resolutely by her husband's decision. Eunice's campaigning was "a daring affront to the unity of the administration"—after all, her husband was still working for Johnson—but even that did not satisfy Kennedy's aides, who wanted Sarge to leave the administration and join the Kennedy campaign. Will you miss the excitement of campaigning once you get to Paris? a *Washington Post* reporter asked Eunice. "Of course," she replied. "But what Mr. Shriver is doing is important too. He'll be working on problems that bear on international peace. You certainly can't have peace [in Vietnam] without France." France had just agreed to serve as host for negotiations between America and North Vietnam. "He made his commitment, a very firm one, to the president before Bobby announced. We think it's a great opportunity."

On April 24 some 2,000 of Shriver's friends, colleagues, and poverty program employees attended a musical revue at the Sheraton Park Hotel in honor of the retiring OEO director. *Au Revoir, Sarge,* written by the OEO public relations director Herb Kramer, was a huge success, featuring songs that gently mocked the Shrivers' predicament. In one song, a character playing Eunice Shriver sang, "My Bobby lies over the ocean, my Bobby lies over the sea, Oh, how can I campaign for Bobby, when Bobby is so far from me?" There was also a song, "Can't I Come Home, Dick Daley?" lampooning Shriver's desire to be governor of Illinois. The columnist Mary McGrory attended the event and sensed "much genuine regret at Shriver's departure." Shriver's new job—trying to sell Charles de Gaulle on American ideas and policy—McGrory wrote, would be "the greatest challenge of his career."

PART FIVE

France (1968–1970)

CHAPTER THIRTY-EIGHT

Springtime in Paris

O n May 7, 1968, Shriver was sworn in as US ambassador to France. The ambassadorship was the oldest diplomatic position in US history: Established during the American Revolution, it had been held by such Founding Fathers as Benjamin Franklin, John Adams, and Thomas Jefferson. But Shriver was inheriting the job at one of the most challenging times in the history of the relationship between the two countries.

In 1968, Franco-American relations had reached a postwar ebb. The problems between the two allies had originated with the Second World War itself. Whereas the Americans had seen France as merely one battleground in the larger war against the Axis, the French Resistance—led by Gen. Charles de Gaulle—saw it as a nation to be liberated. At the liberation of Paris in 1944, US troops graciously had allowed French soldiers to enter the city first, to create the illusion that "Paris had liberated herself." De Gaulle considered this symbolic act patronizing and had spent much of the ensuing quarter-century trying to ensure that France would never again be dependent on another Great Power for its military defense.

Ever since his election to the French presidency in 1958, establishing the Fifth Republic, de Gaulle had been complicating life for the makers of US foreign policy. Unlike the rest of Western Europe, de Gaulle's France had chosen to separate itself from America and pursue what de Gaulle called "independent" foreign and defense policies. In February 1960, France became the first country other than the United States and the Soviet Union to have detonated an atomic bomb. France required a *force de frappe* (a nuclear strike force), de Gaulle argued, to put the country on equal footing with the United States, the Soviet Union, and Britain. Militarily, of course, even with a nuclear arsenal, France was in no position to compete with the Soviet Union or the United States. But de Gaulle's primary purpose was not military but political: to restore French self-confidence and to steer an independent middle way between competing ideological blocs. As early as January 1961, when President Kennedy took office, "what to do about the French" and "understanding de Gaulle" had become obsessions of the State Department. In early 1963 de Gaulle held a press conference in which he renounced cooperation with the Americans on nuclear disarmament and other projects and declared that France would seek its own way. It was, according to one de Gaulle biographer, "an open and undisguised breach with the Anglo-Saxons."

Then, in 1966, after years of threats, de Gaulle officially announced that he was withdrawing France's troops from NATO's joint command, and he asked that all foreign troops—as well as NATO headquarters—be removed from French soil. This baffled the Americans and the other NATO countries, who had argued strenuously that France should remain in the alliance. The United States and its allies were trying to take a firm line against the Soviet Union and the Warsaw Pact; this dissension within NATO only weakened the cause. What purpose was this serving? But Charles "Chip" Bohlen, Shriver's predecessor as ambassador, told LBJ that to continue to argue with de Gaulle would just make matters worse. So Johnson ordered 800,000 tons of military supplies to be removed from France immediately.

The NATO gambit was only one of de Gaulle's provocations. The French president also formally recognized Communist China in 1964; developed relations with East European Communist countries such as Czechoslovakia, Poland, and Romania; and tried to establish France as the leader of all the developing countries not already aligned with either the Soviet Union or the United

States. Most alarming of all to State Department types, de Gaulle repeatedly downplayed the global threat posed by the Soviet Union and made friendly overtures to that country's leadership: France shared as many, if not more, common interests with the Soviet Union, de Gaulle would say, as it did with the United States.

De Gaulle gave Lyndon Johnson fits. He was the first, and for several years the only, Western European leader to question America's Vietnam policy. When Johnson's emissary George Ball met with the French president in December 1964, de Gaulle told him that the United States should withdraw from Vietnam. "You cannot win it," de Gaulle said prophetically. When Johnson declined to heed de Gaulle's advice, the Frenchman cited Johnson's folly as yet one more reason for France to pursue an independent foreign policy from America. Hearing of this, Johnson exclaimed to his aides, "If he wants to jack off, he can."

De Gaulle continued to nettle Johnson. In February 1965 the French president sent a personal letter of sympathy to Ho Chi Minh, leader of the Vietnamese Communists, deploring the US intervention in the East Asian country. And in May 1965 de Gaulle instructed France's UN delegate to vote with the Soviet Union to condemn the US military incursion into the Dominican Republic. By this point, "Washington and Paris were scarcely on speaking terms any longer."

This was the frosty environment in which Shriver would soon find himself as ambassador. Chip Bohlen, a highly respected diplomat who spoke perfect French, was considered one of the most talented people in the whole foreign service. Yet the five years Bohlen spent as ambassador to France had been, according to a de Gaulle biographer, "the most difficult . . . that any American envoy ever spent in the French capital." Bohlen had been impressed with de Gaulle personally and found him unfailingly polite, but when he left his post to become an under secretary in the State Department he wrote to Dean Rusk: "Given the attitude of de Gaulle, there would seem to be very little chance of any real improvement in Franco-American relations. . . . I can offer little encouragement to any belief in a change in our relations with France until after the departure of de Gaulle."

When Shriver called on Bohlen in Washington before leaving for Paris, Bohlen wished him well but then said, as Shriver recalled, "You're not going to have any fun." Explaining that it was impossible to get anything done in

France, Bohlen mused, "I'll tell you what I'd do if I were you. I'd go rent a house outside Paris in the French countryside. Go out there every Thursday afternoon and don't come back until Tuesday morning." To Shriver, burned out after four years at the OEO, the prospect of long weekends in the countryside didn't sound so bad.

Shriver had planned to leave for France on May 11, and he had every intention of following Bohlen's advice and hunting for a country house once he got there. But events intervened. Shriver was asked to depart three days earlier, so that he could greet Averell Harriman and Cyrus Vance when they arrived in Paris to begin negotiations with Xuan Thuy of North Vietnam—the first formal talks between the principal antagonists in the Vietnam War. (The groundwork for these talks had been laid during LBJ's withdrawal speech on March 31, when the president announced that he would be reducing the number of bombing raids over North Vietnam and that he would make Harriman available for peace negotiations anywhere, anytime.) Shriver, as US ambassador, was to serve as host to the American delegation. Over the next two years, although he was not himself an active participant, Shriver had an up-close view of the confidential negotiations. His old friend and Yale classmate Cy Vance would sometimes use him as an informal sounding board, and Shriver was privy to some of the cable traffic that passed between Harriman and the White House. He would later put this privileged access to controversial use when campaigning for the vice presidency in 1972.

Based on Bohlen's briefing, Shriver anticipated an uneventful stint in Paris, a respite from the turmoil engulfing America. In the weeks before Shriver had left Washington, the assassination of Martin Luther King Jr. had set off a wave of riots in 110 American cities; from his office at the OEO, Shriver could see flames against the horizon behind the White House. In New York City, students seized control of Columbia University and made it the headquarters for what threatened to become a general revolt. The 1960s New Frontier-Great Society liberal consensus had become completely unglued, producing a centrifuge of radical extremism that appeared to threaten the basic social order.

But upon arrival in Paris, Shriver quickly learned that things were to be no calmer in France; it seemed the spark of revolt had jumped across the Atlantic and found dry tinder among French students and workers. A general spirit of unrest seemed to be sweeping through the youth of the developed world, many of whom sympathized with the plight of the Vietnamese people and not a few of whom subscribed to newly fashionable Maoist theories about the evils of consumer capitalism. There were disturbances in places as far afield as the London School of Economics and Tokyo University. In France, however, the unrest took firmer hold.

The chaos that was erupting when Shriver arrived in Paris on May 9, 1968, had been triggered by a seemingly innocuous event. In March, students had staged protests at the University of Paris at Nanterre to demand the right of male students to visit female students in their dormitories. Under the leadership of Daniel Cohn-Bendit, a sociology student who would become known as "Danny the Red," the protest grew, and soon students had taken over the campus. The dean responded by shutting the campus down.

This aroused the ire of student activists at the Sorbonne, in the center of Paris's Latin Quarter, who demanded that Nanterre be reopened. When administrators shut down the Sorbonne in an effort to prevent more protests, the students rioted, and on the night of Friday, May 10, they erected barricades and seized control of the campus. The French government responded by sending in the riot police, who engaged in violent fighting with student occupiers. Hundreds of students and policemen were injured. By the morning, 600 arrests had been made. Millions of French people followed the events on radio and television. Given France's history of revolution, the appearance of barricades in the Latin Quarter called to mind previous epochs—1830, 1848, and 1871. Paris braced itself for further upheaval.

To Shriver, who had just arrived for his first day of work at the embassy near the Place de la Concorde, the images of police brutalizing student protesters looked all too familiar. It was a scene he had seen played out many times in the United States in recent years: most recently the riots after Martin Luther King's death but also the riots of previous summers and the brutal clashes between police and civil rights protesters in the South. "It was," Shriver recalled, "the kind of welcome I had come to expect in Watts or Berkeley or Detroit." Since he had not yet presented his diplomatic credentials to de Gaulle, and therefore had little official business to conduct, Shriver decided that "being an ambassador could wait." To the great consternation of his newly inherited staff, he simply walked out the front door of the embassy and went to see firsthand what the students in the Latin Quarter were up to.

Reluctantly accompanied by Nick King, the embassy's press attaché, Shriver drove across the Seine and along the crowded streets of the Left Bank as far as the throngs of people massed everywhere would permit. Near the Latin Quarter, Shriver and King got out and walked amid the chaos, finding themselves eventually among a crowd of some 2,000 students jammed onto the Boulevard St. Germaine near the Sorbonne. Suddenly, a student with a bullhorn bellowed, "Assiez, assiez!"—"Sit down!" Shriver, along with everyone else, sat down. As he recalled, if "at that moment the president of the United States had sought consultation with his newly designated ambassador to France—he would have found him squatting on the macadam of a main thoroughfare in the Latin Quarter—surrounded by the angry perpetrators of the French student rebellion."

Sitting there, Shriver recognized the incongruity of his own position. "To the French people, I would be the very epitome of the American establishment, representing its values, its standards, and its policies. Yet, for the past four years, I had been engaged in a fierce effort to undermine that establishment" through Community Action. Therefore, he decided, he would try to make his ambassadorship the living embodiment of anticlericalism, of antibureaucracy. "My own faith," Shriver wrote not long after his experience in the Latin Quarter, "has always been with the outsider, rarely with the clerk. The rebel rather than the conformist." He therefore declared his allegiance to the youth of France— "I presented my credentials to the French students before I presented them to de Gaulle," as he would say—against the stultifying influence of bureaucracy.

The Paris peace talks, which were to have begun triumphantly that day, opened quietly across town, bumped off the front pages by stories of tear gas and revolution. Meanwhile, the unrest spread as workers joined the students in protest, beginning to strike all over France. On May 13 the French prime minister, Georges Pompidou, began negotiating with the students at the Sorbonne, momentarily calming things down. "The tempest is really over," Pompidou told de Gaulle, urging him to commence a long-scheduled trip to Romania that day.

Practically the moment de Gaulle took off for Bucharest, however, factory workers at a government-owned aviation plant in Nantes staged a sit-in, welding the gates to the factory shut and hoisting a red flag over the roof. Over the next two days, strikes and sit-ins erupted all over the country. Within two weeks, millions of workers had seized control of factories, mines, shipyards, nuclear facilities, and government offices. The banks and the Paris Stock

Exchange ceased operation. All flight and rail service into and out of the country was cancelled (although not before Eunice was able to arrive with the children on May 15). Television and radio stations intermittently went off the air.

De Gaulle returned from Romania on May 18 and, with events threatening to spiral out of control, announced that he would address the country on Friday, May 24. In a cable to the State Department, Shriver wrote, "So many spectacular events have occurred the embassy believes it should warn the dept that . . . there exists the possibility that we could be faced with an insurrectional situation. . . . Not only are extremist elements ready to ignite again the charged atmosphere, but also there is a possibility of spontaneous combustion developing." "I knew Sarge Shriver was a dynamic fellow," LBJ's national security adviser, Walt Rostow, wrote to the president, "but I didn't think all this would come from sending him to Paris."

De Gaulle's speech that Friday evening was a disaster. The great general, the living embodiment of *la gloire de la France*, looked tired and old. He pleaded for everyone to return to work and declared that he would soon hold a national referendum on whether workers should be granted more "participation" in the ownership and management of both private and state-run businesses. Watching the address on television at the embassy—with power supplied by an emergency internal generator, since the strikes had deprived the city of electricity—Shriver was struck once again by the parallels between the struggles convulsing both America and France: the demands for "participation" by the powerless, the violent expressions of bottled-up impotence and rage.

Although the street disturbances ceased briefly while de Gaulle was speaking, they resumed with a vengeance when he was done. Violence erupted once again in the Latin Quarter, and by the following morning the streets around the Sorbonne "looked like scenes out of World War II." Cars had been overturned, trees were uprooted, the streets themselves were ripped up; more than 500 people were hurt and some 800 arrested overnight. On this inauspicious morning, Shriver formally presented his credentials to the French government, wondering as he did so how long this government would last. Shriver alluded to the chaos outside only indirectly in his initial statement to de Gaulle, saying that he was taking up his duties in Paris at a time of "volatile movement" and "profound change." "In many countries," Shriver continued, "the universal search for new structures offering more freedom to individuals" has helped create "the present, fluid situation." That was putting it mildly.

Four days later de Gaulle disappeared, slipping out the back gate of the Elysée Palace and fleeing the city without telling anyone, not even his cabinet, where he had gone. Was he abdicating? Chaos reigned.

A day later de Gaulle returned, having held a secret rendezvous in the Black Forest with Gen. Jacques Massu, the commander of the French forces in West Germany. At 4:30 p.m., de Gaulle made a five-minute address to the nation in which he announced that he was in complete control of the nation, that he was dissolving the national assembly, and that he would fulfill his mandate to the French people. "France is threatened by a dictatorship that could only be from totalitarian communism," he said, before concluding: "Eh bien! Non! The Republic shall not abdicate."

Just like that, the crisis was over. The strikes ended. Half a million de Gaulle supporters marched up the Champs-Elysée, singing his praises in the name of the Fifth Republic. (The next day, just as de Gaulle had instructed, everyone went back to work. In the election a month later, Gaullists won a huge majority in the new National Assembly.) Shriver, watching from the front of the American Embassy as the cheering patriotic throngs flocked past, stood in awe, not only at the power of the seventy-eight-year-old leader's charisma but at everything that had transpired since he had arrived less than three weeks earlier. He decided he wouldn't get that house in the countryside after all.

FAMILY TRAGEDY

Things had scarcely calmed down in Paris when tragedy struck in the United States. A few minutes after midnight on June 5, just moments after he had given a speech in the ballroom of the Ambassador Hotel in Los Angeles celebrating his victory over Eugene McCarthy in the California primary, Robert Kennedy was shot by Sirhan Sirhan while cutting through a kitchen to escape the madding crowd. Despite multiple surgeries and heroic medical efforts to revive him, Kennedy died in the hospital twenty-four hours later. For the day that Bobby's life hung in the balance, the Shrivers called the family in Los Angeles for regular updates. "We sat in the house saying rosary after rosary after rosary," Timothy Shriver recalled. For an unfathomable fourth time, one of Eunice's siblings had died a premature, violent death.

LBJ sent Air Force One to transport Kennedy's body to New York, and the

Shrivers flew—along with Ted Kennedy's wife, Joan, who had been staying with them at the ambassador's residence—to La Guardia Airport to greet Bobby's aides and Kennedy family members. When Sarge attempted to help Bobby's aides unload the casket from the plane, they pushed him away angrily, bitter in their grief, unwilling to forgive his decision to go to France rather than campaign for his now-fallen brother-in-law.

On the morning of Saturday, June 8, some 2,000 luminaries from around the world attended a Pontifical Mass at St. Patrick's Cathedral, said by Richard Cardinal Cushing. The service was followed by a funeral train ride from New York to Washington, which transported Bobby's remains, along with Kennedy family members and friends, to Union Station, from which the casket was delivered to the burial site at Arlington National Cemetery. Hundreds of thousands of mourners stood along the route, while inside the train fifteen-year-old Joe Kennedy, Bobby's eldest son, walked up and down the aisles of the twenty-one cars, shaking hands with people and thanking them for coming. In coming years, Joe would be the first of the next generation of Kennedys to try his hand at the family trade. In the meantime, all eyes turned to Ted Kennedy. Would he pick up the dropped JFK-RFK mantle?

THE FIRST SPECIAL OLYMPICS

A week later, the Shrivers were again in Paris. At least part of their attention, however, was back across the Atlantic, on Chicago. Sarge was thinking about the upcoming Democratic convention, scheduled to take place in the Windy City in late August. With Bobby gone, there were two leading contenders for the Democratic nomination, Eugene McCarthy and Hubert Humphrey. Bobby's former advisers soon dispersed among the various Democratic candidates, but the "Kennedy Movement," as the journalist Theodore White called it, longed for Ted to enter the race, or at least to make himself available as a running mate. For Kennedy supporters outside of Bobby's inner circle, a next-best alternative to Ted was Shriver: a Kennedy by marriage who shared Bobby's commitment to social programs for the down and out and who possessed the appearance—the dash and style—of JFK. By the third week in June, newspapers were reporting that Shriver sat atop Humphrey's list of possible running mates. Talking to reporters on a visit to New York on June 21, Humphrey said he was "very interested" in allying himself with Shriver. Shriver read reports like this with interest but heard no formal word yet from Humphrey himself.

Meanwhile, Eunice was moving forward with a long-planned event: the launching of the Special Olympics. Now that the Shrivers had moved abroad, Camp Shriver could no longer be continued, but Eunice had not slackened her efforts on behalf of the mentally retarded. Since 1964, the Kennedy Foundation had been giving grants every summer to the Chicago Parks District to run programs along the lines of Camp Shriver. In January 1968 Eunice dispatched Kennedy Foundation staff members to Chicago to meet with Parks District staff to work up a proposal for a full-blown track-and-field event. On March 29 Eunice stood alongside Mayor Daley and announced that the foundation would be granting an additional $20,000 to the Parks District for the "Chicago Special Olympics."

On July 19 the Shrivers flew to Chicago and checked into the La Salle Hotel, where hundreds of mentally retarded children from twenty-six states were swarming around the hallways and the lobby. The next morning, nearly 1,000 athletes gathered at Soldiers Field, alongside Lake Michigan, for the opening of the games. At the pre-games press conference, Eunice said: "I wish to announce a national Special Olympics training program for all mentally retarded children everywhere. I also announce that in 1969 the Kennedy Foundation will pledge sufficient funds to underwrite five regional Olympic tryouts." Now, she said, "Let us begin the Olympics."

"I was the original number one skeptic of Special Olympics." Sarge Shriver recalled. "I didn't believe it would ever work." But watching those first games, he found that his appreciation for his wife's vision deepened. Sitting alongside Mayor Daley, Shriver believed he could also feel the mayor's cynicism softening into marvel as he watched the young athletes. At one point, Daley turned to Shriver's wife and said, "You know, Eunice, the world will never be the same after this."

CHAPTER THIRTY-NINE

"Sarjean Shreevair"

⌒

The scene at Soldiers Field may have seemed at the time to have no bearing on life in Paris, but Eunice's work with the mentally retarded would play a crucial role in thawing the relationship between the United States and France. Even as she was planning the inaugural Special Olympic Games in Chicago, Eunice had thrown herself into working with the mentally retarded in Paris. She sought out French experts on mental retardation and brought them in for conversations at the ambassador's residence. She went to work every Monday at the External Médico-Pédagogique, a nearby facility for mentally retarded children, where she taught the children how to swim, helped out with their occupational therapy, and got them to play games and sports. And to the consternation of the French staff at the ambassador's residence, she brought dozens of mentally retarded children into the Shrivers' home on Avenue D'Iena, near the Trocadero Fountain, where they would scamper around with the Shriver children.

The ambassadorial staff had never seen anything like this. In France, even more than in America, mental retardation was a taboo subject; a mentally retarded child was something to be ashamed of. Yet here was the ambassador's wife, not only working openly in a school for the retarded but also regularly busing dozens of retarded children over to her home, where she would let them run amok. It was just too much. Longtime housekeepers and other staff members at Avenue D'Iena quit in disgust.

It wasn't just the retarded children that offended the French staff's sense of propriety; it was the whole Shriver family. They didn't behave the way an ambassador's family should. For one thing they insisted on supplementing the permanent residence staff with their own, imported from America. For another, they completely refurnished the residence. Out went all the ornamental antique furniture and French paintings. In came more comfortable, modern-looking furniture and lots of avant-garde American art—paintings by Jasper Johns, Robert Indiana, Georgia O'Keeffe, and Roy Lichtenstein. In addition the Shrivers hung hundreds of photographs, a museum's worth, of the Kennedy family. (Shriver also hung his favorite crucifix, the one that had lain atop JFK's casket and been blessed by Pope Paul, on the wall of his oak-paneled office at the embassy.) The Shrivers' two dogs, Lassie and Shamrock, scampered underfoot. A guest arriving in the great hall of the ambassador's residence might find all the furniture pushed to one side, the better to accommodate a game of floor hockey among various Shrivers and visiting retarded children, and the carefully manicured backyard being used as a badminton court. (The residence gardeners threatened to quit over this offense.)

Within weeks of their moving in, the Shrivers and their cheerily chaotic household had become notorious on the diplomatic circuit. Soon, the story of the lively new American ambassador and his unusual family made its way to the Elysée Palace, the home of Charles de Gaulle and his famously prim wife, who was known to the French people as "Tante Yvonne" (Aunt Yvonne).

One day not long after his family's arrival in Paris, as Shriver recalled, someone called the ambassador's residence from the Elysée Palace to say that Madame de Gaulle would like a private audience with Mrs. Shriver. Could that be arranged? Shriver was alarmed. This was simply unheard of—an unsolicited invitation from the president's wife? Madame de Gaulle was rarely seen in public and was not known for making casual social calls. Shriver worried that the shake-up of the residence staff had somehow offended the de Gaulles.

On the appointed day, Eunice had lunch with Yvonne de Gaulle. It turned out that Mme de Gaulle had indeed heard about the goings-on at the American ambassador's residence and that she did want to talk to Eunice about them, but not for the reasons Sarge had feared. Although few people knew it, the de Gaulles had had a retarded daughter, Anne, who had died twenty years earlier. Privately, the general and his wife had doted on Anne; publicly, they had scarcely acknowledged her existence. Now Mme de Gaulle, intrigued by the stories of Eunice's work with the mentally retarded, wanted to learn more. So the two women talked about the problem of retardation, Eunice's plans for a Special Olympics program, and their respective family travails.

Not long thereafter, Sarge was invited to the Elysée Palace to meet with de Gaulle for the first time since he had formally presented his credentials. As it turned out, Mme de Gaulle's account of her meeting with Eunice, and her description of the Shrivers' unconventional habits, had struck a chord with her husband. President de Gaulle decided that he wanted to become better acquainted with the new American ambassador.

At the palace, Shriver joined de Gaulle and his minister of culture, André Malraux, for lunch. The president and the ambassador immediately took to each other. De Gaulle was intrigued by this charismatic American who seemed incapable of behaving like a typical career diplomat and who seemed genuinely interested in interacting with the French people, not just with members of the formal diplomatic apparatus. De Gaulle had respected Shriver's predecessor, Chip Bohlen, too, but Bohlen didn't thrill ordinary French people the way Shriver did. Shriver, for his part, was enthralled by de Gaulle: his physical presence, his charisma, the boldness of his conception of France's role in the world.

Several factors contributed to the warming of relations between the United States and France in 1968. One factor was Lyndon Johnson's willingness to send negotiators to talk to the North Vietnamese, an implicit admission that de Gaulle had been right all along: Outright victory in Vietnam was impossible. A second factor was the social unrest that rocked both America and France that year, giving them common ground for discussion. A third was the Soviet Union's invasion of Czechoslovakia that summer, which undermined de Gaulle's conviction that the USSR was not a threat to Western Europe and forced him closer to the United States. Other geopolitical factors, too, helped make the environment more conducive to better Franco-American relations. But without the highly unexpected personal relationship that the Shrivers struck up with the de Gaulles, the healing of the rift between the two countries— culminating with President Nixon's state visit to Paris early in 1969—might not have been possible.

Robert O. Blake, Shriver's deputy chief of mission, worked in the foreign service for forty years. He recalled that "of all the ambassadors I've seen in all the places I've been, Shriver was more original and effective at 'public diplomacy' than anybody we've ever had." He improved the "morale and mood of the foreign service," Blake said, "by inspiring us to reach out to the French with warmth rather than pessimism and restraint." Bob Holliday, a longtime member of the foreign service who worked in the embassy, says that Shriver almost single-handedly "won the hearts and minds of the French people and the heart and mind of de Gaulle." As ambassador, Holliday believes, "Shriver did probably the best job that has ever been done in the history of our foreign service."

Shriver created a youth corps consisting of the embassy's younger staffers, and he instructed them to convey American values to their French counterparts. He established exchange programs for American and French politicians, groundbreaking science-and-technology transfer programs, and (with Eunice) a French Special Olympics.

More than any previous ambassador, Shriver traveled around the country to meet with the French people—not just with government officials or celebrities or top business executives but with fishermen and coal miners and factory workers and students. And he didn't meet them in an arid, press-conference environment but in their milieu. He washed tuna with the fishermen, got his face blackened by soot with the coal miners, sat alongside the barricades with the students. Indeed, it wasn't what he did so much as how he did it—lending US diplomacy "a rare and welcome panache," according to *Time*—that made such a powerful impression. Over the summer of 1968, Shriver traveled around the country and made speeches commemorating the fiftieth anniversary of various World War I battles. At Verdun, for instance, Shriver celebrated the anniversary of a successful American offensive there and gently reminded the French officials in the audience that European security still depended on the forceful presence of the United States. To the surprise of embassy staff members, who had seen similar speeches by Chip Bohlen greeted with a chilly hauteur, Shriver's remarks were followed by enthusiastic cries of "Vive l'Amérique!"

By the fall of 1968, American newspaper columnists were reporting that "everybody had noticed the bouncy cheer at the American Embassy these days after all those years when the diplomatic barometer read nothing but 'glum.'" Shriver's "drastic change in style" had helped bring about a "verbal bombing halt" by the French against the Americans. "It is going to be much more fun being nice to Americans now that Ambassador Shriver is here," declared Prime Minister Georges Pompidou in August.

The French people came to love him as one of their own—"Sarjean Shreevair," as they called him—in a way that President de Gaulle could not fail to notice. It would soon become the consensus view in the State Department and among experts on Franco-American relations that Shriver was the most effective US ambassador to France in fifty years. There was no small irony in this. Several of LBJ's foreign policy aides had strongly advised the president that it was essential to appoint an experienced diplomat who was fluent in French, given the high diplomatic stakes. And now Shriver, with his high-school French and lack of any formal diplomatic training, was doing more to put Franco-American relations on a good footing than his more experienced predecessors. "It's a different ball game now," Shriver said, when a reporter from the *Washington Star* asked him about Franco-American relations. "De Gaulle says things to me he hasn't discussed in years."

Shriver cut a dashing, if sometimes eccentric, figure around the country. He and his family would bicycle together around Paris. On a brief trip to the Riviera, he startled guests at a garden party by showing up in swimming trunks and bathrobe. He played tennis in Monaco with Prince Rainier. In June he was the first American ever to play in the French tennis championships (later to become the French Open). In early July he crossed the English Channel to play in the "gentleman's veterans" doubles draw at Wimbledon, the first American of high diplomatic rank ever to play there—and he even won a match. French newspapers and magazines covered his family as if they were movie stars. French television devoted whole half-hour programs to "un Kennedy à Paris." *Paris Match*, a popular national magazine, listed Shriver as one of the five most popular people in France.

The American ambassador's residence became one of the most exciting social destinations in Paris. As they had in Chicago and at Timberlawn, the Shrivers held regular salons on various topics, where fifty or more people—a mixture of students, diplomats, French officials, and international celebrities—would crowd into their living room for lively discussions. The tennis star Arthur Ashe was a regular guest, as were Donald Dell and America's Davis Cup tennis team. So too were the Aga Khan, Warren Beatty, Harry Belafonte, Yul Brynner, Maurice Chevalier, Julie Christie, Rose Kennedy, Vanessa Redgrave, and Peter Ustinov.

The New Frontier had come to Paris.

CHAPTER FORTY

The 1968 Election

⟋⟍

For all the success Shriver was enjoying in France, a significant part of his attention remained tightly fixed on politics in the United States. The death of Robert Kennedy had dramatically altered the complexion of the 1968 election campaign.

As soon as Humphrey first mentioned him as a possible running mate on June 21, a Shriver-for-VP boomlet began to blossom. Several days later, Warren Hoge, the Washington correspondent for the *New York Post*, wrote that Humphrey was "enthusiastic" about Shriver as a running mate and "eager to pursue him." Hoge observed that it was "a graceful way out of a situation that has grown increasingly more awkward with each suggestion that the slain Senator's brother, Edward, run with Humphrey in 1968." Shriver, Hoge wrote, "spares Humphrey the embarrassment of making an appeal for Kennedy support as obvious as a direct bid to Ted Kennedy. And Shriver spares Kennedy the political discomfort of having to reject such a bid—which he doesn't want—when polls are showing that with him or some other Kennedy representative on the ticket the Democrats are assured of victory in November." Hoge added

that although Shriver had not been formally approached by LBJ's vice president, he was reportedly "receptive" to the idea of joining the Humphrey ticket.

This was true. As much as Shriver enjoyed his work as ambassador, he coveted the idea of winning elected office. Every time over the last nine years that
he had seriously contemplated running for office, his sense of duty to someone
or something had thwarted him: Joe Kennedy in 1960, the Peace Corps in 1962,
the OEO in 1966, and Bobby Kennedy's circle in 1964. Like the Kennedy family, Shriver conceived of public service as almost a religious calling; winning
election to high office seemed to him the best way to serve his country. "It has
never really fascinated me to have a title like governor, ambassador, or senator,"
he told a reporter in 1970. "But I have always felt the greatest public service a
man can give is through elective office."

Many of the people Shriver had worked with over the years believed that
he would be a good president of the United States. Some of them had angled
for years to put him in a position where he might someday have a chance to
make a credible run for the presidency. Now, with Bobby Kennedy gone, Ted
Kennedy reticent, and Hubert Humphrey in need of a running mate, they saw
an opportunity. "A number of us who had worked with Sargent Shriver in the
Peace Corps or the War on Poverty thought a Humphrey-Shriver ticket would
be a good and winning combination," Harris Wofford recalled. As Shriver was
in Paris, "several of us decided to go to [the Democratic convention in] Chicago
to uphold his interests—and our interest in his nomination."

Weeks before the convention, however, it was clear that the road to a
Shriver nomination would be politically tricky, for two main reasons. First,
there was no guarantee that Humphrey would win the Democratic presidential nomination. McCarthy was still stalking him through the later primaries.
Many still hoped Ted Kennedy would allow himself to be drafted. And there
were suspicions that, with Bobby out of the race, Lyndon Johnson would go
back on his word and make himself available at the convention.

Second, of course, was the Kennedy family. No one knew exactly what "the
family" wanted. Actually, it was now becoming increasingly clear that there was
no longer a monolithic Kennedy family—if in fact there ever had been since
Joe Kennedy's incapacitation by stroke in 1961. Polls showed that the American
people, especially Democrats, craved a Kennedy on the 1968 ticket. But whereas
in the past the order of succession had been clear (Joe Jr. to Jack to Bobby to

Ted)—and whereas in the past Joe Sr. had been around to make decisions any time the order of succession was *not* clear—that wasn't true anymore, especially if Ted were not going to step forward. That left a myriad of sometimes competing, sometimes overlapping groups. There were the former aides to Jack Kennedy (Fred Dutton, Ralph Dungan); the Bobby loyalists, some of whom had been first-generation aides to Jack (Arthur Schlesinger, Ted Sorensen, Kenny O'Donnell, and Steve Smith) and some of whom had not (Adam Walinsky, Peter Edelman); and the JFK people who had, against Bobby's wishes, stayed on under Johnson (Larry O'Brien, Robert McNamara, McGeorge Bundy, and Shriver). The group most antagonistic toward Shriver tended to be Bobby's supporters, but even within this crowd were individuals (Donald Dell, Frank Mankiewicz, Mike Feldman) who felt as loyal to Sarge, or nearly so, as they did to Bobby. Then there was the family proper. The politically inclined in-laws, Shriver and Steve Smith, "circled each other like boxers," as someone who was friendly to both recalled.

Although too much can be made of these divisions, Shriver could not simply ignore them. Actually, the early signs were favorable. Bill Moyers, who had left the Johnson administration in 1966 and was now the publisher of *Newsday*, wrote to Shriver on the day Warren Hoge's article appeared. "I had a long and private meeting Tuesday with Fred Dutton and asked him how the hardcore Kennedy people would react to you as vice president," Moyers wrote. "I went over the reasons why your selection would be good for Humphrey and the country, hitting hard on the symbolic meaning it would have for the young, the poor, and the black. He thought this made sense, and expressed the belief that the idea would be accepted by most of the people around [Bobby] Kennedy, himself (Dutton) included." For the time being, though, Moyers advised Shriver to lie low, since appearing to campaign for the vice presidency might antagonize them. "I would advise you, if asked by reporters about the V.P. thing, to say *nothing*—public or private," Moyers wrote. "That goes for what you say to your acquaintances as well, publicly and privately. *Discretion* is the first virtue for the moment."

Bill Josephson, the former general counsel of the Peace Corps, had been in contact with Shriver about these issues for several months. In early July, Josephson met secretly with Max Kampelman, a close adviser to Hubert Humphrey, to discuss the Shriver situation. As Josephson later reported to Shriver, Kampelman "had talked briefly with HHH about you and HHH enthusiastically wants you around but felt that he could not, in terms of his relationship with the President, ask you to drop the new assignment [in Paris]." When Josephson told Kampelman that Shriver and LBJ had agreed that Shriver would stay in Paris only until some better opportunity opened up in the United States, Kampelman replied that "HHH definitely wanted you in the new Administration and then brought up the subject of the Vice Presidency." Kampelman asked if someone would prepare a memo, outlining Shriver's qualifications for vice president and describing what he would bring to the Humphrey ticket. Kampelman also implied that before Humphrey made any official move toward bringing Shriver onto the ticket, Ted Kennedy would have to provide his blessing.

Thus began the period of Waiting for Ted. Kennedy supporters all across the country were waiting for Ted to say he would accept the Democratic presidential nomination. Humphrey and company were waiting to see if Ted would be available for the vice presidency. Shriver and company were waiting to see whether Ted would support Shriver for the vice presidency. But, for the moment, Ted wasn't saying anything.

When Shriver had lunch with Cy Sulzberger, the *Times* foreign affairs columnist, on July 10, Shriver said he would like Humphrey to ask him to run for the vice presidency, but he "thought . . . Ted Kennedy was the obvious choice, provided he was asked and that he had surmounted the psychological shock of Bobby's death."

On July 17 Don Petrie, the business executive who had been close to Shriver since his days at the Merchandise Mart, reported that the Shriver-for-VP trial balloons the Humphrey camp had sent up via leaks to the press had produced "generally favorable comment, generally along the lines of 'that makes a lot of sense.'" Petrie also recounted to Shriver a conversation that a colleague had had with Steve Smith about the Democratic ticket. According to Petrie, Smith had said that while it was obvious that Kennedy could win the nomination, he didn't want it. Nor did he want to be Humphrey's running mate. So, Smith was asked, who would Humphrey pick? "It looks like Sarge," Smith responded. "But the family resents it."

But what, exactly, constituted "the family"? "The Kennedy organization from New York to California is largely in disarray and acts sort of punch-drunk," Petrie wrote. "They are making moves to preserve some semblance of influence and power but they are the instinctive moves of a fighter who took a long count in the previous round. If, as individuals, they weren't so very able it would be apparent to everyone what bad shape they are in. But they're pros. So far no external bickering. That will come when Teddy announces he won't run."

In late July, Ted finally announced that he wouldn't run for president. Richard Daley, breaking with his longtime practice of doing his candidate work entirely behind closed doors, publicly proposed to draft Kennedy for the vice presidency. Kennedy declined that, as well. Newspapers began handicapping the alternate choices, with Shriver usually being one of the top two names on the list. Clayton Fritchey wrote in the *Washington Star*, "Sen. Edward Kennedy's withdrawal has complicated [Humphrey's] problem, for where else can he find what he was looking for in Ted, that is, someone who is young, liberal, dovish, urban-minded, already famous, and, above all a magnet for the Kennedy legions? The able Sargent Shriver is married to a Kennedy, but he is not a hero to the followers of JFK and RFK. Nor does he have a record of peace on Vietnam."

In the first week in August, the Republican convention in Miami nominated Richard Nixon as its presidential candidate. Maryland governor Spiro Agnew was nominated as his running mate. This opened another potential opportunity: If Nixon-Agnew won in 1968, Maryland would need a replacement governor. Why not Shriver? Josephson and Richard Schifter, who was head of the Democratic Party in Montgomery County, Maryland, began exploring this possibility on Shriver's behalf. On the vice presidency, Shriver himself continued to lie low through early August, as his network of influential supporters quietly grew: Coretta Scott King, newspaper columnist Charlie Bartlett, civil rights leader Bayard Rustin, Democratic National Committee vice chair Louis Martin. On August 9, the Senate majority leader, Mike Mansfield, secretly visited Shriver in Paris, to help him strategize. So, too, several days later, did Bill Josephson and Bill Moyers. When newspaper reporters caught wind of Moyers's visit, they speculated that he was delivering an invitation to the ticket from Humphrey. Moyers denied this.

On August 9 Josephson again met with Max Kampelman, who got right to the point: "Let's talk turkey about Shriver." Kampelman told Josephson that for Humphrey to select Shriver, three arguments against his nomination would have to be addressed. First, "selection of Shriver would saddle Humphrey with an easy target for Nixon. Humphrey is trying to run not on the Johnson

Administration's record but on the Humphrey Administration's future. With Shriver as a running mate, Humphrey could be more easily tagged with responsibility for 'OEO's failures,' for the OEO programs that set in motion . . . the riots and so forth."

Second, Kampelman told Josephson, the selection of Shriver "would alienate the Kennedy family and their surrounding politicos." Josephson countered that Humphrey needed to identify someone "who speaks authoritatively for the Kennedy family" and to get "a reliable report of what he or she says." Josephson told Kampelman that "if, for example, Rose Kennedy, Eunice Kennedy or Ethel Kennedy were asked," he was "reasonably sure that they would be strongly positive about Sarge's candidacy." However, "if Steve Smith were asked, he would be negative." But why, Josephson asked, should Smith's views be taken as authoritative?

At this, as Josephson recorded in his notes immediately following the meeting, "Max's eyebrows shot up." Kampelman said that "Steve was negative toward Sarge" and that "Steve and the Vice President had dined together recently." Kenny O'Donnell was "also knocking Sarge." Humphrey was influenced by these opinions, Kampelman said, because of "the importance to the Vice President of not losing the enthusiasm and competence of the Kennedy supporters nationwide."

Josephson responded by suggesting that "probably Ted Kennedy was the only person who could and would speak authoritatively for the family." Kampelman agreed that Ted's views would carry great weight, not only with Humphrey but also with party leaders like Dick Daley, who refused to give up on the idea of Ted for vice president. The challenge was getting Humphrey and Kennedy together for a chat; Ted was still being elusive.

When Kampelman brought up the third argument being made against Shriver, Josephson's "jaw dropped." Shriver, some people were saying, was a "wonderful man," a "great human being"—but "intellectually unqualified to be president." Josephson was aghast. That's incredible, he told Max. Shriver was one of the smartest people he had ever known. "Max repeated soberly that the argument was being made. I asked for an example of who was saying this. Max declined to give one."

In retrospect, it seems quite likely that it was Smith and O'Donnell, along with possible others such as Schlesinger and Sorensen, who were leveling the "intellectually unqualified" charge. Josephson was moved to write to Kampelman, extolling Shriver's intellect.

> I . . . have worked for and known Sarge well for seven years, roughly half of my adult life. I am considered to be a bright guy and an intellectual. Yet, I have always had to run to catch up with Sarge. I have handed him large and small issues, complicated and simple, well staffed out and badly staffed out, and he has rarely handled them other than superbly. Sarge has a way, even in the most complicated of situations, of reaching out and picking up the three or four most salient factors pro and con, measuring them against one another and reaching a result. This may well strike some people as unsophisticated, but it gets the issues resolved well and quickly. Sarge's personality is more receptive to information than any I have ever seen. He will read anything quickly, carefully and understandingly. He is always alert, curious, and questing. Another strength is his ability to participate in the give-and-take that moves ideas down the road to action.

Stirring testimony. But would it be enough to sway Humphrey?

THE PALACE GUARD WITHOUT A PALACE

In his August 15 column for the *Washington Post*, Drew Pearson listed the running mates Humphrey was thinking about: Richard Hughes, the governor of New Jersey; Joseph Alioto, the mayor of San Francisco; Edmund Muskie, the former governor of Maine and a current senator; and Shriver, who, Pearson implied, was the most likely choice because of "his appeal to youth."

In mid-August, Maryland Democratic leader Dick Schifter flew to Paris to talk secretly with Shriver about his chances for the national ticket and about possibilities in Maryland. Schifter and Shriver agreed that if Shriver were to become the vice presidential nominee, he would need the support of two key people: Dick Daley and Ted Kennedy. Shriver asked Josephson and Moyers to see if they could get Louis Martin and Dan Rostenkowski to talk to Daley. Kennedy would be more difficult. After agreeing to make a discreet side trip to Paris during a European vacation in the second week in August, Kennedy never showed up.

Humphrey's people had been told about the planned Kennedy-Shriver meeting in Paris and were hoping this would clear the way for Shriver's

nomination. Kampelman was telling people that the choice was down to
Shriver and Alioto. But when Humphrey and company learned that Kennedy had
returned to the States without talking to Shriver, they got antsy. Was Kennedy's
failure to visit Paris an implicit rejection of a Shriver nomination? Ted's views,
Josephson wrote Shriver on August 17, are still "the crucial point." What those
views were, exactly, needed to be discovered soon. Perhaps, Josephson suggested,
Eunice could contrive a trip home to visit relatives, and *she* could have the necessary meeting with her brother. "It is trickier [for you to come back to the
United States] but perhaps you should. I don't know. *Do* something."

On August 20, Bill Moyers delivered to Humphrey a memo, "Concerning the
Vice Presidency," that he had written with Josephson, Herb Kramer, and others.
The memo made a strong case for Shriver on his own merits, while trying to
finesse the question of his being a "Kennedy candidate" without the support of
certain Kennedy people.

Shriver would appeal to the young, because as director of the Peace Corps,
Head Start, and other programs, he had become "the personal symbol for the
idealism those programs inspired." In the spring of 1968 Shriver, alone among
LBJ's high-ranking cabinet officials, could appear on college campuses without
being picketed. Shriver could also reach out to black voters: Two years ago, the
memo reminded Humphrey, Shriver had ridden through the streets of Watts,
packed with 10,000 spectators, in a car on which his Watts hosts had written
"Sargent Shriver—The Man Who Has Done the Most for the Negro." Also, not
only was Shriver a proven administrator, a forceful campaigner, and a nationally known figure, but he also had not been "a casualty of the Vietnam war."
The memo said:

> As a member of the Administration he could not and did not denounce the war,
> but he appeals to critics of the war because he had been totally involved in the
> two Kennedy-Johnson programs most remote from and opposite to the war: The
> Peace Corps and the Economic Opportunity Programs. He is on record as con-
> sistently demanding a greater share of effort and funds for domestic programs.
> At the same time, as Ambassador to France, he personifies the overwhelming
> desire for peace as it is being sought in the Paris negotiations.

Finally, Shriver got along well with Humphrey and, as the "prototype of the modern American Catholic" (he had already been named America's Catholic layman of the year), he would help win the crucial blue-collar ethnic vote.

Inevitably, however, the memo began with the Kennedy question, devoting more words to that than to any of Shriver's individual traits.

> Shriver appeals to many of the people reached by Robert Kennedy. Not because he is married into the Kennedy family, but because Shriver espouses many of the same causes, embraces many of the same principles, and creates some of the same kind of excitement as the late Senator, he stands in the Kennedy tradition. He is a personality in his own right, but it is a personality with the kind of charisma respected in the New Politics. It is argued by some that Shriver is not acceptable to the "Kennedy people," but it needs to be asked, "Who *are* the 'Kennedy people'"? Are they only the personal staff of the late Senator, or do they not include all those thousands of people, such as those who served in the Peace Corps, who remain loyal to the ideals of John and Robert Kennedy and wish to serve those ideals even though the men who embodied them are gone? They are also "Kennedy People." Furthermore, Kennedy supporters are not monolithic. Some have gone to Eugene McCarthy, some to George McGovern [the South Dakota senator who had recently put himself into contention for the presidential nomination], some to Hubert Humphrey. It is absurd to argue that any one man is unacceptable to all "Kennedy people."

The memo seems to have been leaked to *Washington Post* columnist Drew Pearson, who on August 21 wrote a column, "Shriver Stands out as VP Timber," that strongly promoted Shriver along the lines outlined in the memo. Pearson, too, began by addressing the Kennedy question. "Four years ago when President Johnson considered drafting Shriver to be his 1964 running mate, Mrs. Shriver, who is the eldest of the Kennedy sisters, is reported to have said, 'No, it's Bob's turn.' Ken O'Donnell, JFK's appointments secretary was even blunter. He sent word to Shriver that if any Kennedy were going to run for Vice President it would be Bobby, not a man who was only 'half a Kennedy.' Time and tragedy have changed this. Bobby is gone. Now it may be Sargent Shriver's turn."

Finally, Ted Kennedy spoke up. He telephoned Shriver in France on August 19 and the two brothers-in-law spoke for thirty minutes. On the question of whether "the family" would support Shriver on the Humphrey ticket, Kennedy was ultimately inconclusive. But the substance of the conversation, as Shriver reported it the next day in a letter, was revealing. Shriver wrote: "'Kennedy wing' of Dem. Party most anxious now to keep heat on HHH to change his policy (whatever it is today) on V-N & establish clear-cut position—let's say same as Bobby's—not same as Gene [McCarthy's]. They feel if I were 'available' to HHH now that I would present a way for HHH to circumvent their efforts—an escape route if you will—at the precise time that they are trying to get maximum swing in their direction principally on the war & secondarily on national priorities for spending. I responded that I had no desire or intention of 'circumventing' such an effort and that I had been speaking about changing priorities for 3 years, well before anyone else."

The conversation then turned more specifically to overt opposition to Shriver within the Kennedy camp. "I brought up issue presented to me by Sorensen, O'Donnell, S. Smith talk against me personally etc etc. To which he pointed out the reality that many K boosters really are sore at me—even bitter—because I didn't help more [on Bobby's campaign]." Teddy agreed to "keep in close touch" with Shriver through the convention and said that "if S.S. [Steve Smith] were the source [of the negative comments about Shriver] that he would slow him down or shut him up."

But the fundamental problem, Shriver now realized, was "that most of those who had staked most of their personal hopes on RFK are extremely frustrated—and the prospect of anyone 'in the family' who didn't impale himself— or herself—on a picket fence without regard to the consequence—suddenly being in a position to pick up all the marbles—that prospect is galling!"

His best hope of overcoming Humphrey's nervousness about alienating the Kennedy family, Shriver now decided, was to instigate a lobbying effort on his behalf by other people close to Robert Kennedy. If Bobby's supporters "could be persuaded to speak out publicly for me," Shriver wrote, "that mere fact would start to kill the jazz being circulated by the Ted Sorensen-Arthur Schlesinger self-appointed mouthpieces."

"All I asked Teddie was for neutrality," Shriver continued. "I said frankly I had never asked him or Steve or anyone else in the family for anything—which is true. Now all I suggested was that it brought no credit to anyone for Steve or others to attack me. I can't report that Teddie explicitly stated he would be neutral. My belief is this: He will try to be neutral if he doesn't run himself—but his neutrality would be neutrality *for* Muskie or McGovern or [Maryland senator Joe Tydings] and neutrality *against* [Oklahoma senator] Fred Harris or me."

In Shriver's analysis, at least one of three things would have to happen for Humphrey to select him. One, an alternative Kennedy group (Feldman, Dutton, and company) could come out strongly for him. Two, Humphrey could adopt a strong anti-Vietnam platform at the convention, thereby mitigating the need for the Kennedy wing to apply pressure on him. And three, "if Humphrey really wanted me he could (theoretically) agree to most of the things the Kennedy wing wanted and say he had to have me with all-out support from Teddie. True, that's expecting a lot from HHH but maybe he wants the Kennedy wing that badly!"

Shriver concluded his letter bitingly. "Clearly . . . the same clique who opposed [the Peace Corps] as an independent agency—the same palace guard (now without a palace) (or a pretender) find it hard to accept the prospect of a prodigal in-law (let alone son) sitting down to their feast."

The pique Shriver expresses in this letter is striking—and uncharacteristic. This letter is one of the few tangible pieces of evidence revealing that he ever felt, in fifty years of being a Kennedy in-law, the slightest bitterness about his place in the clan. Many of his closest friends and associates say that in all their time of acquaintance with him, they never heard him express any overt resentment, regret, or frustration at the impositions and demands of the Kennedy family. Indeed, many of these same friends and associates express frustration on Shriver's behalf, saying they can't fathom how he endured so many years of subservience to his brothers-in-law and other family members. (Other of Shriver's friends concede that there were moments when flashes of frustration showed through.) But Shriver himself, although he does not disavow the sentiments this letter expresses, has said for years that, on balance, he has felt blessed—personally and politically—to have been associated with the Kennedy family.

Moreover, Ted Kennedy, the most obvious candidate for Shriver's hostility at this juncture, was a hard man to hate. Shriver had liked and greatly admired Jack, and for the most part respected Bobby. But he felt friendliest toward Ted, who had a warmer personality than either of his brothers, and he had a hard time holding family politics against him. The problem for Sarge in 1968, according to Donald Dell, who worked for both Shriver and Bobby Kennedy, was that "Steve [Smith] was the money guy for both Bobby and Ted. He was always in the middle of everything. He ran the financial side of the foundation. He had a major role in everything the family did. He was running [Bobby's campaign] in early 1968, and later he was running [Ted's campaigns]." This complicated Sarge's dealings with the brothers.

Although there was tension between Bobby's and Sarge's staffs, Dell notes that "the two principals didn't necessarily enter into it. For example: I have *never* heard Sarge criticize Bobby or Ted Kennedy in my presence ever, *ever,* at any time, and I've been damn close to Sarge, in a lot of situations. Having said that, there is no question in my mind that Sarge didn't like some of the people *around* Bobby."

Dell says that there was a "natural human competitiveness or jealousy" that ran both directions between some of Bobby's advisers and Shriver.

> Schlesinger and Sorenson, for instance. They were brilliant writers. One of the smartest guys Bobby ever had was Adam Walinsky. You'll never meet a smarter guy than that. But none of these guys had the people skills, and the managerial ability of Sargent Shriver. Take Bobby Kennedy, whom everybody adored and loved: he had the aura and the Kennedy name and the good looks—but he didn't have the people skills that Sargent Shriver had. Not even close. Don't misunderstand me, I loved Bobby. I'm just saying they were different. And I think that most people in the Kennedy camp thought of Sarge as glib and easy and great with people—they used that to kind of knock him. Because they didn't have his ability!

Such nuances, however, weren't as good copy for the press as blunter accounts of family infighting. Word that the Kennedys had blackballed Shriver was soon reported by the press, with Drew Pearson providing the fullest play-by-play account. "Hubert Humphrey's search for a Vice-President has run into a family feud that could only happen in the Kentucky mountains or with the Kennedy clan," he reported with typical hyperbole several days into the convention.

> Teddy Kennedy doesn't want the Vice Presidency, but the family has turned thumbs down on Ted's brother-in-law, Sargent Shriver, who does. And since one reason for putting Shriver on the ticket would be to get Kennedy family support, this amounts to a firm veto.

Among the Kennedys you play for keeps, and envoys for Hubert Humphrey have found that their views on brother-in-law Shriver are deadly serious. It is based on the family rule of succession and dates back to a meeting held in the White House immediately after the assassination in Dallas at which time it was decided that Robert F. Kennedy would pick up the mantle of his late brother and carry on. . . .

The reason for the family veto of Sargent Shriver now is the argument, first, that he is not really a Kennedy; second, that if he were elected Vice President he might get in the way of Teddy Kennedy's future. The country might get fed up with a chain of Kennedys running for high office; or the Humphrey Administration, of which he would become a part, might become unpopular.

Although Humphrey had determined that Shriver possessed all the qualifications he was seeking in a running mate, he felt he couldn't do anything until the Kennedy family blessed that selection. As Max Kampelman recalled in his memoir, "Hubert was very fond of Sarge, whose genial and charming exterior hid a strong sense of principle, personal integrity, and stubborn independence." But Kenny O'Donnell passed the word to Humphrey that the family would consider it "an unfriendly act" if he were to select Shriver. Humphrey called Shriver in Paris to explain the bind he was in. When Sarge reported the situation to Eunice, she "began serving as her husband's ambassador to remove the veto of the Kennedy family" and recruited her mother to the cause, as well. Still, Pearson observed, "it's doubtful whether Mrs. Shriver can get much effective help from her mother in breaking down the Kennedy clan's taboo on her husband as a candidate for Vice President. Meanwhile, however, Eunice has been wearing a Humphrey button in Paris and has made it unequivocally clear who she is for."

Unfortunately, according to the *Washington Post*'s society columnist Maxine Cheshire (a longtime scourge of the Kennedys and other celebrities), Ethel Kennedy was running a counter campaign against Shriver. "We never took [Ethel's opposition] very seriously, I give you my word," Eunice would tell a reporter in 1972. "I consider Ethel my greatest friend. I've never had any feeling *ever* from her about disloyalty. And if she didn't want Sarge to do something, I have full 100 percent confidence that she would call me and say, 'For God's sake, will you say this or say that to Sargent.' She does not work around 18 people and say, 'Stick it to Sarge.'"

History tends to bear out Eunice's protestations of family harmony. In the

1970s, when some of Bobby and Ethel's children were suffering with various well-publicized psychological problems and drug addictions, Ethel—herself suffering greatly in the aftermath of her husband's assassination—turned to Eunice and Sarge for assistance, and they served for a while as surrogate parents for some of the kids in her large brood. Max Kennedy, for instance, lived with the Shrivers for a year when he began college, and he credits them with helping him to get his life on track.

Another columnist, Marianne Means, raised the question of whether the Kennedy family simply felt that Shriver was jumping his proper place in line ahead of Ted Kennedy and possibly Steve Smith. Smith, she noted, "has ambitions to run in 1969 for mayor of New York, a job [whose] national visibility . . . could easily spawn a presidential candidacy."

With Ted Kennedy apparently neutral to negative on Shriver, the odds that Humphrey would select him were small. But Shriver's loyal crew of supporters persisted nonetheless, and they traveled to the convention in Chicago to press the case for their man. A few days before the convention opened, Oklahoma senator Fred Harris was telling Moyers that Humphrey had narrowed the list to Shriver and himself.

The journalist Theodore White later wrote that as the convention began, on the evening of Monday, August 26, "it was obvious that this promised to be one of the most unusual conventions in American political history." But no one could have foretold just how damaging for the Democrats it would be. Walter Ridder later observed that for the Democratic Party, the convention was like the *Lusitania*, struck by the twin torpedoes of war and race but without anyone yet realizing that the ship was going down.

Through the first day of the convention, the leading rumor was that Ted Kennedy would be drafted into taking the presidential nomination after all. Southern delegates had been defecting from Humphrey, hoping to goad LBJ into jumping into the race. Dick Daley was reported to be holding his delegates back, waiting "to see if something develops." The California delegation pledged all 174 of its delegates to Kennedy. But the Kennedy boom ended as quickly as it began. Southern delegates, fearing that Kennedy would be nominated, moved their support back to Humphrey. More important, Kennedy made clear through Steve Smith that he would not allow himself to be drafted.

By Wednesday morning, it looked as if Humphrey had the nomination sewn up. But as delegates heatedly debated Vietnam (a Humphrey-Johnson resolution favoring continued involvement was competing with a McCarthy resolution in favor of complete withdrawal), all hell was breaking loose outside on the streets. Vietnam protesters, civil rights activists, black power advocates, and various hippies, crazies, and drug-addled college students whipped themselves into an almost insurrectional frenzy—only to find themselves being brutalized by National Guardsmen and the Chicago police under Mayor Daley's direction. Mobs of police clashed with mobs of protesters. It was as if all the pent-up frustrations and revolutionary aspirations loosed by the Great Society were welling up at once—and all the reactionary, counter-revolutionary forces provoked by the Great Society were stirring in response. And all of it was captured on television. "The whole world is watching, the whole world is watching!" the protesters cried. At 8:05 p.m. on Wednesday night, White jotted this sentence in his notebook: "The Democrats are finished." A little more than three hours later, Humphrey was officially nominated by the convention to be the Democratic presidential candidate. "I was a victim of that convention," Humphrey told White after the election, "as much as a man getting the Hong Kong flu. Chicago was a catastrophe."

That the convention gravely wounded Humphrey's election hopes is indisputable. But is there a chance it could have turned out otherwise? What if Humphrey had selected Shriver as his running mate on the final day of the convention, instead of Maine senator Edmund Muskie? Harris Wofford, for one, believes that "if Humphrey had picked Shriver, that week and the ensuing campaign might have ended differently." Listening to radio reports and getting telephone updates in Paris, Shriver was appalled by what Daley's police were doing. He told Wofford that whoever won the nomination should speak out forcefully against the police violence—even at the risk of offending Dick Daley, which any Democratic presidential hopeful would clearly be reluctant to do. "The test is what Humphrey does now," Shriver told Wofford over the phone. "He has about eighteen hours until his acceptance speech to show where he stands on all this."

At the time he spoke to Wofford on Wednesday, Shriver had reason to believe he might be in a position to influence Humphrey significantly. Despite resistance to his nomination from certain quarters, Shriver knew that he was still very close to being named to the ticket. When Dick Daley had decided that there was no chance Kennedy would join Humphrey, he decided that Shriver would give the Democrats the best chance of winning. At breakfast with Humphrey on Wednesday morning, Daley strongly urged that he pick Shriver. The Chicago papers reported that Shriver's selection was imminent.

In Paris, Shriver met with Cy Vance and Averell Harriman to discuss what sort of Vietnam peace plan he would urge on Humphrey if the vice president called to offer him a place on the ticket. Shriver also began preparing an acceptance speech, in which he would attempt to reach out both to the peace movement generally and to the protestors who had been beaten and jailed that week in Chicago in particular. "From 4,000 miles away," Wofford wrote, "Shriver was able to see more clearly the significance of what was happening than Humphrey in his busy suite on the twenty-fifth floor of the Hilton." Shriver's selection to the ticket would have helped defuse the tension and would have controlled the damage the convention caused to the Democratic Party. Humphrey, in contrast, attacked the protestors and publicly supported Dick Daley.

At midnight on Wednesday, Walter Mondale called Wofford from Humphrey's suite to tell him that "Kennedy family opposition to Shriver's nomination was weighing heavily against his selection." Wofford's suspicion was that someone like Larry O'Brien or Kenny O'Donnell was speaking in the family name, "perhaps without prior authority." Wofford told Mondale that this "former palace guard" had "no monopoly on the Kennedy legacy." Besides, Wofford said, you don't really think that a man as decent as Ted Kennedy would impede the aspirations of his own brother-in-law?

In fact, Kennedy already had. Earlier in the day, according to Humphrey's aides, Ted had called and promised him his support. But according to Max Kampelman, Humphrey's words after getting off the phone with Kennedy were, "I sensed Teddy was not adamant [in his opposition to Shriver], but led me to believe better not." On Thursday morning, August 29, Humphrey's people let Shriver's people know that he was out. The VP nomination was down to Edmund Muskie and Fred Harris.

Reflecting on the events some forty years later, Kennedy did not clearly recollect his conversation with Humphrey, but he will never forget his state of mind at the time. His brother Bobby's death had been as devastating to him as John Kennedy's had been to Bobby. Having seen two of his brothers assassinated while campaigning, Ted wanted nothing more than to get as far away from politics as possible until his wounds could heal. He deliberately absented himself from the convention, sending word repeatedly through Steve Smith and others that he would not accept the nomination either for the presidency or the vice presidency. He even left Hyannis Port and went to a hideaway in Maine to avoid political pressures.

Kennedy had been disappointed when Shriver resisted coming back from Paris to participate in Bobby's campaign. In addition, he had been in a state of physical and emotional exhaustion for much of the time since Bobby's funeral. All of this, Kennedy now believes, accounts for the negative vibrations Humphrey may have received when they spoke. Nevertheless, he is adamant that he did not veto his brother-in-law in his talk with Humphrey, and maintains that he has always had genuine affection for Shriver, as well as respect for his abilities and accomplishments.

Shriver, having spilled his bile in his letter of August 20, was philosophical. He recognized that the Kennedys had their own political priorities, which placed blood relatives above in-laws. "In politics, when men are playing for such stakes," he told Wofford, "you can't count on personal ties and shouldn't take these things personally." By the end of the convention—with McCarthy's peace plank defeated, Humphrey defending Daley's police tactics, and the Democrats plummeting in the polls—it seemed that maybe he was best off not getting the nomination anyway.

"We needed the goodwill of the Kennedys more than we needed Sarge," said one of Humphrey's advisers. "His name was effectively vetoed." "For the second time," as Wofford would write in his memoir, "a brother-in-law had put his future political interests above Shriver's immediate opportunity."

Two years later Max Kampelman had lunch with Shriver in Washington. As Kampelman wrote in a letter afterward, "We . . . talked about 1968 and the convention. I again made it clear to [Shriver] that he was knifed and I believe he knows that. I believe he also knows who did it."

THE PEACE TALKS AND THE 1968 ELECTION

Within a day of Shriver's being denied the vice presidential nomination, rumors started circulating about his being considered for the Maryland governor's position that would be abandoned by Spiro Agnew if he and Nixon won the general election. Shriver's political supporters began writing to him about that possibility as well as others in Illinois and New York. "We are ready to attack another hill as soon as the trumpet blares, the whistle blows or even a little finger is raised," Edgar May wrote to him.

Although Shriver felt frustrated to be thousands of miles away from the presidential race, he was in some ways quite near the center of what determined its outcome: the Paris peace talks. As William Bundy later wrote, "Even the slightest movement toward peace might unite the Democratic Party and bring back those of its liberal wing who had opposed the Chicago platform. . . . So it was natural for Nixon to feel that only a breakthrough in the Paris talks could wrest (in his eyes, steal) the election from him at the last minute." After the Chicago convention, Humphrey had plummeted in the polls; at one point in October he had fallen so far that he found himself running practically even with third-party candidate George Wallace. Everywhere Humphrey went, he was heckled by demonstrators protesting the Vietnam War. Meanwhile, GOP nominee Richard Nixon had discovered that his best applause line was, "We will end the war on an honorable basis," and he used it over and over again.

In Paris, meanwhile, Shriver was meeting regularly with Vance and Harriman to discuss progress on the Vietnam peace negotiations. Over the summer, the negotiations had stalled over who exactly should be allowed to participate. The North Vietnamese believed the South Vietnamese government in Saigon had no legitimacy and therefore insisted on negotiating directly with the United States. Also, the North Vietnamese were insisting on bringing the National Liberation Front (NLF), the political arm of the Vietcong guerrillas who had infiltrated the south, to the negotiating table. The United States, in contrast, wanted the Saigon government at the table but not the NLF. All sides were refusing to budge.

In September, however, in the fifth month of negotiations, Vance and Harriman had constructed what they thought was at least the framework for a peace agreement: The Americans would agree to stop the bombing of North Vietnam if Hanoi, in turn, agreed to allow Saigon a role in any governing arrangement. On September 30 Humphrey gave a long-anticipated speech in Salt Lake City in which in announced he would support a bombing halt if it would lead to peace. From that point forward, protestors mostly stopped heckling him; he began to gain on Nixon in the polls.

On October 11 Harriman reported to LBJ that there seemed to have been a breakthrough: The North Vietnamese said that they would permit the South

Vietnamese government to join the negotiations, in exchange for the cessation of US bombing runs.

Over the next several weeks, negotiators worked around the clock in Paris and Saigon and Washington, edging closer to an agreement, all the while trying to keep the progress secret so as not to jeopardize the positive momentum. But journalists began to ferret out what was going on. The State Department briefly considered, then rejected, the idea of bringing Shriver back to the United States for a press conference. Harriman and Vance felt a real urgency in the work they were doing now; in their conversations with Shriver, they discussed their fear that if Nixon won the election he would blow the chance for peace by replacing them as negotiators. They wondered whether they should leak news about their progress, as a means of bringing credit to the Johnson-Humphrey administration and thereby helping the Humphrey-Muskie ticket. ("I simply can't stand Nixon," Harriman told Cy Sulzberger. "I was all ready to quit under Johnson but I won't stay one second under Nixon. I just don't trust him.") Mainly, the negotiators hoped that an agreement could be reached before the election.

On October 16, LBJ held a conference call with Humphrey and Nixon and told them that Harriman was close to securing a deal with the North Vietnamese delegates: a bombing halt in exchange for the South Vietnamese at the table and the possibility of a coalition government in South Vietnam. To the presidential candidates, the implication was clear: If LBJ pulled this off, Humphrey would surely win the election. If something went awry, the election would go to Nixon.

By October 29, a week before the election, newspapers all over the world reported the rumor that the end of the Vietnam War might finally be at hand. Polls showed that the gap between Nixon and Humphrey was now closing rapidly. Two days later, on Thursday night, President Johnson savored his final moment in the limelight, announcing on television to the American people that "I have now ordered that all air, naval, and artillery bombardment of North Vietnam cease as of eight a.m. Washington time, Friday morning. I have reached this decision in the belief that this action can lead to progress towards a peaceful settlement of the Vietnamese war. What we now expect are prompt, productive serious and intensive negotiations in an atmosphere that is conducive to progress." Hanoi would respect the DMZ [demilitarized zone] and stop attacking cities in the south. Expanded peace talks—with both the government of South Vietnam and the NLF at the table—would begin after the election on November 5. Polls taken after Johnson's television appearance showed Humphrey moving even with, and then ahead of, Nixon. With the two major-party candidates now running neck and neck, Nixon announced that "people"—not him, of course—were saying that Johnson's announcement was nothing but a political ploy to give Humphrey the election.

Within thirty-six hours the hope of peace abruptly faded. The South Vietnamese government in Saigon announced that it would not, after all, be joining the Paris peace talks the following week. Threatened by a revolt within his own cabinet, which objected to any official recognition of the NLF, the South Vietnamese president, Gen. Nguyen Van Thieu, had had to back away from the negotiating table.

Or so it appeared. But was there another force at work? Had Richard Nixon, or his operatives, somehow sabotaged the peace agreement? Lyndon Johnson believed that to be the case.

Indeed, it turned out that a prominent Nixon supporter named Anna Chennault had made contact with the South Vietnamese and urged them to back out of the peace agreement, implying that Saigon could win a more favorable peace settlement—if not an outright military victory—after Nixon was elected. The Nixon campaign affected shock and horror when they learned that these overtures had been made in Nixon's name, and it seemed at the time that the saboteurs had carried out their actions without Nixon's knowledge. Estimable journalists such as White and Tom Wicker, for instance, were convinced that Nixon himself had played no part in trying to influence the South Vietnamese government to back out of the talks. Shriver, however, watching from close up in Paris, wasn't so sure; he knew from Vance and Harriman that something very fishy had prompted Thieu's backing away from the negotiations.

In 1972, while campaigning as George McGovern's running mate against Nixon, Shriver would publicly accuse Nixon of having purposely destroyed the chance for peace in 1968. Nixon and the Republicans attacked Shriver mercilessly in response, saying not only that his charge was baseless but that he couldn't possibly have known anything about the status of the negotiations in 1968, because LBJ hadn't trusted him enough to make him privy to anything that important.

It wasn't until the 1980s that historians, journalists, and Anna Chennault herself would reveal that Shriver's charge had been well founded. Chinese-born Chennault had in 1947 married Gen. Claire Chennault, an American who had left the US Air Force to lead a group of volunteers, the Flying Tigers, in defense of the Chinese against the Japanese early in the Second World War. In the 1950s and 1960s, Anna Chennault established herself as a prominent Republican activist and socialite, with well-known ties to Nationalist Chinese leaders in Taiwan and elsewhere in East Asia. She made regular visits to South Vietnam— her sister was married to a Chinese Nationalist diplomat in Saigon—and developed a close personal friendship with Nguyen Van Thieu, who became president of the South Vietnamese government in October of 1967. Through this and other friendships in Vietnam, Chennault had become an ardent supporter of South Vietnam and of US involvement in the war. She, like many Nationalist Chinese, blamed the United States for having lost China to the Communists in 1947, and she greatly feared that Lyndon Johnson or another Democratic US president would similarly abandon South Vietnam to the Vietcong.

By the late 1960s, Nixon and Chennault had known each other for a long time through GOP circles. In the summer of 1968 their interests became naturally allied. Chennault greatly feared a negotiated peace in Vietnam that gave the Communists any power in the government of South Vietnam. Nixon feared a peace settlement in Vietnam, but for a different reason: It would likely give victory to the Democrats. On July 12, apparently at Chennault's instigation, Nixon summoned three people to his apartment in New York City for a meeting: Chennault; Nixon's aide and future attorney general John Mitchell; and Bui Diem, a good friend of Chennault's who happened also to be South Vietnam's ambassador to the United States. The meeting was secret; no one else on Nixon's campaign staff was informed of it. According to both Chennault and Diem, Nixon and his three guests talked for at least half an hour about the upcoming election, and about the need to establish close communication between Nixon and President Thieu. Anna Chennault, Nixon told Bui Diem, "would be the sole representative between the Vietnamese government and the Nixon campaign headquarters." According to William Bundy, in his history of Nixon's foreign policy, "The relationship thus established was hardly a normal or customary one, and may have been unique. The opposition party's candidate for President was setting up a special two-way private channel to the head of state of a government with whom the incumbent President was conducting critically important and secret negotiations!"

Chennault traveled to Saigon, where she told Thieu that she would be the conduit for communications between him and Nixon. She was also in daily contact with John Mitchell, relaying to him the latest information on the negotiations as reported by Saigon.

On October 15 Thieu told Bui Diem that a breakthrough in the Paris talks was imminent. Diem immediately reported this to Chennault, who in turn called Nixon and demanded that he do something to call off the bombing halt. Over the next two weeks, she was in regular contact with Saigon, making clear that Nixon opposed a deal. Thieu, for his part, said that he was reluctant to make a deal, too, and that he "would much prefer to have peace talks after your election." Is this a message to "my party"? Chennault asked. Thieu's reply: "Convey this message to your candidate."

When LBJ announced the bombing halt on October 31, Chennault was watching the speech on television at a private party. Mitchell, who evidently knew how to reach her at all times, called her there and asked her to call him back from a private location. When she did so, a nervous-sounding Mitchell said: "Anna, I'm speaking on behalf of Mr. Nixon. It's very important that our Vietnamese friends understand our Republican position and I hope you have made that very clear to them." (Chennault had her friend Thomas Corcoran, a lawyer, eavesdrop on the conversation and take notes.) Chennault says that she responded by saying she was reluctant to exert "direct influence" on the South Vietnamese; she was, she told Mitchell, only a conduit for information.

Chennault's claim that she never tried to exert "direct influence" was hair splitting. As William Bundy has observed, "repeated inquiries, coming from an authorized Nixon agent like herself, surely conveyed Nixon's fervent desire that Thieu should not go along with the Johnson plan. She may have avoided direct appeals, but her message was hardly subtle or obscure." Ambassador Bui Diem later reported that during the last week of the election he was "regularly in touch with the Nixon entourage"—Chennault, Mitchell, and Texas senator John Tower—who were encouraging him to convey to Saigon the GOP's fervent desire that South Vietnam not agree to join the United States at the negotiating table in Paris.

Lyndon Johnson got wind of these Republican overtures to Saigon and ordered the FBI to tap Anna Chennault's phone, on the grounds of national security. On November 2, the phone tap registered a call from Chennault to Thieu in which she told him that if he resisted coming to the negotiating table until after the election, Nixon would give them a more favorable settlement. Thieu asked her if Nixon knew she was calling him. He does not, she said, but "our friend in New Mexico does." Spiro Agnew was in Albuquerque that day.

The evidence is clear. In short, Richard Nixon secretly tried to derail the Vietnam peace process in order to win the 1968 election. Thus the charges Shriver would level four years later were—despite Nixon's vociferous disavowals and the opprobrium his people heaped on Shriver—substantially correct. Whether Nixon's machinations actually "blew" the chance for peace in 1968 is debatable. Thieu may well have decided to back away from the talks even absent Nixon's pressure. But the key points here are two: First, Nixon *intended* to "blow" the peace (as Shriver would allege in 1972) and took unethical steps in order to carry out that intention. Second, Thieu's decision to pull back from the negotiations at the eleventh hour, whatever caused him to do so, was the crucial determining factor in the outcome of the 1968 election.

On November 5, 1968, Richard Nixon defeated Hubert Humphrey by less than one percentage point of the popular vote (43.40 to 42.72 percent), a matter of less than half a million votes out of 75 million votes cast nationwide. In electoral terms, the margin was greater: Nixon won thirty-two states for 302 electoral votes compared with Humphrey's thirteen states (and the District of Columbia) for 191 votes and Wallace's five states for 45 votes. Given that the combination of the racial demagogue Wallace and the Republican Nixon together beat Humphrey by 56.9 percent to 42.7 percent, the 1968 election can be viewed as a repudiation of Johnson's Great Society. Racial unrest, the riots of 1967 and 1968, the Vietnam War, the unfulfilled expectations of the War on Poverty, and the chaos at the Chicago convention—all had combined to curdle much of the idealism that had prevailed as recently as three years earlier.

And yet it is not so hard to imagine that the 1968 election might have turned out differently. Consider, first, that Humphrey lost Illinois. With Shriver, whom Illinois could plausibly claim as a native son, Humphrey would likely have won that state, instantly narrowing the electoral margin to 276 to 217. Consider, second, that many of the Catholic and ethnic voters who had been so crucial to the Democrats' victory in 1960 now switched their allegiance to Nixon in 1968. Muskie, of course, was a Catholic. But if the Humphrey ticket had included

Shriver—as Catholic layman of the year he was "more Catholic" than Muskie—
the Catholic defection to Nixon would not have been so substantial. A few thousand more votes among the Catholic Poles of Milwaukee, say, or among the
German Catholics of Cincinnati—and Wisconsin and Ohio might have swung
into the Democrats' column. A switch in those three states alone would have
given Humphrey a razor's-edge victory. (Polls also showed that Shriver fared better than Muskie head to head against Agnew among all voters, not just Catholics.)

Moreover, by far the most pressing issue on most voters' minds was the war
in Vietnam. If the peace talks had succeeded, as seemed possible in late
October—or if Shriver had been selected and carried through with his plan to
hold out an olive branch to the peace protesters, backed by the authority of the
negotiators themselves, Vance and Harriman—who knows how many additional votes might have gone Humphrey's way?

Most important, Humphrey had wanted Shriver on the ticket for largely the
same reason he had wanted Ted Kennedy on the ticket. After the deaths of Jack
and Bobby, many American voters were hungry for another Kennedy—not a
Restoration, per se, but a reminder of what the New Frontier had been like
before 1965, before hope and optimism had withered. Yet when Kennedy withdrew himself, Humphrey had to do without the assistance of the "Kennedy
mystique." How many votes would that mystique have been worth? Did the
Kennedys, through their efforts to maintain the line of succession and to wreak
vengeance on Shriver for his decision to go to Paris, give victory to Nixon?

It's impossible to say for sure. Counterfactual history is necessarily shot
through with conjecture; rare is the alternate path that can be deemed as true
to the dictates of historical forces as what actually happened. Still, it is tempting—
and poignant—to think about how vastly different the last years of the twentieth century would have been had a Humphrey-Shriver ticket triumphed over
Nixon-Agnew in 1968.

CHAPTER FORTY-ONE

Nixon in Paris

~

However bitter and disappointed Shriver may have been at the Democrats' defeat, and at his own fate, he didn't show it for long. He and Ted Kennedy quickly mended fences—Teddy, as always, was warm and cordial toward him—and Shriver threw himself back into winning the hearts and minds of the French.

Still, he kept casting sidelong glances at American politics. Should he run for the Eighth Congressional District in Maryland? Senator in Illinois? As avidly as he and his friends followed the domestic scene, they were all caught unawares by the opportunity that materialized in December 1968.

After winning the election in November, Richard Nixon had declared that, as an expression of bipartisanship, he would select at least one Democrat to serve in his cabinet. (There had been two prominent Republicans—Robert McNamara and Douglas Dillon—in President Kennedy's.) At the beginning of December, president-elect Nixon called Shriver in Paris and asked him if he would fly to Washington for a meeting, to talk about the position of ambassador to the United Nations. (Hubert Humphrey, after some deliberation, had

declined to take the position.) Shriver said he would and made arrangements
to fly to the United States on December 7.

Before taking off, however, he placed phone calls to advisers and prominent
Democrats—including Bill Moyers, Senator William Fulbright, Dean Rusk,
Lyndon Johnson, Hubert Humphrey, and Ted Kennedy—and asked for meetings
with each of them to discuss the matter. In 1963 and 1964 Shriver had had no
qualms about staying on under Lyndon Johnson after President Kennedy had
died. It was one Democratic president succeeding another and, no matter what
Bobby Kennedy might say, Shriver believed that continuing to serve was a matter of patriotic duty. Accepting President Johnson's appointment to France after
his brother-in-law had declared he was running in opposition to Johnson's foreign policy, Shriver knew, was a bit more complicated. Nevertheless, he didn't
hesitate to accept the appointment, believing he was serving his country (and at
the same time escaping the LBJ-RFK crossfire). But joining a Republican administration, where, as the token Democrat (and the token "Kennedy"), he might be
used as political cover for all manner of nefarious policies, was different. Shriver
had considerable misgivings.

Still, his interest was piqued. The United Nations was an institution he
respected, and he wondered if maybe he couldn't expand the traditional UN
ambassador's job into something more Shriveresque. It would also keep him in
the public eye while he contemplated other political opportunities.

Shriver flew into New York on the evening of Saturday, December 7, and
the following morning he continued on to Washington to have breakfast with
Henry Kissinger, the Harvard professor of foreign relations whom Nixon had
recently decided would be his national security adviser. Shriver had decided
that, before he took any position, he would need not only to secure the
approval of the Democratic establishment but also to get a sense from Nixon's
team of how much latitude he would have as UN ambassador. Perhaps surprisingly, Shriver and Kissinger got along quite well. Shriver was generally
straightforward, even ingenuous, in a way that tended to make intellectuals suspect that he wasn't that smart or sophisticated. Kissinger, famed for his brilliance and his Machiavellian mind, prized secrecy and indirection. Yet the two
men shared a disdain for the existing foreign service bureaucracy and an admiration for men who could get things done effectively. Shriver and Kissinger each
decided he could work with the other.

Later in the day Shriver met with Secretary of State Rusk and President Johnson. Rusk warned him that the UN job could be frustrating—far more symbolic than powerful—but said he was in favor of Shriver accepting the position. LBJ also warned that the job lacked real power—"Gawd, Sarge," Johnson said at one point, "that is the worst fucking job in the world"—but ultimately advised that Shriver accept it.

After meeting with the president, Shriver called on the president-elect in his suite at the Hotel Pierre in New York City. As expected, Nixon offered him the position of UN ambassador. But the meeting was a strange one. Shriver had had reservations about Nixon ever since he had first met him at Jack and Eunice's Georgetown townhouse in 1948. At that first meeting, Nixon had reminded him of a boxer, always feinting and weaving. More recently, Shriver had entertained suspicions about Nixon's role in the derailment of the Paris peace talks. So he entered his meeting with Nixon warily but with an open mind, hoping to discover in the man some presidential timber.

He didn't find any. A few hours later, Shriver met Bill Josephson for drinks. "Generally [Sarge] is expansive in describing events," Josephson recorded shortly afterward. But Shriver was not at all effusive about his meeting with Nixon. "Mainly," Josephson noted, "Sarge concentrated on the personal impression Nixon had made on him. It seemed to me that Sarge had gone in hoping he would find something in Nixon to like and had come away unsatisfied. He talked about how Nixon appeared to have no real personality and about how insecure Nixon seemed to be, to the point where Sarge noticed Nixon studying Sarge's suit and tie intently as if feeling ill at ease and comparing Sarge's taste to his own."

Both Johnson and Rusk had reminded Shriver of how much trouble there had been between the UN ambassador and the secretary of state when both men were from the *same* party. (Under JFK, for instance, Dean Rusk and Adlai Stevenson had always been butting heads.) Imagine how difficult the relationship would be when the two men were from *different* parties. "That's a good point," Nixon said when Shriver mentioned that concern. He gazed out the hotel window for a few moments, appearing to study the people below. "I think the only solution is for you to meet with my secretary of state and make a resolution about how your relationship should be. If you two think you can get along together and you can explain it to me and to the public, then everything will be fine." Nixon told Shriver in confidence that he was going to name William Rogers, who had served briefly as Eisenhower's attorney general, as his secretary of state.

The next morning Shriver met secretly with Rogers. He was wary going into this meeting. Nixon himself, according to Kissinger, believed Rogers to be "one of the toughest, most cold-eyed, self-centered, and ambitious men he had ever met."

On the basis of his discussions with LBJ, Rusk, Moyers, and Josephson, Shriver decided to make his acceptance of the UN ambassadorship conditional on his being granted power, latitude, and access unprecedented for the position. To Shriver's surprise, Rogers agreed to all his conditions.

Shriver then continued his tour of consultations with prominent Democrats, meeting first with Senator Fulbright, the chair of the Senate Foreign Relations Committee. Fulbright told him, "we have only one government and we have— unfortunately—only one President," so you might as well take the position. Shriver then met for two hours with Vice President Humphrey. Humphrey told Shriver that had he not just lost a campaign for the presidency, he himself would have taken the UN position when Nixon offered it to him. Having run for president, Humphrey said he felt he needed to help rebuild the Democratic Party, which precluded his accepting the ambassadorship. But he saw no reason why Shriver shouldn't take it.

So far, every Democrat Shriver had spoken to had been in favor of his taking the position. But he had yet to speak to the most crucial Democrat. All day, Shriver's friend Bill Mullins, a former colleague from the Peace Corps and the OEO, had been on the phone with Ted Kennedy's office, trying to set up a meeting between Shriver and the senator before Shriver flew back to Paris. Finally, word came that Kennedy was himself meeting with Nixon but would meet with Shriver at National Airport before Shriver flew back to Paris.

The brothers-in-law greeted each other warmly, then retired to a small private room provided by one of the airlines. Shriver outlined for Kennedy what he thought the pros and cons of taking the UN position were and briefly summarized the counsel of the other leading Democrats. Then he got to the point: Please tell me "unambiguously and honestly," he entreated Ted, if you feel that by accepting the post I will be involving you and Eunice too intimately with the Nixon administration. If you feel that I would be, Shriver said, I will decline the position. No need to make up your mind right now, but call me when you've decided.

Back in France, Shriver began preparations to leave his post in Paris. He asked Moyers and Josephson to prepare a press release and speech to accompany the announcement of his appointment as UN ambassador. He also had them prepare a draft of the remarks he hoped Nixon would make when announcing the appointment, clarifying that Shriver had received the blessing of the Democratic leadership before accepting the new post and laying out what the extent of his authority and responsibilities would be. Sometime in the early afternoon, Ted Kennedy called Shriver at the embassy.

What's your decision? Shriver asked. Should I do this? Kennedy responded that he thought Shriver had analyzed all the pros and cons of the situation very astutely, but he declined to take a position one way or the other. A few hours later, Shriver called his brother-in-law back. Before I make a decision, he said, I really want your opinion. Kennedy still declined to take a position. According to Shriver's notes of the conversation, the senator called it "a purely personal decision. That's where I'll come out: You must weigh all aspects and decide for yourself whether you're doing the right thing."

Shriver replied, "Well, when Eunice and I decide, I'm going to telephone you back. I want to be sure that our step—my step—is not going to be an irritant or be looked on as a 'sell-out' by you or by Ethel or anyone else." Kennedy never did take a clear position. But, by circling around the issue, Shriver later observed, his brother-in-law had made it implicitly clear that he was opposed to Shriver's taking the UN job.

The *New York Times* and the *Washington Post*, meanwhile, were already reporting that Shriver was going to be named. He sent Nixon his list of conditions.

Late in the afternoon of December 11, Nixon called the embassy, and he and Shriver spoke for about half an hour. (A Shriver aide listened in and recorded the conversation.) Shriver began by saying that he had given a great deal of thought to Nixon's offer and was "very enthusiastic" about the opportunity and particularly interested in working through the UN to develop more multilateral agreements of various sorts. Nixon said he was amenable to that. Shriver then said that he had discussed some points with Rogers that he and Nixon had not discussed when they met in Washington. "I just want to bring them up with you now," Shriver said, "to make sure there is a meeting of the minds between us."

Shriver went through his list of conditions item by item (control over all of America's UN personnel; selection of the assistant secretary of state for international affairs; and supervisory control over specialized UN agencies) and found Nixon amenable to all of them. When Shriver asked for status in the State Department equivalent to that held by the under secretary of state, Nixon replied, "As you can see, Rogers is not doctrinaire. I'm confident that this can be worked out between you and him." When Shriver asked to be able to report directly to the secretary of state, rather than to an assistant secretary, Nixon said, "I'll get Rogers on the phone to you, and I'll tell him this is what I'm trying to do. I want you and Rogers to reach a firm agreement which gives the UN ambassador that status. Otherwise, you are just going [to have a job where all you do is] read speeches." Nixon also agreed to allow Shriver to have full cabinet status and to have him sit in on all National Security Council meetings.

Finally, Shriver brought up the effect his departure from Paris would have on relations with de Gaulle. "Just say you had to choose between France and the UN," Nixon said. "I would like you to tell de Gaulle that I'm vitally interested in continuing improving relations with France. You should say that the decision was very difficult for you and for me, that we talked for a long time but felt this larger forum is where you are needed." It was agreed that Shriver would stay in Paris until the end of the Johnson administration.

The deal seemed set. But when Shriver spoke to Rogers, he got the impression that the secretary of state–designate was backtracking from his original commitments. So Moyers sent Rogers a draft of the speech he and Josephson had written for Nixon, because it included, in Moyers's words, a "rough outline of the important features which mean something to Sarge and which he related to us as being the basis of his understanding with the President-Elect." Emphasizing Shriver's desire to be something more than "Democratic window-dressing on the shelf of Mr. Nixon's cabinet," Moyers conveyed to Rogers "the hope that the language of the announcement will create the impression of substance and lead to his playing a role that will be more than superficial."

Everything was in place. The next day Shriver cabled President Johnson and Secretary Rusk, saying that everyone he had spoken to had "encouraged me to take the post from viewpoint of our party as well as of service to the country." In addition, Shriver said, "I have negotiated agreement with new secstate and with president-elect under terms of which all perquisites and powers of UN ambassadorship will be retained and for several reasons enhanced. For the above reasons and with the hope and trust that I can count upon your support

. . . I have accepted the offer and my appointment will be announced tomorrow." Shriver also met with President de Gaulle, informing him that he would be leaving Paris for the UN.

Less than twenty-four hours later, Shriver was summoned to take a phone call on one of the secure lines on the third floor of the embassy. It was William Rogers. The line was scrambled and Rogers was hard to hear. "Sarge," he said, as Shriver recalled, "you know I've read your document several times." He was referring to the Nixon speech drafted by Moyers and Josephson. "I can't accept it." Shriver responded that he considered the conditions to be merely a set of ground rules, to help clarify the relationship between the secretary of state and the UN ambassador, which historically had been fraught with tension. "I thought that the document reflected what your opinion was about how we would work together," Shriver said. "Well, Sarge," Rogers said, "I really think you must have misunderstood me because I really can't be Secretary of State successfully if the ambassador to the United Nations has the power and responsibility you think he should have."

"Nixon and Rogers have changed their minds on UN," Shriver cabled to Rusk and LBJ the next morning, "while asking me to continue in Paris indefinitely. Many thanks for your advice and encouragement. Fortunately we love Paris and the job you gave us."

The next day, the White House announced that Nixon had named a sixty-one-year-old career diplomat, Charles Yost, who had previously served in Egypt and Poland, to be US ambassador to the United Nations. (He had also been one of Adlai Stevenson's deputies during the Cuban missile crisis.) When reporters asked what had happened to Shriver, Nixon said he had considered him for the UN post but had ultimately decided that to ensure ongoing good relations with de Gaulle as well as continuity in the Paris peace talks, Shriver would be more valuable remaining in his present post. (In January, when Shriver met again with Nixon in Washington, the new president reiterated this reasoning; Shriver, for his part, believed Nixon's stance had been formulated "at least fifty percent ex post facto.") For the UN position, Nixon said, he preferred to have a "professional diplomat" rather than a "political figure." But the Washington Post reported that in the days before the announcement of Yost's appointment, Rogers had been raising questions about Shriver's fitness for the job, worrying that he was "overly ambitious" and "too much of a political animal." There were also rumors that de Gaulle had personally interceded, asking Nixon to retain Shriver in Paris.

The reality was that Rogers, an accomplished lawyer who had little background in foreign policy, felt his authority as secretary of state was being eroded from several directions at once. Nixon had several times told his aides that he wanted to serve as his own foreign secretary, obviating the need for a true secretary of state. Meanwhile, it was already becoming apparent that the Nixon administration's foreign policy would be formulated in the Kissinger-Nixon nexus, not in the State Department. Nixon even went so far as to tell Kissinger that he wanted to "wall off" the State Department. For Rogers, the additional prospect of an ambitious, activist UN ambassador was simply too much, and he blocked the appointment.

The blackballing was probably to Shriver's advantage. Shriver and Rogers would have clashed regularly, adding weight to the theory that UN ambassadors and secretaries of state rarely get along. With a few exceptions, neither Rogers nor Yost, edged to the margins of relevance by Kissinger and Nixon, accomplished much of import. Perhaps Shriver would have been able to make more of the position; more likely, he would have seethed with frustration. Finally, by remaining in Paris he stayed at a greater remove from the Nixon administration, sparing himself—and the Kennedy family—the taint of that association.

One reason that Nixon genuinely wanted Shriver to stay on in Paris was that he hoped to continue to improve relations between France and the United States by paying an official state visit to de Gaulle. Other than at JFK's funeral, LBJ and de Gaulle had never met face to face; relations between the two countries were so poor that no state visit had occurred between them since Jack and Jackie Kennedy had gone to Paris in 1961. Nixon was eager to put an early imprint on foreign policy and hoped to solidify America's relations with Western Europe. With the Vietnam peace negotiations still going on in Paris, and with the Soviets flexing their muscles in Czechoslovakia, Nixon was keen to get on a good footing with de Gaulle. Shriver's relations with the French president were crucial to making this happen.

As early as November, just after Nixon was elected, Shriver had raised with LBJ's State Department the possibility of an official state dinner for de Gaulle and the American president. Nixon and Shriver discussed the idea further at their meeting in New York in December. By the time the UN imbroglio was playing itself out in late December, the American Embassy and the White House had each begun their initial planning for a meeting to take place sometime in the spring. In early February, de Gaulle told Shriver that he would welcome a visit from the recently inaugurated American president, as part of Nixon's European tour.

Given the symbolic importance of the trip, Nixon wanted to be assured that everything would run smoothly, so in mid-February he dispatched his aides H. R. "Bob" Haldeman and John Ehrlichman to Europe to do advance planning. Haldeman and Ehrlichman's planning went smoothly in every city except Paris, where Nixon was scheduled to stay for two nights. On the first night, de Gaulle was to host a dinner at the Elysée Palace; on the second night, Nixon was to return the favor at the ambassador's residence. But when Ehrlichman arrived at the Shrivers', he was horrified. (When Haldeman arrived a day or so later, he was horrified, too.) The residence was all wrong for a state dinner. To begin with, there was all the clutter: footballs, hockey sticks, and toys everywhere. That, presumably, could be cleaned up. But what could be done about the Shrivers' taste in furnishings? (Four months later, White House aides were still "shuddering" at the memory of the Shrivers' "psychedelic" dining room.) Then there was all the Catholic religious paraphernalia—crucifixes, statues of the Blessed Mother.

But the worst of it was the Kennedy photographs. The residence was a veritable shrine to Jack, Bobby, Kathleen, and Joe Jr. Edgar May, who had accompanied Shriver to Paris as an aide-de-camp, recalled that every time Haldeman and Ehrlichman "saw a picture of President Kennedy, they would recoil, as if to say, 'Ahhh! Monster!'"

Not long after Haldeman and Ehrlichman toured the residence, Shriver got word from the White House that President Nixon would not be hosting the dinner for de Gaulle at the ambassador's residence after all but, rather, in the basement of the embassy itself. "This will be less of an inconvenience to you and your family," Shriver remembered the note said, "and the embassy's location near the Elysée Palace makes it more convenient for President de Gaulle." Shriver immediately contacted the White House and said, as he recalled, "The president of the United States cannot have a dinner for the president of France in the cafeteria in the basement of a goddamned office building! That's not appropriate and the French will be insulted. The dinner must take place at the residence." He went on to say that he realized the residence did not belong to him but rather to the US government. "If you want my family and me to move to a hotel for a few days, we will," Shriver said. "If you don't like the photographs on the wall, we'll take them down. If you want us to get the place a new paint job, we will."

"I was rather unequivocal about that," Shriver recalls. This caused "some kind of agitation" in the White House, while Haldeman and Ehrlichman debated what to do. Soon, word came back from Washington. The dinner would take place at the ambassador's residence, after all. But all the Kennedy photographs would have to be taken down, the Catholic iconography removed, and the mansion refurnished. Removing the pictures and statues was easy enough. (In the end, Shriver's deputy chief of mission Robert Blake persuaded Nixon and Haldeman to allow the family pictures on the piano to remain in place.) Refurnishing the mansion on a week's notice was more challenging. Fortunately, a few months earlier, Shriver had been offered the opportunity to become the head of MGM studios; now, he took advantage of his connections in MGM's European office by ordering a supply of movie-prop furniture to replace the actual furniture, which was moved into temporary storage. Meanwhile, US protocol officers worked feverishly to borrow substitute antiques, some of which had to be shipped in from Washington.

Nixon and his entourage arrived in Paris on Friday, February 28. Shriver and de Gaulle met them at the airport in a ceremony full of fanfare, then proceeded to the Elysée Palace for meetings and an elaborate dinner. As eighty-eight dinner guests took their places at a single very long table, de Gaulle, with Eunice Shriver on his arm, led the president and his entourage into the palace dining room. After dinner, Shriver, Nixon, de Gaulle, and the two presidents' top aides retired to a salon for cigars and $600 brandy.

A full day of meetings scheduled for the next day between Nixon and de Gaulle and their advisers at Versailles was to be followed by a black-tie dinner at the ambassador's residence. The residence boasted a fabulous French chef, who had been working for weeks planning an elaborate, nine-course meal for the evening. But a few days before the event, word came from the White House: President Nixon would prefer to have Kansas beefsteak and baked potatoes. The residence staff was aghast. "The Nixon people brought their own food," Edgar May recalled some thirty years later. "I still can't get over that." (This kind of reaction wasn't lost on Nixon's aides. In his memo on the European trip,

Ehrlichman wrote, "There were some raised eyebrows about the President bringing his own food.")

All things considered, though, the dinner was a success. Shriver established the tone of the evening when, speaking in French, he stumbled over his opening remarks and had to ask jovially for the wife of the French prime minister, Couve de Murville, to assist him, causing the dozens of gathered dignitaries to burst into laughter. From that point forward, the Nixonian spirit of stiff formality was replaced by a Shriverian spirit of general gaiety. "It wasn't pompous any longer," Shriver recalled.

Haldeman and Ehrlichman had decreed that the Shriver children were not to be present. "I just remember my mother being so incensed that we were not allowed to come down to the state floor," Timothy Shriver says. But when the Shriver children appeared cautiously at the top of the stairs, peering down at the proceedings, their father gestured for them to come down, and they scampered into the dining room. Nixon looked peeved, but President de Gaulle greeted them warmly and engaged them in conversation in French. The world-famous violinist Yehudi Menuhin and his pianist sister, Hepzibah Menuhin, played a Franck sonata after dinner.

All in all, the meetings between Nixon and de Gaulle were a great success, everything the American president could have hoped for. De Gaulle advised Nixon to withdraw from Vietnam and to recognize Red China. Nixon "listened politely to the first, avidly to the second," according to William Bundy. "France at once became the bearer, through her ambassador to Beijing, of a general message to the Chinese leadership of Nixon's interest in changing the American relationship to China."

No specific agreements were reached between the two heads of state during the more than ten hours of private and group discussions, but newspapers and foreign policy analysts in both America and France hailed the meeting as a harbinger of improved relations. Several days after Nixon had left, Shriver cabled the State Department to report that French foreign minister Michel Debré had told his staff at the foreign office that "a new era of deeper understanding and cooperation was now opening between France and the United States, and the French should seek to cooperate as closely as possible with us in every area where French and American interests coincide." There had been, Shriver wrote, "an almost audible sigh of relief on all sides, except on the

extreme left, that the two presidents have publicly endorsed improved relations." In subsequent days, Shriver also reported that de Gaulle had been very
pleased with the meetings and was telling his aides that Franco-American relations could now enter an era of "much greater intimacy."

But a new challenge lay on the French political horizon. The possibility remained that ongoing negotiations between the de Gaulle government and the
French labor movement would stall, producing a domestic crisis. One day not
long after Nixon's visit, the novelist André Malraux, de Gaulle's longtime minister of culture, stopped by for one of his periodic visits with Shriver. Ostensibly,
Malraux had requested the meeting so he could discuss his upcoming com-
mencement address to Harvard University. But once he arrived in Shriver's
huge, oak-paneled office at the embassy, he told Shriver that de Gaulle was
secretly planning to resign soon. De Gaulle would call a bogus referendum,
Malraux said, and if the referendum failed to pass, he would be able to leave
the presidency saying, "I am not deserting the people of France; the people of
France have deserted me." The "financial, labor, social, and monetary situation," Shriver subsequently cabled the State Department, was "so fragile that
any serious problem in any direction could bring on political troubles of major
proportions for President de Gaulle. . . . The waves are rising."

Sure enough, de Gaulle, frustrated by a series of small domestic political
setbacks, declared a national referendum—calling for a reorganization of the
regional governments—to be held April 27. On the eve of the vote, Shriver
cabled the State Department. "Odds are so close as to be unmeasurable on the
referendum. Thus it is well within the range of possibility that de Gaulle will
no longer be president of France on Monday morning." A reprise of May 1968
seemed possible.

The referendum was voted down, 53 to 47 percent. Just before midnight on
the evening of April 27 de Gaulle told Prime Minister Murville that he was
resigning. Over the next several weeks, Shriver monitored the situation anxiously. France endured mild chaos and a lot of confusion, but not the feared
breakdown of the social order.

On June 15 Georges Pompidou, de Gaulle's former prime minister—who
had been dismissed not long after the disturbances of the previous May—was
elected to the French presidency. For a few weeks, American newspapers had

been speculating that, having made his visit to Paris, Nixon would seek to replace Shriver as ambassador. If Nixon had in fact entertained such thoughts, he abandoned them now. Shriver and Pompidou got along well, and Pompidou's new prime minister, Jacques Chaban-Delmas, played tennis with Shriver several times each week. Nixon and the State Department could not have asked for better access to the highest levels of French government. In the last week in June, Shriver flew to Washington for a week of meetings with Nixon, Kissinger, CIA director Richard Helms, and various State Department analysts. Nixon urged Shriver to stay in the Paris post as long as he wanted. (Several newspaper reporters pointed out that this was not an entirely selfless gesture. Nixon knew that Shriver had his eye out for political opportunities in the United States, so the president figured it couldn't hurt to keep this popular Democrat overseas as long as possible.)

Back in Paris in July, Shriver visited thirteen cabinet ministers, some of them multiple times, in five days. In a meeting with Pompidou he raised the possibility of the French president's making a state visit to America in 1970, to build on what de Gaulle and Nixon had established a few months earlier.

In July 1969 the Shrivers returned to the United States for a momentous occasion: the launching of the Apollo XI rocket from the newly christened Cape Kennedy. They arrived in Melbourne, Florida, on July 16, having flown from Paris on a chartered airplane that *Paris Match* magazine had hired for the ambassador's family (along with various European royalty). Standing in the grandstands alongside former President Johnson and Vice President Spiro Agnew, Shriver watched through his binoculars as the rocket emerged from a "ferocious orange blaze" and began thundering toward the moon. Two days later, the family was back in Paris, ready to watch the first moon landing. Shriver set up television sets throughout the residence and invited French leaders and the entire diplomatic corps in to watch the event. When the astronauts landed on the moon, at about two in the morning, dozens of ambassadors cheered. (The Soviet ambassador, Valerian Zorin, who in his former role as UN ambassador had squared off against Adlai Stevenson over the Cuban missiles, looked glum and left the party early.)

For the Shrivers, celebration of the event was short lived. That same day, word had come from Massachusetts that Ted Kennedy had driven off a bridge at Chappaquiddick, Martha's Vineyard, and that his passenger in the car, Mary Jo Kopechne, a former aide to Robert Kennedy, had been killed. The Shrivers called off a trip to the Riviera and flew to Boston to give Ted their support and lend their voices to the family council. At the Kennedy compound in Hyannis Port, Eunice helped script Ted's nationally televised statement of contrition the following Friday. At one point, Ted proposed that as a result of the tragedy, he would promise never to run for president; Eunice argued him out of it.

Shriver was never anything other than supportive of his brother-in-law, both publicly and within the family. In a typical television appearance, the following February, an interviewer asked him whether the Chappaquiddick incident had "finished" Ted Kennedy politically. In his response, Shriver observed that "many of the most successful men in history have had episodes like that or occasions like that in their life and they certainly were not finished by them." Noting that Teddy was "quite young still" with "at least twenty years ahead of him," Shriver waxed philosophical: "It's just a stroke of fate you might say, and one of the things that helps a man to mature, I believe, is his capacity to undergo an episode like that and become a better man rather than a worse man as a result of it."

CHAPTER FORTY-TWO

Au Revoir

⌒

By the fall of 1969 Shriver's many political supporters in the United States were telling him it was time for him to come home. There was still a chance he could get on the national Democratic ticket in 1972—perhaps even be the presidential nominee—but he needed to make his presence felt domestically, preferably by running for some kind of elective office in 1970. Political memories are short; the accomplishments of the early 1960s were receding into the distant past.

The national Democratic Party was in disarray. The Democratic presidential ticket had lost in 1968, ending eight years of Democratic reign in the White House, but that was only the most tangible symptom of a deeper malaise. The New Deal liberal consensus that had prevailed since FDR's administration had unraveled. Widespread support for New Frontier-Great Society idealism had dissipated in the riots in inner cities and the jungles of South Vietnam. The chaos of the 1968 convention in Chicago had been an unfortunate advertisement for all that ailed the Democratic Party—its uncertainty, its nostalgic longing for the Kennedy mystique, its kooky and disrup-

tive New Left, its militant black power radicals, its lack of cohesion on
Vietnam, and its clashes between the new forces of revolution (represented
by hippie protesters) and the old forces of reaction (represented by Mayor
Daley and the Chicago police).

In the months following the 1968 election, the prevailing assumption
among political experts was that by 1972 Ted Kennedy would be seasoned
enough—and would have recovered enough from the shock of Bobby's
death—to unite his fractured party, leading a competitive race against Nixon
from the top of the Democratic ticket. The Chappaquiddick tragedy
changed that calculus in an instant. That episode itself—Teddy had left the
scene of the accident and waited until morning before reporting Kopechne's
death to the police—along with rumors of his drinking and womanizing,
had made him radioactive. There were serious questions about whether
Kennedy could continue his career in politics at all, let alone lead the
Democrats to victory in 1972.

Thus, in addition to the Democrats' other problems, they now confronted
a serious leadership vacuum. LBJ had gone off to Texas, where his hair grew
long and his health rapidly declined. Democratic politicians still made pilgrimages to him for consultations, but he was a spent force. Hubert Humphrey
had similarly been pushed to the margins. Many Democratic partisans were
bitter because of the weak campaign he had run in 1968, and liberals in particular could not forget his unwillingness to take a stronger anti-Vietnam stance.
That left Edmund Muskie and George McGovern. McGovern, the South
Dakota senator, had not done well at the 1968 convention; he was not well
known nationally and in any event was perceived as too liberal to compete successfully with the popular Nixon. That made Muskie, the Maine senator and
1968 vice presidential nominee, the de facto Democratic front-runner, but he
was failing to inspire voters. The party remained adrift, its rank-and-file hungry for leadership.

So, many Democrats turned their hopeful eyes to Paris, where they
reposed their aspirations in the American ambassador. Shriver possessed
many of the attributes necessary to bring together a wounded party and to
lead the ticket in 1972. He was nationally known. His association with the
Peace Corps made him popular with young people, and he had also, helpfully,
maintained his ties to the Humphrey-Johnson old guard. His work with the

OEO and civil rights made him attractive to blacks—but his solid personal relationships with many Southern congressmen made him viable (for a liberal, anyway) in the South. Most of all, he had surplus quantities of charisma and optimism, two elements that were in short supply among the Democratic leadership as 1970 approached.

Finally, there was the Kennedy connection. With Ted reeling, Shriver, as a Kennedy brother-in-law and creator of the Peace Corps, was the closest the Democrats could get to capturing the Kennedy mystique. To many, Shriver's style and panache made him the living embodiment of the New Frontier.

Beginning in the spring of 1969 he was inundated in Paris by letters from Democratic leaders all over the country, trying to recruit him for elective office in Illinois, Maryland, New York—even Texas. A group of leading Democrats and business executives in Illinois implored him to run for the Senate seat of Everett Dirksen, who had just died. Senator Joseph Tydings and party boss Richard Schifter asked Shriver to run for Congress in Maryland. Of course, most of these entreaties had an implicit subtext. The job at hand (whatever it turned out to be) was only to be a stepping stone to a higher calling: the presidency of the United States. The obviousness of this subtext would soon cause political problems.

Through most of 1969, Shriver played it coy, denying he was seeking elective office. But in the last week of October he took a weeklong trip to the United States that was clearly an exploratory political expedition: he visited Washington, New York, Baltimore, Chicago, and Los Angeles, meeting with Democratic leaders in each city.

Once again, he found himself plagued by the problem that had dogged him since 1964. Everywhere he went, he had wildly enthusiastic supporters—everyone from high-ranking machine politicians and members of Congress to college students willing to volunteer—most of whom believed him to be, in Ted Kennedy's absence, the carrier of the Kennedy flame. Yet a crucial Democratic constituency—the Kennedy apparatus, mainly Ted and Bobby's advisers and Ted himself—quietly telegraphed their misgivings. The posture they adopted was not unlike the one adopted by Jack Kennedy's White House advisers when Shriver had approached them for help with the Peace Corps after he had insisted on keeping it out of AID: "You wanted your independence—now you're on your own." All this caused consternation among some of Shriver's would-be supporters. How can he be the keeper of the Kennedy flame, if the Kennedys deny him that role?

On the evening of October 29, Shriver met for several hours with Mayor Daley and his Democratic slate makers. The meeting was inconclusive. Daley afterward said that Shriver would "always be welcome in Illinois" but did not specify what office he would run for.

The next day, Shriver took a major public step toward dissociating himself from the presidential administration for which he still worked—and toward restoring his credibility among Robert Kennedy Democrats—by condemning Nixon's policy on the Vietnam War. In a speech at Chicago's Mundelein College, Shriver said that the United States should get out of Vietnam as quickly as possible. Shriver was asked why, if he was so opposed to US policy on Vietnam, he had continued to work for both LBJ and Nixon. "It was a difficult moral decision," he said. He had often thought of quitting in protest, he explained, but "decided I could do more good by staying on." The record shows this to be true; several times Shriver directly confronted Johnson, telling him that if the president did not shift more money from Vietnam to the OEO, he would quit. However, he never carried through on these threats. When Johnson asked him to go to Paris, Shriver said, he had faced "that decision again." But "I decided that my work for the cause of European peace was important—that I should continue that work even though the war is immoral."

The next day Shriver was in Baltimore, where the newspapers reported that Mayor Tom D'Alesandro was close to endorsing Shriver in a Democratic primary fight against Governor Marvin Mandel, the interim governor filling Spiro Agnew's office. (Many Maryland liberals were searching for someone to defeat Mandel in the primary.) Shriver, D'Alesandro said, was a "dynamic personality" who could "catch fire" as a candidate.

In his public statements, Shriver consistently denied that he was actively seeking elective office in the United States. I am keeping my future options open, he would say, but for the moment I'm contentedly serving as ambassador to France. Despite these public disavowals, Shriver's peripatetic wanderings invited the criticism that he was more concerned with establishing a launching pad for the presidency than he was with the problems and issues of the states he was visiting. "There are those who are saying," Josephson wrote to him in Paris, "that you are just a political whore looking for a bed to lie down in."

Stung by these accusations—and lacking the unalloyed support of Mayor Daley, anyhow—Shriver formally withdrew himself from consideration in Illinois and began seriously studying what his prospects would be in a primary challenge against Governor Mandel. Shriver operatives on the ground in Maryland commissioned a poll on his behalf, and Mayor D'Alesandro and state attorney general Francis Burch began helping him to build a political organization there.

Back in Paris, Shriver hosted a dinner for Henry Cabot Lodge, the Republican senator he had helped Jack Kennedy to unseat in 1952 and who was now stepping down as head of the American delegation to the Paris peace talks. The next day, Shriver had lunch with Wayne Hays, a Democratic congressman from Ohio. When Hays returned to Washington, the talk in the Capitol Hill cloakrooms was that Hays had anointed Shriver the Democratic presidential nominee for 1972.

In 1964 it had been a *Washington Post* column by Rowland Evans and Robert Novak that had fueled the brief Shriver-for-vice-president fever—and that had led to Shriver's heated encounter with an angry Robert Kennedy. In 1970 the idea that Shriver might head the Democratic ticket was given establishment validation by another Evans and Novak column. "Shriver Is Boomed by Democrats to Fill '72 Vacuum Left by Kennedy," the *Post* headline said, and the article described how a broad range of prominent Democrats were hoping to make Shriver their man for 1972. It also reported, however, that the cause of Shriver's indecisiveness about whether and where to run in 1970 was "hostility from the Kennedy apparatus." "The Kennedy family and its political outriders," Evans and Novak reported, "still resent Shriver's loyal support for President Johnson and his failure to back Robert F. Kennedy for President in 1968." Shriver, they argued, "is inhibited chiefly by his keen awareness of the resentment from the Kennedy apparatus."

Although Evans and Novak believed that the sorry state of the Democratic Party and the lack of other star-quality candidates could "quickly propel Shriver out of the dark horse category for 1972," they reported that "a close friend" had told Shriver privately that a presidential campaign "would be seen by Kennedyites as taking advantage of Ted Kennedy's discomfiture."

The idea that Shriver would try to "take advantage" of Ted Kennedy's post-Chappaquiddick predicament was preposterous; the idea that some people would *perceive* him to be doing so, however, was not as far-fetched. Thus, although many of Shriver's supporters were recommending that he forget the idea of running for governor or senator, and instead come home and take charge of the Democratic National Committee, or campaign for other Democrats in 1970 (as Richard Nixon had for Republicans in 1966), Shriver decided instead that it would be safer to pursue the Maryland governorship. Surely no one would object to that.

In early January, Shriver told Cy Sulzberger that he hoped "to win the Democratic nomination for governor of Maryland, to win the election, and to go on in 1972 to win the Democratic nomination for the presidency and move into the White House." Sulzberger was impressed by the nature of Shriver's ambition, which was "not for power itself" but rather "to assume direction of government policy and channel its principal emphasis along [domestic] lines, particularly social reform to eliminate poverty and hunger."

By the end of 1969, Shriver was feeling increasingly uncomfortable to be associated with the Nixon administration. He could see firsthand that the Paris peace talks on Vietnam were still going nowhere. Nixon's new policy of "Vietnamization" seemed to be producing neither victory nor significant de-escalation of US involvement. Just before Christmas, Scotty Reston reported in the *New York Times* that Shriver had told his Kennedy in-laws he would resign from his ambassadorship after Pompidou's visit to the United States in March 1970. At that point, Reston wrote, Shriver would confer with leading Democrats about running for president in 1972.

Before he left Paris, however, Shriver wanted to make some final grand gesture, to help build anticipation for Pompidou's trip and to give the French people something to remember him by. One day that fall, he called a meeting of friends and staff to brainstorm about what sort of event might be conducted by the Paris embassy to, in effect, kick off the Pompidou visit the following spring. Various ideas were suggested: a dinner, a symposium, a parade. But the idea that caught Shriver's fancy was proposed by a young Dominican priest, Father Daniel Morrissey, whom Shriver had retained to teach "the spiritual dimension of life" to his children.

At the time, Morrissey was living in a Dominican monastery in Paris. There he had learned a great deal about the history of Sainte Chappelle, the resplendent chapel on the Ile-de-la-Cité in the shadows of the Palace of

Justice and Notre Dame Cathedral. In 1242 Louis IX (Saint Louis) had commissioned the building of Sainte Chappelle to house a holy relic—what was believed to be the crown of thorns that Christ had worn during the Passion—and to demonstrate that the kingdom of France was at the forefront of Western Christianity. Once a year during Saint Louis's reign, the crown and other relics would be brought from the locked treasury at Notre Dame and displayed during a brief religious service. In the years since, Sainte Chappelle had become a tourist destination, noted for its beautiful stained-glass windows tracing the biblical story of humanity, from creation to redemption through Christ. To the French people, Sainte Chappelle was one of the country's most glorious symbols.

One of the older priests at Morrissey's monastery, the Reverend Raymond Leopold Bruckberger, had been a chaplain to the French Resistance. In 1944, after the Allies had retaken Paris from the Germans, Bruckberger had led de Gaulle through Notre Dame and Sainte Chappelle. Why not, Morrissey proposed, hold a special Midnight Mass at Sainte Chappelle? Morrissey knew that the Dominicans had occasionally held Mass there. Wasn't it conceivable, then, that Shriver could get permission from the French government to hold a Mass there for the diplomatic corps?

Shriver loved the idea. A Midnight Mass at Sainte Chappelle had a combination of elements that appealed to him greatly. It had political and historical significance for the French, as well as for Franco-American relations. If done right, a Mass held in such a beautiful setting would have a distinctive grace, beauty, and style. For Shriver, as a devout Catholic, it would have great personal religious significance. Best of all, as Shriver soon learned, it would be unprecedented in modern times. The last time anyone had held a Christmas Midnight Mass at Sainte Chappelle was before Louis XIV had decamped for Versailles in 1682. And no private, much less non-French, person had ever used Sainte Chappelle for a Mass. This would be an event the French would not soon forget.

The first step was securing permission for the Mass, which proved to be more of a challenge than expected. Shriver had to lobby the Ministry of Culture for several weeks before permission was granted. The next step was to plan the event. Shriver wanted everything to be just right, so he and his staff went to great lengths to make sure that it would be. He hired an elite string quartet to play on period instruments dating from the era of the chapel's construction. He had someone go to the Bibliothèque Nationale to track down the manuscript of a trumpet voluntary that had been composed especially to be played in Sainte Chappelle. He engaged Anna Moffo, a leading soprano of the Metropolitan Opera, to sing Christmas carols before the Mass.

Shriver thought it would be appropriate for an American priest to say the Mass, so he asked Father Morrissey to do so. Many of the religious accoutrements brought in for the event had special significance, as well. Morrissey's vestments, retrieved from a museum in Nice, were made partly of gold and had been designed by Henri Matisse. (Matisse's final work had been the design of a chapel—including its priestly garments—for some Dominican nuns.) The stole Morrissey would wear had belonged to a French saint, Vincent de Paul—the same Vincent de Paul to whose society Shriver's father had belonged when Sarge was a young boy. It was decided that Shriver's son Bobby would lead the procession into the chapel. Atop the processional cross Bobby was to carry would be his father's most treasured possession, the crucifix that had lain on JFK's bier and had been blessed by Pope Paul and Patriarch Athenagoras.

There were other logistical challenges that would have deterred someone less determined than Shriver. Paris in winter can be cold and damp; the cavernous, unwinterized chapel would surely be uninviting late on a December night. Also, Sainte Chappelle's most winning feature—its magnificent windows—could be appreciated only on sunny days, when illuminated by natural light from outside. Shriver wasn't daunted. He installed portable heaters two days in advance, so that by midnight of December 24 the Gothic chapel was comfortably warm, and he had floodlights set up all around the perimeter of the building, so that the beautiful stained glass would be illumined from without, despite the nighttime darkness.

The event, on December 25, 1969, was one of transcendent beauty. One guest told *Time* that it was "visually the most beautiful Christmas Eve Mass I've ever been to." Father Morrissey recalled it as "patriotic and beautiful." Cy Sulzberger, the longtime roving foreign correspondent for the *New York Times*, recorded in his diary that "the Mass was absolutely beautiful—above all the glowing Sainte Chappelle." Embassy personnel among the 300 guests—most of whom were French ministers and ambassadors from various countries—tend to recall the Mass as the capstone of the Shrivers' sojourn in Paris.

PART SIX

Democratic Politics (1970–1976)

CHAPTER FORTY-THREE

The Politics of Life

O n January 27 Shriver formally submitted his resignation to Nixon. President Pompidou's visit to the United States would mark "a high point," Shriver wrote, "from which my successor can felicitously begin another period of Franco-American history." As for himself, he told Nixon, "the needs of our own country . . . impinge more and more upon my conscience."

Nixon agreed that Shriver's resignation should not be made public until after Pompidou's visit to the United States in March 1970, so Shriver worked assiduously through the winter to help prepare for the meeting. In his free time, he began to concentrate more of his attention on Maryland and on further dissociating himself from Nixon's foreign policy. In his first appearance on national television after his return to the States, Shriver made clear that he was unhappy with the pace of American de-escalation in Vietnam.

Marvin Mandel's supporters, clearly perceiving Shriver to be a real threat, began trying to disqualify him on grounds that he hadn't voted in Maryland within the last five years. (He had lived in Paris for the previous two years, and for many years before that he had maintained his voting address in Chicago, with the expectation that his political future lay in Illinois.) An amendment to the Maryland constitution was introduced in the state legislature that would have barred him from running for governor on these grounds. Ted Kennedy wrote to Shriver, asking if it would be helpful for him to use his influence on Maryland Democrats to try to block this amendment—thereby signaling the Kennedy family's assent to a Shriver campaign in that state.

Still, the obstacles to attaining the Maryland State House were formidable. First, it is almost always extremely difficult to challenge an incumbent politician in a primary. Mandel had the power of patronage on his side. Second, Shriver's two-year absence from the state and his Illinois voting address made him vulnerable to charges of carpetbagging. One local paper editorialized, "There is something just a little bit wrong about a rich glamour boy rushing home to challenge an incumbent of his own party for a post in which he had previously shown no interest." Finally, Shriver's long period of indecisiveness had begun to hurt him. Some key politicos—such as Montgomery County Democratic chair Dick Schifter and Senator Joe Tydings—got tired of waiting.

Shriver returned from Paris at the end of March and announced that he would make an official decision "within six weeks" about whether to challenge Mandel in the primary. As soon as he was back in Maryland, he began to pull together his team.

The incipient campaign was a disaster, for two main reasons. The first problem was the all-volunteer campaign staff, which although enthusiastic was abysmally organized and not terribly skillful. "A good deal of time and energy has been spent in attempting to structure and organize with volunteers whose political experience is nil," one internal campaign memo reported in frustration. The second problem was Shriver's own ambivalence. For a man who had no trouble throwing himself wholeheartedly into projects he believed in, he was surprisingly diffident about his undeclared campaign. For weeks stretching into months, he wouldn't commit to an open declaration of his candidacy. He kept wanting to wait a little bit longer—to see if his poll numbers improved, to see if he could raise more money, to see if he could line up more blue-chip endorsements, to see if his campaign staff could begin to work more smoothly.

Mainly he wanted to keep his options open. A movement was afoot among Democratic members of Congress to draft Shriver as their leader and spokesman for the 1970 election season, either under the auspices of the Democratic

National Committee or as part of a new Democratic organization. Democrats who had no stake in the Maryland State House were whispering in Shriver's ear that he should skip the governor's race in favor of barnstorming the country with other Democratic candidates, accruing political capital for 1972. In Shriver's other ear, however, he could hear the whispers of disapproval of any national effort from the Kennedy apparatus.

The more time that passed, the worse the Maryland situation became. Shriver's stump speeches could still inflame an audience's passions, but his coyness about his intentions wore badly with voters. His own campaign staff grew desultory and even more disorganized. Meanwhile, Mandel's job approval ratings, previously quite low, had begun to rise. Several prominent supporters, convinced that Shriver would never make up his mind, defected to the Mandel camp. On May 22 Shriver's press secretary wrote to his campaign manager in a state of despair. "The whole picture begins to take on some of the characteristics of a 'Greek Tragedy' situation," he wrote. Some months later, Shriver would say the campaign had been "the worst experience of his life"; he couldn't recall being involved in anything "so badly managed either by him or in his behalf."

As his (still undeclared) campaign floundered, Shriver was summoned to Capitol Hill for a meeting with a group of Democratic members of Congress led by the House majority leader Carl Albert of Oklahoma. Forget Maryland, they told him. We need your help. By Memorial Day, more than 100 representatives had signed a "Draft Shriver" petition, calling on him to take charge of their national reelection campaign. One Democrat told the New York Times that Shriver was the party's only hope, now that LBJ and Humphrey were seen as washed up. "We have no young national figures, no young governors, who can invest the time in this thing that it takes and who can also express . . . half as well as Sargent Shriver the terrible issues before us. We are in that bad shape. But [Shriver] is a guy who appeals to both the Johnson-Humphrey crowd and the Kennedy people—the old Democrats and the youngsters—and I say we've just got to have him."

On June 3, Democratic congressional leaders issued a press release in which they asked Shriver to head a new party council to help revive the party. The names on the press release included the House majority leader, Carl Albert; the Senate majority leader, Mike Mansfield; the Speaker of the House, John McCormack; and the Senate majority whip, Ted Kennedy. The next day, Larry

O'Brien, the former JFK aide who was now chairman of the Democratic National Committee (DNC), attacked the plan for the new party council, saying it would be "yet another source of division and splintering of our precious resources." He claimed he had not been consulted and said that the new council would take valuable fund-raising dollars away from the DNC. Shriver and his supporters could have soothed O'Brien's concerns without too much trouble had it not been for the fact that Ted Kennedy, whose name appeared on the press release, now denied having had anything to do with it.

After an hour-long phone conversation between Shriver and O'Brien failed to settle their differences, O'Brien issued another blistering denunciation of the proposed new council. Three weeks of negotiations ensued. Finally on June 24 Carl Albert and Mike Mansfield announced that Shriver would be heading a newly formed organization—dubbed the Congressional Leadership for the Future (CLF)—that would be independent of, but would coordinate closely with, the DNC. To allay O'Brien's concerns, it was agreed that the CLF would limit its fund-raising activities and concentrate its efforts on campaigning and serving as a speaker's bureau.

Shriver gave a speech declaring the end of his political foray in Maryland. "While I have been evaluating the situation in Maryland," he said, "a national crisis has occurred. The invasion of Cambodia and expansion of war in Southeast Asia; the massacres at Kent State, at Jackson State, and in Augusta; the runaway inflation, rising prices, and growing unemployment—these events have changed the whole atmosphere of our country. They have affected me deeply, more deeply than any political event in my life. Their impact has borne heavily upon me and has made me feel an obligation to focus once again on national and international affairs." Therefore, he said, he was accepting the invitation of congressional leaders to try to build "a new politics and a new patriotism."

Shriver immediately began to build an organization, setting up an office on K Street in Washington. It rapidly became the city's political hotspot, the place with all the sizzle and excitement. Mike Feldman, a former aide to JFK, and Edward Bennett Williams, an influential Washington lawyer, joined the CLF as vice chairmen. Michael Novak, a budding Catholic theologian and political activist, was in charge of formulating policy. (After Shriver had discovered Novak's book *The Experience of Nothingness* earlier in the year, he had read excerpts to his family at the dinner table and then invited Novak to Timberlawn.)

The office was always abuzz with activity, as senators, members of Congress, and celebrities came and went. Drawing on Shriver's deep reservoir of friends and acquaintances, the list of speakers and advisers the CLF offered to Democrats in tightly contested congressional races was a Who's Who of Hollywood (Lauren Bacall, Warren Beatty, Carol Channing, Sammy Davis Jr., Paul Newman, Gregory Peck, George C. Scott, Joanne Woodward), high culture (James MacGregor Burns, William Styron, Kurt Vonnegut), and sports (Arthur Ashe, Asa Parseghian, Brooks Robinson). The most frequent speaker was Shriver himself. Between July and November he gave nearly a hundred speeches for more than eighty candidates in thirty-six states.

The bulk of the CLF's work consisted of identifying close congressional races and providing campaign assistance to the Democrats competing in them. Observers commented that Shriver's speech-making tour was similar to Nixon's of 1966 and predicted he would use the favors he was collecting as a base for a presidential campaign.

The Democratic Party as a whole had seemed moribund, almost dead, for many months. Now it began to stir again. Its pulse was loudest in Shriver's K Street offices. "The White House plods its somber way, Congress creaks on sagging hinge—and the swinging spot on the national political scene today is the crisp bustling headquarters where friends and foe alike think R. Sargent Shriver, liberal Democrat, is launching his drive for the presidency," one political columnist wrote in August. The CLF did have the look of a burgeoning presidential campaign. "The eye-bulging political organization now being put together for Sargent Shriver's 'Congressional Leadership for the Future,'" Evans and Novak wrote, "looks suspiciously to some politicians like the forerunner of a 1972 Shriver-for-President organization." Republicans, Evans and Novak reported, were worrying about how to handle Shriver. Should the GOP attack him and risk building him up, as LBJ's attacks on Nixon in 1966 had inadvertently done? Or should it aim to exploit the fissures between the CLF and the Democratic National Committee, "which already regards Shriver with jealous eyes."

Still, much as many Democrats longed for a Shriver-for-president campaign, Senator Muskie had to be considered the party's heir apparent until proven otherwise. In candid moments with friends, Shriver admitted he would not be averse to running for president if a good opportunity presented itself. But his honest analysis was that such an opportunity was not—the exhortations of various members of Congress and political columnists notwithstanding—likely to arise. People would be wary of rallying around a presidential candidate who had never previously held elective office.

Then, too, there was the Ted Kennedy question. If Kennedy won his Senate reelection race in 1970, Shriver figured there was a good chance that calls of "Draft Ted" would be renewed. Did Sarge really want to run that gauntlet again? Every time he was together with the Kennedys at Hyannis Port during this period, as one of his aides recalled, "Sarge would be carved up." "Why did you say that, why the hell did you say this?" various Kennedy aides would demand, suspicious that Shriver's personal ambitions might impede Ted's in 1972 or 1976.

As the 1970 campaign season wound down, Shriver flew from city to city in a frenzy of speech making. His most popular speech, written by Michael Novak, was called "The Politics of Life." In it, Shriver talked about how coming back from France had been a shock because it seemed to him that, in contrast to the heady idealism of the 1960s, "the hand of death lay heavy upon our society." What followed came to represent a distilled version of the Shriverian creed. "I make a distinction between the politics of life and the politics of death," he would say.

> The politics of death is bureaucracy, routine, rules, status quo; the politics of life is personal initiative, creativity, flair, dash, a little daring. The politics of death is calculation, prudence, measured gestures; the politics of life is experience, spontaneity, grace, directness. The politics of death is currying favor with the rich, toadying to the established and the powerful; the politics of life is helping the poor to dream and to become strong. The politics of death is fear of youth; the politics of life is to trust the young to their own experience.

Some of Shriver's advisers thought the speech was too sentimental ("The politics of death has been carried too far," Bill Moyers said. "We can only die once!"), but by October, Democratic candidates were requesting that speech regularly.

When the CLF was launched in June, the Democrats seemed to be heading for an election debacle. Republicans were calculating they would win control of the Senate and pick up seats in the House of Representatives. The GOP was inspired by the prospect of a big victory and put together the largest, most expen-

sive off-year campaign in history. John Kenneth Galbraith wrote a despairing article, "Who Needs the Democrats?"—to which the reply was, "Apparently no one."

The CLF helped turn election day 1970 into a modest success for the
Democrats. The Democrats won a net gain of twelve seats in the House (restoring the size of their majority to pre-1966 levels) and twenty-two out of thirty-five
governors' races, the largest net gain by either party since 1938. Finally, although
there were more than twice as many Democratic incumbents up for reelection
in the Senate as Republicans, the GOP managed to win only two seats. This was
far better than anyone had been predicting four months earlier. "The Democratic
party came out of the Tuesday elections like a hibernating bear out of a dark
cave, savoring the warm sun of success and stretching political muscle it had suddenly rediscovered," the New York Times reported.

CHAPTER FORTY-FOUR

International Men of Mystery

A fter the election, Shriver turned his attention to deciding what to do next. His political star was twinkling brightly above Washington once again, his travails at the OEO ancient history. If he were serious about a run for the presidency in 1972, now would have been the time to start building his organization. It would have been easy to do using the framework and personnel of the CLF. Instead, Shriver scuttled CLF's operations and—after a trip to Paris for the funeral of Charles de Gaulle—returned after a thirty-year hiatus to the private practice of law.

Shriver's early experience with the law, in 1946 at Henry Stimson's Brahmin law firm, had been dismal: routine, boring, with no outlet for his creative energies. Now Shriver was a national figure, a hero to many Democrats. Many people still believed he would be the Democrats' savior in 1972. Why, then, practice law?

Several factors helped Shriver make his decision. One of them was money. This was not as out of character for the man as it might seem. No one would ever call Shriver greedy; spiritual and religious values were always far more important to him than wealth. It is true that from 1953 onward he had lived in high style—with a sprawling estate in Maryland and a large home on Cape Cod—but this was much more a result of his association with his wife's family, and all their wealth, than of his own money. Working for Joe Kennedy at the Merchandise Mart between 1947 and 1960, Shriver had established himself as a successful businessman. But for the last ten years, he had worked exclusively for the government and on political campaigns. The truth was that although the Kennedy family was rich, Sargent Shriver himself was not.

The opportunity to earn real money in his own right was important to him, for at least two reasons. The first was largely psychological. Having seen his own father laid low by the Depression, Shriver was acutely conscious of how money, or the lack of it, could affect a person. Like many in the generation that grew up in the Depression, he was always aware of the value of a dollar and had a sense of the ephemerality of wealth. Also, Shriver had always been fascinated with self-made men. He was naturally attracted to men who had made their own way through business—like Joe Kennedy—and who had established a powerful place in the world through their work. The model of Joe Kennedy, who had finally passed away in 1969, loomed large for Shriver. Here was a man who had started with little and built an empire—and then who had, for all his faults, used that empire as a platform for public service for his entire family.

Second, Shriver was weary of running into the Kennedy question with each tentative foray he made into the political arena. Going into the private sector was a way for him to escape that for a while—and, significantly, to establish a small financial base independent of the Kennedy family's, in preparation for possible future campaigns.

Although money was important to Shriver, he would never have taken a job solely to get rich, and he sought a firm that offered additional rewards. He ended up selecting Strasser, Spiegelberg, Fried, Frank & Kampelman, a large corporate law firm with offices in Washington, New York, and London. (Upon Shriver's arrival, the firm changed its name to Fried, Frank, Harris, Shriver & Jacobson.) On the face of it, Fried, Frank was just another large corporate law firm. Like many high-end firms, Fried, Frank was stocked with brilliant lawyers in possession of impressive educational pedigrees. Like many firms at the dawn of globalization, it also had a growing roster of international and multinational clients. And like numerous Washington-based firms, many of its attorneys moved easily back and forth between public service and the private sector. But in other ways, Fried, Frank was anything but typical. Some of its partners— Dick Schifter, Max Kampelman, Arthur Lazarus, Sam Harris—were prominent Democrats, and the firm as a whole had a reputation for being much more liberal than other corporate shops. Its Native American practice was the largest in the country. All these attributes appealed to Shriver.

It also appealed to him that most of the firm's partners were Jewish. In Shriver's view, Fried, Frank's Jewishness marked the firm as different, as outside the mainstream of the typical Brahmin firms. As someone who thought of himself as a maverick or an outsider—within the Kennedy family, for instance, and in his approach to government bureaucracy—he believed he would fit in well. Bill Josephson, Shriver's former Peace Corps colleague and one of his closest friends, had joined the firm several years earlier and now helped bring Shriver in for exploratory talks. On February 15, 1971, Fried, Frank announced that Shriver was joining the practice as a named partner, working out of both the Washington and New York offices.

Shriver's principal responsibilities were to bring in new clients and to use his worldwide connections to help companies expand their businesses internationally. He rapidly built a substantial client list and traveled frequently to Europe and Latin America to work on business deals.

Shriver's most prominent client in his first years at Fried, Frank was Armand Hammer, the billionaire industrialist and financier. Hammer was a notorious character. Born in 1898 in New York to Russian immigrants, he had trained to become a doctor—but an unlikely meeting in Moscow with Vladimir Lenin in 1921 had led to Hammer's operating an import-export empire out of Moscow. In May 1922, Lenin wrote a secret letter to Joseph Stalin that designated Hammer as the Soviet Union's official "path" to the American business world. "This path," Lenin wrote, "should be made use of *in every way*." This was the last note Lenin would send to Stalin before the former was incapacitated by a stroke for several months.

With that letter, Hammer's fortune was made: He was to be America's official business representative to the Soviet Union. Over the next fifty years, he would exploit this position to its maximum potential, representing hundreds of companies to the Russians and making millions of dollars in profits for himself.

In making his fortune in this way, however, Hammer was forced to make certain ethical compromises. Throughout much of the 1920s, for example, Hammer laundered money for the Soviet government through American banks. By the time Shriver first encountered him in 1971, Hammer had made and lost his fortune several times, married four women (and divorced three of them), and acquired thick files at the FBI, the Securities and Exchange Commission, the CIA, Scotland Yard, and the KGB. At one point in the 1930s the State Department deemed him a national security risk; for some twenty years, he was not allowed to travel outside of the United States. Hammer had also dabbled in art dealing (he brought Fabergé eggs to America), whiskey distilling and distribution, and Democratic politics.

In 1959, at the age of sixty, Hammer bought a small, Los Angeles–based oil company, the Occidental Petroleum Corporation, and over the next decade turned it into a multibillion-dollar international conglomerate. In 1961 Hammer used his political connections in the Kennedy administration to win permission to return to the Soviet Union, to pursue fertilizer deals there. Although the FBI's J. Edgar Hoover advised Robert Kennedy to bar Hammer from the Soviet Union, adverting to his shady past, Hammer successfully argued that his deals would be "an antidote to communism"—and nearly forty years after his meeting with Lenin he went to Moscow for a summit with Khrushchev.

Not long after Shriver joined Fried, Frank, Hammer retained him as a legal counsel. According to former Occidental employee Carl Blumay, Hammer hired Shriver because he was friendly with a Russian named Dzherman Gvishiani, with whom Shriver had become acquainted while ambassador to France. Gvishiani, in addition to being the deputy chairman of the Soviet State Committee for Science and Technology, happened to be the son-in-law of Soviet premier Aleksei Kosygin and was reputed to have great influence over him. Hammer wanted Shriver to use his relationship with Gvishiani to help expedite some Occidental deals with the Russians.

Why would the idealistic, public-service-minded Shriver enter a professional relationship with a charlatan like Hammer? Partly, he was just doing his job. As long as the work Hammer was asking him to do was not illegal or grossly immoral, Shriver would have had no reason to deny him his services as an attorney. But Shriver also found Hammer to be wonderfully appealing. Hammer, although a small man, was larger than life. He had a colorful personality. He had made millions of dollars. And on top of all that, he could tell stories about Lenin.

In the same way that Shriver had been powerfully drawn to Joseph P. Kennedy, another self-made millionaire, he was drawn to Armand Hammer. And as with Joe Kennedy, although Shriver perceived some of the moral failings behind the charismatic facade, he mostly chose to forgive or overlook them. Men like Joe Kennedy and Armand Hammer had energy; they were exciting to be around; they made things happen. The scope of Shriver's own idealism was such that he was able to focus on their public-spiritedness— Hammer was a philanthropist, and he cast his business dealings with the Soviets (with some justification) as a means to improve relations between the cold war enemies—while ignoring their craven qualities. David Birenbaum, a partner at Fried, Frank says, "Was Armand Hammer a spy for the Russians? Probably so. Did Sarge know that? Absolutely not. Hammer made all kinds of not just shady deals but fraudulent deals, a lot of bad stuff. Did Sarge know any of that? No. I think Sarge thought of him, perhaps naively, as a buccaneer, as a self-made man. That impressed him."

In 1971 Shriver introduced Hammer to another larger-than-life businessman, David Karr. Karr was a brilliant, mysterious, complex figure—like someone out of a novel by Graham Greene or John Le Carré. Born David Katz to Russian-Jewish parents in Brooklyn, Karr had begun his professional life as a writer for the Communist *Daily Worker* in New York in 1936—not, as he would later insist, because of any Communist sympathies but because of his antifascist zeal. Over the next dozen years, Karr worked as a Fuller Brush salesman, an investigator for the Council against Nazi Propaganda, an employee of the Office of War Information, and an aggressive and unscrupulous investigative reporter for the influential columnist and radio personality Drew Pearson. In 1948 he moved into public relations, eventually starting his own company, Market Relations Network. Next, Karr turned himself into an expert on managing proxy fights during corporate takeovers, publishing a book on the subject in 1956. Turning his attention to show business, he produced several movies and Broadway plays before marrying a French woman—his third wife—and moving to Paris, where he set himself up as a financial consultant and entrepreneur.

Shriver and Karr first crossed paths in 1968, when Shriver was ambassador and Karr was involved in a deal to buy three of France's ritziest hotels, which

Charles de Gaulle had decreed should never fall into foreign hands. Karr, Shriver recalled, "was a wheeler dealer. You never knew exactly what the hell he was doing, or who he was with, or what nefarious or glorious thing he was doing. He was an extraordinary, exceptional, brilliant man who didn't play by any rule book. Some people would say he was a crook. Some people would say he would do anything to make money."

Shriver's attraction to Karr was not unlike his attraction to Joe Kennedy and Armand Hammer. When Shriver met Karr he was entranced. "Karr was chiaroscuric," he told *Fortune* magazine in 1979, not long after Karr had been found dead in his Paris apartment under suspicious circumstances. (Karr's widow was convinced he had been murdered by the Russians; others suspected he had been killed by agents of Hammer.) "He sketched out the most imaginative proposals." Here was a man with energy and creative intellect to match Shriver's own. With an IQ allegedly measured at genius level, Karr had taught himself dozens of foreign languages, and he was a fixture of the diplomatic social circuit. Everyone in the American expatriate community knew him, as did most of the important French business executives. Whether Karr was a philanthropist and a patriot or a rogue and a spy depended on whom you asked. Karr's friend Alan Cranston, the liberal California senator, would later say that Karr was devoted to helping Russian Jews and that he "had a strong social conscience that made him an intense promoter of détente" between Russia and the United States. Learning of Cranston's comments, one of Karr's business associates scoffed. "When I hear that David Karr was concerned about Russia's Jews, I smile," he said. "He was interested in only one thing—money."

Karr seems to have been as fascinated by Shriver as Shriver was by Karr. Part of Karr's interest was undoubtedly calculated. Karr attached himself to as many politically powerful people as he could over the years, cultivating relationships with Henry Wallace, Jimmy Carter, Gerald Ford, and Cranston among others. Shriver, as US ambassador and a Kennedy in-law, was in a position to help clear the way with both the French and American governments for some of Karr's myriad business deals. But Karr genuinely seemed to enjoy spending time with the ambassador, who shared his endless energy and passion for ideas. Whatever better angels Karr had in him, Shriver drew them out. The two men had spent hours smoking cigars and talking in the ambassador's office during the years they were in Paris together.

Karr, like Hammer, was pursuing various deals involving Soviet businessmen and in this way had become friends with Vladimir Alkhimov, the Soviet deputy foreign trade minister, who could be helpful in facilitating business matters with the Russian government. Knowing this, Shriver arranged to introduce Karr and Hammer. Instantly perceiving the value of Karr's connections—and also recognizing that Karr's expertise on proxy wars could be helpful to him in averting hostile takeover attempts of Occidental—Hammer hired him as a consultant. For a brief period, Hammer, Karr, and Shriver became a three-man team.

They were an unlikely trio—two Jews and a Catholic; two double-dealing businessmen-spies and a morally upright idealist—but the partnership worked. In 1971 Occidental had fallen on difficult times, largely as a result of a worldwide oil glut. So Hammer turned his attention to a series of blockbuster deals in Russia that he hoped would turn his company's fortunes around. "You're always talking about your old friend Lenin," Karr said to Hammer one day when the three men were together. "Let's go to the Soviet Union and make a deal." Karr and Shriver worked their contacts in the Soviet and American governments to prepare for the trip. "Hammer knew who to see to make the trip worthwhile," Shriver recalled, "but we organized it."

By early July 1972 everything was in order. Hammer had decided that, for symbolic purposes, he wanted to fly to Moscow in his private Gulfstream jet. Shriver and Karr had lunch with Gvishiani in Paris and wrangled permission; it was the first time a foreigner's private plane would be allowed to fly through Soviet airspace. The only stipulation was that a Soviet crew would have to pilot the aircraft. So in mid-July, just as the Democrats were gearing up for their national convention in Miami, Hammer, Shriver, and Karr flew in Hammer's aircraft (which included its own Goya painting) to Copenhagen, where it picked up a Russian crew, and then continued on to Moscow.

Once in Moscow, Hammer and his retinue began a series of meetings that introduced them to the heads of eighteen ministries over the course of five days. For Shriver the trip was revelatory, the beginning of a new chapter in his life. "Karr and I," Shriver recalled, "kind of got pulled along by Hammer like people being dragged along by a high-speed motorboat." Shriver found he rather liked the Communist bureaucrats he met (and they liked him) and was soon convinced that the United States and Russia could overcome their differences in ideology to achieve a full rapprochement.

Over the next three years Shriver would make multiple trips to the Soviet Union, culminating in an influential lecture tour of the country in 1975. He developed deep and lasting friendships with numerous Communist Party members—such as Eduard Shevardnadze (a Communist Party leader who would later serve as Mikhail Gorbachev's foreign minister and, after the dissolution of the Soviet Union, as president of the former Soviet state of Georgia) and Andrei Pavlov (the director of the influential State Committee for Science and Technology)—who found that the irrepressible American lawyer was changing their view of the United States.

Shriver so charmed his Soviet hosts that for a brief period in the mid-1970s he may have had more access to high-level Communist Party officials than any other American. He was always watched by a KGB handler, of course, but he was given astonishing latitude to wander around Moscow and do as he pleased. He would stay in a hotel in Red Square and visit his government contacts in the Kremlin, and on several occasions he was even allowed to sit in on meetings of the Politburo.

Shriver's trip with Hammer in July 1972 seemed at first to be a grand success. At meetings with Communist officials, Hammer would generally begin the proceedings by drawing from his pocket a yellowing piece of paper. "This is one of the letters that Lenin sent to me," he would say, and from that moment forward the party officials would effectively prostrate themselves before him. Shriver recalled that Hammer used his Lenin connection to the hilt. "We went into Lenin's little study in the Kremlin and there on his desk sits the little object"—a sculpture of a monkey—"that Hammer had given him. Well, there aren't many people alive—Russians or non-Russians, Communists or non-Communists—who have a gift sitting on Lenin's desk." At a ceremony sponsored by the Committee for Science and Technology, Karr and Shriver watched as Hammer was feted for signing a preliminary agreement on what would eventually be a $20 billion fertilizer deal.

During that same trip, Shriver was inspired to propose the building of a hotel complex in Moscow that would accommodate Western businessmen and at the same time provide them with office space for their companies. "I had been running the Merchandise Mart in Chicago," Shriver recalled, "and when we were talking about trade, it was almost a knee-jerk reaction for me to make the suggestion." Shriver knew from the Mart that such a building could be good for business; in this case, by establishing ties between East and West, it could also help international relations. Occidental Petroleum soon announced that it would be the contractor for a $180 million, four-building complex that could provide office space for up to 400 companies, plus apartments, a conference center, a movie theater, and 600 hotel rooms. The World Trade Center, as it came to be called, still stands along the Moscow River.

On the way back from Moscow on July 17, Hammer, Shriver, and Karr stopped in London, where Hammer gave a press conference announcing the biggest deal in history between Russia and the United States; Occidental's stock shot up 19 percent that day. (Several days later, when it was revealed that the deal was considerably more tentative than Hammer had implied, the stock plummeted.) While Hammer flew to Washington to begin lobbying President Nixon to give him the concessions he would need to make the deal go through, Shriver traveled to Hyannis Port to join his family.

CHAPTER FORTY-FIVE

Shriver for Vice President

In 1972 global communications were in their infancy. There was a "hotline" between the Kremlin and the White House, but beyond that there wasn't much direct communication between the Soviet Union and the United States. So although Shriver had had a glimmer of major US news events while in Russia—he knew, for instance, that the Democrats had nominated George McGovern for president on July 12—he had not been in contact with his family or with his office. So he was surprised to learn when he returned that on July 13, while he had been meeting with Soviet ministers, both Frank Mankiewicz and Pierre Salinger had placed calls to his office.

Mankiewicz, his former colleague at both the Peace Corps and the OEO, had gone on to work for Bobby Kennedy's campaign in 1968. Now he was chairman of the McGovern campaign. Salinger, who had worked as JFK's press secretary, was also working for McGovern. Calls from them on July 13 likely meant one thing: McGovern had wanted to talk to him about being his running mate. And he had missed the call.

But to have missed being on the 1972 ticket did not seem in late July of that year to be such a terrible thing. The prospects for the Democratic ticket didn't look good. McGovern was trailing Nixon by more than twenty points in the latest polls. And Shriver's law practice, after all, was thriving.

Shriver had supported Edmund Muskie from the early primaries, believing that he offered the best chance (among a somewhat uninspiring group of Democrats) to defeat Nixon. Shriver liked George McGovern personally—they had first gotten to know each other during the early years of the Kennedy administration, when Shriver was running the Peace Corps and McGovern was in charge of Food for Peace—but he believed, along with most of the political experts in early 1972, that McGovern had little chance of winning the Democratic nomination, let alone the presidency. "George is a good guy," Shriver was overheard to say at a dinner party, "but I don't believe he can win."

Along with just about everyone else, Shriver was caught by surprise when McGovern, propelled by his "army" of young campaigners, finished a close second place behind Muskie in the New Hampshire primary and then beat the field in Wisconsin and Massachusetts. After winning a rough showdown with Humphrey in the all-important California primary, McGovern had, against all odds, secured victory. At the convention in Miami, McGovern won the nomination on the opening ballot.

But at what cost? McGovern's campaign, led by Mankiewicz and Gary Hart, had something of the quality of a guerrilla insurgency. Partly this was because McGovern had been such an underdog going in. Before the New Hampshire primary, he was limping quietly along at less than 5 percent in the polls, behind at least four other candidates. Even after he had jumped to the front of the pack, the McGovern campaign had retained its underdog spirit. (This wasn't hard, because Nixon seemed poised to defeat any candidate the Democrats sent his way.)

Many of McGovern's supporters explicitly rejected what they called the "old politics"—the Democratic Party that had supported LBJ on Vietnam and then stood, with Humphrey, on the side of Daley's police force in 1968. They called for a "New Politics" that drew more on youth, on women, and on minorities. McGovern himself had recently chaired a reform commission for the Democratic Party that sought to address the problems that had been so evident in Chicago in 1968. By 1972 McGovern's commission had changed the way Democratic convention delegates were selected, creating a system whereby every state had to have a representation of women, young people,

African Americans, and other minorities proportionate to their numbers in the general population.

The impulse that created this quota system was a noble one, but the short-term effect it had on the party was devastating. It brought radicals of various flavors (New Left, black militant) into the party leadership; more important, it kept many more-experienced Democratic Party regulars out. This had the effect of isolating McGovern from his own party's local machines. Mc-Govern's own campaign managers were later appalled at what they had wrought. "We were always subject to this pressure from the cause people," Mankiewicz recalled. "We reacted to every threat from women, or militants, or college groups. If I had to do it all over again, I'd learn to tell them when to go to hell."

Still, for a brief moment after the nomination had been won, it seemed as though McGovern had a chance. As Theodore White put it, "It seemed barely possible, just faintly possible, in the exhaustion, the giddiness, the evangelical moment, that this George McGovern, the prophet, was indeed a serious candidate for the Presidency."

THE EAGLETON DEBACLE

When Shriver returned from the Soviet Union on July 18, this "evangelical moment" seemed as though it might persist. And had the next two weeks unfolded differently, it just might have. But, unbeknownst to anyone at that point, the forces that would undo McGovern for good—and that would suddenly bring Shriver back onto political center stage—had already been set in motion by the selection of Missouri senator Thomas Eagleton as the Democrats' nominee for vice president.

On Thursday morning, July 13, the day after McGovern was nominated, about twenty-five of his aides gathered in a conference room at Miami's Doral Hotel to discuss the matter of a running mate. Frank Mankiewicz, who chaired the meeting, was dismayed at how many people the candidate had invited. But McGovern had requested that a list of possible running mates be submitted to him by noon, just two hours away, so Mankiewicz pressed ahead, gathering a preliminary list of names. "We had no framework for our discussion," Gordon Weil, one of McGovern's top campaign aides, recalled. "McGovern had indi-

cated no preferences." All they knew was that McGovern's pollster had determined that Ted Kennedy would help the ticket.

When the initial brainstorming turned up twenty-three names, it was
agreed that only those candidates for whom someone in the room was willing to make an aggressive case would be preserved on the list. By the end of
the meeting, the list had been narrowed to seven names. The precise order of
the list (from most highly to least highly recommended) has been disputed over
the years, but according to Theodore White it went: Boston mayor Kevin
White; Sargent Shriver; Connecticut senator Abraham Ribicoff; Wisconsin governor Patrick Lucey; Wisconsin senator Gaylord Nelson; Idaho senator Frank
Church; and, finally, Eagleton. (According to Pierre Salinger, Shriver was first
on the list.) Ted Kennedy was not on the list, but everyone knew that if he
could be persuaded to accept it, the vice presidential nomination would be his.

No one in the room knew Kevin White or Tom Eagleton personally, so aides
set about trying to gather what information they could on these men and to do
quick background checks on all the others. In previous election years, the list
of running mates would have been vetted by a group consisting of the
Democratic Party leadership, spokespeople for different regional blocs, labor
leaders, and the candidate's closest advisers. But McGovern was an avatar of the
New Politics, so he chose to have his list vetted not by the usual suspects but
rather by representatives of the women, blacks, and young people in the party.
Hart, Mankiewicz, Pierre Salinger, and McGovern met with representatives
from each group in the candidate's suite. Salinger repeatedly made the case for
Shriver to each group. "My arguments," Salinger recalled, "were that he was
strongest where McGovern was weakest." Shriver was popular with blacks,
Catholics, and "white ethnics"—and, although he could serve as a useful bridge
to the Old Politicians, he wasn't tainted by association with them, having never
himself held elective office. Also, of course, he would bring the "Kennedy mystique." "Senator McGovern appeared impressed with my arguments," Salinger
later wrote, "and I was strongly supported by Frank Mankiewicz." When the
black leaders indicated their enthusiasm, McGovern halted the meeting and
asked Salinger to call Shriver's office.

Salinger and Mankiewicz called Shriver's Watergate office from the telephone in the living room of McGovern's suite. "Could I speak to Mr. Shriver?"
Salinger asked.

"I'm sorry, but Mr. Shriver is out of the city," someone in Shriver's office said.

"Is there anywhere he can be reached?" Salinger asked.

"Well, he's in Moscow."

Salinger mumbled a discouraged thank you and hung up.

As Salinger recalled, "When I reported to the meeting that Shriver was in Moscow there was a moment of silence. It was already 1:30 in the afternoon in Miami. Everybody agreed that if you couldn't get the candidate back to Miami Beach in time to appear before the convention that evening there was no use pursuing his name."

As there was no easy way to reach him in Moscow—and since it wouldn't do for McGovern, already seen as too liberal by many Americans, to have his running mate fly in from the Kremlin—Shriver's name was dropped from the list. Some thirty years later, McGovern would tell an interviewer that "if we could have somehow located him . . . in the Soviet Union, he'd have been the nominee." "He was a good candidate," McGovern recalled. "If we had started with him, we'd have been just fine."

Kevin White was considered next. Everyone seemed to be in favor, and a preliminary background check found no skeletons in his past. Word was sent to White that he was likely to be selected. But when McGovern called to clear the selection with Ted Kennedy, the Massachusetts senator gently indicated his opposition. He said he wanted some time to "think it over." This raised McGovern's hopes that maybe, after all, Kennedy himself was thinking of joining the ticket. While McGovern waited for Kennedy to call back, he got word from John Kenneth Galbraith that Mayor White was unacceptable to the Massachusetts delegation. White's name was dropped.

McGovern, growing anxious, next called his old friend Gaylord Nelson, the Wisconsin senator, to offer him the nomination. No way, Nelson said; he had promised his wife he wouldn't. But, Nelson said, if you're set on picking a senator, have you thought about Tom Eagleton?

McGovern barely knew Eagleton, but he possessed many of the attributes Shriver would have brought to the ticket. He was youthful and attractive— and Catholic. McGovern consulted with the aides gathered in his suite—Hart, Mankiewicz, Fred Dutton, among others—and found none of them especially enthusiastic about Eagleton. But none of them had anything against him, either; they could see that selecting Eagleton made a certain amount of sense.

"Well, I guess it's Eagleton," McGovern said.

At the morning meeting, someone had mentioned rumors that Eagleton had a drinking problem. But McGovern's aide Gordon Weil had quickly checked these out and found them to be untrue. In his research on Eagleton, Weil did find reference to mental health problems "in his background," but Weil had assumed this meant that someone in the senator's family had had problems, not the senator himself.

When McGovern called Eagleton, the Missouri senator said, "George, before you change your mind, I hasten to accept." McGovern handed the phone over to Mankiewicz, who talked briefly to one of Eagleton's aides. Mankiewicz then had Eagleton come back on the line, so he could ask the senator if he had "any skeletons in his closet" and gave some specific examples of what sort of skeletons he was worried about. Eagleton said he did not. Mankiewicz went downstairs to announce that McGovern had made his selection. The convention endorsed the McGovern-Eagleton ticket by acclamation.

That night, calls from various news outlets began streaming into McGovern's suite, asking about rumors of Eagleton's mental illness. About four o'clock on Friday morning, on his way to a victory party in the Doral's Starlight Lounge, Gordon Weil pulled Eagleton's aide Douglas Bennet aside and asked him if there were any truth to the rumors he had been hearing. Bennet repeated that although the stories of alcoholism were not true, Eagleton had once checked himself into a hospital with "mental exhaustion and depression." Weil alerted Mankiewicz, who talked to Bennet the next day. At this point, Bennet reported that the senator had in fact been hospitalized for mental illness on at least two separate occasions.

The campaign continued, but McGovern was troubled. What was the real story about Eagleton's past? It wasn't until the following Wednesday, July 19, when Hart and Mankiewicz had breakfast with Eagleton in the Senate dining room, that the McGovern campaign finally got a full accounting. Eagleton explained that he had been hospitalized for depression three times, in 1960, 1964, and 1966, that he had been treated with electroshock therapy, and that he still occasionally took tranquilizers. Mankiewicz and Hart urged McGovern to drop Eagleton from the ticket.

For the moment, however, McGovern did nothing. On Sunday, July 23,

McGovern appeared on national television, on *Face the Nation*, and talked about what kind of campaign Eagleton would run. That same day, reporters for the Knight newspaper group approached Frank Mankiewicz and said they had good evidence that Eagleton had been hospitalized for "severe manic depressive psychosis with suicidal tendencies." It was clear the story would break soon. But McGovern evidently believed the story would not have a lasting effect. The next morning in South Dakota, he discussed the situation with Eagleton over breakfast. Immediately afterward, Eagleton held a press conference in which he revealed to reporters his three hospitalizations and his electroshock treatment. With that, Eagleton thought the matter settled, and he took off for Los Angeles and Hawaii to campaign.

But in the days following Eagleton's press conference, McGovern's Senate office was flooded with letters, phone calls, and telegrams urging that Eagleton be dropped from the ticket. By midweek, major newspapers—the *New York Post* and the *Los Angeles Times*, followed by the *Washington Post*, and, finally, the *New York Times*—editorialized in favor of dropping Eagleton. What would McGovern do?

He kept telling his aides privately that he was waiting to gauge public reaction before making a decision one way or the other, but they urged him to do something emphatic soon. The Eagleton affair was becoming a major distraction from the campaign. People were beginning to question McGovern's competence. What did it say about his own intelligence-gathering operations that he had selected a running mate whose background would clearly raise such troubling questions?

On Wednesday night, July 26, it seemed that McGovern had made his decision. "I'm 1,000 percent for Tom Eagleton," he declared in a statement he released to the press. One could argue with the wisdom of this position—and most of McGovern's own staff disagreed with it—but one could not fault McGovern for his boldness and conviction. Despite the doubts and questions, he was going to stand firmly by his man. Party regulars who had once thought McGovern too "soft" to support now wondered if they had gotten him wrong; maybe he had some backbone, after all.

Pressure to drop Eagleton persisted, however, and by Friday, July 28, McGovern's aides had persuaded him to change his mind. On Sunday morning, in an appearance on NBC's *Meet the Press*, Democratic chairs Jean Westwood and Basil Patterson stated that Eagleton should withdraw. Since Westwood acknowledged that she had just talked with McGovern, the meaning was clear:

The candidate had decided he wanted his running mate dropped. Embarrassingly, no one had informed Eagleton—in fact, the night before, McGovern had reiterated his "1,000 percent" support. Thus, at almost exactly the same time that Eagleton was being publicly dumped from the ticket on one network, he was appearing on another network (CBS), on *Face the Nation*, defending his presence on the ticket.

For the moment, though, the axe did not officially fall. On Monday, McGovern flew to Louisiana for the funeral of Senator Allen Ellender. He sat next to Ted Kennedy on the flight back and spent most of the time trying to persuade the Massachusetts senator to join his ticket. Again, Kennedy demurred. Back in Washington that night, Eagleton and McGovern met in Gaylord Nelson's Senate office. McGovern told him that his health had come to dominate the campaign. Eagleton argued that the issue would die down soon, but McGovern responded that he couldn't afford to lose any more time or any more distance in the polls. Eagleton would have to go. All things considered, the meeting was cordial. The two men made separate statements and Eagleton was gone.

But the damage was done. In the mind of the public, not only had McGovern shown astoundingly poor judgment in selecting (what was perceived to be) a defective running mate in the first place, he had also shown himself not to be a man of his word. The about-face could not have been any more dramatic: from "1,000 percent" to "good-bye" in less than five days.

McGovern's campaign was premised on his image as a different kind of politician. Now, with his botched running-mate selection he had shown himself to be as bad as the rest of them. For the next several weeks, the press coverage of the McGovern campaign was not just conventionally negative; it made him "look like a fool." "Lost," Theodore White wrote, "was McGovern's reputation as politician somehow different from the ordinary—a politician who would not, like others, do *anything* to get elected. McGovern by this time had already antagonized many Americans by his stand on issues. For the first time, after Eagleton, he would incur not merely antagonism but—far worse in politics—contempt for incompetence."

THE LUCKY SEVENTH

The Eagleton affair was a disaster. McGovern's long odds were now longer than ever. There was only one thing that might be able to repair the damage: Ted

Kennedy joining the ticket. Again McGovern implored Kennedy to reconsider; again, Kennedy said no. Kennedy had personal reasons for not wanting to run. He was still nervous about the impact of Chappaquiddick, and he was trying to serve as surrogate father to the children of his slain brothers. Even had he been inclined to join the ticket before the Eagleton debacle, there was little incentive for him to do so afterward. McGovern had dug himself a hole so deep, anyone could see it would be impossible to climb out of it.

What politician in his right mind would join the McGovern ticket? This was the Democrats' question as August began, and McGovern made an increasingly frantic series of phone calls to prospective candidates, each of whom turned him down. The Eagleton disaster threatened to become an embarrassment of even more epic proportions: What if no credible candidate could be persuaded to run for the vice presidency? "Who'd take it?" mused one Democratic worker. "It's a suicide mission."

On Wednesday, McGovern tried to get Senator Ribicoff to persuade Kennedy—yet again—to join the ticket. When this didn't work, McGovern asked if Ribicoff himself would join. Ribicoff said no. On Thursday at breakfast, McGovern tried to talk Hubert Humphrey into joining him. Humphrey said no. Later that day, McGovern asked Reubin Askew, governor of Florida. Askew said no. That night, McGovern turned to Edmund Muskie. Muskie said he would think about it.

Earlier in the week, about the time McGovern was making his overture to Ribicoff, Frank Mankiewicz and Pierre Salinger once again began pressing the case for Shriver. At first, McGovern had resisted. (One report had him saying, "*Shriver!* Who wants him? All that Shriver talk is coming from Shriver himself.") McGovern wanted to curry favor with his fellow senators by selecting one of them. An additional concern, as Gary Hart recalled, was that selecting Shriver would alienate the Kennedys, whose support was crucial if McGovern were to make the race competitive. But sometime during the week, according to Hart, the Massachusetts senator signaled to McGovern that it would be okay with him if Shriver were on the ticket.

Meanwhile, a draft-Shriver movement had sprung up among the members of Congress who had recruited him to head the CLF in 1970. Led by George Mitrovich, an aide to New York congressman Lester Wolff, the movement peppered McGovern headquarters with phone calls and telegrams. Shriver himself remained oddly diffident. Once, when Mitrovich called him, Shriver declined to take the call, saying he didn't want to interrupt his dinner with Rose Kennedy. Another time, he refused to come off the tennis court to take a call. Mitrovich left an angry message: "What do you want to be—Wimbledon champ or Vice President of the United States?"

While Muskie mulled whether to join the ticket, McGovern and his staff agreed that if Muskie turned them down, they would turn next to Shriver. They did not want to be rejected by a seventh candidate, however, so they decided that before McGovern called, Mankiewicz would sniff around to gauge Shriver's interest. Shriver got wind of this and asked his friend Donald Dell, who had worked with Mankiewicz on Bobby Kennedy's 1968 campaign, to alert the McGovern team that he would accept the nomination if offered. Dell went down to McGovern's Senate office on Friday and pulled Mankiewicz out into the hall. "Frank," Dell said, "I'm just here to pass a message that if asked, Sarge would accept the vice presidency." As Dell recalls, Mankiewicz explained that McGovern was really scrambling and could not afford to get turned down again. "Is that absolutely clear?" Mankiewicz asked. Dell's reply: "I'm here to tell you that, if asked, Sarge will accept." As Dell recalled, Mankiewicz said, "Donald, just go back and tell Sarge he has a ton of credit in my bank account."

The news that Mankiewicz had encouraged Shriver to be on call in case Muskie said no was reported as the lead story in Saturday's *New York Times*—a fact that may have influenced Muskie finally to decline McGovern's offer.

While Shriver waited to see what Muskie would do, he contemplated his own situation. His main concern was whether Teddy would block him from joining the campaign, as he had in 1968. If Ted wanted to vie for the Democratic nomination in 1976, Shriver's presence on the McGovern ticket could pose a problem, because even if (as seemed likely) McGovern-Shriver lost in November, Shriver would stand to become the de facto Democratic front-runner for 1976, as Muskie had been for 1972.

Shriver sought out his brother-in-law in Hyannis Port and asked him whether he would object to an in-law being on the McGovern ticket and whether "it would affect anything you want to do." Ted said he would not object. It is likely that after the Eagleton scandal, Kennedy believed that McGovern would lose badly—perhaps even very badly, as badly as Goldwater had done in 1964. Such a defeat could turn McGovern into a political leper and his running mate into tainted goods. It seemed unlikely that Shriver could parlay the experience into a viable platform for 1976. And even if he planned to, Teddy figured, the Kennedy family councils could talk Sarge out of it. As one political analyst put it at the time, "This is a slight but not an awesome gamble for the youngest of the Kennedys so long as the McGovern-Shriver ticket seems headed for oblivion." A more charitable view is that Ted felt bad for having helped block Sarge's way in 1968 and was now trying to make amends. Also, he recognized McGovern's desperation; it would be a disservice to the party to block Shriver from the ticket.

The question that must have been running through Kennedy's head was, Why would Shriver *want* the vice presidential nomination? McGovern was trailing badly in the polls and getting abused by the press, and he struck many Democratic Party regulars as a laughingstock. Signing on to the campaign at this point would be political suicide. Besides, everyone knew that five people had already turned McGovern down—Muskie would be the sixth. No self-respecting high school girl would accept a prom invitation if she knew she were her date's seventh choice; why would a self-respecting politician?

But Shriver's mind worked differently from most people's; also, his situation was different from the first six prospects McGovern had asked. Of all the men McGovern approached, Shriver was the only one who had never held elective office. Leaving aside his half-hearted foray in Maryland, he had never even run for one. And after being actively thwarted from joining the presidential tickets in 1964 and 1968, he welcomed the opportunity when it finally presented itself in 1972—especially since the Kennedy family had officially approved it.

Like all politicians, a part of Shriver's mind was shrewdly calculating. Along with everyone else, he could see that the prospects for a Democratic victory in November were tiny. But he perceived that by joining the ticket when no one else would, he would be doing his loyal duty to the party and adding to the bank of gratitude he had built up through his work on the 1970 congressional campaign. That could stand him in good stead for 1976 or beyond. Also, he was confident of his abilities as a campaigner. He believed that showcasing those abilities now, even in a losing effort, might be a good advertisement of his skills. Some of his friends believed that he wanted to show he could campaign as well as, or better than, his Kennedy brothers-in-law.

But compared with the minds of other politicians, the shrewdly calculating part of Shriver's mind was relatively small. The part of his mind that believed that doing the right thing is important, in contrast, was large—as was that part of his mind that believed he could accomplish the impossible. Shriver saw that the McGovern campaign was listing badly, in danger of capsizing. If it did capsize, much of the Democratic Party would go down with it. Shriver saw himself as ballast that could stabilize the ticket and keep the party from self-destructing. He also believed, at least some of the time, that McGovern could win. He could see that the poll numbers were terrible and that the press coverage was awful. But there were still three full months until the election. He had seen Truman defeat Dewey. And he had made a habit of accomplishing what other people said was impossible: making the Peace Corps a success; saving the OEO in 1967; winning over Charles de Gaulle. Defeating Richard Nixon, a man he increasingly believed to be misguided and corrupt, couldn't be any harder than what he had already done.

As Shriver saw it, he had little to lose. If the ticket went down to defeat, well, that was only to be expected. And if somehow it won? *That* would be a victory more impressive than any Kennedy candidate had ever pulled off.

On the morning of August 5, Muskie called McGovern campaign headquarters to say he would not be joining the ticket. McGovern called Shriver in Hyannis Port. A household staff member came out to the tennis court to say that Senator George McGovern was on the phone. Strangely insouciant, Shriver insisted on finishing his tennis game before taking the call; it was as though, having made clear his availability, he was signaling that he was still his own man and would do things his own way. When he picked up, he heard, "Sarge, this is George McGovern. Say, Sarge, we've been going over this vice presidential thing pretty thoroughly for the past few days, as I'm sure you know, and I want you to know that everyone here, including myself, would like very much to have you on this ticket." Shriver accepted the offer.

By this point, McGovern's aides had had more than a week to check out all the prospective candidates *"very* thoroughly," as Gary Hart recalled, so they were confident that Shriver had no "skeletons in his closet." Still, after what had transpired with Eagleton, Shriver felt compelled to bring up the one episode that he worried might be used against him. He explained to McGovern that one night while he was ambassador to France, he and Eunice had gone to a social event at a Paris nightclub. Eunice had gone home early but Sarge had stayed late, dancing the night away with a bevy of female admirers. Nothing untoward had happened, but a photograph of him dancing with a famous young French model, who was wearing a (very) short skirt, had appeared on the cover of a French newspaper, accompanied by a saucy caption. McGovern laughed. "If that's the best you can offer in the way of skeletons," he said, "then I think we're in pretty good shape."

Shriver began his campaign for the vice presidency in typical fashion: by bringing together the best and the brightest minds he could assemble for a free-wheeling, all-day ideas session. "Win or lose," he told Eunice, "we've got to have fun in the campaign." The morning after McGovern called Hyannis Port, as Hart recalled, "Shriver swung into action with the energy for which he is famous, filling his Maryland estate with 'old Kennedy people' by Sunday morning for all day planning and organization meetings." Hart and others came out to Timberlawn to brief Shriver and company on the issues.

It was immediately apparent from the assembled crowd that Shriver might help McGovern rebuild bridges to the old Democratic regulars. "That meeting," Hart recalled, "was generations meeting each other at a crossroad. I tried to talk about grassroots organization, gypsy-guerrilla advance people, and citizen-volunteer canvassers, while the Kennedy people from 1960 and 1968 barked orders, summoned successful lawyers away from lucrative practices, and negotiated heavy salaries. It was like Che Guevara meeting General Patton."

After having had a field day with the protracted Eagleton debacle, the press hailed Shriver's selection. "George McGovern virtually backed into the selection of Sargent Shriver as his ticket-mate but he has latched on to the best that is left of the high aims and high hopes of the New Frontier days," Charlie Bartlett wrote in his column on August 7. Shriver, Bartlett continued, bore little of the taint attached to conventional politicians. "More open in public and more naive in the backrooms, he is atypical of the species. He comes through, at 56, as one who still believes the world can be a better place and wants another chance to work at it. He enters active politics at a high level only because the lower levels were closed off by professionals who sensed he was not one of the usual breed." NBC news declared that "there is a dynamism, an excitement about [Shriver] that turns crowds on in a way that George McGovern just doesn't." Hubert Humphrey told *Time*, "Sarge is just what George needs—

somebody with enthusiasm, somebody with zip." *Time* also reported that Shriver had "quickly made many people wonder why he had not been the first choice all along." And in his "Foreign Affairs" column in the *New York Times*, Cy Sulzberger wrote that the best possible outcome of the 1972 election would be for Nixon to win—keeping the wild-eyed McGovern out of office—while Shriver would get enough public recognition to win the presidency in 1976. "Mr. Shriver has not yet made his mark," Sulzburger wrote, "but, an energetic, intelligent, and compassionate man, he is in some respects the best endowed of any of the Kennedy clan for the Presidency of the United States."

Two days later, the Democratic National Committee met for a special miniconvention at the Sheraton Park Hotel in Washington to officially sanction the replacement of Tom Eagleton. Mike Mansfield and Dan Rostenkowski officially nominated Shriver. The nomination was approved all but unanimously, with only Eagleton's Missouri delegation (and a few individual Oregon delegates) declining to support it. It was the first time in the history of the party that a second vice president had been nominated before election day.

Shriver's acceptance speech on national television that night was not widely seen. By this point the nation, turned off by McGovern's handling of the Eagleton affair, had tuned the Democrats out. Those few million Americans who did watch, however, were treated to a glimpse of the optimistic Shriver spirit—and of the family drama that had played out behind the scenes. Until Shriver spoke, the evening had had a desultory feeling to it. Shriver enlivened the crowd, "his enthusiasm for the task . . . in marked contrast to the gloom that had hung over the McGovern camp." Shriver declared in his speech that "I am not embarrassed to be George McGovern's seventh choice for vice president. We Democrats may be short of money. We're not short of talent. Ted Kennedy, Ed Muskie, Hubert Humphrey, Abe Ribicoff, Tom Eagleton—what a galaxy of stars. Pity Mr. Nixon—his first and only choice was Spiro Agnew."

After saluting Eagleton's courage and grace in handling his exile from the ticket, Shriver unexpectedly made light of his relations with the Kennedy family. "John Kennedy's victory ended discrimination against Catholics," he said. "Lyndon Johnson's victory ended discrimination against Southerners. And now," he continued with a sly grin, "George McGovern has proved there is no discrimination against in-laws." Then, departing from his printed text, he gestured over at Ted Kennedy who was sitting nearby on the platform and cracked, "Look at him with that pensive look. The great Ted Kennedy. I wonder what's he's thinking about."

The vice presidential campaign began in chaos. Shriver had had no time to prepare—he had just returned from the Soviet Union, after all—but now, since more than two weeks had been wasted on the Eagleton affair, he had only days to get a full-blown campaign up and running. He needed to learn McGovern's issues and stances, of course. And because he had no pre-existing political organization, he needed to recruit a staff.

To take charge of the campaign plane, Shriver selected Donald Dell—partly because he liked and trusted Dell, having worked closely with him at the OEO; partly because Dell had been his conduit to the McGovern campaign; partly because Dell had good relations with the other branches of the Kennedy family, having been close to both Bobby and Ethel, and to Ted. But mostly he picked Dell because Don was pretty much the first person to appear on the scene after McGovern's phone call.

Dell's tenure as campaign trip director did not last long. Dell admired and respected Shriver and strongly supported his candidacy. But he had just launched his own business, representing professional athletes as their agent in negotiations, and was ambivalent about abandoning it for three months at such a crucial time. More significantly, he discovered within a few days that he was unable to exert the control over Shriver that was necessary to keep the candidate focused and on schedule.

Few people could have. Shriver worked according to his own internal clock and was forever running late. For most of his professional life, this was not a fatal problem. But national election campaigns are constantly battling the clock, trying (and usually failing) to adhere to a strict schedule of travel and appearances. When the natural clock-battling of the campaign was combined with Shriver's obliviousness to the passage of time, the results were predictably disastrous. For the first week of the campaign, the candidate was constantly showing up in the wrong place, at the wrong time, with the wrong speech. Politically, Shriver seemed to have a perverse sense of priorities: He would spend hours talking to a group of sixteen-years-olds, who weren't even old enough to vote, while keeping influential local Democratic politicians waiting

for hours. It was as if he was refusing to grant any single person more importance than any other—a worthy goal as a Christian, but terrible tactics as a
politician. (This was the sort of thing that made Shriver so widely loved by—
and so exasperating to—his campaign staff.) Among other things, Shriver's late
and unpredictable schedule was hell on the press corps, which was forever missing its filing deadlines. This affected the campaign's press coverage.

Dell, as tough and as smart as he was, simply couldn't keep Shriver on
schedule.

"Everywhere we go Sarge is late," Dell recalled. "We had this one stop in
Cleveland, where Shriver was supposed to meet the head of the labor union,
and we're up in the hotel suite. And I said, 'Sarge, the guy's waiting downstairs.'
And he says, 'I gotta go get a haircut.' I said, 'Sarge, you can't get a haircut.
We're already 30 minutes late on our schedule, and the labor leader's down in
the lobby.' We had this huge argument about his haircut. I go into the bathroom. I come out, he's left. And he's gone somewhere to get this goddamn haircut." When Shriver returned, fifteen minutes later, he and Dell went downstairs
to find that the labor leader had left in a huff. "The McGovern people called me
immediately, and they're furious," Dell recalled. "They all blame me, because
I'm supposed to get him there on time; it's my job."

On the airplane that night, Shriver and Dell got into a screaming argument,
which ended when Shriver banged his hand down on the fold-out tray table and
snapped it in two. That was Dell's next-to-last day on the campaign plane. The
next morning, in the car on the way to a speaking appearance, Shriver turned
to Dell and said, "Donald, how's your business going?" Dell acknowledged that
with all the time he was putting in on the campaign, his business was suffering.
So Shriver, as Dell recalled it, said, "Donald, listen, I've got a great idea. Why
don't you go back to Washington, and you can run your firm, you can help out
with Citizens for McGovern/Shriver." This was, Dell says, Shriver's "nice, polite
way of getting me out of my role."

If Dell couldn't keep a handle on Shriver, then who could?

Bill Josephson. Although still young, in his late thirties, Josephson had worked
with Shriver on and off since 1961, and his years in the Peace Corps had taught
him how to manage his old boss. Plus, he was—as Dell happily concedes—even
smarter, blunter, and tougher-talking than Dell was. In some ways, Josephson

was not unlike Adam Yarmolinsky: He suffered fools poorly; associates at Fried, Frank were afraid of him. Although he had been only twenty-six when he first went to work for Shriver, he had earned his intellectual respect and related to him now as a peer. He was also unfailingly devoted to Shriver, guarding his interests— as one Fried, Frank colleague later recalled—"like a pit bull." So when Josephson received a call from Shriver on August 6, he dropped everything and flew to Washington. He wouldn't return home until after the election.

Once Josephson took over from Dell as trip director—and Mickey Kantor was installed at the Washington headquarters—the campaign ran more smoothly. But it never fully recovered from being thrown together so quickly, and it was always short on funds. The campaign was always scrambling.

Despite the grim picture the poll numbers painted, the campaign plane (which Shriver christened the *Fighting Lucky 7*, a reference to his being McGovern's seventh pick, as well as to the seven—Bobby, Maria, Timmy, Mark, and Anthony, plus Sarge and Eunice—Shriver family members) remained a font of energy, ideas, and creativity, with a typically New Frontierish collection of talent. Mark Shields, a veteran of the defeated Muskie campaign (and today a celebrity pundit), came aboard as political director. Doris Kearns, a Harvard professor and veteran of the Johnson administration (who would later become a best-selling, Pulitzer Prize–winning popular historian), came on as an issues director. Mike Barnicle, now a famous (and controversial) newspaper columnist, was a speechwriter. So was Richard Parker (now a professor at Harvard), who walked in off the street after finishing up his clerkship to Supreme Court justice Potter Stewart. Michael Novak, the Catholic philosopher and veteran of the 1970 CLF campaign, joined up once again.

Running the show at Shriver headquarters in Washington were Mickey Kantor, the former Legal Services attorney; Lee White, a former chairman of the Federal Power Commission who had served as a special counsel to both JFK and LBJ; and Tersh Boasberg, a public interest lawyer and former OEO colleague. Lloyd Cutler, a longtime Kennedy family legal adviser (and later a lawyer for Bill Clinton), headed up the fund-raising operation. Other team members included Baltimore councilwoman Barbara Mikulski (now a US senator) and former *Washington Evening Star* managing editor Burt Hoffman.

Also joining the group was an idealistic young veteran of Bobby Kennedy's 1968 campaign named Jeannie Main, who had been working as a Senate staffer for Walter Mondale for the last few years. She couldn't stand the idea of four more years of Richard Nixon, so she showed up at McGovern headquarters one day to offer her services as a volunteer. Jeannie ended up as a regular on the Shriver campaign plane. (Shriver recognized that she possessed uncommon mettle, and he hired her as an assistant at Fried, Frank following the election. At the end of 2003, Main was finishing her thirty-first consecutive year of service at Shriver's side. "Jeannie Main guarded the gate," one of Shriver's colleagues at Fried, Frank recalled. "She had worked for Bobby Kennedy and was unbelievably smart and loyal and kept Shriver on track.")

The "talented people that Shriver was able to recruit at a moment's notice to join a doomed effort was a testimony to the effect he had on people," Mark Shields recalled. "I mean, we knew going in that this campaign was not likely to be a glowing resume item for any of us. But he got the Mickey Kantors of the world to drop high-paying jobs and show up to work." Shields had never met Shriver before, but he soon understood why so many people were willing to give up so much for him. "I have never been associated with anybody on a daily basis for whom I had more affection or respect," Shields says.

Despite all the assembled talent—this "jolly bunch of amateurs" as one reporter called it—the challenge was enormous. Everyone knew what the polls showed. When McGovern's pollster Pat Caddell broke down the numbers, they seemed even worse. Large percentages of normally Democratic voting groups—Catholics, blue-collar workers, and the "white ethnics"—had gone over to Nixon in droves. McGovern had so alienated the Democratic rank and file that the McGovern-Shriver campaign now had to focus its effort on recapturing a large portion of its core constituency, rather than chasing after Republicans or swing voters. Of all the Democratic constituencies, only African Americans seemed staunchly in the McGovern camp—and this served to alienate much of the George Wallace voter bloc, mainly blue-collar white Southerners who felt threatened by blacks. In a campaign memo on August 24, Mickey Kantor told Doris Kearns and Bill Josephson that they had to start from the premise that fully twenty-six states had to be completely written out of the Democratic column; the only hope was to cobble together enough electoral votes from some of the remaining twenty-four, which fortunately included such large-population states as California, Illinois, Massachusetts, New York, Pennsylvania, and Texas.

The mission of the vice presidential campaign, as Mark Shields recalled, was "to bring home wayward Democrats. I don't think we saw three white Protestants in the whole campaign. Everywhere we went it was ethnic Catholics, Southerners, and union members." A Democratic presidential candidate couldn't hope to carry a state without enlisting various of these groups. What made this especially challenging for the Shriver campaign, according to Shields, was that certain staffers on the McGovern campaign, intent on defining a "new" Democratic politics, viewed any association with those traditional groups "as proof of moral cowardice."

In some ways, Shriver was well equipped to go after these traditional Democratic constituencies. He was a prominent Catholic. And he, unlike McGovern, had not severed his ties to the Daleys and the LBJs of the party. As a Marylander from a Confederate family, he had more credibility than McGovern south of the Mason-Dixon line. He was also a more dynamic campaigner than McGovern and possessed more of what might be called "the common touch." McGovern could go after the Northeastern liberals and the new suburban Democrats, where his support was strongest; Shriver would be sent out to the factories and the slaughterhouses and the wharves to mingle with the working man.

However, Shriver's "common touch" tended to be swaddled in Pierre Cardin suits. Shriver's feeling of fellowship with the blue-collar ethnics was genuine; his powerful innate curiosity about other people was entirely sincere. When he mixed with crowds on the campaign trail, it was as one among equals—not, as so often appears to be the case when candidates meet the throngs, the politically anointed patronizing the unwashed masses. But this genuine feeling of connection to the voters tended to blind Shriver to how different from them he appeared. Rather than seeking to dress and act like the people he was meeting, he dressed and acted like the person he was: an intellectual, and a man of some affluence who liked to dress with fashionable panache. Mingling with factory workers in their standard-issue work shirts, or with coal miners in their soot-stained coveralls, Shriver looked out of place in his double-breasted French suits and his fancy Italian shoes. The people he met liked him. But the images that appeared on television and in press photos showed what looked like a man out of touch with the people he was trying to lure back to the party.

Shriver didn't help matters when, on at least one occasion, he fumbled when explaining to fellow Catholics why he sent his eldest son, Bobby, to Phillips Exeter Academy, an elite WASP preparatory school. Nor did it help that

AFL-CIO president George Meany, believing he had once been snubbed by Shriver in Paris, made no secret of his dislike for both McGovern and Shriver; it looked as though the AFL-CIO was going to forgo its traditional allegiance to the Democrats and stay neutral—or perhaps even endorse Nixon.

The most egregious example of Shriver's apparent disconnection from the blue-collar constituency he was trying to woo occurred in Youngstown, Ohio. In 1972 Youngstown was a classic rust-belt working-class steel town—just the sort of place in which Shriver should be campaigning if he wanted to reach the factory-worker vote. The story of what happened in Youngstown the day Shriver campaigned there has been told so many times over the years that it has achieved the status of myth; it is no longer easy to separate fact from legend. But according to Mark Shields, what happened was this:

Thomas P. "Tip" O'Neill, a longtime Massachusetts congressman (he would soon become House majority leader and then Speaker of the House) with stalwart credentials among working-class ethnic Democrats, agreed to accompany Shriver on a campaign trip to Youngstown. On the plane, Shriver and O'Neill talked about Jack and Bobby Kennedy. "Ya know, your brothers-in-law were cheap bastards," O'Neill said affectionately. "They never bought a round." This, claimed O'Neill, an orotund Irishman with a classic drinker's nose, had hurt them with the white working-class voter. "Here's what we'll do," he told Shriver. "We'll go to the local saloon, right outside the steel mill." Drinking in a bar, O'Neill assured him, is the way to relate to the working man.

O'Neill and Shriver arrived with some aides at a local dive near a Youngstown steel mill and sat down at a table to await the end of the next shift. Soon, the bar was filled. O'Neill was in his element. So, in his way, was Shriver; the rapport between the candidate and the people was good. Then it came time to order another round. Everyone yelled out his choice of beer: Schlitz! Budweiser! Pabst! Then it was Shriver's turn. "Make mine a Courvoisier!" he yelled, calling for an elite and expensive liqueur.

"That's it," O'Neill said. "I'm getting back on the plane and going back to Boston. There's no hope here."

"WE HAVE TO DESTROY SHRIVER NOW"

One of a vice president's jobs is to be his running mate's attack dog, the mudslinger who allows the presidential nominee to remain above the fray. Aggressive personal attacks, generally speaking, were not Shriver's style—this was one reason old-school machine politicians perceived him as lacking an instinct for the jugular. But in this instance, he launched his attacks with evident relish. He called Nixon "Tricky Dicky," a "psychiatric case," "power-mad," "the greatest con artist," and "the number-one bomber of all time." He attacked Nixon for his economic policies, his nuclear policies, and his social policies. These attacks were to be expected from a vice presidential candidate, and although they could arouse partisan crowds, they didn't attract much media attention.

His attacks on Nixon's Vietnam policy, however, did. A few days into his campaign, Shriver told a group of reporters that Nixon had "blown" the opportunity for peace in late 1968 and early 1969. Nixon, Shriver said, had had "peace in his lap" when he took office in 1969 and could have signed an acceptable negotiated treaty ending the war, but he opted instead for his policy of Vietnamization, continuing to support the war but with a declining number of US troops on the ground.

This was a serious charge. Among other things, 20,000 additional American lives had been lost in Southeast Asia between the winter of 1969 and the summer of 1972. Meanwhile, Henry Kissinger's talks with the North Vietnamese in Paris, no longer secret, had increased in frequency through July and August, as Nixon strove (as LBJ had in 1968) to achieve a peace settlement before November, in order to boost his already highly favorable reelection chances. Shriver's allegation added fuel to Democratic claims that Nixon's pursuit of peace was motivated entirely by politics; if the president could have had the same settlement in 1969, as Shriver claimed, why did he wait until he was up for reelection to try to take advantage of it?

Coming from just about anyone else, such a charge would have been predictably inflammatory, but it could have been effectively handled by rote denials from Nixon. But because Shriver had been ambassador to France in 1968 and 1969, and had been privy to State Department cable traffic during the Nixon administration, his allegation was instant front-page news. Why, Nixon's defenders asked, did Shriver accept a position in the Nixon administration if he believed the president had already blown a chance for peace? Because, Shriver said, in January 1969 he still thought Nixon would do what Eisenhower had done when he took over from Harry Truman, ending the Korean War. "It wouldn't have been hard" for Nixon to achieve peace in 1969, Shriver said.

President Nixon immediately dispatched both Secretary of State Bill Rogers and Secretary of Defense Melvin Laird to defend his administration and to ridicule Shriver's claim that he had been privy to any secret information. Rogers went on the attack, telling a press conference that Shriver was engaging in "political fantasy"; the notion that Nixon "blew" the chance for peace was "bunk." Rogers said, "Certainly if the President of the United States is sitting with peace in his lap, as Mr. Shriver says, and Mr. Shriver knows that peace is in his lap, he could pick up the phone and call me, or call the President, or talk to [Henry] Cabot Lodge, or the other negotiators and say, 'My God, peace is in the President's lap.' He didn't mention anything of that kind." Then Rogers cracked up reporters by pretending to be Shriver, holding an imaginary phone up to his ear and saying, "Bill, this is Sarge Shriver. The President has a historic opportunity for peace. Peace is in his lap. Why don't you do something about it?" Rogers's State Department also announced that it had combed through Shriver's own cables from Paris and claimed to find nothing about a "historic opportunity for peace."

But behind the scenes, Nixon worried. He knew that the story of his interventions with the South Vietnamese delegation, if it got out, would be extremely damaging to his reelection chances. Through Anna Chennault and President Thieu, Nixon *had* actively sought to sabotage the chance for a settlement in 1968. If the blown-chance-for-peace story gained momentum, it would add force to a series of stories that had recently been appearing in the *Washington Post*.

The week after Shriver's nomination to the ticket, long articles in both *Time* and *Newsweek* about the Eagleton debacle were immediately followed by much shorter articles about a break-in at the Democratic National Committee headquarters in the Watergate building. On June 17, five men had been arrested when they were found trying to implant bugging devices in the DNC offices. Now evidence was growing that the men had ties to the GOP and specifically to the Committee to Reelect the President.

For Nixon, the Eagleton debacle had been a godsend: not only did it gravely damage McGovern's image but it also pushed the breaking Watergate story off the front pages. Even when the story did appear on the front pages, as it was now doing with some regularity in the *Washington Post*, no one seemed to pay much attention. Although Shriver kept mentioning it in his speeches, voters didn't take an interest.

The Vietnam story, in contrast, had legs. Unfortunately for the Democratic ticket, Shriver didn't quite know what he had stumbled onto yet. He, along with

Humphrey, LBJ, and Johnson's peace negotiators, all knew that Nixon had been involved in some funny business, making direct overtures to the South Vietnamese to impede a peace settlement in late October 1968. But the full story of Nixon and Anna Chennault's skullduggery would not emerge for a decade. So in his attacks on Nixon, Shriver focused more on the situation in Paris—and on the situation on the ground in Vietnam—*after* Nixon took office in January 1969.

Shriver was on solid ground here, as well. At the time Nixon took office, North Vietnamese troops had withdrawn from the two northernmost provinces in South Vietnam, where most of the fiercest combat had taken place. It was the first such withdrawal since full-scale combat engagements had begun in 1965. The Americans, meanwhile, had 500,000 troops on the ground in South Vietnam. This gave the United States the strongest negotiating position it had had for years—and the active withdrawal of North Vietnamese troops seemed to many to signal that they were ready to come to the negotiating table. But when Nixon, already enmeshed in his relationship with President Thieu, took office, he focused more on acceding to South Vietnamese demands than on working toward a settlement.

The day after Rogers mocked Shriver to reporters, Averell Harriman and Cyrus Vance, the two leading American negotiators in 1968, issued a joint statement backing up Shriver's claim of a "blown" peace. "We support completely Sargent Shriver's view that President Nixon lost an opportunity for a negotiated settlement in Vietnam when he took office," they declared. The North Vietnamese withdrawal of troops was a clear signal, Vance and Harriman argued, that Hanoi was ready to talk seriously about peace. When Rogers's State Department again denied this, Harriman told the *New York Times*, "There's no use in the department trying to deceive the American public. This was a fact. We had the same information in Paris that they had in the State Department." Harriman acknowledged that some "hard-liners" may have refused to recognize the troop withdrawal as a peace signal, but he and Vance, as well as Clark Clifford, then secretary of defense, had clearly seen the withdrawal for what it was. The *Times* published an editorial blasting the disingenuousness of Rogers, Nixon, and company in denying that such an opportunity for peace had ever existed.

When reporters asked Harriman why, if the signal from the North had come before November, President Johnson hadn't reached a settlement,

Harriman replied: "We couldn't carry on discussions because President Thieu would not permit his representatives to negotiate." What Harriman did not fully know even in 1972 was that Thieu had refused to negotiate at least partly because of instructions from Nixon, which had been conveyed to him through Anna Chennault and Bui Diem.

Despite the fact that he was still trouncing McGovern in the polls, Nixon became preoccupied with managing the attacks on Shriver. On the morning of August 14, Treasury Secretary John Connally told Haldeman they needed to broaden their attacks on Shriver. "We should make all our responses in the form of an attack, we should not defend against their charges," Connally said, "and . . . we have to destroy Shriver now."

Later that afternoon, Nixon briefly broke off a conversation with his aides Patrick Buchanan and Bob Haldeman about his acceptance speech for the upcoming GOP convention to say, as Haldeman recorded it in his diary, that he was concerned about "how we're handling the Shriver and [former attorney general Ramsey] Clark attacks. Feels we should be hitting Shriver hard on the point that he didn't know what was going on. . . . That he was not told any-thing, because LBJ didn't trust him. . . .We have the chance to destroy Shriver. We should all attack him."

The depth of Nixon's eagerness to "destroy" Shriver here suggests how close the former ambassador had come to drawing real blood. (Never does Haldeman indicate that Nixon ever expressed so much concern about anything McGovern did.) Much of Nixon's own staff was not aware of his role in push-ing Thieu away from the negotiating table in 1968, but they, like the president, recognized that destroying Shriver's credibility on the issue was the best way to render the "blown-peace" question moot. "Need to destroy Shriver and his credibility," Haldeman wrote the next day in his diary. We've "got to keep hit-ting Shriver and build a factual chronology."

One person who might have helped the Democratic ticket by defending Shriver's credibility was Lyndon Johnson. He knew (from FBI wiretaps) about Chennault's interventions with the South Vietnamese on Nixon's behalf; he knew how close he had been to peace before the South Vietnamese backed away from negotiations at the eleventh hour before the elections in 1968. Why didn't he say something now?

Mainly, it was because LBJ disliked George McGovern and everything he stood for. Whatever else Johnson was—a liberal or a conservative, a racist or a civil rights champion (and he was all of these)—he was unquestionably a politician of the old school. He loved the "smoke-filled rooms" of brokered conventions, thrived amid the horse-trading and log-rolling of Congress, lived for politics with a capital P—lived, in other words, for everything that the reformist George McGovern, with his commissions and his quotas and his radical supporters, was against. Johnson also believed McGovern couldn't win. "George McGovern couldn't carry Texas if Dick Nixon were caught fucking a sow in downtown Fort Worth," Johnson was telling reporters off the record.

When McGovern and Shriver flew to meet with LBJ at his ranch on August 22, Johnson insisted that the meeting be short and that there be no press and no pictures—nothing to signal that he approved of the South Dakota senator. (The official reason given for Johnson's reticence was that he wasn't feeling well.) After the meeting, LBJ called Billy Graham to say that Nixon had done much more for him (Johnson) than McGovern ever had. According to Haldeman, LBJ told Graham that "McGovern is associating with amateurs, that he ought to shake up his staff, and he ought to stand up and say what a wonderful place America is." Johnson also—according to Haldeman's notes about what Billy Graham reported—"told Shriver that he didn't know what he was talking about on Vietnam. He had the documents to prove it, and he handed them to Shriver and told him to read them. He also told McGovern that he has letters in the library, and that he should go read them, regarding Vietnam."

Shriver's claims about the blown opportunity for peace "in 1968" indirectly tarred Johnson with the same damning brush that tarred Nixon. Concerned about his historical legacy, Johnson was not happy. He told John Connally he was "mad as hell" about it. But the story that LBJ told Billy Graham about yelling at Shriver and brandishing documents seems to have been a typical Johnson fabrication, concocted with the certainty that it would be conveyed from Graham to Nixon. No one present at the August 22 meeting at the LBJ ranch—including Shriver, McGovern, and their aides—has any recollection of Johnson producing any "documents."

In his memoirs, Nixon wrote that Johnson called Haldeman to say that he had never kept Shriver abreast of what was going on in the Paris negotiations because "I never trusted him, the SOB, not even then." This is most likely apocryphal; Haldeman makes no reference to any such phone call in his diaries and, besides, the source of any distrust Johnson felt toward Shriver had to do with Bobby Kennedy—who had been dead for three months by the fall of 1968. Even if Johnson did say this to Haldeman, Shriver never claimed to have gotten his information from LBJ; he was getting it from Vance and Harriman, who were with him in Paris and who were now staunchly supporting his claims in 1972.

But without Johnson's active and public corroboration, Shriver's Vietnam allegations, although they continued to get front-page attention in the press for a while, failed to have any effect on the electorate. Over the summer, as the administration let it be known that Kissinger and the North Vietnamese negotiators were hastening down the road toward peace, the American public's approval of Nixon's handling of Vietnam rose. With Shriver unable to produce some hard piece of evidence that proved Nixon had blown the peace, the argument seemed to voters to boil down to one party's argument versus the other's. In August 1972 more people were still inclined to trust Richard Nixon than Sarge Shriver or George McGovern.

At summer's end, the McGovern-Shriver campaign appeared to be in dire straits. Polling by the candidate's own staffer Pat Caddell found that McGovern trailed 60–34. (Caddell said that he often felt "like the recreation director on the *Titanic.*") Worse, in some of the states that Kantor had deemed essential to victory, McGovern-Shriver trailed by as much as a 2–1 margin. Shriver had been on the ticket for a month, but everywhere he went he was inevitably asked as many questions about the Eagleton affair as he was about his own positions on the issues. Fund-raising was also a problem: It was hard to persuade even the most loyal Democrats to throw money at a losing cause. The Kennedy family had pledged to make significant contributions, but by the end of August they still had not fulfilled their promise. When Lee White and Bill Josephson met with McGovern at the end of the month, the candidate expressed his frustration that Steve Smith, keeper of the Kennedy purse strings, had yet to deliver any money. Larry O'Brien hinted that this might be because Smith feared Shriver would parlay any success into a campaign in 1976.

Everyone knew that, barring some unforeseen miracle, the McGovern-Shriver ticket would go down to defeat. For the next two months the candidates' campaign staff had to perform the difficult trick of acting as if it would be otherwise, without appearing to have their heads buried deep in the sand. Also, as alluded to by Larry O'Brien, some of McGovern's people resented seeing Shriver apparently using the 1972 campaign to position himself for 1976. "It's incredible what's going on in [Shriver's] outfit," a disgruntled senior staffer on the McGovern campaign said. "It looks as if Sarge is trying to put together his own base for a bid for the Presidency in 1976." Another McGovern aide alleged, "Sarge is out to pull a Muskie. He wants to emerge as the one shining hope of McGovern's debacle, the one guy marked for higher office despite this year's disaster."

Such resentments were natural, given how poorly the Democratic campaign was going—and how much better Shriver's press notices were than McGovern's. "Although there is nothing less prestigious than running for the vice presidency on a weak team, Sargent Shriver is probably the most sparkling of the four candidates in the electoral race," Stanley Karnow wrote in the *Washington Post* in late September. "In contrast to George McGovern, whose nasal piety borders on the self-righteous, Shriver exudes a natural sense of humor that seems to suggest that he considers the election is a game even if he is playing to win." And although the McGovern-Shriver ticket was as many as forty points behind Nixon-Agnew in the polls, when Shriver and Agnew were matched up head to head, voters picked Shriver over Agnew.

One reason the vice presidential campaign had so much energy was the presence of Eunice Shriver. She amazed campaign staffers with her political acumen and her sheer endurance. A reporter who followed her for a day described her "sprinting through all-white suburban neighborhoods and all-black slums, laying campaign literature on anyone who would open a door." Gary Hart recalled,

> Eunice Shriver has been described as the most Kennedy of the Kennedys and the best politician in the family. Although that might be considered too potent a distillation for anyone to achieve, her performance during the fall tended to support both descriptions. She seemed inexhaustible. . . . She also was articulate, but laced her political speeches with anecdotes, improvisations, and spontaneous humor. She also seemed unintimidatable. She would go almost anywhere in search of voters and was not easily put off by precedents or tradition.

Rose, Ethel, Ted, Joan, and various other Kennedy family members and advisers campaigned for the McGovern-Shriver ticket at different times. Rose, Ethel, and Ted all turned out for an "American Family Picnic" for 3,000 people held at Timberlawn in mid-October, where Neil Diamond and other celebrities performed for the crowd. Eunice aside, however, the Kennedy family involvement in the overall campaign effort was tepid. Those close to Ted were wary of associating themselves too closely with a doomed effort. If 1972 turned out to be a debacle, it would be best to keep away from it. Ted and others therefore merely went through the motions of supporting the ticket; they needed to seem like loyal Democrats without going down with the ship.

Jacqueline Kennedy and her new husband, Aristotle Onassis, in contrast, resolutely supported Shriver's political efforts, not only with financial contributions and campaign appearances but with quiet expressions of support. The Shrivers' daughter, Maria, and Jackie's daughter, Caroline, were close friends (Maria spent part of her summers with the Onassises in the Greek Islands); this helped Sarge and Jackie to stay close over the years. Perhaps more than anyone in the family circle, Jackie possessed an acute understanding of how politically difficult it was for Sarge to be a Kennedy in-law. A week after the election in November, Shriver would write to Jackie and Ari, "Both Eunice and I are grateful for all your encouragement and support during these past months and it gives us comfort to know you're thinking of us now." And then, handwritten onto the note, Shriver added: "Jackie: You were so solicitous and sensitive to my situation that I must add a note of special thanks."

"LIKE WATCHING LIGHTNING STRIKE THE FIREWORKS SHED"

Through August and September, Shriver continued to hammer away at Nixon's record on unemployment and inflation. Meanwhile, he escalated attacks on what he alleged was the corruption of the Nixon administration, continuing to try to pin blame for the Watergate break-in on the president directly. "How can the president claim to know what's going on in Peking or the Kremlin," Shriver asked repeatedly, "if he doesn't even know what's going on in his own reelection committee?" He told a crowd in Sacramento, "The Watergate incident will be where Nixon meets his Waterloo."

Briefly, there was the faintest glimmering of hope. The gap between Nixon and McGovern, although still wide, began to narrow dramatically, dropping from thirty-four points behind at the beginning of September to eighteen points behind at the end of it. Back at the office for a day, after weeks on the campaign trail, William Greider, the *Washington Post*'s national political correspondent, told his editors that he believed McGovern would win the election. (Greider's editors looked at him as if he had been smoking something.)

But by the middle of October, Nixon's lead began to widen again, and then widen some more. Three weeks before election day, the race was effectively over. The only questions remaining to be answered on election day were: How badly will McGovern-Shriver lose? and Will the Democratic Party be completely destroyed?

The will of the McGovern staff had "crumbled," but the Shriver staff soldiered on. They could see they were headed for a crushing defeat; all they could aim for was to keep the margin of victory from being "historic." Campaign staffers were weary from three straight months of twenty-hour workdays. Since the beginning of August, Shriver had logged more miles and given more speeches than any of the other three candidates on the two tickets. (Shriver said that because, unlike a senator or a governor, he could deliver no bloc of votes to the ticket as a "bridal dowry," he felt he had to work harder.) Eunice had logged more miles than any of the other candidates' wives.

The mood on the *Fighting Lucky 7* grew bleaker, but it never sank into despair; there was still even some joy. This was largely because Shriver's spirit never seemed to flag. Many on the staff had naturally grown depressed, but the candidate never let his own frustration show through. "I was never depressed during the campaign," Shriver recalled. "Maybe that shows I was dumb. But I really liked the experience."

"I remember the last day," Mark Shields says. "We went from Baltimore to Pittsburgh to Detroit to Madison to Brownsville, Texas. At each stop, we knew we would get our heads handed to us. But at each one, it was almost as though Sarge thought if he could just talk to everyone he could somehow turn it around."

He couldn't, of course. Election day was indeed historic, a disaster for the McGovern ticket. Nixon won 60.7 percent of the popular vote nationally, just missing LBJ's record-breaking 61.1 percent of 1964. In electoral terms, the margin of victory was far greater: 521 votes for Nixon-Agnew, 17 for McGovern-Shriver. Most striking was the almost unimaginable geographic comprehensiveness of Nixon's victory: he won forty-nine states, more than any president in history, losing only Massachusetts.

Sarge and Eunice voted in the early afternoon at a high school near their Maryland home, then returned for a game of touch football with their kids. Friends and campaign staff gathered for cocktails and dinner at Timberlawn to watch the election returns. Everyone knew what was coming. "This will be a hell of a night," Eunice predicted grimly. "The first time a Kennedy loses an election." "It was a horrible night," Donald Dell recalled. "You know we're sitting there, all these returns were coming in and we're getting slaughtered in every state. It was painful because they had done so badly."

Yet even in this crushing defeat, there was some redeeming joy. Herb Kramer and assorted campaign staffers had composed a brief musical revue, the *Lucky Seven Follies*, that was performed for a private audience that night at Timberlawn. Despite the undercurrent of disappointment, it was riotously funny. The Shriver campaign, the narrator intoned, "was a happening, a spectacular, a piece of original Americana, a circus, a parade, an ethnic festival, an Italian wedding, an Irish wake, and a Bris all rolled into one." The *Follies* poked fun at almost every aspect of the campaign: its general chaos and disorganization; the tension between the McGovern and Shriver staffs; the tension between Shriver's staff in Washington and his traveling staff on the airplane; Shriver's problems with George Meany; even Shriver's aspirations for 1976. The performance was recorded on a vinyl record; thirty years after the event, the uproarious laughter on this saddest of election nights can still be heard clearly over the scratches and blips on the record. The most audible laugh is Sargent Shriver's.

"We were having a grand old time," Shriver recalled, "and nobody felt defeated. When the McGovern people called and said I had to go downtown to declare the other side victors, well, nobody wanted me to leave. I didn't want to leave. We were having a real ball. Which maybe tells you that we were all nuts."

Although at times the *Lucky Seven Follies* was merciless in its satire, the last few minutes turned sentimental. "In a campaign of surpassing importance," the narrator said,

> with the opposition in hiding and his running mate 25 percent behind in the polls, Sargent Shriver ran for the vice presidency as if he were running for the Olympic gold—as if it would make a compelling difference to the future of America and the world.

But of course he's right. It will make a difference. Just as the Peace Corps made a difference. And Job Corps. And Head Start. And Legal Services. And health centers. And day care. And medical ethics. And help for the helpless. And compassion for the down and out and the neglected and the rejected.

Sargent Shriver, like sun spots, the boll weevil, or the very air we breathe, does make a difference. And whatever the outcome of this election, he will continue to make a difference in the lives of all of us.

A little anger. A lot of laughs. A little impatience. A world of respect. Being around Sarge is like watching lightning hit the fireworks shed: Brilliant, explosive, unpredictable, but exciting as hell.

And so Sarge, whether it's forward to the Executive Office Building or back to 600 Watergate, we sing our fond farewell to you and the great experience of working with you. The words are different but the melody lingers on, as we hope it will linger on for many years to come.

CHAPTER FORTY-SIX

Shriver for President

Watching the Watergate scandal unfold was frustrating. In the ensuing months, the *Washington Post* and other publications slowly uncovered the president's direct knowledge of the break-ins and political "dirty tricks" operations. A special prosecutor was appointed to investigate the administration's alleged crimes, and within eighteen months, Congress was moving toward impeachment proceedings against Nixon—the first time in more than a century that such an action seemed imminent.

When Shriver himself was not in his law office (which, as it happened, was in the Watergate building and had been bugged by Nixon's "plumbers"), he was busy traveling the world on behalf of his clients. But as the Watergate scandal built to its denouement, he paid close attention. The inevitable thoughts ran through his head: Why couldn't people have paid attention to this earlier, when the Committee to Reelect the President had first been implicated in the late summer of 1972? How humiliating to have been so badly defeated by a crook. And, finally, what will this do to the American spirit?

To the race riots of the 1960s and the enduring angst produced by the

Vietnam War was now added the ignominious resignation of a president, on top of which the country found itself by 1974 entering its worst economic slump since the Depression. Internationally, of course, the United States remained a military and economic colossus, but its credibility had been damaged by its adventures in Vietnam and elsewhere. The threat of nuclear war had been a fixture of the American consciousness since the 1950s. But whereas in earlier years fear of a nuclear holocaust had been but a single dark blot on an otherwise bright horizon, the nuclear threat was now one more cloud on a dark vista.

Americans' faith in their national institutions—the government, the presidency, the military, the economic experts—had fallen far and fast. Less than ten years had elapsed since the high-water mark of the Great Society, and scarcely more than that since the great, early promise of the New Frontier. But those years felt like a century ago, so different was the prevailing mood now. Shriver saw this clearly and worried about it, as he made clear in the public speeches that he continued to deliver regularly.

But whereas the prevailing mood of the nation had become one of corrosive cynicism and resignation, Shriver remained energized, if angry. He still carried around in his head the hopeful idealism of an earlier time. His own temperament jibed much more naturally with the early 1960s than with the mid-1970s, and he took every opportunity he could to declaim publicly the importance of, in effect, "getting America moving again" (as JFK had put it in 1960), to restore to American culture the faith and confidence that had characterized the post–New Deal, postwar era. But the post–World War II era had given way to the post-Vietnam, post-Watergate era; Shriver's voice of hope, and his calls to action, sounded dissonant amid the drift and malaise of the 1970s.

Through the midterm elections of 1974, Shriver once again did a fair amount of campaigning and fund-raising for Democratic candidates. "I felt that I shouldn't just crawl away in defeat" after 1972, Shriver recalled. But because he was busy with his work at Fried, Frank, he could not reprise his full-time Congressional Leadership for the Future campaign of the previous midterm elections.

To outside observers, it must have seemed that Shriver had now turned his back on his presidential ambitions. He was nearly sixty years old, an age when many men begin looking ahead to retirement, and it seemed unlikely that a man approaching old age, and who had never before held elective office, would make an effort to vie for the presidency in 1976. If he had been a senator or a governor, that would have been another matter; he would have had a political base, a built-in constituency, and a preexisting organization. But he had none of that—all he had was the stench of defeat from 1972.

Yet some of the people around him could not let the dream of a Shriver presidency die. Throughout 1973 and 1974, they quietly transformed the Friends of Sargent Shriver Committee—a vehicle set up during the 1972 election season to raise money and now working to retire campaign debt—into an exploratory task force for a Shriver-for-president campaign in 1976. Many of Shriver's close friends and associates, some of them influential Democrats, pressed him to consider a race for the Democratic nomination. They had seen how effective a campaigner he had been on McGovern's behalf and how enthusiastically crowds had responded to him. And they believed that if Sargent Shriver were president, he could put the country back on the right track with the force of his idealism.

Shriver himself was not convinced. After the 1972 debacle, he was a long shot for the president. Moreover, nothing he—or any other prospective Democratic candidate—did would be taken seriously until Ted Kennedy decided what his plans were for 1976. "With the disastrous defeat of George McGovern," wrote Jules Witcover, then a reporter for the *Washington Post*, "1973 saw a seemingly inexorable drift in the party back to the dream of another Kennedy candidacy, with all the political magic it promised." Kennedy led all other contenders in the national polls; "as long as Ted Kennedy was present, no one dared move boldly ahead toward the nomination." Kennedy himself implied strongly that he planned to run. In May 1973 Johnny Apple reported in the *New York Times* that "Mr. Kennedy has given his close friends the impression in recent days, as he never did in 1972, that he believes his moment to strike for the summit has come." Although Senator Henry "Scoop" Jackson of Washington, Senator Walter Mondale of Minnesota, and Congressman Morris Udall of Arizona all began quietly exploring their presidential possibilities, their cautious quasi-candidacies were premised on the gamble that Kennedy would ultimately *not* run. Only Jimmy Carter, a first-term Georgia governor with a folksy manner, and George Wallace, the racial demagogue, began to plan in earnest for a run for the Democratic nomination. Whenever anyone asked Shriver what his plans for 1976 were, he would say that he expected that he would be campaigning for his brother-in-law.

But over the first weekend of September 1974, when the Kennedy clan gathered in Hyannis Port for Labor Day, the family council convened to discuss Ted's situation. Earlier in the year, the assumption within the family had been that Teddy would run. But over the summer, the consensus had shifted. For one thing, there remained the specter of Chappaquiddick. Over the Fourth of July holiday, Kennedy had traveled to Decatur, Alabama, where he made a controversial appearance with George Wallace. Kennedy's intention had been to demonstrate that unity was possible within the party; the liberal, civil rights–supporting Massachusetts senator could coexist in the party with the segregationist Alabama governor. But the appearance had generated a slew of hate mail to Kennedy's Senate office. What alarmed Kennedy and his family was how frequently these letters made reference to Chappaquiddick. However much he might have hoped otherwise, the incident had not been forgotten. A presidential campaign would produce constant reminders of July 19, 1969. Ted did not think the family could withstand that.

Other family problems also militated against a presidential run in 1976. Kennedy's son, Teddy Jr., had developed cancer in 1973, leading to the amputation of his right leg; he still required ongoing treatment and care. Caroline and John Kennedy, the children of Jack and Jacqueline, seemed to be growing up into healthy young adults; that was not true, however of many of Bobby and Ethel's children. Bobby Jr. and David had drug problems. Some of the younger children seemed tormented and confused. Ted, as family patriarch, felt responsible for them; a presidential campaign would interfere with that responsibility and would increase the pressure on Bobby's children. Then, too, there were the struggles of Ted's wife, Joan. Several trips to rehabilitation facilities had failed to cure her alcoholism. "He wasn't going to leave her," a family friend told Jules Witcover, "but she couldn't take a campaign like that. He knew it wouldn't work publicly, and, besides, he wanted to spare her."

Above all was the fear, shared by many within the family, of a third assassination. Once Ted Kennedy declared his candidacy, he and his family worried, he would become a target for all kinds of psychopaths and radicals.

For years the Kennedys had been, as Witcover wrote, "a kind of royal family in exile, awaiting in their Washington and Cape Cod homes an eventual return to the political summit from which they had been so brutally banished on the tragic day in Dallas. They wanted the promise of John and Robert

Kennedy to be realized and fulfilled in Edward Kennedy." But on this weekend, it was decided finally that the exile would continue, at least through 1976. It was agreed that Kennedy would not run.

Teddy tried to keep this decision a secret as long as possible, so that he would be a more effective campaigner for Democratic congressional candidates in the midterm election. But when reporters insisted on interpreting his campaign trips as early barnstorming for his own 1976 campaign, Kennedy decided to make clear his intentions. On September 23, 1974, he held a press conference at the Parker House Hotel in Boston. Standing alongside his wife, Kennedy declared that he would not seek the Democratic nomination in 1976. His decision, he said, was "firm, final, and unconditional." He wanted to be as clear as possible, he said, both "to ease apprehensions within my family about the possibility of my candidacy" and to "clarify the situation within my own party."

The Kennedy family may have been relieved, if regretful, but the situation among the Democrats was hardly clarified. A yawning gap opened up at the center-left of the party, and a large group of contenders rushed in to try to fill it. Whereas before there had been only Ted Kennedy—with just George Wallace, Scoop Jackson, and Jimmy Carter standing barely noticed in his shadow—now there was a clamoring of more than a dozen senators, representatives, governors, and others. Making matters still more chaotic, many Democrats continued to hope that Kennedy—despite his adamant statements to the contrary—would ride to the rescue.

Ted Kennedy's decision not to run instantly changed the political calculus for Sargent Shriver. If his brother-in-law was "firm, final, and unconditional" about not running, that meant the way was clear for him to throw his own hat into the ring. Many people he trusted were telling him he should run. (A few other advisers—most prominently his wife and Bill Josephson—were telling him he should not.)

On balance, as Shriver's law partner David Birenbaum recalled, Shriver seemed "very, very reluctant" to throw his hat into the ring. Nevertheless, a series of informal discussions among Shriver's friends culminated in a dinner one night in late 1974 at the 1789 Restaurant in Georgetown, where Shriver, Birenbaum, Mickey Kantor, Democratic strategist Bob Shrum, pollster Pat Caddell, and others convened to assess Shriver's chances in the 1976 Democratic primaries.

The consensus was that Shriver's prospects were reasonably good. Kennedy's stepping aside had opened the field. That left Scoop Jackson as the likely front-runner with Morris Udall, Jimmy Carter, Oklahoma senator Fred Harris, and Texas senator Lloyd Bentsen as the other declared candidates. (George Wallace remained officially undeclared.)

Surveying the field, the 1789 gang quickly dismissed three of the candidates. The first was Lloyd Bentsen, a freshman senator only two years into his term; he was tall and attractive, but nothing else about him made him seem a viable candidate. The second, George Wallace, had the potential to win a lot of votes, particularly among lower-middle-class white Southerners, but it was a safe bet he would alienate suburban Democrats in the rest of the country. The third was Jimmy Carter, a one-term governor of Georgia; although he had declared his candidacy earlier than anyone else, he was best known for his presumptuous attempt to sell himself to George McGovern as a running mate in 1972. (McGovern's aides had laughed at him and told him to stick to Georgia politics.) Carter's national profile was nonexistent. He was the darkest of dark horses.

According to the polls, Scoop Jackson led the other declared candidates. But Shriver's advisers felt he matched up well against the Washington senator, because Jackson, although not a hard-core conservative like Wallace, tended toward the conservative wing of the Democratic Party, especially on foreign policy. It would be easy to distinguish the liberal Shriver from the conservative Jackson on a range of issues—the most important being relations with the Soviet Union: Whereas Jackson favored taking a harder line with the Soviets, Shriver favored détente.

Harris and Udall would pose more of a problem; both were liberals, like Shriver. All three—along with Indiana senator Birch Bayh and Pennsylvania governor Milton Shapp, who were rumored to be contemplating running for the nomination—would be competing for the liberal voters and the "Kennedy voters" made available when Ted Kennedy exited the race. For Shriver to have any chance at winning the nomination, he would have to distinguish himself from the rest of this liberal crowd.

At the time of the Georgetown dinner, that seemed eminently possible, because Shriver had several points in his favor. First, he was the only Catholic in the race. Although his stance on abortion might complicate his standing with some liberal voters, his religion would surely play well in heavily Catholic Iowa, where the first caucus would be held in January 1976. Second, early polls suggested that, although he was the only candidate not to have held elective office, Shriver had the highest name recognition. Third, as veterans of the McGovern campaign reminded him, he was a highly skillful campaigner. He did well both with live audiences and on television.

Finally—and this was, as always, an unpredictable element—there was the Kennedy connection. For voters disappointed not to be able to support Ted Kennedy, a Kennedy in-law might be a next-best alternative; then again, there was a real danger that if Shriver weren't careful, he might never be able to emerge as an independent candidate in his own right. People might see him merely as a "stalking horse" for Ted Kennedy, collecting delegates through the Democratic primaries only to hand them over to Kennedy at the convention.

At the dinner, as David Birenbaum recalled, Shriver seemed torn: tempted by the opportunity but "clearly concerned about how 'the family' would react to it." He was wary of committing himself before he knew he had the Kennedy's full-fledged support—or at the very least had secured some kind of nonaggression pact in which they would guarantee they would neither impede his progress nor exile him from the family circle. By the end of dinner, the consensus was that Shriver's chances were as good as any of the other candidates' and that it was worth exploring his options further.

Shriver assigned Birenbaum to compile a "Friends of Shriver" advisory committee. Eventually, the list ran to hundreds of names and included the usual New Frontierish array of talent and celebrity: elected politicians, famous actors, professional athletes, Fortune 500 executives, best-selling authors, Nobel laureates, and other public figures. Cyrus Vance was named the chairman of this committee. At first, Shriver didn't ask these "Friends" for money or to campaign for him or even to meet with him. He was just collecting their names, in case he needed them later.

It seemed to Birenbaum, who would later help run the campaign, that Shriver spent an inordinate amount of time making up this list "because he needed to feel that he had all of these important, prestigious people behind him. It was psychologically necessary for him." Part of Shriver's feeling of vulnerability, surely, emanated from perception that some of Robert Kennedy's advisers thought of him as a "lightweight," that he didn't have the intellectual acuity and the political hard edge to hold high office. By lining up academics and novelists and Nobel Prize winners behind him, Shriver was trying to compensate for some perceived deficiency. ("Reading the names," his friend Colman McCarthy wrote not long after the election, "it was clear that . . . he must be the last of the sophomores to believe that many voters would be impressed by his knowing so many of the beautifuls.")

The truth of the matter is that although Shriver may have lacked a hard political edge, he was—according to people who knew both Shriver and all three Kennedy brothers—easily as "smart" as all three of them and more of an "intellectual" than either Bobby or Teddy. Intellect, of course, is an amorphous concept; there are lots of ways to be smart. The three Kennedy brothers (and Eunice, too) had more native political intelligence than Shriver—the instinctive ability to size up voting blocs and make electoral calculations. But Shriver was as quick-thinking as any of them, with perhaps a greater ability to assimilate and contextualize complex ideas and concepts. Shriver was also incredibly creative and imaginative, and he was open to ideas—a fact that Shriver's detractors interpreted as a sign of his intellectual promiscuity.

Shriver's real genius lay in his gift for dealing with people. Jack could inspire people with his style and his rhetoric; Bobby with his moral fervor. But only Teddy approached Shriver in his genuine curiosity about people and his gift for putting them at ease.

Yet for all Shriver's superior acuity and depth of intellect, the lightweight charge stuck. To the socially awkward academics he seemed too smooth; to the policy wonks, too much of a salesman; to the hardened political operators, too much of a naïf. During the 1972 campaign, "Shriver is a lightweight" jokes had become a staple of Johnny Carson's monologues. By 1976 some of this had penetrated Shriver's self-confident exterior, making him feel the need to buttress himself with a star-studded cast of supporters, so that he could say to his detractors, "See who's behind me?"

Father Bryan Hehir had gotten to know Shriver in 1973, when Hehir was working with the National Conference of American Bishops. Shriver had been invited to give a series of lectures at Notre Dame on the subject of religion and civil rights, and he was looking for people to help him compose the speeches. After receiving a typically out-of-the-blue phone call from Shriver, Hehir had ended up writing one of the speeches, and through that experience had become close to the family and a regular dinner guest at Timberlawn. This was a heady experience, as the dinners were often populated not only by senators and other politicians but also by prominent Catholic theologians such as Hans Kung and Charles Curran and by radical priests like the Berrigan brothers.

One day in the spring of 1975, Hehir was invited to one of the Socratic discussions at Timberlawn about whether Shriver should run for president. As Hehir recalls, the evening was a typically perfervid brainstorming session. "We sat down around the dinner table, then we moved into that big family room, where a rambling discussion just raged." Rarely able to sit still in one place for very long, Shriver fidgeted in his chair. At one point, as Hehir recalls, Sarge stood up and walked over to the picture window that looked out over the expansive Timberlawn grounds. "I have kinds of advantages that most people can't even imagine," Shriver said, gesturing at the tennis court and swimming pool and stable of horses. "Doesn't that give me an obligation to do something?" Hehir was struck by this. "This was obviously the way he was thinking about the presidency," Hehir recalled. Not because he was hungry for power, but rather because "he felt an obligation to do good things."

Based on the poll numbers, Shriver's chances continued to look as good as or better than those of any other Democrat in the race. But doubts about his willingness to go for the jugular began to cloud views of his prospects. During the 1972 campaign, a British journalist had expressed doubt that Shriver possessed the necessary "ruthlessness of his good intentions" to be a successful candidate.

As he walked into the warm Maryland evening after one of these long Timberlawn seminars, Hehir recalls falling into conversation with Anthony Lake, a foreign affairs expert who had worked for both Henry Kissinger and Edmund Muskie and who would later serve as Bill Clinton's national security adviser. Lake turned to Hehir and said wistfully, "You know, it's too bad. Basically, Sarge is probably too nice a guy to be president of the United States." Lake was disappointed because, to him, the same qualities that he believed would make Shriver such an effective president made him unlikely ever to get elected. "What I found both very appealing about him, and disqualifying as a politician, is his passion for ideas," Lake recalled—and not just his passion for ideas in an abstract, academic sense, but his passion for translating ideas into action. The problem, as Lake and others recognized, was that "I don't think he ever calibrated these ideas in terms of political effect very well. Which is again why I was for him. Too many of our politicians are too good at that calibration."

Later that summer, as the campaign began to advance beyond the purely theoretical stage, Lake was struck by how different its culture was from any campaign he had ever been associated with, before or since. "In many campaigns, in my experience, the flow of ideas is upwards. Which is to say the staff has ideas, the advisers have ideas, they go to the candidate, and the candidate takes some and rejects others. And occasionally is allowed to have an idea himself. The Shriver campaign was very much the opposite. There would be an explosion of ideas that Sarge would have, and then the role of his staff and advisers was to encourage him to pursue some, while suggesting that others were not politically wise." To Lake, that made Shriver practically unique.

Shriver's passion for ideas at the expense of political calculation gave his strategists fits. One day, he hosted a lunch at Timberlawn for Jewish American leaders. Before the lunch, Lake had spent several hours briefing the candidate on the current state of the Middle East, the status of peace negotiations, and what the other Democratic candidates were saying about Israel. Together, Shriver and Lake worked out all the points he should make to try to win the backing of these Jewish leaders. But as Lake recalled, "When we got into the lunch, rather than launching a discussion of the issues, he starts asking them about [the ancient Jewish philosopher] Maimonides. And so we had a long and fascinating discussion of Judaism and philosophy and Maimonides, and never quite got around to politics." As Lake glanced around the table, he could see Shriver's other political advisers staring at their plates, their faces burning with frustration.

THE RUSSIAN LECTURE TOUR

Throughout the spring of 1975, Shriver moved slowly, reluctantly, ambivalently toward making his candidacy a reality. Carter, Jackson, Udall, and others had already been fund-raising for months and building ground operations in key primary states. Shriver's advisers were telling him that, to have a realistic chance, he needed to declare soon. But two factors inhibited him. The first was the Kennedy family. Teddy's declaration that he would sit out the race notwithstanding, Democrats still (as always) pined for Kennedy to ride to the rescue. As long as there was any chance of that happening, a Shriver candidacy would never fly. He needed to get official family authorization for a campaign from Ted himself.

Second, through his work at Fried, Frank, Shriver had by 1975 made more than a dozen trips to Russia over the past three years. He was well known among the Moscow business community and had developed increasingly friendly relations with government ministers in the Kremlin. Partly as a result, he was invited by the Kremlin to undertake a lecture tour across the Soviet Union in March and April that would culminate with a press conference in Moscow. Shriver happily accepted the invitation.

Of course, the Soviets' invitation was not based entirely on their personal affection for the American. At least two groups in Moscow had vested interests in extending the invitation. The first group consisted of the Russian business community and the Ministry of Trade. Shriver had already been instrumental in bringing billions of dollars in American investment into the Soviet economy—more than from the US government—and in opening the US market to more Russian products.

The second group consisted of Kremlin denizens who were keeping their eye on the upcoming US elections. The Soviet leadership had enjoyed a certain amount of schadenfreude as Nixon resigned and as the Vietnam War sputtered to its unhappy conclusion; in the zero-sum game of the cold war, anything that was bad for the Americans was good for the Soviets and vice versa. But the Soviets also worried about political uncertainty in the United States, because it made it hard for them to know what they would be dealing with in future years. Surveying the American political landscape, they most feared Ronald Reagan and Scoop Jackson, the two presidential candidates who promised to take the hardest anti-Soviet line.

Thus, when word reached the Kremlin that Sargent Shriver was a potential Democratic candidate, the Soviet leadership paid close attention. Shriver, more than the other candidates, was a known quantity. He clearly liked Russia and got along well with his Soviet counterparts, and they liked him, too. The hard-liners in the Kremlin no doubt saw Shriver as appealingly soft, a man they could take advantage of. The moderates in the Kremlin, who were Shriver's friends, saw him as someone they could work with to thaw the cold war and achieve mutual benevolent objectives.

Russia's foreign intelligence was not always terribly accurate. Distracted by the fact that Shriver was an in-law to the famous Kennedy family, many in the Kremlin evidently concluded in early 1975 that he was the likeliest Democratic nominee for the upcoming election. It could only help the cause of US-Soviet relations to have the next president of the United States tour Russia in the year before he was elected. So after some negotiations between Shriver and his Kremlin connections, the Presidium of the Supreme Soviet proposed the extended lecture tour, during which Shriver would be allowed to travel widely across the vast Soviet empire.

So it was that in March 1975 Shriver put his presidential planning on hold and flew to Moscow for a three-week trip. Traveling with him was a large entourage: Eunice; his three oldest children, Bobby, Maria, and Timothy; his nephew John F. Kennedy Jr.; a young Harvard law professor, Larry Tribe, who had been introduced to Shriver by Democratic strategist Bob Shrum and whom Shriver had brought along so he could explain the differences between constitutional law in Russia and the United States; Chris Whitney, a young Fried, Frank associate who was fluent in Russian; and a priest, Father Murphy, who was to administer private Masses for the family everywhere they went.

Andrei Pavlov, of the State Committee for Science and Technology, was the Shriver family's host and tour guide for the entire trip. Pavlov had known Shriver for several years now and considered him a friend. Shriver was fond of Pavlov as well and appreciated the access he provided to the upper echelons of the Soviet leadership. Pavlov had been a member of the Communist Party since he was seven years old and had a corner office in the Kremlin with a huge window. Although this made Shriver suspect that Pavlov was a high-ranking member of the KGB, that didn't make him like the man any less. (In the 1990s, after the fall of communism, Shriver persuaded Pavlov to join the board of the Special Olympics, in which capacity he has been instrumental in helping that organization expand into former Communist countries.)

Traveling in a rickety twin-engine plane, Shriver and company visited not only Moscow, Leningrad, Volgograd, and Stalingrad, but also Ukraine and Uzbekistan, as well as Bratsk and Irkutsk and Yakutsk in the far reaches of eastern Siberia. Shriver gave lectures at various universities and research centers around the country.

According to Tribe, it was evident that the Soviets considered Shriver to be a serious presidential prospect because "everywhere we went, we were received with vodka and Beluga caviar." Tribe recalled serious discussions about various issues with high-ranking Kremlin denizens. "They showed Sarge everything," Tribe said. "They allowed a degree of freedom for him and the rest of us to wander around freely. It was clear the Soviets hoped the trip would give him a feeling of the cultural diversity and the ethnic variety and the governmental system of the country."

In Moscow, Shriver and company stayed in two rather imposing buildings that had been constructed for the 1950s meeting between Khrushchev and Eisenhower that had never taken place. Tribe and Maria Shriver were exploring the buildings when Maria opened a door "and stumbled upon a room full of KGB agents watching TV screens." On one screen Maria saw her father, sitting calmly reading in a rocking chair in his bedroom—clearly the whole entourage was being watched by hidden cameras! Maria and Tribe backed quietly out of the surveillance post, and Maria ran back to her father's room to report what she had seen. He received the news with calm bemusement.

Pavlov recalled that the lecture that made the most powerful impression on the Soviets was the one Shriver gave in Siberia, to the Academy of Sciences of the USSR. While planning the trip, Shriver had told Pavlov he wanted to make a speech that would attract a lot of attention. (Partly, of course, this was with an eye toward getting free press for his incipient presidential campaign back home.) Pavlov told him that the Academy of Sciences was one of the most august intellectual bodies in the country, and that he would try to arrange something there. Many of the scientists at the academy had been among the first political dissidents who had spoken out during the thaw of the early 1970s. Now they had, in effect, been banished to the institute in Siberia. But as scientists and dissidents they were likely to provide the most open-minded audience a Western capitalist could find in the Soviet Union.

Shriver's presentation to the academy, set for March 22, was built up to be a major event: He was the first American, and the first nonscientist, ever to address the body. In the days leading up to the lecture, Shriver made Pavlov nervous by refusing to provide an advance copy of his speech; Pavlov had no idea of what to expect.

Pavlov needn't have worried. "Many Americans have believed that they were ordained by God in history to become a model for all mankind," Shriver said to his audience of some 2,000 Soviet scientists. "You have believed that communism was similarly ordained by history as God. Events have not settled the propriety of either claim, but history has set a priority: that together we must make a détente, so that by perfecting our coexistence, we may achieve a common existence." He continued, arguing that the United States was not out to conquer the Soviet Union, ideologically or otherwise. "Despite the best progress of negotiation, real differences of policy and principle will continue. We will not persuade you to become capitalists—and you will not talk us into communism. But while we each remain what we are, we can both enlist in a larger cause. We must not only make the world safe for diversity; we must also make a safer world by a degree of unity."

To Shriver, it was obvious that communism could not last. The system was creaky. His son, Mark, who did not go on the trip, said, "I remember him coming back home saying how the infrastructure of the country was so decrepit, and that it was really not a military threat to our country. The infrastructure of the country was falling apart."

"Once you spent time there, it was obvious the Soviet menace was a joke," recalled Bobby Shriver, who was twenty years old at the time of the trip. "Everything you saw there from electronic equipment to the finish on cars was poorly made. If they couldn't even make bathroom fixtures, how the hell were they going to make atomic bombs that really worked?" But in his speech, Shriver equated the power of communism with the power of capitalism and emphasized the endurance of each. Neither one was headed for "the ash-heap of history," he argued, so "some mode of coexistence was necessary for peace."

Shriver acknowledged that deep recession, inflation, Watergate, and the first-ever resignation of a US president had all eroded faith in American institutions. But don't— Shriver warned, speaking "very forcefully" and banging his fist dramatically on the lectern—underestimate the strength of the American idea or the resilience of the American people. You cannot defeat us, Shriver said. So you might as well learn to live with us. And if we're going to coexist, we might as well turn our joint efforts and resources toward higher goals. "Perhaps the memory of the blood we shed together against fascism can provide the most fitting metaphor for our future. We fought as one to defeat a common enemy. Now Providence, which you call History and I call God, calls us to join together again, this time with all men, to defeat the most ancient and most recent enemies of mankind: the tyranny of hunger and disease and the poverty of a world stripped bare."

According to Pavlov, the Russian audience "sat rapt and wide-eyed," entranced by this lively American preaching détente. After the presentation, a mob of scientists surrounded Shriver, wanting to speak with him. "You made us realize there are some reasonable Americans," Pavlov recalls them saying. In 1975 most Russians still thought that all Americans were militaristic imperialists who hated the Russian people. (Americans generally thought the same of the Russians.) With no access to Western television or other media, Russians knew nothing of the real America, "only the caricature of our official propaganda," according to Pavlov. "For that reason," Pavlov says, "Shriver's speech was incredibly useful."

On April 11, after touring the country for nineteen days, Shriver held a ninety-minute press conference for the Soviet media in Moscow. Surprising almost everyone in attendance, he announced that a group of Western banks led by the Franco-American investment bank Lazard Freres & Company (where David Karr was then a principal) would be providing the largest private loan in history ($250 million) to the Soviet Union.

While Shriver and most of his entourage flew off for brief visits to Paris and Rome, Bobby Shriver and John Kennedy Jr. prepared to fly to London and then home. When the two young men were seated on their Western commercial airliner, preparing to fly for New York, Bobby noticed his cousin rocking back and forth in his seat "like an autistic child," and murmuring aloud. "What the hell is he doing?" Bobby thought to himself and leaned in to listen. "Solzhenitsyn . . . Solzhenitsyn . . . Solzhenitsyn," John was saying. "Solzhenitsyn . . . Solzhenitsyn . . . Solzhenitsyn!" A year earlier, in February 1974, the Russian novelist Aleksandr Solzhenitsyn had been arrested and deported for his dissident views, and in particular for his devastating account of life under Stalin in *The Gulag Archipeligo*. The dissident author was a sensitive topic for the Soviets, and Shriver and his family had been explicitly instructed never to mention the writer's name. This naturally had the effect of making the young people want to say it. After nineteen days of resisting the impulse, JFK Jr. could contain the urge no longer and, to his cousin's great amusement, the long-repressed "Solzhenitsyn, Solzhenitsyn!" came burbling out.

"I'M WAITING FOR TEDDY"

While the Shriver family was out of the country, the political rumor mill churned. Mayor Daley declared that, with Ted Kennedy out of the race, Shriver was the Democrats' best candidate. But on April 14, while the Shrivers were still abroad, the *New York Times* reported that, although Shriver had indicated he would run for the presidency, at least one labor leader didn't believe it. "I don't want to hear it from Sarge," the labor leader told the *Times*. "I want to hear it from Eunice." In other words, Shriver couldn't be considered a serious presidential candidate until a *real* Kennedy declared that he was one. And for the moment, the Kennedys did not (as usual) seem enthusiastic about the idea. "I can't help it if he runs," Ted Kennedy told *Washington Post* columnist Victor Zorza with evident exasperation. And Eunice, according to what Christopher Lydon wrote in the *Times*, was "just as reserved as her brother with the sort of Kennedy family blessing Mr. Shriver . . . needs."

Ted never said anything overtly hostile about Shriver, nor did Shriver publicly express any resentment over Kennedy's tepid response to his possible candidacy. But to longtime political observers and Kennedy watchers, the tensions were evident. Shriver's aides continually emphasized that if in fact he were to run, it would be "as his own man." Yet in his preliminary explorations, one of the key questions was what kind of boost Shriver could get from exploiting his Kennedy connections. Kennedy, for his part, "revealed just that touch of asperity, barely perceptible" toward Shriver; this suggested to Zorza that the senator "was less than happy about [Shriver's] political ambitions. An old family rivalry, some might say, or resentment at the political complications which the Shriver factor might add to Kennedy's own plans—whatever those might be."

On May 1, after Shriver's return to the United States, a group of some thirty Harvard academics feted him at the Kennedy Institute of Politics, under the pretense of a discussion of "Ethics and Politics." The real purpose, however, was to gauge the support of the Boston-Cambridge intelligentsia, an earlier generation of which had been so integral to John F. Kennedy's election and administration. Shriver came away from the dinner convinced that his support among that group was strong. The prevailing assumption was that he would soon make an official declaration of his candidacy.

But the most important hurdle had yet to be cleared. On June 4, 1975, after consulting extensively with his own advisers and taking soundings from people around Ted Kennedy, Shriver went to visit his brother-in-law in his Senate office. As Jules Witcover reports in his book on the 1976 election, Shriver told Kennedy "he had found a strong consensus among Democrats that the field of men offering themselves for the nomination was unsatisfactory, that Teddy was still the candidate they wanted." This was clearly the case. Most Democratic operatives salivated at the prospect of Teddy's entrance into the race—and if Ted had said at this point he would reconsider running, Shriver would instantly have scuttled any of his own plans. But Kennedy demurred emphatically once again. So Shriver told him he was considering entering the race himself.

As in 1970, however, when confronted with the decision of whether to challenge Marvin Mandel in Maryland, Shriver was having a hard time making up his mind. The clock was ticking: other candidates were already in the race, and the pool of available Democratic funds was getting smaller by the day. But Shriver didn't want to commit until he was absolutely sure that he had the stomach for the race. Also, in order to be taken seriously by party leaders—who could never see Shriver clearly because they perceived Ted Kennedy lurking over his shoulder—Shriver wanted to make sure he could assemble a powerful fund-raising and campaigning apparatus before making any public announcement. So he headed to Florida for a vacation, where he could fish and play tennis and think about what he wanted to do.

His plans for a leisurely contemplation of his options were ruined a few days later when the *Washington Star* published a front-page article headlined "'All Engines Go' for Shriver Bid for Presidency," breaking the story of his clandestine meeting with Kennedy and reporting that his entrance into the race was imminent. Witcover, at the *Washington Post*, felt he had been scooped and tried frantically to catch up by calling Shriver's aides for confirmation. When the aides insisted, accurately, that Shriver had not yet made up his mind, Witcover decided to seek out Senator Kennedy.

As Witcover recalled, Kennedy answered questions about Shriver "with wry amusement." The "Family of Long Memories" had not forgotten that Shriver had gone to Paris rather than campaign for Bobby; thus "Teddy, while not disposed to stand in Sarge's way, wasn't about to become his campaign manager either."

"What did Sarge say to you when he came up here to see you?" Witcover asked Kennedy. "And what did you say to him?"

"He told me he was going to run," Kennedy replied, "and I wished him well." He grinned slightly as he said this.

"Well," Witcover asked, sensing his cue, "if Benito Mussolini walked in here and told you he was going to run, would you wish him well?"

"If he was married to my sister!" Kennedy answered, and laughed heartily.

Some twenty years later, Shriver would recall that Kennedy had given him his blessing but not his official endorsement because, the senator said, he had already promised other candidates (like Morris Udall, Fred Harris, and Birch Bayh) that he would remain neutral.

Once Shriver's visit to the Kennedy family don had been reported publicly, the pressure on Shriver to declare his candidacy escalated. But still he equivocated, taking the necessary steps to move his candidacy forward while declining to say whether he was actually running. On July 15 he announced the formation of a fund-raising committee, to be headed by Cyrus Vance; Arthur Rooney, the owner of the Pittsburgh Steelers; Chesterfield Smith, a former president of the American Bar Association; and Bill Blair, Shriver's old Chicago friend and the former ambassador to Denmark and the Philippines. Shriver also publicized the existence of his large "Friends of Shriver" advisory group, a constellation of talent that included the actor Paul Newman, the novelist Kurt Vonnegut (quotations from whose novels peppered Shriver's speeches), and the tennis player Arthur Ashe, who had just won Wimbledon a few weeks earlier. Still, he declined to say whether he was running for president.

Ronald Reagan, who also announced the formation of his fund-raising committee on July 15, likewise did not say whether he had decided to run against Gerald Ford in the GOP primaries. The press saw Reagan's official reticence as prudent, but they viewed Shriver's as silly. "In his coyness," Witcover wrote, "he had unwillingly gotten off to a comic start"; his campaign was being "openly ridiculed by most politicians and members of the press." In September Shriver finally stated the obvious: He was going to make a declaration of his candidacy soon. But the run-up to that declaration, according to Witcover, "had the subtlety and smoothness of a final scene in a Marx Brothers movie." Part of this clumsiness derived from Shriver's chronic ambivalence about his own candidacy. But much of it also derived from Shriver's having to make absolutely sure that Ted Kennedy would not object before making any kind of definitive move.

The harsh, almost mocking press coverage Shriver received between July and September practically guaranteed that his candidacy would never gain the traction it needed. This was unfortunate. Shriver's record at the Peace Corps, the OEO, and the Paris embassy gave him a résumé at least as impressive as any of the other Democrats. And he had shown his loyalty to the party by heading the CLF in 1970 and, more self-sacrificially, by joining the sinking McGovern ship in 1972. He was also, as Witcover put it, "perhaps the only recognizable 'celebrity' in the pack, the only one who could walk into a political reception and get all the hands out of the shrimp tray to shake his."

Yet he was hemmed into a tight box. He was damned if he didn't try to make use of the Kennedy connection, because it was that connection that in some ways made him the most distinctive candidate in the group; but he was damned if he did, too. When a *Post* reporter asked why the candidate's advisory committee had no Kennedy family names on it, a Shriver aide replied, "There was no effort to get Kennedy family people or those who have a peculiarly close relationship to Teddy. The people we have are friends of Shriver's. He wanted to demonstrate that he personally has the support."

A week later, an account by Christopher Lydon in the *Times* made the Shriver-Kennedy tensions sound dire. "There is trouble in the Kennedy camp and perhaps in the Kennedy family over brother-in-law Sargent Shriver's incipient Presidential campaign," the report began. "In his search for active campaign help [Shriver] has time and again been rebuffed by Kennedy hands." Lydon listed several former aides to Jack, Bobby, and Ted who had supposedly turned Shriver down, or at least deferred giving their support, and reported that the "sharpest turndown" had come from Steve Smith. "I'm waiting for Teddy," Smith reportedly said, when approached by Shriver. When Shriver persisted, pointing out that the senator had repeatedly disavowed any interest in running himself, Smith replied, "I'm still waiting for Teddy." "It seems to be one of those times when people want the genuine thing, not the in-law imitation," said Judge Edmund Reggie, who had been the Kennedy family's man in Louisiana since the 1960 election. Reggie said that he, too, was "waiting for Teddy."

Shriver's predicament was bizarre. He was spending some of his weekends in Hyannis Port, socializing cordially with Ethel's family, Ted's family, Jean's family. His children played happily with all their Kennedy and Smith cousins. Yet for what must have seemed to Shriver like the hundredth time since 1960, alleged tensions and arguments that could have been resolved on one of the porches of the Kennedy compound were being played out in the newspapers.

The press, always hungry for inside dope about the Kennedy clan, made more of the family drama than the participants did. Politics was serious business for the Kennedy family, more serious than any other, and members of the so-called Kennedy apparatus did continue to look askance at Shriver's ambitions. But within the family councils—at Hyannis Port, at dinner parties in Maryland or Virginia—the tension was hard to perceive, especially in contrast to that of 1968, when the wounds to those in Bobby Kennedy's circle still ran deep. What signs of tension existed were subtle. For instance, Bobby Shriver thinks it significant that his father staked out his domain on the tennis court, where he knew he could easily beat any Kennedy, while staying away from the Hyannis Port Yacht Club and the touch football field, where he was more evenly matched. Shriver also sought respite from any family conflict by going to Mass with the family matriarch Rose, with whom he continued to cultivate a warm and close relationship. Relations within the family remained outwardly civil.

This did not change the political reality, however. Paradoxically, Shriver was perceived simultaneously to be the Kennedy family's handmaiden (or stalking horse) and their prodigal in-law, the man whom Ted Kennedy and Steve Smith, among others, had seemed to renounce. None of this was fully accurate, but there was enough truth to it to feed the perception. In politics, perception counts. Shriver's advisers were realizing that it would be an enormous challenge for their man to emerge as a serious candidate in his own right, especially if he wanted to capture the "Kennedy vote."

PICKING UP THE DROPPED KENNEDY MANTLE

But while Kennedy family issues were clouding Democrats' perceptions of Shriver, an influential Republican found himself smitten by this first-time presidential candidate. George Will, a young conservative columnist for the *Washington Post*, had made arrangements to interview Shriver in August. According to David Birenbaum, Will arrived as scheduled at Fried, Frank only to be kept waiting—in typical Shriver fashion—for several hours while Shriver gabbed cheerfully on the phone. Birenbaum and others fretted that this would earn Shriver a negative column; they could see Will burning with the indignity of being kept waiting.

But then, according to Birenbaum, Will noticed some of the books strewn around Shriver's messy law office. It wasn't the law books, or the candidate briefing books that caught his interest; it was the books on philosophy and theology. No doubt suspecting that they had been left lying about for show, to advertise that Shriver was a Serious Thinker, Will began flipping through them. To his surprise, they were all heavily underlined, with lots of comments written in the margin; Shriver clearly had not only read these books by Teilhard de Chardin and Jacques Maritain but had also thought hard about them.

Shriver eventually presented himself for the interview, and the result was a highly favorable column from this most unexpected of sources. "When God designed Shriver," Will wrote in his August 4 *Post* column, "he left out second gear. Shriver does everything at full throttle, and when campaigning he will eat or drink or dance any ethnic specialty at any hour." This, Will said, could make Shriver the man to beat in the Democratic primaries. But Will was clearly more struck by what he called Shriver's "religious seriousness": "It sets him apart in the political profession, most members of which seem to have no inner life beyond an almost heathen enthusiasm for getting on. He reads—he even underlines—theology books and journals." Will also wrote that Shriver "has a proper moralist's intensity which gives him that mysterious quality—call it the 'earnestness factor'—necessary for wooing liberals. McGovern had earnestness seeping from every pore, but he lacked a redeeming sense of fun. Shriver has that sense, and it keeps him from seeming suffocatingly pious."

Will recognized that Shriver's energetic idealism placed him out of sync with the times, and that this could hurt him. Shriver "will be 60 in November, but looks 45; the last dozen dispiriting years didn't happen to him, physiologically or philosophically. These years have left many Americans listless, in no mood for a President who would clap the nation on its slumped back and exhort it to shape up. Shriver is a back-slapper."

Yet Will also located Shriver in exactly the context in which the candidate had sought to be placed. "Much more than his brother-in-law, Ted Kennedy," the columnist wrote, "Shriver evokes the revved-up, wheel-spinning days of the New Frontier. He embodies the political sensibility of 1961. This does not mean Shriver is dated, but that he is the candidate for those people—and they may be legion—whose pulses quicken to the remembered cadences of President Kennedy's evangelical inaugural address. It is altogether right that the Democratic Party should produce in Shriver an evangelical candidate, to discover how many people still call Camelot their political home, and think they can go home again."

At 11:00 a.m. on Saturday, September 20, Shriver held a press conference at Washington's Mayflower Hotel to declare that he would become the ninth active Democratic candidate in the race. Shriver's advisers were confident of his chances. Birenbaum, Tribe, and others had worked hard on the announcement speech. After hours of tinkering they believed that the speech struck the proper balance between Shriver's claiming to be a "Kennedy candidate" and his being an independent agent with credentials and assets of his own. "Don't talk about trying to restore the Kennedys to the throne," Tribe and Birenbaum had admonished the candidate each time he tried to work additional New Frontier references into the speech. You've got to run on your own record, they told him.

Birenbaum and the campaign press secretary Don Pride had left a draft of the speech on the lectern. All Shriver had to do was deliver it, his aides believed, and they would be on their way to the Democratic nomination.

But something went amiss, and at the last minute Shriver's confidence in his ability to run as an independent candidate faltered. Partly it was the setting: a room at the Mayflower Hotel, downstairs from the suite where he and his eager band of New Frontiersmen had hatched the Peace Corps for JFK fifteen years earlier. Partly it was the influence of those who surrounded him as he made his announcement: his wife, Eunice Kennedy, on his right and his sister-in-law Ethel Kennedy on his left; his mother-in-law, Rose Kennedy, and sister-in-law Jackie Kennedy, along with sisters-in-law Jean Smith and Joan Kennedy in the audience; and "old . . . Kennedy faithful hanging from the rafters." And partly, no doubt, he had been intoxicated by George Will's column, which depicted him as the avatar of the New Frontier.

Shriver began his speech as prepared. He was running, he said, because given the state of domestic and foreign affairs, and given the current lack of leadership at home, "I could not stand aside." He continued: "For only the second time in this century, the forward movement of America has been reversed; we have retrogressed as a society. And it is this sudden, overwhelming reversal of momentum that has generated the vast crisis of confidence we face today. . . . Not since the Great Depression has America stood in fear of the future."

He argued that a Shriver administration would cut a middle path between the Republicans' antigovernment cynicism and the Democrats' propensity toward government bloat. "I'm opposed to centralized, rigid, unresponsive bureaucracy," he said. "I worked to combat that kind of bureaucracy in business, as head of Chicago's School Board, and later in Washington and in the Foreign Service. In the Peace Corps, in Head Start, in Legal Services for the Poor, in Foster Grandparents, we created the least bureaucratic public enterprises in modern governmental history. But a purely negative approach to government will get us nowhere."

It was a fine speech. Some quotes from Bobby, an understated reference to Jack: just enough of the Kennedy factor, but not too much, in the calculation of Shriver's speechwriters. And then, to the alarm of his aides who were looking on, Shriver reached into his breast pocket, drew out a small sheaf of papers, and launched into a long encomium to the spirit of JFK. "His legacy awaits the leader who can claim it, "Shriver concluded. "I intend to claim that legacy not for myself alone but for the family who first brought it into being; the millions who joyfully entered public life with him and the millions of people throughout the world . . . for whom the memory of John Kennedy is an inspiration and a lifting of the heart."

It was, Birenbaum and others recalled, a beautiful, stirring conclusion to his announcement—and one that effectively torpedoed Shriver's candidacy. As Shriver's former OEO colleague Colman McCarthy recalled, it looked to some detached observers that "Shriver felt insecure about running on his own record and ideas, so he was hooking jumper cables to John Kennedy to be energized by a winner." And as Jules Witcover observed, the announcement's "boldness in donning the political mantle of the family surprised some of those who knew that some Kennedy family members frowned on Shriver's presidential ambitions."

The next morning Shriver appeared on Meet the Press to talk about his fledgling candidacy. All four interviewers—Bill Monroe, Jack Germond, Marty Nolan, and Robert Novak—"pawed Shriver with legacy questions," grilling him on why he would claim to be "picking up the Kennedy mantle." What had he meant by that, Shriver was asked, and why was the mantle his to claim? Don't you have more claim on the "McGovern legacy"? As Colman McCarthy observed, Shriver was immediately forced on the defensive by newspapermen who found it a bit much that someone would try to ride "the coattails of a man dead 13 years." Shriver was compelled to admit that, yes, brother-in-law Ted was in fact "the logical claimant" of the Kennedy legacy—but Ted had "decided, you know, not to be a candidate." Look, he said, "my success in business" was not solely attributable to the fact that "I married the boss's daughter."

"He never got out from under that 'mantle' business," Birenbaum recalled wistfully.

The campaign operation in 1976 was actually, by Shriver's normal standards of "personal anarchy," quite organized and professional. Still, as *Newsweek* reported, the campaign ran on "pep, hope, and a kind of creative chaos." Dick Murphy, a former assistant postmaster general and a political protégé of Larry O'Brien, was campaign manager. Ed Cubberly, who had been treasurer for RFK's 1968 campaign, and Pat Baldi, a former Peace Corps volunteer who had worked on the 1972 vice presidential campaign, served as Murphy's deputies. Pat Caddell was in charge of polling, as he had been for McGovern in 1972. Two trusted veterans of administration at the Peace Corps and the OEO, Bill Kelly and Bill Mullins, ran the Shriver fund-raising operation. Don Pride, who had formerly served as press secretary to Florida governor Reubin Askew, and Dick Drayne, a former press secretary for Ted Kennedy, were in charge of the media.

The campaign had several overlapping strategies. Aim for primary victories in the industrial states where JFK had scored big in 1960. Force out the other liberal candidates early on by winning the support of black voters and Kennedy voters. Counteract the McGovernite taint of 1972 by reaching out to old party bosses and by espousing fiscally conservative economic policies. Win back the Catholic ethnics who had gone over to Nixon in 1972. Use the New Frontier–like collection of celebrities who tended to cluster around Shriver—the campaign called them "sparklies"—to dazzle voters with excitement and charisma.

Along with all the other candidates, Shriver spent the following months crisscrossing the early caucus and primary states, primarily Iowa and New Hampshire. The Shriver campaign had reason to believe it could do well in both states—Iowa because it was heavily Catholic, New Hampshire because it was just north of Kennedy country. Shriver could hardly afford not to do well in these states. With Harris, Udall, Shapp, Shriver, and now also Birch Bayh, the Indiana senator, all vying for the same liberal constituency, one of them needed to score significant victories early; otherwise, the liberal vote would get divided and Jackson or Carter would prevail.

In October 1975 a debate in Manchester, New Hampshire, served as the "official" kickoff of the primary campaign. Bayh, Carter, Harris, Shapp, Shriver, and Udall all participated. Surveying the competition, Shriver believed the tall Arizonan, Mo Udall, to be his most formidable competition. By far the weakest competition, he thought, was Jimmy Carter. A lot of these guys might be able to beat me, Shriver told his son Timothy, but I can definitely beat *that* guy, pointing to the former Georgia governor.

But the poor reaction to Shriver's Manchester speech revealed some of his key failings as a candidate. One was the degree to which what George Will had called Shriver's "back-slapping"—and what Witcover called his "shrill hucksterism"—rubbed cynical voters the wrong way. Whether audiences perceived him to be a huckster (which would have been an inaccurate perception) or naively idealistic (which would have been closer to the mark), the exhortatory tone of his speeches failed to resonate. "He's a lightweight and I think he's kidding himself," one long-time Kennedy associate reportedly told the conservative *Washington Star*. "He thinks he can just run down the runway and the natural air currents will lift him off the ground. He's still talking and thinking the way we all did in the early 60s but there's a new ball game out there that guys like Jerry Brown in California and Mike Dukakis in Massachusetts are playing. He doesn't see it partly because he's the most politically orthodox one in the family." This analysis seemed to reflect the source's bias more than any effort to see Shriver for what he was: Shriver had considerable failings as a candidate, to be sure, but "orthodoxy" was surely not one of them. (Nor, for that matter, did Brown or Dukakis turn out to be notably successful in their respective presidential forays.)

What did make Shriver seem most like a lightweight, ironically, was the "problem" that Anthony Lake described: his prioritizing of ideas and substance over politics. Rather than spending his time doing what a candidate should do—calibrating his message to appeal to key groups of voters—Shriver spent his time wrestling with real issues, trying to arrive at the most effective or most ethical policy. David Birenbaum recalled a representative discussion among Shriver and his aides in a New Hampshire motel room about abortion policy that lasted for four hours. "What impressed me about that more than anything else was he just never, never allowed himself to talk about anything but the substance of what was the right thing to say. He never let go of his principles." Although this concern for principle and substance impressed his advisers—and might have made him a first-rate president—it struck jaded, post-Watergate voters as a put-on. No real candidate could be as much like the Jimmy Stewart character in *Mr. Smith Goes to Washington* as Shriver sometimes seemed to be.

Nevertheless, Shriver polled well at first in Iowa. An early straw poll put him a close second behind Carter, who had already been campaigning in Iowa on and off for a year, and ahead of Bayh. The other candidates trailed far behind. But because Carter had begun 1975 as the least known of the candidates, the press focused heavily on how unexpectedly well he was doing. In fact, according to Carter biographer Peter Bourne, the crucial turning point of the 1976 campaign occurred on October 27, 1975, when Johnny Apple wrote a front-page story for the *New York Times* annointing Carter the front-runner; this was "an object lesson in the power wielded by the press in the presidential selection process."

Still, Shriver and the rest of the contenders continued to underestimate Carter, believing that his lead would be short lived. Carter had had the advantage of an early start, but surely, they thought, he didn't have the stuff to sustain his lead all the way to the nomination.

In Iowa, particularly, Shriver figured his Catholicism would give him an extra boost, especially because as the January 19 caucus approached, the abortion issue loomed large. Iowa had more than half a million Catholics, including a significant proportion of Democratic voters who considered themselves pro-life on abortion. Neither Carter nor Shriver publicly espoused a strictly pro-life position, but Shriver's position leaned much farther in a pro-life direction than Carter's did.

In truth, both Carter and Shriver over the years had expressed nuanced, and sometimes inconsistent, views on abortion. But whereas for Shriver (and especially for his wife) abortion was one of the most burning issues of the time, more morally urgent than busing or inflation policy or anything else, for Carter it had been just one issue among many that he cared about.

While governor of Georgia, Carter had strongly supported family planning services that provided abortions, and he had even written the foreword to *Women in Need*, a book that endorsed a woman's right to choose. He had supported the plaintiffs who had filed suit to change outdated Georgia laws on abortion and had been a supporter of the Supreme Court's decision in *Roe v. Wade*, which declared it unconstitutional for states to prohibit abortions in the first and generally the second trimesters of pregnancy. After Carter was subjected to some stinging attacks at town meetings for his pro-choice stance, he had begun to moderate his position slightly. Throughout 1975, however, he had expressed his support for *Roe v. Wade* whenever he was asked about it. He also said he opposed the idea, being advanced by a powerful movement of social conservatives in both parties, of passing a constitutional amendment that would in effect overturn the Supreme Court decision. As the Iowa caucus approached, Carter found himself under increasing criticism for his position from pro-life Democrats. For a time, it seemed, his lead in that state might evaporate.

Although Shriver, in contrast, had come out tentatively in opposition to the proposed constitutional amendment, he was in his personal beliefs staunchly opposed to abortion. Eunice was even more strongly opposed. Working with the mentally retarded and expanding the Special Olympics was now her life's work, but since the mid-1960s she had thrown herself with equal moral passion into another project: trying to reduce the number of abortions performed in the United States each year. In 1964, when Bobby was running for election to the Senate in New York and Ted was running for reelection in Massachusetts, Sarge had convened a meeting of the country's leading Catholic theologians at Hyannis Port to brief his brothers-in-law on the latest Catholic thinking about abortion. After states began relaxing their prohibitions on abortion in 1967, Sarge and Eunice had put together the first-ever conference on abortion, jointly funded by the Kennedy Foundation and Harvard Divinity School. Over three days in early September of that year, scores of experts in medicine, law, ethics, sociology, and religion convened to discuss not only abortion specifically but also various developments in medicine and technology. In the early 1970s, the Shrivers had used Kennedy Foundation money to establish the Kennedy Institute of Ethics at Georgetown University, in Washington. "Our idea," Sarge recalled, was to combine "biology with ethics." To describe this notion, he coined the term "bioethics," which is now a full-fledged academic field. Indeed, by 1980, work produced by associates of the Kennedy Institute had changed how the medical profession made many of its ethical decisions.

Abortion, then, was not merely a tactical political issue for the 1976 Shriver campaign, as it may have been for some of the other candidates. After having spent much of the last decade actively thinking about and discussing the moral and legal aspects of abortion, there was no way Shriver could have come up with a position on abortion that was designed purely, or even primarily, to secure a certain bloc of voters.

As the most pro-life candidate in the Democratic field, Shriver should have had a real advantage among some of Iowa's heavily Catholic areas like Dubuque and Carroll counties, especially because Carter was already under attack for being too strongly pro-choice and was in fact being forced to backtrack from his position. But in the week before the Iowa caucus, Carter was quoted in the *Catholic Mirror*, the official paper of the Des Moines diocese, that he would in fact support a "national statute" to outlaw abortion. Whether Carter was misquoted by the *Mirror* or was tailoring his comments to suit his audience is not clear—but his ostensible support for a national statute (which can only have meant a constitutional amendment) was clearly at odds with Carter's previous pro-choice position. Carter would later—when playing to social moderates—say he never actually voiced support for the outlawing of abortion; the misunderstanding reprinted in the *Mirror* had resulted when a group of priests in the basement of a church in Des Moines asked him a series of "improbable" hypothetical questions, the last of which was: "Are there any circumstances under which you might support a national statute against abortion?" To which Carter says he replied: "Yes, I suppose it is possible, although I cannot think of any."

The misunderstanding, if that's what it was, worked distinctly to Carter's advantage in Iowa. After the *Catholic Mirror* quoted him as being in favor of federally outlawing abortion, making him seem the candidate most congenial to Iowa's pro-lifers, word quickly passed from diocese to diocese; on the Sunday before the caucus, Catholic priests (and fundamentalist Protestants) urged their parishes to vote for Carter. Shriver was mistakenly listed on Catholic fliers as the next-to-the-worst candidate (from a pro-life perspective) on abortion. The Church, the *Nation* reported, "through its publication, including a bulletin distributed at many masses on the 18th [the day before the caucus], conveyed an inaccurate account of the public positions of Carter and Shriver, making Carter sound tougher and Shriver sound weaker in their mutual opposition to abortion."

This destroyed Shriver in Iowa. When Don O'Brien, Shriver's regional campaign manager in the state, learned that Carter was trying to blur his real position on abortion, he went to Frank Brady, an influential priest in Sioux City, and explained the situation. Monsignor Brady looked into the record and discovered O'Brien was speaking the truth: Carter had clearly always opposed a constitutional amendment outlawing abortion. Brady went on local television to denounce Carter for his misrepresentation.

But it was too late: Shriver had been counting on the Catholic vote to put him among the top finishers. Now, misled, Catholics went heavily for Carter.

According to Rowland Evans and Robert Novak, Carter's obfuscation of his real abortion position "made the difference between first and second place for Carter in Iowa." The Catholic Church did pretty well at helping [Carter] and hurting Sargent Shriver," the *Nation* reported. Jack Germond, the political correspondent for the *Washington Star*, wrote a piece implying that Carter, who was campaigning on his honesty, had shaded the truth for political expediency. "I think I've been sandbagged by Carter," one priest told Germond.

Shriver told friends he felt he had been robbed. Had he won a larger portion of Iowa's 600,000 Catholic voters, he would have performed much more respectably. As it was, Carter finished with 29.1 percent, Bayh with 11.4, Harris with 9.0, Udall with 3.8, and Shriver with only 3.1 percent. (The remaining candidates—Wallace, Jackson, Shapp, Hubert Humphrey, and a few others—all got less than that.) With Carter the runaway winner, Johnny Apple's *New York Times* piece of late October looked prophetic.

After the Iowa caucus, Shriver released a series of statements that sought to clarify his personal opposition to abortion and to lay out his long record of interest and concern in the bioethics arena. "I am strongly opposed to abortion," he said a few days after the caucus. "I intend to work in and out of government, as I have for the past decade, for the day when abortion will no longer be looked upon by anyone as a desirable or necessary procedure." He talked about his sponsorship of the first international abortion conference in 1967 and about his work with the Kennedy Institute of Ethics. He also pointed to his work with Eunice in establishing a network of what they called "Life Support Centers," which provided prenatal care and child-rearing instruction; helped mothers find jobs; and generally tried to augment the incentives for teenage mothers *not* to abort.

After consultations with Eunice and advisers from the Kennedy Institute, Shriver stopped short of endorsing a constitutional amendment to override *Roe v. Wade* and said he would abide by the Court's decision. "Let me repeat. I am and always have been strongly opposed to abortion—ethically, morally, intellectually, emotionally. I say that without reservation. But as president I must take an oath to uphold the laws the land."

Although it hurt Shriver, Carter's ambiguity on the abortion issue was not the sole cause of his disappointing finish. Carter had done a better job than Shriver (or any of the other candidates) of connecting with Iowa voters, who related to his plainspoken folksiness. Also, despite Shriver's having billed himself as the bearer of the Kennedy torch, there was nary a Kennedy of Jack's generation (besides Eunice) in sight in Iowa. Many of the younger generation of Kennedy cousins—the Lawford children; JFK's daughter, Caroline; and some of the Robert Kennedy children—made appearances, but not the other prominent New Frontiersmen. "The Kennedy clan and its long list of old political and social associates who had turned out in droves for [Shriver's] declaration of candidacy were in short supply in Iowa," Jules Witcover wrote. "Sarge had been given a great bon-voyage party at the pier; now, as he sailed off, most of them stood on the dock and waved."

Despite the fifth place finish in Iowa, Shriver still had hope. The next caucus was to be held five days later in Mississippi, where, of all the candidates, Shriver had by far the strongest rapport with black voters. Thousands of black (and some white) residents of that state had benefited from OEO programs Shriver had launched there. Shriver's bitter battles over the CDGM were by now mostly forgotten, but the thousands of children who had passed through Mississippi's Head Start programs had not been.

As a Southerner himself, of course, Jimmy Carter had something of a favorite son's advantage in Mississippi. The real favorite son, however, was George Wallace, who was sure to win most of the white vote. The crucial battle would be for second place. In the days before the caucus, Carter's wife, Rosalynn, urged him to quickly recruit a group of prominent African Americans with whom he could tour the state, to demonstrate that it was not only Shriver who could reach out to black Southerners.

Shriver had been leading Carter in the polls just a few days before the caucus. But on Saturday, January 24, Wallace won Mississippi, going away with 44 percent of the vote. Carter finished second with 14 percent, narrowly edging Shriver's 12 percent. No other candidate won more than 2 percent of the vote. According to Carter's former aide Peter Bourne, Rosalynn's ploy spelled the difference.

Still, not all was lost for the Shriver campaign. The abortion fiasco had led to a disappointing result in Iowa, but the relatively strong finish in Mississippi demonstrated that Shriver remained at least as viable a national candidate as either Bayh or Udall. The upcoming New Hampshire and Massachusetts primaries would go a long way to determining which of the liberal contingent would continue to the finish, challenging Carter (and maybe Scoop Jackson) for the nomination.

But although Shriver's name recognition was higher among Northeastern voters than Udall's or Bayh's, it wasn't as high as it had been a few years earlier. Many New Hampshirites seemed to know that he had some connection to the Kennedys but weren't sure what it was. One day he made a campaign stop at an insurance company in Manchester. "He was laboring to be taken as his own man, not just the Kennedy brother-in-law," Witcover wrote, "but inquiries among the young women revealed that he wasn't even doing well in that department. Linda Miller, a twenty-three-year-old customer-service representative said, 'He's associated with the Kennedys. . . . Isn't he Ethel Kennedy's brother? No? Joan Kennedy's brother? No? There's so many of them.'"

Shriver remained bedeviled by the Kennedy issue. "He is a stunningly young 60," reported *Newsweek* magazine from the campaign trail in New Hampshire. "He is well bred and lovingly tailored. He is thoughtful in private, charming in a crowd. He has positions on practically everything. He has survived half a lifetime in government without a breath of scandal, political or personal. He has good teeth. He excites. He ought to be a dream candidate—and yet Shriver has been unable to fight clear of the notion that he is only an imitation Kennedy holding the franchise until the real thing comes along."

Shriver also faced a money crunch. After early success in fund-raising, the money stream had tapered off—almost as if the big Democratic funders decided not to waste their money once they saw that the campaign had lost momentum. Shriver had far less to spend in New Hampshire than either Carter or Udall.

The primary results, on February 24, 1976, were gravely damaging to Shriver's candidacy: Carter finished first, with 30 percent of the vote; then Udall, with 24 percent; Bayh, with 16 percent; Fred Harris, with 11 percent; and finally Shriver, with 9 percent.

Shriver remained in the race, despite dwindling campaign funds, because he held on to the hope that the Kennedy connection in Massachusetts and the Daley connection in Illinois would propel him to success in those two crucial primaries. Shriver knew that to resuscitate his candidacy, he would need to perform well in Massachusetts; anything lower than third place would surely finish him. So he poured most of his remaining resources into the Bay State. As recently as early February, polls had shown him leading the Democratic field in Massachusetts. But his poor showing in New Hampshire sapped his momentum, and several factors were now working against him. First, there were no more scheduled debates—and in a year when no single issue (like Vietnam) gal-vanized voters, it was proving difficult for candidates to establish distinct pro-files. Shriver had to distinguish himself not only from the other candidates but from his in-laws (while at the same time exploiting his connection to them).

In Massachusetts, as in New Hampshire, the prevailing view seemed to be that Shriver was merely a "step-Kennedy." One night at a Chinese restaurant in Boston, Ted Kennedy gave a short dinner speech to a gathering of local Democratic operatives. During his remarks, he introduced his sister, Eunice, who was sitting at his table, but without mentioning her husband who, although not present that evening, was campaigning actively in the state. When Ted returned to his table after his speech, Eunice needled him. "You didn't even mention my last name," she said.

In a campaign appearance in Worcester, Massachusetts, in mid-January, Shriver tried to play up his Kennedy connection while also putting some distance between himself and the family. "I think it's a fabulous family, but I'm happy to have a record that antedates my marriage," he said. He also reiterated that he had made his decision to run only after he was sure that Teddy would not run. But voters, and Democratic Party operatives, seemed unable to see him inde-pendently of his wife's family. Twice at a campaign appearance in Lowell, Massachusetts, a local party boss accidentally referred to him as "Eunice."

Another problem for Shriver—and the other liberal candidates—was that Scoop Jackson was concentrating most of his early resources in Massachusetts. A notoriously liberal state, the only one to have gone for McGovern in 1972, Massachusetts might have seemed an unlikely proving ground for the hawkish Jackson. But Scoop had focused heavily on the hot-button issue of forced bus-ing. For several years, competing factions had been locked in bitter combat over the use of busing to forcibly integrate schools. Many poor minorities and lib-eral Democrats were in favor of busing; it was a matter not only of abstract social justice and achieving more racial diversity in schools but of giving poor minority students the same educational opportunities that white students had. But many white ethnics—the Irish of South Boston, the Italians of the North End, even some of the Brahmins on Beacon Hill—violently objected to forcible integration. Whereas most of the liberal candidates, Shriver included, had staked out positions moderately in favor of busing, Jackson had taken a strong antibusing position, which was the electorally stronger stance.

On primary day in Massachusetts it snowed heavily, covering the state in a blanket of white. Shriver's nomination chances were buried as deeply as the cars on Commonwealth Avenue. Jackson won 23 percent, followed by Udall at 18 percent. Wallace, helped by his antibusing stance, garnered 17 percent. Jimmy Carter, suffering his first real setback of the primary season, finished fourth with 14 percent. Behind him were Harris (8 percent), Shriver (7 percent), and Bayh (5 percent).

"There were a number of us," David Birenbaum recalled, "who were counseling him to get out after Massachusetts because we didn't have enough money and he was continuing to run up debts. I didn't want him to be burdened by it. There seemed to be no way he was getting anywhere. Nobody was paying any attention to him. Everyone thought he would do well in Massachusetts, because of the Kennedy connection. In fact, he did very badly in Massachusetts. Where was he going to do well?"

Bayh withdrew from the race the next day. Shriver conferred with Birenbaum and his other advisers about whether to follow Bayh out the exit or make one last-ditch effort in Illinois. Logic, and lack of money, dictated that Shriver was finished after Massachusetts and that he ought to drop out. Ted Kennedy told him, as Shriver recalled, "that my candidacy was in bad shape and maybe the best thing for me to do would be to get out of it." But, largely for sentimental reasons, he decided to press on through Illinois. After all, it was in that state that he had coveted elective office the longest; and with the support of Democratic kingmaker Dick Daley, anything could happen. So Shriver carried on through the March 16 race in Illinois.

Shriver was the only candidate Daley allowed to have a personal audience with the Cook County Democratic Committee, but ultimately the mayor withheld his personal endorsement, remaining neutral so that he could put forward Adlai Stevenson III as a favorite-son candidate at the convention. Although "some elements of the Daley machine helped Shriver behind the scenes," his lack of "money, organization, and power base" prevented him from winning. Shriver finished a respectable third place—behind Carter and Wallace, but far ahead of the rest of the field. Now, however, he was out of money, and Carter's momentum seemed unstoppable. "If I couldn't do any better than [third] in Illinois," Shriver said later, he knew he had no chance. It was time to call an end to this adventure. On March 22, 1976, he withdrew from the race and released his delegates.

"This is not a happy day for me," he said. "I have to face up to the failure of my campaign, and I don't like it. But I blame no one but myself and I make no excuses." He used his withdrawal speech to call on American leaders to put forward a more idealistic vision for the future, something that would help draw the country beyond its cynicism, and "out of such spiritual doldrums." Shriver paraphrased his favorite theologian, Teilhard de Chardin, in deploring those who had mocked his campaign as representing the spirit of the 1960s, the idealism of a more hopeful time. "Down with the cowards and the skeptics, the pessimists and the unhappy, the weary and the stagnant," he said.

He retained his good humor. When a Japanese businessman came to Fried, Frank not long after Shriver had been trounced in both the New Hampshire and the Massachusetts primaries, the visitor tried to offer consolation by saying he had heard that American primary elections were just "beauty pageants." Shriver shocked the businessman by bursting out laughing and replying, "Well, I must be one ugly son-of-a-bitch!"

To many who had worked with Shriver for years, the most infuriating thing about the 1976 campaign was not that he had lost; it was that the loss seemed to have permanently affixed the "lightweight" tag to his reputation. *Newsweek*, for instance, reported that the 1976 campaign had heightened "Shriver's reputation, in the conventional political wisdom, as a lightweight—an overbred dilettante with great exclamation-pointed enthusiasms, notably about himself, and very little bottom." During the campaign, a reporter for the *Washington Star* had written, "Some people, including some old Kennedy hands, consider him something of a lightweight, a Boy Scout with a marshmallow core who isn't tough enough. They see him as a sort of political Willy Loman who married well and is out there with a shoeshine and a smile trying to play Jack and Bobby's game."

Many of Shriver's friends and colleagues—especially those who had known him before he married into the Kennedy family—found this maddening. The idea that Shriver was somehow the weak link in the Kennedy chain, or the prodigal son-in-law horning in on sacred turf, or the inferior of his brothers-in-law, was preposterous to them. Shriver, whose litany of significant personal sacrifices to the Kennedy family extended over twenty years, deserved better than this.

In 1976 Mark Shields, who had worked on the 1972 campaign before becoming a political commentator, said, "Shriver's a bright guy and he's as good a candidate as there is, willing to go sixteen hours a day. He's full of joy and vitality and he likes people. He's not one of these liberals who loves mankind and hates people. But because of this some people unjustly write him off as a lightweight. We make the mistake of equating ponderousness with profundity."

In the aftermath of the 1976 election, the most spirited and eloquent defense of Shriver's intellect was mounted by Colman McCarthy, who wrote a long article for the *Washington Monthly*, titled "Shriver: The Lightweight Label." After his withdrawal speech, McCarthy wrote, "Shriver was characteristically buoyant. . . . That was vintage Shriver: ever the mole, boring his way through piles of defeat and fatigue, and coming up to sun himself on whatever ray was left. It is one of the traits by which Shriver has endeared himself to so many of us who once worked for him. It is also the kind of behavior that has caused him to be dismissed as a lightweight by many reporters."

To McCarthy, as to so many of Shriver's supporters, the death knell of the 1976 Shriver-for-president campaign was sounded as soon as he tried to stake his claim to the Kennedy legacy. Not because he didn't deserve it, but because, in trying to stake that claim, he inevitably obscured what he had achieved in his own right. McCarthy wrote:

> The real irony of Shriver's making himself dependent on John Kennedy was that, of all the Democratic candidates . . . only he had a record of service and innovation that was unique and substantial on its own. Shriver was the only candidate who could go back and say that something he began 15 years ago—the Peace Corps—is still alive today and retains much of the philosophical purity that he originally gave it. He was the only candidate who could point to ten-year-old programs and ideas—Head Start, Job Corps, Legal Services, Upward Bound, among others—and claim that they were still productive and working today. . . .
>
> If there was a legacy crying out to be claimed, it was Shriver's own: one to take immense political pride in and one that separated him in obvious ways from the Jacksons, Carters, and Udalls. None of them could point to something initiated 15 or 10 years ago and say, honestly, that it was functioning today.

PART SEVEN

Private Life, Public Service (1976–2003)

CHAPTER FORTY-SEVEN

Nuclear Politics

~

S hriver's brief, sporadic career in elective politics was over. His dedication to public service was not. He returned to Fried, Frank, remaining as active, passionate, and engaged as he had been at the height of the New Frontier.

He continued to play an active role in determining where the Kennedy Foundation would spend its money. He also spent a great deal of time working with scholars on various projects at the Kennedy Institute of Ethics. In 1979 he spearheaded the Kennedy Institute's launch of what would come to be called Trialogue, a running interfaith colloquium among Christian, Jewish, and Muslim scholars that aimed to mine all three religious traditions in the hopes of finding "a surer basis for peace."

Beginning in the mid-1970s, when Shriver's business trips to Moscow were most frequent, he began campaigning for a more meaningful détente with the Soviet Union and for a reduction in the American stockpile of nuclear arms. After he dropped out of the presidential race in the spring of 1976, Shriver tried to parlay whatever political capital he had left into influencing the eventual Democratic nominee, Jimmy Carter, to work toward the idea he had spelled out on his Soviet lecture tour the previous year—a peaceful "Common Existence" for the United States and the Soviet Union. On September 18 Shriver teamed up with Herbert and Tom Scoville to form the United States Committee for East-West Common Existence, which sought to maximize international exchange between the cold war superpowers and to impress on them the importance of reducing their nuclear stockpiles. Herbert "Pete" Scoville had been an expert on military technology for thirty years; after working in the federal government (the Defense Department, the CIA, and the Arms Control and Disarmament Agency), he had become an arms control activist and went on to found the Arms Control Association. His son, Tom, served as executive director of the Arms Control and Disarmament Agency's advisory committee.

In December 1976 the committee sent Jimmy Carter a letter signed by dozens of the most prominent names in arms control and liberal advocacy, including Father Ted Hesburgh, George Kennan, and Charles Yost. "Dear President-Elect," Shriver and company addressed Carter in Georgia, "We are writing this letter because of our concern that one of the most important challenges confronting America as you take office is to restore momentum to the effort to improve Soviet-American relations."

Conservative hawks—in particular Ronald Reagan, Ford's defeated challenger in the GOP primary—had recently escalated their cold war rhetoric. Détente was a sham, Reagan and others said; we need to abandon peaceful coexistence and strive instead for all-out military supremacy. Shriver and his colleagues on the committee found this deplorable, believing it an "illusion" that security and peace could be won through military build-up alone. Should these militaristic policies regain ascendance, the committee warned Carter, "the U.S. and the Soviet Union would be headed toward disaster, with fear in the driver's seat—not an appropriate fear of nuclear holocaust, not fear of an endless arms race, not fear of atomic weapons in the hands of all nations—but an unreasoning fear of each other. *This fear*—spread by those who say that the United States is weak, spread by those who say that relaxation of tensions is only a trap, spread by prisoners of the Cold War generation—*would become our greatest enemy.*"

The committee argued that America already was Russia's military superior by far. Shriver, based on his own experience in the Soviet Union, strongly believed this to be true. Operating from its position of military strength, Shriver and company told Carter, the United States should substantially reduce nuclear arsenals and delivery mechanisms; formulate a more active policy to block nuclear proliferation elsewhere in the world; and declare a moratorium on *all* nuclear testing.

Carter initially opted for the path charted by the committee: limiting nuclear-arms build-up, negotiating restraints on strategic weapons, and trying to "raise the threshold" on nuclear war planning. But the apparent failure of the "détente experiment" of the 1960s and 1970s seemed to have loosened superpower restraint; by the end of his administration, Carter was tacking in a more hawk-ish nuclear direction. In December 1979 the Soviet invasion of Afghanistan destroyed whatever was left of détente. Carter declared that the Soviet advance into Central Asia had to be stopped; he feared the Soviets would advance all the way to the Persian Gulf, to seize the oil supplies there. Secretary of State Cyrus Vance's nemesis in the administration, the far more hawkish national security adviser Zbigniew Brzezinski, gained in influence. Carter declared that the United States would boycott the 1980 summer Olympic Games in Moscow. Relations between the superpowers were growing more truculent—and more atomically threatening—than they had been since the early 1960s.

Ronald Reagan hewed even farther from détente than Carter had. In 1981, when Reagan took office, Shriver (along with George Ball, William Fulbright, John Kenneth Galbraith, Averell Harriman, Jacob Javits, George Kennan, and others) sent him a letter similar to the one they had addressed to Carter in 1976. It fell on deaf ears.

Shriver now began strategizing to see how the arms-control movement might achieve more leverage over the rabidly hawkish Reagan administration. As usual, he began by seeking out the best and brightest minds he could iden-tify and bringing them to his home for a discussion. In 1981 the Shriver family had moved out of Timberlawn into a house called Avondale, on Foxhall Road in Northwest Washington. On Tuesday, October 20, 1981, a small but influen-tial band of foreign policy experts joined Sarge and Eunice for a secret dinner discussion at Avondale to discuss "what needs to be done" about the Reagan administration's policy on nuclear arms. The dinner guests that night included Pete Scoville; Robert McNamara, who was presently head of the World Bank; Paul Warnke, who had served as Jimmy Carter's chief negotiator during the

Strategic Arms Limitation Talks (SALT); George Kennan, the author of the famous "X" document, which spelled out the policy of containment of communism during the Truman administration, and who was now a scholar at the Institute for Advanced Study in Princeton, New Jersey; William Colby, the former head of the CIA; Gerard Smith, Shriver's boyhood friend, now one of the nation's leading arms-control negotiators; and Father Bryan Hehir, director of policy for the National Conference of Catholic Bishops.

To Hehir, who was the youngest and (at the time) least distinguished of all the guests present, the dinner was a heady experience. "Reagan had made a statement that day, or virtually that day, that you could have a limited nuclear war in Europe and Europe would probably survive," Hehir recalled. "McNamara found that just incomprehensible. And he was apoplectic about that. As the discussion evolved, somebody said, 'We've got to do an article" on the idea that a first-launch nuclear strike was not only immoral but tactically senseless. "Then they had a discussion about who should write it," Hehir recalled. "And we went around the table and of course they all had a hundred names and it was like the Old Boys' School of Foreign Policy. Eventually they settled on Mac Bundy."

Before Bundy would agree to take on the draftsman's role, he told Kennan he needed to know what core principles the statement would be expressing. Shriver agreed that an outline of principles was a necessary first step—and later that day Kennan dictated a rudimentary statement to Shriver's assistant Jeannie Main. The statement read, in part:

1. We are persuaded that there is literally no way that either this country or the Soviet Union could initiate the use of nuclear weapons in combat with ultimate advantage to itself—without incurring, that is, a wholly unacceptable risk of escalation into nuclear war disastrous to all parties.

2. This being the case, we consider that the United States should, while retaining the option of a nuclear response to a nuclear attack, abandon the principles of first use of nuclear weapons in any armed conflict.

3. We recognize that this will necessitate an extensive restructuring of American armed forces in points of strategy, tactics, equipment and training. We urge that such a restructuring be put in hand at once.

To accommodate this restructuring, the statement called for a strengthening of conventional forces by both the United States and NATO. Shriver immediately sent the statement to McNamara, Colby, Hehir, Scoville, and Warnke for their comments.

In a series of further discussions at Avondale over the next several weeks, it was agreed that Bundy, Kennan, McNamara, and Gerard Smith would serve as coauthors of a statement calling on the Reagan administration to promise never, under any circumstance, to launch a nuclear first strike. Shriver served as ringleader and cheerleader, collecting and circulating material and trying to recruit additional troops to the disarmament cause. When Averell Harriman wrote an op-ed column in the *Washington Post*, calling for "decisive leadership" in limiting nuclear arms and for a study on nuclear war options, Shriver forwarded it to McNamara with a letter that sounded the clarion call of the New Frontier. "Decisive leadership," Shriver wrote, "will not be fulfilled . . . just by a call for a study to explore the nuclear war options at this time, especially the first-use option. Useful though such a study might be, it would not meet the current situation. Instead, we need a declaration just like Jack's: 'We'll put a man on the moon in this decade.'" We need, Shriver wrote, to make a forceful statement calling for the US government to renounce the use of a nuclear first strike.

On the day that Harriman's op-ed piece appeared in the *Post*, Secretary of State Alexander Haig announced a "contingency plan" whereby US military forces would detonate a nuclear warhead as a "demonstration" meant to deter the Soviet Union from invading Western Europe. This, Shriver believed, was one step removed from a first strike. "Human beings," he wrote to McNamara, "need their eyes and hearts lifted to an alternative to Haig-ism, 'demonstration blasts,' etc. You all [Bundy, Kennan, McNamara, and Smith] can do all that; and many centrists would join you."

For the next three months, Shriver buzzed like a gnat in the ears of McNamara, Kennan, and company, goading them on, sending them new material, winning new recruits to the "no-first-strike" cause. He got Oregon senator Mark Hatfield, a Republican, to agree to endorse any statement on nuclear arms Kennan's crew made, and Hatfield agreed to introduce his support in the Senate as the "Hatfield Resolution."

In mid-December, Kennan and Bundy were still wrestling over who would serve as primary draftsman, and Shriver was getting impatient. If we're having trouble getting Mac Bundy to write a paper for us, he wrote to McNamara, then why not get someone else to do it? He specifically recommended James Fallows, a young veteran of the Carter administration who had carved out a reputation for himself as a journalist knowledgeable on national defense issues. McNamara wrote back that the problem was not "the paper, but rather how to present it. I am running into a lot of opposition from people who I thought would support a 'no-first-strike' policy."

Shriver refused to relent, and he continued to apply pressure on McNamara, Kennan, Bundy, and others to issue some kind of prominent statement. Eventually, they settled upon *Foreign Affairs*, the most influential and prestigious American journal on foreign policy, as the venue for their statement. (Also, the journal's chief editor happened to be McGeorge Bundy's brother, William.) Bundy and McNamara agreed to serve as primary writers, with Kennan and Smith also appearing as named coauthors.

Through January, Shriver held weekly strategy dinners at Avondale, where he brought nuclear disarmament activists and Kennedy Institute ethicists together with McNamara, Smith, and Kennan. At one dinner Averell Harriman spoke. Anthony Lake, who was present, recalled that the discussion turned to the question of

> whether you could contemplate tactical nuclear exchanges with the Soviet Union. There were various experts around the table, and I think a number of Soviet officials. So Harriman looks around the table, and says there are two kinds of people: "There are people who are insane, and believe that we could fight a limited nuclear war with the Soviet Union. And there are people who are sane, who believe that we cannot. I consider myself sane. Is there anyone here at the table who considers themselves insane?" And then he glared around the table, and of course nobody spoke up.

At an earlier meeting, in October, Bundy had mentioned that it would be useful to have the Catholic Church endorse the no-first-strike position Shriver's group was discussing. In February, Bryan Hehir told Shriver that, partially inspired by the conversations at Avondale, he had begun working up a draft of a pastoral letter—that is, a letter to all the Catholic dioceses in America—on nuclear war, which would echo the moral arguments being made in the *Foreign Affairs* article. "Dear Mac," Shriver wrote in late February. "I do remember at least the semblance of a snicker when you mentioned on the phone, 'Sarge, I understand you are going to deliver the Roman Catholic hierarchy.' That was last October. Now on March 1, I want you to see that I have delivered. What can I do for you and your fellow-authors now?"

For a full month before the article was published, the rumor in foreign policy circles was that it would be "a blockbuster." On April 7, 1982, the spring issue of *Foreign Affairs* was published. In "Nuclear Weapons and the Atlantic Alliance," Bundy, Kennan, McNamara, and Smith spelled out a sensible, centrist argument for a bold departure from current US nuclear policy: a total renunciation of first-strike capability. "We are four Americans who have been concerned over many years with the relation between nuclear weapons and the peace and freedom of the members of the Atlantic Alliance," the article began. "Having learned that each of us separately had been coming to hold new views on this hard but vital question, we decided to see how far our thoughts, and the lessons of our varied experiences, could be put together; the essay that follows is the result. It argues that a new policy can bring great benefits."

The article explained that until 1949, when the Soviets exploded their first nuclear device, the Western military strategy had been based on the assumption of American nuclear superiority. The ensuing thirty years had witnessed the massive arms race between the two superpowers, in which each strove to keep up with the other to maintain nuclear balance. Specific American military doctrine vis-à-vis its responsibilities to its NATO allies had evolved over the years, but "a major element in every doctrine has been that the United States has asserted its willingness to be the first—has indeed made plans to be the first if necessary—to use nuclear weapons to defend against aggression in Europe." But this policy, the authors wrote, had been formulated in the 1940s, when the American nuclear advantage was overwhelming. Now that any nuclear war "would be a ghastly catastrophe for all concerned," it was time to revisit the willingness to use a first strike.

The article could not be dismissed as the plaintive coos of mindless doves. It was written, after all, by four men who, as the *New York Times* reported, "had helped shape America's defense strategy for a generation." McNamara, although he had later turned against the war, had been the primary architect of the Vietnam War under JFK and LBJ. Bundy had been a national security adviser to both presidents and was known for his toughness and analytical rigor. Kennan had been the author of containment policy; although less hard-line than the advocates of "roll-back," he had certainly not been one to underestimate the global Communist threat. And Smith was no namby-pamby liberal; he had served as an arms negotiator on the SALT treaty under Richard Nixon.

The authors made their arguments in both moral and military terms. The idea of global nuclear war was too terrible to contemplate—and the responsibility for loosing such a fate upon the world extremely grave. Yes, the authors conceded, our Western European allies—especially West Germany—relied significantly upon the threat of an American nuclear strike to deter Soviet invasion. But the idea that a "limited" strike, aimed solely at repelling a Soviet ground attack, could be kept from escalating seemed absurd. Thus the solution was to beef up US and NATO *conventional* forces in Western Europe, so that those could be used as a deterrent, while the United States adopted the morally and strategically wise doctrine of no first use.

One reason the article attracted so much attention was that the authors renounced the doctrine of "flexible response" (which gave the US military the option of responding to conventional Soviet aggression with either conventional or nuclear weapons)—a policy that McNamara and Bundy themselves had been instrumental in formulating during the Kennedy administration. "We do not think that deterrence can safely be based forever on a doctrine which more and more looks to the people like either a bluff or a suicide pact."

Shriver's name did not appear on the article. He worried that he was already seen as too much of a peacenik, and he was not, as all of the named authors were, an official expert on foreign policy. Yet his imprint is all over the article; he was its progenitor, the instigator without whom it never would have happened. And the "Gang of Four" (as Bundy dubbed himself, Smith, Kennan, and McNamara) readily acknowledged Shriver's influence. Several days before the article appeared, McNamara wrote to him: "Sarge, as an unacknowledged author of this article, I hope you are pleased with the result. Many thanks for all you did to make it possible." Two months later, Kennan wrote to Shriver, "I must say that you touched off a notable series of events with the hospitality you gave us at your home last fall; and I greatly appreciate the self-effacing but greatly effective support you gave to the most important of all causes."

In the short term, the article had its desired effects: ongoing front-page coverage in major newspapers all over the world and heated public debate about the future direction of America's first-strike nuclear policy. Ted Kennedy seized the opportunity to reintroduce discussion of a "nuclear freeze" on the Senate floor.

Typically, Shriver turned his attention next to mobilizing the Catholic Church to speak out against America's first-strike policy. In June 1982 Bryan Hehir sent Shriver a first draft of a pastoral letter on nuclear war, by the National Conference of Catholic Bishops, "God's Hope in a Time of Fear," which Hehir had cowritten (anonymously) with Bruce Russett, a professor of political science at Yale.

Hehir's draft began by directing Catholics' attention to the Christian vision of peace, as embodied by the life of Christ, but then took up specific questions about "just war theory" and the right of self-defense in the nuclear era. Hehir acknowledged that both Christian tradition and just war theory allowed for limited self-defense and deterrent measures. Yet the advent of nuclear weapons had changed the moral calculus involved in deterrence; the danger of tragic consequences on a massive scale were great. "Christians cannot long live by the sign of the mushroom cloud." Thus, an "ethically acceptable defense policy" required, among other things, adopting the position first developed in Shriver's dining room and expressed in the *Foreign Affairs* article: The initiation of nuclear warfare should be cast out of the American military strategic repertoire.

Shriver sent Hehir a ten-page assessment of the draft. His criticisms were several.

First, he felt that Hehir's "just war" arguments relied too much on St. Augustine without sufficiently noting that when Augustine was theorizing about issues of war and self-defense in the fifth century, he was doing so in a context where wars were fought mainly by professionals, not draftees and conscripts, and where weapons of mass destruction were unimaginable.

Second, he wrote, he didn't "feel a real presence of Jesus of Nazareth penetrating this document." To be effective, Shriver believed, it needed to reflect the spirit of Jesus—and that spirit was more inclusive than what the letter reflected. The draft "seems to me . . . to be too much of a *Roman* document, too constricted by its emanation from our Western Catholic Church, without any note or harbinger of 'the world Church.'"

Hehir incorporated some of Shriver's changes, as well as those proposed by other people who had read the draft, and in early October the bishops publicly released the letter, explaining that it was just a draft and inviting further comment on it from the Reagan administration and from ethicists and military experts.

The circulation of the draft letter became front-page news, producing a furor of public debate. The most controversial part was the idea first broached at Avondale and then circulated in the *Foreign Affairs* article: the bishops' suggestion that the Reagan administration renounce a first-strike nuclear policy. Both Reagan's national security adviser, William P. Clark, and his defense secretary, Caspar Weinberger, responded with letters to the bishops, explaining the strategic necessity of America's retaining the first-strike option. A pledge not to use nuclear arms first, Clark wrote, might lead "the Soviets to believe that Western Europe was open to conventional aggression." Weinberger argued that given that the doctrine of deterrence had worked up until now—and given the horrific consequences should nuclear war break out—"the burden of proof must fall upon those who would depart from the sound policies of deterrence which have kept the peace for so long."

On October 25 the draft letter was excerpted in major national newspapers. "We find the moral responsibility of beginning nuclear war not justified by rational political objectives," the bishops said. The uproar this generated was significant; after all, the Reagan administration had made "flexible response" a cornerstone of its defense policy.

Administration officials and congressional Republicans reacted as angrily as they dared, given America's 55 million Catholic voters, asserting that the release of the draft letter just weeks before the 1982 congressional midterm elections was a political gambit designed to help the Democrats. Some GOP officials also argued that the Catholic Church had no business sticking its nose into public policy, and even that it was violating the constitutional separation of church and state.

As the National Conference of Catholic Bishops prepared to meet in Washington in November to discuss the draft letter, argument raged on the nation's op-ed pages about whether the Catholic Church was meddling where it didn't belong. ("The whole chorus pleads with the bishops to hie them back to the sacristy, where they can speculate ad infinitum on transubstantiation and other pinheaded if angelic topics," was how Georgetown University president Father Timothy Healy characterized the bulk of the criticism.) Shriver was still in active consultation with Hehir and felt strongly that the bishops did have the right and, indeed, the duty to involve themselves in moral questions of nuclear war. So he and Gerard Smith drafted a letter on the subject, and Shriver spent the early part of November recruiting prominent signatories.

On November 17 Shriver and Smith forwarded their letter to Ben Bradlee and A. M. Rosenthal, editors at the *Washington Post* and the *New York Times,* respectively. Acknowledging that some critics believed "that Bishops don't know about nuclear weapons and should leave the matter to military and civilian experts or governments," Shriver and Smith yet noted that "nuclear war could well spell the end of modern civilization." Wasn't it reasonable, then, to conclude that this prospect presented "a moral problem for religious leaders to be concerned about"? In the letter's most striking paragraph, Shriver and Smith wrote, "In pre-war Germany the Nazis charged the Jews were a threat to the German nation. Would it have been meddling in secular affairs had the Bishops of Germany and of the world addressed themselves directly to that abomination?" The letter was reported in the *Times* and sparked an editorial in the *Post* ("The Bishops Discover the Atom").

The next day, November 18, a committee of bishops who were meeting in Washington voted overwhelmingly in favor of endorsing the draft of the pastoral letter and sending it back to the National Conference of Catholic Bishops' committee on war and peace to be revised for presentation to the entire conference for a vote the following May. White House criticism had failed to soften the bishops' stance against a first strike.

Through all this, Shriver himself operated mostly behind the scenes. He was not the principal instigator of the bishops' letter. His byline had not graced the *Foreign Affairs* article the preceding spring. But he was the primary link between Bundy's Gang of Four article and Hehir's pastoral letter, the moral and logistical linchpin as the bishops moved toward a forceful moral statement on nuclear war. And now, although still behind the scenes (because he worried that his dovish reputation would hurt the cause), he had galvanized civilian support for the bishops' right to involve themselves in nuclear policy debates. "Thank you for being the stimulus which produced a very useful contribution to this important issue," former CIA director Colby wrote to him after the *Times* had reported on the statement Shriver and Smith had drafted. "It is a spirit like yours that produces results. The rest of us just go along and react to the people with real drive."

In the spring of 1983, the bishops circulated a third draft of their pastoral letter in preparation for the vote scheduled to take place on May 2. The bishops' letter, George Kennan wrote, "may fairly be described as the most profound and searching inquiry yet conducted by any responsible collective body into the relations of nuclear weaponry, and indeed of modern war in general, to moral philosophy, to politics, and to the conscience of the national state."

As the day of the vote approached, Shriver once again took it upon himself to marshal lay support—and continued to lobby Bryan Hehir for additional modifications to the text of the pastoral letter, right up until the moment of the vote.

The next morning, the bishops voted overwhelmingly (238–9) to endorse the letter, meaning that it would be published in Catholic publications and distributed in dioceses all over the country. Chicago's Joseph Cardinal Bernardin received a standing ovation when he urged his fellow bishops to seize the "new moment" in history to pose a "revolutionary challenge" to outmoded nuclear doctrines.

The only strident opposition from within the Conference of Bishops came from Philip Hannan, archbishop of New Orleans, who had served as a military chaplain to paratroopers in World War II. "You don't have the faintest idea of what you're talking about unless you've been in war," he said exasperatedly after a series of amendments he had proposed had been voted down. "If you're going to speak on weapons, you should know what you're talking about."

Reading Hannan's remarks, Shriver immediately telegrammed the archbishop at the Palmer House, where most of the bishops were staying. "Your Excellency," Shriver wrote, "having been in war like you, I can understand your feelings, but our times are bygone times. Proud as I am of what we did in World War II, I cannot help but agree that Einstein was right, and that the Popes have been right, when they have said that nuclear weapons require us to change our way of thinking about war."

"Isn't it the most wonderful time to be alive?" Shriver continued, with a hint of either facetiousness or profound ingenuousness. "For the first time since Noah, one can seriously think that the world could come to an end, that a new flood could occur nowadays for almost the same reasons the original flood occurred back in Noah's time. Not since the Caesars and the Huns have we had such tyrants to struggle against as the Bolsheviks. So, keep praying for us all, and if you are really desolate, come help me build an ark in Washington."

The pastoral letter was warmly received by the Catholic laity. According to the *New York Times*, "Many of the 50 million Catholics in the United States consider the bishops' action to be the boldest and most decisive step on social issues in the history of the American hierarchy." Historians today consider the document to be "the era's most influential challenge to American nuclear policy."

The nuclear freeze movement had multiple bases (Ted Kennedy, among others, had been promoting a nuclear freeze in the Senate for months, and religious leaders like Ted Hesburgh and Billy Graham had been touting a nuclear freeze since the 1970s), and the no-first-strike policy had been batted around in various academic settings over the years, although it had never found general public expression before the *Foreign Affairs* article. One of the common threads tying everything together and bringing nuclear issues to the fore was Shriver's behind-the-scenes activism. Shriver was the hidden nexus where the bishops and the defense experts came together. When Bundy wrote an essay in the *New York Review of Books* in June 1983, reviewing the pastoral letter along with the just-released Scowcroft Commission's report on strategic forces, he forwarded an advance copy to Shriver with a note. "Dear Sarge," Bundy wrote, "As the invisible hand behind the Gang of Four and probably behind the bishops too, you may enjoy this piece in which one of the former salutes all of the latter."

CHAPTER FORTY-EIGHT

Special Olympics, a Family Affair

⌒

A ll through the 1970s and early 1980s, the Special Olympics had been growing. After the success of the inaugural games at Chicago's Soldiers Field
in 1968, Eunice reprised the event in the same location two years later; this time,
twice as many mentally handicapped children participated, some of them traveling from beyond North America.

By the summer of 1975, as Sarge was preparing to launch his presidential
campaign, Eunice was busy planning the first official International Special
Olympic Games, to be held in Mount Pleasant, Michigan. Some 4,000 athletes
from seventeen countries participated, and the event was broadcast on a prime-
time ABC television special featuring Barbra Streisand. "Special Olympics" was
becoming a household name; Camp Shriver had officially gone national. That
same year, Congress passed a law mandating that "free, appropriate education"
programs—what came to be known as "special education"—for handicapped
children be implemented in America's public schools by 1978. Eunice had revolutionized the way the country dealt with the mentally retarded.

By 1980 the program that had begun in the backyard at Timberlawn had

375,000 annual participant-athletes and 350,000 volunteers each year. Every state had a Special Olympics chapter, as did some thirty foreign countries. In 1968, at the inaugural games, there had been just a few dozen people in the stands; in 1983, there were 65,000 spectators at Louisiana State University for the opening of the fifteenth-anniversary games.

Sarge, the "original number one skeptic" of the Special Olympics, found himself dedicating more and more time to his wife's work. Through the 1950s and 1960s, he had helped her fund research on the subject of the mentally retarded and recruit the best and brightest scientists. In the 1970s, as the program grew into a multimillion-dollar organization, he found himself helping his wife with marketing, fund-raising, and speechwriting, all in an unofficial capacity. Timothy Shriver says he recalls his astonishment when he discovered a bunch of his mother's old notebooks from the 1950s and 1960s—they were all marked up with ideas and suggestions in his father's handwriting.

On March 24, 1984, Ronald Reagan awarded Eunice the Presidential Medal of Freedom, America's highest civilian honor. "With enormous conviction and unrelenting effort," Reagan said,

> Eunice Kennedy Shriver has labored on behalf of America's least powerful people, the mentally retarded. Over the last two decades, she has been at the forefront of numerous initiatives on behalf of the mentally retarded, from creating day camps, to establishing a research center, to the founding of the Special Olympics program. Her decency and goodness have touched the lives of many, and Eunice Kennedy Shriver deserves America's praise, gratitude and love.

As Ana Bueno, a historian of the Special Olympics, has written, "To say that Mrs. Shriver almost single-handedly changed the way an entire world viewed people with mental retardation would not be far from the mark."

Of course, Eunice's "decency and goodness" were sometimes more evident in the abstract than they were to those who worked directly with her. "I think my mother does put the fear of God in most people," Maria Shriver has said. "She's a perfectionist. She's very demanding of herself and therefore, I think, demanding of the people around her. Dozens of people who have worked with Eunice—even those who say they like and respect her—say she can be, at times, impossible to deal with: ruthless, demanding, merciless. To those who couldn't stand up to her, working for her could be absolute misery. She regularly drove employees to exhaustion, tears, drink, or all three. For the uninitiated, merely being in her presence for a few minutes could be a stressful experience. She is so full of nervous energy that even in repose she seems to give off an audible whir, like an overheating computer or a household appliance.

Yet even today, well into her eighties, Eunice can be seen at Special Olympics games running beside handicapped athletes, exhorting them along or tenderly ministering to their wounds when they hurt themselves. Of all the Kennedy siblings, Eunice has always done the most, by far, for her disabled sister, Rosemary. And at fancy Kennedy cocktail parties in Hyannis Port or Washington, Eunice often seeks out the most evidently ill-at-ease or out-of-place guests and tries gently to draw them out of themselves or into the general conversation. Eunice is an extraordinarily complex beast. But she has in spades what her husband's political campaigns sometimes seemed to lack: the ruthlessness of her good intentions.

"I'VE GOT THIS SPORTS PROGRAM"

By the early 1980s Shriver was spending less and less time at his Fried, Frank office at the Watergate building and more and more time at the Special Olympics headquarters on K Street. With the election of Ronald Reagan, the character of Fried, Frank—like the general tenor of the country—began to change subtly. When Reagan was inaugurated in January 1981, down came many of the pictures of the firm's lawyers shaking hands with prominent Democrats; up went the pictures of the same lawyers shaking hands with prominent Republicans. Some of the most active liberal Democrats in the firm began to edge rightward—not into the Republican Party, necessarily, but from the liberal wing of the party toward the center. Max Kampelman, for instance, once a Hubert Humphrey liberal, was becoming more sympathetic to the neoconservatives; so, for that matter, was Dick Schifter. Meanwhile, a youngish, maniacally driven securities lawyer named Harvey Pitt (who would later serve an ill-starred turn as George W. Bush's SEC chief) had taken over the management of the Washington office from Kampelman. In keeping with the ethos of the eighties, Pitt slowly pushed the pro bono work and the Native American practice to the margins.

Shriver's own practice was thriving. But he had less clout in the executive branch of the federal government than he had had since before he moved to

Washington in 1961, and he no longer found the Fried, Frank culture to be as oriented toward public service as it once had been. As his son Timothy said, "His career as an active political leader ended after Carter's election. And after Reagan was elected, my father could see that, 'Okay, my next job's not going to be secretary of state.' So the balance in our family shifted from Daddy's work to Mommy's work."

By the mid-1980s, the Special Olympics had become a national phenomenon. The next step, Eunice believed, was to make it an *international* phenomenon. She had revolutionized the way Americans thought about the mentally handicapped—so why not revolutionize the way citizens of the world thought, too? To successfully expand the Special Olympics overseas, Eunice would need someone to lead the effort. Someone who had traveled widely and who had connections in the governments of many foreign countries; someone who had experience in diplomacy and in selling new concepts to new peoples; someone with experience running a large international program; someone with charisma. Someone, that is, like her husband.

In 1984 the Special Olympics board of directors elected Shriver president of the organization, and in 1986 he retired as a partner at Fried, Frank, Harris, Shriver & Jacobson. In 1990 he was appointed chairman of the Special Olympics Board, a position he held until the spring of 2003.

In the intervening two decades, Shriver—and, later, his son Timothy—were enormously successful in recruiting new countries to start their own chapters of the Special Olympics and in getting them to send their retarded athletes to the International Games. In 1985, Dublin, Ireland, hosted the first European Special Olympics; Austria, Bolivia, Monaco, New Zealand, Panama, Portugal, South Korea, Switzerland, Tunisia, and Yugoslavia all joined the Special Olympics that year, and the People's Republic of China sent observers to the United States to watch the International Games.

As the cold war ended, Czechoslovakia, Estonia, Hungary, Latvia, Lithuania, and Poland all joined the Special Olympics at the coaxing of Sarge Shriver. So, before it collapsed in 1991, did the Soviet Union. In February 1989 the Soviet Union hosted the largest "coaches' clinic" the Special Olympics had ever held. Shriver recruited his old friend and Communist Party leader Andrei Pavlov to become head of the Soviet chapter of the Special Olympics.

Shriver began his work at the Special Olympics as a dutiful husband. "It can't have been easy," his son Timothy says, "at age sixty-five, with his résumé, to be perceived as going to work for your wife at a charity." But he soon became passionate about it. "He became very excited about Special Olympics," Timothy Shriver says, "and he was especially excited about its geopolitical, historical, and political relevance, its ability to unite people from different backgrounds and different political systems. So he spent a great amount of time taking this message to foreign heads of state. He would say, 'I've got this sports program. And you'll probably be like me at first—you'll probably think it's crazy. But just go out and watch the games and you won't believe what happens!'"

Sarge was, Timothy continues, "starting to market the Special Olympics movement as a sort of post–World War II sociocultural paradigm. His rhetoric was almost like Lenin's. 'There's a new system out there and it doesn't have politicians at its head, or kings or queens or palaces. Rather it's got this kind of karmic aura that comes from these children with a mental disability playing sports.' My dad became obsessed with the power of this story he could tell, with the movement."

With Shriver as president and chairman of the board, and Eunice as guiding spirit, the Special Olympics became a Shriver family affair. In 1989 the Shrivers' youngest son, Anthony, founded Best Buddies (which might best be described as a Big Brother/Big Sister mentor program for the mentally retarded), starting the operation out of a small office at the Special Olympics headquarters. In just over a decade, Best Buddies has grown from a single chapter on one college campus into an international organization with 750 chapters serving 750,000 mentally handicapped children.

In 1987 the Shrivers' oldest son, Bobby, produced the first *Very Special Christmas* album, to raise money for the Special Olympics. Working with coproducers Jimmy and Vicki Iovine, Bobby assembled rock stars such as Bruce Springsteen, Whitney Houston, Madonna, Sting, John Mellencamp, U2, Stevie Nicks, Bob Seger, the Pointer Sisters, Bon Jovi, and the Pretenders, all of whom donated their talent. The seven *Very Special Christmas* albums, a *Jazz to the World* album, and a *World Christmas* album together have raised well over $50 million for the Special Olympics.

The Special Olympics became even more of a family affair when Timothy Shriver was hired by the board as president and CEO in 1996. The most devout of the five Shriver children, Timothy had followed his father and his brother Bobby to Yale for his undergraduate education, then went on to attend Catholic University in Washington, DC, where he received a master's degree in religion. He moved back to New Haven to teach in the public school system there and to launch a program called the New Haven Public Schools' Social Development Project. As a result of this work, Timothy was named a fellow at the Yale School Development Program; while there, he started a program that harked directly back to his father's launching of Head Start twenty years earlier: the Collaborative for the Advancement of Social and Emotional Learning at the Yale Child Study Center. The program brought together researchers, teachers, and social workers to promote early intervention programs in public schools across the country.

Timothy's professional and academic accomplishments clearly marked him as a smart and serious young man, but he was so young (still in his mid-thirties) that his being hired as president and CEO of Special Olympics would have been seen as pure nepotism had he not already distinguished himself to the board by saving the International Games in 1995.

The story of why the 1995 games needed saving began several years earlier. Early in 1992, Eunice had told Ted Kennedy that she planned to hold the next International Special Olympics Games in Dallas, in 1995. The city of Dallas had put together a generous, multimillion-dollar invitation to the Special Olympics, and Eunice was eager to accept it. But Ted, bruised by his recent involvement in the highly publicized rape trial of his nephew William Kennedy Smith (Steve Smith's son), and additionally traumatized by the release of Oliver Stone's film *JFK*, which showed—repeatedly and in slow motion—footage of Jack's death, said he wanted nothing to do with Dallas. In fact, Ted (along with many of the other Kennedys, although not the Shrivers) had made it a point never to return to Dallas after 1963. The city just held too many unpleasant memories.

Eunice reopened the search for a site for the 1995 games. The International Special Olympics Games require an enormous amount of planning, so a new site had to be settled upon fast. To the rescue came Timothy Shriver, who assembled a civic group in New Haven, Connecticut, that put together a proposal that the next games be held there. The proposal was accepted, and in 1995 Timothy presided over the New Haven games. With a $34 million budget, Timothy coordinated more than 7,000 mentally handicapped athletes and more than 60,000 volunteers—the largest sporting event in the world that year. The 1995 games were so successful that when the Special Olympics board of directors began searching for a replacement for Sarge as president and CEO, Timothy's name kept coming up. Both Sarge and Eunice expressed their skepticism about this idea—not because they thought Timothy wasn't up to the task, but because they worried about the perception of nepotism and because they didn't want Timothy to have to live in the very large shadows they cast. Yet the search committee, after duly considering his parents' objections, once again concluded that Timothy was the best available candidate. (The committee may also have realized that he was one of the few people on earth who could manage Eunice effectively.) In June 1996 Timothy Shriver succeeded his father as president and CEO of the Special Olympics.

Since 1996—as indeed since its inception in 1968—this multimillion-dollar charity has been run as a family affair. Eunice still serves as "founder and honorary chairman"; Timothy Shriver is president and CEO; and Sarge was chairman of the board. In June 2003, when his father stepped down as chairman of the Special Olympics board, Timothy took on that role as well.

SHRIVER AND SCHWARZENEGGER

Through the 1980s and 1990s, Special Olympics events often featured an incongruous sight: the enormous Arnold Schwarzenegger pumping iron with mentally retarded children.

By the time Schwarzenegger married Maria Shriver, on April 26, 1986, after dating her for nine years, he had already traveled an enormous distance in his life. Born in a small village in Austria in 1947, Schwarzenegger had grown up in relative poverty. Deciding he wanted to transcend his rural origins, Schwarzenegger found his way out through bodybuilding, a then-obscure quasi-sport in which competitors vie to have the biggest muscles and most impressively sculpted physique. Schwarzenegger started competing in Austria and soon was winning competitions throughout Europe.

In London in 1967 Schwarzenegger won the Mr. Universe contest—the bodybuilding equivalent of winning the tennis championship at Wimbledon or being part of the winning football team at the Super Bowl. At twenty years of age, he was the youngest Mr. Universe in the history of the competition. But his ambition was not slaked. In 1968 he moved to the United States to seek greater fame and fortune.

"From the first, Arnold loved America," his biographer Wendy Leigh wrote in 1990. He became a businessman and entrepreneur, setting up a successful mail-order business that sold various bodybuilding products. Already famous in the arcane world of bodybuilding, his celebrity began to seep into the mainstream.

In 1974 the journalist Charles Gaines published *Pumping Iron*, a book about bodybuilding that featured many stories about Arnold. Although the book was ignored by the mainstream media, it went on to become an underground classic and, in 1977, it spawned the documentary movie of the same title, which premiered at the Plaza Theatre in New York on January 18, 1977. "Although the film was billed as a documentary study of bodybuilding," Wendy Leigh writes, "there was no question whatever that it was, in reality, a showcase for Arnold Schwarzenegger." Movie audiences marveled at him—not just at his remarkable physique but at his peculiar blend of ingenuous charm and Machiavellian scheming. America loved him. "He was," Leigh writes, "a charmer, a champion, an endearingly arrogant winner."

It was in August 1977, the year his celebrity began to bloom, that he met Maria Shriver at the Robert F. Kennedy tennis tournament in Forest Hills, New York. In the tournament, Schwarzenegger was paired with Rosie Grier, the actor and former football player who had worked on both of Sarge's campaigns. (Grier had also been at the Ambassador Hotel in Los Angeles in 1968 when RFK was shot, wrestling the assassin, Sirhan Sirhan, to the ground after he had fired his deadly shots.) Sarge and Eunice had no idea who this behemoth on the tennis court with Grier was. When Maria, who had just graduated from Georgetown University, saw him, however, she was intrigued. "I could see that Arnold was, like my father, kind of an outsider," Maria recalled. "I wanted in a husband somebody who was going to deliver me from the madness of the whole Kennedy thing. I looked at Arnold as someone who had his own kind of dream, who was a dreamer, who was different." As Schwarzenegger put it, "I think what made her fall in love with me was that I was the rebel—the opposite of the establishment" that the Kennedy family represented. "Bodybuilding was a sport that was not socially accepted by the Kennedys or Shrivers, like being a golf player or a tennis player. I was a symbol of a different world for Maria. She went for a rebel so she could defy the Washington scene."

In 1977 Schwarzenegger was just beginning to make his mark as an actor, climbing through the ranks in Hollywood. (That same year he acted in his first feature film, a now-forgotten movie called *Stay Hungry*, for which he won a Golden Globe award for "best acting debut.") But the Kennedy family stood for the one major goal he had yet to pursue: political power. Earlier that year, Schwarzenegger had told a German news magazine, "When one has money, one day it becomes less interesting. And when one is also the best in film, what can be more interesting? Perhaps power. Then one moves into politics and becomes governor or president or something."

For this Austrian boy of humble origins, the Kennedy family represented the epitome of American political power. Although he had arrived in the United States after the death of JFK, Schwarzenegger had lived in the country long enough to know that the Kennedy family was political royalty. So when Maria Shriver and Caroline Kennedy invited him back to the Kennedy compound at Hyannis Port after the tennis tournament, Arnold eagerly accepted.

Sarge would later say that he instinctively liked the burly Austrian from the very beginning. Maria recalls that, of all the Kennedys and Shrivers, her father was the most accepting of Arnold when she first brought him to Hyannis Port for weekends. But at first, Sarge was wary of Schwarzenegger. Shriver knew little about the worlds of bodybuilding and Hollywood in which Arnold traveled, and what little he did know made him nervous. "Sargent was not really aware of the latest cutting-edge stars or the best action movies, so when we first met he had definitely been not much aware of me at all, beyond what his kids may have told him," Schwarzenegger said. "So obviously he wasn't thrilled at first, when I began dating his daughter."

Some years later, Maria would tell her father that she had known almost from the moment she met Arnold that he was the man she wanted to marry. Shriver decided he liked the oversized Austrian, but he still wasn't sure how he felt about the man dating his daughter. "I think in the beginning," Schwarzenegger said, "he was worried about my lifestyle." Maria remembers a letter her father had sent her very soon after she started dating Schwarzenegger. Arnold was living in California, building his film career; Maria was in Baltimore, starting her television career. One time, Arnold invited her out to Los Angeles for the weekend and offered to pay her airfare. When Sarge learned of this, he wrote his daughter a long letter explaining, as Maria recalled, "why I should never allow a man to pay for an airline ticket for me, because that signaled to a man that he could 'buy' me." "Men do this sort of thing, they want sex, they're going to pay for your airline tickets, and then you'll feel beholden to them," Maria recalled her father writing. "Don't ever accept that. Be your own woman. Pay for your own stuff."

"I've carried that message from my father my whole life. I always remember my dad saying, 'Make your own way, make your own money. Never let anybody feel that they own you.' Even after I married Arnold and people were telling me I could quit my job, because Arnold was doing so well, I remembered what my father told me."

Sarge wasn't the only one who was initially dubious about Maria's relationship with Arnold. Although "in public neither the Kennedys nor the Shrivers have ever made any negative comments about Maria's relationship with Arnold," Wendy Leigh has written, "in the early days, there were those who declared that he was the Kennedys' worst setback since Chappaquiddick."

Schwarzenegger, for his part, became deeply attracted to her beauty and her indomitable will, which she had inherited from her mother; he also quickly came to respect his girlfriend's parents. He readily allowed Eunice to talk him into becoming the "honorary weight-lifting coach" for the Special Olympics. As it turned out, weight-lifting was a highly effective morale booster for the mentally handicapped, because, starting from very low weights, training can produce rapid improvement.

In 1982 Schwarzenegger starred in *Conan the Barbarian*, which, despite being roundly panned by critics, was a box office bonanza, the top-grossing film of the summer. *People* magazine published a feature titled "Arnold Schwarzenegger Conquers as Conan and Maybe as a Kennedy In-Law." (A family friend recalled looking on in bewilderment as a discussion between Eunice and Arnold about "the theology and ethics of *Conan the Barbarian*" became increasingly heated.) In 1984, the year after he was granted American citizenship, Schwarzenegger starred in *The Terminator*, a movie that not only produced huge box office revenues but also attracted positive critical notice. He was now officially a huge star, an A-list celebrity.

Eunice and Sarge exploited his celebrity fully. Schwarzenegger became a fixture at the International Special Olympic Games every few years, and many of his movie premieres, beginning with *Twins* in 1988, have doubled as fund-raisers for the charity.

Like Eunice and Sarge, Maria and Arnold dated for a long time before becoming engaged. Finally, on August 10, 1985, they announced their engagement. They were to be married on April 26, 1986, in Hyannis Port.

It seemed impossible that any wedding could top the glitz, glamour, and raw celebrity power of Sarge and Eunice's 1953 nuptials. At that wedding, there had been senators and cardinals, Supreme Court justices and gangsters, millionaires and movie stars, all paying their obeisance to Joseph P. Kennedy and the growing political prospects of the Kennedy family.

Thirty-three years later, Joe Kennedy was gone, Rose Kennedy was nearing her 100th birthday, and Jack and Bobby were dead. The family's remarkable political future, in distant prospect in 1953 (when Jack had just been elected senator from Massachusetts), was now a part of still-living history. The story of the Kennedy family had hardened into American political legend. Ted remained an active liberal Democrat, of course, and a fixture of the Senate, and RFK's son Joe Kennedy now occupied Jack's old Massachusetts congressional seat. But after Sarge's defeats in 1972 and 1976, and Ted's failed challenge against Jimmy Carter in the 1980 primary, the New Frontier seemed dead and buried for good. Yet the wedding of Arnold and Maria would recapture the buzz and ferment, if not the substance, of the New Frontier era.

In late April, Arnold flew by private jet to Hyannis Port from Mexico, where he was in the midst of shooting the movie *Predator*. Maria came up from New York City, where she had recently landed one of the most prestigious jobs in television, as anchor of the *CBS Morning News*. On Friday, April 25, Maria's matron-of-honor, Caroline Kennedy, and Caroline's mother, Jacqueline, hosted a luncheon for the wedding party. By Saturday, placid little Hyannis Port was bustling with celebrities; for all the media camped outside the compound, it could have been November 1960.

Of all the disparate red-carpet celebrities present—from Tom Brokaw to Quincy Jones, Queen Noor to Barbara Walters (President Reagan and Pope John Paul II were unable to attend and sent their regrets)—none made more of an impression on the older Kennedy generation than Grace Jones, Schwarzenegger's co-star from *Conan the Destroyer*, and her date, Andy Warhol. Jones, tall, sleek, strong, and black, arrived midway through the ceremony, stepping out of her limousine in a clingy outfit that kept her, just barely, from violating laws against public indecency; at her side, small, frail, owlish, and pale white, was Warhol.

The ceremony was held at the local Catholic church, St. Francis Xavier, the white clapboard structure where Sarge, Rose, and usually Eunice attended daily Mass every summer. Sarge, Eunice, and Ted Kennedy all gave readings from the Bible; Oprah Winfrey, Maria's colleague from her early years in television, read a poem. "It was the most beautiful wedding ceremony I've ever seen in my life," Ethel Kennedy said.

At the reception Stephen Hesnan, the Shriver family's chef, unveiled the wedding cake he had baked, 7 feet tall and 425 pounds, modeled after pictures he had seen of the 8-foot cake at Sarge and Eunice's wedding. Arnold presented his new in-laws with a gift: a silk-screened portrait of Maria done in vivid colors by Andy Warhol. (It hangs in the Shrivers' Potomac, Maryland, living room today, at right angles from a photograph of Pope John Paul II.) After dancing with Eunice and Jackie Kennedy Onassis, Arnold announced to the assembled guests, " I love her and will always take care of her. Nobody should worry."

After his marriage to Maria, Schwarzenegger continued to be active in the Republican Party. He campaigned with George H. W. Bush in 1988, and in 1990 he was named chairman of President Bush's Council on Physical Fitness. It was in the early 1990s that his name started coming up regularly in conversation as a possible GOP candidate for governor in California. "Conan the Republican" the pundits called him. But for more than a decade he remained coy about his political ambitions. His flirtations with California politics were somewhat reminiscent of his father-in-law's in Illinois through the 1950s and 1960s.

When Schwarzenegger's gubernatorial ambitions became more serious, thanks to California's recall initiative in the summer of 2003, his father-in-law encouraged them. "You're making me very happy," Shriver wrote to him on July 11. "I can't think of any person today that I would rather have in office. If I were a resident of California, I hope you realize that I'd be voting Republican for the first time ever!"

In some bizarre, not wholly apt way, Schwarzenegger represents the apotheosis of Shriver's ambition. Sarge genuinely thinks highly of Arnold. He sees in his son-in-law many of the traits he admired in his father-in-law, Joe Kennedy: the intelligence; the boldness verging on brazenness; the charisma; and, above all, the drive to rise far above humble origins. "I would say certainly the biggest influence in Arnold's life has been Daddy and Mummy, which is kind of ironic," Maria says, because although her parents are dyed-in-the-wool Democrats and devout Catholics, her husband is a Republican. "Arnold is interested in ideas and creation and dreaming; he's a force that way, like my dad."

"Eunice and Sargent are like my second parents," Schwarzenegger says, "and I have drawn my deepest inspiration from Sargent's work and advice." Schwarzenegger says that he could tell, when he first started dating Maria, that Sarge believed he should be doing something more substantial with his life than just acting in movies. "I could feel it," he says, "the feeling that, you know, we already have an actor [Lawford] in the family and he didn't do much. 'You're an expert in health and fitness,' Sargent would tell me, 'so why don't you continue your education and work in that area.' I remember him just pushing me and pushing me."

As Schwarzenegger started moving into public service and then into electoral politics, he used Sarge as a sounding board and a principal source of advice. "I would sit there for hours and just pump him for information," Schwarzenegger says, "because I think this is a rare opportunity to talk to someone that has worked with the Kennedy administration, the Johnson administration, and the Nixon administration. Also, he gave me a glimpse of what it's like to work with politicians"—for instance, LBJ and Nixon—"who may not think highly of your family." As a Republican married into America's foremost Democratic family, this was a situation with which Schwarzenegger knew he himself might someday have to contend.

Despite his allegiance to the Republican Party, Schwarzenegger's politics have clearly been affected by his association with the Shrivers. He explicitly credits Shriver with teaching him the value of building partnerships between the public and private sectors, which had been a signature of the War on Poverty. Schwarzenegger's first serious foray into politics in his own right, in 2002, was in support of an initiative to provide after-school programs to all California's children—a policy idea that followed clearly in the pattern of Head Start. And on August 8, 2003, two days after Schwarzenegger declared his gubernatorial candidacy on the *Tonight Show with Jay Leno*, the *Washington Post* quoted one of Schwarzenegger's former movie producers as calling him a "Shriver Republican." "You can't be married to Maria Shriver and spend all that time in Hyannis Port and be a continuous-tax-cuts-for-the-rich monomaniac," Matthew Miller, a prominent Democratic newspaper columnist, wrote a week later.

On October 7, 2003, Schwarzenegger was elected governor of California in a landslide. At his victory party that evening, the governor-elect stood alongside his wife, flanked by Bobby, Timothy, Mark, Anthony, Eunice, and Sarge— the whole Shriver clan had turned out to support Maria and her husband. For his part, Schwarzenegger proudly claimed association with the Shriver family— even though his wife's uncle, Ted Kennedy, had already signaled his dismay with the Republican's victory. "These are all Shrivers standing behind me," Schwarzenegger said during his victory speech, gesturing over his shoulder.

At some level, surely, it must be disappointing to Shriver that the first man into public office from among his children's generation is not his son Anthony (whom Florida Democrats have tried several times to recruit to run for mayor of Miami) or his son Mark (who lost a tough Democratic primary race for Maryland's Eighth Congressional District in 2002) but Schwarzenegger—a Republican and an in-law, not a Shriver by blood.

Yet Shriver knows all about being "only" an in-law. There is a certain fitting irony that, as he fades into the twilight, he should once again find himself being eclipsed by an in-law.

In 1994 President Bill Clinton recognized Shriver for his life's work, awarding him the Presidential Medal of Freedom, making Sarge and Eunice the only husband and wife in history to have each won this highest civilian award individually. "Sargent Shriver," Clinton said at the awards ceremony,

> is the man who launched the Peace Corps thirty-three years ago. Because of his creativity, his idealism, his brilliance, the Peace Corps remains one of the most popular government initiatives ever undertaken. From the time he and his wife, Eunice, helped to organize a Conference on Juvenile Delinquency for the Attorney General in 1947 to his efforts for public education in the 1950s, to his leadership of Head Start and Legal Services and now the Special Olympics, Sargent Shriver has awakened millions of Americans, including many in this administration, to the responsibilities of service, the possibilities of change, and the sheer joy of making the effort.

Yet, despite this recognition, along with dozens of honorary degrees, named buildings, and other such honors (in 2002 Congress appropriated $10 million to start a Sargent Shriver Peace Center), Shriver, when he is remembered at all, is still viewed mainly through the prism of the Kennedy family. In an early episode of *Seinfeld*, the zeitgeist-defining sitcom of the 1990s, the character Elaine asks, apropos of nothing, "Whatever happened to Sargent Shriver? Is he still with the Kennedys? You don't hear much about him these days? Is he out of the loop?"

Mark Shields, the political commentator, has reflected, "I'm one of those (and I'm sure I'm not alone) who believe that if Sarge had married Susie Glotz—and I'm not in any way disparaging his choice of a wife—he would have been governor of Illinois. I think he would have been a national figure in his own right. I think marrying into the Kennedy family really hurt him. And once he was in the family, his own independent ambition was more a curse than a blessing."

Once, on a plane flight during the 1972 campaign, Shriver was reading a newspaper account of an appearance he had made the night before when he dropped the paper onto his lap in frustration. The article had identified him as "the brother-in-law" of Ted Kennedy. "I used to be Jack Kennedy's brother-in-law," he said in exasperation. Then it was Robert Kennedy's brother-in-law. "Now I'm Ted Kennedy's brother-in-law. I suppose in twenty years I'll be the uncle of Robert F. Kennedy Jr." Right idea, wrong in-law: It is not as the uncle of RFK Jr. that he is now primarily known, but as the father-in-law of Arnold Schwarzenegger.

CHAPTER FORTY-NINE

Faith and Hope

In "The Lightweight Question," written after the 1976 election, Colman McCarthy said:

> Shriver was a passionate reader of philosophy, theology, and literature, one who sought to make the connection real between daily politics and the resources of the inner life. It was not a pose of piety, but an effort to go out of himself to seek communion with minds and spirits larger and deeper than his own. It is standard American politics for public men to display their reverent side, but as Nixon exemplified with his White House prayer services, what we get is not religion but religiosity. . . . Shriver, both in 1972 [and 1976] kept his interior life where it should be: hidden and within.

Shriver's deep faith and his salesman's enthusiasm might have led him to become a proselytizer or evangelist. Yet he never traveled that route. Shriver, now in his late eighties, remains serious about his Catholicism. He attends Mass daily, goes to confession regularly, carries rosary beads in his pocket, and reads widely in Catholic literature—everything from Catholic periodicals such as *Commonweal* and the *National Catholic Reporter* to abstruse theological tracts and works of biblical exegesis. Yet he retains an open-mindedness and a curiosity about other faiths—and even the lack of faith—that many of his Muslim, Jewish, Hindu, and atheist friends find disarming. He still thrills to the back-and-forth of theological discourse across faiths and denominations.

But for all his privacy about his own faith, and for all his broad tolerance of other faiths, the root of Shriver's self-concept is as a lay Catholic, as a non-clerical servant of God, who has tried always to model his life after the ethics of Jesus as expressed in the Gospels. This has not been a passive pursuit. Ever since he was a schoolboy, Shriver's bedrock system of values has never changed: "Christian, Aristotelian, optimistic, and American" was how he characterized himself in the *Yale Daily News* in the late 1930s, a description that applies with equal accuracy today. Each of those four qualities is important, but it is the Christian in him—and the Catholic in him—that underlies and inflects the rest. He is always asking himself, "Am I living my life as Christ would want me to?" "You cannot separate Daddy from his faith," Maria Shriver says. "Faith has been the motivating factor in his whole life. Maybe this sounds kind of corny, but he totally looks to Jesus as his role model. In tough times, he looks to Jesus."

There are many breeds of religiosity among the devout, cutting across faiths and denominations: the fire-and-brimstone sermonizer; the zealot; the Puritan; the holier-than-thou; the power-hungry; the ritualistic; the superstitious; the lonely; the desperate; the God-is-a-tool-for-realizing-my-desires instrumentalist; and the skeptic, to name just a few partial variations. Shriver is none of these. Nor, strictly speaking, has he signed on as a man of faith for the most common of reasons—for a ticket to the afterlife or to heaven (although he aspires to get there). Rather, what Shriver gets from his faith is less the solace of the Lord's presence, less the promise of transcendence in the hereafter (although he does derive both of those qualities from his faith), than a mobilizing vision for action here on earth. It is telling that in the 1930s Shriver invited Dorothy Day to speak at Yale. Shriver's Catholicism is in some ways analogous to Day's: rooted in the ethics of the Christian Gospels; dedicated to working toward peace, social justice, and redemption of suffering *here on earth* (as opposed to in the afterlife); and concerned especially with easing the plight of the poor and the disabled.

As Christopher Lydon put it in a *New York Times* article during the 1972 presidential campaign, "Sargent Shriver is a Roman Catholic candidate of an unfamiliar sort, a man who slips quietly out to mass many mornings of the campaign and works a little harder because of the thought that a good day's effort can be a form of prayer." Indeed, much of Eunice and Sarge's endless appetite for work comes from their belief in the Benedictine dictum that "to work is to pray." According to Catholic tradition, one of Shriver's closest Catholic friends says, "you can choose either the contemplative or the active life. In the contemplative life, you try to make yourself a better person through reflecting and praying. In the active life, you emulate Jesus and try to sanctify the world. Sarge has chosen the active life." Almost everything about Shriver—his politics, his moral values, the decisions he made or failed to make, the way he thinks—can be better understood in the context of his powerful and abiding faith.

Sarge has sometimes expressed what might be called a conservative relationship to Catholic tradition: a deep respect for the institution of the Roman Catholic Church, for its hierarchy and traditions. This is expressed most obviously in Sarge's affiliation with Opus Dei, a "zealously orthodox" Catholic lay organization founded in Spain in 1928 that espouses a highly traditional (some would say retrograde or even reactionary) version of Catholic moral values. Many liberal Catholics dislike or are suspicious of Opus Dei, resenting its influence within the Church and considering it more of a secretive fraternal organization, like the Freemasons, than a real Catholic organization. The theologian Hans Kung, one of the progressive theologians the Shrivers gathered around them in the 1960s and 1970s, says that Opus Dei is "medieval" in its outlook; he can't understand how the Shrivers, who were once so progressive in their views, could have become associated with it.

Yet Sarge's association with Opus Dei—he is not a full-blown member—makes some sense. Its retrograde, antifeminist principles aside, the focus of the organization is on "sanctifying the world"—the idea that ordinary Catholic citizens, going about their mundane daily lives, can achieve holiness through hard work and living by Christian ethics. Even for lay people, Opus Dei stresses, work should be a spiritual calling. In its emphasis on energetic action by the laity, Opus Dei naturally appeals to Shriver. Some of its maxims include: "I don't understand how you can call yourself a Christian and lead such an idle, useless life. Have you forgotten Christ's life of toil?"; "Work without resting"; and "To be idle is something inconceivable in a man who has apostolic spirit."

Today, it seems in some ways that Sarge has come full circle: fifty-five years ago, he was working for Eunice in Washington, and now he is doing so again. To those with a cynical view of the Kennedy family, this confirms their worst impression of Sarge's relationship with it. He does the family dirty work—then gets out of the way while others get the credit. In this view, Sarge can never escape being Eunice's hen-pecked husband, the dutiful servant to her overweening needs.

Two images, bookending the Shriver marriage, reflect this point of view. One is of their first apartment. Eunice had a suite of elaborately appointed rooms, which overlooked Lake Michigan. Sarge occupied what used to be the servant's quarters: a small, spare room in the back of the apartment, its only adornment a crucifix hanging over his bed. The second image is of Sarge in his office at the Special Olympics. He is meeting with, say, Hosni Mubarak, the president of Egypt, or with a reporter from the *New York Times*, when a call from Eunice interrupts. His physical bearing shifts from authoritative to deferential. "I'm sorry," Sarge will say. "This meeting is over. I have to do something for my wife." "It's a master-slave relationship," jokes Arnold Schwarzenegger.

To view Sarge as a hen-pecked husband and Eunice as an overbearing Kennedy wife, however, is to succumb to a pinched, narrow view of a rich and complex relationship. It has been, for more than half a century, a political, romantic, and religious partnership. Sarge regards serving Eunice as serving God; Eunice regards Sarge as her spiritual and intellectual anchor. Theirs is a formidable marriage.

In recent years, both Sarge and Eunice have had to deal with health problems. In 1988 Sarge had triple bypass surgery for a heart condition, and he underwent radiation treatment for prostate cancer. Yet he refused to let that slow him down. He continued flying around the world "as if jet lag did not exist." His doctors were concerned about the threat his frenetic lifestyle posed to his health, especially while he was recovering from heart surgery, but they could not persuade him to slow down. Finally his family asked Schwarzenegger to provide a bodybuilder/babysitter, who would forcibly prevent Sarge from overexerting himself. Yet, as soon as his doctors deemed him ready, Sarge was back at work and beating men half his age on the tennis court.

Sarge's health problems pale in comparison to his wife's. Yet Eunice is like the Timex watch in the old advertising campaign: She takes a licking but she keeps on ticking. In recent years, much attention has been directed to the serious health issues her brother Jack suffered, including when he was in the White House. JFK suffered from Addison's disease, colitis, and back trouble. Eunice has endured all these ailments and others as well—plus multiple hospitalizations for injuries suffered in car crashes and other accidents.

At least twice in the last dozen years, Sarge has summoned priests to administer last rites to his wife. And each time not only the priest but the medical doctors have gone away shaking their heads at her seemingly inhuman fortitude.

Part of the problem is that Eunice has no patience with getting from point A to point B; she wants to be at point B instantaneously, and if she is going to have to waste time driving somewhere, she is going to make the most of it, talking on the phone, dictating memos and speeches, and looking through her files. In January 1991, driving south to her office along Canal Road, a narrow, winding route in Washington, DC, she collided at high speed with a van. Her car was destroyed; it took the jaws of life to extract her from the crumpled wreck. When Sarge got the call from the state police, he was told it was doubtful she would live. She suffered two broken arms, a shattered elbow, a crushed hip socket, massive internal bleeding, and lacerations all over her body, but she survived. "By all the laws of time and nature," one Kennedy family biographer has written, the accident should have left the sixty-nine-year-old Eunice "if not a partial invalid then at least relegated to a cautious and sedentary old age." But within days, she was making calls from her bed at Johns Hopkins Hospital to her staff at the Special Olympics, making her usual, impossible-to-satisfy-quickly-enough demands.

In 2000, Eunice's longtime adrenal problems finally necessitated the removal of part of her pancreas. Doctors wanted to do the procedure immediately, but Eunice insisted on delaying the surgery until after the Best Buddies fund-raiser that year, which was held at the Shrivers' home in Potomac, Maryland, so that she could help her son Anthony raise money for his program. She went into Johns Hopkins Hospital for the procedure the next day. She came home after ten days but then ended up back in the hospital with major complications, including a raging infection, and several days later she plunged into a coma. Anticipating her death, television and radio news programs broadcast specials on her life, with the commentators frequently referring to her in the past tense, as though she were already gone. After the coma had lasted for several days, the doctors told Sarge that her chances for recovery were practically nonexistent. Several times in the first week of her coma, she hovered near death. Shriver summoned a priest to administer last rites.

Yet astonishingly, after several weeks, Eunice began to stir. One day, Sarge swore he saw her open one of her eyes. He called for the doctors, but when they examined her they told him he must have imagined it. Her coma persisted. Over the next several days, however, Eunice's eyes began to flutter, and one day they flickered open for a full ten seconds. Her eyes closed again, but the next day they opened again, for longer this time, and within a few days after that she was clearly conscious, although not yet speaking. Within a week after that she was sitting up and talking. The doctors told Sarge they couldn't understand it; it was "miraculous," they said. Several weeks later she was at home and starting to eat solid food.

Eunice's colleagues and employees at the Special Olympics were relieved she had survived, but if they were hoping that her near-death experience would soften her, they were disappointed. Within weeks she was barking orders into the phone and had her secretary working full-time out of the house. Rather than slowing her down, the confrontation with her own mortality had, if anything, caused her to speed up. There was still so much work to be done.

Over the summer of 2001, the day before a planned eightieth-birthday celebration in Hyannis Port, Eunice was involved in another car accident. This time, she shattered one of her legs. The party was cancelled, and she was bedridden for weeks. And still she refused to slow down. Once again her secretarial staff was summoned to her home, and she worked full days from her bedroom, writing memos, receiving visitors, barking orders at her secretary, and yelling into the telephone.

Sarge did his best to keep up with her, but by the end of 2002, at age eighty-seven, he was beginning to have a hard time keeping pace. His memory betrayed him sometimes, and his mind wasn't as sharp as it used to be. In early 2003, he learned he had Alzheimer's disease. "It's great," he said of the diagnosis, typically cheerful. "It finally gives me an excuse for not remembering everyone's name." There was some debate within the family circle about whether to publicize his illness. Shriver himself had no problem being forthright, but there were those who worried about the specter of Ronald Reagan or Charlton Heston, whose Alzheimer's diagnoses seemed to diminish them in the public eye and to cast retrospective doubt on some of their earlier ideas and pronouncements. (When I asked Shriver about this issue, he said it wasn't a concern to him. "Reagan had a much worse affliction than I did," he said. "Hard-core conservatism. Whatever I've got now, I never suffered from that.") But because Shriver wanted to remain actively involved in Special Olympics work, his family deemed it best that he go public with the diagnosis; that way, any statements he made would not necessarily be taken as the official writ of the Special Olympics.

In June, when he officially stepped down as chairman of the Special Olympics, he sent a letter disclosing his illness to dozens of his closest friends. It is a remarkable document, totally representative of its author: cheerful, optimistic, forward looking, and a call-to-arms. "Dear Good Friend," he wrote.

> Please forgive this impersonal correspondence, but time is of the essence! After all, I will turn 88 later this year and in a few short weeks I will retire from what has been a full-time position for me—Chairman of Special Olympics International. Who knows when the next assignment, if any, might be? . . .
>
> The joy, the challenge, and the results of Special Olympics are one of the reasons I consider myself to be "the luckiest man on earth." While I will step down from my formal responsibilities, I will never stop doing my part to encourage the world to see the miraculous power of what Eunice has given to all of us. Her creation, Special Olympics, has given me pleasure and fulfillment beyond description, and I will be grateful for as long as I live.
>
> Nevertheless, it is time to start a new chapter, and at 87, I'm hoping I still have a few chapters left! For all these years, I have done my best to challenge others. Now, I want to *challenge myself!* I want to keep my ideas fresh so I can actively take part in public debate.
>
> But as we all come to learn sooner or later, desire is only part of the equation. To play a role, one needs not only desire, but skills too; not only a vision, but the ability to put it into action; not only a willingness to work tirelessly, but the friends and allies who together can create the results that make a difference. All of these, I have had, but time has brought unwelcome news too, and for me, it's been tough to accept. Recently, the doctors told me that I have symptoms of the early stages of Alzheimer's Disease! From my point of view, this disease means one thing, and one thing only: my memory is poor. It's a handicap, and

it's a challenge. But it does not mean that I am ready to stop challenging myself, *or you*. . . .

I have no doubt that the world needs to be challenged again—challenged to search for the pathways to peace, challenged to overcome the horrors of poverty and neglect in this country and around the world, challenged to build the international institutions of cooperation that we failed to build in the 20th century. Hopefully, I can join others in calling on our leaders to do better. I know in my heart that we can.

Shriver also wrote that he looked forward to spending time with his fifteen grandchildren and to continuing to marvel at his wife's ongoing work. "I would gladly scrap any work of my own simply to watch her in action! Age has neither dimmed her anger at injustice nor her humor in overcoming any obstacles the foolhardy throw across her path. What a joy to be part of her whirlwind!"

"I look forward to being in touch with as many of you as possible," he concluded. "If names are slow to come to me, please forgive me. . . . Remind me of the great times we've had and of the great work waiting to be done. I'm eager to rise to face new challenges, whatever they may be."

On receiving the letter, Mark Shields called Mickey Kantor, President Clinton's former secretary of commerce. After working together on Shriver's 1972 campaign, Kantor and Shields had remained friends and fellow Shriver admirers ever since. Kantor had recently taken a twelve-hour plane flight with Shriver. "In twelve hours," Kantor marveled to Shields, "Sarge never once reminisced about the good old days or the past. Everything was about what we had to do—today and tomorrow—about the challenges all of us still have to meet." Shields recounted this conversation in a column in the *Washington Post*, "A Champion of Life," in which he remarked how Shriver's announcement that he had Alzheimer's had "not so much as a syllable of self-pity."

Shriver's faith, Shields continued,

which he lives, is reflected in the Gospel of St. Matthew in the parable: "I was hungry and you gave me food, I was thirsty and you gave me drink, a stranger and you welcomed me, naked and you clothed me, ill and you cared for me, in prison and you visited me." To which the listeners respond, "Lord, when did we see you hungry and feed you, or thirsty and give you drink? When did we see you a stranger and welcome you, or naked and clothe you? When did we see you ill or in prison and visit you?" And the answer, which has inspired and energized Sargent Shriver well into his ninth decade: "Amen, I say to you whatever you did for one of these least brothers of mine, you did for me."

Sarge was wrong. He is not the luckiest man on the face of the earth. That distinction is shared by all of us whose lives he has touched.

Shriver hasn't stopped moving forward—challenging, exhorting, inspiring. Several days after sending the letter to his friends, announcing his diagnosis, he traveled to Ireland with his family for the 2003 International Olympic Games, where as usual he dazzled everyone with his charm, energy, and good humor. Maria Shriver was amazed. "I do not know how my parents have so much endless energy," she said. "I really do not know."

> [During the International Games], you have to get up at six o'clock in the morning and deal with thousands of people every day and they're pulling on you, and asking for photographs, and making demands, and it's ninety degrees outside. And I found myself tired. But my parents, it's like they're running on batteries. I tried to study what they eat. I mean, most people I know think I have more energy than anybody they know—but my parents have far more energy than me. It would be nine o'clock at night, and my father would be dancing, laughing, intensely talking to people, interested in people, and he's 87 years old. It's not what he eats; it's not a vitamin. I don't know what it is. I can only think that it must be divine.

A month earlier, a banquet had been given in Los Angeles by the National Center of Poverty Law to honor Shriver's role in creating Legal Services. Kantor, former president Clinton, and other speakers were on hand to toast Shriver. On this evening, Shriver treated audience members to a forty-five-minute speech, rousing them to a passionate pitch. As usual, his focus was not on celebrating past achievements but on exhorting the assembled lawyers to do more for the poor. When Bill Clinton got up to speak, after listening to Shriver's speech, he extemporized, "You know, the only reason Sargent Shriver accepted this award tonight was so he could come here and berate us about how we should be doing more!"

"In my lifetime," Clinton said, "America has never had a warrior for peace and against poverty like Sargent Shriver. In 1994, I gave him the Presidential

Medal of Freedom, the highest civilian honor. Ten years later, he's still up here telling us what we should be doing. It's not a coincidence that there are so many former cabinet members and a former President here. Shriver touched us all. . . . His whole life has honored Learned Hand's commandment: Thou Shalt Not Ration Justice. Sargent Shriver gave a lifetime and he's still giving."

Sargent Shriver had many flaws. He was, in the end, a failure as a politician. He suffered from a surfeit of innocence and idealism. He ground good men and women to exhaustion, embittering some of them forever. He at times revealed a salesman's affinity for style over substance. He could be stubborn. He was chronically, pathologically late, betraying at times what seemed to be a lack of respect for those he kept waiting. For all his great interest in the welfare of humankind, he could sometimes seem oblivious to the suffering of the man standing next to him. He made his share of grievous mistakes.

And yet there is always a danger, when writing about someone like Shriver, who has done so much for so many and who is sincerely motivated more by concern for the commonweal than by his own self-interest, of sliding into hagiography. The word *hagiography* has two definitions, the second of which is "an idealizing or idolizing biography." The word's connotation, in this sense, is pejorative; it implies a lack of perspective on the part of the biographer or an unwillingness to apply the same scrutiny to flaws as to strengths, or to defeats as to victories.

This book has tried—and it is up to the reader to judge with what success— to avoid being this kind of hagiography. The first and more historically precise definition of hagiography, however, is "a biography of a saint or venerated person." And in the fullness of time the Catholic Church may render anything written about Shriver to be, in the original sense of the word, hagiography. "I do believe he will be canonized one day as a saint," Colman McCarthy told me recently. "In 2300 or 2400, he and Eunice will be canonized together. I mean, St. Vincent de Paul was canonized after working among the poor in just one village. St. Francis was canonized after working in just Assisi. Sarge and Eunice worked among the poor on a global scale. I don't think any couple in history has had more positive effect on more lives than those two."

In the summer of 2000, Shriver traveled to Beijing for a Special Olympics meeting with top Chinese officials. This was to be a major public relations event for the organization: Shriver's son Timothy, in his role as Special Olympics CEO, would be making the trip, as would Arnold Schwarzenegger, in his role as a celebrity ambassador for the program. (The weekend Arnold was to arrive, the Chinese national television station ran Schwarzenegger movies around the clock.)

Sarge, eighty-five years old, had flown all night, and when he arrived his hosts asked him if he wanted to rest at his hotel before going to the first meeting. No, Shriver said, he wanted to go early to meet with the retarded children at the school where the meeting was to take place. So Shriver and his translator Bill Alford, a Chinese expert at Harvard Law School, were taken to the site.

It was a sweltering day, ninety degrees or higher, and Shriver was wearing what has become, in his later years, his trademark double-breasted suit. The school was packed—not just with students and faculty but with some 50,000 other people, many of whom wanted to meet the leaders of the Special Olympics, far more of whom wanted to meet Arnold Schwarzenegger. Arnold and Timothy weren't scheduled to arrive for an hour or so yet, however, so school officials had arranged for some of the mentally retarded students to put on a show for Shriver and the assembled Chinese crowd, in which they demonstrated some of the skills they had learned through the Special Olympics.

Shriver watched with his typical warmth and enthusiasm, and when the students were done with their performance they swarmed him, grabbing at his arms and indicating that they wanted to play basketball with him. The Chinese hosts, deeply embarrassed to see the distinguished octogenarian harassed in this way, intervened and said, "Oh no, leave him alone. He doesn't want to play basketball." But Shriver interrupted. "Sure, I do," he said, as Alford recalled. "I'd love to play basketball with them. These kids were so nice to perform for me, I would like to do that with them." And to the astonishment of the crowd, this eighty-five-year-old American, just off the airplane from the United States, began happily shooting baskets with the retarded Chinese children, with not a hint of self-consciousness evident.

Eventually Timothy and Arnold arrived and the formal proceedings began. Sarge gave a speech. "It was an unbelievable speech," Alford recalled, "about how grateful he is to learn from retarded people." "When I was younger," Shriver said, "I thought I knew a lot more than these people who were retarded. Well, I began to see that they had some attributes I didn't have. What I learned most from them was the meaning of the word love. When you see someone who is mentally retarded express love it is genuine love; there is no guile. It is pure emotion, what God intended." The message carried even through the translation. The audience was rapt; some of them were crying.

The next speaker was former deputy minister Yan Ming Fu, who had been Mao's translator before spending seven years in prison during the Cultural Revolution and then recovering to become a powerful official in his own right. After the events at Tiananmen Square in 1989, he had briefly fallen out of favor with the party because he had been one of the few officials who had taken a soft stance toward the student revolutionaries, but he had recovered to become vice minister of civil affairs, the rough equivalent of being director of homeland security in the United States. By the summer of 2000, Yan had retired from political life to become the head of a large Chinese charitable organization. But to the Chinese people, he remained a formidable figure.

After Shriver's speech, everyone expected Yan to get up and read some official standard proclamation. But to everyone's amazement, he departed from the official script. Standing up from his chair on the dais, he pointed to Sarge. "Look at this guy," Yan Ming Fu said.

He's eighty-five years old. He's not in great health. Yet he got on an airplane from America yesterday to fly here. He's a rich and powerful and important American, from the Kennedy family. He doesn't have to do any of this. He could just be sitting back in America, enjoying himself. He doesn't have to be here. But he keeps doing this because working for retarded children is important. If we Chinese people have any pride in ourselves, we ought to match this kind of commitment to humanity. This man who has every right to be sitting back in retirement is putting himself through all this to come tell us that these people matter. We ought to treat these children with more respect.

The speech was, Bill Alford recalled, "one of those moments in life when you're really overcome."

After the event was over, the chief school administrator came up to Alford and said, "For years we've been trying to get local political officials to pay attention to us and fund us but they've always ignored us. But now, because of vice minister Yan Ming Fu and this Kennedy family person, we know that when we need something from the local government, we will be well-treated."

Then, the school administrator turned to Shriver. "Thank you, old man," he said.

NOTES

Part 1: Youth (1915–1945)

Chapter 1: States' Rights, Religious Freedom, and Local Self-Government

4 **The first Shrivers:** *Men of Mark in Maryland,* vol. 4.

4 **Andrew and Anna Margareta Schreiber:** Shriver, "The Narrative of Abraham Shriver," 1826, in *History of the Shriver Family,* 13.

5 **The Shriver bloodline's powerful aversion:** Ibid., 19.

5 **On November 8, 1774:** Nead, *The Pennsylvania German,* 187; Shriver, *History of the Shriver Family,* 20.

5 **In 1797, as George Washington served:** Robert Fowler, "AHI Visits the Shriver Homestead, at Union Mills, Maryland," *American History Illustrated,* July 1968.

6 **Until 1826 all the Shrivers in America:** Shriver, *History of the Shriver Family,* 60.

6 **The county that included Union Mills sent:** Klein, *Just South of Gettysburg,* 4.

6 **"Our two families":** Ibid., 17.

7 **"For God's sake, Shriver":** Robert Fowler, quoting William H. Shriver, in *Civil War Times,* February 1962, 2. Much of the foregoing Civil War account is drawn from William H. Shriver's manuscript, reprinted in *Just South of Gettysburg,* and from the recollections of Sargent Shriver, who heard the stories in his youth. Additional detail and corroboration provided by various secondary Civil War sources listed in Bibliography.

8 **"There has been a sort of bitter feeling":** Frederick Shriver to Henry Wirt Shriver, July 12, 1863, Carroll County Historical Society.

8 **The bullet tore:** Louis E. Shriver, "Memoirs," in Klein, *Just South of Gettysburg,* 182–83.

8 **Herbert was shot and wounded:** L. VanLoan Naisawald, "Little Devils with the White Flag," *Civil War Times,* February 1962.

8 **The "hurrahs and songs":** William H. Shriver manuscript, in Klein, *Just South of Gettysburg,* 201–2.

9 **Herbert continued:** Shriver, *History of the Shriver Family*, 81.

9 **In 1908 he was a delegate:** "Hilda Shriver Dies; Political Activist in Md.," *Washington Star*, August 19, 1977.

9 **"Lately [T. Herbert Shriver] has been mentioned":** *Men of Mark in Maryland*, 49.

9 **Superficially, the cousins appeared:** Sargent Shriver, interviews August 10, 1997; December 28, 1997; March 22, 1999. Helen "Babs" Shriver, interview June 22, 2000.

10 **"Catholic capital of the United States":** Ellis, *The Life of James Cardinal Gibbons*, 7–15.

11 **The councils of the American Catholic Church:** Ellis, *The Life of James Cardinal Gibbons*, 7–15.

11 **Upon his discharge from the Confederate army:** Sargent Shriver, interview August 15, 1997; Ellis, *The Life of James Cardinal Gibbons*, 7–15.

11 **"In the simple and dignified atmosphere":** Ibid., 182–83.

13 **Green Street:** Descriptions of Westminster based on Sargent Shriver, interviews August 10, 1997; December 28, 1997; March 12, 1999; June 22, 2000; and on author's visit to Westminster and Carroll County Historical Society, June 22, 2000.

15 **Hilda succeeded early on in converting:** Sargent Shriver, interviews August 10, 1997; December 28, 1997; March 12, 1999. Dorothy Brown, "Maryland Between the Wars," in *Maryland: A History—1632 to 1974*, 687.

16 **great "wet hope":** Ibid., 672–97.

17 **Afterward, Shriver and his cousin:** Mollie Shriver Pierrepont, interview August 14, 2000; accounts of 1924 and 1928 conventions based on Sargent Shriver, interviews August 10, 1997; December 28, 1997; March 12, 1999.

Chapter 2: The Education of a Leader

20 **watching the great Lefty Grove pitch:** Shriver's love of baseball, which he carried into adulthood (between 1988 and 1993 he and his son Bobby were part of the ownership team that ran the Orioles), provides a hint of the leadership style that characterized his years in public life.

   Through high school and college, Shriver's preferred position was always catcher. Although catcher is often considered the most grueling field position to play—the hours of uncomfortable squatting behind the plate, the bruises from foul balls and backswung bats, the cumbersome protective equipment—Shriver loved it. The catcher is the only member of the team who can survey the whole terrain of the field: He is looking at the infield, the outfield, the pitcher, the batter, the base runners—even most of the fans. (The center fielder, who has a similar view from the other direction, can only see the backs of most of the other players.) With his panoramic view of the action, the catcher is the field general. He sees when the second baseman should move closer to first, or when the shortstop should move closer to third. He tells the outfield when to move in or out. He gets the signal from the manager and then conveys to the pitcher what pitch to throw. More than any other player, save perhaps the pitcher, the catcher determines what happens on the field. He's got more responsibility than any other player on the field. Sarge craved that.

   Finally, being a good catcher requires knowing about players' strengths and weaknesses and then minimizing them or maximizing them as the situation dictates. On every pitch, for instance, the catcher needs to balance the strengths and weaknesses of his pitcher against the strengths and weaknesses of the batter he's facing. Shriver found he had a knack for intuiting strengths and weaknesses. Seeing the whole field, being in the thick of every play, knowing how to manage people's strengths and weaknesses: Shriver would later say that he directly translated his experience as a catcher into his style as an organization leader.

22 **On September 24, 1930:** *Tabard*, September 1930, courtesy of Canterbury School.

23 **"the domain of American":** Mack, *The Way It Was at Canterbury*, courtesy of Canterbury School, 3.

23 **"This was a stalemate":** Ibid., 4.

24 **Shriver's parents visited him:** Records of Canterbury School, New Milford, CT.

24 **Shriver quickly established himself:** Issues of *Tabard*, 1934, courtesy of Canterbury School.

24 **"little Jack Kennedy":** Mack, *The Way It Was at Canterbury*, 121.

25 **"the atmosphere of secularism":** Ibid., 17.

26 **In the 1930s, Eleanor's parents:** Accounts of the Hoguets from Sargent Shriver interviews August 24, 1997; March 12, 1999. Eleanor Hoguet DeGive, interview August 11, 2000. Hoguet, *Robert Louis Hoguet (1878–1961)*.

27 **his presence was so large:** Eleanor Hoguet DeGive, interview August 11, 2000.

28 **"That's enough, Ellie!":** Ibid.

28 **"Sargent did such a good job":** Nelson Hume to Robert Shriver, Shriver Papers, JFK Library.

29 **"I was at the SSSIC the other week":** Sargent Shriver, interview August 24, 1997.

29 **"peace on earth, goodwill toward men":** Peters, *Passport to Friendship*, 9.

30 **The first groups of students:** Ibid., 60.

30 **Shriver set sail from New York:** Sargent Shriver to Hilda and Robert Shriver, Shriver Papers, JFK Library.

Chapter 3: A Yale Man

31 **"It seems as though I have been here a long time":** Sargent Shriver to Hilda and Robert Shriver, n.d. [September 1934], Shriver Papers, JFK Library.

33 **"If by chance you all are worried about these bills":** Sargent Shriver to Hilda and Robert Shriver, April 29, 1936, Shriver Papers, JFK Library.

33 **"Money means so awfully, awfully little to me":** Sargent Shriver to Hilda and Robert Shriver, October 6, 1937, Shriver Papers, JFK Library.

34 **"I must tell you":** George Day to Sargent Shriver, August 1, 1935, Shriver Papers, JFK Library.

35 **"Tap Day was the outstanding event":** Sargent Shriver to Hilda and Robert Shriver, May 9, 1936, Shriver Papers, JFK Library.

35 **"We begin work on the twentieth":** Sargent Shriver to Hilda and Robert Shriver, January 1, 1936, Shriver Papers, JFK Library.

37 **"If your real interest is in peace":** Peters, *Passport to Friendship*, 116.

38 **Shriver would listen to the soldiers goose-stepping:** Ibid., 125–26; Sargent Shriver, interview August 24, 1997.

38 **"Thank you for coming to Mass this morning":** Sargent Shriver, interview March 22, 2000.

39 **"That is Buchenwald":** Peters, *Passport to Friendship*, 127–28.

40 **"There were two worlds in Germany":** Ibid., 128.

40 **"armed to every last inch":** Sargent Shriver to Hilda and Robert Shriver, n.d. [July 1937], Shriver Papers, JFK Library.

40 **"I'm afraid I'll have to have some money in Rome":** Sargent Shriver to Hilda and Robert Shriver, July 31, 1937, Shriver Papers, JFK Library.

41 **"Gregory is doing all in his power":** Sargent Shriver to Hilda and Robert Shriver, August 13, 1937, Shriver Papers, JFK Library.

41 **Eleanor Hoguet had also gotten free passage:** Hoguet, *Robert Louis Hoguet (1878–1961)*, 146.

41 **"number one beau":** Eleanor Hoguet DeGive, interview August 11, 2000.

42 **Sarge felt as though he had been punched in the stomach:** Sargent Shriver, interviews August 16, 1997; March 22, 2000. Eleanor Hoguet DeGive, interview August 11, 2000.

42 **"I seem to have recouped some of my lost ability to pray":** Sargent Shriver to Hilda and Robert Shriver, August 22, 1937, Shriver Papers, JFK Library.

42 **"Are you interested in marrying her?":** Sargent Shriver, interviews August 17, 1997; April 22, 2000.

43 **Eleanor announced her engagement:** Hoguet, *Robert Louis Hoguet (1878–1961)*, 154; Eleanor Hoguet DeGive, interview August 11, 2000.

43 **"You will never know till you're in Heaven":** Sargent Shriver to Hilda and Robert Shriver, October 6, 1937, Shriver Papers, JFK Library.

44 **"That ends little Sarge's undergraduate days":** Sargent Shriver to Hilda and Robert Shriver, July 3, 1938, Shriver Papers, JFK Library.

45 **"If you could pay for law school":** Sargent Shriver, interview March 22, 2000.

45 **Sarge and his friend Bob Stuart:** Bob Stuart, interview September 5, 2001.

46 **Stewart grew frustrated:** Ibid.

46 **"I've been riding so high for so long":** Sargent Shriver to Hilda and Robert Shriver, n.d. [fall 1938], Shriver Papers, JFK Library.

46 **"I do feel I should do better":** Ibid.

46 **"I am doing Legal Aid work":** Sargent Shriver to Hilda and Robert Shriver, n.d. [spring 1939], Shriver Papers, JFK Library.

47 **"the mail planes":** Sargent Shriver to Hilda and Robert Shriver, July 19, 1939, Shriver Papers, JFK Library.

48 **"shares the universal fear of German aggrandizement":** Ibid.

49 **"Haven't you heard?":** Sargent Shriver, interview August 24, 1997.

49 **"Open the door":** Ibid.

50 **"The pier was crowded":** Peters, *Passport to Friendship*, 139–40.

52 **"The news from Europe is most depressing":** Sargent Shriver to Hilda and Robert Shriver, December 12, 1939, Shriver Papers, JFK Library.

52 **"The news from Europe this evening is so appalling":** Sargent Shriver to Hilda and Robert Shriver, May 15, 1940, Shriver Papers, JFK Library.

52 **"I have only one week":** Sargent Shriver to Hilda and Robert Shriver, May 26, 1940, Shriver Papers, JFK Library.

54 **"There is nothing lower than I was that summer":** Liston, *Sargent Shriver*, 38.

54 **"just skimming through":** Sargent Shriver to Hilda and Robert Shriver, n.d. [September 1940], Shriver Papers, JFK Library.

54 **"Well tomorrow begins":** Ibid.

56 **Wood had grown increasingly concerned:** Cole, *Charles A. Lindbergh*, 115–16.

56 **"a most attractive guy":** Ibid., 107–8.

56 **Shriver crowded into a packed auditorium:** Sargent Shriver to Hilda and Robert Shriver, n.d., Shriver Papers, JFK Library.

57 **As late as August 1941:** Fleming, *The New Dealers' War*.

58 **"Yes, I did belong to AMERICA FIRST":** Sargent Shriver, n.d., Shriver Papers, JFK Library.

58 **"I wanted to spare American lives":** *Look*, June 16, 1964.

Chapter 4: War

60 **One Sunday morning:** Account of this day based on interviews with Sargent Shriver August 2, 1997; April 4, 2000; plus additional conversations.

60 **Just after 2:22 p.m.:** *New York Times*, December 8, 1941.

62 **"I just got Herbert's telegram":** Sargent Shriver to Hilda Shriver, June 16, 1942, Shriver Papers, JFK Library.

64 **"No ship more eager to fight":** Morison, *The Two-Ocean War*, 193.

64 **"Gatch may not have had much passion for clean fingernails":** Leckie, *Challenge for the Pacific*, 286.

65 **"The ship was like your wife and your girlfriend both":** *USS* South Dakota *Reunion Video* (Norfolk, VA, May 15–17, 1998).

65 **"the best time of my life":** Ibid.

65 **A buzzing noise:** Sargent Shriver, interviews August 2, 1997; April 4, 2000.

66 **"Attack," commanded Gatch:** Leckie, *Challenge for the Pacific*, 290.

67 **"her flaming nose in the battleship's high foaming wake":** Ibid., 291.

67 **"for a single confused minute":** Ibid., 292.

68 **"magnificent shooting by the 'wild men'":** Morison, *The Two-Ocean War*, 195.

69 **"Every confrontation":** Hammel, *Guadalcanal*, 11.

69 **Shriver was recognized for his courage:** J. K. Richards, Commander, US Navy, to Robert Sargent Shriver, November 14, 1945, National Naval Personnel Records Center.

70 **"The psychological effect on the officers":** Frank, *Guadalcanal*, 478.

71 **"tossing out life rafts":** Morison, *The Two-Ocean War*, 205.

71 **"We were going close to 30 knots":** Sargent Shriver, interview August 2, 1997.

72 **like a pack of out-of-control bowling balls:** *USS* South Dakota *Reunion Video* (Norfolk, VA, May 15–17, 1998).

72 **"a loud crash, a rolling explosion":** Frank, *Guadalcanal*, 480.

72 **Shriver winced at the noise:** Sargent Shriver, interviews August 2, 1997; August 4, 1997.

72 **More than half of his division would be killed or wounded:** *Lincoln-Belmont Booser*, November 20, 1955.

72 **"The sight was terrifying":** Sargent Shriver, interview August 2, 1997.

73 **"a shell came through":** Ibid.

73 **"I got up and looked around the deck":** Ibid.

74 **"This can have quite a lasting impact on you":** Ibid.

75 **"I put a nickel in the phone":** Sargent Shriver, interview April 4, 2000.

75 **"Allied ships going to Russia":** Sargent Shriver, interview August 2, 1997.

75 **"being deep under water":** Ibid.

76 **"Good to see you, Shriver":** Ibid; Liston, *Sargent Shriver*, 43–44.

78 **"Save your breath":** Shriver, interview August 2, 1997; Liston, *Sargent Shriver*, 142.

79 **"All of us in the submarine corps":** Sargent Shriver, interview August 10, 1997.

79 **"All I could do was rejoice":** Ibid.

80 **"The war had a profound effect on me":** Sargent Shriver, interview August 2, 1997.

Part 2: The Chicago Years (1945–1960)
Chapter 5: Joseph P. Kennedy

84 **"As a decorated veteran":** Sargent Shriver, interview April 5, 2000.

85 **"there was this breathtakingly beautiful woman":** Sargent Shriver, interview March 30, 1998.

86 **"Never had I met a woman so intelligent":** Ibid.

87 **"that memorable evening outside the Plaza Hotel":** Sargent Shriver to Eunice Kennedy, n.d. [early September 1948], Shriver Papers, JFK Library.

87 **"Eunice Kennedy had far more on her mind":** Sargent Shriver, interview March 30, 1998.

87 **"Shriver—This is Joe Kennedy":** Account of meeting with Joe Kennedy based on Sargent Shriver interview August 10, 1997, and additional interviews.

89 **"For Christ's sake, Sarge":** Sargent Shriver, interview August 10, 1997.

89 **"Don't go anywhere near the bastard":** Ibid.

90 **"I went over things in my mind":** Ibid., plus additional interviews.

90 **"I've just bought this building out in Chicago":** Sargent Shriver, interview August 10, 1997, and additional interviews.

91 **"Sarge, I think you'll enjoy Chicago":** Bob Stuart, interview September 5, 2001.

91 **"Thanks for your letter":** Nelson Hume to Sargent Shriver, December 12, 1946, Shriver Papers, JFK Library.

92 **"I realized I had walked two blocks":** Sargent Shriver, interview August 10, 1997.

92 **In July 1945, he expanded his sights:** Liston, *Sargent Shriver*, 51.

92 **a "thumping bargain":** Whalen, *Founding Father*, 370.

93 **the Mart was a phenomenally successful investment:** Ibid., 371.

94 **"My political life is temporarily shattered":** Sargent Shriver to Eunice Kennedy, October 2, 1948, Shriver Papers, JFK Library.

94 **where Chicago's celebrities came to see:** Liebling, *Chicago: The Second City*, 75.

94 **"I was having a great time":** Sargent Shriver, interview August 10, 1997.

Chapter 6: Eunice

95 **Eunice also displayed a commitment:** Leamer, *The Kennedy Women*, 146.

96 **"Puny Eunie":** Ibid., 225.

96 **"The doctors told my father":** Ibid., 320.

96 **"regressed into an infantlike state":** Ibid., 322.

97 **"as if by sheer will":** Ibid., 376.

97 **"If that girl had been born with balls":** Collier and Horowitz, *The Kennedys*, 159.

97 **"Of all the kids in the family":** Blair and Blair, *The Search for JFK*, 524.

98 **"I think that someone with her training and background":** Tom Clark to Joseph P. Kennedy, December 24, 1946, Shriver Papers, JFK Library.

98 **"Substantial efforts must be made":** *Boston Sunday Post*, July 7, 1998, 392–93.

98 **"You're a lawyer":** Sargent Shriver, interview August 10, 1997.

99 **"Sarge was in love with Eunice":** Liston, *Sargent Shriver*, 55.

99 **"Eunice was not so sure":** Leamer, *The Kennedy Women*, 396.

99 **"He and Eunice saw a lot of each other":** Liston, *Sargent Shriver*, 55.

100 **"If you think you can change Sargent Shriver":** Sargent Shriver to Eunice Kennedy, February 20, 1949, Shriver Papers, JFK Library.

100 **"I ended up alone at a table":** Sargent Shriver, interview August 24, 1997.

100 **"chase you around the Justice Department office":** Sargent Shriver to Eunice Kennedy, February 20, 1949, Shriver Papers, JFK Library.

101 **"Government girls should stick at their jobs":** *Boston Sunday Post*, July 4, 1948.

Chapter 7: The Long Courtship

103 **"I was just so happy":** Sargent Shriver to Eunice Kennedy, September 13, 1948, Shriver Papers, JFK Library.

103 **"This weekend it is Bill Blair's":** Sargent Shriver to Eunice Kennedy, n.d. [early September 1948], Shriver Papers, JFK Library.

103 **"In the middle of a dinner party":** Sargent Shriver to Eunice Kennedy, December 27, 1948, Shriver Papers, JFK Library.

104 **"You who don't cry":** Sargent Shriver to Eunice Kennedy, n.d. [fall 1948], Shriver Papers, JFK Library.

104 **"Your Dad has been here for several days":** Sargent Shriver to Eunice Kennedy, September 28, 1948], Shriver Papers, JFK Library.

104 **"I should have known":** Sargent Shriver to Eunice Kennedy, November 21, 1948, Shriver Papers, JFK Library.

105 **"did your mother say she waited for your Father":** Sargent Shriver to Eunice Kennedy, March 30, 1949, Shriver Papers, JFK Library.

105 **"I'm a way behind time":** Sargent Shriver to Eunice Kennedy, February 19, 1949, Shriver Papers, JFK Library.

105 **"I used to say I'm the only guy":** Leamer, *The Kennedy Women*, 416.

105 **"After going out with her on and off":** Sargent Shriver, interview March 12, 1999.

108 **Shriver had told the Hoguets:** Eleanor Hoguet DeGive, interview August 11, 2000.

109 **"Up here this anti-communist business":** Martin, *Adlai Stevenson of Illinois*, 683.

109 **"my type of guy":** Ibid., 688.

110 **Campaigning at a furious pace:** Whalen, *Kennedy versus Lodge*, 82.

110 **"the Fitzgeralds have evened the score with the Lodges":** Whalen, *The Founding Father*, 423.

Chapter 8: Marriage

112 **"She was blonde":** Sargent Shriver, interviews August 10, 1997; March 30, 1998.

112 **Several of Shriver's friends from the time:** Kay Fanning, interview September 19, 2000; Frances Bowers, interview August 22, 2000; Bob Stuart, interview September 5, 2001; interviews with anonymous sources.

113 **"I met her in the hotel lobby":** Sargent Shriver, interview March 12, 1999; Eunice Kennedy Shriver, interview October 15, 2003.

114 **he had never consciously played matchmaker:** Whalen, *The Founding Father*, 440.

114 **"I don't know what made me decide to marry him":** Eunice Kennedy Shriver, interview September 24, 2001.

114 **"He was relentless":** Ted Hesburgh, interview April 17, 2002.

114 **"Sarge would have emerged":** Bob Stuart, interview September 5, 2001.

115 **"everyone's here except Rin Tin Tin":** Eleanor Hoguet DeGive, interview August 11, 2000.

115 **"Kennedy, Kennedy, Kennedy":** Frances Bowers, interview August 22, 2000.

115 **"The Shrivers were appalled":** Red Fay, quoted in Leamer, *The Kennedy Women*, 426.

116 **"Ten minutes before the plane":** Sargent Shriver, interview March 12, 1999.

Chapter 9: Religion and Civil Rights

117 **famous for the parties they threw:** Leamer, *The Kennedy Women*, 427.

118 **She missed and drenched Kay Field's:** Kay Fanning, interview September 19, 2000.

118 **"blind man's bluff":** Bill Blair, interview October 20, 2000.

118 **"I'd go to the door":** Sargent Shriver, interview March 12, 1999.

119 **"You should have known better":** Mary Ann Orlando, interview September 26, 2001.

119 **more than 6 million African Americans had moved:** Cohen and Taylor, *American Pharaoh*, 30.

120 **"there are today approximately 800,000":** "And Your Brother Shall Live with You," *Interracial Review*, June 1959, 120.

120 **"capital of black America":** Lemann, *The Promised Land*, 64–65.

120 **Samuel Cardinal Stritch:** Ibid., 70.

120 **Many Catholics drew their identity:** Cohen and Taylor, *American Pharaoh*, 34.

121 **Catholics accounted for fully 40 percent:** Lemann, *The Promised Land*, 70, 97–98; Lloyd Davis, interview October 18, 2000.

121 **The institutional Church made little overall contribution:** Lloyd Davis memo to author, "Sarge Shriver in Chicago, 1948–61"; Father Zielinski, *Bridge*, spring 1998.

121 **received approval from Cardinal Stritch:** *Chicago Daily News*, June 1, 1957; Catholic Interracial Council documents, box 17, Chicago Historical Society.

121 **met Lloyd Davis in the Pump Room:** Lloyd Davis, interview October 18, 2000.

122 **"Shriver's scholarship drive":** Liston, *Sargent Shriver*, 83.

123 **"After I married Eunice":** Sargent Shriver, interview August 24, 1997.

124 **"We think the School Board":** *Chicago American*, October 28, 1955.

125 **"As a result of the unanimous action":** Statement by Shriver to Finance Committee, January 16, 1956, Catholic Interracial Council papers, Chicago Historical Society.

125 **praised by the city's editorialists:** Liston, *Sargent Shriver*, 69–70.

125 **"the boldest, most creative":** *The Credit Base of the Board of Education of the City of Chicago: A Factual Historical and Financial Report*, October 15, 1956, 15.

125 **attended White Sox games together:** *Chicago Daily News*, October 26, 1955.

126 **Every week throughout much of the 1950s:** See, for instance, Mayer and Wade, *Chicago*.

126 **"Public high school students":** Catholic Interracial Council papers, Chicago Historical Society.

126 **"A white person takes his life in his hands":** *U.S. News & World Report*, August 9, 1957.

127 **At Shriver's insistence:** "This Year . . . A Story of Achievement: Work of the Catholic Intterracial Council—July through December 1954," Chicago Historical Society.

127 **"Injustices done to Negroes":** *New World*, September 21, 1965.

128 **"The heart of the race question":** Martin Zielinski, "A Movement of Perseverance for Interracial Justice,"

Bridge, spring 1998; "Catholic Bishops Speak on Racial Discrimination and the Moral Law: Statement of Principles and Objectives," Chicago Historical Society.

129 **"a white or Negro Catholic":** Lloyd Davis memo to author, October 18, 2000; Liston, *Sargent Shriver,* 80.

129 **"I congratulate the city of Chicago":** Lyndon Baines Johnson telegram to Chicago Interracial Council, Shriver Papers, JFK Library.

Chapter 10: Chicago Politics

130 **"looms as a 'dark horse'":** "Dems May Run Shriver," *Chicago American,* October 26, 1955.

130 **"almost everyone at my table":** Wofford, *Of Kennedys and Kings,* 44–45.

131 **"As I have often told you":** Lloyd Bowers to Sargent Shriver, October 11, 1960, Shriver Papers, JFK Library.

131 **As the event approached:** See, for instance, Martin, *A Hero for Our Time,* 107.

131 **Shriver was dispatched:** Burns, *John Kennedy,* 183–84.

131 **Stevenson then brought up:** Ibid., 181; Martin, *A Hero for Our Time,* 106.

132 **"It is not the political advantage":** Burns, *John Kennedy,* 184.

132 **"Kennedy, with his clean, 'all-American boy'":** Ibid., 181.

132 **"I had a personal fondness for Jack":** Martin, *A Hero for Our Time,* 106.

133 **"you were 100 percent behind Jack":** Sargent Shriver to Joseph P. Kennedy, July 18, 1956, JPK Files, JFK Library.

133 **"Eunice had become so much a part of Chicago life":** *Chicago Daily News,* August 3, 1956.

134 **"When I got to Jack's hotel room":** Martin, *A Hero for Our Time,* 111–12.

134 **He put his arm around his brother-in-law:** *Chicago Sun-Times,* August 16, 1956.

135 **"Eunice was ambitious as hell":** Leamer, *The Kennedy Women,* 464.

135 **"I'd like to do something for the foundation":** Ibid., 478.

135 **the real motivation for her years of toil:** Eunice Kennedy Shriver, interview September 24, 2001.

135 **"I originally wanted to be a sociologist":** Ibid.

136 **"In a round of handshaking sessions":** Liston, *Sargent Shriver,* 93.

138 **"I don't have any gnawing compulsion":** Ibid., 96.

138 **Mollie recalls coming over:** Mollie Shriver Pierrepont, interview August 14, 2000; Sargent Shriver, interviews August 11, 1997; April 25, 2000. Collier and Horowitz, *The Kennedys,* 212.

Chapter 11: Dawn of the New Frontier

140 **"I'm not sure I'd drop everything":** Liston, *Sargent Shriver,* 96.

141 **"a subaltern in his brother-in-law's":** Ibid., 95.

141 **"knew and respected Sargent's abilities":** Ibid., 97.

141 **"An Unwelcome Resignation":** *Chicago American,* October 12, 1960.

141 **"Along with many Chicagoans":** *Chicago Sun-Times,* October 12, 1960.

141 **Shriver "badly wanted Kennedy's nomination":** Wofford, *Of Kennedys and Kings,* 43.

143 **Ted Hesburgh had written to Shriver:** Sargent Shriver to Lloyd Davis, August 21, 1959, Catholic Interracial Council Papers, Chicago Historical Society.

143 **"As someone who has studied Gandhi":** Wofford, *Of Kennedys and Kings,* 45.

144 **"pleaded with him to get Chester Bowles":** Ibid., 41.

144 **The problem was, however:** Ibid.

144 **"I am campaigning here for Kennedy":** Harris Wofford, remarks, n.d., Shriver Papers, JFK Library.

144 **"to our dismay":** Wofford, *Of Kennedys and Kings,* 42.

145 **"What does it mean?":** O'Donnell and Powers, *Memories of John Fitzgerald Kennedy,* 160.

146 **"My first night in West Virginia":** Sargent Shriver, interview August 24, 1997.

146 **Shriver was a real "ramrod":** Fleming, *Kennedy vs. Humphrey,* 92.

146 "should have been condemned": Mary Ann Orlando, interview September 26, 2001.

146 "We've never had a Catholic president": White, *Making of the President, 1960*, 105.

147 "not a single Protestant minister": Fleming, *Kennedy vs. Humphrey*, 92–93.

147 "They would distribute flyers": Mary Ann Orlando, interview September 26, 2001.

147 "I remember one day": Sargent Shriver, interview August 24, 1997.

148 "We really don't know much about this whole thing": Wofford, *Of Kennedys and Kings*, 47.

148 "weak support from African Americans": Sargent Shriver, interview August 24, 1997.

149 "I had responsibility for all the African American vote": Ibid.

149 "Early each morning": Wofford, *Of Kennedys and Kings*, 51.

150 "All through the night": White, *Making of the President, 1960*, 168.

150 after tracking down Dick Daley: Sargent Shriver, interview August 24, 1997.

151 "They stood apart": White, *Making of the President, 1960*, 171.

152 "never, never, *never* trade": Ibid., 173.

152 "Lyndon will?": Wofford, *Of Kennedys and Kings*, 53; Harris Wofford, interview January 30, 1998.

152 "I was so furious I could hardly talk": O'Donnell and Powers, *Memories of John Fitzgerald Kennedy*, 191.

153 all hell broke loose: O'Donnell and Powers, *Memories of John Fitzgerald Kennedy*, 192.

154 "feeling as terrible as I was": Ibid., 192.

154 "During a lull around midday": Wofford, *Of Kennedys and Kings*, 56.

154 The whole truth: Shesol, *Mutual Contempt*, 50.

156 Shriver's gentleness: Collier and Horowitz, *The Kennedys*, 215.

156 he shunned mortal-stakes intensity: Bobby Shriver, interview May 21, 2003.

157 Jack also gravitated to Smith: Collier and Horowitz, *The Kennedys*, 217.

157 "Jack and Bobby had a couple of guys": Sargent Shriver, interview August 24, 1997.

157 "Bobby always spat on Sarge": Leamer, *The Kennedy Women*, 503.

158 "the house Communist": Wofford, *Of Kennedys and Kings*, 44.

158 "interpreted [Shriver's] cheerfulness as weakness": Redmon, *Come as You Are*, 26.

158 None of this covert hostility: Ralph Dungan, interview May 15, 2003.

160 Shriver enticed Franklin Williams: Wofford, *Of Kennedys and Kings*, 61.

160 "I'm just back from Africa": Ibid., 60.

161 the deed to Richard Nixon's house: Ibid.

161 "Let's not use words": Ibid., 61.

162 "Uncle Tom's Cabin": Ibid.

163 "They are going to kill him": Ibid., 11.

163 "this was not very reassuring": Ibid., 17.

164 "If Jack would just call Mrs. King": Sargent Shriver, interview August 11, 1997.

164 "It's not too late": Wofford, *Of Kennedys and Kings*, 18.

164 "you just need to convey to Mrs. King": Sargent Shriver, interview August 11, 1997.

164 "Negroes don't expect everything will change": Wofford, *Of Kennedys and Kings*, 18.

164 "That's a pretty good idea": Sargent Shriver, interview August 11, 1997.

165 "You just lost us the election": Ibid.

165 Wofford and Martin got blasted by Bobby Kennedy: Wofford, *Of Kennedys and Kings*, 19.

166 "I had expected to vote against Senator Kennedy": Ibid., 23.

167 "You don't need to ask Bobby's permission": Ibid., 23–24.

167 Shriver authorized: Ibid., 24–25.

168 "When 'Ray the Fox'": Ibid., 25.

168 "It is difficult to see how Illinois": White, *Making of the President, 1960*, 354.

168 James Michener later called the King phone call: Wofford, *Of Kennedys and Kings*, 26.

170 **"How many of you"**: "Remarks of Senator John F. Kennedy at the University of Michigan," October 14, 1960. JFK Library, www.cs.umb.edu/jfklibrary/j101460.htm.

170 **The audience was "wildly responsive"**: Rice, *The Bold Experiment*, 20.

171 **"our young men and women"**: Ibid., 15.

172 **"I can still vividly recall the dejection"**: Sargent Shriver, interview August 10, 1997.

Chapter 12: The Talent Hunt

174 **"I want you to help me put the cabinet together"**: Sargent Shriver, interview August 10, 1997.

174 **"Though people were sometimes ruffled"**: Schlesinger, *A Thousand Days*, 146.

174 **"the most outgoing member of the immediate circle"**: Adam Yarmolinsky, "The Kennedy Talent Hunt," *Reporter*, June 8, 1961.

174 **"I had never worked at the higher levels"**: Sargent Shriver, interview August 10, 1997.

175 **"Bundy had been running a 'talent hunt'"**: Sargent Shriver address to Southern Methodist University, Dallas, TX, March 29, 1984, Shriver Papers, JFK Library.

175 **"If you thought you were going on vacation"**: Wofford, *Of Kennedys and Kings*, 68.

175 **This meant, as he told Shriver**: Sargent Shriver, interview August 10, 1997.

176 **"Shriver knew the kind of man"**: Wofford, *Of Kennedys and Kings*, 70.

176 **"One of the things we had to keep in the forefront of our minds"**: Liston, *Sargent Shriver*, 109.

176 **"I was to go after the best people"**: Adam Yarmolinsky oral history, JFK Library.

176 **"the Shriver group began with the positions"**: Schlesinger, *A Thousand Days*, 146.

176 **"state of friendly competition"**: Adam Yarmolinsky oral history, JFK Library.

177 **"I had a candidate for almost every job"**: Wofford, *Of Kennedys and Kings*, 72.

177 **bias *against* Irish Catholics**: Schlesinger, *A Thousand Days*, 148.

177 **"I'm tough"**: Parmet, *The Presidency of John F. Kennedy*, 63.

177 **brought in a consultant from IBM**: Adam Yarmolinsky oral history, JFK Library.

178 **a master of salesmanship**: Liston, *Sargent Shriver*, 106–7.

178 **"a big-game hunter"**: Halberstam, *The Best and the Brightest*, 221.

179 **After meeting with Bell**: Sargent Shriver, interview August 10, 1997; Wofford, *Of Kennedys and Kings*, 71–72.

179 **"Oh, I don't care about those things"**: Schlesinger, *A Thousand Days*, 135.

179 **"Kennedy picked Dillon not only for his government experience"**: Parmet, *The Presidency of John F. Kennedy*, 65–66.

179 **In the end, this arrangement**: Wofford, *Of Kennedys and Kings*, 76–77.

180 **By the second week in December**: Ibid., 84; Sargent Shriver, interviews August 11, 1997; August 30, 1997.

181 **"involved complicated negotiations"**: Schlesinger, *A Thousand Days*, 150.

181 **"Why are you giving me these?"**: Wofford, *Of Kennedys and Kings*, 90.

183 **"With each call made"**: Ibid., 70–71.

183 **"Let's do it"**: Ibid., 71.

184 **"nonpolitical and nonpartisan"**: Sorensen, *Kennedy*, 283.

184 **The "remarkably high quality"**: Ibid., 285.

184 **"[Kennedy's] search succeeded"**: Ibid., 287.

185 **"One by one"**: Wofford, *Of Kennedys and Kings*, 95.

185 **"Shriver was hardly Eleanor Roosevelt"**: Ibid., 97.

Part 3: The Peace Corps (1961–1963)
Chapter 13: The Towering Task

189 **Eunice had recovered**: Leamer, *The Kennedy Women*, 522.

190 **"received more letters from people"**: Wofford, *Of Kennedys and Kings*, 98.

191 **"We were arrogant":** Redmon, *Come as You Are*, 266; Bill Haddad, interview January 4, 2002.

191 **"the difference between a slow march and a jig":** Martin, *A Hero for Our Time*, 262.

192 **"The 16 million young men":** Reeves, *Profile of Power*, 38.

192 **"Man, we's rich now":** Collier and Horowitz, *The Kennedys*, 260.

193 **But the Shrivers had been back:** Sargent Shriver, interview August 16, 1997.

194 **The extent of what he did:** Rice, *The Bold Experiment*, 32.

194 **Rostow contacted his MIT colleague:** Ibid., 34; Wofford, *Of Kennedys and Kings*, 251.

195 **Shriver assumed:** Shriver, *Point of the Lance*, 12.

196 **"The president just asked me":** Wofford, *Of Kennedys and Kings*, 98.

196 **Some ten years earlier:** Rice, *The Bold Experiment*, 36–37.

196 **Shriver took special pleasure:** Sargent Shriver, interview August 16, 1997.

196 **Early in 1960:** Rice, *The Bold Experiment*, 10–11.

197 **"One name soon led to another":** Ibid., 37.

197 **Even if he had wanted to:** Sargent Shriver, interviews August 16, 1997; March 24, 2000.

197 **"My style":** Rice, *The Bold Experiment*, 37.

197 **"Get yourself back here":** Mary Ann Orlando, interview September 26, 2001.

198 **"the only point of unanimity":** Rice, *The Bold Experiment*, 38.

198 **After the first few sessions:** Wofford, *Of Kennedys and Kings*, 253.

198 **"I needed help badly":** "Sargent Shriver Comes Back for a Day," *Peace Corps Times*, December 1978/January 1979.

199 **people "on the inside":** Redmon, *Come as You Are*, 32.

200 **"We've got to have a vehicle":** William Josephson oral history, JFK Library.

200 **"Josephson and I decided":** Redmon, *Come as You Are*, 32.

200 **A "small, cautious Peace Corps":** Warren Wiggins and William Josephson, *The Towering Task*, Shriver Papers, JFK Library.

201 **Now that their report was written:** William Josephson, interview August 5, 2000; William Josephson oral history, JFK Library.

202 **"mimeographed copies of *The Towering Task*":** Redmon, *Come as You Are*, 30.

202 **"Now I've never met this man":** Sargent Shriver, interview August 16, 1997; Redmon, *Come as You Are*, 33.

202 **"If you want to succeed":** Hoffman, *All You Need Is Love*, 43.

202 **Wiggins and Josephson had written:** Warren Wiggins and William Josephson, *The Towering Task*, Shriver Papers, JFK Library.

203 **If they were to wait the six months:** William Josephson memo to Sargent Shriver, February 27, 1961, Josephson Papers, JFK Library.

203 **After Shriver asked him to help:** William Josephson oral history, JFK Library.

204 **"My theory of why the task force was so successful":** Sargent Shriver, interview August 16, 1997.

204 **Probably the most fundamental disagreement:** Sargent Shriver, "Two Years of the Peace Corps," *Foreign Affairs*, July 1963.

205 **As the report neared completion:** William Josephson oral history, JFK Library.

205 **"Having studied at your request":** "Report to the President on the Peace Corps," box 85, President's Office Files, JFK Library.

207 **"This looks interesting":** Sargent Shriver, interview August 2, 1997.

207 **rooting around for historical precedent:** William Josephson to Sargent Shriver, February 19, 1961, Josephson Papers, JFK Library.

207 **if the Peace Corps were not launched immediately:** William Josephson, interview August 15, 2000.

208 **The task force's arguments:** Schlesinger, *A Thousand Days*, 627.

208 **"Our own freedom":** "Statement by the President upon Signing Order Establishing the Peace Corps," March 1, 1961, Shriver Papers, JFK Library.

Chapter 14: Shriver's Socratic Seminar

209 **"Kennedy knew that Shriver":** Rice, *The Bold Experiment*, 51–52.

210 **"It would be a serious mistake":** Sargent Shriver to President Kennedy, n.d., box 85, Peace Corps Office Files, JFK Library.

210 **"take the world by surprise":** *New York Times*, March 6, 1961.

211 **"You guys had a good day today":** Wofford, *Of Kennedys and Kings*, 263.

211 **By March 15:** Shriver, "Five Years with the Peace Corps," *Peace Corps Reader*, 1967.

211 **Since he didn't know how to procure the money:** Bill Haddad, interview January 4, 2002.

211 **Through the first days of the Peace Corps' existence:** Mary Ann Orlando, interview September 26, 2001.

212 **"midnight requisitioning" trips:** Redmon, *Come as You Are*, 77.

212 **"We had been prepared to wait a few days":** Ibid., 33.

212 **"Shriver didn't want anyone around":** Thomas Quimby, quoted in Rice, *The Bold Experiment*, 55.

212 **"Shriver couldn't wait three months for a guy":** Redmon, *Come as You Are*, 46–47.

213 **"He was just enormously impressive":** Ibid., 83.

213 **Shriver "began pounding his desk":** Ibid., 73.

213 **"How much time do I have to decide?":** "Who's Who in Peace Corps Washington," 6, Shriver Papers, JFK Library.

214 **"just come up for about three months":** Charles Peters oral history, JFK Library.

214 **"Wives of staff men":** Wofford, *Of Kennedys and Kings*, 281.

214 **"In my life":** Peters, *Tilting at Windmills*, 121.

214 **"the kind of charisma that makes men charge the barricades":** Ibid., 134.

215 **"Johnson would just come in":** Sargent Shriver, interview August 24, 1997.

215 **"In my Baptist church":** Hoffman, *All You Need Is Love*, 47–48.

215 **"cajoled and begged and pleaded and connived":** Rice, *The Bold Experiment*, 56.

215 **Moyers went directly to President Kennedy:** Ibid.

216 **"the government's usual lethargic pace":** Wofford, *Of Kennedys and Kings*, 281.

217 **"It was like seeing a picture of a cake":** Sargent Shriver, interview December 26, 1997.

217 **"To get an agency going":** Redmon, *Come as You Are*, 36.

217 **"a record for a government agency":** Ibid., 46.

Chapter 15: The Battle for Independence

219 **Josephson had warned him in February:** Williamson Josephson to Sargent Shriver, February 19, 1961, Josephson Papers, JFK Library.

219 **"beginning the Peace Corps as another ICA operation":** "Report to the President on the Peace Corps," box 85, President's Office Files, JFK Library.

219 **"an identifiable, visible body of people":** Gerald Bush papers, quoted in Rice, *The Bold Experiment*, 60.

219 **"wide agreement on the necessity and importance":** Bowles Papers, Yale, quoted in Rice, *The Bold Experiment*, 60.

220 **"The old-line employees of State and AID":** Rice, *The Bold Experiment*, 61.

220 **"There are about twenty people in Washington":** Wofford, *Of Kennedys and Kings*, 263.

220 **Eunice was at this point in the hospital:** William Josephson oral history, JFK Library.

221 **"the Kennedy people didn't have the respect for Sarge":** Redmon, *Come as You Are*, 39.

221 **"a signal to keep pushing":** William Josephson oral history, JFK Library.

221 **the president's aides remained intransigent:** Rice, *The Bold Experiment*, 62.

221 **"The Peace Corps . . . embodies a broader concept":** "The Peace Corps and the Reorganized Foreign Aid Program," confidential memo, Shriver Papers, JFK Library.

222 **"I don't want to go gallivanting":** Sargent Shriver to Henry Labouisse, April 7, 1961, Shriver Papers, JFK Library.

222 **he ratcheted up the pressure:** Rice, *The Bold Experiment*, 63.

224 **"the Peace Corps could not be favored":** William Josephson memo, April 26, 1961, Josephson Papers, JFK Library.

224 **"We had lost":** Liston, *Sargent Shriver*, 123.

224 **Shriver paced back and forth in his hotel room:** Moyers's notes, quoted in Wofford, *Of Kennedys and Kings*, 265.

224 **Talk to Lyndon!":** Liston, *Sargent Shriver*, 123.

225 **Johnson "badgered" Kennedy:** William Josephson oral history, JFK Library.

225 **"All right, Lyndon":** Liston, *Sargent Shriver*, 124.

225 **"extremely annoyed at the unusual methods":** Rice, *The Bold Experiment*, 66.

225 **"Dungan was highly irritated":** William Josephson oral history, JFK Library.

225 **"Ralph called me up":** William Josephson, interview August 15, 2000.

Chapter 16: "The Trip"

227 **"shrewd, learned, utterly unafraid":** Redmon, *Come as You Are*, 135.

227 **"He was swashbuckling":** William Josephson oral history, JFK Library.

227 **"Didn't hear a word from him":** Ibid.

227 **Shriver turned "phosphorescent":** Redmon, *Come as You Are*, 135–36.

227 **"with enough determination and imagination":** Rice, *The Bold Experiment*, 174.

228 **"We were not supposed to fish":** Wofford, *Of Kennedys and Kings*, 268.

228 **"Am I correct, Mr. Shriver":** Redmon *Come as You Are*, 136.

228 **"Sorry, I've lost my voice":** Ibid., 137–38.

229 **Shriver perceived a golden opportunity:** Wofford, *Of Kennedys and Kings*, 270.

229 **over a frenetic three days:** "Report on Visits to Eight Countries by Robert Sargent Shriver Jr., Peace Corps Director," Shriver Papers, JFK Library.

229 **"the hardest and most critical test":** Wofford, *Of Kennedys and Kings*, 271.

230 **"I am sure young Americans":** Ibid., 272.

230 **"my reputation as a strategist in poor condition":** Galbraith, *Ambassador's Journal*, 103.

230 **Nu took Shriver off to the side:** Liston, *Sargent Shriver*, 117.

231 **all eight countries:** "Statement of Robert Sargent Shriver, Jr.," May 17, 1961, Shriver Papers, JFK Library.

231 **"I have never been witness":** Harris Wofford to President Kennedy, May 22, 1961, Peace Corps Office Files, JFK Library.

231 **Shriver's traveling companions at times found the experience trying:** Redmon, *Come as You Are*, 138–39.

231 **Shriver returned to Washington a conquering hero:** Rice, *The Bold Experiment*, 73.

232 **"a lot of important scalps in his belt":** Redmon, *Come as You Are*, 144.

Chapter 17: Storming Capitol Hill

234 **"empire builders":** William Josephson oral history, JFK Library.

234 **"When we returned home":** Wofford, *Of Kennedys and Kings*, 266.

234 **Flying to Cape Cod one weekend:** Ibid., 266–67.

235 **"In wanting to have the Peace Corps have a separate identity":** Redmon, *Come as You Are*, 145.

235 **Josephson disagreed:** William Josephson, interview August 15, 2000.

236 **"a renegade, uncontrollable organization":** Rice, *The Bold Experiment*, 78.

236 **"Forget about talking to women's clubs in Detroit":** Redmon, *Come as You Are*, 147.

236 **"You've got a great asset in Shriver":** Hoffman, *All You Need Is Love*, 51.

236 **"the greatest romance act with Congress":** Redmon, *Come as You Are*, 147.

237 **"You know why I really voted for the Peace Corps?":** Wofford, *Of Kennedys and Kings*, 267.

237 **"I think I'll just go in and ask him":** Redmon, *Come as You Are*, 147–48.

237 a "terrifying scheme": Liston, *Sargent Shriver*, 126.

237 "made such an effort to bring his story personally": Rice, *The Bold Experiment*, 81.

238 "in a sweat": Ibid., 325.

239 "This is how to score": Liston, *Sargent Shriver*, 161.

239 In June he flew to West Africa: "Meeting with Secretary of State," memo, June 20, 1961, Shriver Papers, JFK Library.

240 he wrote to the vice president in July: Hoffman, *All You Need Is Love*, 52.

240 the indifference of Arkansas senator William Fulbright: Rice, *The Bold Experiment*, 83.

241 "cripple the Peace Corps": *New York Times*, August 3, 1961.

241 "Peace Corps appropriation serious danger": Sargent Shriver to John Kenneth Galbraith, August 2, 1961, Shriver Papers, JFK Library.

241 "good to point out to them": Sargent Shriver memo to Lawrence F. O'Brien, August 3, 1961, Shriver Papers, JFK Library.

242 "Bill Moyers and I have been living on the Hill": Sargent Shriver to President Kennedy, August 2, 1961, box 710, White House Office Files, JFK Library.

242 "two hours of verbal bombs": *Washington Post*, August 5, 1961.

242 Kennedy brought his presidential weight to bear: Rice, *The Bold Experiment*, 84.

242 "cut $15 million out of the unnecessary fat": Sargent Shriver memo to President Kennedy, August 29, 1961, Shriver Papers, JFK Library.

243 "Ah lahk you, Saage": Edgar May, interview February 21, 2002; Sargent Shriver, interview August 10, 1997.

243 slash its funding in half: *Washington Star*, September 14, 1961.

243 Shriver . . . continued to lobby individual congressmen: Warren Wiggins memo to President Kennedy, October 12, 1961, Shriver Papers, JFK Library.

243 This effort paid off in an unexpected way: Sargent Shriver, interview August 10, 1997.

244 Of all the bills: *New York Times Magazine*, December 17, 1961.

245 "erased the impression": Ibid.

Chapter 18: Shriverizing

246 Shriver "[projected] himself": Bradley Patterson oral history, JFK Library.

246 "an eagle-scout-on-the-make style": Redmon, *Come as You Are*, 118.

246 "No organization chart": Rice, *The Bold Experiment*, 94.

247 "one hundred percent Shriver": Liston, *Sargent Shriver*, 151.

247 "Shriver's mind churned out thousands": Redmon, *Come as You Are*, 150.

247 "Shriver's most serious fault": Peters, *Tilting at Windmills*, 135.

248 "When you come to work at this place": Liston, *Sargent Shriver*, 151.

248 "Family men abandoned family": Redmon, *Come as You Are*, 202.

248 "When you join the Shriver team": Liston, *Sargent Shriver*, 151.

248 Staff members learned: Edgar May, interview February 21, 2002.

248 "The secretaries were just terrified of the thing": Redmon, *Come as You Are*, 153.

248 "A job on the Peace Corps staff": Rice, *The Bold Experiment*, 91.

248 "Shriver's style of management": Ashabranner, *A Moment in History*, 44.

249 "there was always a winner and a loser": Ibid., 43–44.

249 "The worst possible argument that could be made": Gerald Bush, quoted in Rice, *The Bold Experiment*, 106.

249 "There will be little tolerance": Sargent Shriver to Peace Corps staff, December 1961, President's Office Files, JFK Library.

249 "Working with the Peace Corps": Ibid.

249 "it's a very legitimate question": Bradley Patterson oral history, JFK Library.

250 **"He can be indifferent":** Liston, *Sargent Shriver*, 159.

250 **"hardly anyone on his staff dislikes him":** Ibid., 164–65.

250 **"The thing about the Peace Corps":** Frank Mankiewicz, interview April 5, 2002.

251 **"I used to wake up in the middle of the night":** Sargent Shriver, "Five Years with the Peace Corps," *Peace Corps Reader,* 1967, 20.

252 **Shriver didn't have to wait long:** Ashabranner, *A Moment in History,* 82.

252 **"Dear Bobbo":** *Time,* October 27, 1961.

252 **"No one likes to be called primitive":** Wofford, *Of Kennedys and Kings,* 276.

252 **Within a few hours:** Ashabranner, *A Moment in History,* 82.

253 **"immature young Americans":** Ibid., 82.

253 **"the Peace Corps idea":** Ibid., 86.

253 **"postcard evidence":** *San Francisco Chronicle,* October 20, 1961.

253 **"The Peace Corps could be thrown out":** Redmon, *Come as You Are,* 120.

254 **"It was like a vaccination":** Ibid., 128.

254 **"In the long run":** Wofford, *Of Kennedys and Kings,* 276.

254 **Prime Minister Balewa issued a warm welcome:** *Meet the Press,* December 24, 1961.

254 **"No amount of praise":** Wofford, *Of Kennedys and Kings,* 278.

255 **"to get the *Time* magazine story":** Rice, *The Bold Experiment,* 110.

255 **Haddad in turn hired Charlie Peters:** Peters, *Tilting at Windmills,* 116.

256 **"The advantage of the evaluation process":** Ibid., 117.

257 **"It got to the point":** Redmon, *Come as You Are,* 205.

257 **Shriver began enthusiastically recruiting:** Ibid., 200; Peters, *Tilting at Windmills,* 139.

257 **"you have a duty to raise hell":** Rice, *The Bold Experiment,* 110.

257 **In Pakistan, the entire overseas administrative staff:** Charles Peters oral history, JFK Library.

257 **carried on a long correspondence:** Harris Wofford letters to Sargent Shriver, Shriver Papers, JFK Library.

258 **The Peace Corps representative in Liberia:** Tom Quimby oral history, JFK Library; Charles Peters oral history, JFK Library.

258 **"I doubt that any federal agency":** Ashabranner, *A Moment in History,* 149.

Chapter 19: Timberlawn

259 **When Shriver had first visited the house:** Sargent Shriver, interview August 30, 1997.

260 **"One time it was eleven o'clock":** Edgar May, interview February 21, 2002.

260 **most weekends would find Shriver:** Timothy Shriver, interview April 5, 2002.

261 **"I have seen sights":** *Parade Magazine,* February 2, 1964.

261 **"Behind all Eunice's efforts":** Leamer, *The Kennedy Women,* 577.

261 **"Of all the academics":** Shorter, *The Kennedy Family,* 73.

262 **"Eunice, needling her brother":** Ibid., 83.

262 **"Let's give Eunice":** Ibid., 84.

262 **Her persistence paid off:** Ibid., 82.

262 **"We as a nation":** *New York Times,* October 12, 1961.

263 **"the prime mover":** Shorter, *The Kennedy Family,* 89.

263 **"I see I don't have to draw any pictures":** Leonard Mayo, oral history, JFK Library.

263 **"it was the Shrivers who retained the oversight":** Shorter, *The Kennedy Family,* 90.

263 **"it is actually quite breathtaking":** Ibid., 101.

263 **She would give orders:** Eunice Kennedy Shriver oral history, JFK Library.

263 **"Has my sister been giving you trouble again":** Leamer, *The Kennedy Women,* 531.

264 **But she knew from her experience:** Eunice Kennedy Shriver speech, March 5, 1966, Kennedy Foundation Archives.

264 **"It was really pitiful":** Shorter, *The Kennedy Family*, 113.

265 **"When I'd come home from the office":** Ibid., 114.

265 **camp counselors had raided his liquor cabinet:** Sargent Shriver, interview August 10, 1997; Bobby Shriver, interview May 30, 2003.

265 **"as if it were the most normal thing":** Sargent Shriver, interview August 10, 1997.

265 **"We had no idea of what it would be like":** Shorter, *The Kennedy Family*, 115.

266 **"Aren't you afraid":** Ibid.

266 **In 1963 the Kennedy Foundation supported eleven:** Ibid., 118.

266 **"It was chaos":** Bobby Shriver, interview May 30, 2003.

266 **"There were at least a hundred people":** Maria Shriver, interview July 9, 2003.

Chapter 20: Bigger, Better, Faster

268 **He gave a hint of the scale of his ambition:** "Meeting with the Director on the FY 1964 Budget and the Budget Projections for the Next Five Years," May 8, 1962, Shriver Papers, JFK Library.

269 **When he spoke:** Sargent Shriver memo to President Kennedy, April 10, 1962, Shriver Papers, JFK Library.

269 **"wild and uncontrolled growth":** Ashabranner, *A Moment in History*, 113.

269 **"There is no doubt that":** Ibid., 68–69.

269 **Shriver's May 8 meeting:** "Meeting with the Director on the FY 1964 Budget and the Budget Projections for the Next Five Years" May 8, 1962, Shriver Papers, JFK Library.

270 **"the collection of espionage information":** *New York Times*, March 16, 1961.

270 **"Death to the Yankees":** Warren Wiggins memo to President Kennedy, November 6, 1962, Shriver Papers, JFK Library.

270 **"an old employee of the CIA":** Rice, *The Bold Experiment*, 132.

270 **rife with CIA operatives:** Parmet, *The Presidency of John F. Kennedy*, 213.

271 **"the Treaty":** Josephson oral history, JFK Library.

271 **"We do not want the Peace Corps":** William Josephson memo to Sargent Shriver, September 6, 1961, Records of Government Agencies, Peace Corps, JFK Library.

272 **"I'm getting rather suspicious":** "Kennedy and Shriver on Peace Corps," April 2, 1963, Presidential Recordings, JFK Library.

272 **"All available evidence":** Rice, *The Bold Experiment*, 135.

273 **"It is important that the Peace Corps":** Harris Wofford, "The Peace Corps, Marjorie Michelmore, and the Integration of the World," convocation speech, Los Angeles State College, n.d. [1961 or 1962], Shriver Papers, JFK Library.

273 **"culture-to-culture diplomacy":** Hoffman, *All You Need Is Love*, 91.

273 **"the friend of the colored man":** Rice, *The Bold Experiment*, 89.

274 **"a love-feast":** Sargent Shriver memo to President Kennedy, March 6, 1962, Shriver Papers, JFK Library.

274 **"Shriver, I'm getting suspicious":** Sargent Shriver memo to President Kennedy, March 27, 1962, Shriver Papers, JFK Library.

274 **"You are setting a wonderful example":** Hubert Humphrey to Sargent Shriver, March 27, 1962, Shriver Papers, JFK Library.

275 **"Dear Mr. Shriver":** Georgia Delano to Sargent Shriver, n.d. [April 1962], Shriver Papers, JFK Library.

275 **In June he traveled to Puerto Rico:** Warren Wiggins memo to President Kennedy, June 17, 1962, Shriver Papers, JFK Library.

276 **"Should it come to it":** Hoffman, *All You Need Is Love*, 142.

276 **"It is better to live humbly":** Ibid., 145.

276 **"We are not sorry he went":** Ibid., 146.

Chapter 21: Psychiatrists and Astrologers

278 **Joseph English was wrapping up:** Joe English, interview October 5, 2000.

279 **Peace Corps psychiatrists:** Directors' staff meeting minutes, June 5 and 12, 1962, Shriver Papers, JFK Library.

280 **"I have to have someone to punt to":** Joe English, interview October 5, 2000.

282 **When Shriver returned to Manila:** Warren Wiggins memo to President Kennedy, September 4, 1962, Shriver Papers, JFK Library.

282 **The first group of volunteers:** Fuchs, *"Those Peculiar Americans,"* 132.

282 **He spoke with particular admiration:** Director's staff meeting minutes, September 13, 1962, Shriver Papers, JFK Library.

283 **the reality of the Philippine barrio:** Fuchs, *"Those Peculiar Americans,"* 66.

283 **"It seemed we were being lionized":** Ibid., 129.

283 **"tense, frightening weeks":** Ibid., 113.

283 **"the purposes and successes of the Peace Corps":** Director's staff meeting minutes, September 13, 1962, Shriver Papers, JFK Library.

284 **English joined a search party:** *Peace Corps Memories: Headshrinkers, Astrologers, & Shriver,* n.d., 1972 campaign material.

284 **Thus President Kennedy and the State Department:** Schlesinger, *A Thousand Days,* 532–36.

285 **a personal invitation from Sukarno:** Director's staff meeting minutes, September 13, 1962, Shriver Papers, JFK Library.

285 **"The embassy types were aghast":** *Peace Corps Memories: Headshrinkers, Astrologers, & Shriver,* n.d., 1972 campaign material.

285 **"As we walked":** Ibid.

285 **"Why me":** Joe English, interview October 5, 2000.

286 **As English conversed with the presidential astrologers:** Ibid.

Chapter 22: Growing Pains

288 **"ought to be fired for lunatic stupidity":** Redmon, *Come as You Are,* 205.

288 **"the PDO people *really* hated me":** Ibid.

288 **"You are an inch away from being fired":** Ibid., 206.

289 **"In my shock and panic":** Ibid., 158.

290 **"Hi! I'm Sarge Shriver":** Ibid., 160.

290 **Fortunately, an aide to Arthur Richards:** Ibid., 162.

290 **"What is the line of succession at the Peace Corps, anyway?":** Ibid., 163.

291 **"Tell Peters his reports are right":** Peters, *Tilting at Windmills,* 124.

291 **a "manic drive":** Ashabranner, *A Moment in History,* 149.

291 **"Our country and our times":** "Two Years of the Peace Corps," *Foreign Affairs,* Spring 1963.

292 **Shriver codified this in a policy:** William Josephson, interview August 5, 2000; Rice, *The Bold Experiment,* 112–13.

292 **"administration by rookies":** Bill Haddad, quoted in Rice, *The Bold Experiment,* 114.

292 **"This transient turnover":** *Wall Street Journal,* November 9, 1965.

293 **"Sarge is also concerned to":** Rice, *The Bold Experiment,* 114–15.

293 **"We're almost at the point":** Redmon, *Come as You Are,* 227.

294 **the first week of October 1963:** Sargent Shriver memo to President Kennedy, October 1, 1963, Shriver Papers, JFK Library.

294 **an "enthusiastic crusade":** *Washington Post,* November 10, 1963.

295 **"Sarge is really on the ball":** Rice, *The Bold Experiment,* 136–37.

295 **"How are Sarge's kids doing?":** Ibid., 137–38.

296 **"I'm perfectly capable of looking after myself":** Liston, *Sargent Shriver,* 177.

296 **Shriver "scared" the bureaucrats:** Redmon, *Come as You Are*, 35.

296 **"favorite child":** Rice, *The Bold Experiment*, 137.

296 **Shriver flew into the city on Wednesday:** Redmon, *Come as You Are*, 246.

296 *Time* **had put Shriver on its cover:** *Time*, July 5, 1963.

296 **"Of all the agencies of the federal government":** *New York Times*, March 6, 1963.

Chapter 23: Tragedy

297 **"I'm sorry to tell you this way":** Mary Ann Orlando, interview September 26, 2001.

297 **"Something's happened to Jack":** Sargent Shriver, interview August 16, 1997; Manchester, *The Death of a President*, 143, 208.

298 **"nothing can overcome Eunice":** Sargent Shriver, interview March 21, 1999.

298 **"It doesn't look good":** Joe English, interview October 5, 2000.; Manchester, *The Death of a President*, 247–48.

298 **"Now listen, Eunice":** Joe English, interview October 12, 2000.

298 **the Shrivers sent Timmy home:** Mary Ann Orlando, interview September 26, 2001.

299 **"We didn't want Americans in the field":** Sargent Shriver, interview March 21, 1999.

299 **In his urgency to get there:** Joe English, interview October 12, 2000.

299 **"Right medicine, Doc":** Ibid.

299 **Before leaving for Cape Cod:** Manchester, *The Death of a President*, 255–56.

300 **"I'll get Jackie back to the White House,":** Sargent Shriver, interview March 21, 1999; Joe English, interview October 12, 2000.

300 **Jackie had several reasons for entrusting matters to him:** Sargent Shriver, interviews August 16, 1997; March 21, 1999.

301 **"I'll use Ralph's office":** *True*, April 1964.

302 **"Dungan brooded behind his desk":** Manchester, *The Death of a President*, 380.

302 **Everyone seemed in a daze:** Ibid.; Bishop, *The Day Kennedy Was Shot*, 359.

302 **Shriver then turned his attention:** Manchester, *The Death of a President*, 381.

303 **Shriver believed that as a navy veteran:** Sargent Shriver, interview March 21, 1999.

303 **Jack's children Caroline and John:** When John F. Kennedy Jr. died, thirty-six years later, his ashes were scattered over the Atlantic Ocean, off the coast of Cape Cod.

303 **The next issue Shriver had to worry about:** Manchester, *The Death of a President*, 384.

304 **"as distinguished a tribute as possible":** *True*, April 1964.

304 **"While my husband is there":** Liston, *Sargent Shriver*, 186.

304 **Shriver and Walton agreed:** Liston, *Sargent Shriver*, 187.

304 **"the two most impressive men":** Manchester, *The Death of a President*, 420.

305 **The family will not permit a nonreligious funeral":** Ibid., 422.

305 **"Let's take the low road":** *Miami Herald*, November 20, 1988.

305 **Telephone calls flowed into the White House:** Bishop, *The Day Kennedy Was Shot*, 419.

305 **"We forgot to invite Truman":** Ibid., 474.

306 **"we are not trying to return political favors":** Ibid., 497–98.

306 **"The embalmers":** Joe English, interview October 12, 2000.

306 **As the hour of the dead president's arrival:** *Miami Herald*, November 20, 1988.

307 **everyone deferred instinctively:** Manchester, *The Death of a President*, 437; Liston, *Sargent Shriver*, 188.

307 **"I'll get mine":** Sargent Shriver, interviews August 16, 1997; March 22, 2000.

307 **"Perfect," he declared:** Manchester, *The Death of a President*, 438.

307 **Shriver walked out to the north portico:** Joe English, interview October 12, 2000.

308 **He summoned all the military officers present:** Manchester, *The Death of a President*, 438.

308 **"a scene of indescribable drama":** Ibid.

308 **"This scene":** *True,* April 1964.

309 **Shriver looked around:** Manchester, *The Death of a President,* 439.

309 **"The ambulance doors opened at the back":** Sargent Shriver, interview March 22, 2000; Joe English, interview October 12, 2000.

309 **Seven soldiers:** Manchester, *The Death of a President,* 442.

310 **Climbing the stairs:** Sargent Shriver, interview March 22, 2000.

312 **"a lot of flak":** Manchester, *The Death of a President,* 471.

312 **"I found it was a buzz saw":** *Chicago Daily News,* March 28, 1968.

313 **"I am here if I can be of any help":** Manchester, *The Death of a President,* 317.

313 **regretted leaving the Peace Corps:** Bill Moyers, interview January 30, 1998.

314 **"Well, Sarge, it's a terrible thing":** Sargent Shriver, interviews March 22, 2000; August 16, 1997. Manchester, *The Death of a President,* 478.

315 **"I'll tell Bobby":** Manchester, *The Death of a President,* 479.

315 **"I'd been in the navy":** Ibid.

316 **He's hacking at you:** Ibid., 479–82.

317 **"Except for occasional brief absences":** Ibid., 486.

317 **Jacqueline Kennedy had requested:** Joe English, interview October 12, 2000.

318 **Moyers had asked to be informed:** Sue English, interview October 12, 2000.

319 **"Somebody just shot Oswald":** Manchester, *The Death of a President,* 525.

319 **"a muster of New Frontiersmen":** Ibid., 535.

319 **On Sunday afternoon Rose Kennedy:** Ibid., 558.

320 **Shriver and Sorensen had a common goal:** Ibid., 558–59, 601.

321 **a torrent of praise for the Peace Corps:** Joe English, interview October 12, 2000.

321 **"That's just ridiculous":** Manchester, *The Death of a President,* 575.

322 **"I wasn't there to be seen":** Liston, *Sargent Shriver,* 189.

Part 4: The War on Poverty (1964–1968)
Chapter 24: Shriver for Vice President

325 **"I just don't see any cloud":** Special small staff meeting minutes, November 26, 1963, Shriver Papers, JFK Library.

326 **"I know these days":** "Letter from the President," Shriver Papers, JFK Library.

326 **Shriver refused:** *Washington Daily News,* December 19, 1963.

326 **"For a while there":** *New York Herald Tribune,* December 15, 1963.

326 **After a brief recruiting trip:** Sargent Shriver memo to President Johnson, December 17, 1963, Shriver Papers, JFK Library.

326 **"I need you":** President Johnson to Sargent Shriver, December 2, 1963, Shriver Papers, JFK Library.

327 **the complaints Bobby Kennedy had made:** Lemann, *The Promised Land,* 146.

327 **"I hear you're going to Israel":** Sargent Shriver, interview December 28, 1997; Liston, *Sargent Shriver,* 204.

327 **So it was that on January 3, 1964:** Warren Wiggins to President Johnson, January 7, 1964; Peace Corps staff meeting minutes, February 10, 1964, Shriver Papers, JFK Library.

327 **"almost miraculous":** Sargent Shriver, interview December 28, 1997; *Washington Post,* January 6, 1964.

328 **For 1,400 years:** See, for instance, Küng, *The Catholic Church: A Short History;* McManners, *The Oxford Illustrated History of Christianity.*

328 **"an event of ecumenical significance such as the world had not witnessed in a thousand years":** Sargent Shriver, interview December 28, 1997. This meeting launched a reconciliation. Two years later, on December 7, 1965, the two churches would finally revoke their mutual excommunications, formally ending nine centuries of schism.

328 **Shriver and company arrived in Israel:** *Catholic Living,* March 1, 1964.

328 **At about 10:00 p.m.:** Ibid.

329 **"How many crucifixes":** Sargent Shriver, interview December 28, 1997; *Epistle,* Saints Constantine and Helen Greek Orthodox Church, May 1964, Shriver Papers, JFK Library.

330 **"I regard Sargent Shriver":** Liston, *Sargent Shriver,* 3–5.

330 **"a grand politician":** *New York Times,* March 15, 1964.

331 **"Johnson's going to need Illinois":** Liston, *Sargent Shriver,* 192.

331 **"He hasn't made enemies":** Ibid.

331 **"too young and inexperienced":** Ibid.

332 **"too many enemies as a hatchet man":** Ibid.

332 **Johnson loved the idea:** Bill Moyers, interview January 30, 1998.

332 **"has never been elected to anything":** *New York Times,* March 15, 1964.

Chapter 25: Origins of the War on Poverty

333 **"This administration today here and now":** Lander, *War on Poverty,* 4–5.

334 **the word *poverty*:** Sundquist, *Politics and Policy,* 111–12.

335 **"If the free society cannot help":** Patterson, *America's Struggle,* 122.

335 **"The notion of declaring a war on poverty":** William Capron in "Poverty and Urban Policy," group discussion transcript, 1973, JFK Library.

335 **President Kennedy assigned his brother:** Lemann, *The Promised Land,* 123–25.

336 **"change the institutional life":** Patterson, *America's Struggle,* 133.

336 **"The ultimate aim of community development":** Frank Mankiewicz, interview March 5, 2002; Rice, *The Bold Experiment,* 195.

337 **Harrington began expanding:** Isserman, *The Other American,* 108.

338 **"The extent of our poverty":** *New Yorker,* January 19, 1963.

338 **"a minor American classic":** Bernstein, *Guns or Butter,* 91.

338 **Both men passed copies:** Levitan, *The Great Society's Poor Law,* 14.

338 **He was also struck:** Gillette, *Launching the War on Poverty,* 3.

338 **The results, forwarded to the president:** Walter Heller to President Kennedy, Heller Papers, JFK Library.

338 **The hope was that:** Schlesinger, *A Thousand Days,* 1002–6.

339 **"public services and human beings":** Ibid., 1009.

339 **Kennedy asked Heller:** Robert Lampman oral history, JFK Library; William Capron oral history, JFK Library.

339 **Heller replaced him:** Lemann, *The Promised Land,* 132–33; William Capron oral history, JFK Library.

339 **"Go back and do some more homework":** William Cannon oral history, JFK Library.

339 **"badly in need of the public-policy equivalent":** Lemann, *The Promised Land,* 133.

339 **The cavalry arrived:** William Cannon oral history, JFK Library; William Capron oral history, JFK Library; Jules Sugarman oral history, LBJ Library; Lemann, *The Promised Land,* 133.

340 **Heller had an audience with the president:** Walter Heller oral history, JFK Library.

340 **During his last cabinet meeting:** Weeks, *Job Corps,* 52.

340 **"The time has come":** Schlesinger, *A Thousand Days,* 1012.

341 **"I told him very early in our conversation":** Walter Heller oral history, JFK Library.

341 **"Now I want to say something":** Walter Heller notes, JFK Library.

341 **the journalist Nick Lemann has observed:** Lemann, *The Promised Land,* 142.

341 **"powerful conviction that an attack was right":** Johnson, *The Vantage Point,* 71.

342 **"any more damn new agencies":** William Capron oral history, LBJ Library.

342 **suggested in a memo:** Jim Sundquist oral history, LBJ Library.

343 **"I walked from the main ranch house":** Johnson, *The Vantage Point,* 73.

343 **"It had to be big and bold":** Ibid., 75.

343 **"Look, I've earmarked half a billion dollars":** Walter Heller oral history, JFK Library.

344 **"If he'd said no to it":** Horace Busby, quoted in Lemann, *The Promised Land,* 144.

Chapter 26: "Mr. Poverty"

345 **"Pity the poor soul":** Sargent Shriver, interview December 28, 1997.

346 **"Find Shriver":** William Josephson correspondence with author, July 12, 2003.

346 **"That's great, Sarge":** Sargent Shriver, interview December 28, 1997. Much of the anecdote that follows comes from this interview and from Shriver's oral history in the LBJ Library.

347 **"I'm gonna to announce your appointment at that press conference":** President Johnson's tape recorded conversations are available at the LBJ Library, in Austin, Texas. Transcriptions of many of them have been published in Michael Beschloss's series of books, so far consisting of two volumes, *Taking Charge: The Johnson White House Tapes, 1963–64,* and *Reaching for Glory: Lyndon Johnson's Secret White House Tapes, 1964–65.* Additional Shriver thoughts here are derived from his oral history and from interviews August 2, 1997; December 27, 1997; and December 28, 1997, as well as from his unpublished 1970 manuscript, coauthored with Herb Kramer, "We Called It a War."

350 **He hung up the phone and told Eunice:** Eunice Kennedy Shriver, interview September 24, 2001.

350 **Shriver called the White House:** Beschloss, *Taking Charge,* 208.

350 **"Explain that this is just a study group":** Sargent Shriver oral history, LBJ Library.

350 **Shriver felt:** Kramer and Shriver, "We Called It a War."

351 **Shriver called the White House again:** Beschloss, *Taking Charge,* 208.

352 **Two hours later:** Ibid., 211–14.

353 **"Sarge was not close pal brother-in-law":** Adam Walinsky oral history, JFK Library.

353 **"I think he forced the job on me":** Sargent Shriver, interview December 27, 1997; Sargent Shriver oral history, LBJ Library.

354 **"The President had asked for immediate action":** Kramer and Shriver, "We Called It a War."

Chapter 27: A Beautiful Hysteria

355 **Shriver didn't have much to work with":** Sargent Shriver, interview December 28, 1997.

356 **"one of the most brilliant":** Lemann, *The Promised Land,* 147.

356 **"demolish people with sarcasm":** *Esquire,* February 1965.

356 **Shriver also turned to Frank Mankiewicz:** Frank Mankiewicz oral history, LBJ Library.

357 **That Sunday evening:** William Cannon oral history , LBJ Library.

357 **"I thought community action was absolutely sort of normal":** Sargent Shriver oral history, LBJ Library.

358 **"It'll never fly":** Sundquist, *On Fighting Poverty,* 36; Sargent Shriver oral history, LBJ Library.

358 **"Sarge's focus that night":** William Cannon oral history, LBJ Library.

358 **"That's just false":** Sargent Shriver oral history , LBJ Library.

359 **A great deal of intellectual firepower was present:** "Participants at the February 4, 1964 Meeting on the President's Antipoverty program," Shriver Papers, JFK Library"; "Administrative History of the War on Poverty," 27, LBJ Library.

360 **"this was our Camelot":** Lemann, *The Promised Land,* 149.

360 **"Oh, really, Mr. Harrington":** Harrington, *Toward a Democratic Left,* 8.

360 **"I decided that in the brief time we had":** Kramer and Shriver, "We Called It a War."

360 **"My name is Sargent Shriver":** Edgar May, interview February 21, 2002.

361 **"vintage Shriver":** Edgar May oral history, LBJ Library.

361 **"there were all kinds of millionaires":** Ann Oppenheimer Hamilton oral history, LBJ Library.

361 **"wild brainstorming":** Harold Horowitz oral history, LBJ Library.

361 **"Shriver would bring down people":** Hyman Bookbinder oral history, LBJ Library.

361 **"I've never known anyone as open to ideas":** *New Republic*, March 16, 1964.

361 **"a dilettante":** Levitan, *The Great Society's Poor Law*, 29.

362 **"thin the ranks":** *Esquire*, February 1965.

362 **"Nothing ever seemed very systematic":** Jim Sundquist oral history, LBJ Library.

362 **"three or four nooks and crannies":** Edgar May oral history, LBJ Library.

362 **The poverty program spent:** Christopher Weeks oral history, LBJ Library; Edgar May oral history, LBJ library; Sargent Shriver, interview August 2, 1997; Johnson, *The Vantage Point*, 76; Adam Yarmolinsky "The Beginnings of OEO," in Sundquist, *On Fighting Poverty*.

363 **Movers were constantly losing:** Weeks, *Job Corps*, 105.

363 **$30,000 from the president's contingency fund:** Bill Kelly oral history, LBJ Library; Edgar May oral history, LBJ Library.

363 **"warriors without guns":** Weeks, *Job Corps*, 103.

363 **The atmosphere . . . was like being in the hotel lobby:** Robert Lampman oral history, LBJ Library.

363 **"beautiful hysteria":** *Time*, May 13, 1966.

363 **"I followed closely the work:** Johnson, *The Vantage Point*, 76–77.

364 **"the walls dripped with blood":** *New York Times Magazine*, November 22, 1964.

364 **Shriver instinctively felt:** Sundquist, *Politics and Policy*, 142.

365 **"a way of attempting to test out a variety":** Katz, *The Undeserving Poor*, 99.

365 **"My conception of what it meant":** Yarmolinsky oral history, LBJ Library.

366 **"You have used that phrase four or five times":** Yarmolinsky, "The Beginnings of OEO."

366 **"The disgust of Bobby and his people":** Sargent Shriver, interview June 22, 2000.

367 **"Sarge felt a real loyalty to the programs:** *Life*, August 18, 1972.

367 **"We went to see him early on":** Lemann, *The Promised Land*, 149.

367 **The main instigator in these fights:** Sundquist, *Politics and Policy*, 142.

368 **Wirtz "violently attacked" it:** Daniel Capron, in "Poverty and Urban Policy," Conference transcript of 1973 Group Discussion of the Kennedy Administration Urban Poverty Programs and Policy, 149–50.

368 **"If Wirtz had had his way":** Kramer and Shriver, "We Called It a War."

368 **Shriver had another, more personal reason:** Sargent Shriver, interview August 24, 1997.

369 **"an impractical intellectual":** Lemann, *The Promised Land*, 155.

370 **"an idea that nobody could quarrel with":** Levitan, *The Great Society's Poor Law*, 36.

370 **"can take on anything and everything":** Bernstein, *Guns or Butter*, 104.

371 **"Shriver was of the strong opinion":** See, for instance, Levitan, *The Great Society's Poor Law*, 37.

Chapter 28: Mobilizing for War

372 **One day in February, Vernon Alden:** Vernon Alden, interview February 18, 1998; Vernon Alden oral history, LBJ Library.

373 **Several controversies arose:** Robert McNamara, interview May 15, 2003; Adam Yarmolinsky oral history, LBJ Library.

373 **"their dirty paws on it":** Weeks, *Job Corps*, 78.

373 **"blood vessels began popping in official Washington":** *Washington Post*, February 19, 1964.

374 **"too much of a military flavor":** *Washington Post*, March 13, 1964.

375 **"exactly the kind of innovation that appealed to him":** Weeks, *Job Corps*, 100.

375 **This didn't deter Shriver:** Ibid., 102.

375 **"He swiveled in his chair":** Kramer and Shriver, "We Called It a War."

376 **"no crooks, Communists, or cocksuckers":** Herb Kramer oral history, LBJ Library.

376 **"All of us who had worked so hard":** Kramer and Shriver, "We Called It a War."

377 **Bill Moyers had earlier written a memo:** Bill Moyers, interview January 30, 1998; Evans and Novak, *Lyndon B. Johnson*, 430.

377 **"if you are going to take a Kennedy":** Miller, *Lyndon: An Oral Biography*, 387.

377 **"blood is thicker than water":** Goodwin, *A Voice from the Sixties*, 296.

378 **"The hell he wouldn't":** Wofford, *Of Kennedys and Kings*, 291.

378 **"Robert Kennedy sat in icy silence":** *New York Times*, August 6, 1972.

378 **"At the beginning, I was for Bobby":** *Life*, August 18, 1972.

378 **"Did you plant that story in the paper?":** Sargent Shriver, interviews August 16, 1997; March 31, 2000.

Chapter 29: Wooing Congress

379 **"In no uncertain terms":** Bill Moyers to Sargent Shriver, June 30, 1964, Shriver Papers, JFK Library.

379 **"I know the Republicans thought this to a man":** Sargent Shriver oral history, LBJ Library.

380 **"pull a magnificent rabbit out of a hat":** Johnson, *The Vantage Point*, 77.

380 **"You're talking about the niggers!":** Lemann, *The Promised Land*, 156.

380 **"a few choice words":** Christopher Weeks oral history, LBJ Library.

381 **"Landrum coming aboard":** Larry O'Brien oral history, LBJ Library.

381 **Another of Landrum's assets:** Lander, *War on Poverty*, 16.

382 **"going through menopause for forty years":** Christopher Weeks oral history, LBJ Library.

382 **"I was impressed":** Robert Lampman oral history, LBJ Library.

382 **In the Senate, meanwhile:** Lander, *War on Poverty*, 17.

383 **"Look, this is the problem":** Sargent Shriver oral history, LBJ Library; Kramer and Shriver, "We Called It a War."

383 **Shriver went back to his office:** Sundquist, *Poverty and Policy*, 148.

384 **Shriver paid a call to Smith:** Kramer and Shriver, "We Called It a War."

385 **"what's this about some fellow in your organization":** Ibid.

386 **"Adam looks like he's got a bomb":** *Esquire*, February 1965.

386 **when McNamara told Shriver:** Robert McNamara, interview May 15, 2003.

388 **"Since the New Frontier did not produce a legitimate Alger Hiss":** *Esquire*, February 1965.

388 **Sensing a crisis:** Much what follows is drawn from Evans and Novak, "The Yarmolinsky Affair," *Esquire*, February 1965.

390 **"like an executioner":** Kramer and Shriver, "We Called It a War."

391 **The next day, Friday:** *Congressional Record*, August 7, 1964, 17996.

391 **"the Southern Democrats had asked for and gotten their pound of flesh":** Weeks, *Job Corps*, 16–17.

391 **The next afternoon:** Ibid., 141.

391 **"the most unpleasant experience I ever had":** Sargent Shriver oral history, LBJ Library.

392 **"Well, we've just thrown you to the wolves":** Adam Yarmolinsky oral history, LBJ Library.

392 **Shriver hoped:** Sargent Shriver, interview August 16, 1997.

392 **"There was a lot of feeling":** Christopher Weeks oral history, LBJ Library.

392 **"I came as close to Sarge as anybody":** Don Baker oral history, LBJ Library.

393 **"Sarge was the outside":** Ibid.

393 **"the whole operation began slowly to unravel":** Norb Schlei oral history, LBJ Library.

393 **"just kept him so busy":** Don Baker oral history, LBJ Library.

393 **"As soon as the legislation was passed":** Christopher Weeks oral history, LBJ Library.

Chapter 30: The Law of the Jungle

395 **the "crowded and dilapidated room":** Weeks, *Job Corps*, 184.

395 **"attack these plans":** Andy McCutcheon, interview February 20, 2003.

395 **"the roughest tests":** Weeks, *Job Corps*, 184–86.

396 **By November 25:** "US Opens Drive Against Poverty with $35 Million," *New York Times*, November 26, 1964; OEO press release, November 25, 1964, LBJ Library.

396 **Shriver continued to announce:** "Administrative History of the War on Poverty," 60–62, LBJ Library.

396 **"a kind of euphoria":** Weeks, *Job Corps*, 7.

397 **"Operation 10,000":** Ibid., 203.

397 **"they found a center still half-finished":** Ibid., 204–5.

397 **"didn't know what on earth they were supposed to do":** Christopher Weeks oral history, LBJ Library.

398 **Dramatic problems at some centers:** "Administrative History of the War on Poverty," 92–94, LBJ Library.

398 **"I had the telephone switchboard light up":** Sargent Shriver, interview March 31, 2000.

399 **"You'd go into class:** George Foreman, interview August 15, 2003.

400 **how to construct a radio:** A Job Corps teacher also taught Foreman how to box. Three years later, at the 1968 Olympic Games in Mexico City, Foreman would put what he had learned to good use, winning a Gold Medal in the heavyweight boxing division.

401 **"You'd think that if we took some felons in":** Sargent Shriver oral history, LBJ Library.

401 **"I do not like admonishing the Job Corps":** Weeks, *Job Corps*, 225.

401 **Although this elicited an angry reaction:** Ibid., 216.

Chapter 31: "Political Pornography"

403 **"We weren't quite prepared for the bitterness":** Sargent Shriver oral history, LBJ Library.

403 **"Well, not very much but about as much as was feasible":** John Wofford, "The Politics of Local Responsibility," in Sundquist, *On Fighting Poverty*, 80.

403 **"It was a wild sort of operation":** Don Baker oral history, LBJ Library.

403 **As early as November 1964:** Wofford, John, in Sundquist, *On Fighting Poverty*, 82.

404 **"your plans are being hindered at the federal level":** Lemann, *The Promised Land*, 165.

404 **"Daley was critical to the success":** Califano, *Triumph and Tragedy of Lyndon Johnson*, 72.

405 **"clear there would be no poverty program [in Chicago]":** Lemann, *The Promised Land*, 166.

405 **"What in the hell are you people doing?":** Ibid., 167.

405 **"there are numerous problems":** Hubert Humphrey to President Johnson, March 18, 1964, Watson Office Files, LBJ Library.

405 **"the legal and moral responsibilities of local officials":** Sundquist, *On Fighting Poverty*, 169.

405 **"Mayors all over the United States":** "Administrative History of the War on Poverty," 193, LBJ Library.

406 **"I'm your built-in Special Agent":** Sundquist, *On Fighting Poverty*, 181.

406 **"Shriver's sensitive political antennae":** Ibid., 92.

407 **"activities which do no good":** *The Reporter*, March 3, 1965.

407 **"high-minded . . . innocents":** James Rowe to President Johnson, June 29, 1965, Moyers Office Files, LBJ Library.

408 **The two conceptions of Community Action:** "Administrative History of the War on Poverty," 89, LBJ Library.

409 **"At a stroke":** Davies, *From Opportunity to Entitlement*, 77.

409 **This left the OEO:** Sundquist, *On Fighting Poverty*, 100.

409 **Johnson's hatred of Bobby:** Harry McPherson to President Johnson, June 24, 1965, McPherson Papers, LBJ Library.

410 **"couldn't look at Shriver":** Califano, *Triumph and Tragedy*, 80.

410 **At a meeting at the LBJ ranch:** Sargent Shriver oral history, LBJ Library.

410 **"If you want to wage war on poverty":** Lemann, *The Promised Land*, 170.

410 **"to end poverty in the United States, as we know it today":** Califano, *Triumph and Tragedy*, 79.

410 **every "mayor had a gripe":** Sundquist, *On Fighting Poverty*, 99.

411   "You save money on your programs": Levine, *Lessons from the War on Poverty*, 62.

411   "*We ought not to be in the business*": Califano, *Triumph and Tragedy*, 79.

412   "No such change in OEO's policy": OEO press release, Scottsdale, AZ, November 5, 1965, LBJ Library; Lander, *War on Poverty*, 54.

412   "I didn't bother to clear my statement": Kramer and Shriver, "We Called It a War."

412   "It was overwhelmingly clear": Sargent Shriver to President Johnson, and Charlie Schultze to President Johnson, November 6, 1965, LBJ Library.

413   Grafted onto LBJ's legitimate concerns: Califano, *Triumph and Tragedy*, 7.

413   "bloodbath on Capitol Hill": Ibid., 79–80.

414   Johnson had the Justice Department draw up: Ibid., 80.

414   "you're the only one that's not letting me down": President's daily diary, June 14, 1967, LBJ Library.

414   "the token Kennedy member": *Washington Post*, February 10, 1968.

415   Shriver's "stubborn idealism": Ibid.

415   "Somebody has got to hang in there": Edgar Cahn oral history, LBJ Library.

Chapter 32: Head Start

417   "My God, look at that": Sargent Shriver oral history, LBJ Library.

417   Shriver had been working closely with Eunice: Eunice Kennedy Shriver, interview October 15, 2003.

417   "So we flew down to Gray's research institute": Eunice Kennedy Shriver, interview September 29, 2003.

417   "Like most Americans": Zigler and Valentine, *Project Head Start*, 50.

418   "On the airplane": Eunice Kennedy Shriver, interview October 15, 2003.

418   "a lot of poor kids arrive at first grade": Sargent Shriver, interview August 3, 1997; Zigler and Valentine, *Project Head Start*, 51.

419   "If Joe's not knocking this idea": Sargent Shriver, interview August 11, 1997.

419   "it wasn't until blacks grew up": Zigler and Valentine, *Project Head Start*, 52.

419   "Look, we've got to get a program going": Ibid., 52 –53.

420   "We had to devise programs: Ibid., 54 –55.

420   Shriver asked Dick Boone: "Administrative History of the War on Poverty," 230, LBJ Library.

421   "We deliberately tried to make it an interdisciplinary effort": Jules Sugarman oral history, LBJ Library.

421   "the usually helpful pressure": Mitchell Ginsberg, quoted in Zigler and Valentine, *Project Head Start*, 92.

421   "Okay, let's get it operational": "Administrative History of the War on Poverty," 230, LBJ Library.

421   "How about 'Head Start'?": Zigler and Valentine, *Project Head Start*, 116.

422   "We're going to write Head Start across the face of the nation": Urie Bronfenbrenner, quoted in Zigler and Valentine, *Project Head Start*, 82.

422   "That's such a magnificent idea": Edward Davens, quoted in Zigler and Valentine, *Project Head Start*, 90.

422   Edgar May recalled a meeting: Edgar May, interview February 21, 2002.

423   "Well, if I had wanted a bureaucrat": Julius Richmond, interview February 18, 1998.

423   "The Head Start idea": Johnson, *A White House Diary*, 219.

423   "being bloodied every day on the front page": Jules Sugarman, quoted in Zigler and Valentine, *Project Head Start*, 117.

424   When Richmond began as director: Julius Richmond oral history, LBJ Library.

424   "It was like wildcatting for oil": Zigler and Valentine, *Project Head Start*, 56.

424   Julius Richmond recalled: Julius Richmond oral history, LBJ Library.

424   Once, a courier: Zigler and Valentine, *Project Head Start*, 119.

425   while the applications were being processed: Jules Sugarman oral history, LBJ Library.

425   One study found: Zigler and Muechow, *Head Start*, 26.

425   "the major remaining battalion": Mills, *Something Better for My Children*, 3.

426 **the seventeen-hour workday was standard:** William Phillips oral history, LBJ Library.

426 **"OEO has attracted more bright":** Jules Sugarman oral history, LBJ Library.

426 **"He's a guy that you admired and couldn't stand":** Eric Tolmach oral history, LBJ Library.

426 **"A program as complex as Head Start":** Zigler and Valentine, *Project Head Start*, 128.

427 **"When I first came to OEO":** Jules Sugarman oral history, LBJ Library.

427 **"I've never been in such stimulating staff meetings":** William Phillips oral history, LBJ Library.

427 **"He was tired of the bullshit":** Edgar Cahn oral history, LBJ Library.

427 **OEO originally made a $1.5 million grant:** "Administrative History of the War on Poverty," 66 –68, LBJ Library; Jules Sugarman and Julius Richmond oral histories, LBJ Library.

429 **One faction was led by Bill Haddad:** Robert Clampett to William Haddad, August 4, 1965, OEO Office of Inspection Files, Kennedy Foundation Archives.

429 **"Some of those [Head Start] centers were feeding SNCC":** Don Baker oral history, LBJ Library.

429 **"the headquarters of the project will continue to operate":** Sargent Shriver to John Stennis, August 13, 1965, Shriver Papers, JFK Library.

429 **"a center of civil rights activities":** Senate Appropriation Committee Hearings, October 14, 1965, 515.

429 **"made clear that civil rights work…would not be tolerated":** Sargent Shriver prepared statement to Senate Appropriations Committee, October 14, 1965, Shriver Papers, JFK Library.

429 **Because Head Start was such a popular program:** "Administrative History of the War on Poverty," 69–71, LBJ Library.

Chapter 33: A Revolution in Poverty Law

432 **Before the 1960s:** Johnson, *Justice and Reform*, 3–10.

432 **In most Western European democracies:** Ibid., 14–18.

433 **"It was like Columbus discovering America":** *Washington Post Magazine*, August 18, 1991.

433 **In November 1962, they had:** Johnson, *Justice and Reform*, 22.

433 **their role became controversial:** Ibid., 23.

434 **the Cahns argued:** Ibid., 33.

434 **"watering down the legal services organizations":** Ibid., 42.

435 **But about this time Lowell Beck:** Edgar Cahn oral history, LBJ Library.

435 **When Cahn reported this information:** Dick Boone to Edgar Cahn, November 27, 1964, Shriver Papers, JFK Library.

435 **at an ABA conference in mid-November:** Johnson, *Justice and Reform*, 48–49.

436 **Shriver made that task harder:** *Chicago Daily News*, November 18, 1964.

436 **was deluged with angry letters:** Lewis Powell and Edgar Cahn oral histories, LBJ Library.

436 **On January 12 the Cahns met:** Jean Cahn and Edgar Cahn oral histories, LBJ Library.

436 **Over the next week:** Sargent Shriver, "The Organized Bar and Legal Services," *American Bar Association Journal*, March 1971, 57:223–27; Lewis Powell oral history, LBJ Library.

436 **But just as relations:** Johnson, *Justice and Reform*, 64–65.

437 **Shriver had his own reasons:** Sargent Shriver, interview December 28, 1997.

437 **"if ABA members had visualized":** Lewis Powell oral history, LBJ Library.

437 **Jean Cahn dug in her heels:** Johnson, *Justice and Reform*, 65.

438 **Jean Cahn attacked Shriver publicly:** *Washington Post Magazine*, August 18, 1991.

438 **the Legal Services program was in disarray:** Johnson, *Justice and Reform*, 65–66.

438 **Part of the problem:** Richard Pious, "Policy and Public Administration," *Politics and Society*, 1971, 365–72.

439 **keynote address at the ABA's upcoming annual convention:** Sargent Shriver address to ABA 88th annual meeting, August 11, 1965, Shriver Papers, JFK Library.

439 **Bamberger "was establishment":** Johnson, *Justice and Reform*, 69.

440 "the greatest adventure in the history of the legal profession": Ibid., 70.

440 In a tour de force performance: Pious, *Politics and Society*, 374.

440 In the eighteen months beginning in January 1966: Johnson, *Justice and Reform*, 82–95.

441 "the entire Legal Services program was drifting": Ibid., 26.

441 he quickly signed on to the growing consensus: Stumpf, *Community Politics and Legal Services*, 270.

441 "Equal justice cannot be accomplished": Johnson, *Justice and Reform*, 127.

441 on March 17, 1967: 90th Cong., 1st sess., 1967, S. Rep., 40.

441 During the nine years of the official existence: Lawrence, *The Poor in Court*, 34–35.

441 "caused a lot of trouble": Mickey Kantor, interview March 6, 2002.

442 "maybe the most important thing that we are doing": Don Baker oral history, LBJ Library.

442 "The LSP . . . did seem to increase feelings of political efficacy": Lawrence, *The Poor in Court*, 34–35.

442 "changed whole bodies of law": Edgar Cahn address to National Center on Poverty Law annual dinner, May 1, 2003.

442 "Before the OEO program": Johnson, *Justice and Reform*, 188.

442 "the top people in each law school class": Mickey Kantor, interview March 6, 2002.

443 At one point during the Clinton administration: Clinton Bamberger, interview February 18, 1998.

443 "bought into a whole mess of trouble": Edgar Cahn address to National Center on Poverty Law annual dinner, May 1, 2003.

443 "fondest of Head Start": Kramer and Shriver, "We Called It a War."

444 "We're going to go into health in a big way": Joe English interviews, February 18, 1988; October 12, 2000.

445 Shriver and company decided to research two kinds of programs: Administrative History of the War on Poverty, LBJ Library.

445 "What impressed him most": Clymer, *Edward M. Kennedy*, 86–87.

446 The AMA had on principle opposed: English interviews, February 18, 1998; October 12, 2000.

446 Eunice made a choreographed entrance: Clymer, *Edward M. Kennedy*, 87.

Chapter 34: "Double Commander-in-Chief"

447 "When I look back now": Bobby Shriver, interview May 21, 2003.

447 During the week: Richard Ragsdale, interview October 16, 2000; Andy McCutcheon, interview February 20, 2003.

448 "As the War on Poverty moved into high gear": Kramer and Shriver, "We Called It a War."

448 "Sen. Joe Tydings has a campaign under way": Marvin Watson to President Johnson, February 20, 1965, LBJ Library.

448 "the chief problem for the Peace Corps": Wofford, *Of Kennedys and Kings*, 399.

448 "One of the things I am most interested in making clear": Peace Corps staff meeting minutes, February 10, 1964, Shriver Papers, JFK Library.

449 "It was fascinating to me in those early days": Edgar May, interview February 21, 2002.

449 Early in 1965: Sargent Shriver to President Johnson, March 10, 1965, Shriver Papers, JFK Library.

449 "high-water mark of the Peace Corps": Wofford, *Of Kennedys and Kings*, 302.

449 "the most informal as well as the liveliest": *New Yorker*, March 20, 1965.

450 The day built to a magnificent crescendo: Wofford, *Of Kennedys and Kings*, 302.

450 told Shriver to send the volunteers as soon as possible: Sargent Shriver to President Johnson, October 12, 1965, Shriver Papers, JFK Library.

450 "a tool for political blackmail": Wofford, *Of Kennedys and Kings*, 328.

450 "If you knew the mood the President was in": Ibid., 328–29.

450 sent a blistering memorandum to the president: Sargent Shriver to President Johnson, October 12, 1965, LBJ Library.

451 **the Peace Corps threw a massive anniversary party:** Sargent Shriver to President Johnson, November 2, 1965, LBJ Library.

451 **A Louis Harris poll:** Sargent Shriver to President Johnson, August 24, 1965, LBJ Library.

Chapter 35: The OEO in Trouble

453 **"We sat in his office face to face for the first time in months":** Kramer and Shriver, "We Called It a War."

454 **"I was perplexed":** Ibid.

455 **"a verb that may not be well chosen":** Levine, *Lessons from the War on Poverty*, 63.

455 **"from the very beginning":** Herb Kramer oral history, LBJ Library.

455 **"'Maladministration' may be too harsh a phrase":** C. Robert Perrin oral history, LBJ Library.

456 **Shriver had to compromise from the outset:** *Wall Street Journal*, March 9, 1966.

456 **"ugly problems of the political establishment":** *New York Times*, April 28, 1966.

456 **the staunchest supporter of increasing the OEO's funding:** Donovan, *The Politics of Poverty*, 74.

456 **He told HEW secretary Wilbur Cohen:** Wilbur Cohen oral history, LBJ Library.

457 **Johnson sent a note to his political aide:** Lemann, *The Promised Land*, 188.

457 **"Robert Kennedy was passing Sargent Shriver on the left":** Wofford, *Of Kennedys and Kings*, 421.

458 **"I will not participate in a riot":** *New York Times*, April 15, 1966.

458 **According to Bayard Rustin:** Ibid.

458 **"Shriver was trying to overwhelm them":** *Washington Post*, April 19, 1966.

459 **"irreducible minimum":** Donovan, *The Politics of Poverty*, 77–78.

459 **"A triple blow has been struck":** "Administrative History of the War on Poverty," 559–61, LBJ Library.

460 **When this article was brought to the president's attention:** President Johnson to Bill Moyers, December 2, 1966, LBJ Library.

460 **"shocking and incredible beyond belief":** Kramer and Shriver, "We Called It a War."

460 **Shriver had had enough:** Ibid.

460 **Califano delivered a handwritten note:** Sargent Shriver to President Johnson, December 19, 1966, LBJ Library.

461 **"he hopes that his resignation can be handled":** Bill Moyers to President Johnson, December 19, 1966, LBJ Library.

461 **"During the past ten days":** Hubert Humphrey to President Johnson, December 17, 1966, LBJ Library.

462 **Stennis said the grant would fund "extremists":** Senate Committee on Labor and Public Welfare, 90th Cong., 1st sess., 1967, S. Rep., 782.

462 **On July 7, when the CDGM submitted:** "CDGM Situation Report," September 27, 1966, Office of Inspector General Files, Kennedy Foundation Archives.

462 **he *liked* the fact that the CDGM served mainly African Americans:** Sargent Shriver, interview March 31, 2000; Edgar May oral history, LBJ Library.

463 **The array of problems was substantial:** "CDGM Situation Report," September 27, 1966, Office of Inspector General Files, JPK Foundation.

463 **A week later, Shriver announced:** "Administrative History of the War on Poverty," 76, LBJ Library.

463 **Shriver wrote back:** Ibid., 78–79.

464 **"Say It Isn't So, Sargent Shriver":** *New York Times*, October 19, 1966.

464 **"I'd never really seen him as moved and angry":** Jules Sugarman oral history, LBJ Library.

464 **Shriver fired back:** Sargent Shriver to *New York Times*, October 19, 1966.

465 **"during that period of turmoil":** Zigler and Valentine, *Project Head Start*, 64.

465 **Under pressure from the White House:** Jules Sugarman oral history, LBJ Library.

466 **"agreement in principle" had been reached:** Herb Kramer to Marvin Watson, December 19, 1966, LBJ Library.

466 **At Timberlawn over Christmas:** Kramer and Shriver, "We Called It a War."

Chapter 36: King of the Hill

469 **Califano said that the president planned:** "Administrative History of the War on Poverty," 564, LBJ Library.

470 **"Cutting through the agency's organization chart":** Kramer and Shriver, "We Called It a War."

470 **"single basic issue":** *Congressional Quarterly Almanac,* 1967, 1058.

470 **the bill the White House submitted:** "Administrative History of the War on Poverty," 567, LBJ Library.

471 **Community Action could be pronounced dead:** *New Republic,* March 25, 1967.

471 **call off the War on Poverty:** "Administrative History of the War on Poverty," 575, LBJ Library.

471 **staggering amount of time on Capitol Hill:** Ibid., 578ff.; Sundquist, *On Fighting Poverty,* 176.

472 **"The question at which":** "Administrative History of the War on Poverty," 578, LBJ Library.

472 **Politicians and reporters accused:** Ibid., 579–80.

472 **"I was able to meet a lot of the young cats":** Seale, *Seize the Time,* 35.

473 **"After the riots began":** "Administrative History of the War on Poverty," 581–82, LBJ Library.

473 **"in almost every one":** Ibid., 584–85.

473 **In the House:** House Committee on Education and Labor, *Hearings,* 90th Cong., 1st sess., August 1, 1967, Part 4, 3577–78.

474 **The message these officials sent:** "Administrative History of the War on Poverty," 587, LBJ Library.

474 **the House delivered its most stinging blow:** Special message from Sargent Shriver to all OEO employees, October 12, 1967, LBJ Library.

474 **the OEO had run out of money:** "Administrative History of the War on Poverty," 594–95, LBJ Library.

475 **"I think it would be a gross deception":** *New York Times,* November 6, 1967.

476 **"a sellout to the establishment":** Senate, *Hearings,* 90th Cong., 1st sess., 1967, 2697.

477 **"too much Alinsky in it":** *Congressional Quarterly Almanac,* 1967, 1076.

477 **"The original legislation":** "Administrative History of the War on Poverty," 600–1, LBJ Library.

477 **The ensuing debate:** *Congressional Quarterly Almanac,* 1967, 1076.

477 **Privately, however:** Don Baker and Bertrand Harding oral histories, LBJ Library.

478 **"saving what is worth saving":** Davies, *From Opportunity to Entitlement,* 195.

478 **"nothing but trouble":** C. Robert Perrin oral history, LBJ Library.

478 **deft bit of political jujitsu:** Andy McCutcheon, interview February 20, 2003; Barefoot Sanders oral history, LBJ Library.

478 **"There's going to be an amendment coming up":** George McCarthy oral history, LBJ Library.

479 **"I don't want OEO broken up":** Bill Kelly oral history, LBJ Library.

479 **"The fact of the matter is":** Don Baker oral history, LBJ Library.

479 **"doomed to failure":** Phil Landrum to Sargent Shriver, August 22, 1967, Barefoot Sanders Personal Papers, LBJ Library.

480 **by a larger margin in both houses:** Levine, *Lessons from the War on Poverty,* 76–77; "Administrative History of the War on Poverty," 604–7, LBJ Library.

Chapter 37: What Next?

482 **with no fanfare at all:** *Washington Post,* February 14, 1968.

482 **Shortly after New Year's Day:** *Washington Post,* February 4, 1968.

483 **In his State of the Union address:** Sundquist, *On Fighting Poverty,* 179.

483 **"mass resignation of top officials":** United Press International, February 1, 1968.

483 **"Tell Shriver to trace this leak":** President Johnson to Joseph Califano, February 4, 1968, LBJ Library.

483 **"The real impact of this budget":** *Washington Post,* February 4, 1968.

484 **As the Democratic Cook County Central Committee prepared for its first meeting:** *Chicago Sun-Times,* December 29, 1967, January 14, 1968.

485 **Then, unexpectedly, it did:** *Chicago News,* January 17, 1998.

485 **as far away as Australia:** *Washington Post,* January 19, 1968.

485 **Shriver met with Daley:** *Washington Post,* January 26, 1968.

485 **Shriver began talking to old friends:** See, for instance, Tom King, "Illinois Needs Shriver" letter, n.d; Newt Minow to Sargent Shriver, February 12, 1968, Shriver Papers, JFK Library.

485 **he and some close associates commissioned a secret poll:** Leo Shapiro, "Electing a U.S. Senator from the State of Illinois," Shriver Papers, JFK Library.

486 **"anything Shriver did in the Senate":** *Washington Star,* February 10, 1968.

486 **Shriver declined to show up:** *Chicago Sun-Times,* February 26, 1968.

486 **"Daley's 'Dream Ticket' Fading":** *Washington Post,* February 27, 1968.

487 **"Sarge, I'd like to take a walk with you":** Sargent Shriver, interview August 24, 1997.

488 **by the summer of 1966:** Schlesinger, *Robert Kennedy and His Times,* 739.

488 **Kennedy's "rise in political appeal":** *The Gallup Poll 1935–1971.*

488 **prominent Democrats had warned him:** *Newsweek,* March 16, 1967.

488 **as many as twenty percentage points:** *The Gallup Poll 1935–1971.*

489 **"Bill Moyers called to tell me":** Joseph Califano to President Johnson, December 8, 1967, LBJ Library.

490 **Shriver didn't hesitate:** *Chicago Daily News,* March 23, 1968, March 28, 1968.

490 **"LBJ was tickled":** Califano, *The Triumph and Tragedy,* 266.

491 **Thus he responded noncommittally:** Sargent Shriver, interviews August 24, 1997; March 12, 1999.

491 **"a guy comes barging through":** Donald Dell, interview April 15, 2003.

492 **"Sarge, I've been asked by Bobby's group":** Ibid.

492 **"I know there were feelings":** *Life,* August 18, 1972.

492 **But Sarge believed:** Sargent Shriver, interview August 24, 1997.

493 **"*Your* Daddy didn't come back from France":** Anthony Shriver, interview June 10, 2003.

493 **"Our ambassador supports the positions":** *New York Times,* April 19, 2003.

494 **"That's an iffy question":** Ibid.

494 **"a daring affront to the unity of the administration":** Leamer, *The Kennedy Women,* 627.

494 **"what Mr. Shriver is doing is important too":** *Washington Post,* April 19, 1968.

494 *Au Revoir, Sarge:* *Washington Post,* April 24, 1968.

494 **"the greatest challenge of his career":** *Sunday Star,* April 29, 1968.

Part 5: France (1968–1970)

Chapter 38: Springtime in Paris

497 **sworn in as US ambassador:** State Department press release, May 7, 1968, LBJ Library.

497 **De Gaulle considered this symbolic act patronizing:** Vinen, *France,* 82.

498 **"what to do about the French":** Cook, *Charles de Gaulle,* 347.

498 **"an open and undisguised breach":** Ibid., 360.

498 **in 1966, after years of threats:** Ibid., 382.

498 **The French president also formally recognized:** Vinen, *France,* 181; Cook, *Charles de Gaulle,* 347.

499 **"You cannot win it":** Heath, *The Kennedy-Johnson Years,* 265–66.

499 **"scarcely on speaking terms any longer":** Cook, *Charles de Gaulle,* 370.

499 **"the most difficult . . . that any American envoy":** Ibid., 393.

499 **"Given the attitude of de Gaulle":** Ibid., 393–94.

499 **"You're not going to have any fun":** Sargent Shriver, interview August 16, 1997.

500 **planned to leave for France on May 11:** Robert Barrett datebook, 1968, Shriver Papers, JFK Library.

501 **The chaos that was erupting:** Vinen, *France,* 186–87.

501 **"the kind of welcome I had come to expect in Watts":** Kramer and Shriver, "We Called It a War."

501 **"being an ambassador could wait":** Sargent Shriver, interview August 16, 1997.

502 **Reluctantly accompanied by Nick King:** Kramer and Shriver, "We Called It a War."

502 **"To the French people":** Ibid.

502 **"The tempest is really over":** Cook, *Charles de Gaulle*, 403.

503 **"So many spectacular events":** Sargent Shriver to Secretary of State Dean Rusk, May 24, 1968, LBJ Library.

503 **"I knew Sarge Shriver was a dynamic fellow":** Walt Rostow to President Johnson, May 24, 1968, LBJ Library.

503 **Shriver was struck once again:** Sargent Shriver, interview August 16, 1997.

503 **On this inauspicious morning:** Cook, *Charles de Gaulle*, 404; Robert Barrett datebook, 1968, Shriver Papers, JFK Library.

503 **"In many countries":** Sargent Shriver remarks upon presentation of credentials, May 25, 1968, Shriver Papers, JFK Library.

504 **"France is threatened by a dictatorship":** Cook, *Charles de Gaulle*, 406.

504 **Shriver, watching from the front of the American Embassy:** Sargent Shriver, interview August 16, 1997.

504 **"We sat in the house saying rosary after rosary":** Timothy Shriver, interview March 5, 2002.

505 **When Sarge attempted to help Bobby's aides:** Herb Kramer, cited in Learner, *The Kennedy Women*, 634.

505 **the "Kennedy Movement":** See, for instance, White, *The Making of the President, 1968*.

506 **"very interested" in allying himself with Shriver:** *New York Daily News*, June 22, 1968.

506 **Meanwhile, Eunice was moving forward:** Shorter, *The Kennedy Family* 129–30.

506 **"I wish to announce a national Special Olympics":** Ibid., 134.

506 **"I was the original number one skeptic":** Sargent Shriver, interviews August 10, 1997, August 16, 1997.

Chapter 39: "Sarjean Shreevair"

507 **Eunice had thrown herself into working with the mentally retarded in Paris:** See, for instance, *Vogue*, June 1969.

507 **The ambassadorial staff had never seen anything like this:** Sargent Shriver, interview August 16, 1997; Frances Cook, interview September 25, 2001.

508 **One day not long after his family's arrival:** Sargent Shriver, interview August 16, 1997.

509 **Shriver, for his part, was enthralled by de Gaulle:** Sargent Shriver, interview August 16, 1997.

510 **"of all the ambassadors I've seen":** Bob Blake, interview February 19, 1998.

510 **"won the hearts and minds of the French people":** Bob Halliday, interview March 5, 2002.

510 **"a rare and welcome panache":** *Time*, November 1, 1968.

511 **"Vive l'Amérique":** *Chicago Daily News*, September 25, 1968.

511 **"everybody had noticed the bouncy cheer":** *New York Post*, November 26, 1968.

511 **"It is going to be much more fun":** *Chicago Daily News*, August 28, 1968.

511 **The French people came to love him:** Frances Cook, interview September 25, 2001; Bob Holliday, interview March 5, 2002.

511 **LBJ's foreign policy aides had strongly advised:** Ernest Goldstein to President Johnson, February 24, 1968, LBJ Library.

511 **"It's a different ballgame now":** *Washington Star*, August 4, 1968.

511 **Shriver cut a dashing, if somewhat eccentric, figure:** *Boston Globe*, May 18, 1968; *New York Times*, July 3, 1968; *Time*, November 1, 1968.

Chapter 40: The 1968 Election

513 **"eager to pursue him":** *New York Post*, June 27, 1968.

514 **"It has never really fascinated me":** *Ladies Home Journal*, April 1970.

514 **"A number of us":** Wofford, *Of Kennedys and Kings*, 429.

515   "I had a long and private meeting": Bill Moyers to Sargent Shriver, June 27, 1968, Shriver Papers, JFK Library.

515   Josephson met secretly with Max Kampelman: William Josephson to Sargent Shriver, July 16, 1968, Shriver Papers, JFK Library.

516   "Ted Kennedy was the obvious choice": Sulzberger, *An Age of Mediocrity*, 442.

516   "generally favorable comment": Don Petrie to Sargent Shriver, July 17, 1968, Shriver Papers, JFK Library.

517   "Sen. Edward Kennedy's withdrawal": *Washington Star*, August 2, 1965.

517   his network of influential supporters quietly grew: William Josephson to Sargent Shriver, August 2, 1968, Shriver Papers, JFK Library.

517   Mike Mansfield secretly visited Shriver: Sargent Shriver to William Josephson, August 2, 1968, Josephson Papers, JFK Library.

517   So, too, several days later: William Josephson to Sargent Shriver, August 15, 1968, Shriver Papers, JFK Library.

517   "Let's talk turkey about Shriver": William Josephson memorandum for the record, August 9, 1968, Josephson Papers, JFK Library.

519   Josephson was moved to write to Kampelman: William Josephson to Max Kampelman, August 21, 1968, Josephson Papers, JFK Library.

519   "his appeal to youth": *Washington Post*, August 14, 1968.

520   "the crucial point": William Josephson to Sargent Shriver, August 17, 1968, Shriver Papers, JFK Library.

520   Bill Moyers delivered to Humphrey a memo: Bill Moyers to Hubert Humphrey, "Concerning the Vice Presidency," August 20, 1968, Shriver Papers, JFK Library.

521   "Shriver Stands out as VP Timber": *Washington Post*, August 21, 1968.

522   as Shriver reported it the next day in a letter: Sargent Shriver handwritten note to anonymous source, August 20, 1968, deposited by the author in the Shriver Papers, JFK Library, under certain restrictions, to be unsealed upon the source's death.

523   "Steve [Smith] was the money guy": Donald Dell, interview April 15, 2003.

524   "Hubert Humphrey's search for a Vice President": *Washington Post*, June 27, 1968.

525   "Hubert was very fond of Sarge": Kampelman, *Entering New Worlds*, 167–68.

525   "an unfriendly act": Ibid.

525   "began serving as her husband's ambassador": *Washington Post*, August 29, 1968.

525   "Stick it to Sarge": *Life*, August 18, 1972.

526   served for a while as surrogate parents: Anthony Shriver, interview June 10, 2003; Mark Shriver, interview July 9, 2003.

526   jumping his proper place in line: Marianne Means column, King Features Syndicate, August 25, 1968.

526   Fred Harris was telling Moyers: William Josephson to Sargent Shriver, August 23, 1968.

526   "one of the most unusual conventions in American political history": White, *The Making of the President, 1968*, 276–77.

527   "The Democrats are finished": Ibid., 298.

527   "I was a victim of that convention": Ibid., 303.

527   "The test is what Humphrey does now": Wofford, *Of Kennedys and Kings*, 431.

528   Chicago papers reported: See, for instance, *Chicago Daily News*, August 28, 1968.

528   "From 4,000 miles away": Wofford, *Of Kennedys and Kings*, 432.

528   "no monopoly on the Kennedy legacy": Ibid., 431.

528   "led me to believe better not": Max Kampelman handwritten memo, September 4, 1968, Josephson Papers, JFK Library.

528   Reflecting on the events: Edward M. Kennedy, interview February 16, 2004.

529   "His name was effectively vetoed": *New York Times Magazine*, October 15, 1972.

529   "For the second time": Wofford, *Of Kennedys and Kings*, 432–33.

529   "he was knifed": Max Kampelman to William Josephson, October 7, 1970, Josephson Papers, JFK Library.

530   "We are ready to attack another hill": Edgar May to Sargent Shriver, September 3, 1968, Shriver Papers, JFK Library.

530   "Even the slightest movement toward peace": Bundy, *A Tangled Web*, 28.

530   "We will end the war on an honorable basis": Ambrose, *Nixon*, 190.

531   "I simply can't stand Nixon": Sulzberger, *An Age of Mediocrity*, 478.

531   the negotiators hoped an agreement could be reached before the election: Sargent Shriver to Hubert Humphrey, October 30, 1968, Shriver Papers, JFK Library.

531   By October 29: See, for instance, Bundy, *A Tangled Web*, 28–35; Ambrose, *Nixon*, 211; White, *The Making of the President, 1968*, 378–79.

532   a prominent Nixon supporter named Anna Chennault: Goodman, *The Lost Peace*, 71.

533   "The relationship thus established": Bundy, *A Tangled Web*, 38.

534   "Anna, I'm speaking on behalf of Mr. Nixon": Chennault, *The Education of Anna*, 190–91.

534   "surely conveyed Nixon's fervent desire": Bundy, *A Tangled Web*, 41.

534   "regularly in touch with the Nixon entourage": Diem, *In the Jaws of History*, 239–45.

535   "our friend in New Mexico does": Powers, *Man Who Kept the Secrets*, 199.

535   The evidence is clear: Bundy, *A Tangled Web*, 45–48.

536   A switch in those three states alone: 1968 vote totals, Associated Press statistics.

Chapter 41: Nixon in Paris

537   He and Ted Kennedy quickly mended: Ted Kennedy to Sargent Shriver, November 11, 1998, Shriver Papers, JFK Library.

538   Shriver flew into New York: William Josephson memo for the record, December 16, 1998, Josephson Papers, JFK Library; Ambrose, *Nixon*, 231–34.

539   "Gawd, Sarge": William Josephson memo for the record, December 16, 1998, Josephson Papers, JFK Library.

539   the meeting was a strange one: Sargent Shriver, interview August 24, 1997.

539   Josephson recorded shortly afterward: William Josephson memo for the record, December 16, 1998, Josephson Papers, JFK Library.

539   "That's a good point": Sargent Shriver, interview December 26, 1997.

540   "one of the toughest, most cold-eyed": Kissinger, *The White House Years*, 26.

540   To Shriver's surprise: Sargent Shriver, interview December 26, 1997; Bill Moyers to William Rogers, December 16, 1998, Shriver Papers, JFK Library; William Josephson memo for the record, December 16, 1998, Josephson Papers, JFK Library.

540   "we have only one government": William Josephson memo for the record, December 16, 1998, Josephson Papers, JFK Library.

540   The brothers-in-law greeted each other warmly: Ibid.

541   He also had them prepare a draft: Richard Nixon draft remarks, n.d., Shriver Papers, JFK Library.

541   Shriver later observed: William Josephson memo for the record, January 15, 1969, Josephson Papers, JFK Library.

542   "encouraged me to take the post": Sargent Shriver to President Johnson and Secretary of State Dean Rusk, December 17, 1968, Rostow Papers, LBJ Library; William Josephson memo for the record, January 15, 1969, Josephson Papers, JFK Library.

543   Less than twenty-four hours: Sargent Shriver, interview August 16, 1997.

543   "Nixon and Rogers have changed their minds": Sargent Shriver to Secretary of State Dean Rusk and President Johnson, Rostow Papers, LBJ Library.

543   "at least fifty percent ex post facto": William Josephson memo for the record, January 15, 1969, Josephson Papers, JFK Library.

543   a "professional diplomat" rather than a "political figure": White House press release, December 20, 1968, Shriver Papers, JFK Library.

543 **"overly ambitious":** *Washington Post,* December 21, 1968.

544 **he blocked the appointment:** *Washington Star,* December 20, 1968. In his memoir, Richard Nixon said that he, not Rogers, made the decision to rescind Shriver's appointment. Nixon writes that Shriver "sent me a message stating the conditions for his acceptance. Among other things he required a pledge that federal poverty programs not be cut. It was intolerable to have a prospective ambassadorial appointee making demands relating to domestic policy, so I told Bill Rogers that I had decided against him and to let him know why." Shriver did, of course, want OEO funding to be maintained, and he may at some point have encouraged Nixon not to cut it. But the idea that he premised his acceptance of the UN position on OEO funding is ridiculous. The list of conditions he sent both to Nixon and to Rogers mentioned nothing about the poverty program, nor did he mention the poverty program in his formal conversations about the job with either man.

544 **Shriver had raised with LBJ's State Department:** "President's European Trip," February 3, 1969, Nixon Papers, National Archives.

545 **Nixon wanted to be assured that everything would run smoothly:** Edgar May, interview February 21, 2002; Daniel Morrissey, interviews February 19, 1998; March 3, 2003.

545 **"psychedelic" dining room:** *Washington Post,* May 20, 1969.

545 **Shriver got word from the White House:** Sargent Shriver, interview August 16, 1997.

546 **US protocol officers worked feverishly:** *Washington Post,* May 29, 1969.

546 **Nixon and his entourage arrived in Paris:** President of the United States schedule, February 23–March 3, 1969, Nixon Papers, National Archives; Sargent Shriver, interview August 16, 1997; H. R. Haldeman, February 28, 1969, *The Haldeman Diaries.*

546 **"The Nixon people brought their own food":** Edgar May, interview February 21, 2002.

547 **"There were some raised eyebrows":** John Ehrlichman to H. R. Haldeman, Henry Kissinger, et al., March 13, 1969, Nixon Papers, National Archives.

547 **Shriver established the tone of the evening:** Sargent Shriver, interview August 16, 1997.

548 **"I just remember my mother being so incensed":** Timothy Shriver, interview March 5, 2002.

547 **Nixon looked peeved:** Frances Cook, interview September 25, 2001.

547 **Nixon "listened politely to the first":** Bundy, *A Tangled Web,* 59.

547 **No specific agreements were reached:** *New York Times,* March 2, 1969.

547 **"a new era of deeper understanding":** Sargent Shriver cable to William Rogers, March 4, 1969, Nixon Papers, National Archives.

547 **"an almost audible sigh of relief":** Sargent Shriver to William Rogers, March 6, 1969, Nixon Papers, National Archives.

548 **reported that de Gaulle had been very pleased:** Sargent Shriver to William Rogers, March 7, 1969, and March 17, 1969, Nixon Papers, National Archives.

548 **"I am not deserting the people of France":** Bob Blake, interview February 19, 1998.

548 **"The waves are rising":** Sargent Shriver to William Rogers, March 7, 1969, Nixon Papers, National Archives.

548 **"Odds are so close":** Sargent Shriver to William Rogers, March 29, 1969, Nixon Papers, National Archives.

548 **Shriver monitored the situation anxiously:** Donald Lesh to Henry Kissinger, April 28, 1969, Nixon Papers, National Archives.

549 **could not have asked for better access to the highest levels:** Helmut Sonnenfeldt to Henry Kissinger, June 26, 1969, Nixon Papers, National Archives.

549 **Nixon knew that Shriver:** *Houston Chronicle,* July 20, 1969.

549 **Shriver visited thirteen cabinet ministers:** *Baltimore Sun Magazine,* July 27, 1969.

549 **In a meeting with Pompidou:** Sargent Shriver to William Rogers, July 8, 1969, Nixon Papers, National Archives.

549 **In July 1969 the Shrivers returned to the United States:** Sargent Shriver, interviews August 16, 1997, and March 31, 2000; Sulzberger, *An Age of Mediocrity,* 558–59; *Apollo XI* itinerary, Shriver Papers, JFK Library.

550 **Eunice argued him out of it:** Clymer, *Edward M. Kennedy,* 151.

550 **"they certainly were not finished":** WAYE TV Baltimore, February 28, 1970.

Chapter 42: Au Revoir

553 **A group of leading Democrats:** Bill Gale, William Delano, et al. to Sargent Shriver, September 8, 1969, Shriver Papers, JFK Library.

553 **But in the last week of October:** "Itinerary—USA—October 22 to 31, 1969," Shriver Papers, JFK Library; *Pathersville Telegraph,* October 16, 1969.

554 **"always be welcome in Illinois":** *Chicago News,* October 30, 1969.

554 **"It was a difficult moral decision":** *Chicago Daily News,* October 31, 1969; United Press International, October 30, 1969.

554 **Maryland liberals were searching for someone:** *Baltimore Sun,* October 31, 1969.

554 **a "dynamic personality":** *Sunday Star,* November 2, 1969.

554 **"There are those who are saying":** William Josephson to Sargent Shriver, n.d., Josephson Papers, JFK Library.

555 **Shriver formally withdrew himself from consideration:** See, for instance, Sargent Shriver to Dan Rostenkowski, November 21, 1969, Shriver Papers, JFK Library.

555 **Shriver operatives on the ground in Maryland:** William Josephson to Sargent Shriver, November 28, 1969, Shriver Papers, JFK Library; *New York Post,* November 28, 1969.

555 **Shriver hosted a dinner for Henry Cabot Lodge:** Henry Cabot Lodge to Sargent Shriver, December 9, 1969, Shriver Papers, JFK Library.

555 **"Shriver Is Boomed":** *Washington Post,* December 18, 1969.

556 **Shriver told Cy Sulzberger:** Sulzberger, *An Age of Mediocrity,* 597.

556 **Shriver wanted to make some final grand gesture:** Description of the Midnight Mass from *Time,* January 5, 1970; *New York Daily News,* December 25, 1969. Daniel Morrissey, interviews February 19, 1998; March 3, 2003. William Josephson, interview October 12, 2000. Edgar May, interview February 21, 2002. Frances Cook, interview September 25, 2001. Sargent Shriver, interview August 16, 1997.

558 **"the Mass was absolutely beautiful":** Sulzberger, *An Age of Mediocrity,* 596.

Part 6: Democratic Politics (1970–1976)
Chapter 43: The Politics of Life

561 **President Pompidou's visit to the United States:** Sargent Shriver to President Nixon, January 27, 1970, Nixon Papers, National Archives.

561 **In his first appearance on national television:** *Meet the Press,* April 5, 1979.

562 **Ted Kennedy wrote to Shriver:** Ted Kennedy to Sargent Shriver, n.d., Shriver Papers, JFK Library.

562 **"There is just something a little bit wrong":** *Washington Star,* March 9, 1970.

562 **he began to pull together his team:** Matt Reese, "Proposal III for Ambassador Shriver," Shriver Papers, JFK Library.

562 **"A good deal of time and energy":** Unsigned campaign memo, May 19, 1970, Shriver Papers, JFK Library.

563 **Mandel's job approval ratings:** "A Study of the Political Climate in Maryland" penetration research, April 1970, Shriver Papers, JFK Library.

563 **"The whole picture begins to take on":** Joseph Bailor memo, May 22, 1970, Shriver Papers, JFK Library.

563 **"the worst experience of his life":** Max Kampelman to William Josephson, October 7, 1970, Josephson Papers, JFK Library.

563 **"I say we've just got to have him":** *New York Times,* May 31, 1970.

564 **attacked the plan for the new party council:** *New York Times,* June 5, 1970; *Washington Post,* June 5, 1970.

564 **After an hour-long phone conversation:** *New York Times,* June 25, 1970.

564 **"While I have been evaluating the situation in Maryland:** "Statement by Sargent Shriver," n.d., Shriver Papers, JFK Library.

564 **After Shriver had discovered Novak's book:** *New York Times Magazine*, October 15, 1972.

565 **Between July and November:** "Speeches delivered by Sargent Shriver, July 1970–Nov. 1970," Shriver Papers, JFK Library.

565 **"The White House plods its somber way":** *New York Sunday News*, August 16, 1970.

565 **"The eye-bulging political organization":** *New York Post*, August 8, 1970.

566 **Sarge would be carved up":** *New York Times Magazine*, October 15, 1972.

566 **"the hand of death lay heavy upon our society":** "The Politics of Life," Shriver Papers, JFK Library.

566 **Some of Shriver's advisers:** William Crook to Sargent Shriver, October 29, 1970, and Crook to Citizens Advisory Committee, October 1, 1970, Shriver Papers, JFK Library.

567 **"like a hibernating bear out of a dark cave":** *New York Times*, November 5, 1970.

Chapter 44: International Men of Mystery

569 **Shriver had always been fascinated with self-made men:** David Birenbaum, interview March 4, 2002.

570 **Fried, Frank was anything but typical:** David Birenbaum, interview March 4, 2002; William Alford, interview October 30, 2001.

570 **Lenin wrote a secret letter:** Epstein, *Dossier*, 81.

570 **Over the next fifty years, he would exploit this position:** Ibid., 115.

571 **forced to make certain ethical compromises:** Ibid., 99–110.

571 **he went to Moscow for a summit with Khrushchev:** Ibid., 209.

571 **Hammer retained him as a legal counsel:** Blumay, *The Dark Side of Power*, 146–48; David Birenbaum, interview March 4, 2002.

571 **Shriver also found Hammer to be wonderfully appealing:** Sargent Shriver, interview August 30, 1997.

572 **"Was Armand Hammer a spy for the Russians?":** David Birenbaum, interview March 4, 2002.

572 **Shriver introduced Hammer to another larger-than-life businessman:** Blumay, *The Dark Side of Power*, 148.

572 **Karr was a brilliant, mysterious, complex figure:** *Fortune*, December 3, 1979.

572 **Shriver and Karr first crossed paths:** Sargent Shriver, interview March 31, 2000.

573 **"a wheeler-dealer":** Sargent Shriver, interview August 30, 1997.

573 **"Karr was chiaroscuric":** "The Death of David Karr," *Fortune*, December 3, 1979.

573 **"had a strong social conscience":** Ibid.

573 **"He was interested in only one thing":** Ibid.

573 **The two men had spent hours smoking cigars:** David Karr to Sargent Shriver, December 17, 1969, Shriver Papers, JFK Library.

574 **Shriver arranged to introduce Karr and Hammer:** Blumay, *The Dark Side of Power*, 148.

574 **"You're always talking about your old friend Lenin:** Finder, *Red Carpet*, 227.

574 **Hammer, Shriver, and Karr flew in Hammer's aircraft:** Sargent Shriver, interview March 31, 2000; Bobby Shriver, interview May 21, 2003.

574 **"kind of got pulled along by Hammer":** Sargent Shriver, interview August 30, 1997.

575 **Shriver so charmed his Soviet hosts:** Andrei Pavlov, interview March 31, 2000.

575 **"This is one of the letters that Lenin sent to me":** Bobby Shriver, interview May 21, 2003.

575 **"We went into Lenin's little study":** Finder, *Red Carpet*, 274.

575 **Karr and Shriver watched as Hammer was feted:** Epstein, *Dossier*, 269; "The Death of David Karr," *Fortune*, December 3, 1979.

575 **"I had been running the Merchandise Mart in Chicago":** Finder, *Red Carpet*, 281–82.

Chapter 45: Shriver for Vice President

578 **"George is a good guy":** *New York Times Magazine*, October 15, 1972.

579 **"We were always subject to this pressure":** White, *The Making of the President, 1972*, 44.

579 **"It seemed barely possible":** Ibid., 187.

579 **"We had no framework for our discussion":** Weil, *The Long Shot*, 161.

580 **initial brainstorming turned up twenty-three names:** Ibid., 161–2; White, *The Making of the President, 1972*, 195.

580 **"he was strongest where McGovern was weakest":** *Life*, December 29, 1972.

581 **Shriver's name was dropped from the list:** White, *The Making of the President, 1972*, 195–96.

581 **"if we could have somehow located him":** Koplinski, *Hats in the Ring*, 455.

581 **Kevin White was considered next:** White, *The Making of the President, 1972*, 197–98.

582 **"Well, I guess it's Eagleton":** Weil, *The Long Shot*, 168.

582 **Weil did find reference to mental health problems:** Ibid., 164.

582 **"George, before you change your mind":** Ibid., 169.

582 **Around four o'clock on Friday morning:** Ibid., 171–73.

583 **Eagleton thought the matter settled:** Ibid., 176.

583 **"I'm 1,000 percent for Tom Eagleton":** White, *The Making of the President, 1972*, 204.

584 **"look like a fool":** Ibid., 207.

585 **"It's a suicide mission":** *Newsweek*, August 14, 1972.

585 **Later that day, McGovern asked:** *Time*, August 14, 1972.

585 **"*Shriver!* Who wants him?":** *Newsweek*, August 14, 1972.

585 **McGovern wanted to curry favor:** *Chicago Sun-Times*, August 7, 1972.

585 **the Massachusetts senator signaled to McGovern:** Hart, *Right from the Start*, 267. Adam Clymer's 1999 biography of Ted Kennedy disputes Hart's account. Clymer writes, citing an interview with Ted Kennedy, that "Ted objected to McGovern's final choice, Sargent Shriver, as he had four years before when Humphrey considered his brother-in-law. But McGovern ignored his objections."

586 **"Wimbledon champ or Vice President":** *Newsweek*, August 14, 1972.

586 **Dell went down to McGovern's Senate office:** Donald Dell, interview April 15, 2003.

586 **Shriver sought out his brother-in-law:** *Life*, August 18, 1972.

587 **"This is a slight but not awesome gamble":** *Chicago Sun-Times*, August 7, 1972.

588 **Shriver insisted on finishing his tennis game:** *Time*, August 14, 1972.

588 **"Sarge, this is George McGovern":** Hart, *Right from the Start*, 268.

588 **Shriver felt compelled to bring up the one episode:** Sargent Shriver, interview August 30, 1997.

589 **"we've got to have fun in the campaign":** *Washington Post*, September 25, 1972.

589 **"Shriver swung into action":** Hart, *Right from the Start*, 269.

589 **"Che Guevara meeting General Patton":** Ibid.

589 **"Sarge is just what George needs":** *Time*, August 21, 1972.

590 **Mike Mansfield and Dan Rostenkowski officially nominated Shriver:** Hart, *Right from the Start*, 269.

590 **"his enthusiasm for the task":** *Evening Bulletin*, August 9, 1972.

590 **"I am not embarrassed to be George McGovern's seventh choice":** Sargent Shriver acceptance speech, August 8, 1972, Shriver Papers, JFK Library.

591 **"Look at him with that pensive look":** *Life*, August 18, 1972.

592 **This affected the campaign's press coverage.** Burt Hoffman to Sargent Shriver, September 16, 1972, Shriver Papers, JFK Library. In explaining the importance of catering to preordained news cycles, Shriver's press secretary Burt Hoffman, a former reporter and newspaper editor himself, had some choice observations to make about the nature of the press: "First, some background applicable to both print and radio-tv press. Reporters are terribly insecure people suffering from constant anxiety. Although they are competitive among themselves, their greatest competition is against the inexorable demands of the clock and their editors. As a whole, editors are rather dumb and few have any appreciation of what their reporters are doing or the problems reporters face. Editors exert often unrealistic pressures, and reporters must respond or find themselves out

in the boondocks. . . . Our roadshow must recognize these pressures and assist the reporters in getting their reports to their editors."

592   **"Everywhere we go, Sarge is late":** Donald Dell, interview April 15, 2003.

594   **"Jeannie Main guarded the gate":** William Alford, interview October 30, 2001.

594   **The "talented people that Shriver was able to recruit":** Mark Shields, interview April 16, 2002.

594   **Large percentages of normally Democratic voting groups:** *New York Times*, August 20, 1972.

595   **"I don't think we saw three white Protestants":** Mark Shields, interview April 16, 2002.

595   **why he sent his eldest son, Bobby, to Exeter:** Perry, *Us and Them*, 249.

596   **AFL-CIO president George Meany:** Weil, *The Long Shot*, 153–55; *New York Times*, October 23, 1972.

596   **according to Mark Shields, what happened was this:** Mark Shields, interview April 16, 2002.

597   **Shriver told a group of reporters:** *New York Times*, August 11, 1969.

598   **"historic opportunity for peace":** *New York Times*, August 12, 1969.

598   **The week after Shriver's nomination to the ticket:** *Time*, August 14, 1972; *Newsweek*, August 14, 1972.

599   **Shriver was on solid ground here.** Averell Harriman and Cyrus Vance joint statement, August 12, 1972, Josephson Papers, JFK Library; *Newsweek*, August 28, 1972.

599   **"We support completely Sargent Shriver's view":** Averell Harriman and Cyrus Vance joint statement, August 12, 1972, Josephson Papers, JFK Library; *New York Times*, August 13, 1972.

599   **The *Times* published an editorial:** *New York Times*, August 16, 1972.

600   **"We couldn't carry on discussions":** *New York Times*, August 13, 1972.

600   **Nixon became preoccupied with managing the attacks on Shriver:** H. R. Haldeman, August 13, 1972, and August 14, 1972, *The Haldeman Diaries*.

600   **"we should be hitting Shriver hard":** H. R. Haldeman, August 14, 1972, *The Haldeman Diaries*.

600   **"Need to destroy Shriver and his credibility":** H. R. Haldeman, August 16, 1972, *The Haldeman Diaries*.

601   **"fucking a sow in downtown Fort Worth":** Mark Shields, interview April 16, 2002.

601   **"McGovern is associating with amateurs":** H. R. Haldeman, August 22, 1972, *The Haldeman Diaries*; Weil, *The Long Shot*, 149.

601   **"I never trusted him, the SOB":** Nixon, *The Memoirs of Richard Nixon*, 688.

602   **McGovern trailed 60–34:** *Washington Post*, August 30, 1972.

602   **"recreation director on the *Titanic*":** White, *The Making of the President, 1972*, 319.

602   **When Lee White and Bill Josephson met with McGovern:** William Josephson to Sargent Shriver, August 30, 1972, Josephson Papers, JFK Library; *Washington Post*, August 31, 1972.

603   **"It's incredible what's going on":** *New York Times Magazine*, October 15, 1972.

603   **"Sarge is out to pull a Muskie":** *New York Times*, October 23, 1972.

603   **"Sargent Shriver is probably the most sparkling of the four candidates":** *Washington Post*, September 25, 1972.

603   **when Shriver and Agnew were matched up:** *Washington Post*, October 4, 1972.

603   **"sprinting through all-white suburban neighborhoods and all-black slums":** *Washington Post*, October 9, 1972.

603   **"the most Kennedy of the Kennedys":** Hart, *Right from the Start*, 311.

604   **"American Family Picnic":** *Washington Post*, October 16, 1972.

604   **"Both Eunice and I are grateful":** Sargent Shriver to Jackie Onassis, November 14, 1972, Shriver Papers, JFK Library.

604   **"How can the President claim to know what's going on in Peking":** See, for instance, *Face the Nation*, October 22, 1972.

604   **"where Nixon meets his Waterloo":** *Sacramento Bee*, September 12, 1972.

605   **Back at the office for a day:** Crouse, *The Boys on the Bus*, 362.

605   **the Shriver staff soldiered on:** White, *The Making of the President, 1972*, 335.

605 **"I was never depressed during that campaign":** Sargent Shriver, interview August 31, 1997.

605 **"I remember the last day":** Mark Shields, interview April 16, 2002.

606 **Sarge and Eunice voted in the early afternoon:** "Detailed Schedule—Sargent Shriver—November 7, 1972," Josephson Papers, JFK Library.

606 **"It was a horrible night":** Donald Dell, interview April 15, 2003.

606 **"We were having a grand old time":** Sargent Shriver, interview August 31, 1997.

606 **"In a campaign of surpassing importance":** "Lucky Seven Follies," Timberlawn, November 7, 1972, Shriver Papers, JFK Library.

Chapter 46: Shriver for President

610 **"With the disastrous defeat of George McGovern":** Witcover, *Marathon*, 119.

610 **"Mr. Kennedy has given his close friends the impression":** *New York Times*, May 21, 1973.

611 **over the first weekend of September:** Witcover, *Marathon*, 121.

611 **"He wasn't going to leave her":** Ibid., 121–22.

611 **"a kind of royal family in exile":** Ibid., 124.

612 **"firm, final, and unconditional":** *Boston Evening Globe*, September 23, 1974.

612 **"very, very reluctant":** David Birenbaum, interview March 4, 2002.

613 **McGovern's aides had laughed at him:** Bourne, *Jimmy Carter*, 228–36.

614 **but "clearly concerned":** David Birenbaum, interview March 4, 2002.

615 **"the last of the sophomores":** McCarthy, *One Journalist's Place in the World*, 117.

615 **"Shriver is a lightweight":** Ibid.

616 **"We sat down around the dinner table":** Bryan Hehir, interview March 27, 2003.

616 **"ruthlessness of his good intentions":** *New York Times Magazine*, October 15, 1972.

616 **"Sarge is probably too nice a guy":** Bryan Hehir, interview March 27, 2003.

616 **"What I found both very appealing about him":** Anthony Lake, interview May 13, 2003.

617 **"In many campaigns":** Ibid.

617 **"When we got into the lunch":** Ibid.

619 **Pavlov had been a member of the Communist Party:** Andrei Pavlov, interview March 31, 2000.

619 **Although this made Shriver suspect:** Sargent Shriver, interview March 31, 2000.

619 **Shriver persuaded Pavlov:** Sargent Shriver, interview September 1, 1997.

619 **"everywhere we went":** Larry Tribe, interview February 26, 2002.

620 **"stumbled upon a room full of KGB agents":** Ibid.

620 **Pavlov had no idea of what to expect:** Andrei Pavlov, interview March 31, 2000. This also made the translators very nervous, since they would have to perform simultaneous translation. As Pavlov recalled, Shriver's reference during the lecture to Kissinger's famous remark "power is an aphrodisiac" gave the translators fits, forcing one of them into a frantic digression on the Greek goddess of love.

620 **"Many Americans have believed":** Sargent Shriver lecture paper given before the Institute of USA and Canadian Studies of the Academy of Sciences of the USSR, March 22, 1975, Shriver Papers, Special Olympics International.

621 **"I remember him coming back":** Mark Shriver, interview September 26, 2001.

621 **"Once you spent time there":** Bobby Shriver, interview May 21, 2003.

622 **"rapt and wide-eyed":** Andrei Pavlov, interview March 31, 2000.

622 **Shriver held a ninety-minute press conference:** *New York Times*, April 11, 1975.

622 **his cousin rocking back and forth in his seat:** Bobby Shriver, interview May 21, 2003.

623 **"I want to hear it from Eunice":** *New York Times*, April 14, 1975.

623 **"I can't help it if he runs":** *Washington Post*, March 27, 1975.

623 **"just as reserved as her brother":** *New York Times*, April 14, 1975.

624 **Shriver told him he was considering entering the race himself:** Witcover, *Marathon*, 150.

624 **The "Family of Long Memories":** Ibid., 150–51.

625 **Some twenty years later:** Sargent Shriver, interview August 31, 1997; *Washington Post*, July 16, 1975.

625 **On July 15 he announced:** *New York Times*, July 15, 1975.

625 **"a final scene in a Marx brothers movie":** Witcover, *Marathon*, 151.

626 **"the only recognizable 'celebrity' in the pack":** Ibid.

626 **"There was no effort to get Kennedy people":** *Washington Post*, July 16, 1975.

626 **"There is trouble in the Kennedy camp":** *New York Times*, July 22, 1975.

627 **Bobby Shriver thinks:** Bobby Shriver, interview May 30, 2003.

627 **Will noticed some of the books strewn around:** David Birenbaum, interview March 4, 2002.

629 **"Kennedy faithful hanging from the rafters":** Sargent Shriver would later say that "Ethel's presence showed I was not a heretic [within the family] or something," Koplinski, *Hats in the Ring*, 536; Witcover, *Marathon*, 152.

629 **"I could not stand aside":** Sargent Shriver announcement statement, September 20, 1975, Shriver Papers, JFK Library; Witcover, *Marathon*, 152.

630 **"Shriver felt insecure":** McCarthy, *One Journalist's Place in the World*, 115.

630 **The next morning Shriver appeared on** *Meet the Press*: Ibid.

631 **"He never got out from under that 'mantle' business":** David Birenbaum, interview March 4, 2002.

631 **"pep, hope, and a kind of creative chaos":** *Newsweek*, January 26, 1976.

632 **I can definitely beat** *that* **guy:** Timothy Shriver, interview March 5, 2002.

632 **"He's a lightweight and I think he's kidding himself":** *Washington Star*, n.d.

632 **"What impressed me about that":** David Birenbaum, interview March 4, 2002.

633 **"an object lesson in the power":** Bourne, *Jimmy Carter*, 278.

635 **"Are there any circumstances":** Bourne, *Jimmy Carter*, 279–80.

635 **The misunderstanding:** Ibid; Witcover, *Marathon*, 206–7.

635 **Shriver was mistakenly listed:** Staff meeting minutes, January 19, 1976, Shriver Papers, JFK Library.

635 **"conveyed an inaccurate account of the public positions of Carter and Shriver":** *Nation*, February 7, 1976.

635 **When Don O'Brien:** Witcover, *Marathon*, 207.

636 **"the difference between first and second place":** Ibid.

636 **"I think I've been sandbagged by Carter":** *Washington Star*, January 21, 1976.

636 **Shriver told friends:** Bourne, *Jimmy Carter*, 281.

636 **"I am and always have been strongly opposed to abortion":** Sargent Shriver statement on abortion and telephone conversation—suggestions from people re new draft on abortion, January 27, 1976, Shriver Papers, JFK Library.

637 **Many of the younger generation of Kennedy cousins:** Staff assignment, December 1, 1975, Shriver Papers, JFK Library.

637 **"a great bon-voyage party at the pier":** Witcover, *Marathon*, 206.

637 **Rosalynn's ploy spelled the difference:** Bourne, *Jimmy Carter*, 283.

638 **"He was laboring to be taken as his own man":** Witcover, *Marathon*, 234.

638 **"a stunningly young 60":** *Newsweek*, January 26, 1976.

638 **As recently as early February:** Scripps-Howard News Service, "Shriver Leads in Massachusetts Presidential Polls" February 2, 1976; *Boston Globe*, February 4, 1976.

639 **a "step-Kennedy":** Koplinski, *Hats in the Ring*, 523.

639 **"You didn't even mention my last name":** Witcover, *Marathon*, 250ff.

639 **"I think it's a fabulous family":** *Boston Globe*, February 4, 1976.

640 **On primary day in Massachusetts:** Witcover, *Marathon*, 249.

640 **"counseling him to get out after Massachusetts":** David Birenbaum, interview March 4, 2002.

640 **"my candidacy was in bad shape":** Koplinski, *Hats in the Ring*, 538.

640 **ultimately the mayor withheld his endorsement:** Cohen and Taylor, *American Pharaoh*, 551.

640 **"some elements of the Daley machine":** Koplinski, *Hats in the Ring*, 539.

641 **"This is not a happy day for me":** Sargent Shriver withdrawal statement, March 22, 1976, Shriver Papers, JFK Library.

641 **"I must be one ugly son-of-a-bitch!":** William Alford, interview October 30, 2001.

641 **"Shriver's reputation":** *Newsweek*, January 26, 1976.

642 **"Shriver was characteristically buoyant":** *Washington Monthly*, June 1976.

642 **"The real irony":** Ibid.

Part 7: Private Life, Public Service (1976–2003)
Chapter 47: Nuclear Politics

645 **"a surer basis for peace":** *Washington Post*, October 26, 1979; Sargent Shriver, interview September 7, 1998.

646 **On September 18, Shriver teamed up:** United States Committee for East-West Common Existence press release, September 18, 1976.

646 **"Dear President-Elect":** Sargent Shriver et al. to President-elect Carter, December 6, 1976, Special Olympics Files, Special Olympics Office, Washington, DC.

647 **a small but influential band of foreign policy experts:** Sargent Shriver to George Kennan, September 25, 1981, Special Olympics Files, Special Olympics Office, Washington, DC.

648 **"Reagan had made a statement that day":** Bryan Hehir, interview March 27, 2003.

648 **Shriver immediately sent the statement:** Sargent Shriver to Robert McNamara, October 21, 1981, Special Olympics Files, Special Olympics Office, Washington, DC.

649 **"decisive leadership":** Sargent Shriver to Robert McNamara, November 4, 1981, Special Olympics Files, Special Olympics Office, Washington, DC; *Washington Post*, November 4, 1981.

649 **Haig announced a "contingency plan":** *New York Times*, November 4, 1981.

649 **"Human beings":** Sargent Shriver to Robert McNamara, November 4, 1981, Special Olympics Files, Special Olympics Office, Washington, DC.

649 **Shriver was getting impatient:** Sargent Shriver to Robert McNamara (with handwritten response from McNamara), December 14, 1982, Special Olympics Files, Special Olympics Office, Washington, DC.

650 **At one dinner Averell Harriman spoke:** Anthony Lake, interview May 13, 2003.

650 **"I do remember at least the semblance of a snicker":** Sargent Shriver to McGeorge Bundy, February 26, 1982, Special Olympics Files, Special Olympics Office, Washington, DC.

651 **"a blockbuster":** *New York Times*, April 9, 1982.

652 **"Sarge, as an unacknowledged author of this article":** Robert McNamara, handwritten note to Sargent Shriver, April 1, 1982, Special Olympics Files, Special Olympics Office, Washington, DC.

652 **"I must say that you touched off a notable series of events":** George Kennan to Sargent Shriver, June 30, 1982, Special Olympics Files, Special Olympics Office, Washington, DC.

653 **"Christians cannot long live by the sign of the mushroom cloud":** Pastoral letter on peace and war, confidential first draft, June 11, 1982, Special Olympics Files, Special Olympics Office, Washington, DC.

653 **a ten-page assessment of the draft:** Sargent Shriver to Bryan Hehir, July 1, 1982, Special Olympic Files, Special Olympics Office, Washington, DC.

654 **A pledge not to use nuclear arms first:** *New York Times*, October 4, 1982.

654 **"We find the moral responsibility":** *New York Times*, October 26, 1982.

654 **reacted as angrily as they dared:** Ibid.

654 **spent the early part of November recruiting prominent signatories:** Sargent Shriver to Robert McNamara, Paul Warnke, et al., November 15, 1982; Sargent Shriver to Gerard Smith, November 16, 1982, Special Olympics Files, Special Olympics Office, Washington, DC.

655 **Acknowledging that some critics believe:** Sargent Shriver et al. to Ben Bradlee and A. M. Rosenthal, November 17, 1982.

655 **voted overwhelmingly in favor of endorsing the draft:** *New York Times,* November 19, 1982.

655 **"Thank you for being the stimulus":** William Colby to Sargent Shriver, September 24, 1982, Special Olympics Files, Special Olympics Office, Washington, DC.

655 **"the most profound and searching inquiry yet":** *New York Times,* April 1, 1983.

656 **the bishops voted overwhelmingly:** *Chicago Sun-Times,* May 3, 1983; *New York Times,* May 4, 1983.

656 **Shriver immediately telegrammed the archbishop:** Sargent Shriver telegram to Archbishop Hannan, May 3, 1982, Special Olympics Files, Special Olympics Office, Washington, DC.

656 **"the boldest and most decisive step on social issues":** *New York Times,* May 4, 1983.

657 **"the era's most influential challenge":** McGreevy, *Catholicism and American Freedom,* 285.

657 **"the invisible hand behind the Gang of Four":** McGeorge Bundy to Sargent Shriver, May 25, 1983, Special Olympics Files, Special Olympics Office, Washington, DC.

Chapter 48: Special Olympics, a Family Affair

658 **Eunice was busy planning:** Bueno, *Special Olympics,* 46–47.

658 **By 1980 the program:** Ibid., 53.

659 **"Mrs. Shriver almost single-handedly changed the way:** Ibid., 83.

659 **"my mother does put the fear of God in most people":** Leamer, *The Kennedy Women,* 693.

661 **"His career as an active political leader ended after Carter's election":** Timothy Shriver, interview March 5, 2002.

661 **As the cold war ended:** Andrei Pavlov, interview March 31, 2000; Bueno, *Special Olympics,* 103.

662 **"It can't have been easy":** Timothy Shriver, interview March 5, 2002.

662 **In just over a decade, Best Buddies:** Anthony Shriver, interview June 10, 2003; www.bestbuddies.org.

665 **"Arnold loved America":** Leigh, *Arnold,* 92.

665 **"Although the film was billed":** Ibid., 139.

665 **"a charmer, a champion, an endearingly arrogant winner":** Ibid., 144.

665 **"I could see that Arnold was":** Maria Shriver, interview July 9, 2003.

665 **"I think what made her fall in love with me":** Arnold Schwarzenegger, interview July 29, 2003.

666 **"When one has money":** Leigh, *Arnold,* 178.

666 **her father was the most accepting of Arnold:** Maria Shriver, interview July 9, 2003.

666 **"Sargent was not really aware":** Arnold Schwarzenegger, interview July 29, 2003.

666 **he wrote his daughter a long letter:** Maria Shriver, interview July 9, 2003.

667 **"the Kennedys' worst setback since Chappaquiddick":** Leigh, *Arnold,* 169–70.

667 **quickly came to respect his girlfriend's parents:** Arnold Schwarzenegger, interview July 29, 2003.

667 **"the theology and ethics of *Conan the Barbarian*":** Daniel Morrissey, interview March 3, 2003.

668 **Of all the disparate red-carpet celebrities:** *USA Today,* April 28, 1986.

669 **"It was the most beautiful wedding ceremony":** Ibid.

669 **"I love her and will always take care of her":** Leigh, *Arnold,* 245.

669 **"You're making me very happy":** Sargent Shriver to Arnold Schwarzenegger, July 11, 2003.

670 **"the biggest influence in Arnold's life":** Maria Shriver, interview July 9, 2003.

670 **"Eunice and Sargent are like my second parents":** Arnold Schwarzenegger, interview July 29, 2003.

670 **"I would sit there for hours and just pump him for information":** Ibid.

670 **He explicitly credits Shriver:** Arnold Schwarzenegger, interview July 29, 2003.

670 **"You can't be married to Maria Shriver":** Tribune Media Services, August 13, 2003.

672 **"Whatever happened to Sargent Shriver?":** "The Baby Shower," *Seinfeld,* May 16, 1991.

672 **"if Sarge had married Susie Glotz":** Mark Shields, interview April 16, 2002.

672 **"I used to be Jack Kennedy's brother-in-law":** *New Republic,* January 17, 1976.

Chapter 49: Faith and Hope

673 **"Shriver was a passionate reader":** McCarthy, *One Journalist's Place in the World,* 118.

674 **"You cannot separate Daddy from his faith":** Maria Shriver, interview July 9, 2003.

675 **"a Roman Catholic candidate of an unfamiliar sort":** *New York Times,* September 16, 1972.

675 **"Sarge has chosen the active life":** Mav McCarthy, interview July 30, 2003.

675 **"zealously orthodox":** *Time,* June 11, 1984. Opus Dei, like the Masons, has spawned many conspiracy theories, both in real life and in fiction. Recently, Dan Brown's best-selling thriller novel *The Da Vinci Code* features the sinister side of Opus Dei.

675 **he can't understand how the Shrivers:** Hans Kung, interview May 20, 2003.

676 **"as if jet lag did not exist":** Leamer, *The Kennedy Women,* 755.

676 **forcibly prevent Sarge from overexerting himself:** Sargent Shriver, interview February 18, 1998.

677 **the serious health issues her brother Jack suffered:** See, for instance, Dallek, *An Unfinished Life.*

677 **"By all the laws of time and nature":** Leamer, *The Kennedy Women,* 762.

680 **"A Champion of Life":** *Washington Post,* June 14, 2003.

681 **"I do not know how my parents have so much endless energy":** Maria Shriver, interview July 9, 2003.

681 **"the only reason Sargent Shriver accepted this award tonight":** National Center on Poverty Law annual dinner, May 1, 2003.

682 **"I do believe he will be canonized one day as a saint":** Colman McCarthy, interview July 30, 2003.

682 **In the summer of 2000, Shriver traveled to Beijing:** William Alford, interview October 30, 2001.

BIBLIOGRAPHY

Books

Aaron, Henry J. *Politics and the Professors: The Great Society in Perspective.* Washington, DC: Brookings Institution Press, 1978.

Alden, Vernon R. *Speaking for Myself: The Personal Reflections of Vernon R. Alden.* Athens: Ohio University Press, 1997.

Ambrose, Stephen E. *Nixon.* Vol. 2: *The Triumph of a Politician 1962–1972.* New York: Simon and Schuster, 1989.

Anders, Curt. *Hearts in Conflict: A One-Volume History of the Civil War.* New York: Carol Publishing Group/Birch Lane Press, 1994.

Andrew, John A., III. *Lyndon Johnson and the Great Society.* Chicago: Ivan R. Dee, 1998.

Ashabranner, Brent. *A Moment in History: The First Ten Years of the Peace Corps.* Garden City, NY: Doubleday, 1971.

Associated Press. *The Torch Is Passed . . . : The Associated Press Story of the Death of a President.* New York: Associated Press, 1963.

Auletta, Ken. *The Underclass.* New York: Random House, 1982.

Barta, Russell, ed. *Challenge to the Laity.* Huntington, IN: Our Sunday Visitor, 1980.

Berkowitz, Edward D. *American's Welfare State: From Roosevelt to Reagan.* Baltimore: Johns Hopkins University Press, 1991.

———. *Mr. Social Security: The Life of Wilbur J. Cohen.* Lawrence: University Press of Kansas, 1995.

Bernstein, Carl, and Bob Woodward. *All the President's Men.* New York: Warner Paperback Library, 1974.

Bernstein, Irving. *Guns or Butter: The Presidency of Lyndon Johnson.* New York: Oxford University Press, 1996.

———. *Promises Kept: John F. Kennedy's New Frontier.* New York: Oxford University Press, 1991.

Beschloss, Michael. *Reaching for Glory: Lyndon Johnson's Secret White House Tapes, 1964–1965.* New York: Simon and Schuster, 2001.

———. *Taking Charge: The Johnson White House Tapes, 1963–1964.* New York: Simon and Schuster, 1997.

Biles, Richard. *Richard J. Daley: Politics, Race, and the Governing of Chicago.* Dekalb: Northern Illinois University Press, 1995.

Bird, Kai. *The Color of Truth: McGeorge Bundy and William Bundy: Brothers in Arms.* New York: Simon and Schuster, 1998.

Bishop, Jim. *The Day Kennedy Was Shot.* New York: Bantam Books, 1968.

Blair, Joan, and Clay Blair Jr. *The Search for JFK.* New York: G. P. Putnam's Sons, 1976.

Blumay, Carl. *The Dark Side of Power: The Real Armand Hammer.* New York: Simon and Schuster, 1992.

Bohlen, Charles E. *Witness to History, 1929–1969.* New York: W. W. Norton, 1973.

Bookbinder, Hyman. *Off the Wall: Memoirs of a Public Affairs Junkie.* Washington, DC: Seven Locks Press, 1991.

Bourne, Peter G. *Jimmy Carter: A Comprehensive Biography from Plains to Postpresidency.* New York: Charles Scribner's Sons, 1997.

Brager, George A., and Francis P. Purcell. *Community Action against Poverty: Readings from the Mobilization Experience.* New Haven: College and University Press, 1967.

Branch, Taylor. *Parting the Waters: America in the King Years, 1954–63.* New York: Simon and Schuster, 1988.

———. *Pillar of Fire: America in the King Years, 1963–1965.* New York: Simon and Schuster, 1998.

Bready, James H. *Baseball in Baltimore: The First 100 Years.* Baltimore: Johns Hopkins University Press, 1998.

Bueno, Ana. *Special Olympics: The First Twenty-five Years.* San Francisco: Foghorn Press, 1994.

Bundy, Willam. *A Tangled Web: The Making of Foreign Policy in the Nixon Presidency.* New York: Hill and Wang, 1998.

Burns, James MacGregor. *John Kennedy: A Political Profile.* New York: Harcourt, Brace World, 1959.

Califano, Joseph A., Jr. *Governing America: An Insider's Report from the White House and the Cabinet.* New York: Simon and Schuster, 1981.

———. *The Triumph and Tragedy of Lyndon Johnson: The White House Years.* New York: Simon and Schuster, 1991.

Calvocoressi, Peter, and Guy Wint. *Total War: The Story of World War II.* New York: Pantheon Books, 1972.

Caro, Robert A. *The Path to Power: The Years of Lyndon Johnson.* New York: Vintage Books, 1981.

Chennault, Anna. *The Education of Anna.* New York: Times Books, 1980.

Ciccone, F. Richard. *Daley: Power and Presidential Politics.* Chicago: Contemporary Books, 1996.

Clark, Robert F. *The War on Poverty: History, Selected Programs, and Ongoing Impact.* New York: University Press of America, 2002.

Clifford, Clark. *Counsel to the President: A Memoir.* New York: Random House, 1991.

Clymer, Adam. *Edward M. Kennedy: A Biography.* New York: William Morrow, 1999.

Coffin, William Sloane, Jr. *Once to Every Man: A Memoir.* New York: Atheneum, 1977.

Cohen, Adam, and Elizabeth Taylor. *American Pharaoh: Mayor Richard J. Daley: His Battle for Chicago and the Nation.* New York: Little, Brown, 2000.

Cohen, Richard E. *Rostenkowski: The Pursuit of Power and the End of the Old Politics.* Chicago: Ivan R. Dee, 1999.

Cole, Wayne S. *America First: The Battle against Intervention 1940–1941.* Madison: University of Wisconsin Press, 1953.

———. *Charles A. Lindbergh and the Battle against American Intervention in World War II.* New York: Harcourt Brace Jovanovich, 1974.

Collier, Peter, and David Horowitz. *The Kennedys: An American Drama.* New York: Summit Books, 1984.

Conkin, Paul Keith. *Big Daddy from the Pedernales : Lyndon Baines Johnson.* Boston: Twayne, 1986.

Cook, Don. *Charles de Gaulle: A Biography.* New York: G. P. Putnam's Sons, 1983.

Crook, William H., and Ross Thomas. *Warriors for the Poor: The Story of VISTA, Volunteers in Service to America.* New York: William Morrow, 1969.

Crouse, Timothy. *The Boys on the Bus.* New York: Ballantine Books, 1972.

Dallek, Robert. *Flawed Giant: Lyndon Johnson and His Times, 1960–1973.* New York: Oxford University Press, 1998.

———. *An Unfinished Life.* New York: Little, Brown, 2003.

Danziger, Sheldon H., and Daniel H. Weinberg. *Fighting Poverty: What Works and What Doesn't.* Cambridge, MA: Harvard University Press, 1986.

David, Lester. *Joan: The Reluctant Kennedy*. New York: Funk and Wagnalls, 1974.

Davies, Gareth. *From Opportunity to Entitlement: The Transformation and Decline of Great Society Liberalism.* Lawrence: University Press of Kansas, 1996.

Davis, Harry R., and Robert C. Good. *Reinhold Niebuhr on Politics: His Political Philosophy and Its Application to Our Age as Expressed in His Writings*. New York: Charles Scribner's Sons, 1960.

DiBacco, Thomas V., Lorna C. Mason, and Christian G. Appy. *History of the United States*. Boston: Houghton Mifflin, 1991.

Diem, Bui. *In the Jaws of History*. Boston: Houghton Mifflin, 1987.

Dinnenn, Joseph F. *The Kennedy Family*. Boston: Little, Brown, 1959.

Doenecke, Justus D. *Storm on the Horizon: The Challenge to American Intervention, 1939–1941*. New York: Rowan and Littlefield, 2000.

Donovan, John C. *The Politics of Poverty*. New York: Pegasus, 1973.

Edsall, Thomas Byrne, and Mary D. Edsall. *Chain Reaction: The Impact of Race, Rights, and Taxes on American Politics*. New York: W. W. Norton, 1991.

Ehrlichman, John. *Witness to Power: The Nixon Years*. New York: Simon and Schuster, 1982.

Ellis, John Tracy. *American Catholics and the Intellectual Life*. Chicago: Heritage Foundation, 1956.

———. *The Life of James Cardinal Gibbons*. Milwaukee: Bruce Publishing, 1963.

Epstein, Edward Jay. *Dossier: The Secret History of Armand Hammer*. New York: Random House, 1996.

Evans, Rowland, and Robert Novak. *Lyndon B. Johnson: The Exercise of Power*. New York: New American Library, 1966.

Feldstein, Albert L. *Gone but Not Forgotten: A Biographical Graveside Tribute to Historic Allegany County Figures and Notable Personages from the Past*, vols. 1 and 2. Cumberland, MD: Commercial Press Printing Co., 1988.

Finder, Joseph. *Red Carpet*. New York: Holt, Rinehart and Winston, 1983.

Fischer, Fritz. *Making Them Like Us: Peace Corps Volunteers in the 1960s*. Washington, DC: Smithsonian Institution Press, 1998.

Fleming, Dan B., Jr. *Kennedy vs. Humphrey, West Virginia 1960: The Pivotal Battle of the Democratic Presidential Nomination*. Jefferson, NC: McFarland, 1992.

Fleming, Thomas. *The New Dealers' War: FDR and the War within World War II*. New York: Basic Books, 2001.

Frank, Richard B. *Guadalcanal*. New York: Random House, 1990.

Fuchs, Lawrence H. *"Those Peculiar Americans": The Peace Corps and the American National Character*. New York: Meredith Press, 1967.

Fursenko, Aleksandr, and Timothy Naftali. *"One Hell of a Gamble": Khrushchev, Castro, and Kennedy, 1958–1964*. New York: W. W. Norton, 1997.

Galbraith, John Kenneth. *Ambassador's Journal: A Personal Account of the Kennedy Years*. New York: Signet, 1969.

———. *A Life in Our Times: Memoirs*. Boston: Houghton Mifflin, 1981.

Gallup, George H., ed. *The Gallup Poll (1968)*. Wilmington, DE: Scholarly Resources, 1969.

———. *The Gallup Poll 1935–1971*. New York: Random House, 1972.

Gerber, Michele Stenehjem. *An American First: John T. Flynn and the America First Committee*. New Rochelle, NY: Arlington House, 1976.

Germond, Jack. *Fat Man in a Middle Seat: Forty years of Covering Politics*. New York: Random House, 1999.

Gilbert, Martin. *A History of the Twentieth Century*, vol. 1, 1900–1933. New York: William Morrow, 1997.

Gilkey, Langdon. *On Niebuhr: A Theological Study*. Chicago: University of Chicago Press, 2000.

Gillette, Michael L. *Launching the War on Poverty*. New York: Twayne, 1996.

Ginzberg, Eli, and Robert M. Solow, eds. *The Great Society: Lessons for the Future*. New York: Basic Books, 1974.

Goldman, Eric F. *The Tragedy of Lyndon Johnson*. New York: Dell Publishing, 1968.

Goldstein, Louis L. *Louis Goldstein's Maryland*. Maryland State Archives, 1985.

Goodman, Allan E. *The Lost Peace: America's Search for a Negotiated Settlement of the Vietnam War*. Stanford, CA: Hoover Institution, 1978.

Goodwin, Doris Kearns. *The Fitzgeralds and the Kennedys: An American Saga.* New York: St. Martin's Press, 1987.

Goodwin, Richard N. *Remembering America: A Voice from the Sixties.* Boston: Little, Brown, 1988.

Graham, Frank. *Al Smith, American: An Informal Biography.* New York: G. P. Putnam's Sons, 1945.

Greenberg, Polly. *The Devil Has Slippery Shoes: A Biased Biography of the Child Development Group of Mississippi (CDGM), A Story of Maximum Feasible Poor Parent Participation.* Washington, DC: Youth Policy Institute, 1969.

Gromely, Ken. *Archibald Cox: Conscience of a Nation.* Reading, MA: Addison-Wesley, 1997.

Hackett, Pat, ed. *Andy Warhol Diaries.* New York: Warner Books, 1989.

Halberstam, David. *The Best and the Brightest.* New York: Random House 1969.

Haldeman, H. R. *The Ends of Power.* New York: New York Times Books, 1978.

————. *The Haldeman Diaries: Inside the Nixon White House.* New York: G. P. Putnam's Sons, 1994.

Hamilton, Charles V. *Adam Clayton Powell, Jr.: The Political Biography of an American Dilemma.* New York: Atheneum, 1991.

Hammel, Eric. *Guadalcanal: Decision at Sea: The Naval Battle of Guadalcanal, November 13–15, 1942.* New York: Crown, 1988.

Hammer, Armand. *Hammer.* New York: Perigree Books, 1987.

Hardesty, Robert L., ed. *The Johnson Years: The Difference He Made.* Austin: University of Texas, Lyndon Baines Johnson Library, 1993.

Haring, Hermann. *Hans Kung: Breaking Through.* New York: Continuum, 1998.

Harrington, Michael. *Toward a Democratic Left: A Radical Program for a New Majority.* New York: Macmillan, 1968.

Hart, Gary Warren. *Right from the Start: A Chronicle of the McGovern Campaign.* New York: Quadrangle / New York Times Books, 1973.

Haskins, James. *A New Kind of Joy: The Story of the Special Olympics.* Garden City, NY: Doubleday, 1976.

Haygood, Wil. *King of the Cats: The Life and Times of Adam Clayton Powell, Jr.* Boston: Houghton Mifflin, 1993.

Heath, Jim F. *Decade of Disillusionment: The Kennedy–Johnson Years.* Bloomington: Indiana University Press, 1975.

Heller, Adele, and Lois Rudnick, eds. *1915, The Cultural Moment: The New Politics, the New Woman, the New Psychology, the New Art, and the New Theatre in America.* New Brunswick, NJ: Rutgers University Press, 1991.

Hendrickson, Paul. *The Living and the Dead: Robert McNamara and Five Lives of a Lost War.* New York: Alfred A. Knopf, 1996.

Henggeler, Paul R. *In His Steps: Lyndon Johnson and the Kennedy Mystique.* Chicago: Ivan R. Dee, 1991.

Hersh, Burton. *The Education of Edward Kennedy: A Family Biography.* New York: William Morrow, 1972.

Hersh, Seymour M. *The Price of Power: Kissinger in the Nixon White House.* New York: Summit Books, 1983.

Hesburgh, Theodore M., and Jerry Reedy. *God, Country, Notre Dame.* New York: Doubleday, 1990.

Hess, John L. *The Case for DeGaulle: An American Viewpoint.* New York: William Morrow, 1968.

Heyman, C. David. *RFK: A Candid Biography of Robert F. Kennedy.* New York: Penguin Putnam, 1998.

Hoffman, Elizabeth Cobbs. *All You Need Is Love: The Peace Corps and the Spirit of the 1960s.* Cambridge, MA: Harvard University Press, 1998.

Hoguet, Robert Louis. *Robert Louis Hoguet (1878–1961): An Autobiography.* New York: Vantage Press, 1986.

Humphrey, Hubert H. *War on Poverty.* New York: McGraw-Hill, 1964.

Hung, Nguyen Tien, and Jerrold L. Schecter. *The Palace File: Vietnam Secret Documents.* New York: Harper and Row, 1986.

Hutchinson, Robert. *Their Kingdom Come: Inside the Secret World of Opus Dei.* New York: St. Martin's Press, 1997.

Isserman, Maurice. *The Other American: The Life of Michael Harrington.* New York: Public Affairs, 2000.

Jameson, Colin G. *The Battle of Guadalcanal, 11–15 November 1942.* Washington, DC: Naval Historical Center, Department of the Navy, 1994.

Johnson, Earl, Jr. *Justice and Reform: The Formative Years of the OEO Legal Services Program.* New York: Russell Sage Foundation, 1974.

Johnson, Lady Bird. *A White House Diary.* New York: Holt, Rinehart and Winston, 1970.

Johnson, Lyndon Baines. *The Vantage Point: Perspectives on the Presidency of 1963–1969*. New York: Holt, Rinehart and Winston, 1971.

Jonsen, Albert R. *The Birth of Bioethics*. New York: Oxford University Press, 1998.

Jordan, Barbara C., and Elspeth D. Rostow. *The Great Society: A Twenty-Year Critique*. University of Texas, Austin: Lyndon Baines Johnson Library, 1986.

Kaiser, David. *American Tragedy: Kennedy, Johnson, and the Origins of the Vietnam War*. Cambridge, MA: Harvard University Press/Belknap Press, 2000.

Kaiser, Robert G. *Russia: The People and the Power*. New York: Washington Square Press, 1976.

Kampelman, Max M. *Entering New Worlds: The Memoirs of a Private Man in Public Life*. New York: HarperCollins, 1991.

Katz, Jack. *Poor People's Lawyers in Transition*. New Brunswick, NJ: Rutgers University Press, 1982.

Katz, Michael B. *The Undeserving Poor: From the War on Poverty to the War on Welfare*. New York: Pantheon Books, 1989.

Kearns, Doris. *Lyndon Johnson and the American Dream*. New York: Signet, 1976.

Kennedy, David M. *Freedom from Fear: The American People in Depression and War, 1929–1945*. New York: Oxford University Press, 1999.

Kennedy, John F. *Public Papers of the Presidents: John F. Kennedy, 1961*. Washington, DC: Federal Register Division, National Archives and Records Service, 1962.

Kennedy, Rose Fitzgerald. *Times to Remember*. New York: Doubleday, 1995.

Kessler, Ronald. *The Sins of the Father: Joseph P. Kennedy and the Dynasty He Founded*. New York: Warner Books, 1996.

Kissinger, Henry. *White House Years*. Boston: Little, Brown, 1979.

Kittler, Glenn D. *The Peace Corps*. New York: Paperback Library, 1963.

Klein, Frederick Shriver, ed. *Just South of Gettysburg: Carroll County, Maryland in the Civil War*. Westminster, MD: Historical Society of Carroll County, 1963.

———. *Old Lancaster: Historic Pennsylvania Community*. Lancaster, PA: Early America Series, 1964.

Knox, R. A. *Enthusiasm: A Chapter in the History of Religion*. Oxford: Clarendon Press, 1950.

Koplinski, Brad. *Hats in the Ring*. Bethesda, MD: Presidential Publishing, 2000.

Koskoff, David E. *Joseph P. Kennedy: A Life and Times*. Englewood Cliffs, NJ: Prentice-Hall, 1974.

Kung, Hans. *The Catholic Church: A Short History*. New York: Modern Library, 2001.

Kutler, Stanley I. *Abuse of Power: The New Nixon Tapes*. New York: Free Press, 1997.

Lander, Louise, ed. *War on Poverty*. New York: Facts on File, 1967.

Lawrence, Susan E. *The Poor in Court*. Princeton, NJ: Princeton University Press, 1990.

Lazarus, Edward. *Black Hills, White Justice: The Sioux Nation versus the United States, 1775 to the Present*. New York: HarperCollins, 1991.

Leamer, Laurence. *The Kennedy Women: The Saga of an American Family*. New York: Villard Books, 1994.

Leckie, Robert. *Challenge for the Pacific: Guadalcanal—The Turning Point of the War*. Garden City, NY: Doubleday, 1965.

Leigh, Wendy. *Arnold: An Unauthorized Biography*. Chicago: Congdon and Weed, 1990.

Lemann, Nicholas. *The Promised Land: The Great Black Migration and How It Changed America*. New York: Vintage Books, 1991.

Lens, Sidney. *Poverty: America's Enduring Paradox: A History of the Richest Nation's Unwon War*. New York: Thomas Y. Crowell, 1971.

Leuchtenberg, William E. *Franklin D. Roosevelt and the New Deal*. New York: Harper and Row, 1963.

———. *In the Shadow of FDR: From Harry Truman to Ronald Reagan*. Ithaca, NY: Cornell University Press, 1983.

Levine, Robert A. *The Poor Ye Need Not Have with You: Lessons from the War on Poverty*. Cambridge, MA: M.I.T. Press, 1970.

Levitan, Sar A. *The Great Society's Poor Law: A New Approach to Poverty*. Baltimore: Johns Hopkins University Press, 1969.

Liebling, A. J. *Chicago: The Second City*. New York: Alfred A. Knopf, 1952.

Lincoln, Evelyn. *Kennedy and Johnson*. New York: Holt, Rinehart and Winston, 1968.

Liston, Robert A. *Sargent Shriver: A Candid Portrait*. New York: Farrar, Straus, 1964.

Macdonald, Dwight. *Discriminations: Essays and Afterthoughts, 1938–1974*. New York: Grossman, 1974.

Mack, Edward F. *The Way It Was at Canterbury, 1915–1965*. New Milford, CT: The Canterbury School, 1966.

Manchester, William. *The Death of a President: November 20–November 25, 1963*. New York: Harper and Row, 1967.

———. *The Glory and the Dream: A Narrative History of America, 1932–1972*. Boston: Little, Brown, 1973.

Martin, John Bartlow. *Adlai Stevenson of Illinois: The Life of Adlai E. Stevenson*. Garden City, NY: Doubleday, 1976.

Martin, Ralph G. *A Hero for Our Time: An Intimate Story of the Kennedy Years*. New York: Macmillan, 1983.

———. *Seeds of Destruction: Joe Kennedy and His Sons*. New York: G. P. Putnam's Sons, 1995.

Martin, Ralph G., and Ed Plaut. *Front Runner, Dark Horse*. Garden City, NY: Doubleday, 1960.

Matthews, Christopher. *Kennedy and Nixon: The Rivalry That Shaped Postwar America*. New York: Simon and Schuster, 1996.

Matusow, Allen J. *The Unraveling of America: A History of Liberalism in the 1960s*. New York: Harper and Row, 1984.

May, Edgar. *The Wasted Americans: Cost of Our Welfare Dilemma*. New York: Harper and Row, 1964.

Mayer, Harold M. and Wade, Richard C. *Chicago: Growth of a Metropolis*. Chicago: University of Chicago Press, 1969.

McCarthy, Colman. *Involvements: One Journalist's Place in the World*. Washington, DC: Acropolis Books, 1984.

McGovern, George. *An American Journey: The Presidential Campaign Speeches of George McGovern*. New York: Random House, 1974.

McGreevy, John T. *Catholicism and American Freedom: A History, from Slavery to Abortion*. New York: W. W. Norton, 2003.

McManners, John, ed. *The Oxford Illustrated History of Christianity*. Oxford: Oxford University Press, 1990.

McNamara, Robert S. *In Retrospect: The Tragedy and Lessons of Vietnam*. New York: Vintage Books, 1995.

McPherson, Harry. *A Political Education: A Journal of Life with Senators, Generals, Cabinet Members and Presidents*. Boston: Little, Brown, 1972.

Men of Mark in Maryland. Washington, DC: B. F. Johnson, 1912.

Miller, Merle. *Lyndon: An Oral Biography*. New York: Ballantine Books, 1980.

Miller, Warren E., and Santa Traugott. *American National Election Studies Data Sourcebook, 1952–1986*. Cambridge, MA: Harvard University Press, 1989.

Mills, Kay. *Something Better for My Children: The History and People of Head Start*. New York: Penguin Putnam, 1998.

Morison, Samuel Eliot. *The Two-Ocean War: A Short History of the United States in the Second World War*. Boston: Little, Brown/Atlantic Monthly Press, 1963.

Moynihan, Daniel Patrick. *Family and Nation*. New York: Harcourt Brace Jovanovich, 1986.

———. *Maximum Feasible Misunderstanding: Community Action in the War on Poverty*. New York: Free Press, 1970.

Murray, Charles. *Losing Ground: American Social Policy, 1950–1980*. New York: Basic Books, 1984.

Murray, Williamson, and Allan R. Millett. *A War to Be Won: Fighting the Second World War, 1937–1945*. Cambridge, MA: Harvard University Press/Belknap Press, 2000.

Nead, Daniel W. *The Pennsylvania German in the Settlement of Maryland*. Baltimore: Genealogical Publishing, 1975.

Neal, Steve. *Harry and Ike: The Partnership That Remade the Postwar World*. New York: Charles Scribner's Sons, 2001.

Nixon, Richard M. *The Memoirs of Richard Nixon*. New York: Grosset and Dunlap, 1978.

Nowell, Robert. *A Passion for Truth: Hans Kung and His Theology*. New York: Crossroad, 1981.

O'Brien, Michael. *Hesburgh: A Biography*. Washington, DC: Catholic University of America Press, 1998.

O'Connor, Len. *Clout: Mayor Daley and His City*. New York: Avon Books, 1975.

O'Donnell, Helen. *A Common Good: The Friendship of Robert F. Kennedy and Kenneth P. O'Donnell*. New York: William Morrow, 1998.

O'Donnell, Kenneth P., and David F. Powers. *"Johnny, We Hardly Knew Ye": Memories of John Fitzgerald Kennedy*. Boston: Little, Brown, 1970.

Parmet, Herbert S. *JFK: The Presidency of John F. Kennedy*. New York: Dial Press, 1983.

Patterson, James T. *America's Struggle against Poverty in the Twentieth Century*. Cambridge, MA: Harvard University Press, 2000.

———. *Grand Expectations: The United States, 1945–1974*. New York: Oxford University Press, 1996.

Perry, James M. *Us and Them: How the Press Covered the 1972 Election.* New York: Clarkson N. Potter, 1973.

Peters, Charles. *Tilting at Windmills: An Autobiography.* New York: Addison-Wesley, 1988.

Peters, William. *Passport to Friendship: The Story of the Experiment in International Living.* New York: J. B. Lippincott, 1957.

Poinsett, Alex. *Walking with Presidents: Louis Martin and the Rise of the Black Political Power.* New York: Rowman and Littlefield, 1997.

Powers, Thomas. *The Man Who Kept the Secrets: Richard Helms and the CIA.* New York: Pocket Books, 1983.

Quadagno, Jill. *The Color of Welfare: How Racism Undermined the War on Poverty.* New York: Oxford University Press, 1994.

Quandt, William B. *Peace Process: American Diplomacy and the Arab-Israeli Conflict Since 1967.* Washington, DC: Brookings Institution Press, 2001.

Ralph, James R., Jr. *Northern Protest: Martin Luther King, Jr., Chicago, and the Civil Rights Movement.* Cambridge, MA: Harvard University Press, 1993.

Redford, Emmette S., and Marlan Blissett. *Organizing the Executive Branch: The Johnson Presidency.* Chicago: University of Chicago Press, 1981.

Redmon, Coates. *Come as You Are: The Peace Corps Story.* New York: Harcourt Brace Jovanovich, 1986.

Reeves, Richard. *President Kennedy: Profile of Power.* New York: Simon and Schuster, 1993.

Reeves, Thomas C. *The Life and Times of Joe McCarthy: A Biography.* New York: Stein and Day, 1982.

———. *A Question of Character: A Life of John F. Kennedy.* New York: Free Press, 1991.

Reeves, T. Zane. *The Politics of the Peace Corps and VISTA.* Tuscaloosa: University of Alabama Press, 1988.

Rice, Gerard T. *The Bold Experiment: JFK's Peace Corps.* Notre Dame, IN: University of Notre Dame Press, 1985.

Rorabaugh, W. J. *Kennedy and the Promise of the Sixties.* New York: Cambridge University Press, 2002.

Rusk, Howard A. *A World to Care For: The Autobiography of Howard A. Rusk, M.D.* New York: Random House, 1972.

Russel, Jan Jarboe. *Lady Bird: A Biography of Mrs. Johnson.* New York: Charles Scribner's Sons, 1999.

Ryan, Kevin, and Marilyn Ryan, eds. *Why I Am Still a Catholic.* New York: Riverhead Books, 1998.

Rynne, Xavier. *Vatican Council II.* Maryknoll, NY: Orbis Books, 1999.

Safire, William. *Before the Fall: An Inside View of the Pre-Watergate White House.* Garden City, NY: Doubleday, 1975.

Saunders, Frank. *Torn Lace Curtain: Life with the Kennedys, Recalled by Their Personal Chauffeur.* New York: Holt, Rinehart and Winston, 1982.

Sautter, R. Craig, and Edward M. Burke. *Inside the Wigwam: Chicago Presidential Conventions 1860–1996.* Chicago: Loyola Press, 1996.

Scanlon, Thomas J. *Waiting for the Snow: The Peace Corps Papers of a Charter Volunteer.* Chevy Chase, MD: Posterity Press, 1997.

Scharf, J. Thomas. *History of Western Maryland.* Vol. 2. Baltimore: Regional Publishing, 1968.

Schlesinger, Arthur M., Jr. *Robert Kennedy and His Times.* New York: Ballantine Books, 1978.

———. *A Thousand Days: John F. Kennedy in the White House.* Boston: Houghton Mifflin, 1965.

Schott, Richard L., and Dagmar S. Hamilton. *People, Positions, and Power: The Political Appointments of Lyndon Johnson.* Chicago: University of Chicago Press, 1983.

Schulman, Bruce J. *Lyndon B. Johnson and American Liberalism: A Brief Biography with Documents.* Boston: Bedford/St. Martin's Press, 1995.

Seale, Bobby. *Seize the Time: The Story of the Black Panther Party and Huey P. Newton.* New York: Vintage Books, 1968.

Shesol, Jeff. *Mutual Contempt: Lyndon Johnson, Robert Kennedy, and the Feud That Defined a Decade.* New York: W. W. Norton, 1997.

Shipler, David K. *Russia: Broken Idols, Solemn Dreams.* New York: Penguin Books, 1983.

Shorter, Edward. *The Kennedy Family and the Story of Mental Retardation.* Philadelphia: Temple University Press, 2000.

Shriver, Robert Campbell. *History of the Shriver Family and Their Connections, 1684–1888*. Rev. ed. Privately published, 1976.

Shriver, Samuel S. *History of the Shriver Family and Their Connections, 1684–1888*. Baltimore: Press of Guggenheimer, Weil, 1889.

Shriver, Sargent. *Point of the Lance*. New York: Harper and Row, 1964.

Singer, Daniel. *Prelude to Revolution: France in May 1968*. Cambridge, MA: South End Press, 2002.

Small, Melvin. *The Presidency of Richard Nixon*. Lawrence: University Press of Kansas, 1999.

Smith, Amanda, ed. *Hostage to a Fortune: The Letters of Joseph P. Kennedy*. New York: Viking Press, 2001.

Smith, Charles D. *Palestine and the Arab-Israeli Conflict*. New York: St. Martin's Press, 1988.

Smith, Hendrick. *The Russians*. New York: Quadrangle / New York Times Books, 1976.

Sorenson, Theodore C. *Kennedy*. New York: Bantam Books, 1965.

———. *The Kennedy Legacy*. New York: Macmillan, 1969.

Steel, Ronald. *In Love with Night: The American Romance with Robert Kennedy*. New York: Simon and Schuster, 2000.

Stehle, Hansjakob. *Eastern Politics of the Vatican, 1917–1979*. Athens: Ohio University Press, 1981.

Stimson, Henry L., and McGeorge Bundy. *On Active Service in Peace and War*. New York: Harper and Brothers, 1947.

Stumpf, Harry P. *Community Politics and Legal Services: The Other Side of the Law*. Thousand Oaks, CA: Sage Publications, 1975.

Sulzberger, C .L. *An Age of Mediocrity: Memoirs and Diaries 1963–1972*. New York: Macmillan, 1973.

———. *Seven Continents and Forty Years: A Concentration of Memoirs*. New York: Quadrangle / New York Times Books, 1977.

Summers, Anthony. *The Arrogance of Power: The Secret World of Richard Nixon*. New York: Penguin Books, 2000.

Sundquist, James L., ed. *On Fighting Poverty: Perspectives from Experience*. New York: Basic Books, 1969.

———. *Politics and Policy: The Eisenhower, Kennedy, and Johnson Years*. Washington, DC: Brookings Institution Press, 1968.

Swidler, Leonard. *Küng in Conflict*. Garden City, NY: Doubleday, 1981.

Thomas, James W., and Judge T. J. C. Williams. *History of Allegany County, Maryland*. Vols. 1 and 2. Baltimore: Regional Publishing, 1923, 1969.

Unger, Irwin, and Debi Unger. *LBJ: A Life*. New York: John Wiley and Sons, 1999.

Vinen, Richard. *France: 1934–1970*. New York: St. Martin's Press, 1996.

Warner, David C. *Toward New Human Rights: The Social Policies of the Kennedy and Johnson Administrations*. University of Texas, Austin: Lyndon B. Johnson School of Public Affairs, 1977.

Watt, Donald B. *Intelligence Is Not Enough: The Story of My First Forty Years and of the Early Years of the Experiment in International Living*. Putney, VT: Experiment Press, 1967.

Waxman, Chaim I. *Poverty: Power and Politics*. New York: Grosset and Dunlap, 1968.

Weeks, Christopher. *Job Corps: Dollars and Dropouts*. Boston: Little, Brown, 1967.

Weil, Gordon L. *The Long Shot: George McGovern Runs for President*. New York: W. W. Norton, 1973.

Weinberg, Gerhard L. *A World at Arms: A Global History of World War II*. Cambridge: Cambridge University Press, 1994.

Weinberg, Steve. *Armand Hammer: The Untold Story*. Boston: Little, Brown, 1989.

Whalen, Richard J. *The Founding Father: The Story of Joseph P. Kennedy and the Family He Raised to Power*. New York: Signet, 1964.

Whalen, Thomas J. *Kennedy versus Lodge: The 1952 Massachusetts Senate Race*. Boston: Northeastern University Press, 2000.

White, Theodore H. *The Making of the President, 1960*. New York: Atheneum, 1961.

———. *The Making of the President, 1964*. New York: Atheneum, 1965.

———. *The Making of the President, 1968*. New York: Atheneum, 1969.

———. *The Making of the President, 1972.* New York: Atheneum, 1973.

Whitman, Alden, and the *New York Times. Portrait: Adlai Stevenson: Politician, Diplomat, Friend.* New York: Harper and Row, 1948.

Wills, Garry. *Nixon Agonistes: The Crisis of the Self-Made Man.* Boston: Houghton Mifflin, 1969.

Witcover, Jules. *Crapshoot: Rolling the Dice on the Vice Presidency.* New York: Crown, 1992.

———. *Marathon: The Pursuit of the Presidency, 1972–1976.* New York: Viking Press, 1977.

———. *The Resurrection of Richard Nixon.* New York: G. P. Putnam's Sons, 1970.

Wofford, Harris. *Of Kennedys and Kings: Making Sense of the Sixties.* Pittsburgh, PA: University of Pittsburgh Press, 1980.

Zarefsky, David. *President Johnson's War on Poverty: Rhetoric and History.* Tuscaloosa: University of Alabama Press, 1986.

Zeifman, Jerry. *Without Honor: Crimes of Camelot and the Impeachment of President Nixon.* New York: Thunder's Mouth Press, 1995.

Zigler, Edward, and Susan Muechow. *Head Start: The Inside Story of America's Most Successful Educational Experiment.* New York: Basic Books, 1992.

Zigler, Edward, and Jeanette Valentine. *Project Head Start: A Legacy of the War on Poverty.* New York: Free Press, 1979.

Author's Interviews

Vernon Alden—February 18, 1998

William Alford—October 30, 2001

Clinton Bamberger—February 18, 1998

Bill Blair—October 20, 2000

Frances Bowers—August 22, 2000

Bob Blake—February 19, 1998

David Birenbaum—March 4, 2002

Hyman Bookbinder—February 18, 1998

Frances Cook—September 25, 2001

Bob Cooke—February 18, 1998

Lloyd Davis—October 18, 2000

Eleanor Hoguet DeGive—August 11, 2000

Donald Dell—April 15, 2003; April 17, 2003

Ralph Dungan—May 15, 2003

Joe English—February 18, 1998; October 5, 2000; October 12, 2000

Kay Fanning—September 19, 2000

George Foreman—August 15, 2003

Bill Haddad—January 30, 1998; January 4, 2002

Bob Holliday—March 5, 2002

Phil Hardberger—February 18, 1998

Joe Hakim—April 10, 2002

Bryan Hehir—March 27, 2003

Ted Hesburgh—April 17, 2002

William Josephson—August 5, 2000; October 5, 2000; October 12, 2000

Mickey Kantor—March 6, 2002

Edward M. Kennedy—February 16, 2004

Pat Kennedy—February 18, 1998

Hans Kung—May 20, 2003

Anthony Lake—May 13, 2003

Frank Mankiewicz—February 18, 1998; March 5, 2002

Ed Marciniak—August 21, 2000

Edgar May—February 21, 2002

Colman McCarthy—July 30, 2003

Mav McCarthy—July 30, 2003

Andy McCutcheon—February 20, 2003

Ignatius McDermott—August 21, 2000

Robert McNamara—May 15, 2003

Newt Minow—August 22, 2000

Daniel Morrissey—February 19, 1998; March 3, 2003

Bill Moyers—January 30, 1998

Fred Nadherny—August 21, 2000

Mary Ann Orlando—January 30, 1998; September 26, 2001

Andrei Pavlov—March 31, 2000

Mollie Shriver Pierrepont—August 14, 2000

Richard Ragsdale—October 16, 2000

Julius Richmond—February 18, 1998

Dan Rostenkowski—August 22, 2000

Stan Salette—March 6, 2002

Tom Scanlon—January 30, 1998

Arnold Schwarzenegger—July 29, 2003

Jose Serrano—April 2, 2003

Mark Shields—April 16, 2002

Anthony Shriver—June 10, 2003

Bobby Shriver—May 21, 2003; May 30, 2003

Eunice Kennedy Shriver—January 30, 1998;
    September 24, 26, 2001; September 29, 2003;
    October 15, 2003
Helen "Babs" Shriver—June 22, 2000
Maria Shriver—July 9, 2003
Mark Shriver—September 26, 2001
Sargent Shriver—August 2, 3, 4, 10, 11, 15, 16, 24, 25,
    30, 31, 1997; September 1, 1997; December 26, 27,
    28, 1997; January 30, 1998; February 18, 1998;
    March 30, 1998; September 7, 1998; March 12,
    1999; August 16, 1999; March 3, 4, 5, 22, 23, 24, 31,
    2000; April 4, 5, 25, 2000; June 22, 2000; August
    17, 2000
Timothy Shriver—March 5, 2002
Otis Singletary—February 18, 1998
Bob Stuart—September 5, 2001
Larry Tribe—February 26, 2002
Warren Wiggins—January 30, 1998
Harris Wofford—January 30, 1998

Oral Histories

Don Baker
John A. Baker
Hyman Bookbinder
Edgar Cahn
Jean Cahn
William Cannon
William Capron
Wilbur Cohen
Ann Oppenheimer Hamilton

Bertrand Harding
Walter Heller
Harold Horowitz
William Josephson
Bill Kelly
Herb Kramer
Robert Lampman
Frank Mankiewicz
Edgar May
Leonard Mayo
George McCarthy
Larry O'Brien
Bradley Patterson
Robert C. Perrin
Charles Peters
William Phillips
Lewis Powell
Thomas Quimby
Julius Richmond
Barefoot Sanders
Norb Schlei
Eunice Kennedy Shriver
Sargent Shriver
George Smathers
Jules Sugarman
Jim Sundquist
Eric Tolmach
Adam Walinsky
Christopher Weeks
Adam Yarmolinsky

INDEX

Shrum, Bob, 612, 619

Sims, Albert "Al," 196, 212

Sinatra, Frank, 189

Sinclair, Upton, 338

Singapore, 281, 283

Singletary, Otis, 454

Sirhan Sirhan, 504, 665

Skinner, Richard Dana, 20

Small Business Administration, 371, 455

Smathers, George, 97, 135

Smith, Al, 16–17, 22, 131, 146

Smith, Chesterfield, 625

Smith, Gerard, 40, 648–52, 654–55

Smith, Greg, 40–42, 45

Smith, Howard, 243–44, 274, 384

Smith, Jean Kennedy (sister-in-law): children of, 663; hazing by, 155; JFK funeral, 310; JFK senatorial campaign, 106, 110; marriage of, 156–57; on presidential campaign: (1956), 133–34; (1976), 629; traits, 95

Smith, John Thomas, 40, 45

Smith, Reginald Heber, 432

Smith, Stephen "Steve": children of, 663; JFK funeral, 321; in Kennedy family, 155, 157, 300, 523–24; Kennedy financing, 523–24, 602; marriage of, 156–57; NY mayoral candidate, 526; on presidential campaign: (1960), 161; (1968), 515, 516, 518, 522, 524, 526; (1972), 602; (1976), 602, 626, 627

Smith, William Kennedy (nephew), 663

Smith Fellowship, 443

Social Security, 335, 408

Solzhenitsyn, Aleksandr, 622

Somalia, 270, 291

Sorensen, Theodore "Ted": on antipoverty proposals, 339, 341; Catholicism, political impact of, 131–32; on Community Action, 344; Dell on, 524; JFK aide, 144, 157, 173, 193; on JFK cabinet, 184–85; JFK funeral, 300, 302, 303, 311, 319–20; on LBJ, 311, 316; LBJ on, 352; on McNamara, 184; on "Our Invisible Poor," 338; on Peace Corps, 207, 221; on presidential campaign: (1960), 134, 164; (1968), 515, 523; on Shriver, 158; Shriver on, 157

Southern Christian Leadership Council, 162–63

Southern Illinois University, 398

Soviet Union: Afghanistan, invasion of, 647; business trips to, 574–75, 617–18, 645; Cuban Missile Crisis, 289; Czechoslovakia, invasion of, 509–10, 544; détente, 613, 621, 645–49; foreign policy, 171,

239–40; France and, 499; Hammer import-export, 570–72; on Jackson, 613, 618; lecture tour of, 575, 618–22; loan to, 622; nuclear weapons, 648–51; on Peace Corps, 270, 451; on Reagan, 618; Special Olympics, 619, 661; WWII, 49, 55, 75

Special Olympics: beginnings of, 136, 264–66, 506–7; chairman of, xxviii, 661, 662–64, 679; in Chicago, 506, 658; financing of, 506, 668; in France, 510; international games, 619, 658–59, 661, 681; in Ireland, 661, 681; Maria on, 681; president of, xxviii, 661, 662–64, 676; record albums for, 662; Shriver on, 506, 659, 662, 679–80; in Soviet Union, 619, 661; spokesmen for, 400, 664, 667–668; state chapters, 659; weight lifting, 664, 667

Spellman, Francis, 115

Spiegel, Hart, 45

Springsteen, Bruce, 662

SS *Athenia*, sinking of, 50

Stalin, Joseph, 570

Stanford University, 96

State, Department of: Eunice in, 97; on France, 498; JFK administration, 181, 199–200, 201; JFK critique of, 171, 198, 199, 218–19; Nixon administration, 544; Paris peace talks, 598, 599; Peace Corps, 205, 218–25, 451. *See also* secretary of state

Stennis, John, 428–30, 462

Stevenson, Adlai: for attorney general, 182; gubernatorial campaign, 94; JFK funeral, 302; presidential campaign: (1952), 109; (1956), 131–34; (1960), 142, 144, 145, 149–50; role model, 377; for secretary of state, 180; UN ambassador, 181, 539

Stevenson, Adlai, III, 486, 640

Stewart, Potter, 45, 46, 55, 593

Sting, 662

Stone, Oliver, 663

Stossel, Scott, xxviii–xxx, 682

Strasser, Spiegelberg, Fried, Frank & Kampelman, 569

Strategic Arms Limitation Talks (SALT), 648, 652

Stratton, William, 130

Stritch, Samuel, 120–21, 127–28

Stuart, J.E.B. "Jeb," 6–7, 14

Stuart, R. Douglas, Jr. "Bob," 45–46, 55–57, 91, 93–94, 114

Student Nonviolent Coordinating Committee (SNCC), 429

Student World Federalists, 196

Styron, William, 565

Sugarman, Jules, 421, 426–27, 462, 464